# Bhutan

Lindsay Brown
Bradley Mayhew, Stan Armington, Richard W Whitecross

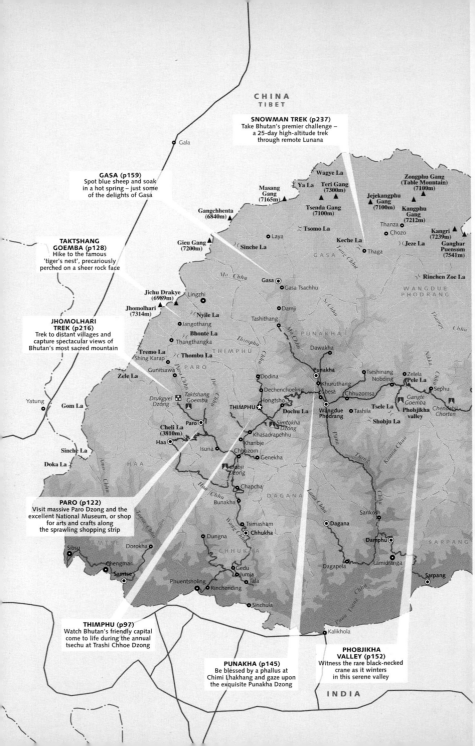

C H I N A
TIBET

Gala

**SNOWMAN TREK (p237)**
Take Bhutan's premier challenge –
a 25-day high-altitude trek
through remote Lunana

**GASA (p159)**
Spot blue sheep and soak
in a hot spring – just some
of the delights of Gasa

Wagye La

Masang
Gang
(7165m) ▲

Ya La

Teri Gang
(7300m) ▲

Zongphu Gang
(Table Mountain)
(7100m)

Gangchhenta
(6840m) ▲

Tsenda Gang
(7100m)

Jejekangphu
Gang
(7100m)

Kangphu
Gang
(7212m)

Thanza

Chozo

Kangri
(7239m)

Ganghar
Puensum
(7541m) ▲

**TAKTSHANG
GOEMBA (p128)**
Hike to the famous
'tiger's nest', precariously
perched on a sheer rock face

Gieu Gang
(7200m)

Laya

Tsomo La

Keche La

Jeze La

Sinche La

Thaga

G A S A

Rinchen Zoe La

Mo Chhu

Gasa

Gasa Tsachhu

W A N G D U E
P H O D R A N G

Jichu Drakye
(6989m)

Lingzhi

Damji

Tashithang

Tang Chhu

**JHOMOLHARI
TREK (p216)**
Trek to distant villages and
capture spectacular views of
Bhutan's most sacred mountain

Jhomolhari
(7314m)

Nyile La

Jangothang

**Bhonte La**
Thangthangka

Tashithang

P U N A K H A

Dawakha

**Tremo La**
Shing Karap

**Thombu La**

Chhuzomsa

Tseshinang
Nobding

Zelela
Pele La

Sephu

Zele La

Gunitsawa

P A R O

Dodina

Dechenchoeling

Punakha

Khuruthang

Lobesa

Gangte
Goemba
Phobjikha
valley

Chendebji
Chorten

**Drukgyel
Dzong**

**Taktshang
Goemba**

Hongtsho

Wangdue
Phodrang

Tashila

Tsele La

Yatung

Gom La

**Cheli La
(3810m)**

Paro

**THIMPHU**

Dochu La

**Simtokha
Dzong**

Shobju La

Haa

Khasadrapchhu

Sinche La

Kharibje

Chhuzom

Genekha

Doka La

H A A

**Babji
Dzong**

D A G A N A

Chapcha

Bunakha

Sankosh

**PARO (p122)**
Visit massive Paro Dzong and the
excellent National Museum, or shop
for arts and crafts along
the sprawling shopping strip

Isuna

Tsimasham

Dagana

Dorokha

C H H U K H A

Dungna

Chhukha

Dagapela

Damphu

Lamidranga

S A R P A N G

Sibsu

Chengmari

Samtse

Gedu
Jumja
Tala

Dagapela

Sarpang

Phuentsholing
Rinchending

Sinchula

Kalikhola

**THIMPHU (p97)**
Watch Bhutan's friendly capital
come to life during the annual
tsechu at Trashi Chhoe Dzong

**PUNAKHA (p145)**
Be blessed by a phallus at
Chimi Lhakhang and gaze upon
the exquisite Punakha Dzong

**PHOBJIKHA
VALLEY (p152)**
Witness the rare black-necked
crane as it winters
in this serene valley

I N D I A

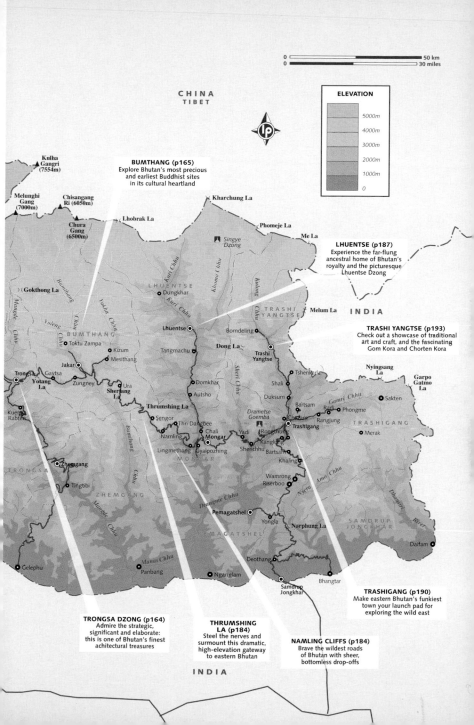

CHINA
TIBET

**ELEVATION**

5000m
4000m
3000m
2000m
1000m
0

0 — 50 km
0 — 30 miles

**BUMTHANG (p165)**
Explore Bhutan's most precious
and earliest Buddhist sites
in its cultural heartland

Kulha
Gangri
(7554m)

Melunghi
Gang
(7000m)

Chisangang
Ri (6050m)

Chura
Gang
(6500m)

Lhobrak La

Kharchung La

Phomeje La

Me La

Singye
Dzong

**LHUENTSE (p187)**
Experience the far-flung
ancestral home of Bhutan's
royalty and the picturesque
Lhuentse Dzong

(Gokthong La)

LHUENTSE

Dungkhar

TRASHI
YANGTSE

Melum La

INDIA

BUMTHANG

Toktu Zampa

Kizum

Jakar

Mesithang

Trongsa

Gaytsa

Yotang
La

Zungney

Ura

Sherjang
La

Kuenga
Rabten

Lhuentse

Tangmachu

Bomdeling

Dong La

Trashi
Yangtse

Domkhar

Autsho

Shali

Duksum

Tshenkurla

**TRASHI YANGTSE (p193)**
Check out a showcase of traditional
art and craft, and the fascinating
Gom Kora and Chorten Kora

Nyingsang
La

Garpo
Gatmo
La

Sakten

Bartsam

Radi

Phongme

**Thrumshing La**

Şengor

Thi Dangbee

Chali

Mongar

Yadi

Rongthung

Drametse
Goemba

Chazam

Trashigang

Rangjung

TRASHIGANG

Namling

Kangtng

Merak

Lingmethang

Gyalpozhing

Shenchhu

Bartsam

MONGAR

Khaling

Zhemgang

Wamrong

Riserboo

TRONGSA

Tingtibi

ZHEMGANG

Pemagatshel

Yongla

Narphung La

SAMDRUP
JONGKHAR

Daifam

PEMAGATSHEL

Gelephu

Manas Chhu

Panbang

Nganglam

Deothang

Bhangtar

Samdrup
Jongkhar

**TRASHIGANG (p190)**
Make eastern Bhutan's funkiest
town your launch pad for
exploring the wild east

**TRONGSA DZONG (p164)**
Admire the strategic,
significant and elaborate:
this is one of Bhutan's finest
achitectural treasures

**THRUMSHING
LA (p184)**
Steel the nerves and
surmount this dramatic,
high-elevation gateway
to eastern Bhutan

**NAMLING CLIFFS (p184)**
Brave the wildest roads
of Bhutan with sheer,
bottomless drop-offs

INDIA

# Destination Bhutan

Bhutan, the Land of the Thunder Dragon, is no ordinary place. This is a country where buying cigarettes is illegal, where the rice is red and where chillies aren't just a seasoning but the entire dish. It's also a deeply Buddhist land, where men wear a tunic to work, where giant protective penises are painted on the walls of most houses, and where Gross National Happiness is deemed more important than Gross National Product.

Tourism in Bhutan is also unique. Visitors famously have to pay a minimum of US$200 per day, making it one of the world's most expensive countries to visit, but this fee is all-inclusive, you don't have to travel in a group and you can arrange your own itinerary. What you won't find in Bhutan is backpacker-style independent travel. This is Nepal for the jet set.

So why spend all your money to come here? First off there are the fantastic monasteries, incredible dzongs and the undisturbed traditional Tibetan-style culture that sets Bhutan aside as the last remaining great Himalayan kingdom. Then there are the textiles, outrageous trekking and stunning flora and fauna of one of the world's biodiversity hotspots. But perhaps most of all, Bhutan offers an opportunity to glimpse another way of living, an alternative vision of what is truly important in life.

It is also a country of surprises. This is not just a nation of saintly, other-worldly hermits. Bhutan is straddling the ancient and modern world and these days you'll find monks transcribing ancient Buddhist texts into computers as traditionally dressed noblemen chat on their mobile phones.

If you do visit Bhutan, you will become one of the few who have experienced the charm and magic of one of the world's most enigmatic countries – the 'last Shangri La' – and you'll be playing your part in this medieval kingdom's efforts to join the modern world, while steadfastly maintaining its distinct and amazing cultural identity.

IZZET KERIBA

# Architecture

STAN ARMINGTON

Subdue your inner demoness at Kyichu Lhakhang (p127)

WES WALKER

Elevate your merit at 'tiger's nest' (Taktshang Goemba; p128)

Catch the cosmos in a glimpse at Kurjey Lhakhang (p173)

NICHOLAS REUSS

# Festivals

See red at the Thimphu tsechu, Trashi Chhoe Dzong (p101), Thimphu

Witness the masterpiece of the Nga Cham drum
dance at the Drametse tsechu (p189)

Dance with the Buddha of the Future at the
annual festival, Jampey Lhakhang (p172)

# Tradition

Make an offering to Buddha at Thimphu's
National Memorial Chorten (p104)

ALISON WRIGHT

LINDSAY BROWN

Watch in wonder at the Voluntary Artists Studio
Thimphu (VAST) studio (p105), Thimphu

Turn your world around with prayer wheels, Cheri Goemba (p115)

LINDSAY BROWN

# Wilderness

Ascend the heights of Mt Jhomolhari (7314m), on the Jhomolhari trek (p216)

Call on your enduring spirit and undertake the
Dagala Thousand Lakes trek (p214)

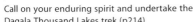

Follow your guide (p201) as they
introduce you to the locals

# Contents

| | |
|---|---|
| The Authors | 11 |
| Getting Started | 13 |
| Itineraries | 19 |
| Snapshot | 24 |
| History | 25 |
| The Culture | 45 |
| Buddhism in Bhutan | 63 |
| Architecture | 78 |
| Environment | 83 |
| Food & Drink | 94 |

**Thimphu** 97

| | |
|---|---|
| Orientation | 98 |
| Information | 98 |
| Dangers & Annoyances | 101 |
| Sights | 101 |
| Activities | 106 |
| Walking Tour | 107 |
| Courses | 107 |
| Festivals & Events | 107 |
| Sleeping | 108 |
| Eating | 110 |
| Drinking & Entertainment | 112 |
| Shopping | 113 |
| Getting There & Away | 114 |
| Getting Around | 114 |
| **AROUND THIMPHU** | **115** |
| North of Thimphu | 115 |
| South of Thimphu | 116 |

**Western Bhutan** 119

| | |
|---|---|
| **PARO DZONGKHAG** | **121** |
| Paro | 122 |
| Around Paro | 127 |
| Paro to Thimphu (53km) | 131 |
| **HAA DZONGKHAG** | **133** |
| Paro to Haa via the Cheli La (68km) | 133 |
| Haa | 133 |
| Around the Haa Valley | 134 |
| Haa to Chhuzom (79km) | 134 |
| **PUNAKHA DZONGKHAG** | **134** |
| Thimphu to Punakha (76km) | 134 |
| Punakha & Khuruthang | 145 |
| **WANGDUE PHODRANG DZONGKHAG** | **149** |
| Punakha to Wangdue Phodrang (21km) | 149 |
| Wangdue Phodrang | 149 |
| Wangdue Phodrang to Pele La | 151 |
| Phobjikha Valley | 152 |
| **CHHUKHA DZONGKHAG** | **155** |
| Thimphu to Phuentsholing (172km) | 155 |
| Phuentsholing | 156 |
| **GASA DZONGKHAG** | **159** |
| Gasa | 159 |
| Laya | 159 |
| Lingzhi | 159 |
| **SOUTHERN DZONGKHAGS** | **159** |
| Tsirang Dzongkhag | 159 |
| Dagana Dzongkhag | 159 |
| Samtse Dzongkhag | 159 |

**Central Bhutan** 160

| | |
|---|---|
| **TRONGSA DZONGKHAG** | **161** |
| Wangdue Phodrang to Trongsa (129km) | 161 |
| Trongsa | 163 |
| Around Trongsa | 165 |
| **BUMTHANG DZONGKHAG** | **165** |
| Trongsa to Jakar (68km) | 165 |
| Jakar | 167 |
| Chokhor Valley | 171 |
| Tang Valley | 177 |
| Ura Valley | 179 |

**SOUTHERN
DZONGKHAGS** **180**
Zhemgang Dzongkhag 180
Sarpang Dzongkhag 180

## Eastern Bhutan 181

**MONGAR DZONGKHAG** **183**
Jakar to Mongar (193km) 184
Mongar 185
**LHUENTSE
DZONGKHAG** **186**
Mongar to Lhuentse
(76km) 186
Lhuentse 187
Around Lhuentse 188
**TRASHIGANG
DZONGKHAG** **188**
Mongar to Trashigang
(92km) 188
Trashigang 190
Far Eastern Bhutan 192
**TRASHI YANGTSE
DZONGKHAG** **193**
Trashigang to Trashi
Yangtse (53km) 193
Trashi Yangtse 195
Around Trashi Yangtse 196
**SAMDRUP JONGKHAR
DZONGKHAG** **196**

Trashigang to Samdrup
Jongkhar (180km) 196
Samdrup Jongkhar 198
**PEMAGATSHEL
DZONGKHAG** **198**
Trekking In Bhutan 199

## Trekking 199

Trekking in Bhutan 199
When to Trek 200
Guides & Camp Staff 201
Trekking Food 202
Clothing & Equipment 202
Maps 206
Treks in this Book 206
Responsible Trekking 210
Health & Safety 210
Druk Path Trek 212
Dagala Thousand Lakes
Trek 214
Jhomolhari Trek 216
Jhomolhari Trek 2 221
Laya–Gasa Trek 222
Gasa Hot Spring Trek 228
Gangte Trek 228
Bumthang Cultural Trek 230
Duer Hot Spring Trek 232
Rodang La Trek 233

Snowman Trek 237
Samtengang Winter Trek 241

## Directory 242

## Transport 257

## Health 267

## Language 275

## Glossary 279

## Behind the Scenes 282

## Index 287

## Map Legend 296

# Regional Map Contents

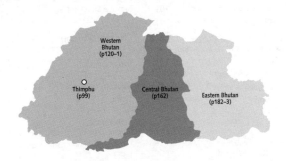

Western
Bhutan
(p120–1)

Thimphu
(p99)

Central Bhutan
(p162)

Eastern Bhutan
(p182–3)

# The Authors

## LINDSAY BROWN
**Coordinating author; Thimphu**

A former conservation biologist and publishing manager of Outdoor Activity guides at Lonely Planet, Lindsay has trekked, jeeped, ridden and stumbled across many a mountain pass and contributed to Lonely Planet's *South India*, *India*, *Nepal* and *Pakistan & the Karakoram Highway* guides, among others. He has still not seen nearly enough of the Himalaya or its peoples.

### Life On The Road

It started at an ungodly hour, when usually only the dogs of Thimphu are awake. This cold, dark morning the canine chorus found a human harmony as hundreds of bleary-eyed tourists and locals sought their allotted lifts, and countless car and bus headlights traced a pilgrimage to Paro. We were off to see the Guru Rinpoche *thondrol* unfurled at the Paro tsechu. To gaze upon the *thondrol* is to have one's sins expunged and to witness such an extraordinary festival is a dramatic highlight of visiting Bhutan. The traffic jam at Paro had to be seen to be believed and it was a relief to set out on foot up towards the dzong. Some strolled, some ran, at least three shortcuts were initiated, but there was no need to rush. The enormous *thondrol* had its own stage and setting separate to the dzong and thousands had already gathered to watch the dances, utter a prayer and attract a blessing.

## BRADLEY MAYHEW
**Western, Central and Eastern Bhutan**

Ever drawn to Himalayan peaks and Tibetan Buddhist communities, Bradley has been travelling to Tibetan areas for over a decade. He coordinated the last two editions of Lonely Planet's *Nepal* and the last three editions of *Tibet*, and has written the Tibetan areas of LP's *China* and *South-west China* guides. British-born and nomadic at heart, Bradley currently lives under the big skies of Montana.

Bradley is also the co-author of Lonely Planet guides *Central Asia*, *Jordan*, *Shanghai* and *Yellowstone & Grand Teton National Parks* and has worked on Lonely Planet guides from *Morocco* to *Mongolia*. He has lectured on Central Asia at the Royal Geographic Society.

### My Favourite Trip

This six-week research trip took me right across Bhutan, from Phuentsholing in the southwest to Trashi Yangtse in the far east. Favourites are hard to pin down in such a remarkable country but I thought the little-visited Haa valley (p133) was great, as was hiking the scenic Phobjikha valley (p152). My nod for favourite dzongs goes to Punakha (p145) and Wangdue Phodrang (p149); the award for 'best drive' goes to Mongar to Lhuentse (p186); 'best discovery' goes to Eundo Chholing (p165). Of the over 100 temples and lha-khangs I got to see, I ache most to go back to Gom Kora (p193) and Kyichu Lhakhang (p127). Oh, and Taktshang (p128), of course!

My favourite place of all? That was a long hike through lush forests, *mani* walls and sudden chortens up to an achingly beautiful and utterly silent hermitage. Where exactly that is, I'm not telling…

## CONTRIBUTING AUTHORS

**Stan Armington**, who also authored Lonely Planet's *Trekking in the Nepal Himalaya,* has been organising and leading treks in Nepal since 1971. A graduate engineer, he has also worked for the US National Park service in the Yellowstone and Olympic parks as well as serving as a guide on Mt Hood in Oregon. Stan is a director of the American Himalayan Foundation, a fellow of the Royal Geographical Society and the Explorers Club, and specialises in opening bars in Himalayan towns. He has travelled extensively in Bhutan and developed a project to train Bhutanese craftsmen in historic building conservation. He lives in Kathmandu, where he runs a trekking company and tries to keep up with all the changes to trekking routes in both Nepal and Bhutan.

**Richard W Whitecross** wrote The Culture and Buddhism in Bhutan chapters. He was raised in southern Scotland and, after encountering several lamas at a young age, developed a lifelong fascination with the Himalayas and, in particular, Bhutan. A former environmental lawyer turned anthropologist, Richard spent a year in a Buddhist monastery preparing for fieldwork. His doctoral thesis, *The Zhabdrung's Legacy: Law and Social Transformation in Contemporary Bhutan* (2002) is the first ethnographic account to focus on law and social change in Bhutan. Following his PhD he was awarded a postdoctoral fellowship and taught courses on political anthropology, ritual and religion, and intends to publish further on Bhutan.

# Getting Started

Bhutan is an extraordinary destination; surrounded by myth and secreted within the mightiest mountain chain, it bumps shoulders with the global giants of China and India. Traditional culture is proudly cherished and natural heritage is equally treasured, and yet modernisation and development is equally conspicuous in this complex and little-known country.

Though it is certainly isolated and remote, Bhutan is not a difficult place to visit. There is no limit to the number of tourists who can visit and there are no restrictions on group size. You can easily organise a journey as a couple or as a solo traveller. The Royal Government of Bhutan requires that foreign visitors travel with a prepaid and preplanned itinerary through a Bhutanese tour company. You can simply buy a space on a group tour or arrange a custom-made program. With some background information and a helpful tour operator you can customise an itinerary that suits your interests, be they culture, wildlife, festivals, trekking, cycling, rafting etc. Generally there is a great deal of freedom as to where you can go and what you can do, though it's sometimes difficult to change your program once you have finalised the arrangements.

English is widely spoken and there are Western-style hotels and food throughout the country. Though as you move further from the capital, Thimphu, expect more simple facilities and less familiar food. The costs seem very steep at first, but factor in what is supplied – accommodation, food, transport, guides – and, of course, Bhutan's unrivalled uniqueness.

## WHEN TO GO

Climate, and therefore season, is certainly a consideration when planning your trip to Bhutan, especially if you are trekking. However, Bhutan's altitude range, from subtropical valleys to alpine peaks, and its busy festival calendar means you can pretty much visit Bhutan at any time of the year to explore its attractions and witness colourful festivals.

The ideal time for trekking and for travelling throughout the country is autumn, from late September to late November, when skies are generally clear and the high mountain peaks rise to a vivid blue sky. While the climate is best in autumn, in Bhutan an umbrella is usually never far from reach, and no matter when you go, there is likely to be rain periods. Autumn is

---

**TOP FIVE CULTURAL EXPERIENCES**

Traditional and modern meld in unexpected ways in a conservative yet rapidly modernising Bhutan.

- Uncovering a fresco, spinning a prayer wheel or peering into a sacred alcove in one of Bhutan's lofty, isolated temples.
- Joining the clamour and crowds of a tsechu (p247) as the masked dancers perform extraordinary feats and playful *atsaras* (masked clowns) swing their whips and wooden phalluses.
- The banter and the boasting, the singing and the skills and the near-misses of an archery tournament (p113).
- Watching artists, young and old, create religious and traditional arts and crafts employing skills passed down from generation to generation (p104).
- The powerful whirr of hundreds of fraying prayer flags reciting in blustery winds at a lonely mountain pass (p199).

also the time of the popular Thimphu tsechu (dance festival) and heralds the arrival of the black-necked cranes to their wintering grounds in central and eastern Bhutan. Not surprisingly, therefore, international visitors also peak in autumn, indeed about half of the total annual tourist numbers arrive between September and November. Avoiding the busiest tourist seasons can save you money (see opposite) and hassle.

The winter is a good time for touring in western Bhutan, bird-watching (p243) in the south's subtropical jungles, and whitewater rafting (p244). The days are usually sunny, cool and pleasant, but it's quite cold once the sun sets and you will need to pack warm clothing. From December to February, there is often snow in the higher regions and occasional snow in Thimphu. The road from Thimphu to Bumthang and the east may be closed because of snow for several days at a time. It would be best not to plan to visit these regions at this time.

Spring, from March to May, is recognised as the second best time to visit Bhutan for touring and trekking. Though there are more clouds and rain than in the autumn, the magnificent rhododendrons, magnolias and other wildflowers are in bloom and birdlife is abundant. You can get occasional glimpses of the high peaks, but these are not the dramatic unobstructed views possible in autumn. Spring is also the time of the magnificent Paro tsechu.

Summer, from June to August, is the monsoon season. And what a monsoon! During these three months 500mm of rain falls in Thimphu and up to a metre falls in the eastern hills. The mountains are hidden, the valleys are shrouded in clouds, and roads disappear in heavy downpours and floods. Summer is still a great time to visit Paro, Thimphu and other parts of western Bhutan. In the mellow monsoon light, the vivid green rice paddies contrast with the dark hills and the stark white dzongs to produce picture-perfect vistas. And the markets are bursting with fresh fruits and vegetables.

A major factor in choosing a time to visit Bhutan, and one that may override considerations of weather patterns, is the festival schedule. These colourful events offer a first-hand glimpse of Bhutanese life and provide an opportunity to see the inside of the great dzongs. It's possible, and highly recommended, to work at least one festival into a tour or trek program. See the boxed text, p247, for details on the calendar. In recent years overcrowding has become an issue during the major tsechus at Thimphu and Paro, which coincide with the best seasons. At these times flights and accommodation are heavily booked and you may find you need to pay a premium for accommodation or settle for lower-standard accommodation. You stand a much better chance of getting flights, accommodation and probably a more intimate and rewarding festival experience if you schedule your trip around one of the other cultural events.

---

**DON'T LEAVE HOME WITHOUT...**

- A compact umbrella and/or rainjacket – for any region at any time of the year.
- Hat, sunscreen, lip balm and sunglasses (especially if trekking; see p199).
- Earplugs (Bhutanese dogs sleep all day and bark all night).
- Walking poles (even if you aren't trekking, you will find these knee savers useful for steep hikes up to dzongs and temples).
- Swimming costume for communal hot-stone baths and hot springs.
- A flashlight for unexpected power cuts and for viewing interiors of dark temples and monasteries.
- Motion sickness medication for the long and winding drives (see p267).

## COSTS & MONEY

Tourism in Bhutan is managed through partnership of government regulators and private travel agencies under a policy summed up by the mantra 'high value, low impact'. There is no restriction on visitor numbers; however, there is a minimum daily tariff fixed by the government. Also your visit must be arranged through an officially approved tour operator (see p263), either directly or through an overseas agent. By dealing through an overseas agent you will avoid complicated payment procedures and also have a home-based contact in case of queries or special needs. On the other hand, if you deal directly with a Bhutanese tour operator you will have more scope to individualise your itinerary, though you'll spend considerable time sending emails and faxes, and learn more than you want to about international bank transfers. For information on visas see p255.

The daily tariff for tourists visiting in a group of three people or more is US$200 per day (US$165 per day in the low season of July to August, whether you stay in hotels (a 'cultural tour') or go trekking.

To encourage trekkers to make longer treks, the Department of Tourism (DOT) allows a 10% discount on days 11 to 20 and 20% from day 21 on.

The daily tariff includes all of your accommodation, food, land transport within Bhutan, services of guides and porters, supply of pack animals on treks, and cultural programs as appropriate. It also includes a US$65 tax, which is used by the government to fund infrastructure, education, health and other programs.

The tour rate applies uniformly irrespective of location or the type of accommodation asked for or provided (with the exception of several premium hotels; see below). This clause means that if things get busy you may get bumped from a better hotel to one of lesser quality, and you have no recourse.

Individual tourists and couples are subject to a surcharge, over and above the daily rate. The surcharge may also be applied if a member of a group arrives or departs on a separate flight from the rest of the party. The surcharge is US$40 per night for one person and US$30 per night per person for a group of two people. Visitors qualifying for any kind of discount still have to pay this small-group surcharge.

Most tour operators expect you to pay separately for all drinks, including liquor, beer, mineral water and bottled soft drinks. You'll also have to pay extra for laundry, riding horses, and cultural splurges such as a Bhutanese hot-stone bath. There are endless potential options that cost extra but provide a means to individualise your itinerary: expert guides, special permits, luxury vehicles, cultural shows and courses, special food and premium accommodation. The availability of these extras will depend on the tour operator and will involve investigating several operators and negotiating prices.

### Premium Hotels

A number of premium hotels have been established in Thimphu, Paro and in a few other locations. These four- to five-star hotels charge accommodation and dining rates in addition to the daily tariff. Details can be found in the relevant Sleeping sections in the destination chapters.

### Discounts & Special Categories

The following categories of visitors are eligible for discounts on the daily rate.

**Children** Up to the age of six, children are free. Kids from seven to 12 accompanied by parents or guardians receive a 50% discount on the daily rates.
**Diplomats** A 25% discount on the rates applies to diplomats from foreign embassies or missions accredited to Bhutan.

---

**HOW MUCH?**

Cup of espresso coffee Nu 25

Bowl of *ema datse* Nu 30

Half-hour of internet access Nu 30

Chocolate bar Nu 20

Prayer wheel Nu 300-500

---

**LONELY PLANET INDEX**

1L of petrol Nu 60

1L of bottled water Nu 15

Bottle of Red Panda beer Nu 80

Souvenir T-shirt Nu 350

Snack of *momos* (dumplings) Nu 25

See Climate Charts (p245) for more information

**Group Leaders** A discount of 50% on the rates is given to one person in a group of 11 to 15 people. A free trip is allowed for one member per group exceeding 15 people.

**Indian Nationals** Because of Bhutan's special relationship with India, Indian tourists are categorised differently from other international tourists. Indians do not require a visa and may pay local rates for food, transportation and accommodation. They may travel independently throughout most of Bhutan, though a special permit is required. DOT recommends that Indian visitors use the services of a Bhutanese tour operator to arrange such permits and to expedite hotel and transport bookings. The initial permit for Indian nationals is for 14 days, and they still need a travel permit to go beyond Paro and Thimphu. Indians may also wander freely into all the border towns of Bhutan, though they must leave by 10pm unless staying in a hotel.

**Students** Full-time students 29 years and younger, with valid identity cards from their academic institutions, are allowed a 25% discount, resulting in a rate of US$150 per night (plus small-group surcharges, if applicable). You should deal directly with a Bhutanese tour operator rather than through a travel agency or tour company at home if you plan to utilise this facility.

**Travel Agents** Tour companies intending to put Bhutan into their programs may apply for a discounted familiarisation tour. It's unlikely that you can manage this arrangement unless you are already a serious player in the travel industry. DOT has an excellent network of connections worldwide and will check your bona fides beforehand. It also requires both a pretrip and a post-trip briefing.

**Volunteers & Project Employees** If you are working in Bhutan, you are not subject to the normal rules for tourists, and the agency employing you will arrange your visa. Soon after you arrive in Bhutan you will be enrolled in a cultural-orientation course for new volunteers. Volunteers are allowed two visitors a year; the visitors must be close relatives and are not subject to the tourist tariff.

## Payment Procedure

If you have arranged your trip directly with a tour operator in Bhutan and are not using an overseas agent, you must make payment directly to DOT in Bhutan. This is not a trivial process.

The most straightforward and efficient procedure is to make a US-dollar transfer to the account of the Bhutan National Bank at Citibank in New York. Transfers into this account are monitored by DOT and credited to the agent in Bhutan. Transfers should be made to **Citibank** (111 Wall St, 19th fl, New York City, NY 10043), account of **Bhutan National Bank** (ABA No 0210-0008-9, account No 36023474, Swift Code Citius 33, Chips Routing No 008). The name of the tour operator should be stated as the 'beneficiary'. If this procedure is not practical for you, contact the tour operator you have chosen to handle your trip for alternative, but more complicated, bank transfer methods.

Once you make the payment, fax a copy of the deposit details to the tour operator in Bhutan so that it can present this documentation to DOT to start the visa process.

In cases of last-minute bookings or other exceptional circumstances it is possible to pay in travellers cheques (but not cash) upon arrival in Bhutan, but this entails a visit to the DOT office to sign documents.

Note that you are paying an agency of the Bhutanese government, not the tour operator directly; therefore you have more protection against default on the part of the tour company.

## Cancellation Charges

Tour programs booked and subsequently cancelled are subject to cancellation charges. Travel insurance is an extremely worthwhile investment given that you must make full payment up front. The fee depends on how many days before the start of the tour program you cancel.

**More than 30 days** No charge
**Within 21 days** 10%
**Within 14 days** 15%

**Within seven days** 30%
**Fewer than seven days** 50%
**Without notice** 50%
**After arrival in Bhutan** 100%

## Cost of Delays

There is no daily tariff for days of delay in your arrival or departure due to weather conditions, Druk Air problems or road blocks. In cases of delayed departure, tour operators will simply charge the actual expenses for accommodation, food, transport and any other services required.

## TRAVEL LITERATURE

Not surprisingly, this little-visited, little-known, out-of-the-way kingdom hasn't generated swathes of literature from travelling wordsmiths. Historical accounts (reprinted in India and available in Thimphu) can be more entertaining than enlightening, sometimes revealing more about colonial attitudes of the writers than the Bhutanese subject. Yet they nevertheless provide an insight into traditional life, past politics and customs. More contemporary accounts reveal the life of 'everyday' Bhutan, usually through the more tolerant eye of an invited guest.

*So Close to Heaven: The Vanishing Buddhist Kingdoms of the Himalayas* by Barbara Crossette is an excellent account of Bhutan's history and culture. The author is a *New York Times* correspondent who has spent considerable time in Bhutan and other Himalayan regions. Published in 1995, the book discusses some of the modern development and political problems facing Bhutan in a geographical and historical context.

*Beyond the Sky and the Earth* by Jamie Zeppa tells the story of a Canadian teacher who fell in love with Bhutan during her teaching assignment in eastern Bhutan. Jamie offers many anecdotes and explanations of strange Bhutanese traditions as she describes her experiences, many of which you may recognise during your travels.

*Dreams of the Peaceful Dragon* by Katie Hickman is a traveller's account of a walk across Bhutan in the 1970s, before the road between Bumthang and Mongar was completed. It provides a good picture of trekking in Bhutan.

---

### TOP FIVE GREAT READS & ILLUSTRATED BOOKS

■ *The Raven Crown* by Michael Aris is the definitive history of Bhutan's monarchy. The late Aris, who lived in Bhutan with his wife (Aung San Suu Kyi) from 1967 to 1972, remains the leading Western authority on Bhutan's history. The book is lavishly illustrated with rare photographs of the early days of Bhutan that help show what a unique civilisation existed in the early 20th century.

■ *Treasures of the Thunder Dragon* by Ashi Dorji Wangmo Wangchuck, Queen of Bhutan, is an appealing and informative personal account of the kingdom from a unique perspective. Part travelogue and part memoir, it introduces Bhutan, its history, culture, tradition, folklore and more.

■ *The Hero with a Thousand Eyes* by Karma Ura is a historical novel. It is based on the life of Shingkhar Lam, a retainer who served in the court of the second, third and fourth kings of Bhutan. It offers extraordinary insight into social conditions in the early days of the 20th century and the reforms and modernisations introduced by the third king, Jigme Dorji Wangchuck.

■ *The Circle of Karma* by Kunzang Choden tells the story of a young woman's journey across Bhutan to find her destiny and rewards the reader with rich detail of everyday life and ritual.

■ *Bhutan, Kingdom of the Dragon* by Robert Dompnier is a superb coffee-table book by a French photographer who has travelled extensively throughout Bhutan.

---

**TOP FIVE MUST-SEE FILMS & DOCUMENTARIES**

These may not be at your local video shop but are worth searching for.

- *Travellers & Magicians* (Khyentse Norbu) is a whimsical tale within a tale tackling the conflict of new and old, delightfully set along twisting roads and in mysterious dark forests, both prominent features of Bhutanese travel.
- *The Cup* (Khyentse Norbu) follows the antics of trainee Tibetan monks obsessed with seeing the finals of the football World Cup.
- *The Other Final* (Johan Kramer) is a nicely crafted record of what happens when the world's bottom team, Monserratt, meets second from bottom, Bhutan; of course football is the winner.
- *Words of my Perfect Teacher* (Lesley Ann Patten) is a documentary that follows renowned reincarnate film maker Khyentse Norbu around the globe as he blesses, teaches and inspires the faithful.
- *Joanna Lumley in the Kingdom of the Thunder Dragon* (BBC) follows the Ab Fab star as she in turn follows the footsteps her grandfather, Lt Col JLR Weir, taken through Bhutan in 1931.

---

*The Blessings of Bhutan* by Russ and Blyth Carpenter is an informative and entertaining account of modern Bhutan based on the authors' intimate knowledge and carefully researched background. It's told with revealing interviews and engaging anecdotes.

*Joanna Lumley in the Kingdom of the Thunder Dragon* is based on a TV program that followed Joanna Lumley as she traced the trek her grandfather, Lt Col JLR Weir, took through Bhutan in 1931. The book is illustrated, conversational and informative.

*A Baby in a Backpack to Bhutan* by Bunty Avieson is her detailed account of spending time in Bhutan with her film-producer partner and their newborn baby. It's a light read, relaying enlightening personal encounters while revealing national characteristics.

*Sikhim and Bhutan, Twenty-one Years on the North-east Frontier* by J Claude White describes with remarkably detailed observation White's 1905 expedition to Bhutan to present the insignia of Knight Commander of the Indian Empire to Sir Ugyen Wangchuck. The book is accessible, despite its vintage.

*Political Missions to Bootan* by Ashley Eden is a pompous Victorian account of the history of Bhutan. Eden disliked the people and their habits intensely, and after reading a few pages you'll have a better idea of why Eden was treated so badly by the *penlop* (governor) of Trongsa when he arrived in Punakha.

*Lands of the Thunderbolt* by the Earl of Ronaldshay is one of the most readable accounts of a British expedition to Bhutan. The earl's full name was Lawrence John Lumley Dundas, Marquis of Zetland. He was president of the Royal Geographic Society from 1922 to 1925.

## INTERNET RESOURCES

The World Wide Web is a rich resource for travellers. You can research your trip, hunt down bargain air fares, book hotels, check on weather conditions or chat with locals and other travellers about the best places to visit (or avoid).

**Bhutan Portal** (www.bhutan.gov.bt) The official government site, with numerous links.

**Bhutan Studies** (www.bhutanstudies.org.bt) The official cultural website.

**Department of Tourism** (www.tourism.gov.bt) For the latest on travel regulations, fees and a list of approved Bhutanese tour operators.

**Druk Air** (www.drukair.com.bt) Bhutan's national airline.

**Kuensel** (www.kuenselonline.com) Bhutan's national newspaper.

**Lonely Planet** (www.lonelyplanet.com) What better place to start exploring.

# Itineraries
## CLASSIC ROUTES

### FOUR DAYS

With just four days you should count on two full days in picturesque **Paro** (p122), visiting Paro Dzong and the National Museum. On the second day, hike up to the dramatic Tiger's Nest at **Taktshang Goemba** (p128) and visit lovely Kyichu Lhakhang. After lunch make the two- to three-hour drive to Thimphu, stopping at the charming **Tamchhog Lhakhang** (p131) en route. Alternatively, move the hike to your last day, when you should be better acclimatised.

On day three you could just about squeeze in a long day trip over the Dochu La to **Punakha** (p145) but you're better off budgeting an extra day for this. The Punakha Dzong is probably the most beautiful in the country. In October and November it's worth getting up before dawn to see the Himalayan views from the pass. In March, budget an hour to walk through the gorgeous rhododendron forests above the pass. On the way back to Thimphu pop into the nearby **Chimi Lhakhang** (p145), the chapel of the 'Divine Madman', Lama Drukpa Kunley.

Day four is in **Thimphu** (p97). Go to the weekend market and visit Cheri or Tango goembas in the upper **Thimphu valley** (p115). If handicrafts are your thing, hit the Textile Museum and National Institute of Zorig Chusum. Late in the afternoon drive back to Paro; most flights depart early in the morning.

If you have limited time or money, you can get a good impression of Bhutan in just four days by concentrating on Thimphu and Paro. Try to arrange to be in Thimphu on a Saturday or Sunday to see the weekend market and avoid Paro on Monday, when the National Museum is closed.

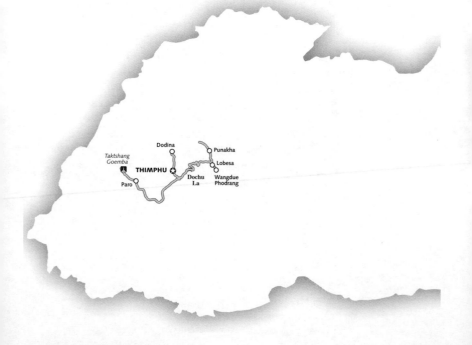

## SEVEN DAYS

For a more comprehensive look at Bhutan, invest in a week and definitely add an overnight trip over the mountains to **Punakha** (p145) and nearby **Wangdue Phodrang** (p149), overnighting at either of these towns. This way you'll have time to make the 1½-hour return hike to the nearby **Khamsum Yuelley Namgyal Chorten** (p147), as well as visit Chimi Lhakhang and the dzong at Wangdue Phodrang.

To get off the beaten track in a short period of time add an overnight trip to the **Haa valley** (p133), en route between Paro and Thimphu. The road goes over the highest motorable pass in Bhutan, the Cheli La, and in October it's worth including a couple of hours hiking to get fine views from just above the pass. Arrive in Haa at lunchtime, and spend an afternoon and maybe the next morning exploring the Juneydrak Hermitage and **Chundu Lhakhang** (p134), before continuing on to **Thimphu** (p97).

Figure on two days in **Paro** (p122), including visits to Taktshang, Kyichu Lhakhang and Drukyel Dzong in the Paro valley, and a full day (or two) in Thimphu. See the previous itinerary for more on what to see in Paro and Thimphu.

If you don't visit Haa, you might be able to add on a day trip to the **Phobjikha valley** (p152), especially worthwhile in winter (October to March) when the valley's black-necked cranes are roosting.

At some point during your trip ask your guide to arrange that quintessential experience, a Bhutanese hot-stone bath, available in most tourist hotels (for a charge). If you're lucky you may also be able to catch a weekend archery tournament, most likely in Thimphu.

A week gives you more time to get a feel for Bhutanese culture and enables you to get off the beaten track in the Haa or Phobjikha valleys, while still seeing the major dzongs and monasteries of western Bhutan. It's worth spending the extra money for another day or two – after all, when are you next going to be in Bhutan?

## TEN DAYS

A 10-day itinerary should allow you two or three days in **Bumthang** (p165), before you have to turn back to Paro. Follow the previous itineraries for the first four or five days.

A night in the **Phobjikha valley** (p152) will give you a chance to see Gangte Goemba and also view the rare and endangered black-necked cranes. If you like explore places on foot then budget an extra half-day's hiking at Phobjikha

From Phobjikha it's a day's drive over the Pele La to the superb dzong at **Trongsa** (p163) and on to Jakar in Bumthang. Leave early, as there's lots to see en route, including the Nepali-style **Chendebji Chorten** (p161).

If you have two days in Bumthang spend one day doing a loop in the **Chokhor valley** (p171), taking in the Jampey Lhakhang, Kurjey Lhakhang and Tamshing Goemba. Day two here should be spent exploring the **Tang valley** (p177), visiting the Burning Lake at Membartsho and Ogyen Chholing Museum. If you have time, overnight in the Ogyen Chholing Guest House and hike back via Gamling.

The Bumthang valley is another good place for some **hiking** (see p170) so budget half a day to stretch your legs after a week's driving. From Jakar it's a two-day drive back to Paro, so sleep at **Wangdue Phodrang** (p149) and visit its impressive dzong.

If you intend to visit India in conjunction with Bhutan, instead of flying consider driving from Thimphu or Paro to **Phuentsholing** (p156), which will add a day to the itinerary. From here you are only a few hours from Darjeeling, Kalimpong and Sikkim, as well as the airport at Bagdogra, which has frequent flights to Delhi and Kolkata.

A longer program of 10 days will allow you two full days in Bumthang with overnight stops in Paro, Thimphu and Wangdue Phodrang and short stops in Punakha and Trongsa as you drive through. Fourteen days will let you see the same places in more detail and at a much more relaxed pace. You could then even include the two-day Bumthang Cultural trek.

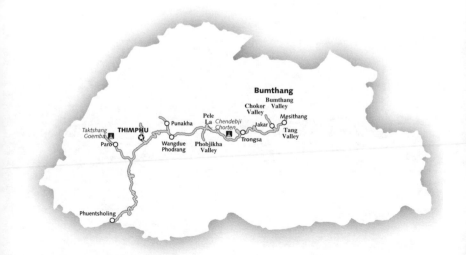

# ROAD LESS TRAVELLED

## THE EAST

This wide-ranging itinerary takes you from one end of Bhutan to the other, well away from the main tourist itineraries. It's a particularly great trip if you're interested in traditional weaving. You'll need to arrange an Indian visa before you arrive in Bhutan.

It takes *at least* two weeks to make a trip out to the little-visited far east. There's certainly a *loooot* of driving involved but then getting there is half the fun! With this itinerary you avoid the long drive back to Paro by exiting Bhutan at Samdrup Jongkhar. Follow the earlier itineraries as far as Bumthang, from where you can see the highlights of the east in five or six days. Expect to be driving for up to five hours a day while in eastern Bhutan.

From Bumthang, day one takes you on a dramatic drive over the **Thrumshing La** (p184) to **Mongar** (p185). Stay here two nights by making a scenic day trip up to remote **Lhuentse** (p187), pausing to visit the dzong and hike 45 minutes up to the traditional weaving village of **Khoma** (p188).

Day three takes you on to **Trashigang** (p190), with a two-or three-hour detour to **Drametse Goemba** (p189), Bhutan's most important Nyingma monastery.

Figure on two nights at Trashigang, with another great day excursion to **Trashi Yangtse** (p195), with stops en route at the pilgrimage site of **Gom Kora** (p193), the old Trashi Yangtse dzong and the Nepali-style Chorten Kora. March and April bring two important pilgrimage festivals to this region.

From Trashigang it's a six-hour winding drive down to the plains at steamy **Samdrup Jongkhar** (p198); stop to check out traditional weaving at Khaling's National Handloom Development Centre. From Samdrup Jongkhar, take a three-hour taxi ride to Guwahati then fly to Kolkata, Delhi or Bangkok, or take the overnight train to West Bengal for Darjeeling and the Nepal border.

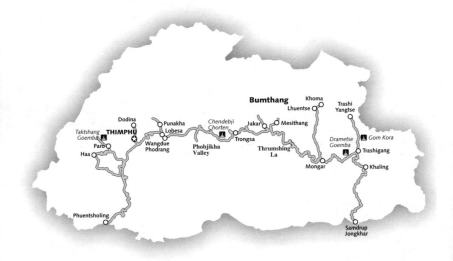

# TAILORED TRIPS

## FESTIVALS

Most people try to time their trip with one of Bhutan's colourful tsechus, or dance festivals. You can expect mask dancing, lots of colourful costumes, and superb photo opportunities, but also lots of tourists and busier than normal flights and hotels. See p247 for the dates of the major festivals.

By far the most popular festival is the spring-time **Paro tsechu** (p122) in March or April. It is perhaps a little too popular with groups, and you'll need to make flight and hotel bookings months in advance.

A less-busy alternative is the **Ura yakchoe** (p179), though the western dates are notoriously changeable here so it's best to include a couple of days' buffer on either side of the predicted date. Camping is a good idea here.

The **Punakha domchoe** (p147) is one of Bhutan's most unusual festivals, in February or March, just after the important Losar new year festival.

The **Jampey Lhakhang drup** (p172) in October/ November coincides with near perfect weather and so is again popular with groups. The **Thimphu** and **Wangdue Phodrang tsechus** also take place during great weather.

The **Kurjey tsechu** (p173) in June/July isn't the best time of year to visit weather-wise (expect lots of rain), but sees few tourists and you can hit the nearby Nimalung tsechu at the same time.

## TREKKING

The best way to experience Bhutan is without doubt on foot, especially if you can combine a trek with a major tsechu and add on a visit to Paro and Thimphu. You really need at least a week if you want to trek in Bhutan. The best months are October and November (for mountain views) and March (for rhododendron blooms).

The six-day **Druk Path trek** (p212) from Paro to Thimphu is a short and relatively simple trek, though it does spend two nights at a high elevation.

The eight- or nine-day **Jhomolhari trek** (p216) offers some of the best high-mountain scenery in Bhutan, crossing a high (4800m) pass. An excellent alternative is to do only the first three days of this trek to Jhomolhari base camp, spend a day exploring, then return to Paro via the same route. This avoids the high passes but still provides spectacular mountain views and visits to highland villages and yak pastures.

Perhaps the best combination of scenery and culture is the 14-day **Laya–Gasa trek** (p222), which offers superb mountain views of Jho-molhari, the historically interesting regions of Lingzhi and Gasa, and the unique culture and people of Laya.

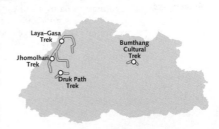

If you are limited for time and don't feel up to a high-altitude trek then the **Bumthang Cultural trek** (p230) can be done in just two days and takes you past several interesting monasteries and through gorgeous forest.

# Snapshot

Change is afoot in Bhutan. Despite centuries of self-imposed isolation, the Himalayan kingdom has opened the Pandora's Box of modernisation and there's no turning back now. Pepsi Cola built a bottling plant in 1997, 60 channels of satellite TV arrived in 1999 and there will soon be more mobile phones in the kingdom than land lines. Bhutanese can even get a Dzongkha font for their Microsoft Windows (though there are still no traffic lights in the country)!

Political change also looms large on the Himalayan horizon. In 2005 Bhutan's much-loved king announced that he would abdicate in 2008 in favour of the crown prince and set about drawing up the country's first ever constitution to prepare for democratic elections that same year. This gradual ceding of royal power in favour of a parliamentary democracy stands in stark contrast to that other Himalayan monarch, Nepal's King Gyanendra.

Yet Bhutan is very aware of the dangers of modernisation and the government continues to assume a very protective role in Bhutanese society. Bhutan was the world's first country to ban not only smoking in public places but also the very sale of tobacco. The wrestling channel and MTV are also banned, as are western-style advertising billboards and plastic bags.

Due to its small size and precarious geopolitical position, squeezed in between the giants of China and India (and with the annexing of Tibet and Sikkim firmly in mind), Bhutan has decided that the only way forward, the only way to ensure its very survival and sovereignty, is to protect its unique culture and environment. Issues of sustainable development, education and health care, and environmental and cultural preservation are therefore at the forefront of policy making, as are the tenets of Buddhism, which forms the base of Bhutan's legal code. Every development project is scrutinised and may be slowed or stopped if it affronts religious faith or adversely affects the environment. Bhutan's strict regulation of limited high-value, low-impact tourism is a perfect example of this. Bhutan is one of the few places on earth so far untouched by the reach of globalisation and where compassion is favoured over capitalism

Still, despite the abundance of hydroelectric power, a large proportion of Bhutanese don't have access to electricity or running water and per-capita income remains one of the world's lowest. In 2004, 6000 Bhutanese troops flushed out militants from Bhutanese jungles bordering India, destroying 30 camps and incurring the wrath of Assamese separatist movements. The issue of the 110,000 refugees languishing in camps in Eastern Nepal is far from being resolved.

Bhutan remains a unique and special country. For better or worse, the next few years, and 2008 in particular, look set to bring profound changes to Bhutan. The challenge ahead for the government is to bring the benefits of the modern world to Bhutan without undermining the very things that Bhutanese cherish about their unique culture.

## FAST FACTS

Population: 634,982 (2005 Census)

Life expectancy: 63

Area: 38,392 sq km – similar size to Switzerland

Number of tourists visiting Bhutan in 2005: 13,600

Human Development Index ranking: 134 out of 177 countries

Forest cover: 72.5%

Percentage of population involved in agriculture: 69%

Percentage of Bhutan's land used for agriculture: 7.8%

Tourism is the third largest provider of foreign exchange in Bhutan, earning it US$18.5 million in 2005

The export of hydroelectricity to India provides 32% of government revenue

# History

Bhutan's early history is steeped in Buddhist folklore and mythology; it features tremendous deeds and beings with supernatural powers. It's said that a saint who had the ability to appear in eight different forms, one of them being Guru Rinpoche, visited Bhutan on a flying tiger and left the imprint of his body and his hat on rocks. School texts describe demons that threatened villages and destroyed temples until captured through magic and converted to Buddhism. Tales abound of ghosts who destroyed temples, and angels who rebuilt them.

Researchers have attached dates to many events, though these often do not seem to fit together into a credible and accurate chronology. When reading Bhutanese history, it's easier to let your imagination flow. Try visualising the spirit of the happenings rather than rationalising events as historical truth. This will, in part, help prepare you for a visit to Bhutan, where spirits, ghosts, yetis, medicine men, and lamas reincarnated in three different bodies are accepted as a part of daily life.

Bhutan's medieval and modern history is better documented than its ancient history, but is no less exotic. This is a time of warlords, feuds, giant fortresses and castles, with intrigue, treachery, fierce battles and extraordinary pageantry

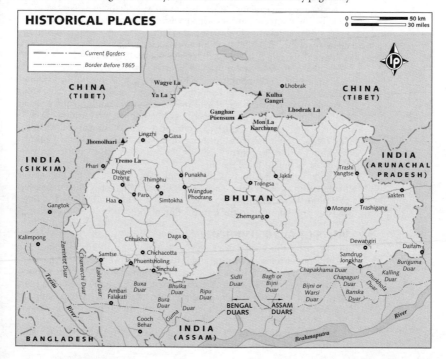

HISTORICAL PLACES

**6th Century**

The animist Bon religion is established in several valleys of what is now Bhutan

**7th Century**

The first Buddhist temples are in Bhutan, such as Kyichu Lhakhang (AD 659), near Paro all playing feature roles. The country's recent history begins with a hereditary monarchy that was founded in the 20th century and continued the country's policy of isolationism. It was not until the leadership of the third king that Bhutan emerged from its medieval heritage of serfdom and seclusion. Until the 1960s the country had no national currency, no telephones, no schools, no hospitals, no postal service and certainly no tourists. Development efforts have now produced all these – plus a national assembly, airport, roads and a national system of health care. Despite the speed of modernisation, Bhutan has maintained a policy of careful, controlled growth in an effort to preserve its national identity. The government has cautiously accepted tourism, TV and the internet and is set to embark on perhaps its biggest challenge – democracy.

## EARLY HISTORY

www.ctf.gov.bt is the Cultural Trust Fund website and is dedicated to the preservation and promotion of Bhutan's rich cultural heritage.

Many of the important events in the country's early history involved saints and religious leaders and were therefore chronicled only in scriptures. Most of these original documents were destroyed in fires in the printing works of Sonagatsel in 1828 and in Punakha Dzong in 1832. Much of what was left in the old capital of Punakha was lost in an earthquake in 1897 and more records were lost when Paro Dzong burned in 1907. Therefore much of the early history of Bhutan relies on reports from British explorers, on legend and folklore, and the few manuscripts that escaped these disasters.

Archaeological evidence suggests Bhutan was inhabited as early as 1500–2000 BC by nomadic herders who lived in low-lying valleys in winter and moved their animals to high pastures in summer. Many Bhutanese still live this way today. The valleys of Bhutan provided relatively easy access across the Himalaya, and it is believed that the Manas River valley was used as a migration route from India to Tibet.

Some of the early inhabitants of Bhutan were followers of Bon (known as Ben cho in Bhutan), the animistic tradition that was the main religion throughout the Himalayan region before the advent of Buddhism. It is believed that the Bon religion was introduced in Bhutan in the 6th century AD.

Buddhism was probably first introduced to parts of Bhutan as early as the 2nd century, although most historians agree that the first Buddhist temples were built in the 7th century AD. See the boxed text, p129, for the story of the construction of these temples.

The kingdom of Cooch Behar, in what is now West Bengal, influenced Bhutan from the early days. The rulers of Cooch Behar established themselves in Bhutan, but their influence faded in the 7th century AD as the influence of Tibet grew along with the introduction of Buddhism.

## VISITS OF GURU RINPOCHE

In AD 746 Sendha Gyab (also known as Sindhu Raja), the king of Bumthang, became possessed by a demon, and it required a powerful tantric master to exorcise it. He sent for the great teacher Padmasambhava, better known as Guru Rinpoche (Precious Master). The Guru captured the demon and converted it to Buddhism. For good measure, he also converted the king and his rival, restoring the country to peace. For a complete description of Guru Rinpoche's efforts, see the boxed text, p173.

The Guru returned to Bhutan via Singye Dzong in Lhuentse and visited the districts of Bumthang, Mongar and Lhuentse. He was returning from

Guru Rinpoche (Padmasambhava) visits Bhutan and is credited with the subduction of evil spirits and further conversions to Buddhism

The Tibetan Buddhist prince Tsangma is banished from Tibet to eastern Bhutan

Tibet where, at the invitation of Trisong Detsen, he had introduced Nyingma Buddhism and overcame the demons that were obstructing the construction of Samye Monastery. At Gom Kora, in eastern Bhutan, he left a body print and an impression of his head with a hat. He flew in the form of Dorji Drakpo (one of his eight manifestations) to Taktshang in Paro on a flaming tigress, giving the famous Taktshang monastery the name 'Tiger's Nest' (see Taktshang Goemba, p128).

It is believed that Guru Rinpoche also made a third visit to Bhutan during the reign of Muthri Tsenpo (764–817), the son of Trisong Detsen.

> The most authoritative and complete history of Bhutan in English is Michael Aris' *Bhutan, the Early History of a Himalayan Kingdom.*

## MEDIEVAL PERIOD

The grandson of Trisong Detsen, Langdharma, ruled Tibet from AD 836 to 842. He banned Buddhism, destroyed religious institutions and banished his brother, Prince Tsangma, to Bhutan. It is believed that many monks fled from Tibet and took refuge in Bhutan during this period. Despite the assassination of Langdharma and the re-introduction of Buddhism, Tibet remained in political turmoil and many Tibetans migrated to western Bhutan.

Between the 9th and 17th centuries numerous ruling clans and noble families emerged in different valleys throughout Bhutan. The various local chieftains spent their energy quarrelling among themselves and with Tibet, and no important nationally recognised political figure emerged during this period.

## THE BHUTANESE FORM OF BUDDHISM

Back in Tibet, Lama Tsangpa Gyarey Yeshe Dorji (AD 1161–1211) founded a monastery in the town of Ralung, just east of Gyantse, in AD 1180. He named the monastery Druk (Dragon), after the thunder dragons that he heard in the sky as he searched for an appropriate site upon which to build a monastery. The lineage followed here was named after the monastery and became known as Drukpa Kagyu.

In the 11th and 12th centuries there was a further large influx of Tibetans into Bhutan. Many Drukpa lamas left Tibet because of persecution at the hands of the followers of the rival Gelug lineage. Most of these lamas settled in western Bhutan and established branches of Drukpa monastic orders. Western Bhutan became loosely united through the weight of their teachings. Charismatic lamas emerged as de facto leaders of large portions of the west, while the isolated valleys of eastern and central Bhutan remained separate feudal states.

One of the most important of these lamas was Gyalwa Lhanangpa, who founded the Lhapa Kagyu lineage. He established the Tango Goemba (monastery; p115) on a hill above the northern end of the Thimphu valley and established a system of forts in Bhutan similar to the dzongs found in Tibet.

Lama Phajo Drukgom Shigpo (1184–1251), a disciple of Lama Tsangpa Gyarey, came to Bhutan from Ralung and defeated Lama Lhanangpa. He and his companions established the small Dho-Ngen Dzong on the west bank of the Wang Chhu and took control of the Tango Goemba. Lama Phajo is credited with establishing the Bhutanese form of Buddhism by converting many people to the Drukpa Kagyu school (see p70). Other lamas resented his presence and success, and they tried to kill him through magic spells. Phajo turned the spells back on the lamas, destroying several of their monasteries.

Between the 13th and 16th centuries, the Drukpa Kagyu lineage flourished and Bhutan adopted a separate religious identity. More lamas from Ralung

| 9th Century | 10th Century |
| --- | --- |
| Many Tibetan Buddhists take up refuge in Bhutan as the Bon-po gain power and Buddhists are persecuted | Further turmoil in Tibet sees various schools of Tibetan Buddhism established in Bhutan |

## GURU RINPOCHE

Guru Rinpoche is also known by the names Padmasambhava, Precious Master and Ugyen Rinpoche. *Padma* is a Sanskrit word meaning 'lotus flower' and is the origin of the Tibetan and Bhutanese name Pema; *sambhava* means 'born from'. He is a historical figure of the 8th century and his birth was predicted by Sakyamuni, the Historical Buddha. He is regarded as the second Buddha and had miraculous powers, including the ability to subdue demons and evil spirits.

Guru Rinpoche is credited with many magical deeds and is regarded as the founder of Nyingma Buddhism. He is one of the most important of Bhutan's religious figures and his visit to Bumthang is recognised as the true introduction of Buddhism to Bhutan. He left an impression of his body on the rock upon which he meditated near the head of the Choskhor valley in Bumthang. On this site the temple of Kurjey Lhakhang was built, and Guru Rinpoche's body print can still be seen there. His statue appears in almost all temples built after his visit to Bhutan in AD 746.

His birthplace was Uddiyana in the Swat valley of what is now Pakistan. Uddiyana is known in Dzongkha as Ugyen, and some texts refer to him as Ugyen Rinpoche. He travelled in various manifestations throughout Tibet, Nepal and Bhutan, meditating in numerous caves, which are regarded as important 'power places'. He preserved his teachings and wisdom by concealing them in the form of *terma* (hidden treasures) to be found by enlightened treasure discoverers called *tertons*. His biographer, Yeshe Chhogyel, urges us not to regard Guru Rinpoche as a normal human being, because by doing so we will fail to perceive even a fraction of his enlightened qualities.

Bhutanese and Tibetans differ over a few aspects of his life; the following description reflects the Bhutanese tradition.

### Eight Manifestations

The Guru is depicted in eight forms (Guru Tshengay). These are not really different incarnations, but representations of his eight main initiations, in which he assumed a new personality that was symbolised by a new name and appearance. Because initiation is equivalent to entering a new life, it is a form of rebirth. The eight forms follow the chronology of Guru Rinpoche's life.

He emerged as an eight-year-old from a blue lotus on Lake Danakosha in Uddiyana, and was adopted by King Indrabodhi. Then he was called Tshokye Dorji (diamond thunderbolt born from a lake). He later renounced his kingdom and went to receive teachings and ordination from the master Prabhahasti in the cave of Maratrika (near the village of Harishe in eastern Nepal), becoming Sakya Senge (lion of the Sakya clan). In this form he is identified with Sakyamuni, the Historical Buddha.

After studying the teachings of the Vajrayana and mastering the sciences of all Indian *pandits*, he obtained full realisation and was able to see all the gods and deities. Then he was called Loden

were invited to Bhutan to teach and build monasteries and many Bhutanese nobles are descended from Lama Phajo.

Among the visitors to Bhutan during this period was Lama Ngawang Chhogyel (1465–1540). He made several trips and was often accompanied by his sons, who established several goembas. They are credited with building the temple of Druk Choeding in Paro and Pangri Zampa and Hongtsho goembas near Thimphu. Another visitor was Lama Drukpa Kunley, the 'divine madman', who established Chime Lhakhang near Punakha (see p136).

Between the 11th and 16th centuries numerous *terma* (sacred texts) hidden by Guru Rinpoche in caves, rocks and lakes were discovered, as he had prophesied, by tantric lamas called *tertons*. The tertons were important

| | |
|---|---|
| Foundation of Druk Monastery in Ralung (Tibet) and beginning of Drukpa Kagyu school | Gyalwa Lhanangpa establishes Tango Goemba in Thimphu valley |

Chogsey (possessor of supreme knowledge). He took as his consort Mandarava, the daughter of the king of Zahor (in the Mandi district of Himachal Pradesh, India). This enraged the king, who condemned them both to be burned, but through his powers the Guru turned the pyre into a lake and converted the kingdom to Buddhism. Then he was called Pema Jugney (Padmasambhava).

He returned to Uddiyana to convert it to Buddhism, but was recognised as the prince who had renounced his kingdom and was burned, along with his consort. He was not consumed by the fire and appeared sitting upon a lotus in a lake. This lake is Rewalsar, also called Tsho Pema (the lotus lake), in Himachal Pradesh, and is an important pilgrimage spot. His father, King Indrabodhi, offered him the kingdom and he became Padma Gyalpo (the lotus king), remaining for 13 years and establishing Buddhism.

When he was preaching in the eight cremation grounds to the *khandromas* (female celestial beings), he caught the life force of the evil deities and he turned them into protectors of Buddhism. Then he was called Nyima Yeozer (sunbeam of enlightenment). Later, 500 heretic masters tried to destroy the doctrine of Buddha, but he vanquished them through the power of his words and brought down a thunderbolt destroying the non-Buddhists in a flash of hail and lightning. He was then called Sengye Dradrok (roaring lion).

When he came to Bhutan the second time and visited Singye Dzong in Kurtoe and Taktshang in Paro, he was in the form of Dorji Drakpo (fierce thunderbolt). He subdued all the evil spirits hindering Buddhism and blessed them as guardians of the doctrine. In this form, Guru Rinpoche rides a tigress.

### Statues of Guru Rinpoche

Most statues of Guru Rinpoche are in his manifestation as Padmasambhava, wearing royal robes and holding the insignia of spiritual realisation. His hat is known as the 'lotus cap' and is adorned with a crescent moon, the sun and a small flame-like protuberance that signifies the union of lunar and solar forces. The hat is surmounted by a *dorji* (thunderbolt) and also an eagle's feather, which represents the Guru's soaring mind, penetrating the highest realms of reality.

Often the statues of Padmasambhava are flanked by statues of two female devotees. These are the Indian princess Mandarava, the lady of wisdom, and the Tibetan khandroma Yeshe Chhogyel, who is regarded as an incarnation of Saraswati, the goddess of knowledge. She was gifted with such a perfect memory that she was able to remember the Guru's every word and became his sole biographer. She is depicted as a white, heavenly being with traditional ornaments and flying scarves; Mandarava is usually depicted as an Indian hill princess.

Guru Rinpoche's celestial abode or paradise is a copper-coloured mountain named Zangto Pelri. The guardians of the four directions guard the four gates, and in the centre is a three-roofed pagoda, with Guru Rinpoche enthroned on the ground level, flanked by his two consorts.

religious figures; the best known of these was Pema Lingpa, who recovered his first *terma* from the lake of Membartsho near Bumthang in 1475. Pema Lingpa constructed several monasteries in Bumthang and is one of the most important figures in Bhutanese history (see p175).

## RISE OF THE ZHABDRUNG

By the 16th century the political arena was still fragmented between many local chiefs, each controlling his own territory and engaging in petty feuds with the others. There were numerous monasteries competing for superiority and the lamas of western Bhutan were working to extend their influence to the east of the country.

*The Divine Madman* by Keith Dowman is a wonderful translation of the poems and works of the extraordinary Lama Drukpa Kunley.

| 1184–1251 | 1433 |
|---|---|
| Lifespan of Lama Phajo Drukgom Shigpo, who establishes Drukpa Kagyu as the dominant school of Buddhism in Bhutan | Thangtong Gyalpo, the Iron Bridge Lama, visits Bhutan from Tibet in search of iron ore and builds eight bridges |

Everything changed in 1616 when Ngawang Namgyal (1594–1651) came to Bhutan from Ralung, the original home of the Drukpa Kagyu in Tibet. In his early years he studied religion and art and is said to have been a skilled painter. He was a descendent of Tsangpa Gyarey, the founder of Ralung. At age 12 he was recognised as the reincarnation of Pema Karpo, the prince-abbot of Ralung Monastery (see p71). This recognition was challenged by the ruler of another principality in Tibet, and Ngawang Namgyal found his position at Ralung very difficult. When he was 23, the protective deity Yeshe Goenpo (Mahakala) appeared to him in the form of a raven and directed him south to Bhutan. He travelled through Laya and Gasa and spent time at Pangri Zampa (Thimphu), which was established by his great-great-grandfather, Ngawang Chhogyel.

As Ngawang Namgyal travelled throughout western Bhutan teaching, his political strength increased. Soon he established himself as the religious ruler of Bhutan with the title Zhabdrung Rinpoche (precious jewel at whose feet one prostrates), thus becoming the first in the line of *zhabdrungs*. He built the first of the present system of dzongs at Simtokha, just south of present-day Thimphu. While the primary function of earlier Bhutanese dzongs was to serve as invincible fortresses, the Simtokha Dzong also housed a monastic body and administrative facilities, as well as fulfilling its defensive function. This combination of civil, religious and defensive functions became the model for all of Bhutan's later dzongs.

The Zhabdrung's rule was opposed by the leaders of rival Buddhist lineages within Bhutan. They formed a coalition of five lamas under the leadership of Lama Palden and attacked Simtokha Dzong in 1629. This attack was repelled, but the coalition then aligned itself with a group of Tibetans and continued its opposition. The Zhabdrung's militia defeated the Tibetans on several occasions, and the influence of the rival lineages diminished. Finally, after forging an alliance with the brother of King Singye Namgyal of Ladakh, the Zhabdrung's forces defeated the Tibetans and their coalition ally. In 1639 an agreement was reached with the Tsang Desi in Tibet recognising Zhabdrung Ngawang Namgyal as the supreme authority in Bhutan.

The Zhabdrung further enhanced his power by establishing relations with neighbouring kings, including Rama Shah, the king of Nepal, and Raja Padmanarayan of Cooch Behar. It was at this time that the king of Ladakh granted the Zhabdrung a number of sites in western Tibet for the purpose of meditation and worship. These included Diraphuk, Nyanri and Zuthulphuk on the slopes of the holy Mt Kailash. The Bhutanese administration of these monasteries continued until the Chinese takeover of Tibet in 1959. Other Tibetan monasteries that came under Bhutanese administration were Rimpung, Doba, Khochag, and De Dzong, all near Gartok. A Bhutanese lama was sent as representative to Nepal, and Bhutanese monasteries were established at Bodhnath (Chorten Jaro Khasho) and Swayambhunath in Kathmandu. Bhutan administered Swayambhunath until after the Nepal–Tibet war of 1854–56, when it was retaken by Nepal on the suspicion that Bhutan had helped the Tibetans.

During his reign, Zhabdrung Ngawang Namgyal ordered the construction of many monasteries and dzongs throughout Bhutan. Of these, the dzongs at Simtokha, Paro, Wandue Phodrang, Punakha and Trongsa are still standing. He established the first sangha (community of monks) at Cheri Goemba near Thimphu. When Punakha Dzong was completed in 1635, the sangha was

> Although known as Bhutan to the outside world, the country has been known as Druk Yul, 'land of the thunder dragon', to its inhabitants since the 13th century.

---

**1450–1521**
The much-heralded life of Pema Lingpa, the most important *terton* (discoverer of sacred texts and artefacts) in Bhutan

**1455–1529**
Lifespan of Lama Drukpa Kunley, who travelled throughout Bhutan preaching an unconventional approach to Buddhism and life

moved there and became the *dratshang* (central monk body), headed by a supreme abbot called the Je Khenpo.

## INVASIONS FROM TIBET

In the meantime, strife continued in Tibet, between the Nyingma (known as 'red hat') group of Buddhists and the Gelugpas ('yellow hat'); the latter are headed by the Dalai Lama. The Mongol chief Gushri Khan, a patron of the Dalai Lama, led his army in an attack on Tibet's Tsang province, where he overthrew the Rinpong dynasty and established the supremacy of the Gelugpas in the region.

In 1644 the Mongols and Tibetans, who were used to the extremely high plains of Tibet, launched an assault from Lhobrak into Bumthang, but found themselves overpowered by the forests and heat of Bhutan. Zhabdrung Nga-wang Namgyal personally led the successful resistance and several Tibetan officers and a large number of horses were captured. Much of the armour and many weapons that were taken during this battle are on display in Punakha Dzong. Drukgyel Dzong was built at the head of Paro valley in 1647 to com-memorate the victory and to prevent any further Tibetan infiltration.

One of the strongest of Tibet's Dalai Lamas was the 'Great Fifth'. During his administration, he became jealous of the growing influence of the rival Drukpas on his southern border and mounted further invasions into Bhutan in 1648 and 1649. Each attempt was launched via Phari in Tibet, from where the Great Fifth's forces crossed the 5000m-high Tremo La into Paro valley. They were repelled, and again the Bhutanese captured large amounts of ar-mour, weapons and other spoils. Some of this booty may still be seen in the National Museum in Paro. Legend relates that the Zhabdrung built a *thos,* a heap of stones representing the kings, or guardians of the four directions, to subdue the Tibetan army. You may not find this one, but similar *thos* can still be seen in the courtyards of many of Bhutan's goembas.

Ngawang Namgyal's success in repelling the Tibetan attacks further consolidated his position as ruler. The large militia that he raised for the purpose also gave him effective control of the country. Mingyur Tenpa, who was appointed by the Zhabdrung as *penlop* (governor) of Trongsa, undertook a campaign to unite all the valleys of the central and eastern parts of the country under the Zhabdrung's rule, which he accomplished by about 1655. At this time the great dzongs of Jakar, Lhuentse, Trashi Yangtse, Shongar (now Mongar), Trashigang and Zhemgang were constructed.

## A BHUTANESE IDENTITY EMERGES

The Zhabdrung realised that Bhutan needed to differentiate itself from Tibet in order to preserve its religion and cultural identity. He devised many of Bhutan's customs, traditions and ceremonies in a deliberate effort to develop a unique cultural identity for the country.

As a revered Buddhist scholar, he had both the astuteness and authority to codify the Kagyu religious teachings into a system that was distinctively Bhu-tanese. He also defined the national dress and instituted the tsechu festival.

The Zhabdrung created a code of laws that defined the relationship be-tween the lay people and the monastic community. A system of taxes was developed; these were paid in kind in the form of wheat, buckwheat, rice, yak meat, butter, paper, timber and clothing. The people were subject to a system of compulsory labour for the construction of trails, dzongs, temples

www.bhutan.gov.bt is the government of Bhutan's portal and has links to the draft constitution, Gross National Happiness (GNH) and background to government operations and policy.

| 1616 | 1627 |
|---|---|
| The first zhabdrung, Ngawang Namgyal, arrives in Bhutan from Ralung, Tibet | Portuguese Jesuits, Fathers Cacella and Cabral are the first European visitors to Bhutan |

and bridges. These practices lasted almost unchanged until the third king eliminated them in 1956.

In the 1640s the Zhabdrung created the system of Choesi, the separation of the administration of the country into two offices. The religious and spiritual aspects of the country were handled by the Zhabdrung. The political, administrative and foreign-affairs aspects of the government were to be handled by the *desi* (secular ruler), who was elected to the post. The office of the Zhabdrung theoretically had greater power, including the authority to sign documents relating to an important matter within the government. Under the system at that time, the Zhabdrung was the spiritual ruler and the Je Khenpo was the chief abbot and official head of the monastic establishment. The Je Khenpo had a status equal to the *desi* and sometimes held that office.

*A Political and Religious History of Bhutan* by CT Dorji chronicles the major personalities in the religious and political spheres Bhutan's history.

The first *desi* was Tenzin Drugyey (1591–1656), one of the monks who came with Ngawang Namgyal from Ralung Monastery. He established a system of administration throughout the country, formalising the position of *penlop* as that of provincial governor. There were initially three districts: Trongsa in the centre, Paro in the west and Dagana in the south. The *penlops* became the representatives of the central government, which was then in Punakha. There were three officers called *dzongpens* (lords of the dzong) who looked after the affairs of the subdistricts of Punakha, Thimphu and Wangdue Phodrang.

Zhabdrung Ngawang Namgyal went into retreat in Punakha Dzong in 1651. He didn't emerge again, and although it is likely that he passed away very early in the period of retreat, his death remained concealed until 1705. It is believed that the four successive *desis* who ruled during this period felt that the continued presence of the Zhabdrung was necessary to keep the country unified and Tibet at bay. Nonetheless, Tibet mounted seven attacks on Bhutan between 1656 and 1730.

In 1668 Mingyur Tenpa was enthroned as the third *desi*. He ruled for 12 years, during which time he extended the boundaries of Bhutan westwards to Kalimpong, which is now part of India.

## CIVIL WARS

When the Je Khenpo finally announced the death of the Zhabdrung in 1705, he said that three rays of light emanated from the Zhabdrung's body, representing the *ku sung thug* (body, speech and mind) of Ngawang Namgyal. This indicated that the Zhabdrung would be reincarnated in these three forms, though only the reincarnation of the Zhabdrung's mind was considered to be the head of state. Because the position of *zhabdrung* was a continuing one, it was necessary for the mind incarnation to be reborn after the death of the previous incarnation.

This structure resulted in long periods when the zhabdrung was too young to rule and the desi often became the de facto ruler. Because the *desi* was an elected position, there was considerable rivalry among various factions for the office. These factions also took advantage of uncertainty over which of the three incarnations of the Zhabdrung was the 'true' incarnation. None of the successive incarnations had the personal charisma or political astuteness of Ngawang Namgyal.

The next 200 years were a time of civil war, internal conflicts and political infighting. While there were only six mind incarnations of the Zhabdrung during this period, there were 55 desis. The longest-serving *desi* was the 13th incumbent, Sherab Wangchuk, who ruled for 20 years; and the most

| 1639 | 1705 |
|---|---|
| Tibet recognises Zhabdrung Ngawang Namgyal as the supreme authority in Bhutan | The much-delayed announcement of the demise of the Zhabdrung Ngawang Namgyal |

important was the fourth, Gyalse Tenzin Rabgye, who ruled from 1680 to 1694. Few of the rulers finished their term; 22 desis were assassinated or deposed by rivals.

The political situation became so unstable that some of the rival factions appealed to the Tibetans for assistance. In 1729 and 1730 Tibet took advantage of Bhutan's instability and invaded the country three times. The lamas in Tibet initiated a truce that eventually ended the hostilities. The rival Bhutanese factions submitted their case to the Chinese emperor in Beijing for mediation. But the issue was only finally resolved when several of the Bhutanese protagonists died, leaving the currently recognised mind incarnation of the Zhabdrung as the ruler. At the same time, formal diplomatic relations were established between Bhutan and Tibet, which the late historian Michael Aris said 'helped to guarantee the fact of Bhutanese independence'.

## RELATIONS WITH COOCH BEHAR

In 1730 the 10th *desi* assisted Gya Chila, the ruler of Cooch Behar, to defeat invaders and to settle a family feud; Bhutan was then allowed to station a force in that southern kingdom. In 1768 the *desi* tried to suppress the influence of the religious establishment in Bhutan and to strengthen his own influence outside of the country. He established alliances with the Panchen Lama in Tibet and with King Prithvi Narayan Shah of Nepal. In 1772 the Bhutanese invaded Cooch Behar to help settle a feud over succession. They won, and kidnapped the crown prince and the queen of Cooch Behar. The Bhutanese also captured Raja Dhairjendra Narayan, the king of Cooch Behar, in the same year.

Several records of the early European exploration and missions to Bhutan have been reprinted by Indian publishers and are readily available in bookshops in Thimphu, Delhi and Kathmandu.

## INVOLVEMENT OF THE BRITISH

In his book, *Lands of the Thunderbolt,* the Earl of Ronaldshay wrote:

> …it was not until 1772 that the East India Company became conscious of the existence, across its northern frontier, of a meddlesome neighbour.

The first contact the British had with Bhutan was when the claimants to the throne of Cooch Behar appealed to the East India Company to help drive the Bhutanese out of their kingdom.

Because the East India Company was a strictly commercial enterprise, its officers agreed to help when the deposed ruler of Cooch Behar offered to pay half of the revenues of the state in return for assistance. In December 1772 the British governor of Bengal, Warren Hastings, sent Indian troops and guns to Cooch Behar and, despite suffering heavy losses, routed the Bhutanese and restored the king to the throne. However, Cooch Behar paid a very high price for this assistance. Not only did its rulers pay Rs50,000, but in 1773 they also signed a treaty ceding substantial powers and future revenue to the East India Company.

The 1774 East India Company expedition led by George Bogle planted potatoes wherever they went, providing a new food crop for Bhutan and a lasting legacy of this mission.

The British pushed the Bhutanese back into the hills and followed them into Bhutan. The British won another major battle in January 1773 at the garrison of Chichacotta (now Khithokha) in the hills east of what is now Phuentsholing. A second battle was fought near Kalimpong in April 1773. The Bhutanese troops were personally led by the 16th *desi* but, after the second defeat, he was deposed by a coup d'état.

| 1772 | 1774 |
| --- | --- |
| Bhutan invades Cooch Behar and kidnaps its king. The British East India company agrees to assist Cooch Behar in return for payment | George Bogle leads a trade mission to Bhutan and Tibet, and plants potatoes in Bhutanese soil |

---

**THE 1897 EARTHQUAKE**

One of the most devastating natural disasters in Bhutan was the great Assam earthquake that occurred at 5.06pm on 12 June 1897. The epicentre was about 80km south of Bhutan in Assam and had an estimated magnitude of 8.7 on the Richter scale. The earthquake destroyed the dzongs in Punakha and Lingzhi and severely damaged the dzongs of Wangdue Phodrang, Trongsa, Jakar and the *utse* (central tower) of Trashi Chhoe. Paro Dzong escaped largely unharmed.

---

## FIRST TREATY WITH THE BRITISH

The new *desi* wanted to make an agreement with the British and appealed to the Panchen Lama in Tibet for assistance. The Panchen Lama then wrote what the British described as 'a very friendly and intelligent letter' that was carried to Calcutta (now called Kolkata) by an Indian pilgrim. The British, although more eager to establish relations with Tibet than to solve the issue of Bhutan, agreed to comply with the Tibetan request. The result was a peace treaty between Bhutan and the British signed in Calcutta on 25 April 1774. In this treaty the *desi* agreed to respect the territory of the East India Company and to allow the company to cut timber in the forests of Bhutan. The British returned all the territory they had captured.

The East India Company wasted no time in sending a trade mission to Tibet. In May 1774 George Bogle led a party through Bhutan to Tibet. The group spent a few weeks in Thimphu waiting for permission to go to Tibet, and eventually reached the seat of the Panchen Lama in Tashilhunpo in October. The written account of this mission provides the first Western view into the isolated kingdom of Bhutan (for more information, see p36).

The British in India attached their own names, derived from Sanskrit, to the titles used by the Bhutanese. They called the *zhabdrung* the '*dharma raja*', and the *desi* '*deb raja*'. Raja is Sanskrit for 'king'; therefore the *dharma raja* was the king who ruled by religious law and the *deb raja* was the king who delivered wellbeing or material gifts. *Deb* is a corruption of the Sanskrit word *deva* or *devata* (the giver).

In the next few years two small expeditions travelled to Bhutan. Dr Alexander Hamilton led a group to Punakha and Thimphu in 1776, and another in 1777, to discuss Bhutanese claims to Ambari Falakati and to consolidate transit rights through Bhutan to Tibet that had been negotiated by Bogle's mission.

## THE PROBLEM OF THE DUARS

*Lands of the Thunderbolt, Sikhim, Chumbi & Bhutan by the Earl of Ronaldshay is a very readable, very British account of regional history and an expedition to Bhutan in the early 20th century.*

The political intrigue and civil wars continued in Bhutan, and there were numerous skirmishes over boundaries and trading rights. The British were engaged in the Burmese war of 1825–26. As a result of this war, the British gained control of Assam, the territory that forms the eastern half of Bhutan's southern border.

The area of plains between the Brahmaputra River up to and including the lowest of the hills of Bhutan was known as the *duars,* which means doors or gates (see p84). The western part of this area, known as the Bengal Duars, had been annexed by the third *desi*, Mingyur Tenpa, in the late 17th century and the Bhutanese considered it their territory. The eastern part, the Assam Duars, had long been administered in a complex rental agreement between Bhutan and Assam.

---

| 1783 | 1826 |
|---|---|
| Captain Samuel Turner leads a grand British Raj expedition to Bhutan and Tibet | Bhutan and Britain start bickering over the sovereignty of the duars (lowest Bhutanese hills) |

After the Burmese war, the British took over the peculiar land rental arrangement for the Assam Duars, along with what were described as 'very unsatisfactory relations of the Assamese with the Bhutanese'. Major disagreements between Britain and Bhutan resulted. In 1826 the British and Bhutanese came into conflict over the ownership of the *duars*. Other than the area's strategic importance, the British were attracted to the *duars* because they were excellent tea-growing country. However, they were also a malarial jungle, and the British had a very difficult time keeping their troops healthy.

Bhutan's existing agreement with the Assamese allowed the British to occupy the region from July to November, and the Bhutanese to occupy it the remainder of the year in return for payment in horses, gold, knives, blankets, musk and other articles. The new arrangement meant that Bhutan sent the payment to the British, who accused the Bhutanese of delivering piebald horses and other defective goods. The Bhutanese insisted that middlemen working for the British had substituted inferior goods.

Disagreements over payments and administration escalated. In 1836 the British mounted an attack on Dewangiri (now Deothang), in the east, to force the surrender of fugitives who had committed crimes in British territory. The *dzongpen* refused to comply and attacked the British detachment. The British won that battle and annexed Dewangiri and the entire Banska Duar. The following year, however, at the request of the *desi,* they agreed to return control of the *duar* to the Bhutanese.

The British annexed the two easternmost *duars* in 1840 and the rest of the Assam Duars in September 1841, agreeing to pay Bhutan an annual compensation of Rs10,000. Lord Auckland wrote to the *deb* and *dharma rajas* that the British were:

> …compelled by an imperative sense of duty to occupy the whole of the duars without any reference to your Highnesses' wishes, as I feel assured that it is the only course which is likely to hold out a prospect of restoring peace and prosperity to that tract of country.

Perhaps more revealing is a letter from Colonel Jenkins, the governor-general's agent, outlining the need for taking over the Assam Duars. He wrote:

> Had we possession of the Dooars, the Bhootan Government would necessarily in a short time become entirely dependent upon us, as holding in our hands the source of all their subsistence.

This was the time of the Afghan War and the Anglo–Sikh wars. The British Indian administration had little time to worry about Bhutan, and major and minor conflicts and cross-border incursions continued. Although the British were making plans to annex the Bengal Duars, they were not able to follow through. Their troops were kept busy trying to suppress the Indian uprising of 1857, which was a movement against British rule in India.

Bhutan took advantage of the instability in the region and mounted numerous raids in the Bengal Duars. To compensate for their losses, the British deducted large sums from payments they owed the Bhutanese. In 1861 the Bhutanese retaliated by raiding Cooch Behar, capturing a number of elephants and kidnapping several residents, including some British subjects.

*Bhutan and the British by Peter Collister is a comprehensive account of the interaction between Britain and Bhutan from 1771 to 1987.*

| 1864 | 1865 |
| --- | --- |
| The ill-fated Ashley Eden expedition sours relations between Bhutan and Britain | Bhutan and Britain go to war over the duars, which was finally resolved with a treaty that saw Bhutan's territory greatly reduced |

## THE TRONGSA PENLOP GAINS CONTROL

At this time the incumbent *zhabdrung* was a youth of 18, and the affairs of state were handled by the Lhengyal Shungtshog (Council of Ministers), which consisted of the Trongsa and Paro penlops, several *dzongpens* and other officials. There was constant infighting and intrigue between the Paro and Trongsa *penlops*, both of whom were vying for power through attacks, conspiracy and kidnapping. When one gained control, he appointed a desi and enthroned him; soon the other penlop gained control, ejected the opposing desi and placed his own representative on the throne.

*Views of Medieval Bhutan* is a coffee-table book by Michael Aris that presents the diary and drawings of Samuel Davis, an artist and member of George Bogle's 1774 expedition to Bhutan.

Through a series of shrewd alliances the Trongsa penlop, Jigme Namgyal (1825–82), gained the upper hand and established effective control of the country. This was the first time peace had prevailed since the time of the first zhabdrung. Jigme Namgyal was working to strengthen his power and that of the central government when he had an inconvenient visitor.

## THE HUMILIATION OF ASHLEY EDEN

The British had managed to extend their influence into Sikkim, making it a British protectorate, and subsequently decided to send a mission to

### EXPLORATION OF WESTERN TRAVELLERS

Some of the most interesting stories of Bhutan, and much of Bhutan's recorded history, came from the descriptions provided by early European explorers. These records provide an insight into what they observed and also reveal the extraordinary attitudes of some of the envoys Britain sent to negotiate with Bhutan.

#### Fathers Cacella & Cabral

The first Western visitors to Bhutan were two Portuguese Jesuit priests. In early 1627 Fathers Cacella and Cabral travelled from Calcutta to Bhutan en route to Shigatse in Tibet. They stayed for a few months in Cheri Goemba, north of Thimphu, with the Zhabdrung. There is no complete account of their journey, but one of their letters provides an insight into Ngawang Namgyal's character:

'He received us with a demonstration of great benevolence, signifying this in the joy which he showed on seeing us and on knowing where we had come from, where we were from, that is from what country or nation, and he asked the other questions normal at a first meeting.'

#### George Bogle

Some 150 years later, the first British expedition arrived in Bhutan in 1774, just after the first British treaties with Bhutan and Tibet were signed. The Court of Directors of the East India Company sent a mission to Tibet via Bhutan to find out about goods, 'especially such as are of great value and easy transportation'. The expedition team, led by George Bogle, planted potatoes wherever they went, providing a new food crop for Bhutan and a lasting legacy of this mission. They spent five months in Thimphu and then travelled on to Tibet.

#### Samuel Turner

The next major venture into Bhutan was in 1783, when Samuel Turner led a grand expedition with all the accoutrements of the British Raj. They travelled through the *duars* in palanquins and

| 1865 | 1885 |
|---|---|
| After the *duar* war, the saying went that Bhutan's border is where a rock rolled down the hill finally stops | After decades of civil unrest, Ugyen Wangchuck emerges as the most powerful figure in the country |

Bhutan to establish a resident British representative and encourage better communication.

Despite reports of political chaos in Bhutan, Ashley Eden, the secretary of the government of Bengal, set out from Darjeeling in November 1864 to meet the *desi*, or *deb raja*. Ignoring numerous messages from the Bhutanese that the British mission was not welcome, Eden pushed on past Kalimpong, through Daling, Haa and Paro, reaching Punakha on 15 March.

It's not clear whether it was more by accident or by design, but Eden's party was jeered, pelted with rocks, made to wait long hours in the sun and subjected to other humiliations. Both Bhutanese and British pride suffered badly. As Eden describes it in *Political Missions to Bootan*:

> The Penlow [penlop] took up a large piece of wet dough and began rubbing my face with it; he pulled my hair, and slapped me on the back, and generally conducted himself with great insolence.

Eden exacerbated the situation by sending the Lhengyal Shungtshog a copy of a draft treaty with terms that he had been instructed to negotiate. His actions

*Political Missions to Bootan* by Ashley Eden is a pompous Victorian account of the history of Bhutan. After reading a few pages, you'll have some idea as to why Eden was treated so badly when he arrived in Punakha.

followed Bogle's route to Thimphu. They also visited Punakha and Wangdue Phodrang before crossing to Tibet.

### Ashley Eden

Minor British expeditions to Bhutan were made in 1810, 1812, 1815 and 1837, for the most part in order to settle border disputes and conflict over the duars. The Ashley Eden mission of 1863 attempted to resolve these issues. He advocated a punitive policy to teach the Bhutanese that they would not be allowed to 'treat our power with contempt'.

### John Claude White

There were no formal expeditions to Bhutan for more than 40 years after Eden's, but the Survey of India sent several agents disguised as lamas and pilgrims to explore Bhutan and Tibet in 1883 and 1886.

By 1905 the Bhutanese and British were friends due to the assistance of the *penlop* of Trongsa, Ugyen Wangchuck, had provided the 1904 Younghusband expedition to Lhasa. White and his large party travelled into Haa and Paro, en route to the investiture ceremony in Punakha, and were guests of Ugyen Wangchuck at his new palace in Bumthang. The expedition returned with the first photographs of *dzongs* and the court of Bhutan.

In 1906 White made a reconnaissance through eastern Bhutan to southern Tibet. He made a third trip, in 1907, when he was invited as the British representative to the coronation of Ugyen Wangchuck as the first king of Bhutan. A summary of White's account appeared in the April 1914 issue of the *National Geographic*, and made Bhutan known to the world for the first time.

### Other British Political Officers

Between 1909 and 1947 the British sent numerous political officers to Bhutan and presented the king with decorations. In 1927 Lt Col FM Bailey attended the coronation of the second king and Lt Col JLR Weir travelled to Bumthang in 1931 to present the king with the insignia of Knight Commander of the Indian Empire.

| 1897 | 1907 |
|---|---|
| On 12 June, the great Assam earthquake destroys the dzongs in Punakha and Lingzhi, and severely damages many others | Ugyen Wangchuck elected the hereditary ruler of Bhutan, the Druk Gyalpo |

implied that this was the final version of the treaty that the Bhutanese were to sign without any discussion. The Bhutanese took immediate exception to Eden's high-handedness and soon presented him with an alternative treaty that returned all the *duars* to Bhutan. One clause in the treaty stated:

> We have written about that the settlement is permanent; but who knows, perhaps this settlement is made with one word in the mouth and two in the heart. If, therefore, this settlement is false, the Dharma Raja's demons will, after deciding who is true or false, take his life, and take out his liver and scatter it to the winds like ashes.

Reading this, it's little wonder that Eden feared for the safety of his party. He signed the treaty, but under his signature added the English words 'under compulsion', which, naturally, the Bhutanese could not read.

## THE DUAR WAR OF 1865 & THE RISE OF UGYEN WANGCHUCK

Although the British considered Eden's mission a failure, and reprimanded him for his conduct, they continued the dispute with Bhutan over payment for the Bengal Duars. The Bhutanese, in turn, were furious the British had renounced the treaty Eden had signed. In November 1864 the British summarily annexed the Bengal Duars, gaining effective control of the entire south of Bhutan. The Trongsa *penlop* mounted a carefully planned counterattack. His troops, protected by shields of rhinoceros hide, captured two British guns and drove the British forces out of Bhutan in January 1865.

The British regrouped and recaptured various towns, including Samtse (then called Chamurchi). A fierce battle at Dewangiri on 2 April essentially ended the war, with the British destroying all the buildings and slaughtering their captives. Negotiations continued through the summer. Eventually the Bhutanese returned the captured guns and accepted a treaty. The treaty of Sinchula was signed, under duress, by the Bhutanese on 11 November 1865. In it the Bhutanese ceded the *duars* to Britain forever and agreed to allow free trade between the two countries.

Through this treaty, Bhutan lost a major tract of valuable farmland and a large portion of its wealth. Its borders became the foot of the hills bordering the plain of India. It is often said that Bhutan's border is where a rock rolled down the hill finally stops. Among the important landmarks the Bhutanese lost were the town of Ambari Falakati, northwest of Cooch Behar, the town of Dewangiri (now called Deothang) in the east and the territory on the east bank of the Teesta River, including what is now the town of Kalimpong.

Back in Bhutan's heartland there were continuing civil wars, but the *penlop* of Trongsa, Jigme Namgyal, retained his power and in 1870 was enthroned as the 51st *desi*. The next 10 years were again a time of intrigue, treachery, power broking and continual strife. The *penlop* of Paro and the *dzongpens* of Punakha and Wangdue Phodrang conspired to challenge the position of Desi Jigme Namgyal and his successor, who was his half-brother. After he retired as *desi*, Jigme Namgyal remained in firm control of the country and in 1879 appointed his 17-year-old son, Ugyen Wangchuck, as Paro *penlop*. Michael Aris' book *The Raven Crown* gives a detailed description of this extraordinary period.

www.bhutanstudies.org .bt is the website for the Centre for Bhutan Studies, a research institute dedicated to promoting research and scholarship on Bhutan; it publishes many detailed historical research articles among other subjects.

**1910**
The Treaty of Punakha is signed, guaranteeing Bhutan's sovereignty and giving Britain a hand in its external relations

**1926**
Ugyen Wangchuck dies and is succeeded by his son Jigme Wangchuck, the second Druk Gyalpo

After Jigme Namgyal died, his son consolidated his own position following a feud over the post of *penlop* of Trongsa. At the age of 20, Ugyen Wangchuck marched on Bumthang and Trongsa and in 1882 was appointed *penlop* of Trongsa, while still retaining the post of *penlop* of Paro. Because his father had enhanced the powers of the office of the Trongsa *penlop,* this gave him much more influence than the *desi.* When a battle broke out between the *dzongpens* of Punakha and Thimphu, Ugyen Wangchuck tried to mediate the dispute.

He sent in his troops after unsuccessful negotiations and his forces defeated the troops loyal to both *dzongpens* and seized control of Simtokha Dzong. The monk body and the *penlop* of Paro tried to settle the conflict and in 1885 arranged a meeting at the Changlimithang parade ground in Thimphu. During the meeting a fight broke out, the representative of the Thimphu *dzongpen* was killed and the *dzongpen* fled to Tibet. Following the battle, Ugyen Wangchuck emerged as the most powerful person in the country, assumed full authority, installed his own nominee as *desi,* and reduced the post to a ceremonial one.

## THE FIRST KING

In order to re-establish Bhutan's sovereignty and help consolidate his position, Ugyen Wangchuck developed closer relations with the British. He accompanied Francis Younghusband during his invasion of Tibet in 1904 and assisted with the negotiations that resulted in a treaty between Tibet and Britain. The British rewarded the *penlop* by granting him the title of Knight Commander of the Indian Empire. In 1906 Sir Ugyen Wangchuck was invited to Calcutta to attend the reception for the Prince of Wales and returned to Bhutan with a better appreciation of the world that lay beyond the country's borders.

In 1907 the secular ruler, the *desi,* died and Ugyen Wangchuck was elected as the hereditary ruler of Bhutan by a unanimous vote of Bhutan's chiefs and principal lamas. He was crowned on 17 December 1907 and installed as head of state with the title Druk Gyalpo (Dragon King). He continued to maintain excellent relations with the British, partly in an effort to gain some security from the increasing Chinese influence in Tibet.

## THE TREATY OF PUNAKHA

British-Bhutanese relations were enhanced in the treaty of Punakha, which was signed in 1910. This treaty stated that the British government would 'exercise no interference in the internal administration of Bhutan'. It was agreed that Bhutan would 'be guided by the advice of the British Government in regard to its external relations'. The compensation for the *duars* was doubled to Rs100,000 per year and Bhutan agreed to refer disputes with Cooch Behar and Sikkim to the British for settlement.

Bhutan still refused to allow the appointment of a British resident, and continued to maintain a policy of isolation aimed at preserving its own sovereignty in an era of colonisation. In 1911 King Ugyen Wangchuck attended the great durbar held by King George V at Delhi and was given the additional decoration of Knight Commander of the Order of the Star of India.

## THE SECOND KING

Ugyen Wangchuck died in 1926 and was succeeded by his 24-year-old son, Jigme Wangchuck. He ruled during the time of the Great Depression and

Michael Aris' book *The Raven Crown* gives a detailed description of Bhutan in the early 20th century; it is lavishly illustrated with rare photographs and provides a perspective based on Bhutanese accounts.

| 1949 | 1952 |
|---|---|
| Bhutan signs a treaty with newly independent India and gains a small concession of land in the *duars* | King Jigme Wangchuck is succeeded to the throne by his son Jigme Dorje Wangchuck |

WWII, but these catastrophic world events did not affect Bhutan because of its barter economy and isolation.

Jigme Wangchuck refined the administrative and taxation systems and brought the entire country under his direct control. He made Wangdich-holing Palace in Bumthang his summer palace, and moved the entire court to Kuenga Rabten, south of Trongsa, in the winter.

After India gained independence from Britain on 15 August 1947, the new Indian government recognised Bhutan as an independent country. In 1949 Bhutan signed a treaty with independent India that was very similar to their earlier treaty with the British. The treaty reinforced Bhutan's position as a sovereign state. India agreed not to interfere in the internal affairs of Bhutan, while Bhutan agreed to be guided by the government of India in its external relations. The treaty also returned to Bhutan about 82 sq km of the *duars* in the southeast of the country, including Dewangiri, that had been annexed by the British.

*Sikhim and Bhutan, Twenty-one Years on the North-east Frontier* by J Claude White describes a 1905 expedition to present the first king, Ugyen Wangchuck with the insignia of Knight Commander of the Indian Empire.

## THE THIRD KING & THE MODERNISATION OF BHUTAN

King Jigme Wangchuck died in 1952. He was succeeded by his son, Jigme Dorji Wangchuck, who had been educated in India and England and spoke fluent Tibetan, English and Hindi. To improve relations with India he invited the Indian prime minister, Jawaharlal Nehru, and his daughter, Indira Gandhi, to visit Bhutan in 1958.

When the Chinese took control of Tibet in 1959, it became obvious that a policy of isolationism was not appropriate in the modern world. The king knew that in order to preserve Bhutan's independence, the country had to become a member of the larger world community. In 1961 Bhutan emerged from centuries of self-imposed isolation and embarked on a process of planned development.

Karma Ura's book *The Hero With a Thousand Eyes* gives a wonderful insight into the protocol and workings of the Bhutanese court in the days of the second king, Jigme Wangchuck, and is available in Thimphu.

Bhutan joined the Colombo Plan in 1962. This gave it access to technical assistance and training from member countries in Southeast Asia. The first 'five-year plan' for development was implemented in 1961 and India agreed to help finance and construct the large Chhukha hydroelectric project in western Bhutan. Not all Bhutanese approved of the pace of change. There were clashes between rival power groups and the prime minister, Jigme Palden Dorji, who was a leading proponent of change, was assassinated on 5 April 1964.

Bhutan joined the Universal Postal Union in 1969 and became a member of the UN in 1971. In the same year, Bhutan and India established formal diplomatic relations and exchanged ambassadors.

The king's domestic accomplishments were also impressive. In 1953, early in his reign, he established the Tshogdu (National Assembly) and drew up a 12-volume code of law. He abolished serfdom, reorganised land holdings, created the Royal Bhutan Army (RBA) and police force, and established the High Court. However, as he led Bhutan into the modern world, he emphasised the need to preserve Bhutanese culture and tradition.

### The National Assembly

The Tshogdu, or National Assembly, meets twice a year. It has 150 members, all of whom serve three-year terms and fall into three categories. The largest group, with 105 members, consists of the *chimis*, representatives of Bhutan's 20 *dzongkhags* (administrative districts; they are marked on the colour map, pp2–3). Each household has a vote in village elections and the *gups* (village

| 1961 | 1972 |
|---|---|
| Bhutan warily emerges from self-imposed isolation and a process of controlled development, undertaking modernisation | King Jigme Dorje Wangchuck is succeeded to the throne by his son, 16-year-old Jigme Singye Wangchuck |

headmen or headpersons) elect the chimi. The *zhung dratshang* (clergy) elect 10 monastic representatives and another 35 representatives are senior civil servants nominated by the government. These appointees include the *dzongdags* (district governors), ministers, secretaries of various government departments and other high-ranking officials.

## THE FOURTH KING & THE INTRODUCTION OF DEMOCRACY

King Jigme Dorji Wangchuck died in 1972 at age 44. He was succeeded by his 16-year-old son, Jigme Singye Wangchuck. Like his father, he was educated in India and England, but he also received a Bhutanese education at the Ugyen Wangchuck Academy in Paro. He pledged to continue his father's program of modernisation and announced a plan for the country to achieve economic self-reliance. This plan took advantage of Bhutan's special circumstances – a small population, abundant land and rich natural resources. Among the development goals set by the king was the ideal of economic self-reliance and what he nicknamed 'gross national happiness' (GNH). GNH is not a simple appraisal of the smiles on the faces of the populace; rather it encompasses explicit criteria to measure development projects and progress in terms of society's greater good. A more sustainable happiness for the individual is believed to derive from such an approach.

The coronation of King Jigme Singye Wangchuck as the fourth Druk Gyalpo on 2 June 1974 was a major turning point in the opening of Bhutan, and was the first time that the international press was allowed to enter the country. A total of 287 invited guests travelled to Thimphu for the event, and several new hotels were built to accommodate them. These hotels later provided the basis for the development of tourism in Bhutan.

The king has emphasised modernisation of education, health services, rural development and communications. He was the architect of Bhutan's policy of environmental conservation, which gives precedence to ecological considerations over commercial interests. He continued the reforms begun by his father in the areas of administration, labour and justice, including the introduction of a secret ballot and the abolishment of compulsory labour. He promotes national identity, traditional values and the concept of 'One Nation, One People'. Bhutan's six development goals, as expressed by the king are: self-reliance; sustainability; efficiency and development of the private sector; people's participation and decentralisation; human-resource development; and regionally balanced development.

In 1988 the royal wedding solemnised the king's marriage to the sisters Ashi Dorji Wangmo, Ashi Tshering Pem, Ashi Tshering Yangdon and Ashi Sangay Choedon.

In 2005 the 49-year-old king announced a plan to abdicate the throne in favour of his eldest son, Crown Prince Jigme Khesar Namgyal Wangchuck, and help move the country from an absolute monarchy to a democratic constitutional monarchy in 2008. At the time of research, a draft, 34-point constitution was being circulated around the country by the crown prince seeking opinion and support and is expected to be ratified by referendum. The constitution reinforces the king's idea of having a democratic government committed to increasing GNH and not just gross national product (GNP). Bhutan's well-planned journey to democracy rests on this constitution's acceptance.

The 1897 earthquake which destroyed and damaged many of the dzongs was the first documentation of a quake producing vertical accelerations greater than 1G, which means that large boulders were lifted from their location and moved to a new spot without touching the ground.

| 1974 | 1974 |
| --- | --- |
| The official coronation of King Jigme Singye Wangchuck | The first 'tourist group' explores the country's sights, paving the way for international visitors to come |

---

**HISTORY OF TOURISM IN BHUTAN**

Until the beginning of King Jigme Dorji Wangchuck's modernisation efforts in 1960, most of the non-Indian foreigners who entered Bhutan were British explorers (p36). A few foreigners were permitted into the country during the 1960s, but only the royal family had the authority to issue invitations, so almost all visitors were royal guests.

Early trekkers included Desmond Doig, a friend of the royal family who trekked in 1961 on assignment for *National Geographic*. In 1963 Professor Augusto Gansser travelled throughout the country studying geology, and in 1964 a group of British physicians, Michael Ward, Frederic Jackson and R Turner, mounted an expedition to the remote Lunana region.

The coronation of the fourth king in 1974 was the first time that a large number of foreign visitors had entered the kingdom. After the coronation, small groups of tourists were allowed into the country and given permission to visit the dzongs and goembas in Thimphu and Paro. From these beginnings, the pattern for Bhutan's tourism industry evolved.

The first group of paying tourists arrived in 1974, organised and led by Lars Eric Lindblad, founder of Lindblad Travel in Connecticut, USA, a pioneer of modern-day group tours. Lindblad encouraged the government to limit tourism and to charge high fees.

Paro airport was opened in 1983 and the newly formed national airline, Druk Air, started operating flights from Kolkata. The airport runway was extended in 1990 and Druk Air began operating jet aircraft, with direct international connections. Until 1991 tourists were handled by the Bhutan Tourism Corporation, a government agency. Tourism was privatised that year and soon numerous agencies were established, most run by ex-employees of the now-disbanded government agency.

---

## NEPALI-SPEAKERS

In the early 20th century many Nepalis migrated to Bhutan and settled in the south of the country. They now comprise much of the population in that region, to the extent that the term Lhotshampa (southern Bhutanese) is almost synonymous with Nepali-speaker.

Although the Nepali-speakers are from many ethnic groups, the majority of them are Hindus, with traditions that are different from those of the Drukpas who live in the north of the country. Some Nepalis asserted that they faced discrimination from the Drukpas and demanded political changes as long ago as the 1950s, when the now-defunct Bhutan State Congress Party was formed.

From the 1950s the Bhutanese government took steps to integrate the ethnic Nepalis. For the first time they were granted citizenship, represented in the National Assembly, admitted into the bureaucracy and Nepali was taught as a third language in primary schools in southern Bhutan. Also, recognition was given to the festivals, customs, dress and traditions of the Lhotshampas. The Nepalis remained culturally distinct from the Bhutanese of the northern valleys. However, up until the 1980s, there seemed to be little or no conflict between the Drukpas and the Lhotshampas.

Major problems didn't really emerge until the late 1980s. At that time, the government began to focus on preserving what it saw as Bhutan's threatened national identity. It introduced a policy of *driglam namzha* (traditional values and etiquette; see p52) under which all citizens had to wear the national dress of *gho* and *kira* at schools, government offices and official functions. At the same time, as part of the implementation of the 'New Approach to Education', study of the Nepali language was eliminated from the school curriculum. Resentment began to stir among some Nepalis in the south,

The year 2007 will mark 100 years of monarchy in Bhutan; however because 2007 is an inauspicious year according to the Bhutanese calendar, Bhutan will wait until 2008 to celebrate the 100 years of Kingdom.

---

**1980s**

Government policies aimed at preserving national identity begin to polarise the Nepali-speaking southerners

**1991**

The start of an eventual mass movement of Nepali-speakers from Bhutan to refugee camps just over the border in Nepal exacerbated by what the government now concedes was overzealous enforcement of the policies by some district officials.

Mindful of the country's extremely porous border – and Bhutan's attractiveness because of its fertile land, low population and free health and education facilities – in 1988 the government conducted a nationwide census. This was aimed partly at identifying illegal immigrants, defined as those who could not prove family residence before 1958. Thousands of ethnic Nepalis lacked proper documentation. A series of violent acts in the south, including robberies, assaults, rapes and murders – primarily against legitimate Bhutanese citizens of Nepali descent – created a sense of fear and insecurity that led to an exodus of Nepali-speakers from Bhutan. How much of the migration was voluntary remains a matter of fierce debate, but tens of thousands of Nepali-speakers left Bhutan between 1988 and 1993.

> www.unhcr.org is the site for the United Nations refugee agency and provides the latest facts and figures on the refugee camps in Jhapa, Nepal.

At the same time, a set of dissident leaders emerged charging human rights abuses in the treatment of Nepalis inside Bhutan, and demanding full democracy and other political changes in the kingdom. This movement received some international attention.

By the end of 1992, some 80,000 Nepali-speakers who said they were from Bhutan were housed in seven camps in the Jhapa district of southeastern Nepal, organised by the office of the UN High Commissioner for Refugees (UNHCR). By early 1993 the exodus had virtually stopped. In June 1993 the UNHCR established a screening centre at Kakarbhitta on the Nepal–India border.

Bhutan and Nepal agreed that they would settle the problem on a bilateral basis. They have held several rounds of talks to try to identify which residents of the camps are legitimate citizens of Bhutan and to find an appropriate solution to this complex problem. After numerous meetings they agreed to a joint verification process which began in March 2001. The process was completed at the first camp, Khudanabari, in December 2001 and the goal was to close the camp on a mutually agreeable basis and continue the verification process at other camps. Unfortunately the findings of the verification process, where only 2.4% of the people in the camp were classified as genuine refugees, did

## BODO GROUPS & THE UNITED LIBERATION FRONT OF ASSAM

The northeastern region of India has suffered years of separatist violence carried out by militants, some of whom have established bases in the jungles of southern Bhutan from which they mount assaults. The actions of these groups have claimed the lives of more than 20,000 people in the Indian state of Assam.

The Bodos are Mechey tribal people that have two militant groups, the Bodo Liberation Tiger Force and the Bodo Security Force, both of which are fighting for a Bodo homeland. The United Liberation Front of Assam, more commonly known as ULFA, is a separatist group formed in 1979 with the goal of an independent Assamese nation. They have staged numerous attacks, including derailing a train with a bomb, and attacking Indian vehicles and, in July and August 2001, buses carrying Bhutanese passengers through India.

In December 2003, after the government felt it had exhausted all peaceful means, the Royal Bhutan Army, led from the front by the king, flushed out the militants from Bhutanese territory. The continued presence of these militants across the border has made travel in the southeastern part of the country risky for both Bhutanese and tourists and is the reason for restrictions on visiting such places as Royal Manas National Park and Pemagatshel.

| 2001 | 2003 |
|---|---|
| A verification process of refugees in the camps is initiated under a bilateral process between Nepal and Bhutan | Disagreements over appeals from the first round of verification escalate and Bhutanese officials are attacked in one of the camps |

*Of Rainbows and Clouds: The Life of Yab Ugyen Dorji As Told to His Daughter* by Yab Ugyen Dorji and Ashi Dorje Wangmo Wangchuck is a fascinating and intimate account of life in Bhutan.

not satisfy the camp population and agreement on the appeal processes was not found after many months of negotiation. Frustration in the camps boiled over into a violent attack on the Bhutanese verification team at Khudunabari in December 2003, stalling the verification process.

At the end of 2005 there were 106,000 people in the camps, 10% to 15% of whom were born there. The status of the people in the camps of Jhapa is protected by the UNHCR, which uses donor support to provide the survival rations and shelter. It is likely that if the support disappears, and if the two countries cannot agree on how to resolve the crisis, those in the camps, most of them former farmers, would enter the larger diaspora of Nepali-speakers in south Asia.

| 2005 | 2006 |
|---|---|
| Announcement of the intended abdication and planned succession of the throne. Draft constitution released for the Kingdom of Bhutan | Circulation of draft constitution and planned referendum for vote on its acceptance |

# The Culture

## THE NATIONAL PSYCHE

Buddhism permeates everyday life in Bhutan and a basic knowledge of Buddhism is essential to understanding the Bhutanese. Prayer flags dot the landscape, prayers wheels powered by mountain streams turn gently at the roadside, images of the Buddha and other religious figures are carved and painted on to cliffs, reminding the visitor that every aspect of daily life is shaped by Buddhist beliefs and aspirations. This can be daunting, even alien, for many Western visitors. The idea of accumulating merit, a deep respect of the natural and often sacred environment, respect for religious practitioners: all central elements of the unique fusion of Buddhism and older non-Buddhist beliefs.

Yet the smiles of the children walking to school in the morning light, the laughter overheard in a family house, the shy greetings from women weaving outside their homes, will quickly entrance the traveller. The Bhutanese are a warm and open people – quick to smile and laughter. As with the other peoples of the Himalayas, the Bhutanese have an infectious sense of humour and quickly overcome barriers to communication. You should not be surprised to be offered a seat and a cup of tea even if you do not speak Dzongkha or one of the other 18 languages of Bhutan. These simple acts are spontaneous and provide the traveller with both fond memories and a brief insight in to the generous nature of the Bhutanese.

*Bhutan: Mountain Fortress of the Gods* (edited by C Schicklgruber and F Pommaret, Serindia), is an excellent introduction to the people and culture of Bhutan.

## DAILY LIFE

The majority of the Bhutanese population lives in central Bhutan, depending on agriculture of crops, and livestock breeding. The main crops grown in this region are rice, buckwheat, barley, potatoes and winter barley. They also grow chillies, which are dried on the roofs of houses before being stored.

There are 19 spoken languages in Bhutan.

Accordingly, daily life revolves around the care of livestock and farm labour. In Bumthang, where the woman is the head of the household, it will be she who decides on the division of farm labour. Bhutanese women are viewed as equal to Bhutanese men and accordingly there are only a few forms of labour traditionally viewed as exclusively male or female. Weaving and spinning have been reserved for women, while harrowing and ploughing were reserved for men. However, it is not uncommon to see a husband and wife working together ploughing their land. Other tasks such as collecting the harvest, threshing and so forth are done by men and women. Usually women brew the homemade alcohol.

Life for most rural households starts around dawn and ends with sunset. Each morning the family will make offerings, typically of water, before the household shrine and a simple breakfast of rice will be prepared. Men and women share equally in the day-to-day care of the children, and although women are usually in charge of the household, men are equally able to, and expected to, assist with the cooking. Meals are eaten sitting on the floor, often with personal bowls for rice and a selection of simple shared dishes set out in front – *ema datse,* perhaps a meat dish or some buckwheat noodles. Children are expected to help with the household and agricultural chores, like collecting water or firewood for the household, cleaning or herding the livestock.

There are approximately 15,000 lay or married monks, called *ngakpa* or *gomchen.*

In the evening, the water from the offering bowls will be poured away and a butter lamp may be lit and left to burn before the household shrine.

Traditionally Bhutanese were very self-sufficient, often making their own clothing, bedding, floor and seat covers, tablecloths, and decorative items for daily and religious use. There remains a degree of self-sufficiency among the

**DOMA**

*Doma* is an integral part of Bhutanese culture. A popular gift throughout Bhutanese society, it is made up of three main ingredients: *doma* or areca nut (Areca catechu), *pani* or betel leaf (Piper betel), and *tsune* or lime (calcium carbonate).

According to Bhutanese tradition, in 1637 a huge gathering of people had come with a variety of food products to offer to the Zhabdrung in Punakha. Deeply touched by their gesture, the Zhabdrung instructed that those present should be served with various gifts of food and *doma pani*. JC White, the British political officer who attended Gongsar Ugyen Wangchuck's enthronement in 1907, reports that *doma* was served to those attending the enthronement.

Eating *doma* was an aristocratic practice, with the various ingredients kept in ornate rectangular silver boxes called *chaka*, while lime had a separate circular box with conical lid called *trimi*. Today, people may keep their *doma* in bamboo *bangchung* or a cloth pouch called a *kaychung*. Young people appear to be turning away from eating *doma*, particularly as it may cause a variety of cancers.

rural Bhutanese, though many day-to-day items are increasingly imported from Bangladesh, India and Thailand.

*In 2003, 46.6% of Bhutanese earned their livelihood from farming. Almost one third of Bhutanese now earn a salary.*

## Marriage

In the past, marriages were arranged. However, since the 1970s the majority of marriages are love matches. The minimum age is sixteen for women and twenty-one for men. In rural areas, it is quite common for the husband to move into his wife's household and if they divorce he will return to live with his own family.

Polyandry, the practice of taking more than one husband, still exists in certain parts of Bhutan and polygamy is restricted. There remains a large number of Bhutanese couples who, although living together as a couple, are not formally married. The divorce rate is increasing and there is legal provision for alimony to be paid to take care of children.

## Death

*The largest monthly expenditures for a Bhutanese family are on food and rent.*

The frescoes of the Wheel of Life show that, to Bhutanese, death is part of the cycle of samsara separating loved ones and leading to rebirth. Accordingly, death is treated as a major life event. Family and friends are informed and monks, *gomchen* (lay or married monks) or nuns begin to recite from the *Bardo Thodrel* to guide the deceased through the intermediate phase.

A *tsip* (astrologer) will be consulted to decide on the most auspicious date and time to hold the cremation. Until the cremation, the deceased is placed in a wooden box and covered in a white cloth and kept separate from the family. At the cremation, the corpse is placed on the pyre facing the officiating lama. The first funeral service is held on the seventh day after death, with other rituals performed on the 14th, 21st and the 49th days. The lama reminds the deceased that they are dead and during the ritual seeks to help them move on to their next and (it is hoped) fortunate rebirth, either as a human being or preferably in a buddha realm.

At the end of the 49 days the ashes of the deceased may be scattered; some are placed in a sacred image and donated to a monastery or temple. The anniversary of the death will be marked for the following three years.

## BHUTANESE SOCIETY

Bhutan was relatively isolated until the early 1950s and traditional Bhutan has changed more in the last 50 years than in the previous 400 years. The country has retained its traditional social structures so far and has actively sought to preserve its cultural identity in the face of modernisation and increasing external influences.

Until the 1960s there were no major urban settlements. Since then Thimphu and Phuentsholing have grown significantly and this has led to pressure on land in these areas. Elsewhere there has been an increase in land acquisition, notably in Gelephu.

As a result of the opportunities created by education and the creation of alternative employment (as civil servants, teachers, armed forces or police), Bhutan has experienced increased social mobility. The rate of rural–urban migration is increasing, particularly as young educated Bhutanese seek employment in offices and other businesses in the capital. There has been growing concern over the increasing unemployment rate among the educated school leavers.

The Living Standard Survey 2003 revealed that 34% of Bhutanese now rely on salaries as their main source of income, and 46% on agriculture. It revealed that in urban areas the average monthly household expenditure was more than Nu 11,100 and about Nu 6,250 in the countryside. For many living in urban areas this figure can represent all or most of their salary which is why many Bhutanese women now work in offices or seek to supplement their husband's income through some form of small business enterprise.

> For more information on education in the Himalayas, and on supporting young students, see www .loden.org.

## Education

Until the introduction of Western-style education by the third king in the 1960s, the only education available in Bhutan was from the monasteries. Prior to this a few students travelled to Darjeeling to receive a secular education. The Western-style education has expanded to cover the whole country.

The educational structure provides for 11 years of basic schooling: one year of pre-primary schooling, six years of primary, two years of junior high school and two years of high school. Students undergo an examination to move from primary to junior high, and another to graduate from junior high to high school.

> The Youth Development Fund promotes a range of educational activities, including scouting and career counselling.

The school system aims to provide basic literacy skills, and knowledge of Bhutan's history, geography and traditions. Most villages have a primary school, though it is not uncommon for children to board at a junior high school or high school. Free education and textbooks are provided to all students until tertiary level. Morning prayers and the national anthem start the day for all students throughout Bhutan. The government provides adult education classes, especially aimed at improving literacy.

A key aspect of Bhutan's development plan involves training doctors, engineers and other professionals. Important trade skills in plumbing, construction and electrics are now being taught to both young men and women. In 2003 the Royal University of Bhutan was established to provide tertiary education in Bhutan. All the existing tertiary institutions were incorporated in the new University.

## Health

Bhutan has made significant progress in its provision of basic health facilities and provides free health care to all its citizens. The main hospital is the National Referral Hospital in Thimphu, and two further regional referral hospitals. There are smaller hospitals in each district. Rural health care is provided through Basic Health Units staffed with a health assistant, nurse midwife and a basic health worker.

> A survey in 2003 revealed that over 80% of food in Bhutan was imported, including rice and dairy products.

Child immunisation is now at almost 100%, and iodine deficiency has been eliminated. Infant and maternal mortality rates have decreased. According to the 2005 census, over 80% of Bhutanese have access to clean drinking water.

## TRADITIONAL MEDICINE

Historically, Bhutan was referred to as the 'Land of Medicinal Herbs' and exported herbs to Tibet. Bhutanese were trained in medicine, known as So-ba Rig pa. It represents a blending of Ayurveda from India – notably the use of the three humours (bile, phlegm and wind) – with Chinese medicine, in the reading of pulses. The earliest medical works date from the 7th and 8th centuries and the main medical teachings are believed to have been transmitted from the Medicine Buddha, Sangye Menlha. They are contained in four volumes, called the Gyuzhi.

When the Zhabdrung Ngawang Namgyal came to Bhutan, he brought with him a highly esteemed physician, Tenzin Drukey, who spread the teachings on So-ba Rig pa in Bhutan. Although the basic texts are the same, the Bhutanese tradition of So-ba Rig pa developed independently from its Tibetan origins. Since 1967 the Bhutanese tradition has been formally incorporated in to the national health system.

The decision about the kind of treatment necessary for a particular condition is made mainly through reading of the pulses. Unlike modern medicine, which only uses reading of pulses to detect anomalies of the heart or the circulatory system, using the So-ba Rig pa method it is possible to detect diseases of organs through the pulses. The eyes, tongue and urine are also examined for signs that will help with the diagnosis, and sometimes the physician will record the patient's medical history.

Several forms of treatment are applied in Bhutanese traditional medicine. Hundreds of medicinal plants, minerals and animal parts form the basic medicines used by the practitioner. These basic ingredients are processed and mixed in different combinations to make 300 medicines in the form of pills, tablets, syrups, powders and lotions. The practitioner may also offer advice on, or treatment for, diet and lifestyle.

There are also procedures that include *gtar* (bloodletting), *bsregs* (cauterisation by herbal compounds), *gser bcos* (acupuncture with a golden needle), *tshug* (cauterisation with instruments of different materials), *dugs* (applying heat or cold to parts of the body), *byugs pa* (medicated oil massage), *sman chu* (stone heated bath), *tsha-chhu* (bath at a hot spring, such as the springs in Gasa), and *lum* (vapour treatment).

Although Bhutan has tackled endemic health problems, it is also facing the emergence of HIV and AIDS. The Bhutanese authorities have taken a proactive stance, emphasising the importance of safe sex and awareness of HIV. Monks and nuns have been trained (in addition to teaching rural communities about basic hygiene) to provide advice on HIV and to act as HIV counsellors for those infected. In August 2004 the King issued a *kasho* (royal command or statement) stressing the threat of HIV and the need to show compassion towards those infected.

The 160 Basic Health Units cover 90% of the population.

### Personal Names

The system of names in Bhutan differs between the north and south of the country. In the north, with the exception of the royal family, there are no family names. Two names are given to children by monks a few weeks after birth. These are traditional names of Tibetan origin and are chosen because of their auspicious influence or religious meaning. Two names are always given, although a few people have three names.

It is often impossible to tell the sex of a Bhutanese person based on their name. A few names are given only to boys, and others apply only to girls, for example Choekyi, Drolma and Wangmo, but most names may apply to either.

In the south, with an evident Hindu influence, a system resembling family names exists. Brahmans and Newars retain their caste name, such as Sharma or Pradhan, and others retain the name of their ethnic group, such as Rai or Gurung.

## TITLES & FORMS OF ADDRESS

Titles are extremely important. All persons of rank should be addressed by the appropriate title followed by their first or full name. Members of the royal family are addressed as 'Dasho' if they are male, and 'Ashi' if female. A minister has the title 'Lyonpo' (pronounced 'lonpo').

The title Dasho is given to those who have been honoured by the king, receiving also the accompanying red scarf. In common practice, many senior government officials are addressed as Dasho even if they have not received the title, but officially this is incorrect.

You would address a senior monk or teacher with the title 'Lopon' (pronounced 'loeboen') or, if he has been given the title, as Lam. A *trulku* (reincarnate lama) is addressed as 'Rinpoche' and a nun as 'Anim'.

A man is addressed as 'Aap' and a boy as 'Busu'; a woman is addressed as 'Am' and a girl as 'Bum'. If you are calling someone whose name you do not know, you may use 'Ama' for women and 'Aapa' for men. In the same situation, girls are 'Bumo' and boys 'Alou'. When Bhutanese talk about a foreigner whose name they don't know, they use the word 'Chilip' or, in eastern Bhutan 'Pilingpa'.

At night, do not shout a person's name, as it's believed this may attract a ghost.

White silk scarves called *kata* are exchanged as customary greetings among ranking officials and are offered to high lamas as a sign of respect, but they are not exchanged as frequently as they are in Tibet and Nepal.

According to the 2005 Census, male literacy is at 69% and female literacy at 51%.

## Traditional Dress

Bhutan's traditional dress is one of the most distinctive and visible aspects of the country. It is compulsory for all Bhutanese to wear national dress in schools, government offices and formal occasions. Men, women and children wear traditional clothing made from Bhutanese textiles in a variety of colourful patterns.

### GHO

The men wear a *gho,* a long robe similar to the Tibetan *chuba.* The Bhutanese hoist the *gho* to knee length and hold it in place with a woven cloth belt called a *kera.* The *kera* is wound tightly around the waist, and the large pouch formed above it is traditionally used to carry a bowl, money and the makings of *doma.* One man suggested that the best part of the day was when he was able to loosen his uncomfortably tight belt.

According to tradition, men should carry a small knife called a *dozum* at the waist. Traditional footwear is knee-high, embroidered leather boots, but these are now worn only at festivals. Most Bhutanese men wear leather shoes, trainers or trekking boots.

*Ghos* come in a wide variety of patterns, though often they have plaid or striped designs reminiscent of Scottish tartans. Flowered patterns are taboo, and solid reds and yellows are avoided because these are colours worn by monks; otherwise patterns have no special significance. Historically, Bhutanese men wore the same thing under their *gho* that a true Scotsman wears under his kilt, but today it's usually a pair of shorts. In winter it's correct to wear thermal underwear, but it's more often a pair of jeans or a track suit, which gives the costume a peculiar look that some people liken to a dressing gown. Formality in Thimphu dictates that legs may not be covered until winter has arrived, which is defined as the time that the monks move to Punakha.

Formal occasions, including a visit to the dzong, require a scarf called a *kabney* that identifies a person's rank. The *kabney* has to be put on correctly so it hangs in exactly the right way. In dzongs, and on formal occasions, a *dasho* or someone in authority carries a long sword called a *patang.*

## DOS & DON'TS

Despite the deep religious belief and the pervasiveness of traditional culture, Bhutanese are quite open and liberal. They have a reputation for being the least complicated Asian people to communicate with. There are many complex customs and traditions in Bhutan, but you are not expected to follow all of these.

If you are courteous and respectful of religious beliefs, you are unlikely to cause offence. Using the word *la* at the end of a sentence in either Dzongkha or English is a sign of respect, eg *kuzo zangpo la* (hello).

You should also follow the normal Asian standards of courtesy and behaviour in Bhutan. These include respect for the monarchy, modest dress and no public displays of affection. Use the right hand or, better yet, both hands to give or receive an object. Don't use your finger to point, especially at deities or religious objects; use an open hand with the palm up. When waving someone towards you, keep your palm pointing down. Never touch the crown of the head, for example of a young child; this is considered a special part of the body.

Most lakes are the abode of gods or spirits. Don't swim, wash clothes or throw stones into them.

### Visiting Temples

Himalayan Buddhism has a generally relaxed approach to religious sites, but you should observe a few important rules if you are invited to enter a lhakhang or goemba. It is customary to remove one's shoes and hat upon entering the important rooms of a temple. You will most likely be escorted by a caretaker monk, and you can follow his example in removing your shoes at the appropriate doorway. Leave cameras, umbrellas and hats outside. Always move in a clockwise direction and do not speak loudly. If there is a ceremony being performed inside, always check before entering that it's OK.

Followers of Himalayan Buddhism will prostrate themselves three times before the primary altar and occasionally before secondary shrines to important saints. You may approach the central altar, and in Bhutanese goembas you will often find a cup containing three dice. Bhutanese roll these dice and the monk interprets the auspiciousness of the result. It is customary to leave a small offering of money (Nu 10) on the altar. When you make this offering, the monk accompanying you will pour a small amount of holy water, from a sacred vessel called a *bumpa,* into your hand. You should make the gesture of drinking a sip of this water and then spread the rest on your head. While male visitors may be permitted (please ask before entering) to enter the *goenkhang* (shrine dedicated to protector deities), this is off-limits to all women. Do not walk behind an altar set before the *goenkhang.*

### KIRA

*Driglam Namzhag* (Bhutanese Etiquette) is a manual published by the National Library of Bhutan and is a good introduction (available in English).

Women wear a long floor-length dress called a *kira.* This is a rectangular piece of brightly coloured cloth that wraps around the body over a Tibetan-style silk blouse called a *wonju.* The *kira* is fastened at the shoulders with elaborate silver hooks called *koma* and at the waist with a belt that may be of either silver or cloth. Over the top is worn a short, open, jacket-like garment called a *toego.* Women often wear large amounts of jewellery. The whole ensemble is beautiful and Bhutanese women are very elegant in their finery.

The *kira* may be made from cotton or silk and may have a pattern on one or both sides. For everyday wear, women wear a *kira* made from striped cloth with a double-sided design, and on more formal occasions they wear a *kira* with an embellished pattern woven into it. The most expensive *kira* are *kushutara* (brocade dresses), which are made of hand-spun, hand-woven Bhutanese cotton, embroidered with various colours and designs in raw silk or cotton thread. Lhuentse is known for its *kushutara* designs.

The Laya women are particularly noted for their distinctive conical bamboo hats and long black wool dresses.

### Feet & Face

As in all Asian countries, you should never point your feet at someone. If you are sitting on the floor, cross your legs or kneel so that your feet are pointed behind you. If you happen to sleep in a room where there is an altar or statue, ensure your feet do not point towards it.

The Asian concept of keeping face also applies in Bhutan. Try to suggest instead of insist. When things go wrong, as they are certain to do at some stage, be patient while your guide figures out a solution. Remember, Asian people dislike saying 'no'. If your request to visit a certain landmark, order a particular dish in a restaurant or depart at a specified time is met with an obviously lame excuse, this probably means that it is impossible.

### Photography

A camera is still a curiosity in most of Bhutan, particularly in remote villages, and your camera may draw a curious crowd. See p251 for advice on photographing people. Photography is not allowed inside any temples; don't embarrass your guide by asking. If you are attending a festival, do not let your picture-taking interfere with the dancers or block the view of the spectators.

### Dress

Asian standards of modesty apply. Both men and women should avoid wearing revealing clothing, including short shorts, halter-neck tops and tank tops. Nudity is completely unacceptable.

Resident expatriates in Thimphu are adamant that visitors should dress up when attending a tshechu or other festival. Bhutanese are too polite to suggest it, and would not openly criticise those who did not dress correctly, but they do appreciate the gesture. Bhutanese are flattered if foreigners wear traditional dress, and are more than happy to help you buy, and put on, a *gho* or *kira* – which is not an easy process.

If you have an appointment with a government official, correct dress is required. Policemen at the entrance to dzongs will refuse admission to anyone who is improperly dressed.

### Social Occasions

If you are invited to a Bhutanese home, it's appropriate to bring a small gift, perhaps a bottle of wine or box of sweets. Social occasions tend to start late and involve extended rounds of drinks before dinner, often with several visitors dropping by for a short time. The evening is quickly concluded once dinner is finished.

When visiting dzongs, women wear a cloth sash called a *rachu* over their shoulders or simply over their left shoulder in the same manner as men wear a *kabney*.

## POPULATION

Western Bhutan, stretching from Haa to Wangdue Phodrang, is inhabited by the Ngalong, who are thought to be descended from Tibetan immigrants who moved to the region in the 9th century. and in the east are the Sharchop (literally, 'the people from the east). The Sharchop are believed the first inhabitants of Bhutan, with their own distinctive language. These three groups comprise about approximately 75% of the population.

In the cold high mountains to the north lie Lingzhi, Laya, Gasa and Lunana. The inhabitants of these remote regions are descended from Tibetan immigrants. In winter, due to the remoteness and the heavy snow falls, many of the families from Lingzhi move down to stay with host families in Paro, and similarly families from Laya move to the Punakha area. On the eastern border of Bhutan with Arunachal Pradesh in India are the seminomadic communities of the Brokpa in Merak Sakteng, who still practice polyandry.

The Centre for Bhutan Studies has an excellent website with online access to the Journal of Bhutan Studies. See www .bhutanstudies.org.bt.

Along the southern border of Bhutan, immigrants from Nepal began settling in the late nineteenth and early twentieth centuries. They began clearing and cultivating the dense jungle and sought to break free from the rigid caste system of Nepal. They are called Lhotshampa (literally, 'the people of the southern border') and represent numerous Nepali-speaking ethnic groups – primarily Brahman, Chettri, Gurung, Rai and Limbu, but also Newars. They are mainly Hindu and form approximately 25% of the population.

In 1971, when Bhutan applied for UN membership, the population was estimated at just less than one million. No census data existed and government officials estimated the population as best they could, choosing to err on the high side in order to help gain world recognition. Over the years, this figure was adjusted upwards in accordance with estimates of Bhutan's population-growth figures, finally reaching the 1.2 million figure. In some publications this total has even been listed at 2.3 million!

According to the 2005 Census, the current population of Bhutan is 672,425. The Census revealed that the number of urban dwellers has increased to 31%. As a result of a family-planning advocacy campaign the population growth rate is 1.3% per year, down from 3.1% in 1994, which was then one of the highest in the world. As in many non-industrialised countries, the high infant-mortality rate in the past induced people to have more children. With the introduction of better medical facilities, many more children now survive.

As a result of both improved infrastructure and rural–urban migration, 58% of the population now lives within an hour's walk from the nearest motorable road. This marks a significant change from the last census when an estimated 80% of the population lived more than an hour's walk from a road and as much as 50% lived more than one day of walking from a motorable road.

A good website for additional information and news on Bhutan is www.bhutansearch.com.

## LANGUAGES

For more information on the languages of Bhutan see George Van Driem's *Dzongkha* (1998), which contains a clear overview of the different languages spoken.

There are 19 languages spoken in Bhutan. The Ngalong people speak Dzongkha, which became the national language in 1960. It is related to Tibetan, but is sufficiently different that Tibetans cannot understand it. Dzongkha is written in the same script as Tibetan, but the orthography has been made more Bhutanese.

Nepali is spoken amongst the Lhotshampa communities in the southern districts and is often spoken by northern Bhutanese. Nepali and English are the two most widely used *lingua franca* whenever Bhutanese have a com-

---

**DRIGLAM NAMZHA**

The Zhabdrung Ngawang Namgyal established a code of etiquette for monastic and government officials. Over the centuries this system of etiquette spread to lay people. Called *driglam namzha,* the code of conduct specifies how to dress when visiting a dzong, the polite way to greet one's boss and officials, the correct way to sit, eat and so forth. Many of the ceremonies one sees performed at the start of an official event *(chipdrel, marchang)*, or an archery match are part of *driglam namzha.*

The government has actively promoted *driglam namzha* since 1989 in an attempt to preserve Bhutanese traditions, notably enforcing the requirement to wear *gho* and *kira* when visiting government offices, dzongs and temples.

Closely linked to *driglam namzha, thadamthsi* refers to the Bhutanese belief in respect towards ones' parents, elders, and other members of the community. Based on the Buddhist teachings on devotion, *thadamtshi* is an important concept in Bhutanese society. It is often illustrated by the story of the Four Friends (see the boxed text, p57).

Linked to *thadamtshi* and less formal than *driglam namzha* is the concept of *bey cha*. Bey cha emphasises the aesthetics of performing everyday tasks gracefully and with care and consideration for others.

munication problem. For more on Dzongkha, and language in Bhutan, see p275.

## RELIGION

Buddhism is practised throughout the country though, in the south, most Bhutanese people of Nepali and Indian descent are Hindu. Relations between Buddhists and Hindus are very good, with major Hindu festivals marked by national holidays. Minority groups practise various forms of ancient animistic religions, including Bon, which predates Himalayan Buddhism. Bhutanese Buddhism is discussed in more depth on p63.

There are approximately 5,500 monks in Bhutan, half under the patronage of the Je Khenpo, the other half subsidised by private patronage.

## MEDIA

In 1999, to mark the 25h anniversary of the coronation of King Jigme Singye Wangchuck, TV and satellite channels were permitted in Bhutan. Since then there has been rapid growth in the number of small cable providers throughout Bhutan. There have been deep concerns expressed about the negative impact of satellite TV on Bhutanese society. It is too early to say if it is damaging Bhutanese society. Rather, those problems which are arising perhaps reflect the problems of urbanisation and changing material aspirations.

There was a recent move to increase the diversity of independently run media in Bhutan. *Kuensel* was, until recently, the only national newspaper. Originally government owned, *Kuensel* was privatised in 1992. Since April 2006 the *Bhutan Times* and the *Bhutan Observer* are have become available. A media act passed by the National Assembly in 2006 caused a great deal of comment in editorials and from Bhutanese film makers (for more on this issue, see www.kuenselonline.com).

The Bhutan Broadcasting Service is government run and provides both TV and radio services. It is worth tuning into the TV channel to hear the news in English and to catch locally produced features and foreign documentaries. The radio channel does not operate all the time and has a schedule printed in *Kuensel*. Since the official introduction of satellite TV in 1999 Bhutanese have been learning about WWF – not the World Wildlife Fund, rather the World Wrestling Federation (and other novelties). Various sections of Bhutanese society expressed concern over the impact of TV on young Bhutanese and, in 2005, several channels were blocked.

Internet is available in Bhutan and is gradually being introduced throughout the country. In Thimphu there are a growing number of internet cafés which are popular with young Bhutanese. Druknet originally attempted to screen certain sites but found that it was too expensive to maintain. A second internet provider, Drukcom, began operation 2004. Since then, the internet has been unrestricted.

You can read current and archived stories at www .kuenselonline.com.

## WOMEN IN BHUTAN

Compared to other areas of south Asia, Bhutanese women enjoy greater equality and freedom with men. The right to inherit often passes property to women rather than men.

In rural areas women often inherit the house and the family land. Traditionally, women look after the household, preparing food and weaving textiles for family use and for sale. However, they also work in the fields, notably at harvest times when all available labour is required. Decisions affecting the household are jointly made. Travelling in Bhutan you will notice that Bhutanese women are independently minded and possess a strong entrepreneurial spirit. In Thimphu and the emerging urban centres such as Trongsa, Gelephu and Phuentsholing, women may seek to boost family income by engaging in trade, selling goods from home or renting a small shop.

HM Ashi Sangay Choden Wangchuck is the UN Goodwill Ambassador in Bhutan.

Rural women are often presented as the custodians of traditional values, while urban women face a different set of challenges. Urbanisation and increasing rural-urban migration have brought new challenges for women separated from their families and social networks.

The introduction of education in the 1960s enabled Bhutanese women to become literate and to seek employment outside of both their homes and their local villages. Teaching, the civil service and other office positions provided important opportunities for young, educated Bhutanese women.

However, there are areas in which Bhutanese women are still not equal with their male counterparts. Levels of literacy remain higher among men than women, though this is being tackled by the government through adult learning classes. Although some women have been appointed to higher positions in the government and NGOs, including the first female district court judge appointed in 2003, there do still appear to be barriers preventing educated and able women access to all levels of government. During the first universal suffrage *gup* (elected village leader) elections in 2002, there were no women candidates in any *gewog* (the lowest administrative level), and the proportion of women who voted compared to the number eligible to vote was significantly lower than for male voters.

More information on RENEW can be found at www.renew.org.bt.

The major women's organisation in the country is the National Women's Association of Bhutan. It was established in 1981 and headed by Dasho Dawa Dem, one of the few women to have received the honorific title of Dasho from the king. In 2004 Respect, Educate, Nurture and Empower Women (RENEW), a new NGO for women, was established by HM Ashi Sangay Choeden Wangchuck. RENEW is highly respected and tackles major issues facing contemporary Bhutanese women. In the same year a National Commission on Women and Children was established to promote the rights of women and children.

## ARTS

All Bhutanese art, dance, drama, music and even architecture have their roots in Buddhism. The highly distinctive architecture of Bhutan is discussed on p78. Paintings are traditionally done not for sale, but for specific purposes – though this is slowly changing. Festivals are not quaint reinventions staged for tourists, but are living manifestations of a long tradition and national faith. Almost all representation in art, music and dance is a dramatisation of the Buddha's teachings about the path to liberation and the constant struggle to overcome the delusions that lead to the cycle of rebirth in samsara. Bhutanese arts are concerned with interpreting values rather than describing facts.

The non-state-funded Choki Traditional Art School in Kabesa offers free training to young students from poor families. See www .chokischool.com.

### The Artistic Tradition in Bhutan

The development of Buddhist arts and crafts in Bhutan can be traced to the 15th-century *terton* (discoverer of sacred texts) Pema Lingpa, who was an accomplished painter, metal worker, sculptor and architect. The country's artistic tradition received a further boost when, in 1680, the fourth *desi* (secular ruler), Gyalse Tenzin Rabgye (1680–94), opened the School of Bhutanese Arts and Crafts, which has evolved into the National Institute for Zorig Chusum.

Traditional Bhutanese artistry is maintained through the support of all levels of society. The royal family, nobility and clergy continue to provide important patronage. Meanwhile, the common people support the arts because they depend on artisans to provide the wide variety of wooden and metal objects indispensable to typical Bhutanese households and painting, both inside and outside of homes.

Bhutanese art has two main characteristics: it is religious and anonymous. The Bhutanese consider commissioning paintings and statues as pious acts, which gain merit for the *jinda* (patron). The name of the *jinda* is sometimes written on the work so that their pious act may be remembered. However, the artist's name is rarely ever mentioned, although there are some artists whose names do become well-known due to the exceptional quality of their work.

There are strict iconographical conventions in Bhutanese art and the Bhutanese artists observe them scrupulously. However, artists do express their own personality in minor details (eg the shading of clouds or background scenes). Paintings and sculptures are executed by monks or laymen who work in special workshops. The disciples of a master, as part of their training will do all the preliminary work, while the fine work is executed by the master himself.

## The Thirteen Arts

The Thirteen Arts are the 13 traditional arts and crafts (Zorig Chusum) believed to have been categorised during the reign of the fourth *desi*, Tenzin Rabgye. Zorig Chusum refers to those physical activities which assist, teach or uplift others.

### SHINGZO (CARPENTRY)
Skilled carpenters are involved in a range of activities ranging from building dzongs and temples, houses and palaces, to making tools and other practical instruments.

### DOZO (MASONRY)
This covers the building of stupas, dzongs and temples as well as making the heavy millstones and stone pestles.

### PARZO (CARVING)
The Bhutanese are highly skilled at wood, stone and slate carving. Examples of their work are evident throughout Bhutan, from the slate carvings depicting the Buddha and other religious figures inserted in stupas, to the wooden printing blocks used for printing sacred texts.

### LHAZO (PAINTING)
Lhazo encompasses drawing and painting in Bhutan. It includes the painting of *thangkas* (religious pictures), murals and frescoes in temples and dzongs as well as the colourful images on the exterior walls of Bhutanese homes. Drawing and painting are governed by strict geometric rules of proportion and iconography. For more on *lhazo* see p56.

### JINZO (SCULPTURE)
Perhaps one of the arts in which the Bhutanese excel is the creation of delicate clay sculptures, occasionally set in amazing landscapes. These sculptures, ranging from small- to large-scale statues, are generally created around a hollow frame with the mud or clay built up to form the image. In 1999 the King awarded the Druk Thugsey medal (Heart Son of Bhutan) to sculptor Lopen Omtong, which reflects the high Bhutanese esteem for sculpture.

As well as statues, *jinzo* includes the production of a range of ritual items, notably the moulded offerings *(torma)* and masks worn during tsechu, and the more prosaic activity of preparing mud walls on new buildings.

### LUGZO (CASTING)
Casting, usually in bronze, refers to the production of musical instruments, statues, tools and kitchen utensils, as well as slip casting for pottery and jewellery.

If you are interested in actually creating your own Bhutanese art, look out for *Tibetan Thangka Painting: Methods and Materials* by David P Jackson and Janice A Jackson.

The 2005 Census revealed that Thimphu is the most populated *dzongkhag*, with 98,676 people, and Gasa the least populated, with 3,116 people.

### GARZO (BLACKSMITHING)
Generally, these craftsmen produce axes, plough blades, chains, knives and swords and other practical items.

According to a survey in 2001, 60% of rural land-owners are women and 45% of urban property and business is owned by women.

### TROKO (GOLD- AND SILVERSMITHING)
This includes all ornaments made from gold, silver or copper. They are often cut out, beaten, drawn or engraved.

### TSHAZO (BAMBOO WORK)
There is a wide variety of these products, as seen in the Sunday market. They include *bangchung* (covered bowls with intricate designs, used to carry food), long *palang* (used to store beer or other liquor), the *tshesip* (box), *belo* (small hat worn for sun protection), *redi* (floor mat), *luchu* (used for storing grain), *balep* (bamboo thatch) and of course, the bow and arrow.

### THAGZO (WEAVING)
*Thagzo* covers the whole process: from the preparation of the yarn, dyeing and the numerous designs. This is the largest craft industry in terms of the variety and number of craftspeople involved throughout Bhutan. See opposite for more on *thagzo*.

### TSHEMZO (EMBROIDERY)
There are two special categories within this craft. The first are those items which are sewn and embroidered (ranging from clothing to intricate and rare embroidered *thangkas*). The second refers to appliqué and patchwork items made from stitching cloth together. This includes the large *thondrols* displayed in the dzongs during tsechu, as well as hats and the elaborate boots worn with the *gho* on official occasions.

### SHAGZO (WOODTURNING)
Skilled wood turners produce a range of delicate wooden bowls, turned with expertise from special parts of a tree or roots. The large wooden *dapa* (serving dishes), wooden plates, buckets, ladles and *phop* (small cups), as well as the various small hand drums beaten during religious ceremonies, are among the products of this craft.

Written works by non-Bhutanese are available as well – notable among them is *Beyond the Sky and the Earth* by Jamie Zeppa.

### DEZO (PAPERMAKING)
The art of making paper from the daphne plant, and more recently bamboo and rice stalks, is under threat from the loss of skilled craftsmen.

## Painting
Aside from spectacular architecture, the most visible manifestation of Bhutanese art is painting. There are three forms of painting: *thangkas,* wall paintings and statues. A painting is invariably religious in nature depicting a deity, a religious story, a meditational object or an array of auspicious symbols (such as the Tashi Tagye or Four Friends).

Paintings, in particular the portrayal of human figures, are subject to strict rules of iconography. The proportions and features must be precise, and there is no latitude for artistic licence in these works. The initial layout is constructed with a series of geometrical patterns, using straight lines to lay out the proportions of the figure, which are defined in religious documents called *zuri pata*. In other cases the initial sketch is made with a stencil of the basic outline, which is transferred to the canvas by patting the stencil with a bag filled with chalk dust. Traditionally, paints were made from earth, minerals and vegetables, though now chemical colours are also used. The

**THE FOUR FRIENDS**

One of Bhutan's favourite fables is that of the four friends. In Dzongkha the name of the story is *Thuenpa puen shi* (Cooperation, relation, four) and it illustrates the concept of teamwork. You will see paintings illustrating this story on temples, homes and shops throughout the country.

The story tells how the elephant, monkey, peacock and rabbit combined forces to obtain a continual supply of fruit. The peacock found a seed and planted it, the rabbit watered it, the monkey fertilised it and the elephant guarded it. When the fruit was ripe the tree was so high that they could not reach the top. The four animals made a tower by climbing on one another's back, and plucked the fruit from the high branches.

material is first reduced into powder and then mixed with water, glue and chalk. The brushes are handmade from twigs and animal hair.

*Thangkas* are painted on canvas that is stretched and lashed to a wooden frame. When the work is completed it is removed from the frame and surrounded by a border of colourful brocade, with wooden sticks at the top and bottom used for hanging. Although some *thangkas* are hung permanently, most are rolled up and stored until they are exhibited at special occasions. This applies particularly to the huge appliqué *thondrols* that are displayed briefly in the early morning during the annual tshechus. The same iconographical rules apply to the *thondrol* which demonstrate the skills of the Bhutanese tailors.

The inner walls of dzongs and lhakhangs are usually covered with paintings. In Bhutan most wall murals are painted on a thin layer of cloth applied to the wall using a special paste. Nowadays, old paintings are treasured because of their historic and artistic value; however, until quite recently old wall paintings were often repainted or even painted over during restoration work.

Most statues are finely painted to sharply define the facial features, which are individualised for each figure. Many religious statues in lhakhangs, especially the larger statues, are made from unfired clay. In addition to the face, the entire surface of these large figures is painted, often in a gold colour, giving them a bronze aspect. Examples of these statues can be seen in Punakha dzong. On bronze statues, some of which are quite small, only the face is painted.

The focus for the contemporary art scene is the Volunteer Artist Studio in Thimphu (VAST), a voluntary organisation that provides art classes to young Bhutanese, which seeks to combine traditional styles with western art techniques and subjects. In Paro, the local artist Chime Dorji has opened the Vajrayana Art Gallery.

## Textiles

Weaving, more than the other Zorig Chusum, is the most distinctive and sophisticated of the arts and crafts. The richness of this art form can be seen at the permanent exhibition in the National Textile Museum in Thimphu. Everyday articles such as clothing, wrappers for goods, and cushion covers are stitched from cloth woven at home. Until the mid-20th century, certain taxes were paid in cloth and collected at the regional dzong. The authorities distributed the cloth as 'payment' to monastic and civil officials and to monasteries. Until quite recently, it was common to present cloth as a gift to mark special occasions or promotions. Bhutanese women still have trunks filled with fine fabrics which may be sold when money is required.

Although some men do practice weaving, the majority of weavers are women. Unlike *thangka* painting, which has very precise religious rules, weaving provides the weaver an opportunity to express herself. Designs, colours, sizes and even the finish have always reflected the materials available and the changes in technology and fashion. Bhutan's weavers specialise in working additional decorative warps and wefts into the 'ground' fabric. The most elaborate weavings are usually for the traditional *kira* and *gho* and these garments may take up to a year to weave in silk.

Thomas Slocum wrote *In His Majesty's Civil Service,* a collection of short stories set in Bhutan.

Each region has its own weaving traditions and designs, with that of Lhuentse, the ancestral home of the royal family, being the most renowned. The weavers in Lhuentse specialise in decorating *kira* and other textiles with intricate patterns that resemble embroidery. Other parts of eastern Bhutan are famous for their distinctive striped garments woven from raw silk. Bumthang weavers produce another popular fabric – *yathra,* hand-woven strips of woollen cloth, stitched into blankets, jackets, cushion covers and even car seats.

Though *yathra* was traditionally produced on back-strap looms, pedal looms were introduced from Tibet in the mid-20th century, whilst Indian spinning wheels are faster than the drop spindle. Today, all these technologies can be seen being used by weavers in their homes.

More recently, with assistance from the government, new items such as bags, decorations and even bed and table linen have been developed both for the local and international markets.

## Literature

The development of *jo yig,* the cursive Bhutanese script, as distinct from a Tibetan script, is credited to a monk by the name of Lotsawa Denma Tsemang. However, the Bhutanese script is based on the Tibetan script introduced by Tonmi Sambhota during the reign of the Tibetan king, Songtsen Gampo. For the most part, the literary culture of Bhutan has been dominated by Buddhism; first as a means of translating Buddhist scriptures from Sanskrit, and second as local scholars began to emerge, as a means of developing Himalayan Buddhist thought.

Wood-block printing has been used for centuries and is still the most common form of printing in the monasteries. Blocks are carved in mirror-image, then the printers working in pairs place strips of handmade paper over the inked blocks and a roller passes over the paper. The printed strip is then set aside to dry. The printed books are placed between two boards and wrapped in cloth. There is an excellent exhibition in the National Library showing the printing process as well as examples of rare texts.

The development of a modern, nonreligious literary culture is still emerging in Bhutan. In recent years local presses have published a range of popular religious works, notably the biographies of *delog.* These biographies retell the experiences of women who have 'died' and visited the various hell and pure realms described in Buddhist teachings. These women then 'return' to life and encouraged people to lead good lives and follow the teachings of Buddha. Other contemporary works published in Dzongkha are on Bhutanese history, notably the work by Lopon Pemala, *Druk Karpo* (White Dragon) and an excellent biography of the Zhabdrung Ngawang Namgyal. The Centre for Bhutan Studies, established in 2000, publishes a range of academic studies on Bhutan in both English and Dzongkha.

*Delog: Journey to realms beyond Death* by Delog Dawa Drolma is a good example of these biographies. *Les Revenants de l'Au-de-là dans le Monde Fibétain,* by Françoise Pommaret, is an excellent academic study of the *delog.*

Contemporary Bhutanese writers, usually writing in English, such as Kunzang Choeden, have produced short stories and collections of folktales from throughout Bhutan. Kunzang Choeden's book *Bhutanese Tales of the Yeti* has an excellent selection of local stories about the *migoi,* or yeti. She recently published *The Circle of Karma.* Sonam Kinga has written a few short plays in Dzongkha and translated the *Songs of Sorrow* by Gyalong Sumdar Tashi. Karma Ura published two excellent books in the 1990s. The first is a translation of the popular Dzongkha *loze* (ballad), The *Ballad of Pema Tshewang.* It tells the tale of Tshewang Tashi, a chamberlain to the governor of Wangdue Phodrang, who is chosen to lead a campaign against the governor of Trongsa. He does so with a sense of deep foreboding and dies after being surrounded by enemy forces. Ura's version contains wonderful illustrations of key scenes. The more recent work, *The Hero of a Thousand Eyes,* is a biography of Dasho Shingkarlam from Bumthang. It is simultaneously an engrossing personal tale and an insight into Bhutanese life prior to the reforms of the third king. HM Ashi Dorji Wangmo has written a fascinating biography of her father and his family, *Of Rainbows and Clouds.* In 2006 she published *Treasures of the Thunder Dragon,* a personal view of Bhutan and reflection on the changes during Her Majesty's lifetime.

Rinzin Rinzin, a young Bhutanese writer from Lhuentse, has published *The Talisman of Good Fortune and Other Stories from Rural Bhutan,* a collection of nine short stories that give the reader a sense of rural life. There is an interesting mix of stories and poems by Tshering C Dorji in *Shadow around the Lamp.*

## Cinema

Film-making is relatively new to Bhutan. The first feature film produced by a Bhutanese film-maker for a non-Bhutanese audience was *The Cup* by Khyentse Norbu, which was nominated as best foreign-language film for the 2000 Academy Awards. *Travellers and Magicians* (2003), also produced by Khyentse Norbu, is the first Dzongkha-language film to be made for an international audience. The film contains two parallel tales and its main theme is very pertinent to contemporary Bhutan. The main story focuses on a young frustrated civil servant, Dhundup, who dreams of leaving Bhutan for the United States. He likes rock'n'roll and western clothes. Yet on the road to the capital, he encounters a series of people who suggest that contentment can be found among his own people.

> The world's largest book, entitled *Bhutan: a Visual Odyssey Across the Last Himalayan Kingdom,* weighs 59kg

Bhutanese of all ages enjoy these films, and part of the enjoyment for many is identifying friends and relatives, as well as the locations. Bhutanese films such as *Khorwa,* made for a Bhutanese audience, often tackle contemporary social problems such as domestic violence, the issues facing stepchildren, alcoholism and more recently, unemployment. Presently, the production values and acting are of varying quality, yet a stronger sense of Bhutanese film-making is gradually appearing, with annual awards recognising local film-makers. One recent film, *Muti Thrishing,* swept the prizes for best actor (Tshering Gyaltshen), actress (Sonam Choki), film, director (Pelden Dorji) and script at the Fifth National Film awards in Thimphu 2006.

## Music

The music scene in Thimphu is small; popular music, *rigsar,* is still evolving. *Rigsar* is typically performed on modern instruments, notably electric piano and synthesiser. *Rigsar* blends elements of traditional Bhutanese and Tibetan tunes, and is influenced by Hindi film music.

> The website http://www .bhutan.ethno-museum .ac.at is an excellent online source of information about Bhutanese culture.

Popular male and female performers are emerging. Lhamo, Dechen Pem and Rinchen Namgay often appear in locally produced films. There is a range of music now available from little booths (notably on Norzin Lam near the traffic island) in Thimphu and throughout Bhutan. New tapes appear regularly and may be music from a Bhutanese film. Cassettes are not expensive (Nu 60 to 80).

In addition to *rigsar* performers, there are various performers who specialise in folk or religious songs, like Am Thinlay. Jigme Drukpa *(Folk Songs from Bhutan)* performs a wide selection of the two main styles of folk singing: *zhungdra,* which developed in Bhutan in the seventeenth century and *boedra,* influenced by Tibetan folk music.

There are four main traditional instruments in Bhutan, beyond the ritual instruments used in religious ceremonies: the ornate *draymen* or Bhutanese lute, the *pchewang,* with has only two strings, *lyem* (bamboo flute) and the *yangchen,* made from hollow wood, with 72 strings which are struck lightly with two thin bamboo sticks.

There is a series of four CDs from the Monasteries of Bhutan, with the misleading title *Tibetan Buddhist Rites* (John Levy, Lyrichord). This collection includes a wide range of sacred and folk music, including a hauntingly beautiful recording of a *manip* (an itinerant ascetic) reciting a song recollecting the Zhabdrung Ngawang Namgyal's arrival in Bhutan.

The website www .raonline.ch/pages/bt has examples of Bhutanese music and further information on Bhutanese culture.

## Theatre and Dance

The main form of dance is the *cham,* performed at the tshechus and other festivals held throughout Bhutan. Usually the tshechus are performed in the dzong courtyards. The tsechu is a social event, drawing people from the surrounding districts, and it's also an opportunity to be immersed in Buddhist teachings. The Bhutanese believe that they will create merit by attending the tshechus and watching the performances of ritual dances. Tshechus are not solemn occasions, but are marked by a holiday atmosphere as people put on their finest clothing and jewellery, share their food and exchange news with friends and relatives.

The tshechur are based on a series of dances performed in honour of Guru Rinpoche. The dates and duration of the tshechus vary from one district to another and always take place on or around the 10th day of the Bhutanese calendar, which is dedicated to Guru Rinpoche.

There are three broad categories of dance; the main dances performed are described here.

### PACHAM (DANCE OF THE HEROES)

An energetic dance based on a vision by Pema Linga and is believed to lead believers directly to the presence of Guru Rinpoche.

*Cressida's Bed* by Desmond Barry is a fictional account of the murder of the last Zhabdrung at Talo Dzong.

### SHAWA SHACHI (DANCE OF THE STAG AND HUNTER)

Based on the story of Milarepa's conversion of the hunter Gonpo Dorji to Buddhism, the dance is split into two parts. The first part is comic, with the hunter preparing to set out on a hunting expedition and his servants joking very irreverently with him. The second part is more serious. The hunter and his dog are in pursuit of a deer when the deer seeks shelter with the yogi Milarepa. Milarepa, identifiable by his white cotton robe, sings a song that converts all three to Buddhism. The conversion is symbolised by a rope that both the dog and hunter must jump over.

### DRANYEO CHAM (DANCE WITH THE DRANYEN)

This dance celebrates the diffusion of the Drukpa lineage in Bhutan by the Zhabdrung Ngawang Namgyal. The dancers carry swords and wear a circular headdress, felt boots and heavy woollen clothes. One dancer carries a *dranyen,* a string instrument similar to a guitar.

### SHA NA CHAM (BLACK HAT DANCE)

This dance, on one level, commemorates the killing of the anti-Buddhist Tibetan king, Langdarma in 842 by the Buddhist monk, Pelkyi Dorji. It also represents the transformation of the dancers into powerful tantric yogis, who take possession of the dancing area and drive out all evil spirits as they stamp the ground.

### PHOLAY MOLAY (DANCE OF THE NOBLEMEN AND LADIES)

This is less a dance than a crude play about the two princesses left with an old couple by two princes who leave for war. The two princesses and an old woman are corrupted by some *atsaras* (clowns). On their return, the princes are furious and punish the women by cutting off their noses. Eventually, everybody is reconciled and the princes marry the princesses.

### DRAMETSI NGA CHAM (DANCE OF THE DRAMETSI DRUMMERS)

Based on a vision by Kunga Gyeltshen, the son of Pema Lingpa, this dance depicts 100 peaceful and wrathful deities. The dancers wear animal masks and knee-length yellow skirts, and carry a large hand drum in their left hand and a drumstick in their right.

### DUNGTAM (DANCE OF THE WRATHFUL DEITIES)

In this dance, the deities are the entourage of one of the eight manifestations of Guru Rinpoche, Dorji Drolo. Dorji Drolo and his entourage are armed with *phurba* (special daggers) which execute and thereby redeem an evil spirit (represented by a small mannequin). This represents Buddhist teachings on the liberation of consciousness from the body.

### RAKSHA MANGCHAM (DANCE OF THE RAKSHAS AND THE JUDGEMENT OF THE DEAD)

This is one of the highlights of the tshechu. It represents a spiritual drama as two newly deceased men are brought before the Lord of the Underworld, represented by a large mannequin surrounded by an entourage of *raksha* (a figure or spirit of the underworld). The first to be judged is a sinner, dressed in black. After hearing from Black Demon and White God, the prosecution and defence, his sins outweigh his good actions and he is dragged to the hell realms. The second figure is dressed in white; again the Lord of the Underworld hears about his good and bad actions, and he is found to be virtuous. After a brief attempt by Black Demon to grab the virtuous man, he is led to the pure lands.

### GURU TSHENGAY (THE EIGHT MANIFESTATIONS OF GURU RINPOCHE)

The eight manifestations are different forms of Guru Rinpoche, who is accompanied by his two consorts, Yeshe Tshogyel (on his right) and Mandarava (on his left). This is both a dance and a drama and starts with Dorji Drolo entering the dance area, followed by a long procession with the eight manifestations. For more on the eight manifestations, see p26.

### CHHOESHEY (RELIGIOUS SONG)

This commemorates the opening of the eastern gate to the pilgrimage site at Tsari in Tibet by Tsangpa Gyarey, the founder of the Drukpa Kagyu.

Folk dances are performed in schools, villages and households, as well as by professional dancers during breaks in the tshechu performance. The dancers form a circle or a line and move in an intricate series of steps accompanied by graceful arm movements. One person may lead the singing, with the other dancers picking up the song or answering with a refrain.

In Thimphu, the Royal Academy for the Performing Arts (RAPA) trains young Bhutanese dancers and musicians in religious and folk dances. The quality of the dancing is exceptional and the program they offer is breathtaking in its colour and vitality.

Until recently there has been no tradition of acting beyond the masked dances and comic skits performed at the festivals, but with the development of modern education, school performances include Shakespeare or locally written plays. These are aired regularly on BBS. Although there was no tradition of writing plays in Bhutan, recently there have been moves to produce plays in Dzongkha. One young playwright, Sonam Kinga, has written several award-winning plays in Dzongkha, loosely based on classical Greek works.

For a blend of traditional and modern music, look out for the beautiful recording of chants by Lama Gyurme and Jean-Philippe Rykiel, *The Lama's Chants – Songs of Awakening* (Sony, 1994) and *Rain of Blessings* (Real World Records, 2000).

*Zangtho Pelri* (Tashi Nyencha, 2000), available in Bhutan, has a good selection of traditional songs.

Finally, wherever there is dancing you should be willing to take part. Traditionally, everybody, including visitors, enthusiastically takes part in the final dance *(Tashi Lebey)*, which concludes all festivities or dance performances. Don't feel shy, just follow the person in front of you and smile!

## SPORT
### Traditional Games

Bhutan's national sport is archery *(datse)*. It is played wherever there is enough space and remains the favourite sport for all ages. There are archery tournaments held throughout the country. In the countryside you will see the traditional wooden bows, while in Thimphu modern imported bows are often now used.

Archery contests act as both an affirmation of Bhutanese cultural identity as well as popular entertainment. The tournaments begin with a short ceremony and breakfast. The targets are placed 140m apart. Players often stand close to the targets and call how good or bad the aim of their opponent is – if the contestant hits the target, his team mates will perform a slow dance and sing his praises, while he slips a coloured scarf into his belt. If he misses, the opposition mock his ability.

Women, usually wearing their finest clothes and jewellery, often stand to ·one side of the archery field and act as cheerleaders. They dance and sing during breaks from the shooting. Their songs and shouts can be quite ribald!

Monks are forbidden to participate in archery, so they often play a stone-throwing game called *daygo*. A round, flat stone rather like a discus is tossed at a target and the winner is the one that gets the closest.

The Bhutanese version of shot put is called *pungdo*, and is played with large heavy stones.

*Khuru* is a darts game played on a field about 20m long with small targets similar to those used by archers. The darts are usually homemade from a block of wood and a nail, with some chicken feathers for fins. If a chicken can't be found, bits of plastic make a good substitute. Teams compete with a lot of shouting and arm waving, designed to put the thrower off his aim. The game is a favourite of monks and young boys; beware of dangerous flying objects if you are near a *khuru* target or archery field.

### Modern Sports

Bhutan first sent an archery team of three men and three women to participate in the 1984 Olympics. Since then Bhutan has participated in the Olympics and in a series of regional sporting competitions. It earned a gold medal for tae kwon do in the South Asia Federation games in 2004.

Modern sports, notably basketball, football, golf, tae kwon do, shooting and tennis, are rapidly growing in popularity. Basketball is a favourite, especially since the king used to play basketball in public on a regular basis. Football teams such as DrukStar in Thimphu have emerged in the main urban areas, and you may see matches taking place on the playing fields at Changlimithang. Bhutan came to the attention of filmmakers during the 2002 World Cup when they arranged for Bhutan to play against the football team of the small island of Montserrat. The documentary film, *The Other Final* produced by Johan Kramer narrates the events leading up to the football match and the enthusiastic participation of the crowd.

There is a small golf course lying between Trashi Chhoe dzong and the National Library, plus another at India House. Golf competitions are popular among the emerging middle class. Cricket has recently gained popularity despite the current lack of suitable cricket pitches and there are currently 12 cricket clubs in Thimphu alone.

Until the mid-twentieth century there were no large urban settlements in Bhutan. By 2005, the population of Thimphu was over 50,000.

The population growth rate has been reduced from 3.1% in 1994 to 1.3% now.

In the 2005 Census 96% of Bhutanese declared themselves to be happy.

# Buddhism in Bhutan

Buddhism is inscribed into the landscape of Bhutan – prayer flags, white-and-red chortens and images of Buddhist saints carved into the rock dot the countryside. To understand Bhutan and its peoples, it is essential to have a basic understanding of Buddhism. Buddhist values are central to Bhutanese daily life. The experience of entering a dzong or monastery, or even a private household shrine room will be enriched by understanding the core Buddhist concepts, and how these are encapsulated in some of the common religious images and practices encountered in Bhutan. The Buddhism of Bhutan has a complex and rich visual tradition that can seem overwhelming. The bright and intricate mandalas decorating temple porches, wrathful protective deities and the Wheel of Life all serve the same purpose: to encapsulate basic Buddhist teachings.

Buddhism is perhaps the most accommodating of the world's religions. As Buddhism has spread, it has adapted to local conditions, creating new schools of thought. However, its basic tenets have remained the same and all schools of Buddhism are united by their faith in the value of the original teachings of Sakyamuni (Sakya Thukpa), the Historical Buddha.

Vestiges of Bon, the pre-Buddhist beliefs of Tibet, can still be found in Bhutan. Moreover, Bhutan has a rich folk religion *(luso)* and Bhutanese folk beliefs are primarily concerned with a range of spirits, like *nep* or local deities who act as the custodian of particular valleys such as Chungdu in Haa, or Radak in Wangdue Phodrang. Other spirits reside in rocks or groves of trees; there are *tshomen,* goddesses who inhabit the lakes; *lu,* or *nagas* – snake-bodied spirits who dwell in the lakes, rivers and wells. *Sadak* are lords of the earth and *tsen* are air spirits who can bring illness and death.

Not all Bhutanese are Buddhist. Many of the Lhotshampas, the descendants of Nepalese migrants, are Hindu – as are the majority of the casual labourers from Assam and Bengal. There are still traces on the earlier pre-Buddhist beliefs in the countryside and a small number of Christian converts. Bhutan is tolerant of all religions but does not permit proselytisation. The draft constitution upholds freedom of belief and does not make any religion the official religion of Bhutan. It does, however, recognise the importance of Bhutan's Buddhist heritage to Bhutan's cultural identity.

> 'Buddhism is perhaps the most accommodating of the world's religions'

## HISTORY

Buddhism originated in northern central India around the 6th or 5th century BC, from the teachings of Sakyamuni Buddha (at present, some historians consider that he lived in the 6th century and others in the 5th century). When he was born the local religion was based on Brahmanism. Some Brahmins (in order to purify themselves before performing rituals to their gods) would wander in remote areas and engage in ascetic practices – fasting, practising yogic techniques and meditation. The young Siddhartha Gautama, who would become known as the Buddha, was one of many such wandering ascetics. His teachings became the basis for a new religion, Buddhism.

Little is known for certain about the young Siddhartha Gautama. According to legend his parents, King Suddhodana and Queen Maya, lived in a small kingdom, Sakya, which lay on the border between the present-day states of Nepal and India. Shortly after his birth a wandering ascetic prophesied to King Suddhodana that the young prince would either be a world-conquering king or a liberator of living beings from suffering. The King took various precautions to ensure that his son would never have cause to follow a spiritual path. However, the young prince grew restless and during various excursions from his palace Siddhartha Gautama saw various examples of suffering that inspired him to escape from his palace life.

After fleeing the palace, Siddhartha became a wandering ascetic, fasting and meditating. Finally at Bodha Gaya in Bihar, India, Siddhartha began meditating beneath a bo (papal) tree, declaring that he would not stop until he had achieved enlightenment. He had realised there must be a middle path between the extremes of his former life in the palace and the ascetic practices he had been taught. As dawn broke on the morning of his third night of meditation Siddhartha became a buddha (an awakened one).

## BUDDHIST CONCEPTS

Shortly after gaining enlightenment, the Buddha gave his first public teaching in the Deer Park at Sarnath. For the remainder of his life, the Buddha continued to give teachings and established the early Buddhist monastic community. These early teachings by the Buddha, who is known in Bhutan as Sakyamuni Buddha or Sakya Thukpa, are collected in the sutras and form the basis for all later Buddhist thought. The Mahayana school, which developed later, diverged from these earlier teachings in some respects, but not fundamentally.

The Buddha started his teachings by explaining that there was a middle way that steered a course between sensual indulgence and ascetic self-torment. The Middle Way can be followed by taking the Eight Fold Noble Path, underpinned by the Four Noble Truths. The Four Noble Truths set out the laws of cause and effect. These basic concepts are the core of early Buddhist thought. In Bhutan, these are contained in a series of meditations that lamas and religious teachers view as the foundation for spiritual growth leading to enlightenment: the Four Mind Turnings.

### Four Noble Truths

The Four Noble Truths underpin Buddhist philosophy and are the basic facts about ignorance and enlightenment, suffering and freedom set forth by the Buddha in his first formal discourse in Sarnath, following his attainment of enlightenment at Bodha Gaya.

The first Noble Truth is that life is suffering, the Truth of Suffering. This suffering is the misery of an unenlightened life and the constant process of rebirth in the different realms of existence. At its root is the inherent imperfection of life – the inability to find true satisfaction in samsara. The suffering of life is inherent in the pain of birth, ageing, sickness and death, in having to associate with the unpleasant things of life and to lose that which brings us pleasure.

The reason for this dissatisfaction and suffering is contained in the Second Noble Truth, True Origins. This refers to our desire for things to be other than they actually are. The Buddha taught that in order to gain liberation from suffering, we need to abandon our delusions and selfish actions which are the cause for our rebirth in samsara. Due to our ignorance, we create the causes for our rebirth and maintain the cycle.

The third Noble Truth was described by the Buddha as True Cessation. True Cessation is the stopping of all delusions, our desires and attachment to samsara. With the cessation of desire and attachment, we are able to break the cycle of rebirth and suffering and reach the state of nirvana, the ultimate goal of Buddhism. The final Noble Truth is the truth of the path leading to cessation.

The doctrine of the Four Noble Truths is the foundation on which the whole path to liberation and enlightenment is built. Therefore a deep understanding of these truths, cultivated through reflection and meditation, is an indispensable basis for following the Buddhist path.

**TASHI TAGYE**

Many homes and temples are decorated with *tashi tagye,* the eight auspicious signs of Himalayan Buddhism. Each has a deep symbolic meaning and represents an object used in religious observances.

**PRAYER FLAGS**   *Kunzang Dorji*

Prayer flags are ubiquitous in Bhutan, found fluttering on mountain passes, ridges, mountain meadows, rooftops, dzong and temple courtyards and in front of houses.

The prayer flags are in five colours – blue, green, red, yellow and white – symbolising the elements of water, wood, fire, earth and iron, respectively. They also stand for the five *dhyani* or meditation Buddhas; the five wisdoms; the five directions; and the five mental attributes or emotions.

They may all look similar, but prayer flags have several important variations. Some prayer flags are hung from strings near holy places, especially passes, but most traditional Bhutanese prayer flags are mounted on vertical poles. The text for the flag is carved into wooden blocks and then printed on the cloth in repeating patterns. Each of the four varieties of prayer flag has a specific function, but they all serve the same basic purpose – to invoke the blessings and protection from the deities for conscious beings, living or dead.

## Goendhar

The smallest prayer flags, *goendhars,* are those mounted on the rooftops of Buddhist homes. These white banners have small blue, green, red and yellow ribbons attached to their edges. They invoke the blessings and patronage of Yeshe Goenpo (Mahakala), the main protective deity of the country, to ensure the family's welfare and prosperity. A purification ceremony is performed and the goendhar is erected once a house has been completed. The flags are replaced annually during a ceremony that honours the family's personal local deities.

## Lungdhar

The *lungdhar* (wind flag) is erected on hillsides or ridges and can be for good luck, protection from an illness, the achievement of a personal goal, or the acquisition of wisdom. These flags are printed with the Wind Horse, or Lungta, which carries a wish-fulfilling jewel on its back.

The name and age of the person is printed on the flag along with the text pertaining to the exact need. Astrological charts are used to determine the direction, colour and location of the flag, and a consecration ceremony is performed when it is erected.

## Manidhar

The *manidhar* is erected on behalf of a deceased person, and features prayers to the Bodhisattva of Compassion, Chenresig. When a family member dies, such flags are commissioned to cleanse the sins of the deceased. The *mani* prayer banner takes its name from the mantra '*om mani peme hum*' ('hail to the jewel in the lotus'), which is the special sacred mantra of Chenresig. These prayer flags are generally erected in batches of 108 and invoke Chenresig's blessing and immeasurable compassion for the deceased.

Both the *lungdhar* and the *manidhar* flags are placed at strategic high points from which a river can be seen. In this way, the belief is that the prayers will waft with the wind to the river, and be carried by the river on its long and winding journey.

## Lhadhar

The largest flag in the country is the *lhadhar* (god flag). These huge flags can be seen outside dzongs and other important places and represent victory over the forces of evil. There is normally no text on these flags; they are like a giant version of the *goendhar*. The only difference, apart from size, is at the top, where the *lhadhar* is capped by a colourful silk parasol. You must be formally dressed in traditional Bhutanese attire for Bhutanese and in appropriate dress for foreigners to enter any place where a *lhadhar* stands.

## Pole

At the top of the pole is a *redi*, a wood carving of a traditional knife. It is joined to the flagpole by a *khorlo*, a wooden wheel. The redi represents the god of wisdom, Jampelyang, and the khorlo represents the lotus, which is associated with the birth of Guru Rinpoche.

## Eight-Fold Path

The Fourth Noble Truth, True Paths, set out by the Buddha refers to the correct means through which an individual is able to overcome attachment and desires in the pursuit of liberation from samsara. These are often described as the Eight-Fold Path: with dedication and practice it may lead to accumulation of merit, then enlightenment and liberation. The eight components of the path to enlightenment are: right understanding, right thought, right speech, right action, right livelihood, right effort, right mindfulness and right concentration.

## Karma

As beings are reborn in samsara their rebirths in the different realms of existence are determined by their karma. Rebirth is not haphazard. Karma is often simplified in translation as meaning 'action' *(las)*. The Buddha states that 'for every action we perform we experience a similar result'.

Karma in Buddhist doctrine refers to three important components: actions, their effects and their consequences. Actions are divided into those of the body, speech and mind and the main concern is with the imprint of each action on the mind or mental continuum which follows each being from rebirth to rebirth. Buddhist teachings liken karma to a seed (action) which ripens into a fruit (effect).

Merit *(sonam)* refers to the wholesome tendencies imprinted in the mind as a result of positive and skilful thoughts, words and actions that ripen in the experience of happiness and well being. According to ancient texts, the Tibetan king Srongtsen Gampo set out the ten virtuous and non-virtuous actions in order to help guide people to lead virtuous lives. The Ten Virtuous actions *(gewa cu)* are to refrain from: killing, stealing, inappropriate sexual activity, lying, engaging in gossip, cursing, sowing discord, envy, malice and wrong view.

Mahayana teachings say it is important to dedicate the merit of one's wholesome actions to the benefit of all living beings, ensuring that others also experience the results of one's positive actions. Therefore, in Bhutan and elsewhere in the Himalayan region, the accumulation of merit is not a selfish act. Rather, it is dedicated to all living beings with the aspiration that they gain liberation from samsara, demonstrating the belief that through action all beings, as one, affect each other.

## Rebirth

In Buddhism, life is a cycle of rebirth, and these rebirths are countless as living beings 'wander' in samsara. There is not just one world but a myriad of worlds in which beings may be reborn – according to Buddhist doctrine there are six different realms of existence. Rebirth, or cyclic existence, emerges from fundamental ignorance through a process known as the twelve links of dependent origination. When this fundamental ignorance is reversed, cyclic existence itself can be reversed and nirvana attained, free from suffering and the processes of rebirth. The six realms of existence and the twelve links of dependent origination are commonly depicted in the Wheel of Life and according to Buddhist teachings it is important during one's lifetime to accumulate enough merit to avoid being reborn in one of the three lower realms. This emphasises the preciousness of a human life and the importance of engaging in virtuous actions.

## Impermanence

Along with suffering and the absence of the self, impermanence is regarded in Buddhism as one of the three marks or characteristics of causally conditioned phenomena. Although Buddhist literature mentions various degrees of impermanence, in general it can be defined as the momentarily changing nature of all things. Buddhist teachings say change is dynamic and never ending, reflecting the nature of flux and fluidity in conditioned existence. This fundamental quality of impermanence includes our bodies, the world around us and also our perceiving minds.

## Four Mind Turnings

In Bhutan, as in Tibet, the teachings of Buddha are presented with an emphasis on developing a strong faith through reflection, and in exhorting the practitioner to take the teachings to heart. Many lamas and teachers start by setting out the Four Mind Turnings (or Four Preliminaries). These are undertaken by an aspiring Buddhist practitioner of the tantras before they receive instruction on more advanced meditational practices. All lamas and teachers emphasise the importance for the practitioner to carefully test the teachings, not simply to accept them.

## SCHOOLS OF BUDDHISM

Shortly after the death of Sakyamuni, disputes began to arise among his disciples over the interpretation of his teachings. The sutras were composed after his death and subsequently different schools of thought appeared, leading to a schism and the emergence of the two principal schools of Buddhism, Hinayana and Mahayana.

Hinayana, sometimes known at Theravada, focused on pursuing liberation for the individual. Mahayana took Buddhism in a different direction, emphasising compassion and the liberation of all living beings. The Hinayana teachings retreated to southern India before becoming established in Sri Lanka, Thailand, Burma and Cambodia. The Mahayana teachings were developed in the new Buddhist universities in northern India before being transmitted northwards through the Himalayas, to China, Japan and Korea.

### Mahayana

The Mahayana school emerged in the 1st and 2nd centuries. It teaches that the bodhisattva ('hero of enlightenment') seeks enlightenment for the sake of all living beings, out of heartfelt compassion and self-sacrifice, rather than seeking liberation from samsara for her or himself. This altruistic attitude is referred to as *bodhicitta*, or mind of enlightenment, and involves cultivating love and great compassion towards others through the practice of the six perfections: generosity, moral discipline, patience, effort, concentrations and wisdom.

The Mahayana teachings on compassion permeate the religious beliefs and practices of the Bhutanese.

### Tantrism (Vajrayana)

A new school emerged from the Mahayana in about AD 600. Both the Hinayana and Mahayana schools studied the sutras that recorded the teachings of Sakyamuni; however, the followers of Tantrism believed that he had left a collection of esoteric teachings to a select few of his early disciples. These were known as Tantra *(gyu)*.

Tantra (Sanskrit meaning 'continuum') has two meanings in Buddhism. It refers to the literature dealing with tantric teachings and secondly to the continuum of development from ignorance to enlightenment. Tantra involves identifying with a tutelary deity through deep meditation and the recitation of mantra. The two most well known mantras are *om mani padme hum* of Chenresig (Avalokiteshvara) and *om vajra guru padme siddhi hum* of Guru Rinpoche (Padmasambhava).

In Bhutan many of the ritual objects and the imagery in the monasteries and temples are derived from tantric teachings. They display the many different aspects of enlightenment – at times gentle as in the image of Chenresig

**GOLDEN FISH**

The *sernga* represents the auspiciousness of all beings in a state of fearlessness without drowning in the ocean of suffering.

**VASE OF TREASURE**

The *bumpa* represents long life, wealth and prosperity.

**VICTORY
BANNER**

The *gyeltshen* represents the victory of the Buddhist doctrine over harmful forces.

or the Medicine Buddha, at times wrathful as in the image of Dorje Drolo. The meditational deities sit at the centre of an elaborate mandala, a representation of the pure land where the deity resides. Through years of careful meditation the tantric practitioner identifies with the deity by visualising in detail the three-dimensional mandala.

## BUDDHISM IN BHUTAN
### Arrival of Buddhism in Bhutan

The introduction of Buddhism occurred in the seventh century, when Tibetan king Srongtsen Gampo (r 627–49), a convert to Buddhism, ordered the construction of two Buddhist temples, at Bumthang in central Bhutan and at Kyichu in the Paro valley. Buddhism replaced, but did not eliminate, the Bon practices that were also prevalent in Tibet until the late 6th century. Instead, Buddhism absorbed Bon and its believers. As the country developed in its many fertile valleys, Buddhism matured and became a unifying element. It was Buddhist literature and chronicles that began the recorded history of Bhutan.

In AD 746, Guru Rinpoche came to Bhutan from India at the invitation of one of the numerous local kings. After reportedly subduing eight classes of demons and converting the king, Guru Rinpoche moved on to Tibet. Upon his return from Tibet, he oversaw the construction of new monasteries in the Paro valley and set up his headquarters in Bumthang. According to tradition, he founded the Nyingmapa sect – also known as the old 'red hat' sect – of Mahayana Buddhism, which became for a time the dominant religion of Bhutan. Guru Rinpoche plays a great historical and religious role as the national patron saint; for more on his influence and history, see p26. Following the guru's sojourn, Indian influence played a temporary role until increasing Tibetan migrations brought new cultural and religious contributions.

By the 10th century, Bhutan's political development was heavily influenced by its religious history. Following a period in which Buddhism was in decline in Tibet, contention among a number of subsects emerged. Among these monks was the founder of the Lhapa subsect of the Kargyupa school, to whom is attributed the introduction of the strategically built dzong. Although the Lhapa subsect had been successfully challenged in the 12th century by another Kargyupa subsect (the Drukpa), led by Tibetan monk Phajo Drugom Shigpo, it continued to proselytise until the 17th century.

**ENDLESS KNOT**

The noose of eternity, *pelgibeu,* represents the mind and the union of wisdom and compassion.

The Drukpa teachings spread throughout western Bhutan and eventually became a dominant form of religious practice. In central and eastern Bhutan the older form of Nyingmapa Buddhism was predominant during this period. The three main schools of Himalayan Buddhism who spread Buddhist teachings in Bhutan were the Nyingmapa, the Kagyupa and the Sakyapa. A fourth school, the Gelugpa, emerged in Tibet in the fifteenth century. This school had no impact on the spread of Buddhism in Bhutan and was viewed by the Bhutanese from the 17th century onwards as hostile to Bhutan.

### NYINGMAPA

Nyingmapa is the oldest school of Himalayan Buddhism. The distinction between the old and new schools of Tibetan Buddhism is made on the basis of the break that followed the persecution of Buddhism during the 9th century in Tibet by King Langdarma and preceded the second or later phase of Buddhist propagation when a further corpus of Buddhist literature was introduced from India by Marpa, Atisa and Rinchen Zangpo during the eleventh century. The religious lineages derived from the earlier phase and works translated before the interregnum are known as Nyingma or the Ancient Translation school, while those that emerged thereafter are known at the New Translation school (Sarma).

The Nyingma school did not develop as a strong centralised school following the revival of Buddhism in Tibet. However, the Nyingma did experience a revival through the discovery of *terma* or hidden texts believed to have been buried by Guru Rinpoche in various sacred sites throughout Tibet and Bhutan. These hidden texts were found in the earth or under water as in the case of Pema Linga the great Bhutanese treasure finder *(terton)*, or they might arise in the mind of the yogi. Religious texts were not the only items discovered by *tertons* – ritual implements and figures of Guru Rinpoche were also discovered.

**LOTUS FLOWER**

The *pema* is a symbol of the purification of the body, speech and mind.

## KAGYUPA

The Drukpa Kagyu lineage was established by Tsangpa Gyarey at Ralung Monastery in central Tibet, and was brought to Bhutan by Phajo Drukgom Shigpo. The lineage stems from the great accomplished masters Tilopa, Naropa and Maitripa through to Marpa the Translator, who formed the Dagpo Kagyu lineage. Of importance for Bhutan is the Drukpa Kagyu lineage. All of these traditions integrate practise derived from sutras and the tantras.

The great yogi Milarepa (1040–1123) was the disciple of Marpa the Translator (1012–93) and his spiritual songs remain very popular today. The influence of Milarepa's own disciple, Gampopa (1079–1153) led to the establishment of monasteries that developed into major teachings centres. Eventually, these monasteries overshadowed the ascetic yogi origins of the Kagyupa, although the yogic tradition did continue. Kagyu religious practices emphasise solitary meditation in the Milarepa style, combined with vajrayana practices.

## SAKYAPA

One of the four principal schools of Tibetan Buddhism, named after Samye monastery in western Tibet founded by Khon Konchok Gyalpo in the 11th century at a site that has a slightly whitish rock surface. Sakya literally means 'pale earth'. The widespread influence of the early Sakya masters soon evolved into a whole new school of Tibetan Buddhism, the school reaching its full maturity in particular through the influence of Sakya Pandita. Sakya Pandita's renown as a Buddhist scholar led him, and subsequent abbots, to be recognised as a manifestation of Manjushri (the bodhisattva of wisdom and learning). During the 13th and 14th centuries, the Sakya school became involved in the politics of Tibet. The essence of the Sakya school's thought and practice is enshrined in the set of instructions called 'the path and the fruit', which presents the entire Mahayana path together with a collection of meditative practices focused on the tantric tutelary deity, Hevajra.

**GOLDEN WHEEL**

The *khorlo* is the precious wheel of the Buddha's doctrine.

# Development of Buddhism in Bhutan

The first record of Buddhism in Bhutan is marked by the building of Buddhist temples by the Tibetan king, Songsten Gampo, in the 7th century at Kyichu Lhakhang in Paro and Jampe Lhakhang, Bumthang. The arrival of Guru Rinpoche is viewed as defining the real introduction of Buddhism. According to Bhutanese tradition, Guru Rinpoche arrived in Bhutan en route to Tibet and subdued local gods and demons, as well as saving the life of a local king of Bumthang, Sendha Gyab (sometimes referred to as Sindhu Raja) from a local spirit that had taken his life essence, thereby leading the king to convert to Buddhism. For more on Guru Rinpoche, see p26.

From the 11th century, with the second diffusion of Buddhism in the region, different religious schools appeared in Tibet and viewed the lands of Bhutan as areas suitable for conversion. Gradually, especially in western Bhutan, the Drukpa Kagyupa school steadily increased its influence.

## Phajo Drukpa

Phajo Drugom Zhigpo was born in Kham, eastern Tibet, in about 1184. He received religious instruction from the nephew of Tsangpa Gyarey and set out for Bhutan in 1222.

After staying in Lingzhi, Phajo meditated at Paro Taktshang where he had a vision of Guru Rinpoche. In a later vision, Phajo learned that he would meet his spiritual consort in Wang. Arriving in Wang, he saw Sonam Peldon with a group of girls and sang to them. She replied and they met each other at the Lungten Zampa bridge (this bridge was located near the one that lies on the modern approach to Thimphu). There is a cave below a chorten underneath the bridge which is said to be where Phajo and Sonam stayed. After settling at Dodeyna, near Tango Goemba, he and Sonam had a daughter and seven sons. One day when Sonam and her daughter were gathering food, Phajo took his seven small sons to a bridge over a fast-flowing river and prayed to the deities to show him the way forward for him and his family. Then he threw the seven infants into the river in the belief that those who survived would help him promote the Drukpa teachings and those that died were demons. Sonam, on returning, was furious. Learning that four sons had been swept off in four different directions, she ran to find them and bring them back to Dodeyna. These four surviving sons were to play a significant role in the promotion of the Druk Kagyu teachings in western Bhutan.

'They viewed Phajo with deep suspicion and attempted to remove him and his family from the area'

At the same time as Phajo's arrival in western Bhutan, a large part of that region was under the influence of the Lhapas. The Lhapas were the followers of the Lhapa Kagyu, another sect from Tibet. They viewed Phajo with deep suspicion and attempted to remove him and his family from the area. Over time, local people came to lose faith in the Lhapa and Phajo's spiritual authority increased steadily.

After Phajo's death in 1251 his descendants maintained close ties with the Gya clan, the ruling family of Ralung (the seat of the Drukpa Kagyu in Tibet). Between the 14th and 16th century, several important Druk Kagyu teachers were invited to preach and establish monasteries in western Bhutan. Perhaps the most famous Druk Kagyu teacher was the colourful and unconventional Drukpa Kunley (1455–1529; p136). He is remembered today with immense affection and faith by the Bhutanese and is closely associated with the beautiful temple of Chimi Lhakhang between Lobesa and Punakha. The annual festival held there is attended by couples wanting to conceive a child, and men visit the temple to receive blessings from Drukpa Kunley.

In central and eastern Bhutan, the Nyingma school was the main presence. In the 14th century, the great Buddhist scholar and teacher Longchen Rabjam spent about 10 years in exile from Tibet in Bumthang and Kurtoe. During this time, Longchen Rabjam established three important monasteries at Tharpaling, Ugyencholing and Kunzangling in Kurtoe. Through his efforts, the Nyingma tradition was strengthened in central and eastern Bhutan.

Probably the most famous Bhutanese religious figure is Pema Lingpa (1450–1521; p175). He is referred to as a *terton* or treasure finder for he located *terma* (treasure) hidden by Guru Rinpoche many centuries earlier. The treasures were spiritual treasures – texts and dharma objects that Pema Lingpa used in his teachings.

As well as giving religious teachings and discovering spiritual treasures, Pema Lingpa composed religious texts and sacred dances, and sponsored temple building and decoration. His descendents, like the descendants of Phajo, were to spread to various parts of Bhutan and formed the noble families of the country.

## Zhabdrung Ngawang Namgyal

The arrival in 1616 of the Zhabdrung Ngawang Namgyal marks the transformation of Bhutan and the ascendancy of the Druk Kagyu sect. Born in Tibet in 1594, the Zhabdrung belonged to the Gya family who effectively ruled the Druk Kagyu school at Ralung. His grandfather, Mipham Chogyal ruled as the seventeenth abbot of Ralung monastery and from an early age Ngwang Namgyal was trained to succeed his grandfather.

When Mipham Chosgyal died in 1606, the Zhabdrung became the eighteenth abbot at the age of 12. However, his ascension as abbot was not uncontested and was complicated by the fact that he was also recognised as the reincarnation of a famous Druk Kagyu scholar, Pema Karpo. The son of a Tibetan prince, Pagsam Wangpo came forward claiming to be the reincarnation of Pema Karpo. The dispute escalated and the ruler of Tsang was asked to recognise the Zhabdrung as the true reincarnation. Unfortunately, the rule of Tsang supported the other claimant. Returning from an unsuccessful attempt to resolve matters the Zhabdrung and his followers quarrelled with some supporters of the Tsang ruler. Some of them died when their yak-skin boat capsized. A court case was raised against the Zhabdrung and he was ordered to return the Rangjung Karsapani, a relic from Ralung. The Zhabdrung refused, since the return of the relic would mean that the other claimant would be recognised as the reincarnation of Pema Karpo.

The Zhabdrung dreamt of the two protective deities, Mahakala and Palden Lhamo, who presented him with the land of Bhutan. A latter dream showed a raven, associated with Mahakala, flying south towards Bhutan. He then received an invitation from a Druk lama in Gasa to go to Bhutan. According to his biographer, the Zhabdrung intended to create a religious state based on the religious laws encapsulated in the concept of the Dual System – the balance of religious and secular laws. The Zhabdrung left Ralung in 1616 and took the Rangjung Karsapani with him. At first he stayed in Gasa and then moved on to the upper Thimphu valley where he stayed at Pangri Zampa lhakhang.

The flight of the Zhabdrung to Bhutan did not end his problems with his rivals. In 1617 the Tsang Desi sent a Tibetan army into Bhutan and it was defeated in Paro. The Zhabdrung then visited Tango Goemba, where he was welcomed by the grandson of Drukpa Kuenley, Tshewang Tenzin, who offered the monastery and its lands to the Zhabdrung. Here the Zhabdrung meditated in a cave and performed various rituals to overcome his enemies. He also composed the famous Sixteen I's, a poem which sets out his powers and is inscribed in his seal. A copy of the seal can be seen in the National Museum, Paro.

Although he had defeated the Tsang Desi, other religious groups viewed his arrival in Bhutan with unease. These groups, known in Bhutan as the Five Groups of Lamas, attacked the Zhabdrung when he was constructing Simtokha dzong in 1629. The leader was killed but the threat was not crushed. The lamas sought Tibetan assistance and in 1634 the Tibetans invaded again and were once more defeated. A third invasion occurred in 1639 and after their defeat, the Tibetans recognised the authority of the Zhabdrung over Bhutan. There were later, unsuccessful attacks by the Tibetan and Mongol forces. Henceforth the Zhabdrung set about consolidating his power and extending the control of the new Druk Kagyu state throughout Bhutan.

The Zhabdrung's vision for his new state combined the promotion of the Druk Kagyu teachings with a particular vision of how to administer the state. Religion and secular administration were closely intertwined in the new Drukpa state. At the pinnacle of the new structure was the Zhabdrung. Below him he created the Je Khenpo, or chief abbot, who was responsible for all religious matters. His secular counterpart was the *desi,* who was responsible for all political matters.

'The Zhabdrung dreamt of the two protective deities, Mahakala and Palden Lhamo, who presented him with the land of Bhutan'

**PROTECTIVE DEITIES**

Buddhism has numerous important deities and protectors of the faith, but there are also many other deities that have special significance only within a certain region. These local protector or guardian deities, as well as *yidam* (tutelary deities), may be wrathful manifestations of enlightened beings, spirits or malevolent beings that were subdued and converted by tantric forces. They are an important element of Bhutan's spiritual beliefs and they occupy a special place in lhakhangs. A locally crafted statue, which is often terrifying or wrathful, of a protective deity is found in a corner or in the *goenkhang* of most of Bhutan's lhakhangs.

The deity Mahakala assisted Zhabdrung Ngawang Namgyal all his life and is recognised as the guardian deity of Bhutan. He is also known as Yeshe Goenpo, is often described as the overlord of all the mountain gods and is a Tantric Buddhist form of the Hindu god Shiva. Mahakali (Wisdom Defender) is the female form, also known as Palden Lhamo (Great Black One), the dark-blue protector.

Most of Bhutan's valleys have a local protective deity. Statues of Thimphu's protector, Gyenyen Jagpa Melen, appear in Dechenphug Lhakhang near Dechenchoeling and in Ney Khang Lhakhang next to the dzong. He is also seen as a national protective deity, with Bhutanese visiting his temple to seek his blessings before a new venture or if leaving the country for any length of time. Among the other regional protective deities are Jichu Drakye in Paro, Chhundu in Haa, Talo Gyalpo Pehar in Punakha, Kaytshugpa in Wangdue Phodrang and, in Bumthang, Keybu Lungtsan and Jowo Ludud Drakpa Gyeltshen. These deities are gods who have not left the world and therefore have not gained enlightenment. For more on protective deities, see p76.

## Organisation of the Religious Community

The *dratshang* (central monk body) refers to the government-supported monks who are under the authority of the Je Khenpo. He is assisted by five *lonpons* (masters), each in charge of religious tradition, liturgy, lexicography, or logic. The Je Khenpo moves between Punakha dzong in winter and Thimphu dzong in summer. On these occasions the roads are lined with Bhutanese seeking his blessings and the journey by road takes two days.

Each dzong has a *lam neten,* who is responsible for the monk body in the each *dzongkhag.* Each dzong will have a master of grammar, master of liturgy, master of philosophy, an *umdze* (choirmaster) and a *kundun* (disciple master), who carries a rosary of large beads and a whip.

Traditionally, Bhutanese families would, if they were able, send one son to join a monastery. This was viewed as creating merit for the family and household and a blessing for the child. The fourth *desi,* Tenzin Rabgye, introduced a monk tax in the late 16th century. The reason for this tax, which required one child to be sent to become a monk, was to promote the Drukpa Kagyu sect. *The Songs of Sorrow* by Gelong Sumdar Tashi, dating from the late 18th century, describe how he had to leave his family, including his young wife and son, to become a monk.

There is no longer a monk tax, and young boys continue to enter the monasteries. Any visitor to Bhutan will see long snakes of maroon-robed boy monks walking near the dzongs in Paro and Punakha. Often they come from poor rural families and may or may not have expressed an interest to become a monk. Once in the monastery, their daily lives revolve around learning to read and write.

Typically, the young monks will sit in class with a monk-teacher in the mornings and in the afternoon sit with friends in small groups, reciting their texts. Throughout a monk's education there is an emphasis on memorisation. So each day the monk will memorise a set amount of text and prayers, and will be tested by his teacher. When they are still young the monks do not understand the meaning of the texts. Once they are in the mid-teens they will be examined individually and they will either proceed to the *shedra* (philosophy school) or perhaps join the ritual school. The *shedra* develops the young monk's knowledge and understanding of a range of Buddhist texts and teachings, while the ritual college trains the monk in the correct procedures for a wide range of rituals. Some monks may be trained as painters or sculptors, or as tailors and embroiderers for the various items required for the monastery.

While the government currently provides basic needs (accommodation, food and clothing), the monks are permitted to keep money received from lay people for performing rituals. They may be requested to attend the blessing of a new house, the consecration of a new chorten or to conduct prayers for the well-being of the household. These events take a great deal of preparation for the sponsor, who will need to ensure that all the necessary ritual items are available. The sponsor will provide food to the monks and often the household will be filled with neighbours attending the ceremony. These events renew and strengthen the bonds between the lay and religious community. The monastic life itself revolves around the performance of rituals in the dzongs and monasteries. Additionally, the monks are busy studying and memorising religious texts and practising skills.

Monks continually take vows, as they progress from novice to fully ordained monk. They are celibate and must abstain from smoking and drinking alcohol, but they are not required to be vegetarian and may eat in the evening, unlike their counterparts in Southeast Asia.

A few monks join monastic orders after adolescence, but they are not the norm. Monks may renounce or return their vows at any time in order to return to lay life, often to start a family, and have to pay a token fine. These former monks are called *getre* or 'retired' monks and there is no social stigma attached to this choice. Some may even act as lay religious figures, called *gomchen,* and perform prayers and ceremonies for a range of daily activities, especially if there is no monastery nearby.

## Domestic Rituals

Every house has a *choesham* (altar or shrine room). Each altar usually features statues of Sakyamuni, Guru Rinpoche and the Zhabdrung. In most homes and temples, devotees place seven bowls filled with water on altars. This simple offering is important because it can be given without greed or attachment. If offerings are made to the protective deities, such as Mahakala, then there are only five offering bowls. As all Himalayan Buddhists do, Bhutanese devotees prostrate themselves in front of altars and lamas, first clasping hands above the head, again at throat level and then at the chest. This represents the ultimate desire to attain the body, speech and mind of a buddha.

On special occasions monks prepare *torma* (ritual cake), white and pink sculptures made from *tsampa* (barley flour) and butter, as symbolic offerings to deities. Each deity is associated with a particular form of *torma*.

Rites are performed for events and crises in life such as birth, marriage, promotion, illness and death. The rituals take place in front of the household shrine, or outside with an altar erected with an image of Buddha (representing the Buddha's body), a religious text (representing the Buddha's speech) and a small stupa or chorten (representing the Buddha's mind). The basic rituals of initiation, purification, consecration and the offering of a *torma* are included. For example, a water or incense purification ceremony is performed after a birth, while more elaborate rituals involving the offering of the eight lucky signs (ie Tashi Tagye) may be offered at a promotion or marriage. Astrology maybe used to decide the timing of the rituals. Bhutanese often consult *tsip* (astrologers) before embarking on a journey or a new undertaking. Astrology

'The monastic life itself revolves around the performance of rituals in the dzongs and monasteries'

plays an important role in overcoming misfortune and deciding the most appropriate time to perform rituals to avert misfortune.

Each ritual, irrespective of its purpose, will include prayers for the lineage gurus and the Buddhas, taking refuge in the Three Jewels (Buddha, Dharma and Sangha), a short verse to generate compassion for all living beings (cultivating *bodhicitta*), invocation of the deity, offering of *torma,* meditation on the deity with recitation of the appropriate mantra, closing prayers with dedication of merit and apologies for any shortcomings in the ritual or its recitation. Ordinary men and women do not typically engage in meditation or Buddhist philosophical studies, though many will attempt to complete the preliminary practices and will seek the blessings of lamas before embarking on new ventures, for their children and prosperity.

### LUSO (FOLK RELIGION)

The invocation of local and protective deities, and the offering of incense to the mountain deities, are everyday rituals in Bhutan. Every locality, mountain, lake, river or grove of trees has its deities and they are worshipped by the local communities. In the morning, leaves or aromatic herbs (juniper) are burned as an offering to the mountain deities. On certain days, a single flag is raised on every house and particular deities are invoked. Many of the local deities are believed to have originally been Bon deities converted to Buddhism by Guru Rinpoche. Bon traditions and rituals are still practised in parts of Bhutan during the celebration of local festivals. Bon may have spread to Bhutan from Tibet prior to the arrival of Guru Rinpoche.

Each locality has its own local practices and often women play a major role in these local ceremonies and celebrations. An interesting, if rare, category of female religious figures is the *delog. Delog* are women, occasionally men, who have died and travelled to the other side, where they have watched the judgment of the dead and encountered various buddhas (eg Chenresig or Guru Rinpoche), before returning to life. The *delogs* stress the importance of leading virtuous lives and refraining from causing harm to living beings. The anthropologist Françoise Pommaret encountered several *delog* in eastern Bhutan during the 1980s and the biographies of historical *delog* remain popular in Bhutan.

### OTHER FAITHS

The minority religion of Bhutan is Hinduism, whose adherents – those of Nepalese origin – officially constitute 28% of the population. Although Buddhism has played a central role in the history of Bhutan it has not been made the official state religion and Hindus have de facto freedom of religion. The Druk Gyalpo decreed Dasain as a national holiday, and the royal family participate in its celebration. As the draft constitution stresses, all Bhutanese have freedom of religion and foreign religious personnel are permitted to work in Bhutan, primarily as educators, but are not allowed to proselytise.

### DZOE – SPIRIT CATCHER

Sometimes you will come across a strange construction of twigs, straw and rainbow-coloured thread woven into a spider-web shape. You may see one near a building or by a roadside, with flower and food offerings. This is a *dzoe* (also known as a *tendo*), a sort of spirit catcher used to exorcise something evil that has been pestering a household. The malevolent spirits are drawn to the *dzoe*. After prayers the *dzoe* is cast away, often on a trail or road, to send away the evil spirits it has trapped.

# IMPORTANT FIGURES OF BUDDHISM IN BHUTAN

This is a brief guide to the iconography of some of the main figures of Buddhism in Bhutan. The images are divided into Buddhas, Bodhisattvas, Protective Deities, and Historical Figures. This guide is neither exhaustive nor scholarly; rather it seeks to enable you to identify the main figures on altars and in the temple murals encountered during your trip. The Bhutanese names are given first with the Sanskrit (where applicable) in parenthesis.

## Buddhas

### SAKYAMUNI

Sakyamuni is the Historical Buddha (of the present age), whose teachings are the foundation of Bhutanese Buddhism. Typically in Bhutan, as in Tibet, Sakyamuni is represented as seated with his legs crossed in the adamantine (diamond/*vajra*) position on a lotus-flower throne. His hair is bluish black and there is a halo of light around his head. His right hand touches the ground in the 'witness' *mudra* (hand gesture) and his left rests on his lap, usually with a begging bowl in the left palm. His body is marked with 32 signs of enlightenment.

Sakyamuni

### OPAGME (AMITABHA)

The Buddha of Infinite Light is one of the five *dhyana* (meditational or cosmic) buddhas and resides in the Blissful Pure Land of the West (Sukhavati). He is closely associated with Tsepame and Chenresig and represents the transformation of lust into wisdom. He is depicted seated cross-legged on a lotus throne, with his hands resting on his lap in meditative pose and holding a begging bowl. His body is red in colour.

### DHYANI BUDDHAS

The Dhyani Buddhas are a group of five Transcendent Buddhas and represent five clans: the Vajra, Buddha, Jewel, Lotus and Action clans. Each clan is associated with one of the five wisdoms of the enlightened mind and is headed by a Transcendent Buddha – one of which is Opagme (described above).

Jampa

### TSEPAME (AMITAYUS)

The Buddha of Infinite Life is associated with practices connected to longevity. He has a red-coloured body and holds a precious vase, filled with the nectar of immortality.

### JAMPA (MAITREYA)

The Future Buddha is said to be residing as a bodhisattva in Tushita heaven until his time to incarnate on earth as a buddha. He is shown seated with his feet on the ground and hands in front of his chest, in the 'turning the wheel' *mudra*.

### SANGYE MENLHA

According to Mahayana tradition, Sakyamuni transformed himself into a deep-blue Buddha who emanates healing rays of light and teaches the science of medicine. Buddhism values medicine as a means to alleviate suffering and prolong human life, thereby improving the opportunity to attain enlightenment. Sangye Menlha is seated cross-legged on a lotus throne, deep-blue in colour, with a begging bowl containing three medicinal fruits. He may be surrounded by a group of eight other medicine buddhas.

Chenresig

## Bodhisattvas

### CHENRESIG (AVALOKITESHVARA)

The bodhisattva of compassion is probably the best-known deity in Bhutanese Buddhism, outside Bhutan. Chenresig appears in a variety of forms. He is the 'glorious gentle one' – one of the four great bodhisattvas and the special guardian of Bhutanese religion – pictured sitting in a lotus position, with the lower two (of four) arms in a gesture of prayer. He also appears with 11 heads and 1000 arms arranged in a circle.

### JAMPELYANG (MANJUSHRI)

Jampelyang

The 'princely lord of wisdom' – the embodiment of wisdom and knowledge – carries a sword in his right hand to destroy the darkness of ignorance. He is the patron of learning and the arts.

### CHANA DORJE (VAJRAPANI)

'Thunderbolt in hand' – the god of power and victory – whose thunderbolt represents power and is a fundamental symbol of Tantric faith; it is called a *dorji* in Tibetan and *vajra* in Sanskrit. He is pictured in a wrathful form with an angry face and one leg outstretched.

### DROLMA (TARA)

Chana Dorje

There are many different emanations of Drolma, and a popular prayer recited daily mentions 21 different activities that she performs to protect people and to enable them to gain enlightenment. The two most common representations are as Drolma, a green, female bodhisattva seated on a lotus flower with her right leg extended, ready to leap down to assist. Green Tara is said to have been born from Chenresig's tears of compassion and from her determination to achieve enlightenment in the body of a woman. She is a dynamic bodhisattva. Popularly seen as a saviour, she represents the miraculous activities of all the buddhas. The other form, known as Drolkar (White Tara), is seated in the full lotus posture and with seven eyes, including one in her forehead and two on her palms and soles of her feet.

## Protective Deities

### CHOKYONG (LOKAPALAS)

#### Nagpo Chenpo (Mahakala)

Mahakala appears in a variety of forms in Bhutan and is one of the fiercest protective deities. Most Bhutanese monasteries and temples have a shrine dedicated to him (*goenkhang*; not open to women). Mahakala may be invoked to help remove obstacles to a new undertaking, or in times of danger. His worship in Bhutan was popularised by the Zhabdrung Ngawang Namgyal, whose personal protective deity he was. According to legend, Mahakala appeared to the Zhabdrung in his raven form (Gompo Jarodanden) and advised him to go to Bhutan. The Raven Headed Mahakala is the basis for the Raven Crown worn by the Bhutanese monarchs.

Drolkar

Mahakala is black with reddish hair which rises upwards. He has three eyes and is surrounded by fire and smoke. He wears various bone ornaments and a skull garland. He carries a curved *vajra* knife in his right hand and a skull cup in his left. Depending on the form depicted he may have two, four, six or more arms.

#### Palden Lhamo (Mahakali)

The Glorious Goddess is a fierce protective deity and is closely associated with Yeshe Gompo. She is an important protector of the Kagyu order and is equally important to the other sects of Nyingma, Sakya and Gelugpa (in Tibet). Palden Lhamo is invoked in times of difficulty and special pujas are performed to avert misfortune, like natural disasters and wars. She has a ferocious appearance and is quite distinctive. Her body is dark blue, while the palms of her hands and the soles of her feet are red. She wears a crown

Green Tara

of five skulls and her long hair rises upwards. She carries a skull cup in her left hand and brandishes a club in her right. She rides on a wild ass and her saddle cloth is a flayed human skin.

## Historical Figures
### GURU RINPOCHE (PADMASAMBHAVA)

'The Lotus Born', is an Indian Buddhist Great Adept who, according to Bhutanese tradition, arrived in Bhutan before he went to Tibet in the eighth century. Popularly known as Guru Rinpoche, he is viewed as the Second Buddha by the Nyingma sect. He is depicted seated in a half-lotus position on a lotus throne, wearing a red five-pointed hat with vulture feathers at the top. He wears a blue inner robe with a golden robe and an outer red cloak. He has long flowing hair and a curly moustache. In his extended right hand he holds a *vajra* and in his left hand, resting on his lap, is a skull cup filled with nectar. A staff topped with a freshly severed head, a decaying head and a skull rests in the crook of his left arm. A ritual dagger, for subduing demons, is tucked into his belt. He may be accompanied by his two female disciples, Yeshe Tshogyal and Mandarava, one on either side. Guru Rinpoche also appears in eight manifestations (see p26).

Guru Rinpoche

### MILAREPA

A great Tibetan magician (1040–1123) and poet of the Kagyu lineage, he is believed to have attained the supreme enlightenment of Buddhahood in the course of one life. He travelled extensively throughout the Himalayan border lands and is said to have meditated at Taktshang in Bhutan, where he composed a song. Most images of Milarepa picture him smiling and holding his hand to his ear as he sings.

### DRUKPA KUNLEY

The wandering ascetic, Drukpa Kunley (1455–1529), is one of the main figures of the Druk Kagyu. His ribald songs and poems were unconventional and have earned him the affection of the Bhutanese. In Bhutan he is often depicted with a bow-and-arrow case and accompanied by a small hunting dog. In Chimi Lhakhang, Drukpa Kunley is depicted dressed similarly to the great Mahasiddhis, with a bare torso and a loin cloth. Elsewhere he is shown wearing normal lay dress with boots. For more on Drukpa Kunley, see p136.

Milarepa

### PEMA LINGPA

The *terton* (treasure finder) Pema Lingpa (1450–1521) was born in Tang valley, Bumthang. The best-known statue of Pema Lingpa was made by Pema Lingpa himself and is kept at Kunzangdrak Goemba, Bumthang. Usually depicted in the *vajra* position, Pema Lingpa holds a *bumpa* (vase symbolising long life) in his hands and wearing a hat similar to that worn by Guru Rinpoche, with the notable addition of two *vajras* crossed at the front of it. For more on Pema Lingpa, see p175.

### ZHABDRUNG NGAWANG NAMGYAL

The Zhabdrung Ngawang Namgyal (1594–1651) is regarded as the founder of Bhutan, where he arrived from Tibet in 1616. The Zhabdrung has a distinctive white, pointed beard and wears monastic robes, and is seated in the lotus posture. In his left hands he holds a *bumpa* and his right hand is in the 'witness' mudra. Over his right shoulder is a meditation belt. The Zhabdrung wears a distinctive ceremonial hat of the Druk Kagyu order.

Zhabdrung Ngawang Namgyal

# Architecture

Bhutanese architecture is one of the most striking features of the country. Massive dzongs (fort-monasteries), remote goembas (monasteries) and lhakangs (temples), as well as the traditional houses all subscribe to a characteristic Bhutanese style. The lack of written plans, however, means there are many variations and very few structures sharing the same design. There are also regional variations dictated by local topography and available building materials.

## HOUSES

The style of Bhutanese houses varies depending on the location, particularly the elevation. Thatched bamboo houses predominate in the lower altitudes in the south of the country, whereas at very high altitudes most homes are simple stone structures or even yak-hair tents. Houses in the inner-Himalayan zone, such as those around Paro and Thimphu, are built in a characteristically Bhutanese style oddly reminiscent of Swiss chalets.

A typical Bhutanese house is two storeys high with a large, airy attic used for produce storage. In rural areas the ground floor is always used as a cattle barn and the upper floor as the living quarters. In most houses, one elaborately decorated room called a *choesum* serves as a chapel.

The foundation is made from stones placed in a trench and built up to a height of about 50cm above the ground. In central and eastern Bhutan the walls are usually made of stone. In the west the walls are 80cm to 100cm thick and are made of compacted earth, which provides an extremely strong, rigid and durable structure. To build these walls, a wooden frame is constructed then filled with damp mud. The mud is compacted by being pounded with wooden poles to which a flat ram is attached. When the wall reaches the top of the frame, the frame is shifted upwards and the process begins again.

The pounders are usually teams of women, who sing and dance as they beat the walls. Although Bhutanese women are usually shy and modest with outsiders, they traditionally loosen their inhibitions and exchange ribald comments with men as they perform the pounding, which can take several weeks for a large house. Once the mud wall is finished, it is either left in its natural colour or is whitewashed.

On the lower floor, an opening for a door, and perhaps some windows, is left in the mud wall that forms the front of the house, which traditionally faces south. The upper floor is supported by wooden beams that fit into holes in the mud wall. Central columns are used to support the beams, because it is difficult to find a single piece of timber to span the entire width of the house. The earthen walls for the upper floor form only the back of the house and the back half of the two side exterior walls. The front portion of the living area is always built of timber, which is sometimes elaborately decorated, with large divided windows facing south. The wooden portion of the house extends out over the front and side mud or stone walls.

Following tradition, and also structurally logical, the windows on the lower floor are small; larger windows are built on upper floors. In older houses the windows are sliding wooden panels, not glass. Above all, windows in Bhutan comprise a cut-out of a curved trefoil motif, called a *horzhing*. In Bhutan there are often several explanations for everything, and this motif is said to be either of Persian influence or simply a practical design which allows a person to look out of the window while the smoke blows out through the opening above their head.

Many houses are decorated with carved wooden phalluses, often crossed by a sword, which are hung at the four corners or over the door to ward off evil.

Building regulations insist all windows in a building (with the exception of toilet windows) must incorporate a *horzhing*, the very characteristic trefoil cut-out at the top of all Bhutanese windows.

An elaborate wooden cornice is usually built along the top of the wall directly under the roof of the house. Traditional roofs are pitched and covered with wooden shingles. Often the roofs leak because the pitch is insufficient or the shingles have been badly prepared. Shingles need to be replaced frequently and many people now choose corrugated sheet metal for their roofs. A feature missing in all Bhutanese architecture is a gutter – expect a soaking when you enter or leave a house during rain.

The internal walls, and often parts of the external walls, are built with a timber frame that is filled in with woven bamboo and plastered with mud. This construction is called *shaddam* (weave-mud).

The heavy wooden doors are made from several planks held firmly together using a tongue-and-groove technique. This technique is used to fit together all the woodwork, and not a single nail is used in a traditional structure. The door hinge is a pair of wooden pegs that fit into round holes above and below the door frame.

A large space is left below the roof. This serves as a place for storing hay or for drying animal skins and chillies. In winter the hay helps insulate the house. Sometimes woven bamboo mats are placed around the attic, but often it is simply left uncovered.

The stairways to the upper floor and attic are ladders made by carving steps into a whole tree trunk. If you find yourself climbing one of these ladders, reach around behind the right edge and you may find a groove cut there to serve as a handrail.

After a house is built, the all-important decoration begins. Wooden surfaces are painted with various designs, each with a special significance. Swastikas, floral patterns representing the lotus, cloud whirls and the *tashi tagye* (eight auspicious symbols) are the most common (see p64). Beside the front door are larger paintings, often of mythical animals such as the *garuda*, or large red phalluses. The phallus is not a fertility symbol; it is associated with the Lama Drukpa Kunley (see p136) and believed to ward off evil. A prayer flag called a *goendhar* is erected on the centre of the roof of all Buddhist homes.

> Wooden roofing shingles typically last about three years before they need replacing, hence the practical and ecological, but not necessarily aesthetic, shift to corrugated iron roofing.

> The word *dzong* is of Tibetan origin and translates as 'fortress'. The dzong system is believed to have been introduced into Bhutan in 1153 by Gyelwa Lhanangpa, a monk from Dresung in Tibet.

## DZONGS

Bhutan's dzongs are perhaps the most visibly striking architectural aspect of the kingdom. They are outstanding examples of grand design and construction. These huge, white citadels dominate the major towns and serve as the administrative headquarters of all 20 *dzongkhags* (districts) and the focus of secular and religious authority in each. As well as the large, active district dzongs, there are a few dzongs that have been destroyed or abandoned, or are now used for other purposes, such as Simtokha Dzong (p116), south of Thimphu, and Dobji Dzong, south of Chhuzom. Not all dzongs are ancient monuments; for example, a new dzong was built in Trashi Yangtse in eastern Bhutan in 1997.

Many dzongs had a *ta dzong* (watchtower), which was either part of the building, as in Jakar Dzong (p122), or a separate structure, as in Paro (p168) and Trongsa Dzongs (p164). This structure was also used as an ammunition store and dungeon. Many dzongs were accessed by cantilever bridges as an additional protective measure. Most dzongs have inward-sloping walls, an architectural feature known as battered walls, which can fool the eye and make the building look imposing and larger than its actual dimensions. They usually have only one massive door, which leads into a small passage that makes two right-angle turns before it enters the main courtyard. This is a design feature to keep invaders from storming the dzong.

During the time of Zhabdrung Ngawang Namgyal (1594–1651), the dzongs served their primary function as fortresses well and each was the stronghold of a *penlop* (regional governor). Many of the feuds and battles for control during

> According to tradition, no woman can be in a dzong between sunset and sunrise. This tradition has only been broken once, when the former Indian prime minister, Indira Gandhi, stayed in Trashi Chhoe Dzong, in Thimphu, after receiving special permission from the Je Khenpo.

**GUARDIANS OF THE FOUR DIRECTIONS**

Paintings or statues of the guardians, or kings, of the four directions appear on the *gorikha* (veranda) to guard the entrance to most lhakhangs. The guardians have an origin in ancient Mongolian tradition, and each one holds a different object. They are warriors who guard the world against demons and earthly threats.

Chenmizang, the red king of the west, holds a *chorten* and a snake, and is the lord of the *nagas* (serpents).

Yulkhorsung, the white king of the east, plays the lute and is the lord of celestial musicians.

Namthose, the gold king of the north, holds a mongoose and a banner of victory. He is a god of wealth and prosperity.

Phagchepo, the blue king of the south, holds a sword in his right hand.

the 17th to 20th centuries were waged by *penlops* whose troops attacked neighbouring dzongs. The key to success in these battles was to capture the dzong of the opposing *penlop*, thereby gaining control of that district.

Bhutan's dzongs were built of stone or pounded mud, and a considerable amount of timber, including massive beams and wooden shingle roofs. This, combined with the large number of butter lamps used in temples, has caused fires in almost all dzongs. Most of Bhutan's dzongs suffered severe damage during the 1897 earthquake and were repaired or rebuilt in their original style. All important dzongs have been (or are being) rebuilt using traditional construction methods, though in many places corrugated-iron roofs have replaced wooden shingles.

Bhutanese proclaim proudly that no nails are used to construct dzongs. Furthermore, dzong architects don't prepare any plans or drawings. They rely only on a mental concept of what is to be built, and this was how Thimphu's Trashi Chhoe Dzong was reconstructed in 1966.

Each dzong has unique details, but most follow the same general design principles. Most dzongs are divided into two wings: one containing temples and monks' quarters and one for government offices. The monastic wing of many dzongs actually serves as a monastery, with the resident monk body called a *rabdey*. In early days, most dzongs had a *rabdey*, but today only the dzongs of Thimphu, Punakha, Paro, Mongar, Trongsa, Jakar and Trashigang serve as monasteries. The *dratshang* (central monk body) maintains monastic schools in the dzongs of Punakha, Trongsa and Paro. Punakha Dzong is the seat of the chief abbot, His Holiness the Je Khenpo.

The main courtyard of the dzong is the *dochey*, which is paved with large flagstones. Along the outer walls of the dzong are several storeys of rooms and galleries overlooking the paved courtyard; these rooms are the monks' quarters and classrooms. Because the monastic wing of the dzong is physically separate from the secular wing, many dzongs have two docheys, the second being surrounded by administrative offices.

The central structure of the dzong is a tower-like building called the *utse*. In most dzongs, the *utse* has a series of chapels, one on each floor. On the ground floor of the *utse* is the lhakhang.

## GOEMBAS & LHAKHANGS

Bhutan has an enormous number of religious buildings. According to the National Commission for Cultural Affairs there are 2002 such buildings – 437 are owned by the state in the custody of the *dratshang* and another 127 are in the care of reincarnate lamas. In addition, there are another 870 village lhakhangs and an estimated 568 that are privately owned. Each was designed for a different purpose to suit the wishes of the founders, architects or sponsors.

Entry to dzongs is through a single gate controlled by a policeman who restricts entry and enforces dzong protocol. Bhutanese are required to wear formal dress (*gho* for men and *kira* for women) and scarf (*kabney* and *rachu*) at all times within the dzong.

Often the entire population of the valley sought refuge in the dzong during a war.

In Dzongkha, a monastery is called a goemba, and the word is pronounced quite differently from the corresponding Tibetan word, *gompa*. A primary reason for selecting the location of a monastery is to have a remote location where the monks can find peace and solitude. This is particularly evident in Bhutan where goembas are built atop rocky crags or on remote hillsides.

Several goembas in Bhutan were built at sacred caves that had previously been places of meditation. Taktshang in Paro (p128) and Kurjey in Bumthang (p173) are two famous examples that were built around caves where Guru Rinpoche is believed to have meditated for extended periods.

All Bhutanese goembas are different, but they all possess certain common features. They are self-contained communities, with a central lhakhang and separate quarters for sleeping. The lhakhang is at the centre of a dochey, similar to that of the dzongs, which is used as a dance arena during festivals.

On all religious buildings in Bhutan, and on dzongs too, a painted red band called a *khemar* runs just below the roof. One or more circular brass plates or mirrors representing the *nima* (sun) are often placed on the *khemar*. The golden deer sometimes seen above the entrance of a goemba, particularly Nyingma goembas, are symbols of the deer park at Varanasi where the Buddha did his earliest teachings.

The term lhakhang is a bit confusing because it may be used to refer to both the building itself and to the room inside the building that is the primary chapel. Furthermore, some goembas have several lhakhangs within the central building.

A typical lhakhang has a cupola and a gilded ball-shaped ornament, called a *serto*, on the roof. Most have a paved path around the circumference of the building. On the outside wall are racks of prayer wheels, which monks and devotees spin as they circumambulate the building.

The entrance to the lhakhang is through the *gorikha*, which is covered with murals, usually depicting the guardians of the four directions or a wheel of life. Entry is via a large painted wooden door that is often protected by a heavy cloth or yak-hair curtain. The door opens to a *tshokhang* (assembly hall), also called a *dukhang* or *kunre*. The hall is usually so large that it has rows of pillars to hold up the roof, and on its walls are paintings that describe the life of Buddha.

At the far end of the *tshokhang* is an elaborately decorated altar *(choesham)* that can be part of the main room or else be housed in a separate room or lhakhang. The two-tiered *choesham,* with its large gilded statue, is a focal point of the lhakhang, and depending on when and why the lhakhang was built, the statue may be of Śakyamuni, Guru Rinpoche or another figure. Jampa is the central figure in many lhakhangs built before Guru Rinpoche's visits to Bhutan, particularly those attributed to Songtsen Gampo. The central statue is usually flanked by two smaller figures, sometimes the consorts of Guru Rinpoche, and other deities related to the central image. (See p75 for the description of key deities.)

On the upper level of the *choesham* are *torma* (colourful sugar-and-butter ornaments) and various objects used in worship, such as a *dorji*, conch shells, trumpets made of thighbone, small drums and bells. On the lower tier are butter lamps and offerings of rice, flowers, water and money. Frequently, a silk parasol hangs over the altar. Often just a single butter lamp burns on the altar, unlike temples in Tibet where there may be hundreds of lamps burning. On auspicious occasions in Bhutan, however, 108 or even 1000 butter lamps are lit.

In most lhakhangs, often on the upper floor, is a room called a *goenkhang,* which is devoted to the protective and terrifying deities (see p76). The statues in these rooms are usually covered except when rituals are performed.

To prevent potentially destructive fires in goembas, arrays of ritual butter lamps are often burned in a separate small building.

One way that lhakhangs in Bhutan differ from those in Tibet is that they feature a pair of elephant tusks alongside the altar to symbolise good. Buddhists revere the elephant because when the Buddha was born, his mother had a vision of a white elephant.

Because dzongs were usually placed on ridges, a tunnel was often constructed to the nearest water supply so that those in the dzong could survive a long siege.

Weapons are stored in this room and may include old muskets, armour, and round shields made from rhinoceros hide. Teams of archers sometimes sleep in a *goenkhang* (chapel housing deities) before a major match, but women are never allowed to enter and the monks are reluctant to allow entry to any visitors.

When approaching a chorten or *mani* wall always walk to the left.

If the lhakhang is in a monastery, then opposite the altar, facing the central image, is a throne upon which the abbot, or *khenpo*, sits during ceremonies. Between the *khenpo's* throne and the altar are rows of cushions on which monks sit during prayers and ceremonies.

## CHORTENS

A chorten is literally a receptacle for offerings, and in Bhutan all chortens contain religious relics. Chortens are often situated in locations considered inauspicious – river junctions, cross roads, mountain passes and bridges – to ward off evil. The classical chorten shape is based on the ancient Indian form of a stupa. Each of the chorten's five architectural elements has a symbolic meaning. The square or rectangular base symbolises earth. The hemispherical dome symbolises water. The conical or pyramidal spire symbolises fire (the spire has 13 step-like segments that symbolise the 13 steps leading to Buddhahood). On top is a crescent moon and a sun, symbolising air, and a vertical spike symbolising ether or the sacred light of the Buddha. Inside is placed a carved wooden pole called a *sokshing*, which is the life-spirit of the chorten.

www.ahf-bhutan.com documents the restoration of Buli Lakhang and the training of Bhutanese in building conservation techniques sponsored by the American Himalayan Foundation.

Some chortens, such as the National Memorial Chorten in Thimphu (p104), are built in memory of an individual. Others commemorate the visit of a saint or contain sacred books or the bodies of saints or great lamas. Bhutan has three basic styles of chorten, usually characterised as Bhutanese, Tibetan and Nepali.

The Nepali-style chorten is based on the classical stupa. On Nepali chortens the four sides of the tower are painted with a pair of eyes, the all-seeing eyes of Buddha. What appears to be a nose is actually the Sanskrit character for the number one, symbolising the absoluteness of Buddha. The prototypes for the Nepali chortens in Bhutan are Swayambhunath and Bodhnath in Kathmandu. The large Chorten Kora in Trashi Yangtse (p195) and Chendebji Chorten near Trongsa (p161) are two examples of the Nepali style of chorten.

The Tibetan-style chorten has a shape similar to the stupa, but the rounded part flares outward instead of being a dome shape. Thimphu's National Memorial Chorten is an excellent example of this style.

Another structure common in Bhutan is the *mani* wall. As its name implies, this is a wall with carved *mani* stones placed in it. Bhutanese *mani* walls are usually quite short, but long *mani* walls can be found in Bumthang.

The Bhutanese design comprises a square stone pillar with a *khemar* near the top. The exact origin of this style is not known, but is believed to be a reduced form of the classical stupa, with only the pinnacle and square base. Some Bhutanese chortens have a ball and crescent representing the moon and sun on top.

Several other types of chorten are also found in Bhutan. The *khonying* (two legs) is an archway that forms a gate over a trail. Travellers earn merit by passing through the structure, which is decorated with interior wall paintings and a mandala on the roof. The *mani chukor* is shaped like a Bhutanese chorten but is hollow and contains a large prayer wheel. It is built over or near a stream so that the water turns a wooden turbine below the structure, which then turns the prayer wheel.

# Environment

Bhutan occupies a fascinating corner of the globe. Scientists have long considered the eastern Himalaya to be an area critically important in terms of global biological diversity. Add to this the legacy of isolation, the sheer inaccessibility of much of the country, low human population and a traditional reverence for nature, and you have the ingredients for a singular showcase of nature conservation within a region increasingly impacted by overpopulation and indiscriminate development.

## THE LAND

Bhutan is a landlocked country about 300km long and 150km wide, encompassing 46,500 sq km. It is bounded on the northwest and north by Tibet and the rest of the country is surrounded by India: on the east by the state of Arunachal Pradesh; on the south by Assam and West Bengal; and on the west by Sikkim. Tibet's Chumbi valley, the old trade and expedition route from India to Lhasa, lies between the northern parts of Bhutan and Sikkim.

Virtually the entire country is mountainous, and ranges in elevation from 100m to the 7541m Gangkhar Puensum peak on the Tibetan border. It can be divided into three major geographic regions: the high Himalaya of the north; the hills and valleys of the inner Himalaya; and the foothills and plains of the south.

### Greater Himalaya

A range of high Himalayan peaks forms part of the northern and western borders of the country. These are the thrones of the gods; almost none has been climbed, many are virtually unexplored and some are not even named. There are several high mountain passes that cross the Himalaya, but for the most part it remains an impenetrable snow-clad barrier (20% of the country is under perpetual snow). The Himalayan range extends from Jhomolhari (7314m) in the west to Kulha Gangri (7554m), near the centre point of the northern border. A chain of lower peaks extends eastwards to the Indian state of Arunachal Pradesh.

The Lunana region, just south of the midpoint of Bhutan's border with Tibet, is an area of glacial peaks and high valleys that are snowbound during the winter. A range of high peaks forms the southern boundary of Lunana, isolating it from the rest of the country.

### Inner Himalaya

South of the high peaks lies a maze of broad valleys and forested hillsides ranging from 1100m to 3500m in elevation. This is the largest region of Bhutan and all the major towns, including Thimphu, are here. This part of Bhutan is cut by deep ravines formed by fast-flowing rivers that have their source in the high Himalaya. The hillsides are generally too steep for farming; most have remained covered in virgin forest.

The greater part of Bhutan's western border is formed by the Himalayan range, including the peaks of Jhomolhari and Jichu Drakye (6989m). Several forested ridges extend eastwards from this range, and these define the large valleys of Thimphu, Paro, Haa and Samtse. Between Punakha and Thimphu lies a well-defined ridge that forms the watershed between Thimphu's Wang Chhu and Punakha's Puna Tsang Chhu. The east–west road crosses this ridge through a 3050m pass, the Dochu La.

*Geology of the Bhutan Himalaya* by Augusto Gansser is a large-format book that comprehensively describes Bhutan's geology.

Millions of years ago the space Bhutan now occupies was an open expanse of water, part of the shallow Tethys Sea. The Tibetan plateau, or 'roof of the world', was beachfront property.

*Trees and Shrubs of Nepal and the Himalayas* by Adrian and Jimmie Storrs is the best field guide to the forests of Bhutan.

A range called the Black Mountains lies to the east of the Puna Tsang Chhu watershed, forming the major barrier between eastern and western Bhutan. Pele La (3500m) is the most important pass across the Black Mountains.

A north–south range of hills separates the Trongsa and Bumthang valley systems. The road crosses this ridge via Yotong La (3425m). Further east, the Donga range of hills follows the border that separates the Bumthang and Lhuentse districts, with Thrumshing La (3780m) as the crossing point for the road. Eastern Bhutan, which encompasses most of the Manas Chhu watershed, lies to the east of this range.

Thrumshing La provides the only road access across the Donga range, which drops precipitously on its eastern side to the Kuri Chhu. The steep Rodang La crosses the northern part of this range and there are few lower passes in the south that are still used by herders. The northern region just east of the Donga range is known as Kurtoe. In the far east, another range of hills runs south from the Himalayan slopes to separate the Lhuentse and Trashi Yangtse valleys.

## Southern Foothills

The foothills rise swiftly from the plains (known as the Terai), and except for a very narrow band of flat land, this part of the country is either forest or terraced farmland.

### THE DUARS

The fertile valleys that extend 15km to 30km from the hills to the Indian states of Assam and Bengal are known as the duars, as is the lower portion of Bhutan's foothills. *Duar* is a Sanskrit word meaning 'passes' or 'gates', and is the origin of the English 'door'. Before the British annexed Bhutan's southern regions each *duar* was under the control of a Bhutanese *dzongpen* (lord of the dzong), but as they were malaria-infested they were largely unoccupied by the Bhutanese, who stayed in the northern hills.

Each *duar* is named after a river valley that leads out of Bhutan, though the *duar* itself is actually the land between two rivers. The land ranges from an elevation of about 100m to almost sea level at the Brahmaputra River, and the slope is barely perceptible. The fertile land now supports tea gardens, rice paddies and a few protected areas such as the Buxa Tiger Reserve.

Seven of the *duars* abut the border of Assam between the Dhansiri (Durlah) and Manas Rivers. The remaining 11, from the Manas River to the Teesta River in the east, border on the state of West Bengal.

## Rivers

Rivers, or *chhus,* play an important role in Bhutan's geography, and their enormous potential for hydroelectric power has helped shape the economy. Flowing south, they have created deep valleys, making all east–west travel a tedious process of steep winding descent followed by an equally steep, equally winding climb to the next ridge. There are four major river systems in Bhutan, most known by several names as they flow through the country.

Most of the rivers have their headwaters in the high mountains of Bhutan, but the Himalaya range is not a continental divide, and there are three rivers that actually flow through the mountains into the country. The Amo Chhu flows from Tibet's Chumbi valley across the southwestern corner of Bhutan, where it becomes the Torsa Chhu, and exits at Phuentsholing. Two tributaries of the Manas, in eastern Bhutan, originate outside the country. The Kuri Chhu has its headwaters in Tibet (where it is known as the Lhobrak Chhu) and crosses into Bhutan at an elevation of only 1200m; the other tributary, the Gamri Chhu, rises in India's Arunachal Pradesh.

*Birds of Bhutan* by Carol Inskipp, Tim Inskipp and Richard Grimmett is a comprehensive, illustrated guide to Bhutan's avian treasures.

Conservation International's website on biodiversity (www .biodiversityhotspots .org) includes facts and figures on biodiversity in the Himalaya hotspot, including Bhutan. Although these hotspots collectively occupy 2.5% of the earth's space, they are home to 50% of the world's plant species and 42% of the world's vertebrates.

*Wild Rhododendrons of Bhutan* by Rebecca Pradhan is a beautiful guide to Bhutan's rhododendrons, with photographs of all 46 species.

The Thimphu Chhu, known in its lower reaches as the Wang Chhu, powers the Chhukha and Tala hydroelectric projects and eventually becomes the Raidak River in India. The Pho Chhu and Mo Chhu join at Punakha to form the Puna Tsang Chhu, which drains the area between the Dochu La and the Black Mountains. This river is known as the Sankosh when it reaches India. The Manas is Bhutan's largest river, draining about two-thirds of the country; in its upper reaches it is known as the Drangme Chhu. The Mangde Chhu flows from Trongsa and joins the Manas Chhu just before it flows into India. Unlike most other rivers that flow from Bhutan into India, the Manas retains its name when it crosses the border. All of Bhutan's rivers eventually flow through the duars to become part of the Brahmaputra, which is known in Tibet as the Yarlung Tsampo, with a source near Mt Kailash in the far west.

The most authoritative and complete guide to Bhutan's mammals, their identification, behaviour and distribution is *A Field Guide to the Mammals of Bhutan* by Tashi Wangchuk.

Because the central Himalaya of Bhutan receives the full brunt of the monsoon, Bhutan's rivers are larger and have created much broader valleys than rivers further to the west in Nepal and India. In their upper reaches, most Bhutanese rivers have created large fertile valleys such as those of Paro, Punakha, Thimphu, Haa and Bumthang. As the rivers pass through the centre of Bhutan, the valleys become steeper and narrower, and roads have to climb high on the hillside. In eastern Bhutan the Manas valley is generally broader, and some roads run alongside the river itself.

When they reach the plains, the rivers drop much of the glacial silt they have collected and follow a meandering course over gravel stream beds. There are several oxbow lakes in the plains where rivers have changed their course over the years.

# WILDLIFE

Bhutan features a tremendous diversity of plants and animals living in a range of ecosystems from subtropical jungle barely above sea level to snowbound mountains above 7500m. The country's various habitats are believed to contain over 5500 species of plants, and close to 200 species of mammals and over 600 species of birds.

## Animals

Large mammals abound in the wilds of Bhutan, but unless you are trekking or until Royal Manas National Park is opened up you will be very lucky to see more than a few examples. The neighbourhood of Royal Manas is home to a large variety of well-known south Asian game species: water buffalo, gaur, serow, wild pig and several species of deer: sambar, muntjac, chital, and hog. It is also the best place to see Asian elephants and the very rare greater one-horned rhinoceros.

The musk deer is a primitive deer that has no antlers; both sexes have oversized canine teeth that protrude from its mouth, in males these protruding teeth can be 7cm long and are used in territorial battles.

On the high trails you may well be lucky enough to spot herds of blue sheep, or bharal. Blue sheep are goat-antelopes, taxonomically somewhere between goats and sheep, that turn a bluish-grey in winter and are found from 1800m to 4300m. Other mammals that prefer the high life include wolves, yaks and the diminutive, unusual musk deer. The male's musk gland is a highly valued perfume ingredient and this secretive deer is a target for indiscriminate poaching. Fat marmots whistle as you pass their burrows in the high alpine pastures and the curious takins (see p87) can be seen in northwestern and far northeastern Bhutan. However, the most likely place to see a takin is in the Motithang Takin Preserve in Thimphu (see p106).

The grey, golden and capped langurs have a specially adapted stomach for digesting leaves and are not an agricultural pest.

### MONKEYS

Several species of monkey are found in Bhutan and some of these are active throughout the day and may be seen not far from villages or a main road – so keep an eye on the roadside trees on those long drives. Most common are the

Assamese macaques: reddish brown, stumpy-tailed monkeys travelling on the ground in troops of 10 to 50 individuals. They are found throughout Bhutan up to 2900m. Rhesus macaques are similar and are the dominant monkey of the Indian planes. In Bhutan the bold rhesus is confined to the southern foothills.

Langurs are elegant, arboreal monkeys with graceful limbs and extraordinarily long tails and a charismatic presence. Three species of langur make a home in Bhutan's forests – up to 3600m in altitude, and usually high up in the forest canopy. The common grey or Hanuman langur is found west of Pele La; the capped langur is found east of the Manas Chhu in eastern Bhutan, while the famous golden langur is only found from the Puna Tsang Chhu in the west to the Manas Chhu in the east. This beautiful primate's existence was not even known to the scientific community until the 20th century. Not surprisingly, its distinctive feature is its golden coat.

### BIG CATS

Several species of cat, ranging from the moggy-sized jungle cat to the powerful tiger, prowl the forests, valleys and mountains of Bhutan. The other cats are the Asiatic golden cat, marbled cat, pallas cat, leopard cat, fishing cat, lynx, clouded leopard, common leopard and the enigmatic snow leopard.

With its extraordinarily beautiful dappled silver coat, the snow leopard has been hunted relentlessly throughout its range (see below) and is now in danger of extinction. This elusive cat is almost entirely solitary, largely because a single animal's hunting territory is so vast and its prey is so scarce throughout its high-altitude habitat. However, when its favourite prey, the blue sheep, migrates to lower valleys in winter, the snow leopard follows. It is then that the sexes meet.

The essentially solitary tiger is a symbol of great reverence in Bhutan. They number probably around 100 animals, mostly concentrated in and around Royal Manas National Park, though tigers may be found throughout Bhutan, even at high altitudes (3900m), and as far north as Jigme Dorji National Park.

Several tiger conservation measures have been implemented in Bhutan and, coupled with the strong protected-areas system, has provided a favourable environment for the animal. It is believed the protected regions of Bhutan and India provide sufficient habitat to sustain viable breeding populations.

### BEARS & PANDAS

There are two species of bear found in Bhutan. The omnivorous Himalayan black bear is a bane to farmers growing corn and fruit near the temperate

Though able to reach 80 years of age, elephants' life spans are determined by their teeth: their molars are replaced as they wear down, but only up to six times. When the final set is worn, the elephant dies of starvation.

---

**THE LEOPARD & THE FUNGUS**

A tragedy is being played out in and beyond the mountains of Bhutan, featuring an exotic cast, high-stakes fashion and a plot that defies imagination. Some Chinese swimming coaches and practitioners of traditional Chinese medicine have talked up the value of Bhutan's *yartsa goenbub* (winter-worm summer-plant), also known as caterpillar fungus, *Cordyceps sinensis,* associating this peculiar fungus with powers matched only by rhino horns, elephant tusks and tiger penises. Tibetan yak herders wandering in and out of Bhutan traditionally scooped up fungus to augment their meagre living, but the increased demand for *Cordyceps* has brought sudden wealth. And the knock-on effect has been felt most keenly by the big cats of Asia. Increasing numbers of new-money Tibetans with a hankering for traditional garb are providing a growing market for cat skins, particularly tiger and snow leopard, which adorn their *chuba* (cloaks). Bhutanese rangers in Jigme Dorje National Park are faced with increasing numbers of fungus gatherers; meanwhile, already endangered big cats across south Asia are enduring a new wave of poaching activity.

### THE TAKIN – BHUTAN'S NATIONAL ANIMAL   *Tashi Wangchuk*

The reason for selecting the takin as the national animal is based both on its uniqueness and its strong association with the country's religious history and mythology. When the great saint Lama Drukpa Kunley, the Divine Madman, visited Bhutan in the 15th century, a large congregation of devotees gathered from around the country to witness his magical powers. The people urged the lama to perform a miracle.

However, the saint, in his usual unorthodox and outrageous way (see p136), demanded that he first be served a whole cow and a goat for lunch. He devoured these with relish and left only the bones. After letting out a large and satisfied burp, he took the goat's head and stuck it onto the bones of the cow. And then with a snap of his fingers he commanded the strange beast to rise up and graze on the mountainside. To the astonishment of the people the animal arose and ran up to the meadows to graze. This animal came to be known as the *dong gyem tsey* (takin) and to this day these clumsy-looking animals can be seen grazing on the mountainsides of Bhutan.

The takin continues to befuddle taxonomists. The famous biologist George Schaller called it a 'beestung moose'. In summer, takins migrate to subalpine forests and alpine meadows above 3700m and graze on the luxuriant grasses, herbs and shrubs found there. By migrating they escape the leeches, mosquitoes, horseflies and other parasites of the monsoon-swept lower valleys. This is also the time when the vegetation in the alpine region is richest in nutrition. Thus, takins gain several kilograms of storable energy: some males become massive, weighing as much as 1 tonne or more. Summer is also the time when takins mate. The gestation period is between seven and eight months, and young – usually a single calf – are born between December and February. These are black, in contrast to the adults with golden yellow and brownish coat. Sometimes the Himalayan black bear will follow a pregnant female takin and immediately after she has given birth, chase her away and eat the calf.

In late August takins start their slow descent to the lower valleys where the herds begin to break up. They arrive at the winter grazing grounds in temperate broadleaf forests between 2000m and 3000m by late October.

Hunting is banned by law and poaching is limited since there is no high economic value placed on the body parts of the takin. In traditional medicine, however, the horn of the takin, consumed in minute amounts, is supposed to help women during a difficult childbirth.

The major threats that the takin faces are competition with domestic yaks for food in the alpine regions and loss of habitat in the temperate regions. In the temperate zones, logging may have detrimental effects on the takin's survival.

forests (1200m to 3500m) it frequents, whereas the sloth bear is principally a termite eater and honey pirate found at lower altitudes. Bears do occasionally attack humans, probably because their poor eyesight leads them to interpret that a standing person is making a threatening gesture.

The red panda is known in Bhutan as *aamchu donkha* and is most commonly found near Pele La, Thrumshing La and parts of the Gasa district. It is bright-chestnut coloured, about 50cm long, including its bushy, banded tail, and has a white face. The red panda is nocturnal, sleeping in trees during the day and coming to the ground to forage on bamboo and raid birds' nests at night.

### BIRDS

Each year Bhutan's extensive bird list grows longer, a consequence of Bhutan's rich biodiversity and the small amount of systematic birding that has been done in the kingdom. Nevertheless, over 600 species have been recorded and bird-watching tours are extremely popular.

Bhutan is rightly famous for its wintering populations of the vulnerable black-necked crane (see p88). Less well known are the winter populations, mainly as solitary individuals, of the endangered white-bellied heron, for

## THE BLACK-NECKED CRANE

The rare and endangered black-necked crane occupies a special place in Bhutanese hearts and folklore. Its arrival every autumn from Tibet inspires songs and dances; it usually heralds the end of the harvesting season and also the time when farm families start migrating to warmer climates.

Many legends and myths exist about the bird, which the Bhutanese call *thrung thrung karmo*. Wetlands of the high mountain valleys of Phobjikha, Bomdeling and Gaytsa serve as the winter habitat for 400 to 500 birds. Like other cranes, these have an elaborate mating ritual, a dance in which pairs bow, leap into the air and toss vegetation about while uttering loud bugling calls. It can be difficult to distinguish the sexes because the coloration is so similar, but the females are slightly smaller. The crane's preferred delicacies include fallen grain, tubers and insects.

The world's entire population of 5600 to 6000 black-necked cranes breed in Tibet and Ladakh. As well as in Bhutan, they winter in south-central Tibet and northeastern Yunan province in China.

The Royal Society for Protection of Nature (www.rspn-bhutan.org) is committed to conservation, education and inspiring the Bhutanese populace. RSPN annually monitors the endangered black-necked cranes in the Phobjikha and Bomdeling valleys, and has produced documentary videos on the cranes.

which there were about 15 records in 2005, in the vicinity of Punakha and Wangdue Phodrang.

Some bird species are even more transient, migrating through Bhutan between Tibet and northern India in autumn and spring. Pailas' fish eagle, which is considered rare, is regularly seen migrating up the Punak Chhu near Wangdue Phodrang in spring. It is often in the company of ospreys, a wide range of ducks, waders such as the pied avocet, and other species that breed in Tibet.

Winter brings numerous species down to lower altitudes, including accentors, rosefinches, grosbeaks, snow pigeons and pheasants such as the satyr tragopan, the Himalayan monal and the blood pheasant. Observant early-morning walkers can often find these on the mountains and passes around Thimphu. In summer many lowland species move to higher altitudes to breed; these species include the exotic-looking hoopoe, various species of minivets, cuckoos (one can commonly hear at least five different species calling), barbets, warblers, sunbirds, fulvettas and yuhinas.

Given the density of forest cover and the steep vertical descents, the road is often the best place from which to spot birds. Recommended stretches include the road down from Dochu La to Wangdue Phodrang (the adventurous can take the old trail, which is even better), from Wangdue Phodrang to Nobding (on the way to Pele La), and before Trongsa. For those who go east, the 2000m descent between Sengor and Lingmethang is spectacular: Ward's trogon and the Rufous-necked hornbill have been recorded in this area. Trekking will provide you with a greater chance of seeing high-altitude birds, including the lammergeier, the Himalayan griffon, the raven, the unique high-altitude wader – the ibisbill – and colourful pheasants.

The global conservation organisation, WWF (www.wwfbhutan.org .bt), has a branch in Thimphu where it funds, manages and communicates with several conservation projects in Bhutan.

## Plants

An astonishing array of plants grow in Bhutan: over 5000 species, including more than 600 species of orchid, 300 species of medicinal plants and over 50 species of spectacular rhododendrons. Few countries could boast the variety of habitats from tropical jungle to alpine tundra in such a compact area. Because glaciation had no impact on the lower reaches of the Himalaya, these foothills remain repositories of plants whose origins can be traced back before the ice age. This area is home to some of the most ancient species of vegetation on earth.

Forests are found up to 4500m and serve not only as a source of fuel, timber and herbs, but also as a cultural resource, as they form the basis of many folk songs and ritual offerings. Though the government policy is to maintain at least 60% of the land as forest, the present ratio is higher, with a remarkable 72% of the country covered in forests of mixed conifers and broadleaf species.

---

### THE BLUE POPPY

The blue poppy, Bhutan's national flower, is a delicate blue- or purple-tinged bloom with a white filament. In Dzongkha it is known by the name *euitgel metog hoem*. It grows to nearly one metre tall, on the rocky mountain terrain found above the tree line (3500m to 4500m). The flowering season occurs during the early monsoon, from late May to July, and the seeds yield oil. It is a monocarpic plant, which means that it blooms only once. It grows for several years, then flowers, produces seeds and dies. Poppies can be found atop some high passes from the far eastern parts of the country all the way across to the west.

At one time the blue poppy was considered to be a Himalayan myth, along with the yeti. In 1933 a British botanist, George Sherriff, who was in Bhutan studying Himalayan flora, found the plant in the remote mountain region of Sakten in eastern Bhutan. Despite this proof that the flower exists, few people have seen one; a mystique surrounds the species in the same way it does the snow leopard.

---

### TROPICAL & SUBTROPICAL

Tropical evergreen forests growing below 800m are unique repositories of biodiversity, but much of the rich vegetation at these lower elevations has been cleared for pasture and terraced farmland. In the next vegetation zone (900m to 1800m) are the subtropical grasslands and forests of chir pine, oak, walnut and sal. Above groves of bamboo, numerous varieties of orchid and fern grace the branches of forest giants.

### TEMPERATE

The temperate zone (1800-3500m) is a region of great diversity. The tropical vegetation of the lower zones gives way to dark forests of oak, birch, maple, magnolia and laurel. On most hills, the sunny south side is forested with broadleaf species such as oak, and the damp, shady north side with rhododendron and conifers, particularly blue pine. Spring is the time to see the magnificent red- or cream-flowering rhododendrons of Bhutan. In the autumn you will see the mauve or pinkish blooms of the Himalayan wild cherry.

The two plants that produce the ingredients in *doma* (betel nut) grow in the *duars* in southern Bhutan. The nut comes from the *khair*, a palm, and the leaf used to wrap it comes from the betel-leaf vine.

### SUBALPINE & ALPINE

Between the tree line and the snow line at about 5500m are low shrubs, dwarf rhododendrons, Himalayan grasses and flowering herbs. Junipers are also found in a dwarfed form at altitudes over 4000m. Their distinctive foliage, short prickly needles and fleshy, berry-like fruit, is unmistakable.

As the snows begin to melt at the end of the long winter, the high-altitude grazing lands are carpeted with a multitude of wildflowers, which remain in bloom until early summer. After the onset of the monsoon, in July, a second and even more vibrant flowering occurs, which extends until the end of the monsoon in late August. Some of the varieties found at these higher elevations include anemones, forget-me-nots, dwarf irises, dwarf rhododendrons, primulas, delphiniums and ranunculus.

## NATIONAL PARKS & PROTECTED AREAS

There are four national parks, four wildlife sanctuaries and one nature reserve, which together constitute about 26% of the country, or 10,758 sq km. In 1999 an additional 3800 sq km was designated as a network of biological corridors linking all nine protected areas.

All but three of the protected areas encompass regions in which there is a resident human population. Preserving the culture and fostering local tradition is part of the mandate of Bhutan's national-park system. The government has developed zoning policies and an integrated conservation and development program to allow people living within a protected area to farm, graze animals, collect plants and cut firewood.

Bhutan established its national-park system to protect important ecosystems, and for the most part they have not been developed as tourist attractions. Apart from one or two exceptions, you won't find the kind of facilities you may normally associate with national parks, such as entrance stations, camping grounds and visitor centres. In many cases you won't even be aware that you are entering or leaving a national park.

## Jigme Dorji National Park

Jigme Dorji National Park is the largest protected area in the country, encompassing an area of 4329 sq km. It protects the western parts of Paro, Thimphu and Punakha Dzongkhags (districts) and almost the entire area of Gasa Dzongkhag. Habitats in the park range from subtropical areas at 1400m to alpine heights at 7000m. The park management has to cope with the needs of both lowland farmers and seminomadic yak herders, and three of the country's major trekking routes pass through the park. Villagers are also allowed to harvest a wide variety of indigenous plants for use in incense and traditional medicines.

The park is the habitat of several endangered species, including the takin, snow leopard, blue sheep, tiger, musk deer, red panda, Himalayan black bear and serow. Other mammals to be found are leopards, wild dogs, sambars, barking deer, gorals, marmots and pikas. More than 300 species of birds have been catalogued within the park.

## Royal Manas National Park

The 1023-sq-km Royal Manas National Park in south-central Bhutan adjoins the Jigme Singye Wangchuck National Park to the north and India's Manas National Park and Manas Tiger Reserve to the south. Together they form a 5000-sq-km protected area that runs from the plains to the Himalayan peaks.

The area has been protected as a wildlife sanctuary since 1966 and was upgraded to a national park in 1988. It is the home of rhinos, buffalos, tigers, leopards, gaurs, bears, elephants and several species of deer. It is also home to several rare species, including the golden langur, the capped langur and the hispid hare. The 362 species of birds in the park include four varieties of hornbills. Unfortunately, because of security concerns related to separatist groups in India, at the time of research it was not possible to visit Manas.

## Jigme Singye Wangchuck National Park

The 1400-sq-km Jigme Singye Wangchuck National Park protects the range of hills that separates eastern and western Bhutan – the Black Mountains. It is important because it protects virgin forests of the Himalayan foothills, which have been largely cleared in neighbouring Nepal and India.

Plant life in the park includes a wide range of broadleaf species, conifers and alpine pastures. Animals include tigers, Himalayan black bears, leopards, red pandas and golden langurs, and an amazing 449 species of birds have been catalogued. The Phobjikha valley, wintering place of black-necked cranes, is included in the park.

## Phibsoo Wildlife Sanctuary

A 278-sq-km area was set aside in 1974 as a wildlife reserve and upgraded to the Phibsoo Wildlife Sanctuary in 1993. On the southern border of Bhutan, about 50km east of Phuentsholing, it was established to protect the only remaining natural sal forest in Bhutan. Several protected species thrive in the sanctuary, including chital deer, elephants, gaurs, tigers, golden langurs and hornbills.

## Thrumshing La National Park

The 768-sq-km Thrumshing La National Park lies between Bumthang and Mongar. It was set aside to protect old-growth temperate forests of fir and chir pine. It is also home to red pandas and several endangered bird species including the Rufous-necked hornbill, the Satyr tragopan and the chestnut-breasted partridge.

## Bomdeling Wildlife Sanctuary

The 1545-sq-km Bomdeling Wildlife Sanctuary protects most of the area of Trashi Yangtse Dzongkhag. Within the reserve is a large area of alpine tundra. The sanctuary protects the habitat of blue sheep, snow leopards, red pandas, tigers, leopards, Himalayan black bears and musk deer. It also protects the Bomdeling area, which is an important wintering ground of the black-necked crane.

## Sakten Wildlife Sanctuary

The Sakten Wildlife Sanctuary protects several species endemic to the east; it is also renowned as the only reserve in the world created to protect the habitat of the yeti. It's in the easternmost part of the country, where 650 sq km of temperate forests of blue pine and rhododendron are protected.

## Khaling Wildlife Sanctuary

In far southeastern Bhutan, 273 sq km have been set aside as the Khaling Wildlife Sanctuary. Wild elephants, gaurs, pygmy hogs, hispid hares and other tropical wildlife are protected here. This sanctuary adjoins a comparable reserve in India.

Between March and May the hillsides are ablaze with the deep red flowers of the *etho metho*, the country's most famous rhododendron. There are 46 species of rhododendron that occur throughout the country at altitudes between 1200m and 4800m, ranging from small shrubs to 20m trees.

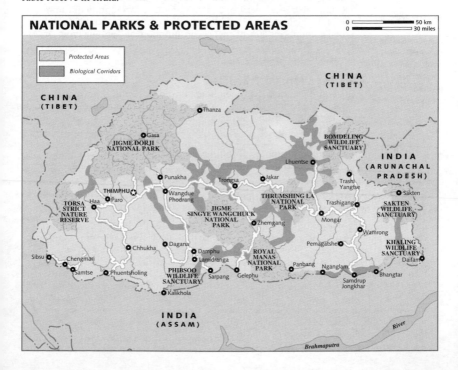

NATIONAL PARKS & PROTECTED AREAS

### Torsa Strict Nature Reserve

The Torsa reserve is in the western part of the Haa district, where the Torsa river enters from Tibet. The 644-sq-km reserve was set aside to protect the temperate forests and alpine meadows of far west Bhutan and is the only protected area with no resident human population.

## ENVIRONMENTAL ISSUES

Bhutan emerged into the 20th century with much of its forests and ecosystems intact. But now, with an increasing population, improved roads and communication and limited farming land, a major effort is required to protect the country's natural heritage.

Natural-resource utilisation now has equal, if not more, ecological pressures from urban populations as from rural consumers. However, growing awareness of environmental issues has prompted appropriate conservation measures. Among these are requirements for environmental assessments for all new public or private investment projects, and nationwide bans on the commercial export of raw timber and the use of plastic bags. Bhutan has consciously decided to forego immediate economic gain from exploitation of its natural resources in order to preserve its environment for long-term sustainable benefits.

### Firewood

Wood is used as fuel in rural areas and in most monasteries (in urban areas cooking gas or kerosene is used), and it was probably only Bhutan's low population that spared the forests before conservation planning was introduced. Managing firewood harvesting is a major problem. At almost 2.8 cubic metres per person, Bhutan's annual consumption of firewood is one of the highest in the world – and that represents about 375,000 trees. Wood accounts for 80% of energy consumption, and although the government is promoting electricity as an alternative source of energy, few rural households have electricity.

You can easily distinguish the chir pine from its relative, the blue pine, because the needles of the chir pine are in groups of three and those of the blue pine are shorter and in groups of five.

### Grazing & Farming Practices

Conservation issues centre on human–wildlife conflicts, such as crop and livestock depredation by wild predators, and the deterioration of high-altitude wildlife habitat from grazing pressure. There are now programs under way to balance the needs of traditional herders and farmers with wildlife protection.

A significant amount of shifting cultivation ('slash and burn', called *tseri* in Dzongkha) is practised in Bhutan, particularly in the east. The practice

---

**GLOBAL WARMING'S FIRST CASUALTIES?**

According to those with vested interests, global warming from human activity has yet to be proven. Meanwhile small villages in Bhutan and other regions of the Himalaya, which hardly contribute to the greenhouse gas surplus, are preparing to be the first casualties of the very real rise in global temperatures. Across the Himalaya, glacier lakes are filling up with melt water, and in recent decades scientists have documented a tenfold jump in glacier-lake outbursts. In Bhutan there are currently 24 lakes poised to burst.

In 1994 a glacier-lake outburst in Bhutan swept 10 million cubic metres of water down the Pho Chhu. It flooded a number of villages and killed 23 people in Punakha, 80km away. While too much water is pouring from the mountains now, a probable longer term consequence of the shrinking Himalayan glaciers is a significantly reduced water supply to almost a quarter of the world's population in India, China and Pakistan.

is officially banned and several methods, including education and fertiliser supply, are being implemented to change this practice.

## Poaching

While the Bhutanese generally observe their own conservation policies, the open southern and northern borders offer opportunities for poaching of both plant and animal life. Many species are sought for their alleged medicinal or other valuable properties. Killing and poaching are unacceptable in Buddhist tradition, but the high prices that wildlife products such as rhino horn, tiger bone, musk and *Cordyceps sinensis* command outside Bhutan present major challenges to conservationists.

The Department of Forestry Services (DFS) operates effective antipoaching programs designed to protect endangered plants and animals, enforce forestry rules and control trade in wildlife parts and products. A national network of foresters regulates timber harvesting, and road checkpoints are operated throughout the country to monitor the transportation of forest products.

*Bhutanese Tales of the Yeti* by Kunzang Choden describes Bhutanese beliefs about where and how this mysterious creature may live.

# Food & Drink

If you haven't eaten Bhutanese cuisine before then you are in for a surprise. The Bhutanese love chillies; there are dishes where chillies are the main ingredient and these mouth-scorching meals may well be accompanied by chilli-infused condiments. It will bring tears of joy to the eyes of chilli lovers – all others beware! Of course, most travellers will not necessarily experience local food at its fiery zenith. All-inclusive travel means hotel-restaurant food (see p247), where toned-down Bhutanese is offered along with continental, Indian and Chinese dishes. Although chillies are ubiquitous, don't expect the aromatically spiced dishes so typical of the subcontinent. These can only be found in the Nepali-influenced south of Bhutan or in an Indian restaurant.

All large towns have restaurants, and in Thimphu you can find Indian, Thai, Italian and other cuisines, as well as a plethora of local cafés. In remote villages the fare is likely to be the national dish, *ema datse* (chillies and cheese), and meat of questionable vintage. If you are ordering from a menu, don't be surprised if many of the offerings are not available.

## STAPLES & SPECIALITIES

If you bite into a bunch of hot chillies, a few mouthfuls of plain rice will often help ease the pain. Also a spoonful of sugar seems to absorb some of the fiery oil.

Traditional Bhutanese food always features devilish red or green chillies. *Ema datse* comprises large green (sometimes red, but always very hot) chillies, prepared as a vegetable, not as a seasoning, in a cheese sauce. The second-most popular dish is *phak sha laphu* (stewed pork with radish). Other typical dishes, always served with chillies, are *no sha huentseu* (stewed beef with spinach), *phak sha phin tshoem* (pork with rice noodles) and *bja sha maroo* (chicken in garlic and butter sauce).

One dish that is frequently available is *dal bhat* (rice and lentils), the traditional mainstay of Nepal. Hotel and trekking cooks make some excellent nonspicy dishes, such as *kewa datse* (potatoes with cheese sauce) and *shamu datse* (mushrooms with cheese sauce). *Tohsey* is a delicious salty, spicy mixture of vegetables and rice made gluggy with cheese. More seasonal are the delicious asparagus and unusual *nakey* (fern fronds), the latter typically smothered in the ever-present *datse*.

Pork fat is a popular dish in the wilds because of its high energy content. Western visitors find it almost inedible because it is usually quite stale or is just fat with lumps of hairy skin attached – no meat whatsoever!

Meat is frequently dry and stringy. There are no slaughterhouses, and only a few cold-storage facilities. Beef and fish come from India, often travelling long distances in unrefrigerated trucks. Avoid beef during the monsoon season, and be very wary of pork at any time. During the summer you are usually limited to chicken, or a vegetarian diet. Yak meat is sometimes available, but only in the winter. You will rarely find mutton or lamb served in Bhutan.

members.tripod.com /thinley/recipe/is a concise website with several traditional recipes and some background to Bhutanese cuisine.

Several Tibetan-style dishes are common in Bhutan. Small steamed dumplings called *momos* may be filled with meat or cheese – delicious when dipped in a chilli sauce. Fried cheese momos are a speciality of several Thimphu restaurants. *Barthu* is a Bhutanese version of another typically Tibetan dish, *thukpa* (noodles), which may be fried or served in soup. Village people also eat *tsampa*, the Tibetan-style dish of roasted-barley flour mixed with salt and yak-butter tea and kneaded into a paste. Look for the strings of rock-hard, dried yak cheese, *chugo*, hanging from shop rafters, but be careful of your teeth.

Although there is plenty of white rice, the Bhutanese prefer a locally produced red variety, which has a sl`ghtly nutty flavour. At high altitudes where rice is not available, wheat and buckwheat are the staples. *Zow* is rice that is boiled and then fried. It's sometimes mixed with sugar and butter and is commonly carried in a *bangchung* (covered basket). In Bumthang *khule* (buckwheat pancakes) and *puta* (buckwheat noodles) replace rice as the foundation of many meals. A common snack food in the east is *gesasip*, corn (maize) that has been fried and beaten.

## DRINKS
### Nonalcoholic Drinks

Indian-style sweet milky tea *(ngad-ja)* is widely available and may be served in a pot, but more often it appears as a cup with a tea bag. Bhutanese frequently drink *sud-ja*, Tibetan-style tea with salt and butter, which is more like soup than tea, and surprisingly tasty and warming on a cold day. Filter coffee and espresso is available in the top-end hotels and a few restaurants in Thimphu, but elsewhere 'coffee' is invariably of the instant variety.

Avoid drinking tap water anywhere in Bhutan and remember that the flasks in hotel rooms are sometimes filled with untreated water. Bottled mineral water is widely available and most restaurants will give you boiled water to drink if you ask for it. For advice on water purification, see p272.

> Bhutan has 28 beekeepers employing European honeybees. In spring look for white transparent honey produced from white clover, while in winter enjoy the very dark honey from buckwheat flowers.

### Alcoholic Drinks

The only beer brewed in Bhutan is the very good Red Panda *weissbier*, an unfiltered wheat beer bottled in Bumthang. Throughout the country there's an ample supply of imported canned beer – Tiger from Singapore and Singha from Thailand, or several brands of Indian beer, which comes in large (650mL) bottles. The most popular brands are Black Label, Golden Eagle and Dansberg from Sikkim. If you want a cheap high, try one of the brands with 8% alcohol content: Hit, Volcano or 10,000.

There are several brands of whisky, including Special Courier, Black Mountain Whisky (better known as 'BMW'), Royal Supreme and Changta, the cheapest. The better brands compare favourably with good Scotch whisky. There are local rums: XXX Bhutan Rum is the strongest, and gins such as Crystal and Pacham. Most hotels also have a stock of international brands.

Wine is available at the duty-free shop in Thimphu, though it is likely to be expensive and disappointing.

The most common local brew is *bang chhang*, a warm beerlike drink made from wheat. The favourite hard drinks are *arra*, a spirit distilled from rice, and *sinchhang*, which is made from millet, wheat or rice.

> Throughout the country alcohol is not served before 1pm and after midnight. Tuesday is a 'dry day' when hotels and restaurants don't serve alcohol.

## VEGETARIAN & VEGANS

There is a good variety of vegetarian food available, although much of it is made using a liberal amount of chilli and a smothering of cheese sauce. Ingredients such as nettles, fern fronds, orchids, asparagus, taro and several varieties of mushrooms appear in traditional Bhutanese vegetarian dishes. Vegans should ask if a dish contains cheese (or eggs) when ordering.

## HABITS & CUSTOMS

Mealtime is a typically relaxed time in Bhutan. It is a social event and family get-together; however, the time spent eating may depend as much on how much is put on the table as the need for conversation. Three meals a day is typical, and it is not unusual for those three meals to all consist of rice and *ema datse*. At a hotel restaurant the full cutlery ensemble will be provided, but in a local café you may be limited to the option of a spoon or using your right hand and bowl of rice to mop up the meal.

One of the great Bhutanese vices is chewing *doma*, also known by its Indian name, *paan*. The centrepiece is a hard *Areca catechu* nut that is chewed as

> Look for fresh asparagus from April to June, and wild mushrooms, apples and peaches later in the summer when mangoes and avocados from the south also appear. Papaya hits the stalls in March and April.

a digestive. The nut is mixed with lime powder (the ash, not the fruit), and the whole collection is rolled up in a heart-shaped betel leaf and chewed slowly. It's a bittersweet, mildly intoxicating concoction and it stains the mouth bright red. When the remains are spat out, they leave a characteristic crimson stain on the pavement.

## EAT YOUR WORDS
### Useful Phrases

There is an array of accoutrements associated with chewing *doma* that many men carry in the pouch of their *gho*. The ingredients are carried in ornate boxes and there are special knives designed to slice the nuts.

| Where is a ...? | ... gâti mo? |
|---|---|
| local bar | changkha |
| restaurant | zakha |

| I don't eat meat. | nga sha miza |
|---|---|
| This is too spicy. | di khatshi dû |
| I don't like food with chillies. | nga zhêgo êma dacikha miga |
| Is the food good? | zhêgo zhim-mä ga? |
| This is delicious. | di zhim-mä |
| Please give me a cup of tea. | ngalu ja phôp gang nang |
| Do you have food now? | chö dato to za-wigang in-na? |
| It's enough. | digi lâm-mä |

### Food Glossary

| beer (local) | bang chhang |
|---|---|
| whisky (local) | ârra |
| tea | ja |
| water | chhu |
| boiled water | chhu kököu |
| cold water | chhu khöm |
| hot water | chhu tshatom |
| | |
| cabbage | banda kopi |
| cauliflower | meto kopi |
| cheese | datse |
| chicken (meat) | bja sha |
| chilli | êma |
| cooked vegetable | tshöse tsotsou |
| corn (maize) | gäza/gesasip |
| egg | gongdo |
| fish | ngasha |
| food | zhêgo/to |
| meat | ha |
| mushroom | shamu |
| mustard | päga |
| noodles | bathu/thukpa |
| potatoes | kewa |
| radish | laphu |
| rice (cooked) | to |
| salad | ezay |
| slices | pa |
| turnips | öndo |
| vegetable | tshöse |
| hot | tshatom |
| hot (spicy) | khatshi yömi |
| tasty | zhimtoto |

# Thimphu

You approach Thimphu along a winding, single-lane access road, little wider than the trucks that suddenly emerge around each curve. Each blind bend promises a glimpse of your destination; however, for most of the journey all that is revealed is another curve followed by another. The steep hillsides are dotted with houses, some abandoned, their massive earthen walls slowly crumbling, and the occasional white-washed temple. Suddenly the road drops to a modern expressway on the valley floor, whisking you through paddy fields to the capital of one of the world's most intriguing countries.

Established as the capital in 1961, Thimphu has a youthful exuberance that constantly challenges the country's conservatism and proud tradition. The ever-present juxtaposition of old and new is just one of its appealing qualities. Crimson-robed monks, Indian labourers, *gho*- and *kira*-clad professionals and camera-wielding tourists all ply the pot-holed pavements, skirt packs of sleeping dogs, and spin the prayer wheels of Clocktower Square, and nobody, it seems, is in a hurry. Thimphu is the world's only capital without traffic lights. A set was installed, but the residents complained that it was impersonal, and so gesticulating, white-gloved police continue to direct the ever-increasing traffic. As well as being a classic Bhutanese anachronism, it may well be the city's most photographed spectacle.

Thimphu offers the best opportunity to do your own thing. It's relaxed, friendly and pretty informal, and is most rewarding if you can be the same.

## HIGHLIGHTS

- Savour the serenity of the powerful yet peaceful architecture of **Trashi Chhoe Dzong** (p101)
- Immerse yourself in the pungent, colourful, bustling **weekend market** (p103) – a gastronomic wonderland and gaudy artefact bazaar
- Stretch your legs and climb through whispering pines to the peaceful solitude of either **Tango Goemba** or **Cheri Goemba** (p115)
- Bend your elbow at one of Thimphu's friendly bars, such as **Om Bar** (p112), and meet the locals over *momos* and beer
- Marvel at the skill and artistry of Bhutanese youth at the **National Institute for Zorig Chusum** (p104)
- Spot an incongruous takin at the **Motithang Takin Preserve** (p106)

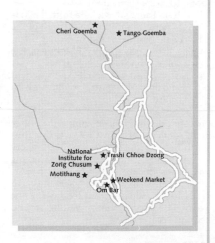

■ ELEVATION: 2320M　　■ POPULATION: 98,676　　■ TELEPHONE CODE: 02

## ORIENTATION

The road from the south (and Paro) is met by the new expressway 11km from the Thimphu. As it races along the valley floor it passes below Simtokha Dzong, before entering Thimphu CBD, marked by an elaborately decorated petrol station. The city sprawls north and west in the lightly wooded valley of the Wang Chhu.

The road leading north from the petrol station is Norzin Lam, Thimphu's main drag, which takes you through the town centre past several major hotels and the pretty Clocktower Sq, the city's heart. Not far north of the square is the famous traffic circle with the arm-waving police. From the traffic circle, Norzim Lam continues uphill past the cinema, the Bank of Bhutan and the government handicraft emporium. At the northern end of Norzin Lam, Desi Lam leads to the National Library, Folk Heritage Museum, the golf course and Trashi Chhoe Dzong. A turn to the west back at the traffic circle puts you on Chorten Lam, which intersects with Doendrup Lam near the Swiss Bakery, before heading south towards the Memorial Chorten. The road leading east from the traffic circle, Wogzin Lam, takes you either to Clocktower Sq or you can continue east on Gatoen Lam past Benez Restaurant to Chang Lam, a north–south thoroughfare that runs beside and above the Changlimithang archery ground and sports stadium.

Doebum Lam makes a loop from the Memorial Chorten above and to the west of the CBD to the northern end of Norzin Lam, passing the Drichu Drakey Bakery and the sports complex on the way. Numerous smaller streets weave their way uphill to government offices and the posh suburb of Motithang west of the centre.

The east and west banks of the Wang Chhu are connected by Lungten Zampa, the bridge at the south end of town. Chhogyel Lam runs north beneath the bridge, past the archery ground, sports stadium, Zangto Pelri Lhakang and the weekend market. On the eastern bank, Dechen Lam leads to several hotels and eventually to the monasteries at the head of the valley. For information on getting around the city, see p114.

### Maps

City maps (Nu 100) are available in bookshops and handicraft shops. The Department of Survey & Land Records publishes the *Thimphu City Map*, which shows all the ministries, other government offices and religious buildings. The similar, glossy *Thimphu/Paro City Map* has an inset showing many of the hotels and shops, plus a small map of Paro on the reverse side.

Although usually well signposted, very few locals, including taxi drivers, actually know and use street names; landmarks and building names will serve you better when asking for or giving directions. To add to the confusion, several of the street names on signposts differ from those on city maps. For more on maps, see p249.

You can download maps of hiking trails around Thimphu from www.bhutan-trails.org /index.html. For more information on these trails see p117).

## INFORMATION

### Bookshops

Thimphu's bookshops carry Bhutanese and Indian newspapers, periodicals and a selection of books on Bhutan, Tibet and Buddhism. Prices are quite reasonable, especially for Indian editions, which are cheaper than overseas editions.

**Book World** (Map pp102–3; ☎ 323386; bookworld@ druknet.bt; Clocktower Sq) At the southwestern end of the square next to Jimmy Bros Stationery, this tiny shop has a good selection of coffee-table books and posters as well as internet access.

**DSB Books** (Map pp102–3; ☎ 323123; dsb@druknet .bt; Chang Lam) Probably Thimphu's best selection of coffee-table and other books on Buddhism, Bhutan and the region. Particularly good for Bhutanese and Indian newspapers. On the ground floor of Jojo's Shopping Complex; enter from the lane behind Chang Lam.

**Megah Books** (Map pp102–3; ☎ 321063; Wogzin Lam) Has a smaller selection that includes some dusty, hard-to-find-elsewhere books on Bhutan.

**Pekhang Bookshop** (Map pp102–3; ☎ 323094; Norzin Lam) Somewhat hidden in the same building as the Luger Cinema; carries lots of stationery supplies.

### Emergency

**Ambulance** ( ☎ 112)
**Fire** ( ☎ 110)
**Police** ( ☎ 113)

### Internet Access

There are a dozen or so internet cafés spread around town, all charging Nu 50 to 70 per hour. Several hotels have rudimentary

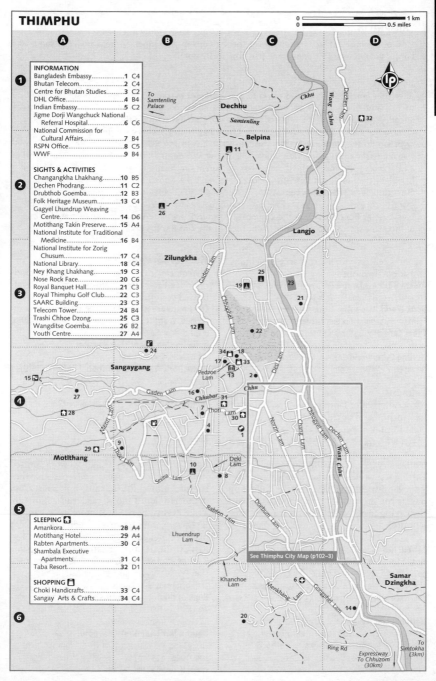

# THIMPHU

0 —————— 1 km
0 —————— 0.5 miles

**INFORMATION**
Bangladesh Embassy...............1 C4
Bhutan Telecom.......................2 C4
Centre for Bhutan Studies.......3 C2
DHL Office..............................4 B4
Indian Embassy.......................5 C2
Jigme Dorji Wangchuck National
   Referral Hospital.................6 C6
National Commission for
   Cultural Affairs...................7 B4
RSPN Office............................8 C5
WWF.....................................9 B4

**SIGHTS & ACTIVITIES**
Changangkha Lhakhang.........10 B5
Dechen Phodrang..................11 C2
Drubthob Goemba.................12 B3
Folk Heritage Museum............13 C4
Gagyel Lhundrup Weaving
   Centre..............................14 D6
Motithang Takin Preserve.......15 A4
National Institute for Traditional
   Medicine...........................16 B4
National Institute for Zorig
   Chusum............................17 C4
National Library.....................18 C4
Ney Khang Lhakhang..............19 C3
Nose Rock Face.....................20 C6
Royal Banquet Hall................21 C3
Royal Thimphu Golf Club........22 C3
SAARC Building......................23 C3
Telecom Tower......................24 B4
Trashi Chhoe Dzong...............25 C3
Wangditse Goemba................26 B2
Youth Centre........................27 A4

**SLEEPING**
Amankora.............................28 A4
Motithang Hotel.....................29 A4
Rabten Apartments................30 C4
Shambala Executive
   Apartments........................31 C4
Taba Resort...........................32 D1

**SHOPPING**
Choki Handicrafts..................33 C4
Sangay Arts & Crafts..............34 C4

To Samtenling Palace

Dechhu

Samtenling

Belpina

Langjo

Zilungkha

Sangaygang

Motithang

Dechhu

Wang Chhu

Chhu

Dechen Lam

Garden Lam

Chhokhel Lam

Desi Lam

North Lam

Chang Lam

Chhoghel Lam

Dechen Lam

Wang Chhu

Chubachu

Chhubar

Thori Lam

Gaden Lam

Mipari Lam

Thori Lam

Sevina Lam

Rabten Lam

Deki Lam

Doebum Lam

Lhuendrup Lam

Khanchoe Lam

Menkhang Lam

Gongphel Lam

Samar Dzingkha

Ring Rd

Pedzoe Lam

Chhubar Chhu

To Samtenling Palace

See Thimphu City Map (p102–3)

To Simtokha (3km)

Expressway To Chhuzom (30km)

THIMPHU

---

**THIMPHU IN...**

Most of the major attractions will already be included in your itinerary. Here are a few suggestions if your itinerary includes some free time in Thimphu.

**24 hours**

After your hotel breakfast head down to the **weekend market** (p103) and soak up the sights,
sounds and smells of the produce stalls before crossing the atmospheric cantilever bridge,
Kuendeyling Baazam, to the trinkets, artefacts and clothing stalls on the east bank of the Wang
Chhu. If the market isn't on, check out the **Chamlimgithang Archery Ground** (p105) for activity
or drop into the **National Textile Museum** (p105), **Painting School** (p104) or **VAST** (p105) to
watch artisans at work or find that unique souvenir. Wander back to your hotel for lunch or visit
a local *momo* (steamed or fried dumpling) restaurant on Norzim Lam, the famed **Swiss Bakery**
(p112), or the trendy **Art Cafe** (p112) for coffee and cake. Round off the afternoon by checking
out the numerous **shopping centres** (p113) for handicrafts, books, trekking equipment or Bhutan's
extravagant postage stamps. As beer o'clock approaches head towards one of Thimphu's friendly
bars, such as **Benez** (p112) or the **Zone** (p112). After-dinner entertainment can be found in one
of the many discos or a late-night haunt such as the **Om Bar** (p112).

---

business centres with internet access, charging
considerably more.

**Atsara Business Centre** (Map pp102-3; City Centre
Complex, Wogzin Lam; ⏰ 9am-10pm)

**Book World** (Map pp102-3; Clocktower Sq; ⏰ 9am-
6pm) Comfy and fast, but only two terminals.

**Cyber Café** (Map pp102-3; Chorten Lam; ⏰ 9am-8pm)
Upstairs, next to Plums Café.

**Norling Cyberworld** (Map pp102-3; Norling Centre,
Norzin Lam; ⏰ 9am-10pm)

## Laundry

Most hotels offer laundry services, but none
has in-house dry-cleaning facilities. Dry-
cleaning takes two days at **Kelly Dry Cleaners**
(Map pp102-3; ☎ 326434; Centre Mall, Norzin Lam), next
to the Luger Cinema. The larger hotels have
clothes dryers and provide same-day service.
During wet weather smaller hotels may return
your laundry damp, or even the following
day. If you are on a tight schedule, ask about
the drying facilities before you hand in your
laundry.

## Libraries

**Jigme Dorje Wangchuck Public Library** (Map
pp102-3; ☎ 322814; Norzin Lam; ⏰ 12.30-5.30pm
Mon-Friday, 9am-1pm Sat) This small library has a
dog-eared collection of paperback novels as well as a few
reference books.

**National Library** (Map p99; ☎ 322885; Pedzoe Lam;
⏰ 9.30am-1pm & 2-5pm Mon-Fri) A better resource for
books about Bhutan. Though the selection of books in
English is small, this is also a worthwhile cultural sight. See
p104 for more details.

## Medical Services

Pharmacies can supply medications, including over-the-counter antibiotics, for travel-
related conditions:

**City Pharmacy** (Map pp102-3; ☎ 321382; City Centre
Complex, Wogzin Lam) A well-stocked pharmacy, upstairs
in the back of the complex.

**India Bhutan Friendship Hospital** (Map p99;
☎ 322485; Chorten Lam)

**Jigme Dorji Wangchuck National Referral Hospi-
tal** (Map pp102-3; ☎ 322496, 322497; Gongphel Lam)
The best hospital in Bhutan.

**Norling Medical** (Map pp102-3; Norling Centre, Norzin
Lam) Opposite the Hotel Tandin.

## Money

Most hotels can change money at government
rates, although they usually have a limited
supply of cash. A few places advertise that they
accept Amex and Visa cards but, apart from
in the handicraft shops, card transactions are
a rare event (see p250 for more information).
If you're planning to use a credit card to pay a
bill in a hotel, settle the bill between 9am and
5pm, while the authorisation office is open.

**Bank of Bhutan** (Map pp102-3; ☎ 322266; Norzin
Lam; ⏰ 9am-1pm Mon-Fri, to 11am Sat) The main
branch; it tends to be busy.

**Bank of Bhutan** (Map pp102-3; Wogzin Lam; ⏰ noon-
2pm Mon, to 4pm Wed-Sat) Smaller city branch only two
blocks away from main branch.

**Bhutan National Bank** (Map pp102-3; ☎ 322767;
Chang Lam; ⏰ 9am-3pm Mon-Fri, to 11am Sat) In the
same building as the main post office. Money-changing is
straightforward at this branch.

## Post

Many hotels and shops sell stamps. Be assured that it is safe to simply drop cards and letters into post boxes here.

**Post office** (Map pp102-3; ☎ 322381; Chang Lam; ✆ 9am-5pm Mon-Fri, 10am-1pm Sat) This main office is a well-organised facility with a postcard and philatelic shop.

## Telephone

Dotted throughout the city there are public call offices (PCOs) that have direct international dialling. You can also make cheaper internet calls at most internet cafés (see p98). For details on making calls see p254.

## Tourist Information

You will find most of your information needs are met by your Bhutanese tour company and guide. There is no visitor information centre in Thimphu, however, English-language newspapers, handicraft shops and your hotel staff are all useful sources for up-to-date, what's-on information.

In the event of a problem with your Bhutanese tour company, the **Department of Tourism** (DOT; Map pp102-3; ☎ 323251; fax 323695; www.tourism .gov.bt; Doebum Lam) can provide advice and assistance.

## DANGERS & ANNOYANCES

There's almost nothing in Thimphu to cause concern. Extraordinary numbers of stray dogs roam at will and bark across town at each other all night, but earplugs solve that problem quite easily. Beware of steep/missing/broken steps and open drains on the pavements. Be careful crossing roads and don't trust cars to stop when you are on a pedestrian crosswalk.

## SIGHTS

Thimphu's attractions are clustered to the north of the city (where you will find the dzong (fort-monastery), library, painting school and folk museum), in the hilly suburb of Motithang overlooking the town, and of course in the city's central district.

### Trashi Chhoe Dzong

This large dzong, north of the city on the west bank of the Wang Chhu, manages not to impose on the valley or the city as a dominating, impenetrable fortress; rather, its splendid proportions and modest setting bestow a subtle, monastic magnificence. The whitewashed outer structure is two storeys high with three-storey towers at the four corners projecting out over the walls and capped by red-and-gold, triple-tiered roofs. The outer walls are built of trimmed, neatly fitted granite blocks, unlike other dzongs, which were made of roughly dressed stones. Similarly, the *dochey* (courtyard) is paved with rectangular stone slabs. The dzong housed the original National Assembly and now houses the secretariat, the throne room and offices of the king and the ministries of home affairs and finance.

Trashi Chhoe has two main entrances on its eastern side. One leads to the administrative section towards the south, and another, towards the north, leads to the monastic quarter, the summer residence of the *dratshang* (central monk body), and where the dances of the annual tsechu festival (see p60 and p107) are performed. The dzong's Sangay Tsokhorsum Thondrol (the immense *thangka* – painted or embroidered religious picture – that is unfurled at the climax of the tsechu) depicts the Buddha Sakyamuni and his two disciples.

Entering the dzong you are greeted by lively sculptures of the Guardians of the Four Directions (see p80), the wrathful gatekeepers Chana Dorje and Hayagriva, and the popular 'Divine Madman', Drukpa Kunley (see p136). Look for the mural of the Four Friends (see p57), depicting a much-loved Bhutanese fable. Upon entering the courtyard you are taken by the splendid proportions of the architecture and the vast courtyard; the enclosed silence only broken by the flight of pigeons, the shuffle of feet and the whirr of prayer wheels. A large *utse* (central tower) separates the northern monastic courtyard, which surrounds the highly decorated Lhakhang Sarpa (New Temple), from the southern courtyard. The northern monastic assembly hall houses a large statue of Sakyamuni, the Historical Buddha (see p75), and meticulous murals illustrate the life of Buddha and portray mystical mandalas.

This is not the original Thimphu dzong. In 1216 Lama Gyalwa Lhanangpa built Dho-Ngen Dzong (Blue Stone Dzong) on the hill above Thimphu where Dechen Phodrang now stands. A few years later Lama Phajo Drukgom Shigpo, who brought the Drukpa Kagyu lineage to Bhutan, took over the dzong. In 1641 the Zhabdrung acquired the dzong from the descendants of Lama Phajo and renamed it Trashi Chhoe Dzong (Fortress of

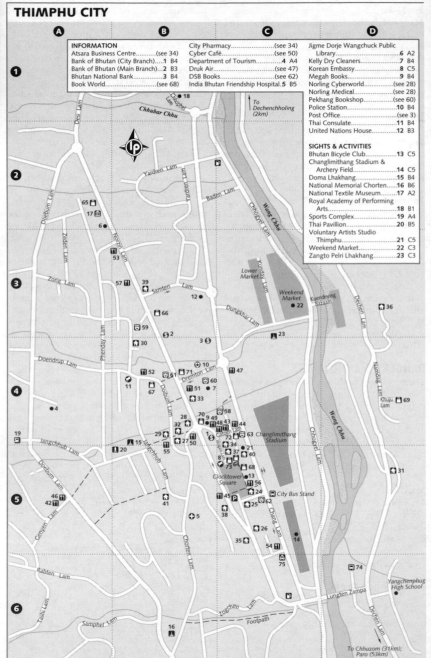

# THIMPHU CITY

## INFORMATION
Atsara Business Centre............(see 34)
Bank of Bhutan (City Branch)....**1** B4
Bank of Bhutan (Main Branch)...**2** B3
Bhutan National Bank...............**3** B4
Book World.............................(see 68)
City Pharmacy........................(see 34)
Cyber Café.............................(see 50)
Department of Tourism...............**4** A4
Druk Air................................(see 47)
DSB Books.............................(see 62)
India Bhutan Friendship Hospital.**5** B5
Jigme Dorje Wangchuck Public
    Library..................................**6** A2
Kelly Dry Cleaners....................**7** B4
Korean Embassy........................**8** C5
Megah Books...........................**9** B4
Norling Cyberworld..................(see 28)
Norling Medical.......................(see 28)
Pekhang Bookshop....................(see 60)
Police Station.........................**10** B4
Post Office.............................(see 3)
Thai Consulate........................**11** B4
United Nations House..............**12** B3

## SIGHTS & ACTIVITIES
Bhutan Bicycle Club.................**13** C5
Changlimithang Stadium &
    Archery Field........................**14** C5
Doma Lhakhang........................**15** B4
National Memorial Chorten......**16** B6
National Textile Museum..........**17** A2
Royal Academy of Performing
    Arts....................................**18** B1
Sports Complex........................**19** A4
Thai Pavillion.........................**20** B5
Voluntary Artists Studio
    Thimphu................................**21** C5
Weekend Market......................**22** C3
Zangto Pelri Lhakhang............**23** C3

Chhubar Chhu

To
Dechenchholing
(2km)

Chhogyel Lam

Wang Chhu

Lower
Market Area

Weekend
Market
**22**

Kuenseling
Bazaam

Kundey Lam

Dungkhar Lam

Samten  Lam

Yardren Lam

Baden  Lam

Zorig  Lam

Zeden  Lam

Desi  Lam

Doebum  Lam

Phenday  Lam

Norzin  Lam

Chubachu

Doendrup  Lam

Dremton  Lam

Changlimithang
Stadium

Dechen  Lam

Namdag  Lam

Wang  Chhu

Chhogyel  Lam

Khuju
Lam

Jangchhub  Lam

Doebum  Lam

Dechen  Lam

Clocktower
Square

City Bus Stand

Chorten  Lam

Genyen  Lam

Changlam  Lam

Yangchenphug
High School

Rabten  Lam

Tashi  Lam

Samphel  Lam

Zorchen  Lam

Footpath

Lungten  Zampa

Dechen  Lam

To Chhuzom (31km);
Paro (53km)

```
0 ├─────────────■ 200 m
0 ■────────────┤ 0.1 miles
```

**SLEEPING** 🏠
Centre Lodge..........................(see 51)
Druk Hotel...................................**24** C5
Hotel Dragon Roots.................**25** C5
Hotel Druk Sherig.....................**26** C5
Hotel Galingkha.........................**27** B4
Hotel Norling.............................**28** B4
Hotel Pedling..............................**29** B4
Hotel Phentsholling Pelri..........**30** B4
Hotel Riverview..........................**31** D5
Hotel Taktsang...........................**32** B4
Hotel Tandin...............................**33** B4
Hotel Yoedzer............................**34** C4
Hotel Zey Zang...........................**35** C5
Jambayang Resort......................**36** D3
Jumolhari....................................**37** C5
NT Hotel.....................................**38** C5
Taj Tashi Hotel...........................**39** B3
Wangchuk Hotel........................**40** C5
Yeedzin Guest House.................**41** B5

**EATING** 🍴
All Stars Disco.........................(see 54)
Art Café.......................................**42** A5
Benez Restaurant.......................**43** C4
Bhutan Kitchen..........................**44** C4
Boomerang...............................(see 70)
Chasa Café...............................(see 64)
Hotel New Grand.......................**45** C5
Jichu Drakey Bakery...................**46** A5
Khamsa Coffee House................**47** C4
Mendayla Sweets........................**48** C4
Mid Point Restaurant.................**49** B4
Plums Café..................................**50** B4
Rice Bowl....................................**51** B4
Seasons Restaurant....................**52** B4
Sharchhogpa Grocery.................**53** B3
SNS Restaurant..........................**54** C5
Swiss Bakery..............................**55** B4
Tashi Supermarket......................**56** C5
Terdzor Hotel.............................**57** B3
Thai Cuisine..............................(see 27)

**ENTERTAINMENT** 🎭
Buzz Club....................................**58** C4
Gravity.........................................**59** B3
Luger Cinema..............................**60** B4
Mila Restaurant..........................**61** B4
Om Bar........................................**62** C5
Space 34....................................(see 62)
Tashi Nencha Music Studio....(see 23)
Zone.............................................**63** C4

**SHOPPING** 🛍
Art Shop Gallery.........................**64** C5
Bhutan Archery Shop...............(see 28)
Druk Handicraft........................(see 70)
Druktrin Rural Handicrafts......(see 40)
Duty Free Shop...........................**65** A2
Handicrafts Emporium...............**66** B3
Hong Kong Market.....................**67** B4
Jimmy Bros Stationery................**68** C5
Jungshi Handmade Paper
  Factory....................................**69** D4
Kelzang Handicrafts....................**70** B4
Kuenphen Colour Lab................**71** B4
Namgyel Tyres.............................**72** C4
Norling Audio............................(see 28)
Philatelic Bureau........................(see 3)
Zangmo Handicrafts...................**73** C5

**TRANSPORT**
Bus Station..................................**74** D6
Taxi Stand...................................**75** C6

the Glorious Religion). He arranged to house both monks and civil officials in the dzong, but it was soon found to be too small. The Zhabdrung then built another dzong, known as the lower dzong, for the civil officials and used the original building for the monks. The 13th Druk Desi, Chhogyel Sherab Wangchuck (1744–63), later enlarged Trashi Chhoe Dzong so that it could again accommodate both civil officials and monks.

The original dzong was destroyed by fire in 1771 and was abandoned in favour of the lower dzong, which was expanded. That dzong itself suffered a fire in 1866 and twice since then. The five-storey *utse* was damaged in the 1897 earthquake and rebuilt in 1902.

When he moved the capital to Thimphu in 1962, King Jigme Dorji Wangchuck began a five-year project to completely renovate and enlarge the dzong. The royal architect performed the repairs without touching the *utse*, Lhakhang Sarpa or any other of its chapels at the centre. Other than these structures, the entire dzong was rebuilt in traditional fashion, without nails or written plans.

Below the dzong is an excellent example of a traditional cantilever bridge. To the south of the dzong is a set of low (and unattractive) administration buildings (for which there are demolition plans). West of the dzong is the small tower of Ney Khang Lhakhang, which houses a statue of Sakyamuni flanked by the protective deity Gyenyen Jagpa Melen and Dorje Daktshen, the female guardian deity of Phajoding.

## Weekend Market

The weekend market is crammed into a set of stalls on both banks of the Wang Chhu, just north of Changlimithang Stadium. Vendors from throughout the region arrive on Thursday and Friday and remain until Sunday night. It's an interesting place to visit, where village people jostle with well-heeled Thimphu residents for the best and cheapest vegetables and foodstuffs.

Depending on the season, you may find potatoes, garlic, numerous varieties of chillies, red and white rice, cauliflowers, cabbages, lettuces, eggplants, asparagus, peas, several kinds of mushrooms and the young, curly fern fronds known as *nakey*. Fruits come from local orchards and from southern regions. You will find oranges, apples, bananas, mangoes, apricots, peaches and plums. If you wander off into one corner of the market, you'll find an odoriferous collection of dried fish, freshly slaughtered beef and pork, and balls of *datse* (homemade soft cheese). During the winter you can even pick up a leg of yak (with the hoof still attached).

Across the newly constructed cantilever footbridge, Kuendeyling Bazaam, to the west bank is a collection of stalls housing clothing, fabric and handicrafts. Here you will find locally produced goods (as well as plenty of stuff from Nepal), including prayer wheels, cymbals, horns, cloth, baskets and remarkable hats from various minority groups. Bargaining is very much in order and you may find your guide or a local can advise you on the quality of your intended purchase.

## National Institute for Zorig Chusum

The **National Institute for Zorig Chusum** (Map p99; ☎ 322302; izc@druknet.bt; Pedzoe Lam; ☼ 9am-5pm Mon-Sat) is commonly known as 'the painting school'. It operates under the auspices of the National Technical Training Institute and offers four- to six-year courses that provide instruction in many of Bhutan's traditional arts to students from throughout the country whose aptitude is more artistic than academic. The students follow a comprehensive course that starts with drawing and progresses through painting, woodcarving, embroidery and statue-making.

Most tour operators include a visit to the school in their sightseeing program. Though large groups of visitors disrupt the classes, you will be astounded at the skill and discipline of the young students. The images of the Buddhist deities on p75 were painted by senior students of the school.

Don't be surprised if you are accosted by one or two entrepreneurial types selling their wares. If you want to peruse a wider selection of the students' art, see Shopping (p113).

## National Memorial Chorten

This large Tibetan-style **chorten** (Map p99; Chorten Lam) was built in 1974 to honour the memory of the third king, Jigme Dorji Wangchuck. The whitewashed chorten is decorated with richly carved annexes facing the cardinal directions, and features elaborate mandalas, statues and a shrine dedicated to the popular third king. There are numerous religious paintings and complex tantric statues housed inside reflecting both peaceful and wrathful aspects of Buddhist deities.

The memorial chorten, with its sun-catching golden finial, is one of the most visible religious structures in Thimphu, and for many people it is the focus of their daily worship. Throughout the day people circumambulate the chorten, whirl the large red prayer wheels and pray at a small shrine inside the gate. The early morning is particularly tranquil as elderly people shuffle in, and spruced-up kids on their way to school whiz in and out to pay homage.

## Folk Heritage Museum

A restored three-storey, rammed-earth and timber building houses the **Folk Heritage Museum** (Phelchey Toenkhym; Map p99; ☎ 327133; Pedzoe Lam; SAARC national/adult Nu 25/150; ☼ 9am-5pm Tue-Sat). The house replicates a traditional farmhouse and is furnished as it would have been about a century ago. A guided tour of this almost-living museum is included in the admission and provides a glimpse into traditional Bhutanese life. The house design and many of the implements are also reminders of how many rural Bhutanese still live today. Bring a torch (flashlight) as some of the rooms are quite dimly lit.

## National Library

West of the golf course is the **National Library** (Map p99; ☎ 322885; Pedzoe Lam; ☼ 9.30am-1pm & 2-5pm Mon-Fri). It was established in 1967 to preserve many ancient Dzongkha and Tibetan texts, and is a lavishly decorated and vibrant example of Bhutanese architecture.

Pride of place on the ground floor is a copy of the largest published book in the world. Entitled *Bhutan*, this mega tome would crush any coffee table and defy any bookshelf. Its illustrated pages are turned one page per month. Details on the book and how to buy a copy can be found at www.friendlyplanet.org. Also on the ground floor are the English-language books. There are a few travel books about India and Tibet, and many about Buddhism and Himalayan history, but it's an eclectic collection where you might find anything. There is a collection of bound volumes of *Kuensel* and another collection of the many reports produced by agencies that have undertaken development or research projects. There is also a small collection of books about Bhutan on a shelf behind the checkout desk.

Traditional books and historic manuscripts are kept on the top floor – it's worth the climb. Many of these books are Tibetan-style, printed or written on long strips of handmade paper stacked between pieces of wood and wrapped in silken cloth. There are displays of several significant documents which are well labelled in English. In another section is an old printing press and wooden blocks used for printing books and prayer flags.

Sometimes you will see people circumambulating the National Library building and chanting mantras. This is because the building houses many holy books. An altar on the ground floor, with statues of Bhutan's most important historic figures, Zhabdrung Ngawang Namgyal, Pema Lingpa and Guru Rinpoche, also contributes to the building's sacred importance. Other displays include a model of Punakha Dzong and an exhibit of Chorten architecture. The library has a branch at Kuenga Rabten palace south of Trongsa in central Bhutan.

## SAARC Building

The large traditional Bhutanese-style building across the river from Trashi Chhoe Dzong was built in the early 1990s to provide a venue for a meeting of the heads of state and government from the South Asia Association for Regional Co-operation (SAARC). That meeting was never held in Bhutan but plans are in the pipeline now that Bhutan boasts several hotels that meet the five-star needs of the SAARC officials. The impressive structure now houses the planning and foreign ministries, and the National Assembly was relocated to this building in 1993. Long 'corridors of power' lead to the elaborately decorated National Assembly (held twice a year), while nearby is the Royal Banquet Hall.

## National Institute of Traditional Medicine

Established in 1978, one of the more interesting facilities in Thimphu is the **National Institute of Traditional Medicine** (Map p99; ☎ 324647; www .health.gov.bt/indigenous/index.htm; Serzhong Lam; ☻ 9am-3pm Mon-Fri, to 1pm Sat). The EU provides funding for this project, which prepares and dispenses traditional herbal and other medicines. There is an impressive laboratory and production facility that manufactures quality products, the components of which may include plants, minerals, animal parts, precious metals and gems. All kinds of pills, tablets, ointments and medicinal teas from here are distributed to regional health-care units around the country.

There is a day-care facility and clinic where doctors diagnose patients and prescribe appropriate medicines or treatments. Tour operators can arrange visits to the institute. There is a small museum and gift shop where you can purchase *tsheringma,* a safflower-based herbal tea.

The institute also researches the use of medicinal herbs and plants and has a trial plot on the premises. It has field units that collect medicinal plants from far away places such as Lingzhi in western Bhutan, where a number of significant medicinal species grow in abundance.

## National Textile Museum

Thimphu's **National Textile Museum** (Map pp102-3; ☎ 321516; Norzin Lam; SAARC national/adult Nu 25/150; ☻ 9am-4pm) is worth a visit to get to know the living national art of weaving. Exhibitions introduce the major weaving techniques, styles of local dress and textiles made by women and men. There is usually a small group of weavers working their looms inside the shop, which features work from the renowned weaving centres in Lhuentse Dzongkhag, the ancestral home of the royal family in northeastern Bhutan. Each item is labelled with the name of the weaver, at prices ranging from Nu 1500 to 25,000.

## Changlimithang Stadium & Archery Ground

The national stadium occupies the site of the 1885 battle that helped establish the political supremacy of Ugyen Wangchuck, Bhutan's first king. It is now the site of the national archery ground, a large football stadium and parade ground, basketball, tennis and squash courts, as well as the headquarters of the Bhutan Olympic committee. It's always worth checking to see what event is taking place when you are in town.

## Voluntary Artists Studio Thimphu

The impressive **Voluntary Artists Studio Thimphu** (VAST; Map pp102-3; ☎ 325664; www.vast-bhutan.org; Chang Lam) is hidden away on the top floor of a not-so-impressive building on Chang Lam. After negotiating several flights of betel-stained stairs you emerge at the study, which can be incredibly busy with after-school and weekend classes in drawing and painting for young artists. The goal of the studio (which accepts donations) is to use Bhutanese artistic values to create both traditional and contemporary works and to provide vocational training. There's a small library and coffee shop where budding artists are encouraged to congregate. Art by the students and instructors is sold in the exhibition spaces in the studio and in the Art Shop Gallery (see p113) in Clocktower Sq.

## Motithang Takin Preserve

A short distance up the road to the telecom tower is a trail leading to a large fenced area that was originally established as a mini-zoo. The king decided that such a facility was not in keeping with Bhutan's environmental and religious convictions, and it was disbanded some time ago. The animals were released into the wild but the takins, Bhutan's national animal, were so tame that they wandered around the streets of Thimphu looking for food, and the only solution was to put them back into captivity. It's worthwhile taking the time to see these oddball mammals. The best time to see them is early morning when they gather near the fence to feed. It's a five-minute walk from the road to a viewing area where you can take advantage of a few holes in the fence to take photographs. For more about this curious creature see p87.

## Telecom Tower

There's a wonderful view of Thimphu valley from the hillside below the telecommunications tower (2685m), high above the town at the end of a road that branches off from the approach to the youth centre. The complex also houses the broadcasting studios of Bhutan TV and is festooned with prayer flags. Don't photograph the telecommunications installation, but the valley is worth a few snaps particularly in the afternoon. The area is known as Sangaygang and the access road attracts fitness fanatics after work and becomes a lovers' lane after dark.

## Royal Academy of Performing Arts

The home of the Royal Dance Troupe is the **Royal Academy of Performing Arts** (Map pp102-3; ☎ 322569; Chhophel Lam; ☉ 8.45am-4.30pm Mon-Fri). It provides formal training for masked dancers and also works to preserve Bhutan's folk-dancing heritage. Unless there's a practice session on, there's little to see here. The professional dancers from this school perform several of the dances at the Thimphu tsechu. With advance notice they will provide a one-hour performance for visitors.

## Changangkha Lhakhang

This is an old fortresslike **temple** and monastic school perched on a ridge above Thimphu, southeast of Motithang. It was established in the 12th century on a site chosen by Lama Phajo Drukgom Shigpo, who came from Ralung in Tibet. The central statue is Chenresig in an 11-headed, thousand-armed manifestation. There are enormous prayer wheels to spin and even the prayer books in the temple are larger in size than usual Tibetan texts. Don't leave without taking in the excellent view from the courtyard.

## Drubthob Goemba

After you drive down the road from the telecom tower, you will find yourself on Gaden Lam, the road that runs high above the golf course. There are some great views of the town, and of Trashi Chhoe Dzong, and above you can see Drubthob Goemba, which now houses the Zilukha nunnery.

## Dechen Phodrang

At the end of Gaden Lam is Dechen Phodrang, the site of Thimphu's original Trashi Chhoe Dzong (see p101 for a brief history). Since 1971 it has housed the state monastic school, and a long procession of monks often travels between here and the dzong. A team of 15 teachers provides an eight-year course to more than 450 students. On any regular day the grounds hum with assorted recitations emanating from the windows. The 12th-century paintings in the goemba's Guru Lhakhang have been restored and the upper floor features a large figure of Zhabdrung Ngawang Namgyal as well as the *goenkhang* (chapel devoted to protective and terrifying deities). The central figure in the downstairs chapel is the Buddha Sakyamuni.

## Zangto Pelri Lhakhang

This private chapel, built in the 1990s by Dasho Aku Tongmi, a musician who composed Bhutan's national anthem, is south of the weekend market. It's beside the older Yigja Dungkhar Lhakhang and is a replica of Guru Rinpoche's celestial abode. It is Bhutan's tallest lhakhang and houses many large statues, including a 4m-high image of Guru Rinpoche.

# ACTIVITIES

You will probably be too busy sightseeing, trekking or shopping to swim, cycle or go rock climbing, but these activities are available if you want them.

There are two tennis courts, squash courts and a basketball court at the north end of the Changlimithang Stadium.

## Golf

The **Royal Thimphu Golf Club** (Map p99; ☎ 325429; www.golfbhutan.com; Chhophel Lam; green fees & club hire per day US$50) has a nine-hole course beautifully situated above Trashi Chhoe Dzong. Indian Brigadier General TV Jaganathan, posted in Bhutan between 1968 and 1973, got permission from King Jigme Dorji Wangchuck to construct a few holes. The king later granted permission to expand the course to nine holes, recognising that it would provide an attractive green area adjacent to Trashi Chhoe Dzong. The course was formally inaugurated in 1971 as the Royal Thimphu Golf Club.

Caddies are available for Nu 200 to 300, but since they are mostly schoolboys, they are usually not on site until late afternoon. You can buy lost balls from kids for Nu 20 to 50. You don't need to make an appointment to play, but weekends are busy and you may have to wait to tee off.

## Cycling

The **Bhutan Bicycle Club** (Map pp102-3; ☎ 321905; www .bhutanmtb.com; Clocktower Sq) organises rides and has bikes for hire (US$30 per day, including helmet). A helmet is required within Thimphu city limits and, of course, is highly recommended elsewhere. The club can arrange to have you and the bike transported to the start of several rides (see p244 for more information).

## Rock Climbing

Bhutan's only rock-climbing club, **Vertical Bhutan** ( ☎ 322966; verticalbhutan@hotmail.com), gathers most weekends to climb on The Nose, a rock face high above the southwest part of Thimphu. There are several prepared routes with names such as 'Wedding Present' and 'Reach and Preach'. Contact the club via email or call the club secretary, Dilu Giri, for the climbing schedule.

## Swimming

You can swim in the pool at Thimphu's **Sports Complex** (Map pp102-3; ☎ 322064; Doebum Lam; Nu 50; ☿ 4-8pm Mon-Fri, 1-6pm Sat & Sun Feb-Nov). There is also a basketball court and gym.

## WALKING TOUR

A young city, Thimphu is not crowded with historical sights but its size makes it ideal for a wander, turning into lanes and following your nose. It's impossible to get lost; if you get confused just head downhill towards the river and you will soon come across something you recognise. See the map on p108.

For a slightly strenuous excursion, start at **Clocktower Square (1)**, head up the stairs to Norzin Lam and turn north to reach the **traffic circle (2)** with the arm-snapping police. Walk uphill along Chorten Lam past the **Art Café (3**; p112) – why not drop in for excellent coffee and cake – to observe the circumambulations of the **National Memorial Chorten** (4; p104). Backtrack along Chorten Lam and turn left at Jangchhub Lam, which takes you north to the rather neglected **Doma Lhakhang (5)** and **Thai Pavillion (6)**. Head down a footpath (northeast) to Doendrup Lam, and turn left towards bustling **Hong Kong Market (7)** and, after perusing the shops, take the narrow alley lined with vegetable sellers to Norzin Lam. From here it's an easy stroll downhill back to Clocktower Sq and continue up Norzin Lam past the **Handicrafts Emporium (8**; p113) to the **National Textile Museum (9**; p105), both worthwhile detours. Head back south down Norzin Lam and drop into the opulent **Taj Tashi Hotel (10**; p110) to check out the ambience, restaurants and bars. Continue east along Samtem Lam to Chang Lam and then further east down Dungkhar Lam to the market area, which has permanent shops but really comes to life during the **Weekend Market (11**; p103). Head along Chhogyel Lam while keeping an eye out at **Changlimithang Stadium (12**; p105) for any sport activity before heading back along Chang Lam to Clocktower Sq.

## COURSES

Some Bhutanese tour companies offer specific tours to cater for special-interest groups, such as bird-watchers, and it is by no means impossible to organise instructive courses in cooking, religion, meditation etc, which can be worked into your itinerary. Of course you will need to organise this with the tour company well in advance.

## FESTIVALS & EVENTS

Thimphu really comes alive during the annual tsechu, held consecutively over eight to ten days in September/October, corresponding to the eighth lunar month in the Bhutanese

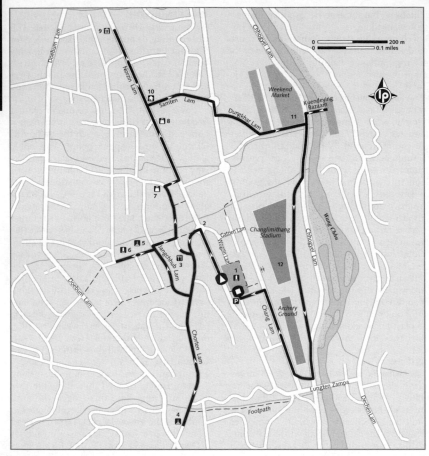

calendar. For dates and more information see p247. Another colourful and entertaining event that is uniquely Bhutanese is a good archery competition; see p113 for details.

## SLEEPING

If you are on a normal tourist visa, you will probably be booked into one of the comfortable midrange hotels unless you have payed a premium for a top-end hotel. Also, if you have scheduled your trip during the Thimphu tsechu, you may find yourself 'bumped' into budget digs, a smaller guesthouse or even a private home. If you end up as a house guest, you will get the chance to make new friends and will have found the perfect recipient for the bottle of duty-free liquor you bought en route.

If you are an Indian national or are working in Bhutan on a project, you have the option to choose a more moderately priced hotel. The budget hotels listed here are not as comfortable as the tourist hotels, but they're all quite adequate. For those paying their own way, hotels will charge 10% sales tax and 10% service on the rates shown. Many of the smaller hotels make no distinction between double or single occupancy and simply charge by the room.

### Budget

All the hotels listed below have hot water and heating, but you may have to turn on your hot water service yourself (and don't forget the tap as well) and request a portable room heater.

**Hotel Zey Zang** (Map pp102-3; ☎ 334707; Norzin Lam; s/d Nu 600/800) The recently established Zey Zang is a comfortable and secure hotel at the top of the budget range. The rooms are rather characterless (save for the bright curtains), airy, carpeted, spotless and equipped with cable TV and heater. The small bathrooms have a shower but no tub. There's a large restaurant-bar and very attentive staff.

**Centre Lodge** (Map pp102-3; ☎ 334331; fax 324709; Centre Mall, Norzin Lam; d Nu 800-1200) Most of this hotel's rooms are bright and sunny, heated, have a TV and are very well kept. The name is apt for this central location. The down side is the seemingly endless staircase to access the rooms.

**Hotel Tandin** (Map pp102-3; ☎ 322380; Norzin Lam; s/d/ste Nu 350/450/650) The Tandin is in the centre of the city, near the cinema, and boasts a bar, restaurant and a nifty little philatelic shop. The rooms are plain and not immune to noise, but have the all-important heater plus the less necessary TV.

**Hotel Yoedzer** (Map pp102-3; ☎ 324007; fax 325927; City Centre Complex, Wogzin Lam; s/d from Nu 400/500) This friendly hotel is conveniently located near Clocktower Sq. The rooms are a little tired but clean enough and there are larger suites available. The restaurant does great Indian food and the chef's shepherd's pie has attracted a small appreciation society.

**Hotel Norling** (Map pp102-3; ☎ 322997; fax 324447; Norling Centre, Norzin Lam; s/d Nu 500/550) The Norling is central, cheap and noisy and the basic rooms are clean and the staff friendly.

## Midrange

All hotels in this range have TV (cable or satellite), heating, phones and private bathrooms with 24-hour hot water. Prices given are usually for standard rooms; a smaller number of deluxe rooms and suites are also usually available for a higher tariff, and some hotels have apartments for long-term rental.

**Druk Hotel** (Map pp102-3; ☎ 322966; fax 322677; druk hotel@druknet.bt; Wogzin Lam; s/d/ste Nu 2700/3000/6000; 🖳) This hotel has long been considered the best in Thimphu. With the arrival of the big boys in the form of Taj and Aman, the friendly Druk will settle for a lower profile – which will suit many of its fans. It is in the centre of town, overlooking Clocktower Sq and boasts a bar, a multicuisine restaurant noted for its Indian food, a business centre with wireless internet, a hair salon and a health club with a gym, sauna and steam bath.

**Jumolhari Hotel** (Map pp102-3; ☎ 322747; fax 324412; www.hoteljumolhari.com; Wogzin Lam; s/d Nu 2500/2900; 🖳) This centrally located hotel bills itself as a boutique hotel and boasts a classy ambience and stylish décor. The rooms are tasteful, carpeted and comfortable; there is a health club with spa, and an excellent restaurant serving Indian, Continental, Chinese and Bhutanese dishes.

**Hotel Druk Sherig** (Map pp102-3; ☎ 322598; fax 322714; Wogzin Lam; s/d/ste Nu 950/1200/1500) The rooms in this former guesthouse are brightly decorated in Bhutanese décor and feature lots of polished wood. A vivid *ghori* hangs over each entrance to the spacious rooms, and the multicuisine restaurant specialises in local dishes.

**Hotel Riverview** (Map pp102-3; ☎ 323497; fax 323496; Dechen Lam; s/d Nu 1500/1800; 🖳) On the east bank of the Wang Chhu is this hefty, pseudo-Bhutanese-style hotel. All of the spacious, carpeted, well-appointed rooms have a balcony with a river and town view. It's a little inconvenient if you want to stroll around town but there's a restaurant, business centre, conference room and handicraft shop on the premises.

**Jambayang Resort** (Map pp102-3; ☎ 322349; fax 323669; jambayangs@druknet.bt; Dechen Lam; s/d Nu 1200/1800; 🖳) High above the Wang Chhu on the east bank is the charming Jambayang Resort. This sprawling old-fashioned guesthouse has 16 individual rooms, some with balcony and views, and four private apartments with kitchens. Many Bhutanese recommend the restaurant here with its great view.

**Hotel Phuentsholling Pelri** (Map pp102-3; ☎ 334970; fax 323392; phuetshopelri@druknet.bt; Phenday Lam; s/d Nu 1625/2000; 🖳) This new hotel was still receiving its finishing touches when we visited. The huge doubles had polished floorboards, thicker-than-usual mattresses, and tea and coffee facilities. The elevator, business centre and top-floor apartments were still works in progress, whereas the swish restaurant and bar were up and running.

**Hotel Dragon Roots** (Map pp102-3; ☎ 332820; fax 332823; droots@druknet.bt; Wogzin Lam; s/d Nu 1800/2200; ♿) The oddly named Dragon Roots boasts an elevator which, although small, should make this hotel relatively wheelchair friendly. The well-equipped rooms are cosy with wooden floors and carved furniture, and there is a large restaurant serving Bhutanese, Indian, Chinese and Continental dishes, with plenty of vegetarian options.

**Wangchuk Hotel** (Map pp102-3; ☎ 323532; htlwchuk@druknet.bt; Chang Lam; s/d Nu 1530/1950) This hotel

**THIMPHU**

overlooks the stadium and is a favourite of many expatriates. The wood-panelled, carpeted rooms are spacious, light and comfortable so don't be put off by the gloomy lobby. The nightly rates include breakfast and the restaurant has a good reputation.

**Hotel Pedling** (Map pp102-3; ☎ 325714; fax 323592; pedling@druknet.bt; Doendrup Lam; s/d Nu 1450/1800; 🖳 ) The double rooms are comfy and well appointed with computer plug-in points, but show their age and are overdue for sprucing up. There is a good restaurant with the usual multicuisine menu and a business centre.

**Yeedzin Guest House** (Map pp102-3; ☎ 325702; fax 324995; yeedzin@druknet.bt; Jangchhub Lam; s/d/ste Nu 700/1000/1200) This delightful guesthouse overlooks central Thimphu and oozes old-world charm. For long-staying guests there are five suites, each with a kitchen. The appealing restaurant is warmed by an open fire and dishes up continental, Chinese and Bhutanese fare at tables or on local-style benches.

**Motithang Hotel** (Map pp102-3; ☎ 322435; Thori Lam; s/d Nu 1020/1290) Looking older than its 1990s heritage, the rustic, wood-panelled Motithang is quite a distance above the business district, in a peaceful rural setting. The appealing rooms are lined in warm wood and there's a multicuisine restaurant.

**Hotel Galingkha** (Map pp102-3; ☎ 328126; fax 322677; Doebum Lam; s/d Nu 1000/1500) Opposite the Swiss Bakery, the rooms of the Galingkha are spacious with basic facilities and furnishings. The fascinating aspect over the southern traffic circle is a bonus for the view but also a curse when the canine opera commences at night. The Thai restaurant downstairs (see opposite) is good for a change of cuisine.

**Hotel Taktsang** (Map pp102-3; ☎ 322102; fax 323284; Doibum Lam; s/d Nu 1100/1300; 🖳 ) Tucked in behind the Galingkha, the rooms at the Taktsang are spacious and carpeted and share the dogs after dark. There is a multicuisine restaurant and a salon.

### APARTMENTS

A couple of the hotels above have apartments for long-term guests. Alternatively there are specialist providers of self-contained accommodation.

**Shambala Executive Apartments** (Map p99; ☎ 323363; fax 323600; Thori Lam; apt per month Nu 32,500) These spacious two-bedroom, two-bathroom, fully furnished, fully serviced apartments boast polished floorboards, wood panelling

and other nice touches. Nightly rates for short-term guests are available on request.

**Rabten Apartments** (Map p99; ☎ 323587; rabten@ druknet.bt; Thori Lam; apt per month Nu 18,000) Long-term guests can stay in these fully furnished (including TV) apartments and the rent includes cleaning and laundry. The restaurant specialises in Bhutanese banquets, where you must call ahead for a reservation.

## Top End

**Taj Tashi Hotel** (Map pp102-3; ☎ 322966; fax 322677; Norzim Lam; holidays@tajhotels.com; s/d/ste US$300/300/500; 🖳 ) At the time of research, the finishing touches were being applied to this centrally located, 66-room hotel that towers over Thimphu but cleverly incorporates traditional architecture. There are several categories of luxury accommodation, with all rooms beautifully appointed with traditional art and contemporary comfort. Guests can choose to dine in three restaurants, take tea in the tea lounge or sample the bar. One's ingestion sins can be expunged in the gym, spa or heated indoor pool.

**Amankora** (Map p99; ☎ 8272333; www.amanresorts .com; Thori Lam; s/d US$925/1000; 🖳 ) On the 'less is more' theme comes this five-star resort on the outskirts of town, far from the dogs and traffic of Norzin Lam. The only sounds to penetrate the vertical breaches in the stone walls are the whispers of the surrounding pine grove. Amankora looks like a mini dzong, its stone-paved passageways inspiring hushed tones in the reverential guests. Inside the open-plan rooms, plenty of wood and tan-coloured textiles mellow the monastery asceticism. The traditional *bukhari* wood heater is a nice touch; so is the altar-like bath tub. If you can leave the bath, you can spa yourself silly, have a massage or take in one of the cultural programs. Airport transfers, meals in the immaculate restaurant (Bhutanese and Continental menu), and beverages are included in the tariff.

## EATING

Thimphu's dining scene is dominated by the hotel restaurants, but there's a handful of cosy cafés and restaurant-bars that hint of epicurean evolution in progress.

Hotel restaurants tend to be a predictable multicuisine compilation of Indian, Bhutanese, Chinese and Continental. Not surprisingly one kitchen rarely excels in all cuisines and we have used locals', expats' and our own gluttonous adventures to source what's good and where. Bhutanese cuisine is widely available, but beware the hot chillies that are an essential, omnipresent ingredient. Other ingredients are seasonal, including meat, so don't be surprised to find some menu items unavailable.

## Restaurants

When tour groups are in residence most hotels have a buffet at Nu 300 to 500, but it's usually possible to order from the à la carte menu too.

**Seasons Restaurant** (Map pp102-3; ☎ 327413; Doendrup Lam; mains Nu 150-200 ⏲ lunch & dinner) This deservedly popular restaurant specialises in pizzas – excellent veg and non-veg varieties – and pasta. There's also a balcony overlooking the bustling Hong Kong Market where you can enjoy a Red Panda wheat beer. And from December to March ask about the yummy yak roast.

**Benez Restaurant** (Map pp102-3; ☎ 325180; Gatoen Lam; mains Nu 40-120; ⏲ lunch & dinner, closed Tue) Benez is a lively and inviting restaurant in the centre of town, with a cosy bar in the back that is popular with locals and expats, especially on Fridays. In addition to the multicuisine mains there are excellent bar snacks of *momos*, samosas, fried cheese balls, etc.

**Druk Hotel** (Map pp102-3; ☎ 322966; Wogzin Lam; mains Nu 75-150; ⏲ breakfast, lunch & dinner) This spacious restaurant caters to tour groups as well as Thimphu's business and who's-who crowd (at least until the Taj Tashi gets going). The Indian menu is excellent and the multicuisine business lunch is top value at Nu 90.

**Jumolhari Hotel** (Map pp102-3; ☎ 322747; www.hotel jumolhari.com; Wogzin Lam; mains Nu 50-150; ⏲ breakfast, lunch & dinner) This delightful restaurant in one of Thimphu's most appealing hotels is notable for its delicious tandoori and curries, delicate naans, cold beer and relaxed atmosphere.

**Bhutan Kitchen** (Map pp102-3; ☎ 331919; Gatoen Lam; mains Nu 100-300; ⏲ lunch & dinner) This elegant restaurant showcases Bhutanese cuisine (in addition to a multicuisine menu) in a spacious but warm setting that features traditional seating, a traditional kitchen and store room. It was designed with tour groups in mind, so you can dive into *ema datse* (chillies and cheese) and other local dishes without calling for the fire brigade. Finish off with a warm *arra* – the local firewater.

**Plums Café** (Map pp102-3; ☎ 324307; Chorten Lam; mains Nu 60-120; ⏲ lunch & dinner Mon-Sat) A small sign above a door points patrons upstairs to this popular restaurant which offers conti-

nental food as well as an extensive range of Chinese and Bhutanese. It's another ideal place to try *ema datse* or a dish of local mushrooms or *nakey*.

**Rice Bowl** (Map pp102-3; ☎ 333844; Centre Mall, Norzin Lam; mains Nu 70-150; ⏲ lunch & dinner) Excellent chilli pork, Sechuan chicken or the recommended crispy sesame chicken, are just some of the numerous spicy offerings best enjoyed by sharing.

**Thai Cuisine** (Galingkha Hotel; Map pp102-3; ☎ 328126; Chorten Lam; mains Nu 60-80; ⏲ lunch & dinner) Local, fresh ingredients are given the Thai touch and presented with flair in this spacious restaurant overlooking the southern traffic circle. Peruse the menu by all means but it's better to ask the chef what she recommends on the night.

**Mid Point Restaurant** (Map pp102-3; ☎ 321269; Wogzin Lam; mains Nu 30-60; ⏲ lunch & dinner) This is a favourite restaurant of many Bhutanese for its generous local, Chinese and Indian dishes, particularly *dosas* and other south Indian cuisine, at very reasonable prices.

**S.N.S. Restaurant** (Map pp102-3; ☎ 326177; Chang Lam; ⏲ breakfast, lunch & dinner) Conveniently located next to All Stars Disco, S.N.S. is a busy place on disco nights and is the only restaurant in town where you might get a late-night snack. It has the only Japanese food around.

**NT Hotel** (Map pp102-3; ☎ 323458; Norzin Lam; mains Nu 30-70; ⏲ breakfast, lunch & dinner) Don't bother checking out the rooms, but the restaurant is a recommended, basic, inexpensive, hot curry and cold beer haunt. Don't inspect under the tables but do enjoy the Tuesday special.

Most hotel restaurants can put on decent meals, and a few have other charms: **Jambayang Resort** (Map pp102-3; ☎ 322349; Dechen Lam; mains Nu 70-180; ⏲ breakfast, lunch & dinner) is noted for its olde worlde charm and superb view over town; on the other hand, the **Amankora** (Map p99; ☎ 8272333; set menu US$50) boasts international fare and five-star service. Not surprisingly the hotels that primarily cater to Indian guests serve up good-value curries. Try the **Hotel Yoedzer** (Map pp102-3; ☎ 324007; Wogzin Lam; mains Nu 40-90; ⏲ lunch & dinner), which also does a mean shepherd's pie; the **Terdzor Hotel** (Map pp102-3; ☎ 334453; Norzin Lam; mains Nu 30-50, buffet per person Nu 130; ⏲ lunch & dinner), which has outstanding Nepali (Friday) and Punjabi (Saturday) buffets; or the **Hotel New Grand** (Map pp102-3; ☎ 324290; Norzin Lam; mains Nu 30-50; ⏲ lunch & dinner), an unsophisticated vegetarian restaurant with south Indian delicacies.

## Cafés

**Art Café** (Map pp102-3; ☎ 327933; Doebum Lam; cakes & soups Nu 50-150; ⏰ 7.30am-7pm, closed Mon) Smart, bright and cosy best describe this Thimphu trendsetter. Great coffee and wicked cakes (such as the addictive chocolate tart) will have you returning again and again, and the small mains selection – hearty soups, pasta, noodles – make for an ideal lunch.

**Swiss Bakery** (Map pp102-3; ☎ 322259; Chorten Lam; ⏰ 8am-7pm Wed-Mon) On a hill above the southern traffic circle, this was Bhutan's first attempt at a fast-food joint. It was opened in 1970 by one of Bhutan's first expatriates and despite its well-worn appearance it's a much-loved institution with expats and locals. It serves great cheese omelettes, plastic-wrapped sandwiches and hamburgers, and a small selection of 'homemade' cakes.

**Chasa Café** (Map pp102-3; Clocktower Sq; ⏰ 8am-7pm) Tiny Chasa has minuscule tables and cheap Bhutanese dishes (all under Nu 70), such as eye-watering ema datse and soothing fried rice.

**Khamsa Coffee House** (Map pp102-3; ☎ 333652; Changlam Plaza, Chang Lam; snacks Nu 25-65; ⏰ 10am-8pm) Upstairs (lots of stairs) is this modern coffee shop where you can get espresso, milkshakes, pancakes and other snacks, as well as a view.

## Quick Eats

**Jichu Drakey Bakery** (Map pp102-3; ☎ 322980; Doebum Lam; from Nu 15; ⏰ 7am-noon & 1.30-7.30pm) Stroll up the hill for first-rate takeaway (there are no tables) cakes and pastries. Small items include pear cakes, cream rolls and tarts, and you can also order apple pie, strudel and larger cakes.

**Mendayla Sweets** (Map pp102-3; Chang Lam; ⏰ 8am-8pm) For Indian sweets, ice cream, yogurt, chocolate, even samosas and pizza, head to this bright sweets shop.

## Self-Catering

For fresh produce, remember the busy weekend market, which kicks off on Thursday, and the semi-concealed stalls in Hong Kong market.

**Tashi Supermarket** (Map pp102-3; Clocktower Sq; ⏰ 8am-7.30pm) Huge supermarket with vast range imported and local groceries, ice creams and refrigerated chocolates.

**Sharchhogpa Grocery** (Map pp102-3; ☎ 323280; Norzin Lam; ⏰ 7am-9pm) Friendly grocery shop with cereals, bread and plenty of packaged foodstuffs.

## DRINKING & ENTERTAINMENT

Thimphu has numerous bars, but only a handful could be recommended for outsiders looking for more than a game of snooker and a swig of whisky. Entertainment can also be a bit of a challenge – unless it's tsechu time. Occasional concerts and video shows at the sports complex will be well advertised by posters and in the newspapers.

### Bars

As well as the hotel bars, there are numerous small bars throughout the town. Alcohol won't be served until after 1pm and most bars are closed on Tuesday, the national dry day. Bars close at 11pm weekdays and midnight on Friday and Saturday.

**Om Bar** (Map pp102-3; ☎ 326344; www.changkhang .com; Jojo's Shopping Complex, Chang Lam; ⏰ from 5pm, closed Tue & Sun) Thimphu's 'in' bar and a quiet gathering spot early in the evening that becomes busy with a diverse collection of locals and expats after 10pm. It's on the 2nd floor of the shopping complex.

Favourite after-work bars (which double as restaurants) include cosy **Benez Restaurant** (Map pp102-3; ☎ 325180; Gatoen Lam; ⏰ 11am-11pm), with its talking points such as coasters and cash from around the globe and designer rums, and the **Zone** (Map pp102-3; ☎ 331441; Chang Lam; ⏰ noon-midnight), with its modern décor and great chips, burgers and pizzas for late-night munchies.

### Nightclubs & Live Music

For a small town there's a fair bit of competition in this scene with live music replacing disco and vice versa and places running hot and cold. Ask around for the latest vibe. Don't expect the discos to kick off much before midnight. Depending on the entertainment and the time you rock up, a cover charge may be applicable. Nightclubs and discos close at midnight weekdays and at 2am Friday and Saturday.

Here are a few on offer:

**All Stars Disco** (Map pp102-3; Chang Lam; ⏰ 10pm-2am Wed, Fri & Sat)

**Boomerang** (Map pp102-3; Yarkay Central, Norzin Lam; ⏰ 9pm-2am Wed, Fri & Sat) A bright venue with big-screen TV, try-out bands and a young crowd.

**Buzz Club** (Map pp102-3; Chang Lam; ⏰ 11pm-2am Wed, Fri & Sat) Big, bold and popular.

**Gravity** (Map pp102-3; Zangto Pelri Shopping Complex, Norzin Lam; ⏰ 10pm-2am Wed, Fri & Sat) Hidden, but follow the signs.

**Space 34** (Map pp102-3; ☎ 323497; Jojo's Shopping Complex, Chang Lam; ☽ 10pm-2am Wed, Fri & Sat) Cosy and thumping and right next to the Om Bar.

## Cultural Programmes

If you are in a group of more than four, your tour operator can arrange a dance performance at the Royal Academy of Performing Arts (see p106). A more relaxed atmosphere prevails at **Tashi Nencha Music Studio** (Map pp102-3; ☎ 322804) near the Zangto Pelri Lhakhang. The studio can provide a Bhutanese meal and an evening of classical and folk music around a bonfire.

**Mila Restaurant** (Map pp102-3; ☎ 325519; Dragon Shopping Complex, Norzin Lam) features singers and a Dzongkha comedian most nights. There is a largely local audience and the performers, both amateur and professional, sing traditional Bhutanese songs. When there are professional acts expect a Nu 50 cover charge. After 8pm members of the audience can request songs at Nu 100 each.

## Cinemas

The usually crowded and always uncomfortable **Luger Cinema** (Map pp102-3; ☎ 322317; Norzin Lam) screens Hindi and Bhutanese movies as well as the occasional ancient English/foreign-language movie.

## Sport

### ARCHERY

Tournaments (see p62) are scheduled on many weekends at the Changlimithang Archery Ground. Whether it's the traditional bamboo or the high-tech carbon-fibre bows, the skill, antics and camaraderie are always entertaining. For dates of events check the papers. Archers practise at the target field at the south end of Changlimithang Stadium on most mornings.

### FOOTBALL

The national football tournament takes place in August at Changlimithang Stadium, with teams from schools throughout the country competing. At major matches the Royal Bhutan Army band provides the half-time entertainment.

# SHOPPING

Thimphu has a plethora of general shops containing a hodgepodge selection such as light bulbs, stationery, farm implements, shampoo, computer disks and canned fish. To provide even more variety, shops may sell drinks by

the glass and their sign may read 'shop cum bar' or the all-encompassing 'general cum bar shop'.

Many items on sale are made in India, but there are lots of interesting Bhutanese products, especially textiles, baskets, jewellery, incense, books and religious items.

At the **Duty Free Shop** (Map pp102-3; ☎ 322167; Norzin Lam) you can buy imported liquor, wine, biscuits and other 'luxury' items, but you have to pay the full price, including duty, unless you're a diplomat or a senior government official.

## Archery

Catering to the large community of Bhutanese archers, **Bhutan Archery Shop** (Map pp102-3; ☎ 332100; Norling Centre, Norzin Lam) specialises in American-made Hoyt brand bows that range in price from US$600 to US$1100. Arrows are the steel-tipped Easton brand, which sell for Nu 280 to 500. It's a relatively expensive sport. The traditional bamboo bows are usually homemade and the bamboo arrows can be picked up at the weekend market.

## Contemporary Paintings & Handmade Paper

**Jungshi Handmade Paper Factory** (Map pp102-3; ☎ 323431; Khuju Lam; ☽ 8.30am-5pm, Mon-Sat) This small factory produces watermark paper as well as cards, lampshades, envelopes, calendars and other items made from traditional Bhutanese paper.

Located near the Clocktower, **Art Shop Gallery** (Map pp102-3; ☎ 325664; Wogzin Lam) has art supplies, traditional paper and handicrafts, and contemporary paintings from the **Voluntary Artists Studio Thimphu** (VAST; Map pp102-3; ☎ 325664; www.vast-bhutan.org; Chang Lam), which also sells art during regular exhibitions.

## Gho & Kira

If you want to wear Bhutanese dress, there are many shops in Thimphu's shopping complexes that have ready-made *gho* and *kira* in a variety of sizes, patterns and quality. **Kelzang Handicrafts** (Map pp102-3; ☎ 321353; Yarkay Central, Norzin Lam) and the **Handicrafts Emporium** (Map pp102-3; ☎ 322810; Norzin Lam) are two to try.

A handmade cotton *kira* costs around Nu 4000 while a silk *kira* sells for Nu 50,000 to 80,000. A *gho* costs about Nu 2000 if it's made from machine-woven cloth and Nu 4000 to 6000 for hand-woven cotton cloth. A silk *gho* can cost from Nu 12,000.

In the industrial estate at the south end of Thimphu, the **Gagyel Lhundrup Weaving Centre** (Map pp102-3; ☎ 327534; Changzamtok; ☺ 9am-5pm) produces hand-woven textiles on site and has a selection of cloth and ready-made garments for sale. This is one of the few places where you can watch weavers at work.

## Handicrafts, Traditional Arts & Jewellery

Don't neglect the handicraft section at the weekend market, where you can put your bargaining prowess to the test. To purchase the excellent works by students of the National Institute for Zorig Chusum visit **Sangay Arts & Crafts** (Map p99; ☎ 327419; Pedzoe Lam), in a building on the road below the school. Behind the school, a narrow lane leads through a garden to a small house where a traditional craftsman makes and sells drums and Tibetan violins.

There a numerous handicraft shops selling *thangkas*, masks, brassware and jewellery, including the following.

**Handicrafts Emporium** (Map pp102-3; ☎ 322810; Norzin Lam; ☺ 9am-1pm & 2-5pm Mon-Sun) This is a large government-run emporium with fixed prices.

**Druktrin Rural Handicrafts** (Map pp102-3; ☎ 324500; Clocktower Sq) At the rear of the Wangchuk Hotel (enter from Clocktower Sq), this shop offers a great variety and has a small museum with antique jewellery and textiles.

**Druk Handicraft** (Map pp102-3; ☎ 322258; Yarkay Complex, Norzin Lam) Good range of 'antiques', handicrafts and earrings.

**Choki Handicrafts** (Map p99; ☎ 324728; fax 323731; Pedzoe Lam) Near the National Institute for Zorig Chusum, this establishment manufactures and sells masks, thangkas, paintings and painted lama tables called *choektse*.

**Zangmo Handicrafts** (Map pp102-3; Wogzin Lam) Sells work from the National Institute for Zorig Chusum and sometimes has students practising there.

## Music

CDs and tapes of Bhutanese and Hindi songs are available for Nu 200 to 400 in numerous shops, including **Norling Audio** (Map pp102-3; Norling Centre, Norzin Lam).

## Postage Stamps

Bhutan Post occupies the northern half of a large building on Dremton Lam, a back road north of the cinema. The **Philatelic Bureau** (Map pp102-3; ☎ 322296; Dremton Lam) here has a counter that sells stamps and souvenir sheets of Bhutanese stamps. There is also a tiny shop on the ground floor of Hotel Tandin (p109), which has a small selection of postcards and unusual stamps.

## Trekking Equipment

If you are missing a piece of gear for your trek, try **Sachak Enterprise** (Map pp102-3; ☎ 333880; Centre Mall, Norzin Lam) for good Nepalese copies of brand-name gear. **Namgyel Tyres** (Map pp102-3; ☎ 325311; Gatoen Lam) stocks hiking boots and is your best bet for larger sizes. There are also a few shops around town that sell Bangladeshi-made fleece jackets, hats and pants at bargain prices – look for the shops full of cardboard boxes stacked with clothes.

## GETTING THERE & AWAY

The journey to/from Phuentsholing took up to 10 days before the road was completed in 1962. It now takes six hours. See p155 for details of the drive.

## Bus

The long-distance bus station is below the east end of the bridge (*zampa*) at the southern end of town. Here you can find numerous crowded buses (vomit comets) to Paro (Nu 35), Phuentsholing (Nu 110; Coaster Nu 170) and other destinations throughout the country (see p265 for more details).

## GETTING AROUND

If you are on a normal tourist visa, you will have a car/minibus, driver and guide available throughout your stay in Bhutan, and you'll have little trouble getting around. Most shops and points of interest are within easy walking distance of Thimphu's major hotels; it's easy to pop out for a drink or a round of shopping on foot.

### To/From the Airport

You can book a taxi at the tea stall outside Paro airport at a fixed rate of Nu 800 to Thimphu. It is 53km from the airport to Thimphu; the journey takes less than two hours.

If your tour operator has not arranged transport for your departing flight, the most reliable way is to have your hotel arrange a vehicle. Arrange your transport well in advance. If you have an early-morning flight from Paro (and most are), you're recommended to spend the night in Paro. Druk Air closes the counter an hour before flight time and won't reopen it if you're late.

### Bus

A public bus service operates throughout Thimphu between 7.30am and 7.30pm from a starting point at the parking area on Chang Lam. Fares are Nu 1 to 9 depending on the distance travelled. In addition to several city routes, the buses also operate to Dechench-oeling in the north and Simtokha and Babesa to the south. Routes, fares and timetables are available at www.bhutanpost.com.bt.

### Taxi

Most of the taxis are tiny Maruti minivans with meters that the drivers rarely use. The taxi stand is on Chang Lam, although you can flag down an empty taxi in the street. Taxi drivers have a habit of charging foreigners, including Indians, as much as they can – one of Bhutan's few flagrant rip-offs. You should be able to hire a taxi for the whole day for about Nu 500, and local trips should cost between Nu 40 and 60 in a shared taxi.

# AROUND THIMPHU

## NORTH OF THIMPHU

As you travel up the east side of the Wang Chhu, north of Lungten Zampa and past the Riverview Hotel, you'll eventually pass the SAARC building (National Assembly), which overlooks the dzong. On the opposite side of the river you may catch a glimpse of Samten-ling Palace, the cottage that is the king's residence. A short distance north is the suburb of Taba where the Forestry Institute has its offices and you can stay at the atmospheric **Taba Resort** (Map p99; ☎ 323532; htlwchuk@druknet.bt; off Dechen Lam; s/d from Nu 1530/1950). The resort is associated with the Wangchuk Hotel in town and boasts a restful, pine-forest location, mineral spring, hot-stone baths and a private goemba built on the ruins of a former palace. There are great valley views from the balconied rooms.

The large **Dechencholeing Palace** is some distance north of the dzong. It was built in 1952 and is the official residence of the queen mother. North of the palace is the Royal Body Guard (RBG) facility.

### Pangri Zampa

North of Dechenchoeling and east of Dechen-phu Lhakhang is **Pangri Zampa**, two imposing white buildings in a grove of giant cypress trees. Founded in the early 16th century,

Zhabdrung Ngawang Namgyal lived here after he arrived in 1616 because this temple appeared in the vision that directed him from Tibet to Bhutan. A well-respected astrologer is in residence and frescoes here are said to have been painted by the Zhabdrung.

### Dechenphu Lhakhang

Dechenphu Lhakhang is a 2km drive on a rocky road up a side valley from a turn-off near Dechenchoeling, then a short climb up a stone staircase to an elevation of about 2660m. The imposing, tall red *goenkhang* is dedicated to the powerful deity Gyenyen and is said to be able to supply armour and weapons for an endless number of soldiers. Unesco financed a project to restore many of the paintings in the adjoining goemba.

### Tango Goemba & Cheri Goemba

Continuing up the valley the road crosses to the east side of the Wang Chhu at Begana, near a training facility operated by the electricity department and a large gold-painted petroglyph of Chenrisig on a rock beside the road. There are no restaurants or shops

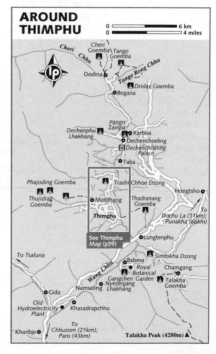

THIMPHU

nearby. If you plan a full-day excursion to either Tango Goemba or Cheri Goemba, bring a water bottle and a packed lunch.

A few kilometres beyond Begana, 12km from Thimphu, a road leads east and climbs a short distance to a parking lot. The trail to **Tango Goemba** is a climb of 280m and takes about half an hour if you follow the steeper shortcut, or about an hour if you take the longer, more gradual trail. Lama Gyalwa Lhanampa founded the goemba in the 12th century. The present building was built in the 15th century by the 'divine madman', Lama Drukpa Kunley (see p136). In 1616 Zhabdrung Ngawang Namgyal visited Tango Goemba and meditated in a cave nearby. The head lama, a descendent of Lama Drukpa Kunley, presented the goemba to the Zhabdrung, who carved a sandalwood statue of Chenresig, which he installed in the monastery.

The picturesque three-storey tower and several surrounding buildings were built in the 18th century by the eighth *desi* (secular ruler), Druk Rabgye. The Zhabdrung Jigme Chhogyel added the golden roof in the 19th century. Tango is the residence of an important young *trulku* (reincarnate lama) who is recognised as the seventh reincarnation of the highly respected fourth *desi*, Gyalse Tenzin Rabgye, whose previous incarnation passed away in 1830.

A short distance beyond the turn-off to Tango Goemba the road ends at Dodina (elevation 2600m). A walk of about one hour leads to **Cheri Goemba** (Cheri Dorji Dhen). The trail starts by crossing a lovely covered bridge that spans the Wang Chhu, and then climbs steeply to the monastery where there are tame deer and soaring birds. Zhabdrung Ngawang Namgyal built this goemba in 1620 and established the first monk body here. A silver chorten inside the goemba holds the ashes of the Zhabdrung's father.

## SOUTH OF THIMPHU

A road leads uphill from Babesa to the Royal Botanical Garden at Serbithang, which was inaugurated in 1999 and has a collection of 500 species of plants. It's a favourite picnic spot of Thimphu residents and has an information centre that sells seedlings and medicines from the medicinal-plants project.

South of Babesa a steep gravel road leads 1.3km uphill to the Gangchen Nyezergang Lhakhang, an ancient lhakhang that was re-built and reconsecrated in 2001 under the sponsorship of Lyonpo Jigme Thinley.

### Simtokha

Simtokha is about 5km south of Thimphu on the old road to Paro and Phuentsholing. The junction with the road to eastern Bhutan is just before Simtokha.

In the valley below the road are the EU-funded plant-and-soil-protection project and the large, red-roofed Royal Institute of Management.

#### SIMTOKHA DZONG

Officially known as Sangak Zabdhon Phodrang (Palace of the Profound Meaning of Secret Mantras), Simtokha Dzong was built in 1629 by Zhabdrung Ngawang Namgyal. It is often said to be the first dzong built in Bhutan. In fact, there were dzongs in Bhutan as early as 1153, but this is the first dzong built by the Zhabdrung, is the oldest dzong that has survived as a complete structure, and is the first structure to incorporate both monastic and administrative facilities. It is the home of the Institute for Language and Culture Studies; the students are both monks and lay people.

The site is said to have been chosen to guard over a demon that had vanished into the rock nearby, hence the name Simtokha, from *simmo* (demoness) and *do* (stone). Conveniently, the site is also an excellent location from which to protect the Thimphu valley and the valley leading to the Dochu La and eastern Bhutan. The dzong is about 60m square and the only gate is on the south side. (Though the original gate was on the west side.)

The *utse* is three storeys high and behind the usual prayer wheels around the outside there is a line of more than 300 fine slate carvings with painted faces depicting saints and philosophers. The large central figure in the central lhakhang is of Sakyamuni; he is flanked by images of eight Bodhisattvas: Jampelyang, Chana Dorje, Chenresig, Jampa, and the less-familiar Sai Hingpo (Shritigarva), Dupa Nampasel, Namkhe Hingpo (Akash Garva) and Kuentu Zangpo. The paintings inside this lhakhang are said to be some of the oldest and most beautiful in Bhutan. One of the lhakhangs, Gen Khang, may be visited only by the lamas. In the west lhakhang chapel are paintings of Chenresig, green and white Taras, and an early painting of Zhabdrung Ngawang Namgyal, which was restored and cleaned in 1995. Large

## DAY WALKS AROUND THIMPHU

In addition to the walks to Tango Goemba (p115) and Cheri Goemba (p115), there are good day walks to monasteries and lookout points near Thimphu. You cannot go into the monasteries, but most are architecturally interesting and command good views of the valley. The Royal Society for Protection of Nature (RSPN) has published Mild and Mad Day Hikes Around Thimphu by Piet van der Poel & Rogier Gruys, with details of 27 hikes as well as numerous alternatives and side trips. You can also download it from www.bhutan-trails.org/index.html. As the title suggests, the hikes range from easy walks to the 25km Thimphu to Paro 'Punishment Trail'. It is important to remember that many of these hikes pass meditation cells near monasteries. Don't shout, disturb them or knock on the door to ask for directions.

### Drolay Goemba

It's a two- to three-hour round trip from the parking lot below Tango Goemba to Drolay Goemba at 3400m. The walk offers amazing views of the Thimphu valley and you can combine it with a walk to Tango Goemba.

### Lungchuzekha Goemba

The best easy walk in the area is a three- to four-hour round trip from Dochu La to Lungchuzekha Goemba. It affords excellent views of the Bhutan Himalaya and you can return via the same route or descend to Trashigang Goemba and Hongtsho. From the 108 chortens the trail gradually climbs into red, white and pink rhododendron forest for 1½ hours with some steep sections, before branching left to Longchuzekha Goemba and right to Trashigang. Combine with dawn views from Dochu La for a great half-day excursion or do it after a morning visit to Punakha.

### Phajoding Goemba

It is a 5km walk uphill from the youth centre in Motithang to Phajoding Goemba (3640m), a large monastic complex with 10 lhakhangs and 15 monastic residences, many of them used for extended meditation retreats. It was founded in the 13th century by Togden Pajo, a yogi from Tibet, who was searching for a place of meditation. Most of the buildings were constructed in 1748 through the efforts of Shakya Rinchen, the ninth Je Khenpo, whose image is the central figure in the main Khangzang Lhakhang here. The monastic school is housed in the Jampa Lhakhang and offers a more secluded environment than the Dechen Phodrang School in Thimphu.

From Phajoding you can ascend another 300m to Thujidrag Goemba. This is the last day of the Druk Path Trek in reverse. See p212 for details.

### Talakha Goemba

The 15th-century Talakha Goemba (3080m) offers spectacular views of the Bhutan Himalaya and Thimphu valley. You can drive part way and then set out on foot. From the small goemba you can make a strenuous six- to nine-hour hike up to the 4280m Talakha peak.

### Thadranang Goemba

Another strenuous two-hour uphill hike leads to Thadranang Goemba (3270m). Start at the Yangchenphug High School and climb steeply up the ridge through a blue-pine forest.

### Trashigang Goemba

It's two hours from the hillside below Hongtsho to Trashigang Goemba (3200m). This goemba was built in 1786 by the 12th Je Khenpo. It is an important meditation centre and there are numerous small houses for pilgrims near the goemba. In addition to about 16 monks, there are a few *anims* (Buddhist nuns). Inside the lhakhang there are statues of several Je Khenpos who meditated here.

### Wangditse Goemba

An easy one-hour walk with great views of Thimphu that takes you from the telecom tower to Wangditse Goemba, which was founded in 1750 by the attendants of Bhutan's eighth *desi*, Druk Rabgye, and renovated in 2001. The lhakhang houses the statues of the guardian deities Yeshey Goenpo (Mahakala), Palden Lhamo (Mahakali) and Tsheringma (the goddess of longevity).

paintings of mandalas and the guardians of the four directions adorn the *gorikha* (porch).

During its construction Simtokha Dzong was attacked by a coalition of Tibetans and five Bhutanese lamas who were opposed to the Zhabdrung's rule. The attack was repelled and the leader of the coalition, Palden Lama, was killed. In 1630 the Tibetans again attacked and took control of the dzong. The Zhabdrung regained control when the main building caught fire and the roof collapsed, killing the invaders. Descriptions of the original Simtokha Dzong were provided by the two Portuguese Jesuit priests who visited here in 1629 on their way to Tibet.

Expansion and restoration of the dzong was performed by the third Druk Desi, Mingyur Tenpa, in the 1670s after Tibetan invaders attacked it in 1630. It has been enlarged and restored many times since, most recently by a Japanese team of builders and architects.

# Western Bhutan

Whether you arrive by air at Paro or by road at Phuentsholing, your first impression of Bhutan is one of stepping into a world that you thought existed only in storybooks or your imagination. Vertical prayer flags flutter in the breeze and men dressed in a traditional *gho* (tunic) and Argyle socks stroll past yellow-roofed shrines and wooden slate-roofed houses. It soon becomes clear that you are well off the beaten path of mass tourism.

As with the rest of country, western Bhutan is a collection of valleys. The remote Haa valley in the far west is separated from the Paro valley by the 3810m Cheli La. The relatively built-up Thimphu valley to the east is divided from the historical centres of Punakha and Wangdue Phodrang by the 3140m Dochu La. East of here the rugged Black Mountain range forms an even greater barrier that separates western Bhutan from the rest of the country. North of here, the upper valleys are trekking territory, leading to the sacred peak of Jhomolhari, the Tibetan border and the fascinating and remote regions of Laya and Gasa. To the south are the lush foothills and the all-important road to the Indian border at Phuentsholing.

This is the region of Bhutan that most tourists see and for good reason. It's the heartland of the Drukpa people, home to the only airport, the capital and the largest, oldest and most spectacular dzongs in the kingdom. Whether it's the beginning of your trip or the all of your trip, it's a spectacular introduction to a magical land.

## HIGHLIGHTS

- Visit the spectacular dzongs of **Paro** (p122), **Wangdue Phodrang** (p149) and **Punakha** (p145).
- Admire the rhododendrons and mountain views on an early-morning drive to the **Dochu La** (p134)
- Immerse yourself in Bhutanese culture and history at Paro's **National Museum** (p124)
- Spot black-necked cranes or just do some great hiking in the remote **Phobjikha valley** (p152)
- Hike uphill to the dramatic cliff-hanging **Tiger's Nest** (p128), Bhutan's most famous sight
- Make a pilgrimage to the **Kyichu Lhakhang** (p127), one of Bhutan's oldest and most beautiful temples
- Explore little-visited monasteries and hermitages in the **Haa valley** (p133)
- Be blessed with a 10-inch penis, if only for a day, at **Chimi Lhakhang** (p145), the monastery of the Divine Madman!

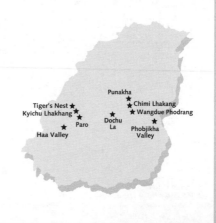

# WESTERN BHUTAN

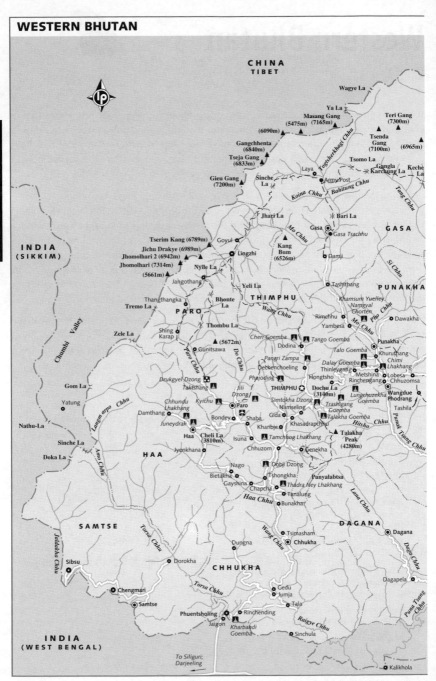

**CHINA**
TIBET

Wagye La

Ya La
Masang Gang (7165m)
(5475m)

Teri Gang (7300m)

(6090m)

Gangchhenta (6840m)

Tsenda Gang (7100m)

(6965m)

Tseja Gang (6833m)

Tsomo La

Gangla Karchung La

Keche La

Gieu Gang (7200m)

Sinche La

Laya
Army Post

Koina Chhu

Bahitung Chhu

Togtsherkhagi Chhu

Tang Chhu

Jhari La

Bari La

Gasa
Gasa Tsachhu

**GASA**

Tserim Kang (6789m)
Jichu Drakye (6989m)
Jhomolhari 2 (6942m)
Jhomolhari (7314m)
(5661m)

Goyul

Lingzhi

Kang Bum (6526m)

Damji

Si Chhu

Nyile La

Mo Chhu

Tashithang

**PUNAKHA**

Jangothang

Yeli La

Khamsum Yueley Namgyal Chorten

Thangthangka

Bhonte La

**THIMPHU**

Rimchhu

Mo Chhu

Phu Chhu

Dawakha

Tremo La

**PARO**

Wang Chhu

Yambesa

Thombu La

Cheri Goemba

Dodina

Tango Goemba

Talo Goemba

**Punakha**

Khuruthang

Zele La

Shing Karap

(5672m)

Pangri Zampa

Dalay Goemba

Chimi Lhakhang

Gunitsawa

Do Chhu

Dechenchoeling

Thinleygang

Metshina Rinchengang

Lobesa
Chhuzomsa

Drukgyel Dzong

Phajoding

Hongtsho

Dochu La (3140m)

Wangdue Phodrang

Taktshang

Jili Dzong

**THIMPHU**

Lungchezekha Goemba

Chhundu Lhakhang

Kyichu

**Paro**

Simtokha Dzong

Trashigang Goemba

Tashila

Damthang

Juneydrak

Bondey

Shaba

Gida

Namseling

Talakha Goemba

Hitsho

Chhu

Chheli La (3810m)

Kharibje

Khasadrapchhu

Talakha Peak (4280m)

**HAA**

Jyenkhana

Isuna

Tamchhog Lhakhang

Genekha

Nago

Chhuzom

Dobji Dzong

Panyalabtsa

Bietakha

Tshongkha

Gayshina

Chapcha

Thadra Ney Lhakhang

Tanalung

Lana Chhu

**DAGANA**

Dagana

Haa Chhu

Bunakha

Punat Tsang Chhu

Dago Chhu

**SAMTSE**

Torsa Chhu

Dungna

Wang Chhu

Tsimasham

Chhukha

Dagapela

Jaldakha Chhu

Sibsu

Dorokha

**CHHUKHA**

Chengmari

Torsa Chhu

Gedu
Jumja
Tala

Samtse

Phuentsholing

Rinchending

Raigye Chhu

Punn Tsang

Jaigon

Kharbandi Goemba

Sinchula

**INDIA**
(WEST BENGAL)

To Siliguri; Darjeeling

Kalikhola

**INDIA**
(SIKKIM)

Gom La

Yatung

Nathu-La

Sinche La

Doka La

Langa arpo Chhu

Amo Chhu

**SAMTSE**

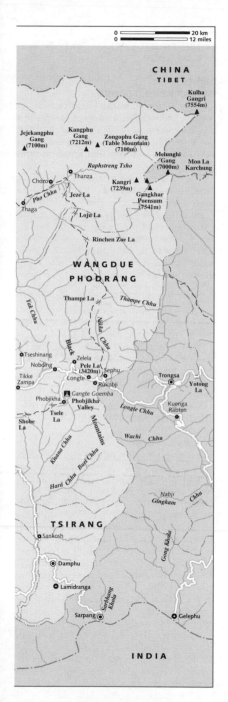

## History

The history of western Bhutan is reflected in the history of Bhutan as a whole. Punakha was the capital of a unified Bhutan from the 17th to the 19th century. The seat of government was later moved to Paro, which then became the commercial, cultural and political centre of the country. Before the construction of roads, most of Bhutan's trade came through Paro, either from Tibet via the Tremo La or from the south via Haa and the Cheli La.

# PARO DZONGKHAG

With our passage through the bridge, behold a curious transformation. For just as Alice, when she walked through the looking-glass, found herself in a new and whimsical world, so we, when we crossed the Pa-chhu, found ourselves, as though caught up on some magic time machine fitted fantastically with a reverse, flung back across the centuries into the feudalism of a mediaeval age.

Earl of Ronaldshay, *Lands of the Thunderbolt* (1923)

The Paro valley is without doubt one of the loveliest in Bhutan. Willow trees and apple orchards line many of the roads, whitewashed farmhouses and temples complement the green terraced fields and forested hills rise on either side to create a beautiful, organic and peaceful whole.

The broad valley is also excellent agricultural land and the people of Paro are better off than many elsewhere in Bhutan. One indication of their affluence is the preponderance of metal roofs throughout the valley, which have largely replaced the traditional wooden shingles. Red and white rice, apples, strawberries and asparagus (wonderful in April) all thrive in the fertile soil.

Several treks begin in or near Paro. The Druk Path trek climbs over the eastern valley wall, crossing a 4200m pass before descending to Thimphu. The Jhomolhari, Laya–Gasa and Snowman treks all lead west from Drukgyel Dzong on to Jhomolhari base camp and the spectacular alpine regions of Gasa and Laya beyond (for more on these regions, see p199).

WESTERN BHUTAN

## PARO

☎ 08 / elev 2280m

The charming small town of Paro lies in the centre of the valley on the banks of the Paro (or Pa) Chhu, just a short distance northwest of the imposing Paro Dzong. The main street, built only in 1985, is lined with colourfully painted wooden shop fronts and restaurants, though a modern concrete extension is taking root to the side.

Some of the older shops in Paro have doors at the back; a strange ladder system provides access through the front window. An unusual local regulation has, for a while, prohibited bicycle riding within Paro town.

## Orientation

The road from Thimphu and the airport enters the town from the south, near the archery ground. The town square is marked by the tower-like Chhoeten Lhakhang. North of the centre, by the Dumtse Lhakhang, a paved side road gives vehicle access to Paro Dzong and the National Museum.

If you follow the main street southeast, you'll pass five *chortens* (stone Buddhist monuments), the Ugyen Pelri Palace and the covered bridge that provides foot access to the massive Paro Dzong. Up on the forested hill above town is Zuri Dzong, home to the valley's local protector gods and therefore off-limits to tourists.

Most of the hotels are on the hillsides west and southeast of town, giving great views over valley.

## Information

### INTERNET ACCESS

**ITSS** (Map p123; ⊙ 9am-9pm; per min Nu 1.33) You can burn digital photos onto a CD here.

**Papu's Internet Café** (Map p123; ⊙ 8.30am-8.30pm; per min Nu 3) Also offers telephone calls.

**Post Office** (Map p123; per min Nu 1.25)

### MEDICAL SERVICES

**Kuen Phuen Medical Shop** (Map p123) Stocks basic medical supplies, opposite Made in Bhutan.

**Hospital** (Map p123; ☎ 271571) On a hill to the west of town and accepts visitors in an emergency.

### MONEY

**Bank of Bhutan** (Map p123; ☎ 271230; ⊙ 9am-1pm & 2-4pm Mon-Fri, 9am-1pm Sat)

**Bhutan National Bank** (Map p123; ⊙ 9am-3pm Mon-Fri, to 11am Sat)

### POST

**Post Office** (Map p123; ⊙ 8.30am-1pm & 2-5pm Mon-Fri, 8.30am-1pm Sat)

## Sights

### PARO (RINPUNG) DZONG

The Paro Dzong is one of Bhutan's most impressive and well-known dzongs, and perhaps the finest example of Bhutanese architecture you'll see. The massive buttressed walls tower over the town and are visible throughout the valley.

The dzong's correct name, Rinchen Pung Dzong (usually shortened to Rinpung Dzong), means 'fortress on a heap of jewels'. In 1644 Zhabdrung Ngawang Namgyal ordered the construction of the dzong on the foundation of a monastery built by Guru Rinpoche. The fort was used on numerous occasions to defend the Paro valley from invasions by Tibet. The British political officer John Claude White reported that in 1905 there were old catapults for throwing great stones stored in the rafters of the dzong's veranda.

The dzong survived the 1897 earthquake but a fire severely damaged the dzong in 1907. It was formerly the meeting hall for the National Assembly and now, like most dzongs, houses both the monastic body and district government offices, including the local courts.

Scenes from Bernardo Bertolucci's 1995 film *Little Buddha* were filmed here.

### Visiting the Dzong

The dzong is built on a steep hillside, and the front courtyard of the administrative section is 6m higher than the courtyard of the monastic portion. A road climbs the hill to the dzong's northern entrance, which leads into the *dochey* (courtyard) on the 3rd storey. The *utse* (central tower) inside the *dochey* is five storeys tall and was built in the time of the first *penlop* (governor) of Paro in 1649. To the east of the *utse* is another small lhakhang dedicated to Chuchizhey, an 11-headed manifestation of Chenresig. The richly carved wood, painted in gold, black and ochres, and the towering whitewashed walls serve to reinforce the sense of power and wealth.

A stairway leads down to the monastic quarter, which houses about 200 monks. In the southeast corner (to the left) is the *kunre*, which is where the monks eat their communal meals. Look out for the mural

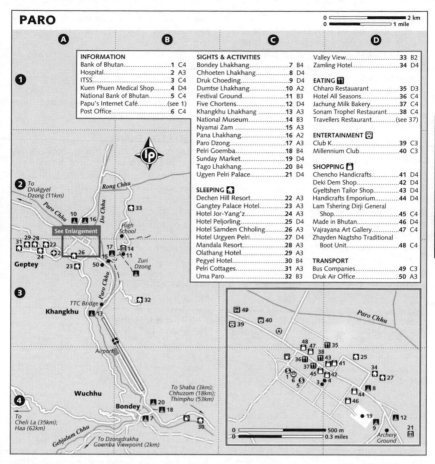

## PARO

0 ——————— 2 km
0 ——————— 1 mile

**INFORMATION**
Bank of Bhutan.....................1 C4
Hospital.................................2 A3
ITSS.....................................3 C4
Kuen Phuen Medical Shop....4 D4
National Bank of Bhutan........5 C4
Papu's Internet Café..............(see 1)
Post Office...........................6 C4

**SIGHTS & ACTIVITIES**
Bondey Lhakhang..................7 B4
Chhoeten Lhakhang..............8 D4
Druk Choeding......................9 D4
Dumtse Lhakhang................10 A2
Festival Ground...................11 B3
Five Chortens......................12 D4
Khangkhu Lhakhang............13 A3
National Museum.................14 B3
Nyamai Zam .......................15 A3
Pana Lhakhang....................16 A2
Paro Dzong.........................17 A3
Pelri Goemba......................18 B4
Sunday Market....................19 D4
Tago Lhakhang....................20 B4
Ugyen Pelri Palace...............21 D4

**SLEEPING**
Dechen Hill Resort...............22 A3
Gangtey Palace Hotel...........23 A3
Hotel Jor-Yang'z..................24 A3
Hotel Peljorling...................25 D4
Hotel Samden Chholing.......26 A3
Hotel Urgyen Pelri...............27 D4
Mandala Resort...................28 A3
Olathang Hotel....................29 A3
Pegyel Hotel.......................30 B4
Pelri Cottages.....................31 A3
Uma Paro............................32 B3

Valley View.........................33 B2
Zamling Hotel......................34 D4

**EATING**
Chharo Restauarant ............35 D3
Hotel All Seasons................36 C4
Jachung Milk Bakery............37 C4
Sonam Trophel Restaurant....38 C4
Travellers Restaurant...........(see 37)

**ENTERTAINMENT**
Club K................................39 C3
Millennium Club..................40 C3

**SHOPPING**
Chencho Handicrafts............41 D4
Deki Dem Shop....................42 D4
Gyeltshen Tailor Shop..........43 D4
Handicrafts Emporium..........44 D4
Lam Tshering Dirji General
    Shop..............................45 D4
Made in Bhutan..................46 D4
Vajrayana Art Gallery...........47 C4
Zhayden Nagtsho Traditional
    Boot Unit.......................48 C4

**TRANSPORT**
Bus Companies....................49 C3
Druk Air Office....................50 A3

**WESTERN BHUTAN**

of the 'mystic spiral', a uniquely Bhutanese variation on the mandala. The large *dukhang* (prayer hall) opposite has lovely exterior murals depicting the life of Tibet's poet-saint Milarepa. The first day of the spring Paro tsechu is held in this courtyard, which fills to bursting point.

Outside the dzong, to the northeast of the entrance, is a stone-paved area where masked dancers perform the main dances of the tsechu. A *thondrol* (huge *thangka*, painted or embroidered religious picture) of Guru Rinpoche, more than 18m square, is unfurled shortly after dawn on the final day of the tsechu – you can see the huge rail upon which it is hung. It was commissioned in the 18th century by the eighth *desi* (secular ruler of

Bhutan, also known as *druk desi*), Chhogyel Sherab Wangchuck.

Below the dzong, a traditional wooden covered bridge called Nyamai Zam spans the Paro Chhu. This is a reconstruction of the original bridge, which was washed away in a flood in 1969. Earlier versions of this bridge were removed in time of war to protect the dzong. You can walk from the parking area near the Ugyen Pelri Palace across the bridge up to the dzong. The most picturesque pictures of Paro Dzong are taken from the west bank of the river, just downstream from the bridge.

The dzong courtyard is open daily but on weekends the offices are deserted and most chapels are closed.

## NATIONAL MUSEUM

At the top of the hill above Paro Dzong is an old watchtower that was renovated in 1968 to house the **National Museum** (Gyelyong Damtenkhang; ☎ 271257; nmb@druknet.bt; locals/SAARC nationals/adult Nu 10/50/100, monks free; ☷ 9am-4.30pm Tue-Sat, closed Sun, Mon & national holidays). The unusual round building is said to be in the shape of a conch shell, with 2.5m thick walls; it was completed in 1656 and was originally the *ta dzong* (watchtower) of Paro Dzong. There is said to be an underground tunnel that leads from the watchtower to the water supply below.

There is a specific route to follow through the entire building that ensures that you walk clockwise around important images. Cameras are not allowed inside the museum but you can photograph the grounds. The museum is an attraction for locals as well as tourists and you may be accompanied by Bhutanese from remote villages or groups of school children on an outing.

You start off on the fourth floor with a description of early history that perfectly illustrates how magic and science are inseparable in Bhutan. Early stone implements are described as the weapons of the *naga* (snake) spirits; early rock carvings and inscriptions are labelled as 'self-created'.

The fifth floor has an impressive collection of *thangkas*, both ancient and modern, depicting all of Bhutan's important saints and teachers. The sixth floor reveals the eclecticism of Bhutan's philatelic collection, including some stamps that you can listen to on a record player.

At the end of the gallery a doorway leads to the Tshozhing Lhakhang, the Temple of the Tree of Wisdom, a complex four-sided carving depicting the history of Buddhism, with its schools and lineages. The four branches represent the Sakya (with images of Sakyamuni), Nyingma (Guru Rinpoche), Gelug (Atisha, Tsongkhapa and Nagarjuna) and Drukpa Kagyu (Channa Dorje, Marpa, Milarepa, Naropa and Tilopa) lineages. Clean your shoes on the yak-hair squares when entering the temple and walk clockwise around the room.

Back down on the fifth floor is the Namse Lhakhang, with a collection of religious statues and stone carvings. The lower-floor galleries highlight teapots, clothes, musical instruments, stuffed animals, religious ritual objects and a display of ancient weapons and shields, many captured during various Tibetan invasions. Look out for the astrological water clock, rhino shield, frog-skin saddle and fish-scale hat! Displays even show you how to make a poisoned arrow from the *mangsut* flower. It's great stuff.

After visiting, you can walk down a path from the museum to the dzong and back to the town, enjoying good views of the valley and of Ugyen Pelri Palace.

## UGYEN PELRI THANG

The Ugyen Pelri Palace is in a secluded wooded compound on the south side of the river just west of the dzong. This palace was built by the Paro *penlop*, Tshering Penjor, in the early 1900s and is now a residence of the queen mother, thus closed to the public. It is designed after Guru Rinpoche's celestial paradise, Zangto Pelri, and is one of the most beautiful examples of Bhutanese architecture. You can get views of the palace from above from the dzong.

On the road beside Ugyen Pelri Palace are five square **chortens** that were built in memory of the first king, Ugyen Wangchuck.

## CHHOETEN LHAKHANG

The tower-like Chhoeten Lhakhang is south of the town square. The caretaker may allow you to visit the upstairs chapel, which features a central Jowo Sakyamuni, with Guru Rinpoche and Chenresig to the side.

## DRUK CHOEDING

Also known as Tshongdoe Naktshang, the quiet and peaceful Druk Choeding is the town temple. It was built in 1525 by Ngawang Chhogyel (1465–1540), one of the prince-abbots of Ralung in Tibet and an ancestor of the Zhabdrung Ngawang Namgyal. The main statue is of a seated Jampa (Future Buddha). Also present is the Bhutanese protector deity Gyenyen (see p115), surrounded by a fearsome collection of old Bhutanese shields and weapons.

## DUMTSE LHAKHANG

To the west of the road is Dumtse Lhakhang, an unusual chorten-like temple that was built in 1433 by the iron-bridge builder Thangtong Gyalpo (see the boxed text, p131). Its three floors represent hell, earth and heaven, and the murals inside are said to be some of the finest in Bhutan. It's essential to bring a good torch. Your travel agency will need to get a special permit to visit the interior so mention this in advance.

WESTERN BHUTAN

Beyond Dumtse Lhakhang, to the east of the road, the tiny privately-maintained Puna Lhakhang is said to date from the seventh century.

### SUNDAY MARKET

Paro's weekly vegetable market isn't all that expansive but it's a fine introduction to some of Bhutan's unique local products. You'll see strings of *chugo* (dried yak cheese), either white (boiled in milk and dried in the sun) or brown (smoked). The fruit that looks like an orange egg is actually fresh husky betel nut, imported from India. The jars of pink paste contain lime, which is ingested with the betel nut. There are also exotic-looking ferns, powdered juniper incense, squares of dried jellied cow skin known as *khoo* (a local snack!) and slabs of *datse*, cheese used in almost every Bhutanese dish. The market is busiest between 6.30am and 10am.

## Sleeping

Most of Paro's accommodation options were built before the town was developed and are in resort-style hotels scattered around the valley, not in the town itself. Most hotels increase their rates significantly during the spring Paro Tsechu, when every hotel and even many local farmhouses are full to bursting point. Some hotels stage dance performances around a campfire when there are enough guests to warrant it.

### BUDGET

Several small hotels near the town square cater to Bhutanese and Indian clientele, including the **Hotel Urgyen Pelri** (Map p123; s/d Nu 250/350) and the basic five-roomed **Zamling Hotel** ( ☎ 271302; s/d 400/600), which offers private bathrooms but no hot water.

**Hotel Peljorling** (Map p123; ☎ 271365; s/d Nu 750/850) Operated by the same group as the Peljorling in Phuentsholing, this four-room local-style hotel and restaurant is in the centre of town. The mattresses are thin.

**Hotel All Seasons** (Map p123; ☎ 271295; s/d with common bathroom Nu 350/450, with bathroom Nu 550/650) Gets a few late-booking tourists during tsechu time.

### MIDRANGE

**Dechen Hill Resort** (Map p123; ☎ 271392; dchncot@druknet .bt; www.dechenhillresort.com; Geptey; old rooms s/d Nu 1300/1600, new rooms s/d Nu 1500/1800) This hotel, in a secluded area below the road and 2km from the centre, is a favourite with expats. It's not

flash but the Indian food is some of the best in Bhutan and the new block has good valley views. A pair of friendly dogs adds to the homey atmosphere.

**Hotel Jor-Yang'z** (Map p123; ☎ 271747; joryangz@druk net.bt; Geptey; standard s/d Nu 1400/1800, deluxe s/d 1600/2000, ste 3500; 🖳 ) Next door and similar, this friendly modern place has good staff, excellent food and some nice balcony seating. It's named after the owners' two children.

**Gangtey Palace Hotel** (Map p123; ☎ 271301; hgpp@ druknet.bt; s/d cottage Nu 1000/1200, standard s/d 1700/2200, deluxe s/d 2200/2500) This 19th-century, traditional Bhutanese courtyard-style building was once the residence of the *penlop* of Paro and it oozes musty historical charm. The spacious deluxe rooms in the main tower come with creaking wooden staircases and a few antique pieces. The comfortable modern main block rooms are not as exotic but you can get a more traditional flavour by spurning the shower and arranging for a hot-stone bath (Nu 650). The views from the restaurant balcony are great and there's a cosy bar. Outside the gate is the small Gangten Lhakhang.

**Hotel Samden Chholing** (Map p123; ☎ 271449; samden _choling@druknet.bt; s/d Nu 1200/1400) Opened in 1999, the simple Samden Chholing has a family feel, with rooms in the main Bhutanese-style building or in the modern block below. You can follow your hot-stone bath (Nu 350) with drinks or dinner on the basic terrace overlooking Paro.

**Kichu Resort** (Map p128; ☎ 271468; intkichu@druknet .bt; www.intrektour.com; s/d Nu 1800/2400, deluxe s/d Nu 2250/3000) Just 700m past the Kyichu Lhakhang and 5.5km away from Paro, this collection of concrete cottages on the banks of the Paro Chhu is popular with trekking groups, Indian tourists and expats from Thimphu looking for a weekend getaway. There's a quiet rural air but the rooms and grounds could do with some freshening up. The deluxe rooms are worth the extra money.

**Pelri Cottages** (Map p123; ☎ 272473; s/d Nu 1800/2000, deluxe s/d 2000/2500) On a hill above the Olathang Hotel, the Pelri is a low-key collection of concrete cottages and rooms, with a private stupa on site. Rooms are decorated with carved wood and Tibetan carpets to give a cosy feel and the small wooden balconies are pleasant.

**Mandala Resort** (Map p123; ☎ 271997; mandala@druk net.bt; s/d Nu 1200/1500) A steep paved road winds its way up to this small concrete block below the Olathang Hotel. Upper-storey rooms come with a balcony, and the dining room offers great views of the valley. Run by the travel company Bhutan Mandala Tours, it's more home-style than glamour.

**Valley View** (Map p123; ☎ 272541; valleyview@druknet .bt; attic rooms s/d Nu 1200/1500, s/d Nu 2000/2500; 🖳 ) Bizarrely, none of the rooms in this superbly located new hotel actually takes advantage of the touted views! Apart from this criminal lack of foresight, the pine-clad rooms are comfortable and there's a cosy bar and restaurant. The pokey third-floor attic rooms won't do for anyone over 6ft tall. It's on the road to Paro Dzong.

**Tiger Nest Resort** (Map p128; ☎ 271310; fax 271640; 9km from Paro; s/d Nu 1300/1500) Just past the turn-off to Taktshang in the upper valley, this small resort is the only one with a view of Taktshang Goemba (see p128) and, on clear days, the snow-capped peak of Jhomolhari. It has 15 cosy rooms in four cottages, with a restaurant accessed by a private bridge.

Other decent tourist hotels in the valley include **Rinchen Ling Lodge** (Map p128; ☎ 1711 1503; nawangd@druknet.bt), **Namsey Choling Resort** (Map p128; ☎ 272080; namseyresort@druknet.bt) and **Pegyel Hotel** ( ☎ 271472; fax 272769; s/d Nu 1200/1500), in a rural setting among rice fields in Shaba, 9km from Paro town.

### TOP END

**Olathang Hotel** (Map p123; ☎ 271304; ohotel@druknet .bt; s/d Nu 1625/2000, cottage s/d Nu 2125/2500, deluxe cottage s/d Nu 3000/3500; 🖳 ) This grand dzong-like hotel was built in 1974 for guests invited to the coronation of the present king and, though getting on a bit, it still maintains a whiff of that grandeur. The main building rooms are set around a lovely interior courtyard and come with elaborate Victorian furniture. Look for the stuffed yak guarding the entrance to the conference hall. For comfortable facilities in a traditional setting, ask to stay in one of the tastefully decorated wooden cottages. Always bustling with groups, it's now managed by the Bhutan Tourism Corporation Limited (BTCL).

**Uma Paro** (Map p123; ☎ 271597; www.uma.como .bz; superior/deluxe r US$280/450, ste US$575-1200; 🖳 ) Kudos goes to the Uma for tastefully combining traditional Bhutanese architecture with top-of-the-line facilities to create the best hotel in town. Nice touches include a CD/ DVD player in all of the rooms, plus a gym, indoor pool and plenty of pampering at the spa and herbal hot-stone bath, with all bath products supplied by Como. Try to request a deluxe room with a view and balcony. Activities include mountain biking, archery lessons, day hikes and a visit to a local farmhouse, at extra cost. While here, check out the world's biggest book, on display in the library! Low-season discounts are from 10% to 20%.

**Zhiwa Ling** (Map p128; ☎ 271277; www.zhiwaling.com; s/d from US$180/200) This impressive new luxury place, 8km from Paro, consists of an echoing, central lodge surrounded by a collection of stern-looking stone towers. It's certainly grand but it's not yet all that cosy, despite some nice antique touches, underfloor heating, a spa (Thai, Shiatsu and Swedish massage) and even a temple on the 2nd floor, built with pillars from the Gangtey Palace. Bizarrely, they manufacture fishing flies here for export to the US. It's 3km past the Kichu Resort.

**Amankora Paro Lodge** (Map p128; ☎ 272333; www .amanresorts.com; s/d full board US$925/1000; 🖳 ) 'Designer dzong' is the architectural theme here, with the half-dozen sleek and severe rammed-earth buildings calling to mind the elite campus of the world's coolest university. The rooms benefit from calming natural woods and homespun fabrics, an open-plan bathroom, *bukhari* (traditional Bhutanese stove) and divan. The spa has a wide range of treatments (book in advance) and there's an intimate restaurant and reading room. It's certainly sleek and stylish but you can't help but feel a bit disconnected from your surroundings out here. The resort is in pine forest near Balakha village, 14km from Paro and not far from Drukyel Dzong. The tax alone is US$289 a night!

## Eating

Most tourists eat dinner in their hotels but you can ask to try the following for lunch.

**Sonam Trophel Restaurant** (Map p123; ☎ 271287) Upstairs, Sonam has excellent home-style Bhutanese cooking adapted to foreign tastes (ie without the chilli) and is popular with small groups. *Momos* (dumplings) are a speciality at Nu 25 to 40 and the *shamu datse* (mushroom, cheese and chilli) is excellent. No MSG is used here.

**Chharo Restaurant** (Map p123; ☎ 272642) This pleasant tourist restaurant (*chharo* means friendship) has a good range of Indian, Chinese and Bhutanese dishes and can prepare Bumthang-style buckwheat pancakes and noodles with some advance warning. The owner is very accommodating.

Two other good local restaurants that are above shops along the main street are **Travellers Restaurant** (Map p123; ☎ 271896) and **Hotel All Seasons** (Map p123; ☎ 271295), both with dishes from Nu 30 to Nu 70. The **Peljorling Hotel** (Map p123) also has a good wide-ranging menu, including fried fish and even baked beans!

You can load up on local bread and pastries at the **Jachung Milk Bakery** (Map p123). *Jachung* means '*garuda*'.

## Entertainment

**Club K** (Map p123; ☎ 271287; cover women/men Nu 100/200, beer Nu 80; ☻ from 9pm) Check out another of Bhutan's many faces at this swanky basement nightclub, which boasts a bouncer (normally it's the female owner, Sonam), a mirrorball and a fairly upper crust crowd. Ladies get in for free on Wednesdays. The Sonam Troephel Hotel is being built above the club.

**Millennium Club** (Map p123; ☎ 271934; cover Nu 200; ☻ from 10pm Sat) You're more likely to get chatting to locals at this older local disco, normally open Saturday nights only.

## Shopping

There are numerous handicraft shops throughout the valley and most open daily and take credit cards. **Chencho Handicrafts** (Map p123; ☎ 271633), on the corner of the town square, has probably the most interesting selection. **Made in Bhutan** (Map p123; ☎ 272886) is a slick operation, with a wide selection of crafts.

The government-run **Handicrafts Emporium** (Map p123; ☎ 271211; ☎ 9am-1pm, 2-6pm), on the main street, has books and modern souvenirs at tourist prices.

There are several interesting local shops. **Deki Dem Shop** (Map p123) and **Lam Tshering Dirji General Shop** (Map p123), both marked by a row of colourful prayer wheels, sell prayer flags, incense and other religious items.

**Gyeltshen Tailor Shop** (Map p123) has a selection of mounted *thangkas*, Bhutanese flags and T-shirts and Buddhist accoutrements.

**Zhayden Nagtsho Traditional Boot Unit** (Map p123; ☎ 272345) is the place for a pair of traditional handmade Bhutanese boots, retailing around US$60.

**Vajrayana Art Gallery** (Map p123; chhidorj@hotmail.com) features art by self-taught Bhutanese artist Chimmi Dorje, who incorporates Buddhist themes such as prayer flags and mandala motifs into his abstract art. There's also some fine photography by his brother. The gallery is often closed out of high season.

## Getting There & Away

Paro airport is 7km from Paro town and 53km from Thimphu. If you have not arranged for a vehicle to meet your flight, you can book a taxi at the tea stall outside the airport. The cost is Nu 300 to Paro or Nu 800 to Thimphu.

Daily buses to Thimphu and Phuentsholing leave from a temporary stand by Dawa Transport at the northwest end of town.

## AROUND PARO
### Upper Paro Valley

Though the Paro valley extends west all the way to the peaks on the Tibetan border, the road only goes as far as Drukgyel Dzong, 11km beyond Paro. En route it passes half a dozen resorts, some lovely rural scenery and some of Bhutan's most famous sights. Beyond the dzong a side valley leads to the Tremo La, the 5000m pass that was once an important trade route to Tibet and also the route of several Tibetan invasions.

There are several options if you are interested in a day hiking in the Paro valley. Southeast of Kyichu Lhakhang in the direction of Paro is Kenchu Goemba and Drongja Goemba, both of which can provide an excuse for a short hike. From here you could continue back to Paro via Loma Lhakhang, just above Paro town, which is visited by Bhutanese whose children are ill. More ambitious is the cardio day hike up to Dorena Goemba, high on the ridge behind the Olathang Hotel.

### KYICHU LHAKHANG

A short drive from Paro is Kyichu Lhakhang, one of Bhutan's oldest and most beautiful temples. This temple is popularly believed to have been built in 659 by King Songtsen Gampo of Tibet, to pin down the left foot of an giant ogress who was thwarting the establishment of Buddhism into Tibet (see the boxed text, p129). Additional buildings and a golden roof were constructed in 1839 by the *penlop* of Paro and the 25th Je Khenpo.

As you enter the intimate inner courtyard you'll see a mural of King Gesar of Ling, the popular Tibetan warrior-king, whose epic poem is said to be the world's longest. Pride of place in the courtyard is a pile of iron links forged by the famous bridge builder Thangtong Gyalpo (see p131). Outside the courtyard,

WESTERN BHUTAN

a band of pilgrims almost as old as the temple itself haul away on ropes and pulleys that are rigged up to turn prayer wheels.

The queen mother, Ashi Kesang Wangchuck, sponsored the construction of the **Guru Lhakhang** in 1968. It contains a 5m-high statue of Guru Rinpoche and another of Kurukulla (Red Tara), holding a bow and arrow made of flowers. Also here is a chorten containing the ashes of Dilgo Khyentse Rinpoche, a revered Nyingma Buddhist master and spiritual teacher of the queen mother who passed away in 1992 and was cremated nearby. There is a statue of him here, as well as some old photos of the queen grandmother and the first king of Bhutan.

The inner hall of the main **Jowo Lhakhang** conceals the valley's greatest treasure, an original 7th-century statue of Jowo Sakyamuni, said to have been cast at the same time as the famous statue in Lhasa. In front of the statue you can feel the grooves that generations of prostrators have worn into the wooden floor. King Songtsen Gampo himself lurks up in the upper niche. Lovely metal plaques line the floor and the main door is superbly gilded. The former quarters of Dilgo Khyentse to the left are closed to visitors.

The outer hall has a large statue of Chenresig with 11 heads and 1000 hands.

Further north, outside the temple and up a side road by the huge Zhiwa Ling hotel, is the site where Dilgo Khyentse was cremated. It's closed to visitors but is still used for high-profile cremations. The small and inconspicuous **Satsam Chorten** by the turn-off once marked the border between Bhutan and Tibet.

Across a bridge on the far side of the valley is the Kunga Choeling Goemba, below the hilltop *shedra* (Buddhist college) of Tsacho Chukor. The dirt road that leads from Satsam Chorten back to Paro is an option for mountain bikers.

### TAKTSHANG GOEMBA

Taktshang is the most famous of Bhutan's monasteries, miraculously perched on the side of a sheer cliff 900m above the floor of Paro valley, where the only sounds are the murmurs of wind and water and the chanting of monks. The name means 'tiger's nest'; it is said that Guru Rinpoche flew to the site of the monastery on the back of a tigress, a manifestation of his consort Yeshe Tsogyal, to subdue the local

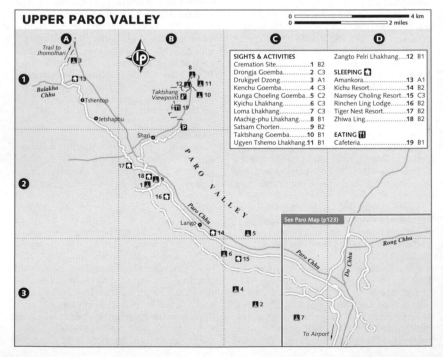

**UPPER PARO VALLEY**

0 — 4 km
0 — 2 miles

| SIGHTS & ACTIVITIES | | Zangto Pelri Lhakhang....**12** B1 |
|---|---|---|
| Cremation Site...................**1** B2 | | |
| Drongja Goemba.............**2** C3 | **SLEEPING** | |
| Drukgyel Dzong...............**3** A1 | Amankora.......................**13** A1 |
| Kenchu Goemba..............**4** C3 | Kichu Resort....................**14** B2 |
| Kunga Choeling Goemba...**5** C2 | Namsey Choling Resort...**15** C3 |
| Kyichu Lhakhang..............**6** C3 | Rinchen Ling Lodge.........**16** B2 |
| Loma Lhakhang................**7** C3 | Tiger Nest Resort............**17** B2 |
| Machig-phu Lhakhang......**8** B1 | Zhiwa Ling......................**18** B2 |
| Satsam Chorten................**9** B2 | |
| Taktshang Goemba.........**10** B1 | **EATING** |
| Ugyen Tshemo Lhakhang.**11** B1 | Cafeteria.........................**19** B1 |

## SUBDUING THE DEMONESS

When the Tibetan king Songtsen Gampo married the Chinese princess Wencheng in 641, her dowry included the Jowo Sakyamuni, a priceless Indian statue of the Buddha as a small boy. As the statue was transported through Lhasa, it became stuck in the mud and no-one could move it. The princess divined that the obstruction was being caused by a huge supine demoness, lying on her back with her navel over a lake where Lhasa's main temple, the Jokhang, now stands.

In 659 the king decided to build 108 temples in a single day to pin the ogress to the earth forever and, at the same time, convert the Tibetan people to Buddhism. Temples were constructed at her shoulders and hips, which corresponded to the four districts of central Tibet, and her knees and elbows, which were in the provinces. The hands and feet lay in the borderlands of Tibet, and several temples were built in Bhutan to pin down the troublesome left leg.

The best known of these temples are Kyichu Lhakhang in Paro, which holds the left foot, and Jampa Lhakhang in Bumthang, which pins the left knee. Other lesser-known temples have been destroyed, but it is believed that, among others, Konchogsum Lhakhang in Bumthang, Khaine Lhakhang south of Lhuentse, and two temples in Haa may have been part of this ambitious project.

demon, Singey Samdrup. He then meditated in a cave here for three months.

The site has long been recognised as a *ney*, or holy place. It was visited by Zhabdrung Ngawang Namgyal in 1646 and pilgrims from all over Bhutan come here. Milarepa is also said to have meditated here, while Thangtong Gyalpo revealed a *terma* (treasure text) at Taktshang. The primary lhakhang was built in 1692 around the Dubkhang (also called the Pelphu), the holy cave in which Guru Rinpoche meditated, by the *penlop* of Paro, Gylse Tenzin Rabgye.

On 19 April 1998 a fire (which some say was arson) destroyed the main structure of Taktshang and all its contents. It had suffered a previous fire and was repaired in 1951. Reconstruction started on an auspicious day in April 2000 at a cost of 130 million ngultrum and the rebuilt site was reconsecrated in the presence of the king in 2005. Tradition says that the original building was anchored to the cliff-face by the hairs of *khandroma* (*dakinis*, or female celestial beings), who transported the building materials up onto the cliff on their backs. The renovation team had only a cable lift for assistance.

### The Hike

The only way up to the Tiger's Nest is to walk, ride a horse or fly on the back of a magic tiger (the latter generally reserved for Tantric magicians). The 1¾ hour hike is a major part of any tourist itinerary and is unmissable for the spectacular views. It's also a good warm-up hike if you are going trekking. If the full hike sounds a bit tough you can walk (or ride horses) to the 'caféteria', a wooden teahouse-restaurant, which offers a good view of the monastery. If you require horses, be sure to mention this to your guide a day or two in advance. Wear a hat and bring water.

A new road, built to facilitate the reconstruction of the monastery, branches off 8km north of Paro and climbs 3km to the trailhead at 2600m.

The trail climbs through blue pines, then switchbacks steeply up the ridge, where a sign exhorts you to 'Walk to Guru's glory! For here in this kingdom rules an unparalled benevolent king'! If you have just flown into Paro, walk slowly because you are likely to be affected by the altitude.

Once you reach the ridge there are excellent views across the valley. To the southwest is the area around Drukgyel; you can see the large school below the village and the army camp above it. After a climb of about one hour and a gain of 300m from the parking lot you will reach a small chorten and some prayer flags on the ridge. Be watchful here as the trail crosses an archery ground. It's then a short walk to the caféteria (2940m), where you can savour the impressive view of the monastery over a well-deserved cup of tea. The caféteria also serves full meals; if you arrange your schedule accordingly, you can have breakfast or lunch here.

The trail continues up for another 30 minutes to a spring and basic monastery guesthouse, used by some Buddhist groups. A cave and plaque marks the birthplace of the previous Je Khenpo; his former residence is just up the hill. A short walk further along the main trail brings you to a spectacular lookout at 3140m that puts you eyeball to eyeball with the monastery, which looks like it is growing out of the rocks.

From this vantage point Taktshang seems almost close enough to touch, but it's on the far side of a deep chasm, about 150m away. The trail descends to a waterfall and the Singye Phu Lhakhang (Snow Lion Cave), a meditation retreat jammed dramatically into a rock crevice, before climbing back up to the monastery entrance.

### The Monastery

Since 2005 it has been possible for tourists to enter the monastery, but only if your guide has arranged a permit in advance. Bags and cameras generally have to be deposited at the entrance and you must register with the army.

As you enter the complex you pass underneath images of the Rigsum Goempo (Jampelyang, Chenresig and Channa Dorje). The first chapel on the left has connections to Dorje Phagmo, with a rock image of the goddess hidden in a recessed hole in the floor. The inner chorten belongs to Langchen Pelgyi Tsengay, a 9th-century disciple of Guru Rinpoche, who meditated in the cave. Behind the chorten is a holy spring.

The **Guru Lhakhang** has a central image of Pema Jungme, one of the eight manifestations of Guru Rinpoche. This statue replaced a famous 'talking' image that was lost in the 1998 fire. Various demonic animal-headed deities, several manifestations of the deity Phurba, and the protector Tseringma (riding a snowlion) decorate the walls.

From here you descend to the **Dubkhang**, the cave where Guru Rinpoche meditated for three months. Outside the cave is a statue of Dorje Drolo, the manifestation the Guru assumed to fly to Taktshang. Inside the cave, behind a spectacularly gilded door, is a chorten stuffed with lots of miniature *phurba* (thunderbolt symbols) with carved heads. Thangtong Gyalpo sits above the door holding his iron chains. Murals of the Guru Tsengye, the eight manifestations of the Guru, decorate the walls.

Further on inside the complex is the **Guru Tsengye Lhakhang**, which features an image of the monastery's 17th-century founder, Gyelse Tenzin Rabgay. Ask a monk to show you the trap door!

### Above the Monastery

After visiting the Tiger's Nest it is possible to take a side trail uphill to the **Machig-phu Lhakhang**, where Bhutanese pilgrims come to pray for children. Head to the cave behind the chapel and select the image of the Tibetan saint Machig Labdron on the right (for a baby girl), or the penis print on the cave wall to the left (for a boy). The main statues inside the chapel are of Machig (see also p134) and her husband Padampa Sangye.

Just above here the trail branches right to the **Ugyen Tshemo Lhakhang**, while the left branch climbs up to the **Zangto Pelri Lhakhang**, named after Guru Rinpoche's heavenly paradise and perched on a crag with great views down to the Tiger's Nest. Roll the dice inside the chapel to double your chances of conceiving more kids. From here the trail descends past a charming holy spring (behind a wooden door) and down to the monastery guesthouse mentioned earlier.

### DRUKGYEL DZONG

At the end of the road, 14km from Paro, stand the ruins of Drukgyel Dzong. This dzong was built in 1649 by Zhabdrung Ngawang Namgyal in a location chosen for its control of the route to Tibet. The dzong was named '*Druk*' (Bhutan) '*gyel*' (victory) to commemorate the victory of Bhutan over Tibetan invaders in 1644. One of the features of the dzong was a false entrance that was designed to lure invaders into an enclosed courtyard. This is said to have worked successfully during the second attack by Tibetan invaders in 1648.

The dzong sits at the point where the trail from Tibet via the Tremo La enters the Paro valley. Once the Tibetan invasions ceased, this became a major trade route between Bhutan and the Tibetan town of Phari. A small amount of informal trade continues to the present day. On a clear day (most likely in October or November) there is a spectacular view of Jhomolhari from the area near the dzong.

Drukgyel Dzong was featured on the cover of the US *National Geographic* magazine when an article was published about Bhutan by John Claude White in 1914. The building was used as an administrative centre until 1951, when a fire caused by a butter lamp destroyed it. You can still see the charred beams lodged in the ruined walls.

Now the dzong is in ruins. There have been a few attempts at renovation, but all that has been accomplished is the installation of some props to keep the roof of the five-storey main structure from collapsing. You can walk up a short path into the front courtyard of the dzong, past the remains of the large towers and the tunnel that was used to obtain water from the stream below during a long siege. At the back are two *ta dzongs*.

On the way to the dzong you pass Jetshaphu village, with its important school, several army training camps and the Amankora resort.

## Southeast of Paro

Twin roads leads south from Paro to Bondey, where roads head west to Haa and southeast to the confluence at Chhuzom, 24km from Paro and 18km from Bondey.

### PARO TO BONDEY (6KM)

The west-bank road south of Paro passes above the airport and Khangkhu Lhakhang to Bondey, which straddles the Paro Chhu to the southeast of the airport.

Beyond the turn-off to the Cheli La is the 400-year-old **Bondey Lhakhang**, on the west bank of the river. On the east side of the Paro Chhu, near the Bondey Zam, is the charming and unusually-shaped **Tago (Walnut) Lhakhang**, founded by Thangtong Gyalpo. A short but steep climb above Bondey is the small **Pelri Goemba**. From here roads lead north to the airport and south to Chhuzom.

An unpaved road leads west from Bondey through fields to the small, recently constructed Changchi Lhakhang. A short walk, bumpy drive or, better, a mountain-bike ride further up this road affords a view of **Dzongdra-**

**kha Goemba**, four chapels and a large white chorten hanging on the side of a cliff. You also get views of the goemba from along the road to the Cheli La.

### CHELI LA

If you don't have time to visit the Haa valley, the 35km drive up to the 3810m Cheli La makes an interesting day excursion from Paro and is an excellent jumping-off point for day walks. On a clear day from the pass there are views of Jhomolhari as well as down to the Haa valley.

For details of the drive over the pass to the Haa valley see p133.

## PARO TO THIMPHU (53KM)

Figure on two hours driving from Paro to Thimphu, longer if you stop en route.

### Bondey to Chhuzom

**18km / 30 mins**

If you're coming from the airport you'll first reach the settlement of Bondey, where there are some lovely old traditional Bhutanese houses and chapels (see left).

About 3km from Bondey is Shaba, a small settlement with an army and road camp. At Isuna, 12km from Bondey, the road crosses a bridge to the south bank of the Paro Chhu. Drak Kharpo, a mountain cave *(drak)* where Guru Rinpoche meditated, clings to the rocks high above, a tough three-hour hike from the road.

About 5km before Chhuzom, the road passes **Tamchhog Lhakhang**, a private temple

**THE IRON-BRIDGE BUILDER**

Thangtong Gyalpo (1385–1464) was a wonder-working Tibetan saint who is believed to have originated the use of heavy iron chains in the construction of suspension bridges. He built 108 bridges throughout Tibet and Bhutan and became known as *Lama Chazampa* (the Iron Bridge Lama).

In 1433 he came to Bhutan in search of iron ore and built eight bridges in places as far removed as Paro and Trashigang. You can see some of the original iron links at the Paro Museum and at Kyichu Lhakhang in the Paro valley. Sadly, the only surviving Thangtong Gyalpo bridge, at Duksum on the road to Trashi Yangtse in eastern Bhutan, was washed away in 2004.

This medieval Renaissance man didn't stop at engineering. Among his other achievements was the composition of many folk songs, still sung today by people as they thresh wheat or pound the mud for house construction, and also the invention of Tibetan *lhamo* opera. He was an important *terton* (discoverer of *terma*) of the Nyingma lineage and attained the title Drubthob (Great Magician). In Paro he built the marvellous chorten-shaped Dumtse Lhakhang. His descendants still maintain the nearby Tamchhog Goemba Lhakhang.

Statues of Thangtong Gyalpo depict him as a stocky shirtless figure with a beard, curly hair and topknot, holding a link of chains.

owned by the descendants of the famous Tibetan bridge-builder Thangtong Gyalpo (see p131). The traditional iron bridge here was reconstructed in 2005 using some of Thangtong's original chain links from Duksum (see p194) in eastern Bhutan. The red soil around the temple contains low-grade ore that once supplied the raw material for iron works.

You can almost feel the clocks slowing down as you step into the 600-year-old temple. A 100-year old mandarin tree dominates the courtyard. The lovely murals have been darkened by centuries of yak-butter lamps. A *kora* (circumambulation) path in the main chapel leads around central murals of Thangtong Gyalpo and his son Dewa Tsangpo. The doorway of the upper floor *goenkhang* (protector chapel) is framed by rows of skulls and a hornbill beak and is dedicated to the local protector Maza Damsum.

Chhuzom, better known as 'the Confluence' is at the juncture of the Paro Chhu and the Wang Chhu (*chhu* means 'river', *zom* means 'to join'). Sometimes this confluence is considered a union of a mother and father river, similar to that of the Pho Chhu and Mo Chhu at Punakha. The Paro Chhu represents the father, and is sometimes called the 'Pho Chhu', and the Wang Chhu is the 'Mo Chhu', or mother river.

Because Bhutanese tradition regards such a joining of rivers as inauspicious, there are three **chortens** here to ward away the evil spells of the area. Each chorten is in a different style – Bhutanese, Tibetan and Nepali.

Chhuzom is also a major road junction, with roads leading southwest to Haa (79km), south to the border town of Phuentsholing (141km) and northeast to Thimphu (31km).

A checkpoint here keeps track of vehicle movements. Dantak, the Indian road-construction organisation, operates a simple coffee shop next to the checkpoint. People from nearby villages often sit by the side of the road south of the checkpoint selling vegetables, apples and dried cheese.

## Chhuzom to Thimphu
### 31km / 1 hour
As the road ascends the Wang Chhu valley, this hillsides become unusually barren. At 1km past Chhuzom there is a rough, unpaved side road that leads to Geynikha and

---

**NOT AS OLD AS YOU THINK**

At several places along the road to Thimphu you will see what look like ancient ruins. These are the remains of houses that either burned down or were abandoned. It is considered unlucky to move into the house of a family whose members have died out or a house that has been abandoned, therefore there are numerous derelict houses scattered around the country. The rammed mud walls are so tough that they survive for years after the rest of the structure has disappeared.

---

the start of the Dagala Thousand Lakes trek (see p214).

The road passes **Kharibje**, a village in a valley on the opposite side of the river. This village is inhabited by *bja-wap* (goldsmiths) who make jewellery and brass trumpets, as well as butter lamps and other items used in goembas. A small bridge across the Wang Chhu provides road access to the village.

Soon comes the small settlement of Khasadrapchhu. On the opposite side of the river is the hydro plant that served Thimphu before the large Chhukha hydroelectric project came on line in 1988.

The valley widens near the small village of Namseling. Below the road are extensive rice paddies. Rice is planted in mid-June and harvested in October. Terraces are barren during the winter. Above the road are numerous apple orchards. Much of the fruit is exported, particularly to Bangladesh. In the autumn people sell apples and mushrooms from makeshift stalls at the side of the road.

The new 'expressway' to Thimphu drops off the road towards the valley floor and travels along the east side of the river. The large ponds by the riverside are part of Thimphu's sewage treatment plant, which uses a microbiological system to treat urban waste from Thimphu so that no polluted water flows to communities downstream.

After passing below the army helipad at Lungtenphu the road crosses the river and enters Thimphu from the south. A second, older road travels via Babesa and Simtokha, enabling you to visit the Simtokha Dzong or bypass Thimphu completely on the way to Punakha.

# HAA DZONGKHAG

The isolated Haa valley lies south of the Paro valley. The Haa Chhu flows from the head of the valley to join the Wang Chhu, by the road to Phuentsholing. Though there is easy access to Tibet from Haa, the remote valley has always been off the major trade routes. It is the ancestral home of the Dorji family, to which the queen mother, Ashi Kesang Wangchuck, belongs.

Not many tourists get to Haa, only opened to tourists in 2001, but it's a picturesque valley that is ideal for mountain biking and hiking, and there is plenty of scope for getting off the beaten track here. We saw at least a dozen monasteries in the valley and doubtless there are many more. The best way to visit is to overnight here and spend a day biking to the sights.

It is a large fertile valley and the staple crops are wheat, potatoes, barley and millet. People also raise yaks and Haa yak meat is regarded as some of the best in the country. Many people from Haa move to Samtse in winter.

There are two roads into Haa. One climbs from Paro, crossing the Cheli La. The other diverges from the Phuentsholing–Thimphu road at Chhuzom and travels south, high above the Wang Chhu, before swinging into the Haa valley.

## PARO TO HAA VIA THE CHELI LA (68KM)

From the turn-off at Bondey, south of Paro, it's 62km to Haa over the high Cheli La, claimed to be the highest motorable road in Bhutan. As you start to climb you can see Dzongdrakha Goemba (see p131) to the left.

About 32km from the turn-off is a herders' camp marked by prayer flags. From here hiking trails lead up for 45 minutes to **Kila Nunnery**, established as a meditation site in the 9th century and reputedly the oldest nunnery in Bhutan. There are 32 nuns resident here.

From here, it's 4km to the pass. At the Cheli La a sign says the elevation is 3988m, but it's really 3810m. If it's raining in Paro it's likely snowing here, even as late as the end of April. Join the Bhutanese in a hearty cry of *'lha-gey lu!'* (May the gods be victorious!) as you cross the pass. During the clear skies of October and November it's worth taking the hiking trails that lead up the mountain ridge for 1½ hours to spectacular mountain views.

It's a 26km descent from the pass to Haa, passing through areas of burnt forest. Many fir trees here were killed by bark beetles, and the only way to prevent the spread of these pests was to burn the trees.

## HAA

☎ 08 / elev 2670m

The town of Haa sprawls along the Haa Chhu and forms two distinct areas. Much of the southern town is occupied by the Indian Military Training Team (IMTRAT) camp (complete with a golf course that has sand 'greens') and a Bhutanese army training camp. Near here is the dzong and monastery. In the central bazaar to the north are the main shops and eating places.

The three hills to the south of town are named after the Rigsum Goempo, the trinity of Chenresig, Channa Dorje and Jampelyang, and also represent the valley's three protector deities.

The scenic road to the north passes the Talung valley and Chhundu Lhakhang, and ends at Damthang, 15km from Haa town. But it would be prudent to turn around before you reach the gates of the large Bhutanese army installation.

### Sights

Haa's **Wangchulo Dzong** is one of Bhutan's newest, built in 1915 to replace a smaller structure. It is inside the Indian army compound but there's not much to see.

The 60-strong monk body is housed not in the dzong but in the **Haa Dratshang**, also known as the Lhakhang Kharpo (White Chapel), at the southern entrance to town. An annual tsechu is held in the large courtyard. A ten-minute walk behind the *dratshang* is the grey Lhakhang Nagpo (Black Chapel).

### Sleeping & Eating

**Risum Resort** ( ☎ 375350, fax 375405; s/d Nu 1000/1500) Good accommodation is available here in cosy, pine-clad rooms with clean hot-water bathrooms, heaters and, on the upper floors, balconies. The excellent information book in the restaurant has lots of information on trips to outlying monasteries, including Wantsa Goemba, a short walk behind the resort. The hotel is located on the east side of the road, between the two sections of town.

**Hotel Lhayul** ( ☎ 375251; tgytaugay@yahoo.com; s/d Nu 550/850) This is a good place for lunch,

WESTERN BHUTAN

with comfy sofas and a bar. There are also eight basic rooms, with four deluxe rooms planned. It's in the central bazaar area of town.

## AROUND THE HAA VALLEY

### Juneydrak

About 1km north of Haa, by the Two Sisters Hotel and hospital and just before the main bridge, a 4WD track branches east to Katsho village, from where you can make a lovely three-hour return hike to **Juneydrak hermitage** (also known as Juneydrag). The cliffside retreat contains a footprint of Machig Labdrom (1055–1132), the female Tibetan Tantric practitioner who perfected the *chöd* ritual, whereby one visualises one's own dismemberment in an act of 'ego annihilation'.

A trail follows the stream past a *mani* wall to a two-legged archway chorten (known as a *khonying*). Cross the bridge and ascend through a charming rhododendron forest. At a red sign in Dzongkha, take the trail to the left and climb up to a chorten that marks the entry to the hermitage. A sign here asks visitors not to disturb the hermits so don't try to enter the lhakhang.

From here a set of exposed log ladders ascend the cliff and the trail curves round the exposed bluff. Don't attempt this if you are afraid of heights or if it's raining. The trail curves round to Katsho Goemba, which is normally closed, but there are fine views down to Katsho village. Follow the switchbacked path back down to the village.

### Chhundu Lhakhang

North of Katsho the main road crosses to the river's south bank and passes several traditional settlements as it heads up the lovely upper Haa valley, past the village of Ingo (Yungo). The large village in the side valley to the north is Talung; Yangthang Goemba is high on the eastern ridge of this side valley and Jangkhaha village is in the valley floor, between Yangthang and Talung villages. Further up the valley is Tsenkha Goemba. You'll need a 4WD to visit Yangthang Goemba.

Three kilometres further along the main road (11km from Haa) is the delightful **Chhundu Lhakhang**, one of several shrines dedicated to the valley's protective deity. The timeless chapel is a five-minute walk down a concrete path below Gyechukha village, which is itself just past the Yakchu Zam bridge at

Haley. The blue-faced Chhundu and his red-faced cousin Jowya glower in glass cabinets on either side of the main altar.

Troublesome Chhundu was banished to Haa by the Zhabdrung after an altercation with Gyenyen, Thimphu's protector. He also had a quarrel with Jichu Drakye of Paro, with the result that the Paro guardian stole all of Haa's water – and that's why there is no rice grown in Haa. Annual sacrifices to Chhundu are still carried out in nearby Jangkhaha village, highlighting how deeply Bhutan's roots run to its pre-Buddhist animist past.

## HAA TO CHHUZOM (79KM)

From Haa village it's 6km to Karnag (also called Karna), and then Jyenkana. After a long stretch of forest the road reaches Nago, with its picturesque water prayer wheels. It's 4km to Bietakha, past a small landslip area and then another 5km to the two small restaurants at Rangshingang and then the large village of Gayshina.

Now high above the river, the road swings into a huge side valley, passing below the village of Susana en route to Mendegang. Near the houses and basic restaurants of Tshongkha is a road leading to a radio tower and a trail leading uphill to Phundup Pedma Yowzing Goemba. The road traverses in and out of side valleys, passing above Dobji Dzong, and then descends into Wang Chuu valley to join the main road at Chhuzom. From Chhuzom it's 24km (45 minutes) to Paro or 31km (one hour) to Thimphu.

# PUNAKHA DZONGKHAG

## THIMPHU TO PUNAKHA (76KM)

The 2¾-hour drive from Thimphu to Punakha, along the National Hwy and over the Dochu La, leads from the cool heights of Thimphu to the balmy, lush landscapes of the Punakha valley.

### Thimphu to Dochu La

#### 23km / 45 mins

From Thimphu the road goes south to Simtokha (2250m). The route to the east leaves the road to Paro and Phuentsholing and loops back over itself to become the east–west National Hwy. About a kilometre past the turnoff there is a good view of Simtokha Dzong (see p116). The route climbs past the forestry research station at Yusupang, then through apple orchards and forests of blue pine to the village of **Hongtsho** (2890m). Ngawang Chhogyel founded a goemba and meditation centre here in the 15th century; he was a cousin of Lama Drukpa Kunley and also founded Druk Choeding in Paro. At the village of Hongtsho there is an immigration checkpoint that controls all access to eastern Bhutan. You must have a restricted-area travel permit to proceed; this is arranged as a matter of course by all tour operators.

High on a ridge across the valley to the south is **Trashigang Goemba** (see p117); you can make a nice half-day hike from the Dochu La to the goemba, ending at Hongtsho (see p117).

The road climbs to **Dochu La** (3140m), marked by a large array of prayer flags and an impressive new collection of 108 chortens. On a rare clear day (only really likely between October and February) the pass offers a panoramic view of the Bhutan Himalaya and some groups make special pre-dawn trips up here to catch the views. The collection of chortens were built in 2005 as atonement for the loss of life caused by the flushing out of Assamese militants in southern Bhutan. A new Zangto Pelri Lhakhang is under construction at the pass.

The hill above the chortens is covered in lovely rhododendron forest, part of the royal botanical park. If you are here between mid-March and the end of April it's well worth taking some time to wander in the forest and take in the wonderful blooms. The forest is also a good area for bird-spotting. If you have more time, you can make an excellent half-day hike to Hongtsho via Lungchuzekha and Trashigang goembas – see p117 for details.

On the hill just below the pass is the **Dochu La Hotel** ( ☎ 02-390404; breakfast/lunch Nu 130/260), actually a restaurant, where many people break for tea. The proprietor also has a business making embroidered *thangkas*, including some large *thondrols* for tsechus, and there's a small gift shop here.

There is a powerful binocular telescope here, a gift from the Kyoto University Alpine Club after members made the first ascent of Masang Gang (7165m) in 1985. A photograph on the wall above the telescope labels the peaks on the horizon (with different spellings and elevations from those used in this book). Gangkhar Puensum (7541m) is the highest peak that is completely inside Bhutan; Kulha Gangri (7554m) is higher, but it is on the border with Tibet. Using the telescope, it's also possible to see the distinctive shape of **Gasa Dzong** (see p226), a small white speck almost 50km to the north.

The area near the pass is believed to be inhabited by numerous spirits, including a cannibal demoness. Lama Drukpa Kunley, the 'Divine Madman', built **Chimi Lhakhang** (see p145) in the Punakha valley to subdue these spirits and demons.

## Dochu La to Metshina
### 42km / 1½ hours

The vegetation changes dramatically at the pass from oak, maple and blue pine to a moist mountain forest of rhododendron, alder, cypress, hemlock and fir. There is also a large growth of daphne, a bush that is harvested for making traditional paper. The large white chorten a few kilometres below the pass was built because of the high incidence of accidents on this stretch of road. It's a long, winding descent past Lumitsawa to **Thinleygang**, during which the air gets warmer and the vegetation becomes increasingly tropical with the appearance of cactus, oranges and bamboo. About 11km below the pass is a government botanical garden.

As you descend from the pass monasteries start to appear on the surrounding hills. First is the striking hilltop Jakar Goemba, near Baekub village. Further along and high on

---

**ROYAL PROCESSIONS**

Thinleygang (1860m) is an interesting village. Every November (on the first day of the 10th month) the Je Khenpo and *dratshang* (central monk body) pack up their robes and move from their summer residence in Thimphu to their winter residence in Punakha, taking their holiest relics with them. The procession takes two days and thousands of locals line the road to catch a glimpse of the Je Khenpo. The entourage overnights here en route, on what is the biggest day of the sleepy Thinleygang calendar. The Je Khenpo lodges in the lhakhang just below the village. The monk body returns to Thimphu in May (the 1st day of the 4th month), but this time overnights in Hongtsho.

## THE DIVINE MADMAN

Lama Drukpa Kunley (1455–1529) is one of Bhutan's favourite saints and a fine example of the Tibetan tradition of 'crazy wisdom'. He was born in Tibet, trained at Ralung Monastery and was a contemporary and disciple of Pema Lingpa. He travelled throughout Bhutan and Tibet as a *neljorpa* (yogi) using songs, humour and outrageous behaviour to dramatise his teachings to the common man. He felt that the stiffness of the clergy and social conventions were keeping people from learning the true teachings of Buddha.

His outrageous, often obscene, actions and sexual antics were a deliberate method of provoking people to discard their preconceptions. Tango Goemba is apparently the proud owner of a *thangka* that Kunley urinated on! He is also credited with having created Bhutan's strange animal, the takin, by sticking the head of a goat onto the body of a cow.

His sexual exploits are legendary, and the flying phalluses that you see painted on houses and hanging from rooftops are his. Kunley's numerous sexual conquests often included even the wives of his hosts and sponsors. On one occasion when he received a blessing thread to hang around his neck, he wound it around his penis instead, saying he hoped it would bring him luck with the ladies.

He spoke the following verse on one occasion when he met Pema Lingpa:

I, the madman from Kyishodruk,
Wander around from place to place;
I believe in lamas when it suits me,
I practise the Dharma in my own way.
I choose any qualities, they are all illusions,
Any gods, they are all the Emptiness of the Mind.
I use fair and foul words for Mantras; it's all the same,
My meditation practice is girls and wine;
I do whatever I feel like, strolling around in the Void,
Last time, I saw you with the Bumthang trulku;
With my great karmic background, I could approach.
Indeed it was auspicious, to meet you on my pilgrim's round!

For a biography and collection of songs and bar-room anecdotes concerning Drukpa Kunley, try Keith Dowman's *The Divine Madman*.

the hill across the valley is Dalay Goemba, with Talo Goemba just above and to the west. The road passes a chorten that flows with holy water, said to have its source in a lake far above.

Three kilometres from Thinleygang, below Mendigang village, is the small **Dechen Hill Resort** ( ☎ 02-322204; s/d Nu 1050/1400), which was closed during our visit. It's a short but steep drive up an unpaved road up to the secluded collection of cottages, which are used mostly by birding enthusiasts. Advance reservations for the resort are a must, as is a 4WD vehicle.

The road continues its descent, looping in and out of a side valley, to the road junction at Metshina, where the road to Punakha branches off from the National Hwy. The Zam Restaurant offers snacks and drinks and a petrol station allows your driver to fill up. If you are continuing to Wangdue Phodrang, stay on the main road.

## Metshina to Punakha
### 11km / 30 mins

The road to Punakha makes a switchback down past a collection of shops and houses at Sopsokha, from where you can visit the Chimi Lhakhang. Beyond here, the road crosses the small Tabe Rong Chhu and swings round a ridge into the valley of the Punak Tsang Chhu. Watch for black great cormorants sitting on rocks beside the river looking for fish. The dirt road on the other side of the valley offers several mountain-biking options (see p148).

*(Continued on page 145)*

Monks performing during a puja, Phajoding Goemba (p117), Motithang

Student sculpting at the National Institute for Zorlg Chusum (p104), Thimphu

Woman weaving fabrics and textiles (p57), Thimphu

JEFF CANTARUTTI

Silk fabrics for sale at the Thimphu weekend market (p103)

Fruit at Thimphu's weekend market (p103)

SALLY DILLON

The traffic circle (p97) of central Thimphu

ALISON WRIG

NICHOLAS REUSS

Trashi Chhoe Dzong (p101), Thimphu

ALISON WRIGHT

Lunghdar prayer flags (p65), Thimphu

Traditional archery tournament (p62), Thimphu

LINDSAY BROWN

ALISON WRIC

Young school children, Thimphu

Women at work in the fields of the Paro
valley (p121)

IZZET KERIBAR

WES WALKER

Young monks with procession flags for the
tsechu, Drametse Goemba (p189)

Holy man at the Thimphu weekend market (p103)

RICHARD I'ANSON

JULIA WILKINSON

Shopkeepers, Paro (p122)

Dance of Black Hat Magicians, Wangdue Phodrang (p149)

NICHOLAS REUSS

Phokpey campsite (p233), Bumthang Dzongkhag

JULIA WILKINSON

Plank bridge across the Bumthang river, Bumthang Dzongkhag (p165)

JULIA WILKINSC

STAN ARMINGTON

Pack horses, Phobjikha valley, at the start of the Gangte trek (p228)

STAN ARMINGTON

Trekkers approaching Nylie Lo on the Jhomolhari trek (p216), with Tserim Kang (6789m) looming up behind

Penis painted on the side of a home (p136)

Wheel of Life painting, Trongsa Dzong (p164)

Punakha Dzong (p146), Punakha

(Continued from page 136)

After another 2km or so, by the village of Wolakha, a road peels off to the left and climbs to the Meri Phuensom and Zangto Pelri hotels (see p148). High upon the hillside this side road continues a relentless uphill for 15km to **Talo Goemba**. You need a permit specifying Talo in order to visit the monastery. Up on the nearby ridge, the village of Norbugang reportedly has several fine lhakhangs but is closed to visitors since it is home to the family of the king's four wives. A 1km side road branches off 5km before Talo to **Dalay Goemba**, a *lobdra* (monastic school) which is home to 30 students and a young *trulku* (reincarnated lama). The monastery was founded by the seventh Je Khenpo and is also known as Nalanda, after the famous Indian Buddhist university.

Back on the main road, just under 2km from the junction and 6.5km from Metshina is the new town of Khuruthang. All of Punakha's shops were relocated to this uninspiring concrete grid in 1999. There are several restaurants and hotels and a Saturday vegetable market.

To the side of the road is the new **Khuruthang Goemba**, built by the queen's mother and consecrated in 2005. The main Zangto Pelri Lhakhang here has excellent ceiling mandalas. The murals on the far wall depict the Zhabdrung and the various dzongs he established. The large Nepali-style chorten here was built by the Indian guru Nagi Rinchen (see p147) and is said to enshrine a speaking image of Guru Rinpoche known as Guru Samzhung.

It's a further 3km to a high school and an excellent viewpoint over the Punakha Dzong. A kilometre further on is a parking area and the footbridge leading across the Mo Chhu to gorgeous Punakha Dzong.

### CHIMI LHAKHANG

On a hillock in the centre of the valley below Metshina is the yellow-roofed **Chimi Lhakhang**, built in 1499 by the cousin of Lama Drukpa Kunley, in his honour after he subdued the demoness of the nearby Dochu La with his 'magic thunderbolt of wisdom'. A wooden effigy of the lama's thunderbolt is preserved in the lhakhang, and childless women go to the temple to receive a *wang* (blessing or empowerment) from the saint.

It's a 20-minute walk across fields from the road at Sopsokha to the temple. The trail leads across rice fields to the tiny settlement of Pana, which means 'field'. It then follows a tiny stream downhill to Yoaka (which means 'in the drain') and across an archery ground before making a short climb to Chimi Lhakhang. During the wet season, this is an especially muddy and slippery walk. Kunley characteristically likened the shape of the hillock to that of a woman's breast.

There are a few monks at the temple, which is surrounded by a row of prayer wheels and some beautiful slate carvings. No permit is required for entrance to the temple, so you may visit and see the central statue of the lama and his dog Sachi, as well as statues of the Zhabdrung, Sakyamuni and Chenresig. Make a small offering and you'll be rewarded with a blessing from the lama's wooden and bone phalluses and his iron archery set. Mothers-to-be then select their future baby's name from a collection of bamboo slips. The small chorten on the altar is said to have been crafted by Drukpa Kunley himself. Murals to the right of the chapel depict events from Kunley's colourful life.

## PUNAKHA & KHURUTHANG

☎ 02 / elev 1250m

Punakha sits in a fertile, warm and beautiful valley at the junction of the Mo Chhu (Mother River) and Pho Chhu (Father River). Commanding the river junction is the gorgeous Punakha Dzong, one of Bhutan's most impressive buildings. Punakha served as Bhutan's capital for over 300 years and the first king was crowned here in 1907. The third king convened the new Bhutan National Assembly here in 1952.

From Punakha, the Punak Tsang Chhu continues past Wangdue Phodrang, dropping away into southern Bhutan, where it is known locally as the Sankosh. The low altitude of the Punakha valley allows two rice crops a year, and oranges and bananas are in abundance.

All of Punakha's shops and facilities are in the unappealing new town of Khuruthang, 4km to the south. The older village opposite the dzong has only private homes, a hospital and an antique-looking fire engine.

Punakha also has one of the most famous festivals in the country, dedicated to the protector deity Yeshe Goenpo (Mahakala).

WESTERN BHUTAN

## Sights

### PUNAKHA DZONG

**Punakha Dzong** was the second of Bhutan's dzongs and until the mid-1950s it served as the seat of the government. It's arguably the most beautiful dzong in the country, especially in spring when the lilac-coloured jaracanda trees bring a rare sensuality to the dzong's characteristically towering whitewashed walls. Elaborately painted gold, red and black carved woods add to the artistic lightness of touch.

The construction of Punakha Dzong was foretold by Guru Rinpoche, who predicted that '…a person named Namgyal will arrive at a hill that looks like an elephant'. The Zhabdrung visited Punakha and chose the tip

of the trunk of the sleeping elephant at the confluence of the Mo Chhu and Pho Chhu as the place to build a dzong. It's not obvious, but with a bit of imagination you may be able to visualise the hill as an elephant.

As early as 1326 a smaller building called Dzong Chug (Small Dzong) housed a statue of the Buddha here. It is said that the Zhabdrung ordered the architect, Zowe Palep, to sleep in front of the statue. While Palep was sleeping, the Zhabdrung took him in his dreams to Zangto Pelri and showed him the palace of Guru Rinpoche. From his vision, the architect conceived the design for the new dzong, which, in keeping with tradition, was never committed to paper.

Construction began in 1637 and was completed the following year, when the building was christened Pungthang Dechen Phodrang (Palace of Great Happiness). Later embellishments included the construction of a chapel to commemorate the victory over the Tibetans in 1639. The arms captured during the battle are preserved in the dzong.

The Zhabdrung established a monk body here with 600 monks from Cheri Goemba in the upper Thimphu valley and he lived out the rest of his life here. Punakha is still the winter residence of the *dratshang*.

Punakha Dzong is 180m long and 72m wide and the *utse* is six storeys high. The gold dome on the utse was built in 1676 by the *dzongpen* (lord of the dzong), Gyaltsen Tenzin Rabgye. Many of the dzong's features were added between 1744 and 1763 during the reign of the 13th desi, Sherab Wangchuk. One item he donated was the *chenmo* (great) *thondrol*, a large *thangka* depicting the Zhabdrung that is exhibited to the public once a year during the tsechu festival. A brass roof for the dzong was a gift of the seventh Dalai Lama, Kelzang Gyatso.

Frequent fires (five between 1750 and 1849) damaged the dzong, as did the severe 1897 earthquake. A glacial lake burst on the Pho Chhu in 1960 and again in 1994, causing damage to the dzong that has since been repaired. Outside the dzong is a memorial to the 23 people killed in that flood. The latest fire, in 1986, damaged the residence of the Je Khenpo in the southwest corner of the dzong.

Cantilever bridges across the Mo Chhu and the Pho Chhu were constructed between 1720 and 1730. They have both been destroyed, however, and the Mo Chhu is now spanned by

**KHURUTHANG**

0 — 200 m
0 — 0.1 miles

**INFORMATION**
Bank of Bhutan...................1  A3
Post Office..........................2  A3

**SIGHTS & ACTIVITIES**
Khurutang Goempa.............3  B3

**SLEEPING**
Damchen Lodge.................4  B3
Damchen Resort.................5  B3
Hotel Welcome...................6  A3
Kunga Hotel.......................7  A3

**TRANSPORT**
Bus & Taxi Stand.................8  A3

To Punakha Dzong (4km)

Junior High School

Urgyen Academy

Vocational Training Institute

Football Field

Vegetable Market

To Zangto Pelri Hotel (3km);
Meri Puensum Resort (3km);
Wangdue Phodrang (21km);
Punakha

Tsang Chhu

a cable suspension bridge that stands next to the remains of the original cantilever bridge.

### Visiting The Dzong

In addition to its strategic position at the river confluence, the dzong has several features to protect it against invasion. The steep wooden entry stairs are designed to be pulled up, and there is a heavy wooden door that is still closed at night.

The dzong is unique because it has three *docheys* instead of the usual two. The first (northern) courtyard is for administrative functions and houses a huge white chorten and bodhi tree. In the far left corner is a collection of stones and a shrine to the queen of the *nagas* (snake spirits), whose image is to the side. The second courtyard houses the monastic quarters and is separated from the first by the *utse*. In this courtyard are two halls, one of which was used when Ugyen Wangchuck, later the first king, was presented with the Order of Knight Commander of the Indian Empire by John Claude White in 1905.

In the southernmost courtyard is the temple where the remains of the *terton*, Pema Lingpa, and Zhabdrung Ngawang Namgyal are preserved. The Zhabdrung died in Punakha Dzong, and his body is still preserved in Machey Lhakhang (*machey* means 'sacred embalmed body'), which was rebuilt in 1995. The casket is sealed and may not be opened. Other than two guardian lamas, only the king and the Je Khenpo may enter this room. Both come to take blessings before they take up their offices.

At the south end is the 'hundred-pillar' assembly hall (which actually has only 54 pillars).

The exceptional murals, which were commissioned by the second *druk desi*, depict the life of Buddha. The massive gold statues of the Buddha, Guru Rinpoche and the Zhabdrung date back to the mid-18th century, and there are some fine gold panels on the pillars.

Bhutan's most treasured possession is the Rangjung ('Self-Created') Kharsapani, an image of Chenresig that is kept in the Tse Lhakhang in the *utse* of the Punakha Dzong. It was brought to Bhutan from Tibet by the Zhabdrung and features heavily in Punakha's famous *domchoe* (type of festival).

After you exit the dzong from the north you can visit the *dzong chug*, which houses a statue of Sakyamuni said to have the ability to talk. North of the dzong is a cremation ground, marked by a large chorten.

### THE UPPER PUNAKHA VALLEY

The road up the west side of Mo Chhu valley passes several country houses owned by Bhutan's nobility, including the Phuntsho Pelri palace, a summer residence of the king, and a former residence of the queen mother, now the Amankora resort (see p148). The current queens' father built many of the lhakhangs in the valley and owns several hotels, including the Zangto Pelri.

Just 1km north of the dzong is the **Bhutan Souvenir Production Training Centre** ( ☎ 584664; ✆ Sun–Fri), a program that trains 20 disadvantaged girls in a one-year course to produce souvenir handicrafts. Products include handwoven bags, embroidered purses, Bhutanese paper products, dolls and Christmas decorations. It's a worthy cause and worth a stop.

---

### PUNAKHA FESTIVAL

The Punakha festival in February/March is unusual because of its dramatic recreation of a 17th-century battle scene. In 1639 a Tibetan army invaded Bhutan to seize Bhutan's most precious relic, the Rangjung Kharsapani, a self-created image of Chenresig. The Zhabdrung concocted an elaborate ceremony in which he pretended to throw the relic into the Mo Chhu, after which the disappointed Tibetans withdrew.

On the final day of the five-day Punakha Domchoe the *thondrol*, which features an image of the Zhabdrung, is displayed. Later a group of 136 people dressed as *pazaps* (warriors) perform a dance in the main courtyard, then shout and whistle as they descend the front stairs of the dzong. Next, a procession of monks led by the Je Khenpo proceeds to the river to the accompaniment of cymbals, drums and trumpets. At the river the Je Khenpo throws a handful of oranges symbolising the Rangjung Kharsapani into the river. This is both a recreation of the Zhabdrung's trick and also an offering to the *naga* (*lu* in Dzongkha), the sub-surface spirits in the river. The singing and cheering warriors then carry their generals back into the dzong as firecrackers explode around them. Mask dances then celebrate the Zhabdrung's construction of the dzong.

On the left side of the road, 4.5km from Punakha, look out for the **Dho Jhaga Lam Lhakhang**, whose pretty gardens shelter a huge boulder split miraculously in two. It is said that the Indian guru-magician Nagi Rinchen sent lightning and hail to split the rock to liberate his mother who was trapped inside. The chapel houses a statue of the guru (to the far right), who is recognisable by the scriptures in his top knot. Rinchen meditated in a cave across the river (marked by prayer flags next to the Sona Gasa, the former palace of the third king), and so is depicted here as a long-haired *drubthob* (hermit-magician). To the far left is a statue of the local female protector Chabdrab, riding a snowlion.

In Yambesa, 7km from Punakha, is the huge **Khamsum Yuelley Namgyal Chorten**, perched high on a hill on the opposite bank of the river. The 30m-tall chorten, which took eight years to build, was consecrated during a three-day ceremony in December 1999. The chorten is dedicated to the crown prince and serves to protect the country so is stuffed with every form of protector deity imaginable, including a yeti with characteristically pendulous breasts. You can ascend up to the roof for superb views of the valley. A side road leads down to a parking lot by the river, where a bridge provides access to a steep 45-minute hike uphill to the chorten. Ask your guide to point out the wonderfully fragrant *tingye* (flower pepper) plants that grow along the trail.

The bridge is a put-in spot for relaxing rafting and kayaking float trips down the Mo Chhu to Punakha Dzong (see p244).

Beyond the chorten the road leads up to Tashithang and then Damji, a half-day walk from Gasa (see p159). This is the jumping-off point for treks to Gasa and the hot springs below it; it's also the ending point of the Laya–Gasa trek (see p222 for details).

## Activities

Punakha's mountain-bike trails offer one of the best chances to break out the fat tyres, though you'll have to bring your own bike as there's nowhere to rent locally.

A 27km loop route from Kuruthang crosses the bridge there and heads up the east side of the valley along a feeder road to Samdingkha (14km), then returns along a trail to Punakha Dzong (7.5km), finally coasting back to Khurutang along the paved road.

A longer 40km loop starts from Bajo, just north of Wangdue Phodrang, and heads up the east side of the valley to Jangsabu (14km), before climbing a trail to Olodama and Tschochagsa (9.5km). From here you can detour to Lingmukha or coast down 10km to the Aumthekha junction, across the river from Chimi Lhakhang, and then pedal back to Bajo and Wangdi.

## Sleeping

Many people visit Punakha as a day trip from Thimphu or visit en route to Wangdue Phodrang, where there are several more hotels (see p151). An **Uma** (www.uma.como.bz) resort is planned above Punakha Dzong.

**Meri Puensum Resort** (Map p146; ☎ 584195; mpuensum@druknet.net.com; s/d Nu 1100/1300, deluxe s/d Nu 1250/1450; 🖳 ) This privately-run place next door to Zangto Pelri is smaller, cosier and has much better service. Rooms are in a central building and cottages that hug the steep hillside overlooking the rice terraces of the Punakha valley. The garden gazebo is a great place to have breakfast or relax after a long day's touring. If you stay here (or at the Zangto Pelri), consider getting up at dawn and driving 8km up the paved road to Laptshaka (1900m) for a beautiful view of the mountains.

**Hotel Zangto Pelri** (Map p146; ☎ 584125; hotzang@druknet.bt; s/d Nu 1100/1320, cottage s/d Nu 1200/1440) Named after the paradise of Guru Rinpoche, this hotel is 6km south of Punakha, 1.2km up a side road, on a hill above the Punakha valley. There are 45 rooms in the central building and quieter surrounding cottages (upper-floor rooms are best), with a neglected swimming pool on the grounds below the hotel. Service is lacklustre at best.

**Amankora** (Map p128; ☎ 584222; www.amanresorts.com; s/d full board US$925/1000; 🗷 ) This is the smallest and most intimate of these über-luxury resorts, with only eight rooms in three buildings (rooms are identical in all Bhutan's Amankoras). The main farmhouse (now the restaurant and reading room) was the former residence of the queen mother and has some charming touches, including a traditional altar room. The spa reception area is in the former farmhouse kitchen. The lovely outdoor dining area is surrounded by rice fields and orchards. Park at the suspension bridge over the Mo Chhu and take a golf cart up to the resort (ring in advance to arrange this).

**Damchen Resort** (Map p146; ☎ 584354; s/d Nu 1200/1400) On the banks of the Punak Chhu, below Khuruthang, this riverside resort was being rebuilt and expanded in 2006. It has a good location near the Khuruthang Goemba but on Saturdays brace yourself for the disco in the underground Blue River Club.

In Khuruthang there are several basic local guest houses, including **Hotel Welcome** (Map p146; ☎ 584106; s/d Nu 200/300) and the better **Kunga Hotel** (Map p146; ☎ 584128; r without/with private bathroom Nu 300/450). Best is the **Damchen Lodge** (Map p146; ☎ 584650; d Nu 1400), where some rooms have balconies overlooking the goemba.

**Hotel Y.T.** ( ☎ 376012; hotelyt@druknet.bt; s/d Nu 1300/1500) Above the road department complex in Lobesa, 2km from Metshina en route to Wangdue Phodrang, this intimate family-run hotel has great views of the valley and a comfortable Bhutanese-style sitting room. The friendly owner is an ex-forester, which is why the gardens are stuffed with mango, avocado and papaya trees. He is planning a new hotel 1km along the road towards Wangdi.

### Eating

You can get curries, *momos*, rice and dal at several small restaurants in Khuruthang, of which the best are at the Kunga Hotel and Hotel Welcome. Otherwise, your guide will book lunch at one of the tourist hotels.

# WANGDUE PHODRANG DZONGKHAG

The scenic dzongkhag of Wangdue Phodrang is centred on the town and dzong of that name and stretches all the way to the Pele La and Phobjikha valley.

## PUNAKHA TO WANGDUE PHODRANG (21KM)

It's a half-hour drive from Punakha to Wangdue Phodrang. Follow the road back to Metshina and drive 1.5km to Lobesa, following the Punak Tsang Chhu.

Soon the dramatic Wangdue Phodrang Dzong comes into view, draped along the end of a ridge above the river. There is a police and immigration checkpoint before the bridge across the Punak Tsang Chhu. A road leads from the bridge south to the Basochhu hydroelectric project and the southern region of Tsirang.

The original bridge over the Punak Tsang Chhu is said to have been built in 1685. Old photos show a wooden cantilever structure with massive turrets. Floods washed it away in 1968, and now a two-lane Swiss-engineered bridge spans the river downstream of the remains of the original structure.

## WANGDUE PHODRANG
☎ 02 / elev 1240m

Legends relate that the Zhabdrung Ngawang Namgyal met a small boy named Wangdi playing in the sand on the banks of the Punak Chhu and was moved to name his new dzong Wangdi – later Wangdue – Phodrang (Wangdi's Palace). The town is still known colloquially as Wangdi.

The small town of whitewashed wooden shops and restaurants has a ramshackle but untouched air. Many houses in town have roofs made from slate that was mined at Tashi Chholing and Tseshinang, on the hills above Wangdi. Sadly, this looks all set to change, as plans are afoot to demolish the wooden shacks and relocate the old town 4km to the north. There's no timeline for this as yet (2006 and 2007 were divined as inauspicious years for such a move) but the concrete grid of the new site is waiting expectantly.

Because it is on an exposed promontory overlooking the river, Wangdi is usually windy and dusty, particularly in the afternoon.

### Orientation

The town's only hotel and the dzong are down a side road to the southwest of the central bazaar. Nearby is the Radak Naktshang, the town temple. The weekly vegetable market is far below the bazaar on a side road.

### Information

**Bank of Bhutan** ( ☯ 9am-1pm Mon-Fri, to 11am Sat) Changes cash and travellers cheques. It's in Bajo village, just north of the planned new town, 2.5km from Wangdue Phodrang.

**Post Office** ( ☯ 8.30am-1pm & 2-5pm Mon-Fri, 8.30am-1pm Sat) In a courtyard just off the main traffic circle.

### Sights
#### WANGDUE PHODRANG DZONG

**Wangdue Phodrang Dzong** was founded by the Zhabdrung in 1638. It sits atop a high ridge between the Punak Tsang Chhu and the Dang Chhu. It is obvious that the site was selected for its commanding view of the valleys below. Legend relates another reason for choosing this spot: as people searched

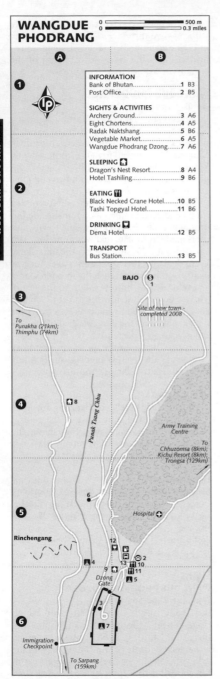

**WANGDUE PHODRANG**

0 _____ 500 m
0 _____ 0.3 miles

**INFORMATION**
Bank of Bhutan........................1 B3
Post Office...............................2 B5

**SIGHTS & ACTIVITIES**
Archery Ground........................3 A6
Eight Chortens..........................4 A5
Radak Naktshang......................5 B6
Vegetable Market......................6 A5
Wangdue Phodrang Dzong.......7 A6

**SLEEPING**
Dragon's Nest Resort................8 A4
Hotel Tashiling.........................9 B6

**EATING**
Black Necked Crane Hotel.......10 B5
Tashi Topgyal Hotel................11 B6

**DRINKING**
Dema Hotel.............................12 B5

**TRANSPORT**
Bus Station.............................13 B5

BAJO

Site of new town -
completed 2008

To
Punakha (21km);
Thimphu (74km)

Punak Tsang Chhu

Army Training
Centre

To
Chhuzomsa (8km);
Kichu Resort (8km);
Trongsa (129km)

Hospital

Rinchengang

Dzong
Gate

Immigration
Checkpoint

To Sarpang
(159km)

for a site for the dzong, four ravens were seen flying away in four directions. This was considered an auspicious sign, representing the spreading of religion to the four points of the compass.

Wangdi is important in the history of Bhutan because in the early days it was the country's secondary capital. After Trongsa Dzong was established in 1644 the *penlop* of Wangdue Phodrang became the third most powerful ruler, after the *penlops* of Paro and Trongsa. The dzong's position gave the *penlop* control of the routes to Trongsa, Punakha, Dagana and Thimphu. It was repaired after a fire in 1837 and again after it was severely damaged in the 1897 earthquake.

The dzong's complex shape consists of three separate narrow structures that follow the contours of the hill. The buildings are refreshingly unrestored, with a wooden roof still held in place by large stones, and the occasional lost chicken wandering across the empty courtyards.

There is only one entrance, fronted by a large *darchen* (prayer pole) and reached by a road that leads downhill from the bazaar. The cacti that cover the hillside below the dzong were planted long ago to discourage invaders from climbing the steep slope.

The administrative portion surrounds a large flagstone-paved *dochey* at the north end of the dzong. The *utse* divides the two portions of the dzong. The Guru Tshengye Thondrol, depicting Guru Rinpoche, is unfurled here each year in the early hours of the final day of the autumn tsechu festival. As you detour around the *utse* you can peer through arrow slits into the valley below. The main assembly hall in the far south of the dzong features a central Dusum Sangay – the past, present and future Buddhas.

### RADAK NATSHANG

Just behind the bazaar, by the tall cypress trees of the district court, is this timeless 17th-century **temple**. The temple is dedicated to an ancient warrior king and there's a large collection of helmets, arrows and shields in the anteroom. Inside are five versions of the local protector deity, as well as a statue to the far right of a *tshomen* (mermaid), who lived in the river and was an obstacle to the construction of this building. Make an offering and roll the chapel dice and the resident monk will read your future.

## RINCHENGANG

From the dzong you can clearly see the compact village of **Rinchengang** on the opposite side of the river. Many of the people who live in this traditional village work as stonemasons, and the services of Rinchengang's craftsmen are sought after for the construction of dzongs and lhakhangs. While Rinchengang is believed to be one of the oldest villages in Bhutan, electricity, water and schools only arrived here in the early 1990s. There's a small lhakhang at the top of the village.

## Sleeping

There's not a great deal of demand for hotel rooms in Wangdi. Many travellers just make a day trip to see the dzong or stay in Punakha (30 minutes' drive away) and drive straight through to Gangte, Trongsa or Bumthang. At tsechu time in autumn, however, the town is packed and rooms are at a premium.

**Dragon's Nest Resort** (Map p150; ☎ 480521; nest@druknet.bt; s/d from Nu 1400/1700; 🖳) This trusty place is on the west side of the river, 4km below Wangdi and diagonally across from the new town. The spacious rooms overlook the river and are safely away from the nocturnal canine hullabaloo of the town. The hot water takes time to kick in so let it run for a while before you call for help. The restaurant staff seem to be in a competition to see who can ignore the guests the longest. Apparently our waiter won.

**Kichu Resort** (Map p128; ☎ 481359; fax 481360; s/d Nu 1650/2400) In Chhuzomsa, 8km east of the town, this tranquil hotel has 22 well-appointed rooms in a lovely landscaped garden overlooking the rushing Dang Chhu. The son of the resort's owners is a *rinpoche* (title given to a revered lama) and so the restaurant serves only vegetarian food. Ask for a riverside balcony room and pack insect repellent against the sand flies.

**Hotel Tashiling** (Map p150; ☎ 481401; fax 481682; s/d Nu 1200/1500; Dzong Lam) This place sits somewhere between a tourist and local hotel, with 16 pine-walled rooms and strings of meat drying from the balconies. It's a decent option if for some reason you want to stay in the town.

## Eating & Drinking

The **Black Necked Crane Hotel** (Map p150) is a decent local-style place for a lunch of Nepali-style *dal bhat* (rice and lentils). The **Tashi Topgyal Hotel** (Map p150) is run by a friendly family and has simple food. The **Dema Hotel** (Map p150) has overstuffed chairs and a sofa so you can relax with a beer and watch the world pass by the front window.

## WANGDUE PHODRANG TO PELE LA
**61km / 1¾ hours**

The beautiful drive east to the Pele La offers access to central Bhutan and the Phobjikha valley, known for its winter population of black-necked cranes. The pass itself takes you over the Black Mountains, the boundary between western and central Bhutan, before dropping down to Trongsa (p163).

Leaving Wangdue Phodrang, the road traverses bare hillsides high above the Dang Chhu. The large building far below the road, alongside the river, is a jail.

By the time the road reaches Chhuzomsa at the confluence of the Pe Chhu and the Dang Chhu, 8km from Wangdi, it is level with the river (Chhuzomsa means 'meeting of two rivers'). There are a few shops and a charming lhakhang here, and the Kichu Resort (see left) lies below the road on the idyllic banks of the river.

Just beyond Chhuzomsa is a ropeway that climbs 1340m in 6km to Tashila. The ropeway is primarily used to carry goods up to the village and to bring logs back down the hill, but it makes two special trips daily to carry people. Passengers sit in an open wooden box and dangle high above the trees for 45 minutes (if there is no breakdown) to the top. The price is Nu 60 for locals and Nu 250 for tourists, who are only allowed to ride in cases of emergency. The Gangte trek (p228) passes the top of the ropeway, and some tired trekkers declare an emergency and ride down from Tashila.

At Tikke Zampa, 4km past Chhuzomsa, the road crosses to the south bank of the Dang Chhu and begins a long climb to the Pele La. You may see horsemen here waiting for their trekking groups to arrive. A further 10km and you'll see a superbly located monastery on a hillock to the left. The valley gets steeper as the road ascends along the edge of the valley, following a spectacular, and occasionally frightening, route. In many places the way for the road has been blasted out of the side of the cliff and the road hangs high above the deep forests of the valley below.

The road detours frequently into side valleys, passing the Phama Hotel at Kalekha (or Khelaykha), the end of an interesting hike from the Phobjikha valley (see p153). From here it's 12km to the village of Nobding

(2640m), and then another 7km to Dungdung Nyelsa, where there are a few basic local-style restaurants. In spring the upper hillsides are covered with red, white and pink rhododendron blossoms. The road climbs steeply up the hillside for 5km to a turn-off that leads 6km to Gangte in the Phobjikha valley (see p154).

From the turn-off, it's 3km through forests to the top of Pele La (3420m), which is marked by a chorten and an array of prayer flags. On a clear day (which is rare in these parts) there is a view of Jhomolhari (7314m), Jichu Drakye (6989m) and Kang Bum (6526m) from a viewpoint 500m down the old road between Nobding and the Pele La. There are no mountain views from the pass itself. The Pele La marks the western border of the Singye Wangchuck (formerly the Black Mountains) National Park and the gateway to central Bhutan.

## PHOBJIKHA VALLEY

☎ 02 / elev 2900m

Phobjikha is a bowl-shaped glacial valley on the western slopes of the Black Mountains, bordering the Jigme Singye Wangchuck National Park. Because of the large flock of black-necked cranes that winters here, it is one of the most important wildlife preserves in the country. In addition to the cranes there are also muntjacs (barking deer), wild boars, sambars, Himalayan black bears, leopards and red foxes in the surrounding hills. The Nakey Chhu drains the marshy valley, eventually flowing into the lower reaches of the Punak Tsang Chhu.

Some people refer to this entire region as Gangte (or Gangtey), after the goemba that sits on a ridge above the valley. The three-day Gangte trek takes off from this valley (see p228).

The road from Gangte Goemba winds down to the valley floor and passes extensive russet-coloured fields of potatoes that contrast with the rich green of the valley. Gangte potatoes are the region's primary cash crop and one of Bhutan's important exports to India.

The valley is snowbound during the height of winter and many of the valley's 4500 residents, including the monks, shift to winter residences in Wangdue Phodrang during December and January, just as the cranes move in to take their place. The local residents, known as Gangteps, speak a dialect called Henke. Pockets of the Bon religion reputedly exist in the Taphu Valley.

## Sights

### GANGTE GOEMBA

Gangte Goemba enjoys the valley's prime chunk of real estate, on a hill overlooking the green expanse of the entire Phobjikha valley. The extensive complex consists of the central goemba and outlying monks' quarters, meditation centres, schools and a small guesthouse.

During a visit to the Phobjikha valley, the 15th-century treasure-finder Pema Lingpa prophesied that a goemba named *gang-teng* (hill top) would be built on this site and that his teachings would spread from here. A Nyingma temple was founded here in 1613 by Gyalse Pema Thinley, the grandson and reincarnation of Pema Lingpa, and the goemba was built by Tenzing Legpai Dhendup, the second

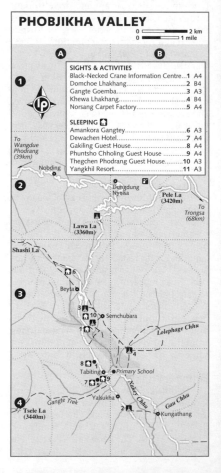

**PHOBJIKHA VALLEY**

| SIGHTS & ACTIVITIES | |
|---|---|
| Black-Necked Crane Information Centre...1 | A4 |
| Domchoe Lhakhang...................................2 | B4 |
| Gangte Goemba.......................................3 | A3 |
| Khewa Lhakhang.....................................4 | B4 |
| Norsang Carpet Factory............................5 | A4 |

| SLEEPING | |
|---|---|
| Amankora Gangtey....................................6 | A3 |
| Dewachen Hotel.......................................7 | A4 |
| Gakiling Guest House................................8 | A4 |
| Phuntsho Chholing Guest House...........9 | A4 |
| Thegchen Phodrang Guest House.......10 | A3 |
| Yangkhil Resort........................................11 | A3 |

reincarnation. The current abbot, Kunzang Pema Namgyal, is the ninth *trulku* of the mind of Pema Lingpa (see p175). The monastery is looked after by 100 or so lay monks, known as *gomchen*.

The *tshokhang* (prayer hall) is built in the Tibetan style with eight great pillars, and is one of the largest in Bhutan. Much of the interior and exterior woodwork of the 450-year-old goemba has been replaced over the last couple of years due to a beetle infestation and a major renovation project is still under way, with all the wood carved on site. A three-day tsechu is held here from the 5th to 10th day of the eighth lunar month (October).

A nearby *shedra* offers a nine-year course in Buddhist studies. The long white building on the hill to the north of the goemba is Kuenzang Chholing, a *drubdey* (retreat and meditation centre for monks) that was started in 1990 by the Je Khenpo. The normal period of meditation is three years, three months and three (sometimes seven) days, during which time the monks remain inside and eat food that is passed in to them by another monk.

### THE VALLEY

The beautiful glacial valley bowl below the goemba is peppered with villages, hiking trails, potato fields, lhakhangs and, if you time your visit right, nesting pairs of black-necked cranes. It's a great place to hike and explore surrounding valleys and it's a good idea to budget an extra day here for that.

Your first stop should be the Royal Society for Protection of Nature's (RSPN) **Black-Necked Crane Information Centre** (Map p152; ☎ 490002; ⏰ 9am-5pm Mon-Fri), which has informative displays about the cranes and the valley environment. You can use the centre's powerful spotting scopes and check what you see against its pamphlet 'Field Guide to Crane Behaviour'. If the weather's iffy you can browse the library and handicraft shop, and watch videos at 10am and 3pm (Nu 200). This is also the centre of the valley's fledgling ecotourism initiative and they can arrange mountain-bike hire (Nu 700 per day), a local guide (Nu 300), an overnight stay in a local farmhouse (Nu 500) or lectures on the local ecosystem.

A further 1.5km is the village and hotels at Tabiting. Behind the Phuntsho Chholing Guest House is the small **Norsang Carpet Factory**. Established in 1992 by a local woman, Dorji Wangmo, it has a small hall housing eight weavers, who produce about 90 carpets a year.

Further on the road becomes a rough 4WD track as it continues past Yalsukha village to the small Domchoe Lhakhang, a 45-minute walk from Tabiting.

WESTERN BHUTAN

---

### HIKING THE PHOBJIKHA VALLEY

There's some great hiking in the valley and surprisingly for Bhutan it's mostly flat going! The information centre has suggested the following walking routes and you can get information on these and other trails there (though take their trail maps with a pinch of salt).

A good short walk is the **Gangte Nature Trail** (1½ hours), which leads downhill from the *mani* stone wall just north of the Gangte Goemba to the Khewa Lhakhang. The trail descends to Semchubara village and keeps straight at the chorten into the edge of the forest, before descending to a square chorten and the lhakhang. From here you can cross over the metal bridge to the local school.

You could add on a half-day hike into the valley behind Khewa Lhakhang along the **Tenkhor Yuetshe Sum trail**, linking up the villages of Gophu, Dogsena, Pangsa and Jangchu Goemba in a loop back to Khewa.

Another option is the one-hour **Kilkhorthang Trail**, from the small lhakhang at Kungathang across the valley to the Damchoe Lhakhang, south of Tabiting. Alternatively, drive further south from Kungathang to the lovely side valley of Lawog and explore on foot from there.

The tougher half-day **Shashi La Nature Trail** leads up the valley behind Beyta school, though the trail is easier to follow from the track behind the Amankora resort. The path leads through rhododendron forests to the village of Ramgokha, a collection of chortens and then Shashi La pass, before descending through old-growth forest to the Phama Hotel at Kalekha on the main Wangdue Phodrang road. Arrange to get picked up here and continue on to Wangdi. This is the traditional route taken by the Gangte *trulku* and local farmers when they leave the valley for the winter. A local guide would be sensible for this route.

## WATCHING THE CRANES

The marshy centre of the Phobjikha valley means it's best avoided on foot but it's a perfect winter residence for the flock of 350 (up from 212 a decade ago) rare and endangered black-necked cranes that migrate from the Qinghai-Tibet Plateau to Bhutan in late autumn, typically between 23 and 26 October. The Bhutanese have great respect for these 'heavenly birds', and songs about the cranes are popular among village folk. In mid-February, the cranes circle Gangte Goemba and fly back across the Himalaya to their summer homes in Tibet. One of the most popular folk songs of the people of Phobjikha laments the time when the cranes leave the valley.

The best months to spot cranes are between October and March, with the best chance between November and January. The best times for viewing are at dawn or dusk, when all the birds in the valley congregate for the night. The RSPN removed a viewing hide in 2005 out of concern for the bird's well-being but you can watch the birds from the centre's viewing area or from the valleyside hiking trails. Wear dull-coloured clothes, keep your distance and refrain from flash photography. For more on black-necked cranes see p88.

The RSPN initiated and sponsors the annual **Black-Necked Crane Festival** on 12 November, the day following the king's birthday. It's primarily an effort to instil conservation values into the people of Phobjikha, but tourists are welcome to watch the festivities, most of which are folk dances staged by school children.

Across the valley from Tabiting is the **Khewa Lhakhang**, which has a tsechu on the first day of the ninth month, when local men (not monks) do the dancing.

## Sleeping

Telephone connections are patchy in this sparsely populated valley and most of the electricity is solar-powered. Bring warm clothes and a torch.

**Dewachen Hotel** (Map p152; ☎ 490007; s/d 1900/2400) Built in conjunction with a US travel company, this huge stone-and-wood building in Tabiting village has large and stylish rooms and a good restaurant with floor-to-ceiling bay windows that offer great valley views. There's electricity between 6pm and 9pm. Dewachen is the 'Pure Land' paradise of the Buddha Amithaba.

**Gakiling Guest House** (Map p152; ☎ 490003; r Nu 900) For something more intimate, try this new wooden guest house just behind the Black-Necked Crane Information Centre. Family run, it's the only locally-owned guesthouse in the valley. There are *bukharis* in all the rooms, plus attached bathrooms and great views from the upper-storey balconies.

**Phuntsho Chholing Guest House** (Map p152; ☎ 490011; s/d Nu 800/1100) Next to the Dewachen, this large Bhutanese-style house was converted to a hotel in 1994. It has creaking wooden floors, traditional wall paintings, a cosy sitting room and even a chapel on the 2nd floor, though the rooms themselves are pretty basic

for the money. Still, if you value experience over mod-cons this is a good opportunity to get a close-up look at the traditional architecture and domestic lifestyle of rural Bhutan. Hot water comes in buckets.

**Thegchen Phodrang Guest House** (Map p152; ☎ 490024; s/d Nu 700/800) Opposite Gangte Goemba, this concrete monastery guesthouse is a last-ditch option, though rooms do come with a private bathroom and renovations are planned.

**Amankora Gangtey** (Map p152; ☎ 490049; www.aman resorts.com; full board s/d US$925/1000) A side road branches 1km to this top-of-the-line lodge from just below the goemba. Rooms are identical to Bhutan's other Amankoras and the views, service and style won't disappoint.

A new resort, possibly called the Yangkhil Resort, is being built by the bridge at the base of the Gangte hill.

## Getting There & Away

The road to Phobjikha diverges from the main road below the Pele La. It's then a 1.5km drive through forests to the Lawa La (3360m), where you may encounter a few stray yaks. There are also barking deer and serows in this area. After the pass the trees disappear and the scenery switches dramatically to low-lying marsh bamboo as the road descends to Gangte Goemba. From the goemba junction the road switchbacks down, past the turn-off to the Amankora resort, to the green expanse of the valley floor.

# CHHUKHA DZONGKHAG

For travellers Chhukha district effectively consists of the winding road that drops from the mountains through the lush tropical foothills of southern Bhutan to Phuentsholing, the primary land crossing into India. There's little reason to take this route unless you are headed to or from India, but it's a dramatic ride and gives you a sense of geographical continuity that flying into Paro doesn't. En route you'll pass gigantic 'Lost World' ferns that spill into the road and dozens of silver-threaded waterfalls, cascading off high cliffs into the mist.

Along this winding and dangerous 1½-lane highway you may want to point out to your driver the superbly cheesy Indian signboards that remind travellers, for example, that 'Speed is the knife that kills life', 'Speed thrills but kills', and 'Impatient on Road, patient of Hospital'. You can't say you haven't been warned…

## THIMPHU TO PHUENTSHOLING (172KM)

The trip by car from Thimphu to Phuentsholing takes about six hours. The route follows the first road in Bhutan, built in 1962 by Dantak, the Indian border-roads organisation, and it's still the most important road in the country. Road crews will be widening the road until 2010, eventually cutting travel time to around four hours.

The first stage of the trip is from Thimphu to Chhuzom (31km, one hour). See p131 for a description of this route (as travelled in the opposite direction, ie from Chhuzom to Thimphu).

### Chhuzom to Chapcha
23km / 45 mins

The road drops quickly, following the Wang Chhu south from Chhuzom. You can see the road to Haa climbing on the opposite side of the valley. The road passes beneath Dobji Dzong, which sits atop a promontory high above the river. Staying near the banks of the river, the road passes the settlement of Hebji Damchu (2020m). About 4km further on is the tiny Hotel Damchu, which has a huge parking lot and almost no business. Here the road starts climbing away from the river, making several switchbacks as it makes its way out of the valley.

Finally the road crests a ridge and passes the Chapcha Bjha (Chapcha Rocks), as you squeeze between a vertical rock face to the left and an equally vertical sheer drop to the right. Cross the Chapcha La to reach the Dantak road construction camp at Chapcha (2450m).

### Chapcha to Chhukha
34km / 1 hour

As you wind around the huge side valley from Chapcha look back to see the small Chapcha Dzong and, on a cliff far above to the right, the dramatic-looking Thadra Ney Lhakhang, built into the side of a rock face. The road switchbacks steeply down through lovely forest to the large Tachhong Zam (Most Excellent High Bridge) and the immigration checkpost of Tanalung. It then climbs the side of a steep forested slope 10km to Bunakha (2270m), where the **Tourist Hotel Bunagu** ( ☎ 08-460522; set meal Nu 260) caters to travellers who have booked in advance. The restaurant has a log-cabin feel, pleasant balcony seating and clean toilets.

From Bunakha the road passes a lovely waterfall to the goemba of Chhukha Rabdey. There is a large monk body here, which is expected to move into the district dzong when it is built in 2008. The monks perform the Chhukha tsechu each April. A few kilometres further on, in the lower part of Tsimasham (formerly Chimakothi) at 2210m, is the **Karma Hotel** ( ☎ 08-478221; r Nu 150), which has food and, across the road, renovated rooms. The Karma Transport buses stop here for lunch.

As the road switchbacks down to the Chhukha hydroelectric project the air gets thicker and warmer. Several side roads lead down to the dam site and the intake structures that divert the river into seven tunnels bored though the hill. The Chhukha and nearby Tala hydroelectric projects produce electricity for all of western Bhutan, with enough surplus to export to India.

Beyond the basic Deki Hotel & Bar there is an immigration checkpoint at the Thegchen Zam (Strong High Bridge), which takes the road to the west side of the Wang Chhu. This is the mid-point between Thimphu and Phuentsholing, both around 95km away.

### Chhukha to Gedu
38km / 1 hour

The road climbs to a lookout over the Chhukha project. The turbines are hidden inside the hillside (the entry is marked by a white needle-like monument), but you can see the transformers and the transmission station. Beside the distribution station is the yellow-roofed Zangto Pelri Lhakhang and the old Chhukha Dzong. Beyond the lookout is the first of several roads leading to the new (2007) 1020MW Tala hydroelectric project. This road leads 8.5km to the intake structure where water is diverted into a 22km-long tunnel.

The rest of the climb is over the ridge that separates the Wang Chhu valley from the Torsa Chhu drainage. The road passes the unfortunately named road construction camp of Wangkha, then climbs to a memorial chorten that commemorates an important official who died here in a road accident. Look out for the spectacular high waterfall visible to the east across the valley. There's then a short bridge over what's left of Toktokachhu Falls (also known as Takti Chhu), much diminished after a flood brought down a collection of huge boulders.

Atop the next ridge at 2020m is a Dantak canteen that specialises in *dosa*s (paper-thin pancakes made from lentil flour). It also has public toilets ('officers only'). Beyond a second road to the Tala project is another road-crew camp at Makaibari (Cornfield), then Asinabari (Field of Hailstones) and the small settlement of Chasilakha (*la kha* means 'grazing field'). About 9km before Gedu is the *shedra* of Tsatse Lhakhang.

Another climb leads to Gedu, a fair-sized village with several small restaurants near the road. The best bet for a meal is the **Lhamu Restaurant & Bar** ( ☎ 05-272332) at the south end of town, with great Nepali-style food and cheese *momos*. The nearby Laptshakha Lhakhang has some nice new murals.

Beyond Gedu a side road leads downhill to Mirching and the Tala power station and will eventually be completed all the way to join the Phuentsholing road just north of Rinchending.

## Gedu to Rinchending
**41km / 1¼ hours**
A short distance on from Gedu is a chorten that marks Jumja village at 2050m. Farmers here sell bottles of buttermilk and squares of local *datse* (cheese), wrapped up in banana leaves. The road makes a sharp bend and gingerly crosses the huge Jumja slide that often wipes away the road during the monsoon, closing the road for up to a week at a time. A sign apologises for

'inconvenience regretted'. Passing the Kuenga Chholing Lhakhang in the village of Kamji, the road turns a corner and starts to drop like a stone, winding its way down to the plains.

At Sorchen a road construction camp houses the workers who continually repair damage from the huge landslides that frequently close this section of road. A diversion ('bye pass') was built in 2001 to provide an alternative road for when the main road is blocked. A new road from Jumja to Phuentsholing via Pasakha should soon provide a short cut around this volatile section of road.

From the bottom of the slide area it's a 12km drive past an industrial area and army camp to the checkpoint at Rinchending.

## Rinchending to Phuentsholing
**5km / 10 minutes**
Rinchending is the former immigration checkpoint, where you may have to register. If you are heading northwards invest in the fruit stalls here as the price of bananas rises almost as quickly as the altitude.

Below Rinchending is the small **Kharbandi Goemba**, built in 1967 by the late royal grandmother Ashi Phuentso Choedron, who has had a winter residence here. The modern temple houses large statues of Sakyamuni, Zhabdrung Ngawang Namgyal and Guru Rinpoche. In the lush grounds are examples of eight different styles of Tibetan chortens.

Below Kharbandi the road switchbacks down to Phuentsholing, offering spectacular views over the Torsa Chhu valley as it bursts out from the hills onto the plains.

## PHUENTSHOLING
☎ 05
The small, sweltering border town of Phuentsholing sits opposite the much larger Indian bazaar town of Jaigaon, separated only by a flimsy fence and a much-photographed Bhutanese-style entrance gate. Coming from India you will notice an instantaneous change in the degree of cleanliness and organisation. Coming from Bhutan the new air is thick with the smells of the subcontinent. There's not a great deal to do here but keep cool and soak up the border atmosphere, as Bhutan blurs into India.

Just to the west of town is the wide flood plain of the Torsa Chhu, which in its upper reaches is known as the Amo Chhu and has its headwaters in Tibet's Chumbi valley. Several hours' walk away, on the opposite side of the Torsa Chhu, is the home of the Doya minority group.

## Orientation

The busy bazaar, called the upper market, is close to the border. From here the truck-clogged main road leads uphill to the post office, banks and government offices, then starts immediately climbing towards the capital, 172km away.

## Information

See p261 for information about visa and other formalities upon arrival in Phuentsholing for foreigners and Indian nationals. All the banks will swap Bhutanese ngultrums for Indian rupees, and vice versa.

**Bank of Bhutan** (Map p157; Samdrup Lam; ☽ 9am-1pm & 2-4pm Mon-Fri, 9am-12pm Sat) Only the main branch changes foreign currency, including travellers cheques.

**Bhutan National Bank** (Map p157; Samdrup Lam; ☽ 9am-3pm Mon-Fri, to 11am Sat)

**Bhutan Photo Studio** (Map p157; Gatoen Lam) One of several studios here for instant passport photos (Nu 20-50).

**DSB Books** (Map p157; ☎ 251898; Gechu Shopping Mall; ☽ 9am-9pm) Paperback novels, Indian newspapers and books about Bhutan.

**GPY Cyber Café** (Map p157; per hr Nu 40; ☽ 9am-9pm) Printing, photocopying and long-distance calls also possible; in the back of the Gechu Shopping Mall.

**Phuentsholing General Hospital** (☽ 254825) A new hospital is due to be completed in the north of town by 2007.

**WESTERN BHUTAN**

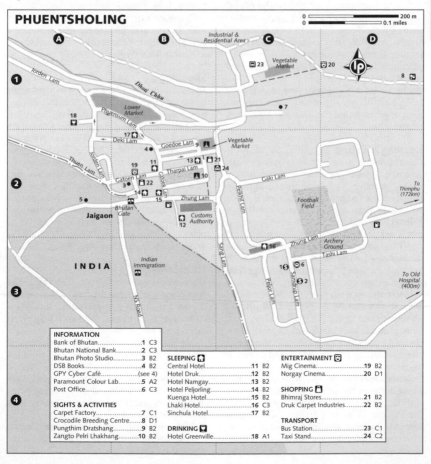

| INFORMATION | | |
|---|---|---|
| Bank of Bhutan | 1 | C3 |
| Bhutan National Bank | 2 | C3 |
| Bhutan Photo Studio | 3 | B2 |
| DSB Books | 4 | B2 |
| GPY Cyber Café | (see 4) | |
| Paramount Colour Lab | 5 | A2 |
| Post Office | 6 | C3 |

| SIGHTS & ACTIVITIES | | |
|---|---|---|
| Carpet Factory | 7 | C1 |
| Crocodile Breeding Centre | 8 | D1 |
| Pungthim Dratshang | 9 | B2 |
| Zangto Pelri Lhakhang | 10 | B2 |

| SLEEPING 🛏 | | |
|---|---|---|
| Central Hotel | 11 | B2 |
| Hotel Druk | 12 | B2 |
| Hotel Namgay | 13 | B2 |
| Hotel Peljorling | 14 | B2 |
| Kuenga Hotel | 15 | B2 |
| Lhaki Hotel | 16 | C3 |
| Sinchula Hotel | 17 | B2 |

| DRINKING 🍷 | | |
|---|---|---|
| Hotel Greenville | 18 | A1 |

| ENTERTAINMENT 🎭 | | |
|---|---|---|
| Mig Cinema | 19 | B2 |
| Norgay Cinema | 20 | D1 |

| SHOPPING 🛍 | | |
|---|---|---|
| Bhimraj Stores | 21 | B2 |
| Druk Carpet Industries | 22 | B2 |

| TRANSPORT | | |
|---|---|---|
| Bus Station | 23 | C1 |
| Taxi Stand | 24 | C2 |

**Post Office** (Map p157; Samdrup Lam; ⏰ 9am-5pm Mon-Fri, Sat to 1pm) Next to the Bank of Bhutan on a hill above the town.

## Sights

The modern **Zangto Pelri Lhakhang** is a replica of Guru Rinpoche's celestial paradise, though we're guessing the original isn't made out of concrete. There's not much to see but the surrounding garden is pleasant and there are always lots of pilgrims spinning prayer wheels.

If you have half an hour to kill, you can visit the sleepy collection of marsh mugger and gharial crocodiles at the **Crocodile Breeding Centre** (Map p157; free; ⏰ dawn-dusk), a 10-minute walk north of the bus station. The crocs are fed every other day at noon.

For an afternoon stroll, follow the prayer flag–lined Dhoti Chhu down to its confluence with the Torsa Chhu. In 1999 monsoon floods caused the river to jump its banks and submerge much of the town. An extensive embankment system now protects against a repeat performance.

The new **Pungthim Dratshang** is currently being built on the site of the former vegetable market to house the local *rabdey* (monk community).

## Sleeping & Eating

The following hotels all have rooms with attached toilets. The smaller hotels have a limited number of air-con rooms and fill up quickly with Indian extended families and businessmen, so book in advance.

**Hotel Druk** (Map p157; ☎ 252426; www.drukhotels .com; Zhung Lam; s/d Nu 2000/2500, deluxe s/d Nu 2900/3200; ✷) This old hotel is in a secluded spot near the Bhutan gate and has excellent rooms, with hot water in the mornings and evenings. The restaurant serves decent Indian food.

**Lhaki Hotel** (Map p157; ☎ 257111; lhakihotel@druknet .bt; Pelkhil Lam; s/d Nu 1800/2300, ste Nu 2800-4500; ✷ 🖳) The other main tourist place is this newly-built modern and marbly place, with clean and spacious rooms. There's a good restaurant here, plus a shopping arcade and a snooker hall in the basement.

**Hotel Namgay** (Map p157; ☎ 252374; hotel_namgay@ yahoo.com; Tharpai Lam; s/d Nu 1100/1300, deluxe s/d Nu 1300/1500; ste Nu 1750-2500; ✷ 🖳) Overlooking the Zangto Pelri Lhakhang, the Namgay is a step down in quality but still pleasant, with tropical plants in the lobby, and money exchange.

**Sinchula Hotel** (Map p157; ☎ 252589; hotelsinchula@ yahoo.com; Phuensum Lam; s/d Nu 450/650, deluxe Nu 550/750, AC 750/1000; ✷ 🖳) This older local hotel has clean, tiled rooms with hot-water bathroom, a good restaurant and a rooftop terrace bar. It's next to an old peepul tree.

Two hotels popular with Indian tourists are the **Central Hotel** (Map p157; ☎ 252172; central hotel@druknet.bt; cnr Tharpai & Gatoen Lams; s/d Nu 450/675, ste Nu 1000; ✷) and the old-fashioned **Kuenga Hotel** (Map p157; ☎ 252293; 5-53 Gatoen Lam; s/d Nu 200/360, deluxe s/d Nu 300/400). Only a few rooms at the Kuenga have hot water but the lobby restaurant is popular with locals.

Another local place is the noisy **Hotel Peljorling** (Map p157; ☎ 252833; Zhung Lam; s/d Nu 225/300, deluxe s/d 400/600), with a good restaurant and bar but basic rooms.

The main hotels all have good restaurants, with Indian and Bhutanese dishes the best bet. The Peljorling menu boasts sizzlers and a 'Macdonalds Burger'.

## Shopping

Phuentsholing has the cheapest consumer goods in Bhutan and many Bhutanese come here especially to load up on shopping trips. It's also one of the cheapest places to have a *gho* made. **Bhimraj Stores** (Map p157), in the bazaar, sells a range of cloth from Nu 120 to 200 per metre; you'll need about 3.75m for a *gho*.

**Druk Carpet Industries** has a factory in north of town where you can see Bhutanese carpets being woven by hand from imported New Zealand wool. The **showroom** (Map p157; ☎ 252004; ⏰ 9am-8pm Wed-Mon) in town is the place if you are looking to buy. An 18in-by-48in carpet costs around US$400.

## Entertainment

If you like Hindi movies, you are in luck. The **Mig Cinema** (Map p157) in the centre of town and the **Norgay Cinema** (Map p157) near the Dhoti Chhu at the north end of town offer several three-hour screenings daily.

For a cold beer, watch the border traffic over a bottle of Indian Fosters (Nu 50) in the terrace of the Hotel Peljorling or star gaze on the roof terrace of the Sinchula Hotel. More earthy is the funky bar at the Bhutan Hotel, though you might get more attention than you can handle here.

The garden bar at the **Hotel Greenville** (Map p157; Jorden Lam) is a good place to get some peace and quiet.

### Getting There & Away

For details on getting to and from India see p261.

Companies like Dawa Transport, Karma Transport and De-Keeling run morning Coaster minibuses from the new bus station to Thimphu (Nu 171) and Paro (Nu 165), with a few weekly services to Haa and Punakha. There are early-morning buses to Siliguri (3½ hours) but these aren't really set up for foreigners as you would have to detour via immigration en route. Bhutan Post has one 3pm bus to Kolkata (Nu 300), arriving the next morning.

There is talk of building an international airport in Phuentsholing but there are no concrete plans at present.

# GASA DZONGKHAG

Gasa is in the far north of the country. Previously a subdistrict of Punakha, it was upgraded to a dzongkhag in 1993, with headquarters in Gasa's Trashi Thongmoen Dzong.

The only way to get here is on foot. The Gasa Hot Springs and Jhomolhari treks touch on the region but only the epic Laya–Gasa and Snowman treks take you through all three districts. For more on the region see p222.

### GASA

The village of Gasa is north of Punakha on the old trade route to Tibet and has a renovated 17th-century dzong. There is a road from Punakha to Damji in Gasa dzongkhag, but the final 18km is not yet complete.

### LAYA

Laya is a large, isolated region in the far northwest of the Gasa district near the Tibetan border. The roughly 800 people of this area are from a group called the Layap, who have their own distinct language, customs and, most famously, conical bamboo hats with a bamboo spike at the top, which makes Laya women instantly recognisable.

The region is believed to be one of Bhutan's *bey-yul* (hidden lands).

### LINGZHI

In the far northwestern corner of the country, Lingzhi is a very isolated region, mostly above 4000m. From whatever direction you approach it, it's necessary to trek for days and cross a 4500m-plus pass to reach it.

The Lingzhi La at the head of the valley was a trade route between Punakha and the Tibetan town of Gyantse and was also used by Tibetan armies during various attacks on Bhutan.

# SOUTHERN DZONGKHAGS

The following dzongkhags are generally closed to tourists.

### TSIRANG DZONGKHAG

This district (previously spelt 'Chirang') is in the south of the country, but is separated from the southern border by Sarpang Dzongkhag.

The major town is Damphu, reached by a road leading south from Wangdue Phodrang. The road passes through Sankosh, said to be the hottest place in the country, then continues southeast from Damphu to the border town of Sarpang.

### DAGANA DZONGKHAG

This dzongkhag, previously known as Daga, is accessed from Wangdue Phodrang. The administrative headquarters is in Dagana and the region is noted for farming and cattle production. It is said that the people of 17th-century Dagana were lawless and out of control, and Zhabdrung Ngawang Namgyal sent Donyer Druk Namgyal with soldiers to conquer them. Druk Namgyal built the dzong in 1655 and gave it the name Daga Trashi Yangtse Dzong.

### SAMTSE DZONGKHAG

Samtse (previously spelt 'Samchi') is in the far southwest. Access is from India, though a road is under construction from Phuentsholing. The Teachers' Training College is here, as is the factory that produces the ubiquitous Druk-brand tinned fruit and jams.

Early British expeditions used a route through Samtse to travel to the centre of Bhutan. From Darjeeling they crossed over the hills of Samtse to Haa, then over the Cheli La to Paro.

# Central Bhutan

There is a great variety of people, architecture and scenery in central Bhutan. Because it takes a little extra time to get here, the countryside and hotels see fewer tourists than in Thimphu, Paro and Punakha. In fact, until the 1970s the only way to reach this part of Bhutan was on foot or atop a sure-footed horse.

Across the 3420m-high Pele La and the Black Mountains is the large, fertile Mangde Chhu valley and the great Trongsa Dzong. Commanding the junction of three major roads, Trongsa has long been the glue that holds the country together. Even today the Crown Prince must serve as the *penlop* (regional governor) of the dzong before he can rule as king.

A short drive over the mountains from Trongsa leads to the four valleys of Bumthang, a magical region of saints and treasure-seekers, great demon-subduing struggles and fabulous miracles, rich with relics from the visits of Guru Rinpoche and Pema Lingma. This forested landscape is Bhutan's cultural heartland. For the visitor it offers several of Bhutan's best and oldest monasteries, some great day hikes and short treks and spectacular festivals, primarily at Jampey Lhakhang and nearby Ura. Bumthang is one of the real highlights of Bhutan.

In the south the Royal Manas National Park protects a region of tropical vegetation and rich biodiversity. It's hoped that the park will soon reopen to foreigners.

## HIGHLIGHTS

- Explore sprawling **Trongsa Dzong** (p164), one of the most dramatic examples of traditional Bhutanese architecture
- Stretch your legs on one of the many excellent hikes in the **Bumthang valley** (p171)
- Pay a visit to **Kurjey Lhakhang** (p173), **Jampey Lhakhang** (p172) and **Tamshing Lhakhang** (p176), Bumthang's most spectacular ancient temples
- Pause at **Chendebji Chorten** (opposite): smaller, but patterned after, Swayambhunath in Kathmandu, en route to Trongsa
- Head up the Tang Valley to the hundred-year-old **Ogyen Chholing Palace** (p178), now home to a fine museum and guesthouse retreat
- Time your visit to take in the **Ura festival** (p179) or leave the groups behind and linger in the nearby traditional village of **Shingkhar** (p179)

## History

Central Bhutan is believed to be the first part of Bhutan to have been inhabited, with evidence of prehistoric settlements in the Ura valley of Bumthang and the southern region of Khyeng. These and many other valleys were separate principalities ruled by independent kings. One of the most important of these kings was the 8th-century Indian Sindhu Raja of Bumthang, who was eventually converted to Buddhism by Guru Rinpoche (see p173). Bumthang continued to be a separate kingdom, ruled from Jakar, until the time of Zhabdrung Ngawang Namgyal in the 17th century.

During the rule of the first *desi* (secular ruler), Tenzin Drugyey, all of eastern Bhutan came under the control of the Drukpa government in Punakha. Chhogyel Mingyur Tenpa unified central and eastern Bhutan into eight provinces known as Shachho Khorlo Tsegay. He was then promoted to Trongsa *penlop* (governor).

Because of Trongsa Dzong's strategic position, the *penlop* exerted great influence over the entire country. It was from Trongsa that Jigme Namgyal, father of the first king, rose to power.

Bumthang retained its political importance during the rule of the first and second kings, both of whom had their principal residence at Wangdichholing Palace in Jakar. Several impressive royal residences and country estates remain in the region, including at Kuenga Rabten, Eundu Chholing and Urgyen Chholing.

# TRONGSA DZONGKHAG

## WANGDUE PHODRANG TO TRONGSA (129KM)

It takes about four hours to drive between the windswept town of Wangdi (Wangdue Phodrang's colloquial name) in western Bhutan, and Trongsa. The route crosses the Black Mountains over the Pele La (3420m) before entering the broad, heavily cultivated Mangde Chhu valley. See p151 for details of the drive from Wangdi to the Pele La.

### Pele La to Chendebji
#### 27km / 1 hour

From Pele La the road drops through hillsides of a strange dwarf bamboo called *cham*. This bamboo never gets large enough to harvest for any useful purpose, but when it is small it is a favourite food of yaks and horses. The

area near Pele La is probably the best place in Bhutan to see yaks from the road. Be alert, though, as these great shaggy beasts are skittish and likely to run off into the forest when your vehicle approaches.

The road drops into the evergreen forests of the Longte valley, passing Kgebji village and the Tashi Choeling Restaurant below the high village of Longte. The groups of small white numbered houses along the road here are quarters for road-maintenance crews.

Lower down into the valley the vegetation changes to broadleaf species and bamboo. The road passes opposite **Rukubji** village with its big school and goemba at the end of a huge alluvial fan believed to be the body of a giant snake. The houses in this village are clustered closely together, an unusual layout for Bhutan. Surrounding the village are extensive fields of mustard, potatoes, barley and wheat.

About 16km from the pass keep an eye open on the left for the roadside rock inscription and mural that was left here in 2002 for the filming of the Bhutanese movie *Travellers and Magicians*. After the Buddhist blessing come the words 'Scene 112, take 101'!

The road enters a side valley and drops to **Sephu** (2610m), next to the bridge that spans the Nikka Chhu. This is the end point of the 25-day Snowman trek that starts from Paro and passes through the remote Lunana district (see p237). You could stop briefly to examine the bamboo mats and baskets for sale here, though most of the products are functional items. The larger baskets, called *zhim*, are tied to horses' pack saddles to transport goods. Tsering's Restaurant cum Bar beside the bridge offers *momos* (dumplings), tea and a clean toilet.

The road follows the Nikka Chhu to two chortens that mark the river's confluence with the Nyala Chhu. It is then a gentle, winding descent through rhododendrons, blue pines, spruces, oaks and dwarf bamboo to the village of Chendebji, recognisable by the yellow roof of its *lhakhang* (chapel), on the far bank. This was a night halt for mule caravans travelling from Trongsa during the reign of the second king.

Two kilometres beyond Chendebji village is **Chendebji Chorten**, at a lovely spot by a river confluence. The large white chorten is patterned after Swayambhunath in Kathmandu and was built in the 19th century by Lama Shida, from Tibet, to cover the remains of an evil spirit that was killed here. The proper name of this structure is Chorten Charo

Kasho; it is the westernmost monument in a 'chorten path' that was the route of early Buddhist missionaries. (The easternmost monument in this path is Chorten Kora in Trashi Yangtse.) The nearby Bhutanese-style chorten was constructed in 1982. Bring some insect repellent to fight off the persistent flies.

Just 500m past the chorten is the **Hotel Chandbjee/Urgyen Dorji Tabdea Restaurant** ☎ 490052; lunch buffet Nu 285, a popular lunch spot and gift shop run by the owners of the Dochu La Hotel.

## Chendebji to Trongsa
41km / 1¼ hours

From the chorten the road passes a few farms, crosses a side stream and climbs again to a ridge, passing above the village of Tangsibji. The valley widens and the road turns a corner into the broad Mangde Chhu valley. The shrubs along this part of the road are edgeworthia, which is used to make paper. The brown monkeys you will probably see are rhesus macaques.

At Tashiling, next to the 'Thinley Zangmo Shop And Bar', you'll see the new **Potala Lhakhang**, consecrated in late 2005 by the Je Khenpo. Inside is a fine 9m-tall statue of Chenresig, alongside a wrathful Guru Rinpoche.

After the road weaves in and out of side valleys for another 5km you finally get a view of Trongsa and the huge, sprawling white dzong that seems to hang in space at

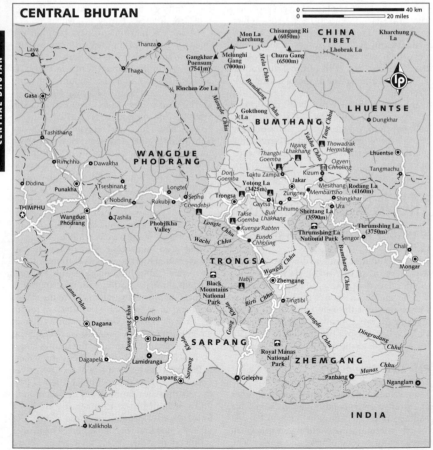

CENTRAL BHUTAN

the head of the valley. On the opposite side of the huge Mangde Chhu valley you can see the road that heads south to Zhemgang and Gelephu near the Indian border. A **viewpoint** next to a small chorten by the road offers a good place for a picnic and photo stop. The dzong looks almost close enough to touch but is still 14km away. There are plans to restore the old footpath between here and Trongsa Dzong.

To reach Trongsa, you switchback into the upper reaches of the Mangde Chhu valley, cross the raging river at the Bjee Zam checkpost, and then climb again above the north bank of the river, past a waterfall and the Yangkhil Resort, before pulling into town.

## TRONGSA

☎ 03 / elev 2180m

Trongsa is smack in the middle of the country, a seven-hour drive from Thimphu, and separated from both east and west by high mountain ranges. The dzong and surrounding town is perched above a gorge, with fine views of the Black Mountains to the southwest. It's a relaxed and pleasant town, lined with the whitewashed wooden façades of shops decorated with potted plants.

Trongsa Dzong has a rich history dating back to the 16th century. The first construction on the site of the dzong was carried out by Lam Ngagi Wangchuck, son of Ngawang Chhojey, who established Pangri Zampa in Thimphu (see p115). He came to Trongsa in 1541 and built a *tshamkhang* (meditation room) after discovering self-manifested hoofprints belonging to the horse of the protector deity Pelden Lhamo. Trongsa ('New Village' in the local dialect) gets its name from the retreats, temples and hermit residences that soon grew up around the chapel.

The town received a large influx of Tibetan immigrants in the late 1950s and early 1960s, and Bhutanese of Tibetan descent run most shops here. The Tibetans are so well assimilated into Bhutanese society that there is almost no indication of Tibetan flavour in the town.

## Orientation

The main road from the west traverses above the dzong and passes the weekend vegetable market and small Thruepang Palace (closed to visitors), where the third king, Jigme Dorji Wangchuck, was born in 1928.

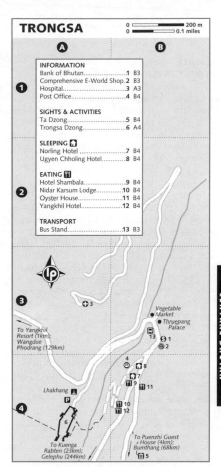

**TRONGSA**

0 — 200 m
0 — 0.1 miles

**INFORMATION**
Bank of Bhutan.........................1 B3
Comprehensive E-World Shop.2 B3
Hospital...................................3 A3
Post Office..............................4 B4

**SIGHTS & ACTIVITIES**
Ta Dzong.................................5 B4
Trongsa Dzong........................6 A4

**SLEEPING**
Norling Hotel..........................7 B4
Ugyen Chholing Hotel.............8 B4

**EATING**
Hotel Shambala.......................9 B4
Nidar Karsum Lodge..............10 B4
Oyster House.........................11 B4
Yangkhil Hotel.......................12 B4

**TRANSPORT**
Bus Stand.............................13 B3

To Yangkhil Resort (1km); Wangdue Phodrang (129km)

Vegetable Market
Thruepang Palace

Lhakhang

To Kuenga Rabten (23km); Gelephu (244km)

To Puenzhi Guest House (4km); Bumthang (68km)

**CENTRAL BHUTAN**

The road climbs to a cluster of shops and hotels that form the bazaar. A traffic circle marks the junction of the road that leads south to Gelephu. A short walk down this road offers good views back to the dzong.

The road east goes uphill from the traffic circle. A short walk on this road leads to a steep, narrow path that will take you to the Ta Dzong watchtower.

## Information

**Bank of Bhutan** (Map p163; ☎ 521123; ☷ 9am-1pm Mon-Fri, to 11am Sat) You need a photocopy of the cheque to change travellers cheques here.
**Comprehensive E-World Shop** (Map p163; ☷ 8.30am-noon & 1-6.30pm Thu-Tue; per min Nu 2) Internet access.

**Post Office** (Map p163; ☙ 8.30am-5pm Mon-Fri, to 1pm Sat)

## Sights

### TRONGSA DZONG

This commanding dzong, high above the roaring Mangde Chhu, is perhaps the most spectacularly sited dzong in Bhutan, with a sheer drop to the south that often just disappears into cloud and mist. The rambling collection of buildings trails down the ridge in a remarkable succession of streetlike corridors, wide stone stairs and beautiful stone courtyards.

The southernmost part of the dzong, Chorten Lhakhang, is the location of the first hermitage, built in 1543. The actual dzong was built in its present form in 1644 by Chhogyel Mingyur Tenpa, the official who was sent by the Zhabdrung to unify eastern Bhutan. It was then enlarged at the end of the 17th century by the *desi*, Tenzin Rabgye. Its official name is Chhoekhor Raptentse Dzong, and it is also known by its short name of Choetse Dzong.

The dzong's strategic location gave it great power over this part of the country. The only trail between eastern and western Bhutan still leads straight through Trongsa and used to run directly through the dzong itself. This gave the Trongsa *penlop* enviable control over east–west trade and the tax revenue to be derived from it. Today visitors enter through the main eastern gate but there are plans to renovate and revive the old footpath and cantilever bridge over the Mangde Chhu, allowing tourists to hike up to Trongsa (two hours) from the current viewing area by the chorten (see p161) and enter the dzong via the eastern gate, in traditional fashion.

Trongsa Dzong is the ancestral home of Bhutan's royal family. The first two hereditary kings ruled from this dzong, and tradition still dictates that the crown prince serve as Trongsa *penlop* before acceding to the throne. When the current crown prince became *penlop* in 2004 the yellow roof was repainted red. The Trongsa *rabdey* (monastic body) migrates between winter (Trongsa) and summer (Bumthang) residences, just as the main *dratshang* (monk body) does between Thimphu and Punakha (see p135).

There are 23 separate lhakhangs in the dzong, though what you get to see depends on which keys are available. The dzong was severely damaged in the 1897 earthquake and repairs were carried out by the *penlop* of Trongsa, Jigme Namgyal, father of Bhutan's first king. Most of the existing fine decoration was designed during the rule of the first king, Ugyen Wangchuck. The dzong was recently renovated by the Austrian team that is currently working on the nearby Ta Dzong.

The atmospheric northern **assembly hall** is still preserved as it was during his reign. There is a painting of the court as it was then, and other paintings of the guardians of the four directions and the deity Phurba in the main hall. There is also a 17th-century mural depicting Swayambhunath in Nepal and another with a pictorial map of Lhasa. The main chapel to the south, the **Chorten Lhakhang**, houses the funerary chorten of the founder Ngagi Wangchuck.

The five-day Trongsa tsechu is held in the northern courtyard in December or January.

### TA DZONG

This watchtower on the hill above the dzong has been converted to a state-of-the-art museum by the same Austrian-financed team that renovated the excellent Patan Museum in Nepal. The displays, which should open in mid-2008, will focus on Buddhist art and the history of the monarchy. Views from the fifth-floor roof will be unrivalled. A café is planned.

A chapel inside the tower is dedicated to the 19th-century *penlop* of Trongsa, Jigme Namgyal. Two British soldiers are said to have been kept in the dungeon here for several months during the Duar War.

## Sleeping & Eating

**Amankora** (www.amanresorts.com; s/d full board US$925/1000) plan to open a hotel above the dzong by 2008.

**Yangkhil Resort** (Map p163; ☎ 521417; yangkhilresort@druknet.bt; s/d Nu 1600/1800, deluxe s/d Nu 1900/2300; ☐ ) This resort, 1.5km west of town, should be your first choice, with rooms lined on a terrace to look back toward the dzong. Rooms are spacious and comfortable with a nice balcony and extremely comfortable beds. The pleasant grounds and sitting areas make it a great place to relax, so arrange your itinerary to ensure an early arrival or late departure. Request one of the six view rooms in advance, as some rooms have only partial views.

**Puenzhi Guest House** (Map p163; ☎ 521197; puenzhi@druknet.bt; s/d Nu 800/1000, deluxe r Nu 1500) A 4km drive above the town leads to this place, run by the former governor of Trongsa. The simple but cosy new rooms at the top are the best and come with a private balcony; next best are the rooms below the restaurant. Literally bottom of the heap are the cottages below. The restaurant balcony offers great aerial views of Trongsa Dzong and steep footpaths lead down to the Ta Dzong.

**Norling Hotel** (Map p163; ☎ 521171; fax 521178; s/d Nu 1050/1200) This concrete hotel occupies a spot somewhere between a local and tourist hotel. The food in the pleasant dining room is quite good and there's BBC World on the TV.

**Ugyen Chholing Hotel** (Map p163; ☎ 521400; r Nu 250-400) This family-run inn is probably the best of the cheapies, with a decent restaurant, western-style bathroom and hot-water geyser.

Several small, friendly places offer simple wooden rooms upstairs and Tibetan-style restaurants and a shop downstairs. These include the **Yangkhil Hotel** (Map p163; ☎ 521126), **Nidar Karsum Lodge** (Map p163; ☎ 521133) and **Hotel Shambala** (Map p163; ☎ 521135). Expect to pay about Nu 60 for a meal of rice, curry and vegetables or Nu 250 for a double room.

**The Oyster House** (Map p163 ☎ 521413) This new upper-floor restaurant is popular with young Bhutanese attracted to its full-sized snooker table. The Indian and Bhutanese dishes are good but they only really serve a fraction of the stuff on the menu. There are a few basic rooms out back.

## AROUND TRONGSA
### Kuenga Rabten

The winter palace of the second king, Jigme Wangchuck, is 23km (one hour) south of Trongsa. It's an interesting drive, passing below Takse Goemba (after 17km), several huge waterfalls, and the fertile rice terraces of the lower Mangde Chhu valley. It's a good half- or three-quarter-day side trip from Trongsa and could even make for a fine bike trip if you can arrange to be picked up at Kuenga Rabten. Traffic is light and it's all downhill from Trongsa!

The palace is under the care of the National Commission for Cultural Affairs so you don't need a special permit to enter. The first storey of the U-shaped building was used to store food; the second was the residence of royal attendants and the army; and the third housed the royal quarters and the king's private chapel. Part of this floor has been converted into a library and books from the National Library are stored here. Sandwiched between the king's and queen's quarters is the Sangye Lhakhang, with statues of Sakyamuni, the Zhabdrung and Guru Rinpoche (take your shoes off for this chapel).

A 15-minute hike uphill from the building is the **Karma Drubdey Nunnery**, which is currently being expanded by its 85 hard-working *anim* (nuns).

A further 25km down the valley is **Eundu Chholing**, the winter palace of the first king, Ugyen Wangchuck. From Kuenga Rabten the road drops down in huge loops, past Refey village to the river and road camp at Yourmu, and then 2km later branches up a dirt road to the palace. The building belongs to a local *dasho* (nobleman) but is looked after by the *dzongpen* (master of the dzong) and tourists can normally visit. The second-floor *goenkhang* (chapel devoted to protective deities; men only) has a highly venerated chorten of Pema Lingpa, as well as a fabulous collection of arms and a lovely *dramnyen* (lute). The entry chapel has some of the finest murals you'll see, depicting the mythical kingdoms of Zangto Pelri and Sukhavati.

# BUMTHANG DZONGKHAG

The Bumthang region encompasses four major valleys: Chokhor, Tang, Ura and Chhume. Because the dzongs and the most important temples are in the large Chokhor valley, it is commonly referred to as the Bumthang valley.

There are two versions of the origin of the name Bumthang. The valley is supposed to be shaped like a *bumpa,* the vessel of holy water that is usually found on the altar of a lhakhang. *Thang* means 'field' or 'flat place'. The less respectful translation relates to the particularly beautiful women who live here – *bum* means 'girl'.

For a more detailed map of the region, see p230.

## TRONGSA TO JAKAR (68KM)

The 2½-hour run between Trongsa and Jakar, the main town in Bumthang, is one of the easier and more interesting drives in Bhutan because it passes numerous villages and goembas as it winds through the Chhume valley.

### Trongsa to Yotong La
**28km / 1 hour**
The road quickly switchbacks up the ridge above Trongsa, climbing steeply for 7km

past the Puenzhi Guest House to a viewpoint where you can look down on the town and dzong. It's then a 5km climb past the small Dorji Goemba to the head of a valley. Finally the road traverses across the top of the valley to a Tibetan chorten and array of prayer flags atop the **Yotong La** (3425m). The old trade route to eastern Bhutan parallels the modern road as it crosses the pass.

## Yotong La to Zungney
### 24km / 1 hour

The descent from the pass is through firs, then blue pines and bamboo. The road enters the upper part of the Chhume valley, marked by the small roadside Chuchi Lhakhang at Gaytsa. On a hill 10 minutes' walk to the north of Gaytsa is the Nyingma school **Buli Lhakhang**, built by Tukse Chhoying, the son of Dorji Lingpa (1346–1405) and recently renovated with assistance from the American Himalayan Foundation (see www.ahf-bhutan.com for details). On the ground floor is the Jowo Lhakhang, with some impressive 12-sided pillars, or *kachens,* and on the upper floor is the Sangay (or Sangey) Lhakhang, named after images of the past, present and future Buddhas. The mural by the window depicts Dorji Lingpa. Look above the stairs to the upper story for a slate carving of the local protective deity. A few black-necked cranes winter in the fields to the northeast of the village.

The red roofs of **Tharpaling Goemba** are visible above the trees on a cliff to the northeast. Nyingma (Dzogchen) philosopher and saint Longchen Rabjampa (1308–63) founded Tharpaling in the 14th century as part of eight *lings* (outlying temples) and lived here for many years, fathering two children. It has several temples, and houses about 100 monks. It's possible to visit the goemba by driving 10km up a rough road just past the turn to Buli

Lhakhang or by trekking over the hill from Jakar (see p170). After heavy rain the road turns to the consistency of butter tea but it's currently being upgraded. Above Tharpaling, at about 3800m, is the large white hermitage of Choedrak Goemba, which consists of two ancient chapels separated by a chorten and a sacred spring. The Thukje Lhakhang to the right has a central 1000-armed statue of Chenresig, whose offerings include Glenfiddich whisky and Coke. The Lorepa Lhakhang contains a stone footprint of Guru Rinpoche and the stone skull of a *dakini* (khandroma, or female celestial being)! Further uphill is the Zhambhala Lhakhang, named after the popular God of Wealth. Pilgrims ask for boons here at a set of circular grooves in the rock behind the lhakhang, which contains the surprisingly grand funeral chorten of Nyoshul Khen Rinpoche. Pema Lingpa revealed several *terma* (sacred texts and artefacts) near these monasteries.

From Gaytsa the road follows the Gaytsa Chhu gently down the valley for 2km to Domkhar. A dirt road branches south for about 900m to **Domkhar Trashi Chholing Dzong**, the summer palace of the second king. It was completed in 1937 and is a replica of Kuenga Rabten (see p165). It served for years as the residence of the grand queen mother, and now serves as a guesthouse for the crown prince, and so is closed to visitors. The monastic school to the south was built in 1968 by the previous reincarnation of the Karmapa, the head of the Karmapa lineage, but it is not currently in use.

Beyond Domkhar village, past Hurjee, is the settlement of Chhume, with two large schools alongside more than 500m of straight road, perhaps the longest stretch of its kind in the hills of Bhutan. Speed bumps have been strategically placed to ensure that your driver does not take advantage of this to make up time!

---

### YATHRA

Hand-spun, hand-woven wool strips with patterns specific to the Bumthang region are called *yathras*. They mostly have geometric designs, sometimes with a border. Three strips may be joined to produce a blanket or bed-cover called a *charkep*. In earlier days *yathras* were often used as shawls or raincoats to protect against the winter cold of Bumthang. *Yathras* were once made from wool from Tibet; nowadays some of the wool is imported from New Zealand and some wool is used from nearby Australian-supported sheep-breeding projects.

Since Bhutan does not have the carpet-weaving tradition of Tibet, *yathra* pieces have often served the same function as Tibetan rugs. Today *yathras* are fashioned into *toegos,* the short jackets that women often wear over the *kira* in cold weather.

A further 1km on is **Sangay Arts and Crafts**, a crafts shop that has a great cartoon mural of three phalluses above the entry. At nearby Zungney you pass the 1.5MW Chhume mini-hydro plant, which supplies electricity to Trongsa and Bumthang. Just before Zungney a new paved road branches off to Nimalung Goemba (see below).

Stop at the two shops at the eastern end of Zungney village to watch the weavers. The speciality here is *yathra,* distinctive strips of woven woollen fabric in numerous colours and patterns. You can buy single strips of cloth or woollen jackets and blankets. Zungney Lhakhang is the small building to the west of the first *yathra* shop. Just past Zungney look out for some unusual two-storey prayer wheels.

## Zungney to Jakar
### 16km / 30 mins
East of Zungney, **Prakhar Goemba** is visible on a promontory on the opposite side of the river. It's a charming 10-minute walk to the three-storey goemba, which was built as a residence by Dawa Gyaltshen, a son of the famous Pema Lingpa (see the boxed text, p175). On the ground floor is a statue of Sakyamuni crafted by artists from Nepal. On the middle floor are statues of Guru Tshengay, one of the eight manifestations of Guru Rinpoche. The top floor contains nine small chortens and murals that are as old as the goemba. The Prakhar tsechu is held in autumn (middle of the ninth month) in the courtyard of a nearby newer building.

A stiff 20-minute walk uphill from Prakhar leads to **Nimalung Goemba**, a Nyingma monastery that was founded in 1935 by Dorling Trulku. It now houses more than 100 monks who study here in the *shedra* (monastic school). The ground-floor inner chapel contains a venerated statue of Drolma (Tara) inside an amulet. Walk behind the cabinets full of statues to see the collection of black hats used during the tsechu in the fifth month (around July). Also here are large metal boxes, one of which holds a large festival *thondrol* (huge *thangka*, painted or embroidered religious picture) that was donated to the monastery in 1994. The upper floor is a *goenkhang* (chapel devoted to protective deities). Outside you might catch the monks playing *kuru*, a game that is part darts, part archery.

The road follows the valley down past the apple orchards of Mangar and into blue-pine forests. A new road is being built from here to Ura, bypassing Bumthang. It's a short climb to the Kiki La, a crest at 2860m marked by a chorten and many prayer flags. Once over the side ridge, the road descends into the Chokhor valley.

## JAKAR
☎ 03 / elev 2580m
Near the foot of the Chokhor valley, Jakar (or Chakkar) is the major trading centre of the region. This will probably be your base for several days as you visit the surrounding valleys.

Jakar itself is a fairly interesting one-street town, with a goldsmith, tailor, several butchers and a hardware store, and it's worth a quick wander. As with other towns in Bhutan, Jakar plans to shift location to a new town, just north of the Sey Lhakhang, though no date has been given as yet for the move.

Bumthang has some important festivals, of which the most important is the Jampey Lhakhang Drup, in the ninth month (October). The recently introduced three-day Bumthang tsechu, a week earlier, features mask dancing in the dzong. Tamshing, Nyang and Ura monasteries all have large festivals. See p247 for dates.

There is a strong wind from the south every afternoon, which makes Jakar nippy in the evenings.

## Orientation
The road from Trongsa enters Jakar from the south, passing a football field that doubles as an army helipad. A traffic circle and the 14th-century Jakar Lhakhang mark the centre of the town

The main street leads east from here to a bridge over the Chamkhar Chhu. Just before you cross the bridge to leave the town, a small chorten marks the spot where a Tibetan general's head was buried after the defeat of a 17th-century Tibetan invasion force. From the bridge roads lead north to the Swiss Guest House and the east bank of the Chamkhar Chhu, and south to Mongar and eastern Bhutan.

## Information
**Bank of Bhutan** ( ☎ 631123; 🕘 9am-1pm Mon-Fri, to 11am Sat)
**Bhutan Broadcasting Service** ( 🕘 9am-5pm Mon-Fri, 9am-1pm Sat; per min Nu 1) Slow but cheap internet access on a hill at the south end of town.

CENTRAL BHUTAN

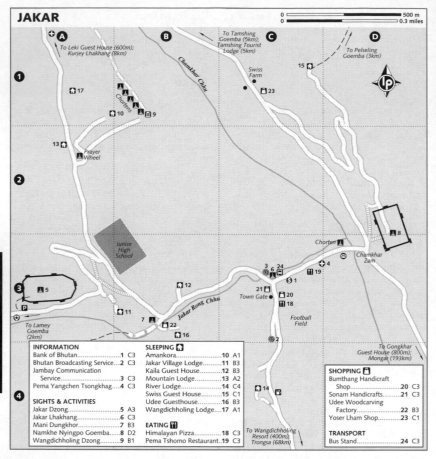

**JAKAR**

INFORMATION
Bank of Bhutan.............................1 C3
Bhutan Broadcasting Service....2 C3
Jambay Communication
  Service.....................................3 C3
Pema Yangchen Tsongkhag....4 C3

SIGHTS & ACTIVITIES
Jakar Dzong...............................5 A3
Jakar Lhakhang...........................6 C3
Mani Dungkhor...........................7 B3
Namkhe Nyingpo Goemba....8 D2
Wangdichholing Dzong...............9 B1

SLEEPING
Amankora....................................10 A1
Jakar Village Lodge...........11 B3
Kaila Guest House............12 B3
Mountain Lodge...............13 A2
River Lodge......................14 C4
Swiss Guest House...........15 C1
Udee Guesthouse.............16 B3
Wangdichholing Lodge...17 A1

EATING
Himalayan Pizza...............18 C3
Pema Tshomo Restaurant.19 C3

SHOPPING
Bumthang Handicraft
  Shop..............................20 C3
Sonam Handicrafts.........21 C3
Udee Woodcarving
  Factory.........................22 B3
Yoser Lham Shop............23 C1

TRANSPORT
Bus Stand.......................24 C3

**Jambay Communication Service** (⏰ 8am-7.30pm; per min Nu 2) Internet access.
**Pema Yangchen Tsongkhag** For medical supplies.

## Sights
### JAKAR DZONG
According to legend, when the lamas assembled in about 1549 to select a site for a monastery, a big white bird rose suddenly in the air and settled on a spur of a hill. This was interpreted as an important omen, and the hill was chosen as the site for a monastery and for **Jakar Dzong**, which roughly translates as 'castle of the white bird'. The Zhabdrung's great-grandfather, Ngagi Wangchuck, founded the monastery.

Jakar Dzong is in a picturesque location overlooking the Chokhor valley. The current structure was built in 1667 and has a circumference of more than 1500m. Its official name is Yuelay Namgyal Dzong, in honour of the victory over the troops of Tibetan ruler Phuntsho Namgyal. The *utse* (central tower) is unusually situated on the outside wall, so there is no way to circumambulate it. A covered passage leads from the dzong down the hill to a nearby spring – a feature that ensured water could be obtained in the event of a long siege.

The approach to the dzong is made on foot along a stone-paved path. The entrance leads into a narrow courtyard surrounded by administrative offices. The *utse* is on the east side of the courtyard and beyond that is the monks' quarters and the district court. At the west end of the dzong is a slightly larger courtyard surrounded by administrative offices. Behind here, outside the main dzong, is a half-round *ta dzong,* or watchtower.

Compared to other dzongs, there are relatively few wood carvings here; most of the timber is decorated with paintings.

Even if the chapels are closed it's a worthwhile climb for the views of the Chokhor valley from the front courtyard.

### WANGDICHHOLING DZONG

The extensive **palace** of Wangdichholing was built in 1857 on the site of a battle camp of the *penlop* of Trongsa, Jigme Namgyal. It was the first palace in Bhutan that was not designed as a fortress. Namgyal's son, King Ugyen Wangchuck, the first King of Bhutan, chose it as his principal residence. The entire court moved from Wangdichholing to Kuenga Rabten (see p165) each winter in a procession that took three days. Wangdichholing was also for a time the home of the third king, before he moved the court to Punakha in 1952.

Wangdichholing was inherited by Ashi Choeki Wangchuck, an aunt of the present king, and the grand but rather neglected building is now used as a *lobdra* (school for younger novices). There are five giant prayer wheels inside square chortens just to the north. The impressive building next door is the Amankora resort.

### NAMKHE NYINGPO GOEMBA

On the hill to the east of Jakar is the **Namkhe Nyingpo Goemba**. This Nyingma monastery was founded in the 1970s and has more than 300 monks in residence. The new prayer hall has massive statues of Guru Rinpoche, Chenresig and Sakyamuni. If you're here between 4.30pm and 6pm check out the mass debating in the courtyard of the *shedra,* behind the main monastery, where monks reinforce their theological arguments with a stamp of the foot and a victorious slap. Don't disturb the debating with your photography.

### LAMEY GOEMBA

High on a hill sits **Lamey Goemba**, a large palace and monastery built in the 1800s as a residence for King Ugyen Wangchuck. Its design is in the palace style of the time, and is similar to Wangdichholing. It is now being used by the Integrated Forest Development Project and isn't formally open to visitors.

## Sleeping

All of Bumthang's guesthouses follow a similar design, with pine-clad rooms and cosy separate dining rooms, and the majority are family run. Most guesthouses have *bukharis* (wood stoves) to heat the rooms. If you're cold, ask the room attendants to light the stove – they start it with a dollop of kerosene and a *whump*! The efficient *bukharis* heat the room quickly, but don't burn for very long.

### JAKAR

The following hotels are either in Jakar town or on the outskirts.

**Jakar Village Lodge** (Map p168; ☎ 631242; gyeldup@ druknet.bt; s/d Nu 1100/1200, deluxe r Nu 1600; 🖳 ) Said to have some of the best food in Bumthang, this hotel situated below the dzong is run by an ex-*dzongdag* (district administrator) who will regale you with stories as you sample his assortment of teas and real freshly ground coffee (!) in the lounge/dining room. The terrace enjoys great views over the valley. Major renovations added new rooms in 2006.

**Mountain Lodge** (Map p168; ☎ 631255; mtnlodge@ druknet.bt; s/d Nu 1500/1700) The lodge has wood-panelled rooms in a large two-storey building overlooking Wangdichholing Palace. Good staff, tasty food and good rooms make this a good choice.

**Swiss Guest House** (Map p168; ☎ 631198; swissguest house@druknet.bt; s/d without bathroom Nu 1000/1100, s/d with bathroom Nu 1300/1500, deluxe r Nu 2000; 🖳 ) It doesn't get more bucolic than this wooden farmhouse surrounded by apple orchards on a hillside above the valley floor. The pine-panelled rooms are rustic but cosy and some have verandas. In 1983 this was the first guesthouse in Bumthang and 10 of the 30 rooms still share bathrooms. Check out the bearskin in the main lodge (the bear was caught raiding the farm's honey hives in 2000). The water supply in the main building is from a rock spring; this is probably the only place in south Asia advertising that you can safely drink the tap water. The bar is the only place in Bhutan where you can get Red Panda beer on draft, guaranteed fresh, since it's brewed just down the road!

**River Lodge** (Map p168; ☎ 631287; pemadawa@druknet .bt; s/d Nu 800/950; 🖳 ) This popular place above the road has rooms in a converted farmhouse, in motel-style cottages or in deluxe rooms below the restaurant. A few rooms share bathrooms. The lodge has helpful management, a small library and hot-stone bath (Nu 295 to

---

### WALKING THE BUMTHANG VALLEY

There are plenty of opportunities for day hikes in the Bumthang region, many involving visits to remote goembas. If you are on a tourist visa, take advantage of the vehicle at your disposal and arrange for the driver to pick you up at the end of a walk.

From Swiss Guest House to **Pelseling Goemba** is a favourite half-day walk, descending a different route to Thamshing Goemba in a total of about four hours' walking. The first half is all uphill (2½ hours) but is more varied than the hike to Tharpaling, through a mix of forest, meadows and villages, and you are rewarded with great views. The monastery is a great place for a packed lunch or flask of tea.

You can also walk from Lamey Goemba over the ridge to **Tharpaling Goemba**, at 3500m in the Chhume valley, and meet your vehicle there. The trail branches off a logging road 1km past the goemba. The first two hours are a hard uphill slog through rhododendron and bamboo, before you finally cross a pass and descend across the bare hillsides of the Chhume Valley to the Zhambhala Lhakhang, Choedrak Hermitage and finally Tharpaling. The hike offers less in the way of views but more the feel of a pilgrimage, taking in several sacred sites. Check for ticks along this route.

A good full-day excursion is to hike up the valley from **Thangbi Goemba** (p174) to **Ngang Lhakhang** (p174). This is the first day of the Bumthang Cultural trek (see p230).

A longer day hike leads from the Swiss Guest House over the ridge to **Kunzangdrak Goemba** (see p178).

The best short walk is between **Kurjey** and **Tamshing** goembas via the Dozam and rock paintings of Lha Kharpo (see p175). You can also walk down the east valley road from Konchogsum Lhakhang to the Swiss Farm (5km) for fine views of Jakar and the Chokhor Valley.

---

495 per person). Irritants include dim lights, small bathrooms and a lack of electrical plugs, and the food's not brilliant, but most people seem to enjoy the stay.

**Kaila Guest House** (Map p168; ☎ 631219; kailaguest house@druknet.bt; s/d Nu 1300/1500; 🖳 ) This is the closest hotel to Jakar and is frequented mostly by NGO workers, who get a 40% discount. The rooms open onto the parking lot, motel style, so get an upper-floor room. The owner was the cook at the Swiss Guest House for many years, so the food is good. In retrospect, the Hello Kitty bedspreads were probably a mistake.

Several new hotels are planned, including a branch of the **Druk Hotel** www.drukhotels.com near Namsey Goemba, and an as yet unnamed hotel just north of the River Lodge.

The **Wangdichholing Lodge** (Map p168) is a new BTCL luxury option next to Wangdichholing Dzong. The new **Amankora** Map p168; www.aman resorts.com; s/d full board US$925/1000; 🖳 is just next door. Both places are due to open in 2007.

### BUMTHANG VALLEY

The following hotels are outside Jakar in the Chokhor valley but still within easy reach of the town and with quiet rural locations.

**Gongkhar Guest House** (Map p172; ☎ 631288; tshering gong@druknet.bt; s/d Nu 850/1000; 🖳 ) This excellent hotel, 1.5km southeast of Jakar, has spacious and comfortable rooms with *bukharis* and abundant hot water in super clean bathrooms. There's a good view of the dzong, garden seating, excellent service and the food is some of the best and most varied in the valley.

**Lodge Rinchenling** (Map p172; ☎ 631147; jampel@ druknet.bt; s/d Nu 1500/1750; 🖳 ) This recommended place, run by Dasho Jampel Ngedup, has spacious rooms, with comfortable mattresses and large bathrooms, either in the main farmhouse or the modern 'L' block out back.

**Yangphel Guest House** (Map p172; ☎ 631191; fax 631176; s/d Nu 1100/1300; 🖳 ) Near the Jampa Lhakhang, Yangphel is a lovely guesthouse in traditional style with a large hot-stone bath, cosy open-plan dining hall and balcony seating. The carpeted rooms vary in size and the shared bathrooms are clean. Some stylish decorative touches add a boutiquey feel.

**Wangdicholing Resort** (Map p172; ☎ 631452; wangdic holingresort@druknet.bt; s/d Nu 1200/1300) This is another good place, on a bluff overlooking the valley to the south of town. The main building has a relaxing balcony festooned in climbing flowers. Rooms are a bit old-fashioned but fine.

**Leki Guest House** (Map p172; ☎ 631231; lekilodge@druk net.bt; s/d Nu 1200/1500) The Leki is one of the oldest hotels in the valley and is showing its age. There are 20 rooms, in a three-storey house or separate cottages, and a dining room decorated with homemade weavings (for sale). Some rooms have shared bathrooms. Some Japanese dishes are available.

Other places are used mostly during tsechu time. These include **Udee Guesthouse** (Map p168; ☎ 631139; udee@druknet.bt; s/d without bathroom 850/1000, with bathroom s/d Nu 1200/1300), a small family-run farmhouse with simple rooms; **Sidhartha Guest House** (Map p172; ☎ 631774; s/d Nu 1400/1600), a place whose pine walls make it look like a giant sauna; and the secluded **Tamshing Tourist Lodge** (Map p172; ☎ 631184; s/d Nu 850/950), on a bluff overlooking the valley, with great views but so-so rooms.

## Eating

Because of the altitude, buckwheat is the crop of choice in Bumthang and buckwheat noodles and pancakes are a Bumthang speciality. The Bumthang Chhu is also famous for its large stock of trout, and despite Buddhist prohibitions on the taking of life, fish do mysteriously appear on hotel dinner plates.

There are plenty of small bars and local restaurants along Jakar's main street, the best of which by a long way is **Pema Tshomo Restaurant** (Map p168; ☎ 631128), with excellent Bhutanese dishes.

There are a few places to try if you're craving Western-style food.

**Himalayan Pizza** (Map p168; ☎ 631437; pizza slice Nu 30) At the south end of town, this place produces decent pizza as well as spaghetti and *roesti*. There is no menu and the owner speaks fluent Swiss-German but no English. Give your order an hour or more in advance if possible.

With prior notice the **Swiss Guest House** (Map p168; ☎ 631198; swissguesthouse@druknet.bt) can produce Swiss specialities such as *roesti* (crispy, fried, shredded potatoes), fondue and *racklette* (a melted-cheese dish).

## Shopping

As in most towns in Bhutan, the shops in Jakar contain a surreal hodgepodge of goods, many of which are brought over the border from China. A typical shop may sell shoes, pens, nails, soap, toy cars, locally made baskets, dried fish and prayer flags, as well as 'foreign fancy items'. One item in good supply in Jakar is *chugo,* dried cheese. Unless you want to break your teeth, let a piece soften for a long time in your mouth before you bite into it.

Udee Woodcarving Factory (Map p168) employs a few woodcarvers who turn out traditional lama tables and painted carvings.

---

**SWISS FARM**

The Swiss Farm is a development project established by Fritz Maurer, one of the first Swiss to work in Bhutan, and now run by his son. The project introduced brewing, farming machinery and fuel-efficient, smokeless wood stoves to the valley, as well as its first tourist guesthouse (p169). The milk from large Jersey cattle is used in Bhutan's only commercial cheese factory and Bhutan's only native beer, Red Panda, is brewed here. It's possible to visit the farm but your guide needs to arrange this in advance.

---

The **Yoser Lham Shop** (Map p168; ☎ 631193) is the main outlet for the Swiss Farm. The shop sells the farm's cheese, apple juice, peach brandy and apple or honey wine, as well as soft Gouda or hard Emmenthal cheese at Nu 250 per kg. This cheese is made for eating off the block, unlike the soft Bhutanese *datse*, which is used only in sauces. Honey is available in July and August.

**Sonam Handicrafts** (Map p168; ☎ 631370) has pricey but nice pieces, including *chang* (barley beer) holders and ornate *gau* (amulets). Credit cards incur a surcharge of 5%. The Bumthang Handicraft Shop, also in the centre, is strong on textiles from eastern Bhutan.

**Handicrafts Emporium** (Map p172; ☎ 631576) is the showroom of a government-supported handicraft project and sells textiles, wooden bowls, tables runners and *ghos*. It's 250m down a dirt road just past the Leki Guest House.

## Getting There & Away

**Gari Singye Express** has Coasters to Thimphu (Nu 267, 12 hours), daily except Monday, leaving at 5.30am.

# CHOKHOR VALLEY

To most people the Chokhor valley *is* Bumthang and the Chokhor valley is often called the Bumthang valley or just simply Bumthang. It's possible to visit Jampey and Kurjey lhakhangs in the morning, cross the river and have a packed lunch at Do Zam, and then visit Tamshing and Konchogsum lhakhangs in the afternoon.

## Western Side of the Valley

The road that leads up the western side of the valley connects a string of interesting temples which are connected in one way or another

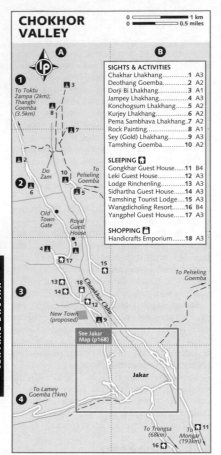

**CHOKHOR VALLEY**

0 ————————— 1 km
0 ————————— 0.5 miles

To Toktu Zampa (2km); Thangbi Goemba (3.5km)

Do Zam

To Pelseling Goemba

Old Town Gate

Royal Guest House

New Town (proposed)

See Jakar Map (p168)

Jakar

To Lamey Goemba (1km)

To Pelseling Goemba

To Trongsa (68km)

To Mongar (193km)

**SIGHTS & ACTIVITIES**
| | |
|---|---|
| Chakhar Lhakhang....................1 | A3 |
| Deothang Goemba....................2 | A2 |
| Dorji Bi Lhakhang....................3 | A1 |
| Jampey Lhakhang....................4 | A3 |
| Konchogsum Lhakhang............5 | A2 |
| Kurjey Lhakhang....................6 | A2 |
| Pema Sambhava Lhakhang....7 | A2 |
| Rock Painting....................8 | A1 |
| Sey (Gold) Lhakhang............9 | A3 |
| Tamshing Goemba............10 | A2 |

**SLEEPING**
| | |
|---|---|
| Gongkhar Guest House......11 | B4 |
| Leki Guest House............12 | A3 |
| Lodge Rinchenling............13 | A3 |
| Sidhartha Guest House......14 | A3 |
| Tamshing Tourist Lodge....15 | A3 |
| Wangdicholing Resort......16 | B4 |
| Yangphel Guest House......17 | A3 |

**SHOPPING**
| | |
|---|---|
| Handicrafts Emporium.......18 | A3 |

with the visit of Guru Rinpoche to Bumthang in 746. A mountain bike would offer a great way to link up the monasteries and continue over to the east bank.

### SEY (GOLD) LHAKHANG

Beyond the hospital north of Jakar is the **Sey (Gold) Lhakhang**, properly known as Lhodrak Seykhar Dratshang. This is a monastic school, established in 1963, with about 25 students. The central figure in the lhakhang is Marpa Lotsawa, a great teacher and translator of the Kagyu lineage. The chapel is open to visitors.

### JAMPEY LHAKHANG

This fabulous **temple** is up a short side road about 1.5km past Sey Lhakhang. It is believed

to have been built in the year 659 by the Tibetan king Songtsen Gampo, on the same day as Kyichu Lhakhang in Paro, in order to subdue a Tibetan demoness (see the boxed text, p129).

The temple was visited by Guru Rinpoche during his visit to Bumthang and was renovated by the Sindhu Raja after the Guru restored his life force (see the boxed text, opposite). It has been repaired several times, and a golden roof built over time by various *penlops* of Trongsa.

Inside the main Jampey (or Jampa) Lhakhang are three stone steps representing ages. The first signifies the past, the age of the Historical Buddha, Sakyamuni. This step has descended into the ground and is covered with a wooden plank. The next age is the present, and its step is level with the floor. The top step represents a new age. It is believed that when the step representing the present age sinks to ground level, the gods will become like humans and the world as it is now will end.

The central figure in the ancient inner sanctum is Jampa, the Buddha of the Future, with his feet on an elephant. This is the oldest part of the oldest chapel in Bhutan. The statue is protected by an iron chain mail that was made by Pema Lingpa. Look up into the alcove above the entry to see a statue of Guru Rinpoche. He sat in this alcove and meditated, leaving behind a footprint. It is said that under the lhakhang there is a lake in which the Guru hid several *terma*.

The inner *kora* (circumambulation) path around the chapel is lined with ancient-looking murals. There are more lovely murals in the atrium. On the right side of the wooden wall divider is an image of Kim-lha, the goddess of the home.

On the northern side of the courtyard is the Kalachakra Temple (Dus-Kyi-khorlo), added by Ugyen Wangchuck when he was *penlop*. Chimi Dorji, the administrator of Jakar Dzong, added the Guru Lhakhang, on the south side of the *dochey* (dzong's inner courtyard), which features Guru Rinpoche, Tsepame and Chenresig. Above the entryway is the Sangay Lhakhang.

Behind the main temple are two large stone chortens; one is in memory of the second king's younger brother, Gongsar Dorji. Nearby is a chorten in memory of Lama Pentsen Khenpo, spiritual adviser to the first and second Bhutanese kings. The four corners of the complex are anchored by four more chortens, coloured yellow, red, white and blue.

CENTRAL BHUTAN

The pile of carved *mani* stones in the parking lot in front of the goemba is called a *thos* and represents the guardians of the four directions.

Each October one of the most spectacular festivals in Bhutan, the Jampa Lhakhang Drup, is staged here. The festival ground and VIP viewing platform is to the left (south) of the chapel. On one evening, after the lama dances, the monastery is lit by a bonfire for a *mewang* (fire blessing), when pilgrims jump through a burning archway. Another late-night rite is the *tercham* (treasure dance), also referred to as the 'naked dance', normally performed at midnight. Both dances serve as fertility rites.

Tourists need a Cultural Affairs permit to visit the lhakhang, which your travel agency will arrange for you.

### CHAKHAR LHAKHANG

Beside the main road, a short distance beyond Jampa Lhakhang, is **Chakhar (Iron Castle) Lhakhang**. Although it is easy to mistake it for a house, this is an interesting temple and worth a short visit. It is the site of the palace of the Indian king Sendha Gyab, better known as the Sindhu Raja (see below), who first invited Guru Rinpoche to Bumthang. The original palace was made of iron, hence the name Chakhar; it was said to have been nine storeys high, holding within it all the treasures of the world.

The current building was built in the 14th century by the saint Dorji Lingpa and its correct name is Dechen Phodrang. The main statue is of Guru Rinpoche, and there are dozens of masks and black hats that are used during the Jampey Lhakhang Drup festival.

Opening hours are a bit hit and miss, and you may have to pay several visits to find the caretaker in.

### KURJEY LHAKHANG

This large, active and important temple complex is named after the body *(kur)* print *(jey)* of Guru Rinpoche, which is preserved in a cave inside the oldest of the three buildings that make up the temple complex. It is at the end of the paved road, 2.5km from Chakhar Lhakhang.

As you enter the complex, there are three large lhakhangs against a hillside on the right.

---

### THE STORY OF KURJEY LHAKHANG

In 746 the saint Padmasambhava (Guru Rinpoche) made his first visit to Bhutan. At this time, the Indian Sendha Gyab had established himself as the king of Bumthang, with the title Sindhu Raja. He was feuding with Naochhe (Big Nose), a rival Indian king in the south of Bhutan, when Naochhe killed the Sindhu Raja's son and 16 of his attendants. The raja was so distraught that he desecrated the abode of the chief Bumthang deity, Shelging Kharpo, who then angrily took revenge by turning the skies black and stealing the king's life force, bringing him near to death.

One of the king's secretaries thus invited the tantric master Padmasambhava to Bumthang to use his supernatural powers to save the Sindhu Raja. The Guru came to Bumthang and meditated, leaving a *jey* (imprint) of his *kur* (body) in the rock, now surrounded by Kurjey Goemba. Guru Rinpoche was to be married to the king's daughter, Tashi Khuedon. He sent her to fetch water in a golden ewer. While she was away the Guru transformed into all eight of his manifestations and, together, they started to dance in the field by the temple. Every local deity appeared to watch this spectacle, except the stony-faced Shelging Kharpo who stayed hidden away in his rocky hideout above the present temple.

Guru Rinpoche was not to be set back by this rejection, and when the princess returned he changed her into five separate princesses, each clutching a golden ewer. The sunlight flashing off these ewers finally attracted Shelging Kharpo, but before he ventured out to see what was going on he first transformed himself into a white snowlion. On seeing the creature appear the Guru changed into a *garuda*, flew up and grabbed the lion and told Shelging Kharpo in no uncertain terms to behave himself. He thus recovered Sendha Gyab's life force, and for good measure converted both the rival kings to Buddhism, restoring the country to peace.

Shelging Kharpo agreed to become a protective deity of Buddhism; to seal the agreement the Guru planted his staff in the ground at the temple where its cypress tree descendants continue to grow. Furthermore, Guru Rinpoche made the king, Sendha Gyab, and his enemy from the south make peace; a stone pillar at Nabji (see p180) in the Black Mountains marks the spot where the agreement was made.

The first temple, the **Guru Lhakhang**, is the oldest and was built in 1652 by Mingyur Tenpa (see p183) when he was *penlop* of Trongsa. Tucked just below the eaves is a figure of a snowlion with a *garuda* above it, which represents the famous struggle between Guru Rinpoche (appearing as the garuda) and the local demon, Shelging Kharpo (as the snowlion).

At the entrance to the lower-floor Sangay Lhakhang is a small crawl-through rock passage; Bhutanese believe that in crawling through a narrow tunnel like this you will leave your sins behind. Behind the statues of the three Buddhas is a secret passageway which is said to have once led to Tharpaling.

The upper-floor sanctuary is the holiest in the complex, and has an image of Shelging Kharpo in a shrine just inside the door. There are a thousand small statues of Guru Rinpoche neatly lined up along the same wall, plus statues of Guru Rinpoche, Pema Lingpa and Drolma (Tara). The main statue in this sanctuary is again of Guru Rinpoche, flanked by his eight manifestations and eight chortens. Hidden behind this image is the **meditation cave**, where he left his body imprint. The far wall has paintings of Guru Rinpoche, his manifestations, his 25 disciples and various other figures connected with the Guru. The big cypress tree behind the lhakhang is said to have sprouted from the Guru's walking stick.

Ugyen Wangchuck, the first king of Bhutan, built the second temple, the **Sampa Lhundrup Lhakhang**, in 1900, when he was still *penlop* of Trongsa. On the entrance porch are paintings of the guardians of the four directions and of various local deities who were converted to Buddhism by Guru Rinpoche. The white ghostlike figure on the white horse to the top right is Shelging Kharpo. Inside the temple is a statue of Guru Rinpoche, this one 10m high, flanked again by his eight manifestations. A smaller image of the Guru sits facing the entrance.

The third building in the complex is a recent three-storey lhakhang built by the queen mother, Ashi Kesang Wangchuck, in 1984 under the guidance of Dilgo Khyentse Rinpoche. She also had the courtyard in front of the three temples paved with stones and built a wall with 108 chortens around the whole complex. On the porch in front of the temple is a large wheel of life depicting various hells and heavens. At the bottom you can see a man being judged, with black and white stones representing his good and bad deeds. There's a mystic spiral mandala

on the opposite wall. Interior murals illustrate various monastic rules and regulations, including the strict dress codes.

The elaborately decorated **Zangto Pelri Lhakhang** is under construction a short distance south of the Kurjey Lhakhang compound and features a 3D depiction of the paradise of Guru Rinpoche.

A five-minute walk up the hillside near the entrance is the **Khurjey Drupchhu**, a sacred spring where monks come to wash their socks.

The popular Kurjey tsechu is held in June and includes a masked dance that dramatises Guru Rinpoche's defeat of Shelging Kharpo. A large *thangka*, called Guru Tshengye Thondrol, depicting the eight manifestations of Guru Rinpoche, is unfurled in the early morning before the dances, which are performed by the monks from Trongsa.

### DEOTHANG GOEMBA

This little-visited but charming private monastery, just north of Kurjey Goemba, was founded in 1949 by Dasho Phuntsok Wangdi. The surprisingly large main hall has a large image of Guru Rinpoche, with 12 more interesting metal statues to the side. A small, dark-skinned image of Thangtong Gyalpo stands to the left. The goemba has a basic four-roomed guesthouse.

### THANGBI GOEMBA

The yellow-roofed Thangbi (or Thankabi) Goemba was founded in 1470 by Shamar Rinpoche and, after a dispute, was taken over by Pema Lingpa. The main chapel of the Dusum Sangay (Past, Present and Future Buddhas) is entered under another of Pema Lingpa's famous chainmails. Just over 20 *gomchen* (lay or married monks) live here, celebrating a *drup* (festival) in October.

The goemba is a 3.5km drive north of Kurjey Lhakhang on an unpaved road, branching across the river at Toktu Zampa. It's worth a visit if you are headed to Ngang Lhakhang but isn't really worth a special visit in its own right. This is also the starting point for the Bumthang Cultural trek (see p230).

### NGANG LHAKHANG

Several hours' walk up the Chokhor Chhu from Thangbi Goemba is the small region known as Ngang-yul (Swan Land). The site was visited by Guru Rinpoche, but the present **Ngang Lhakhang** (Swan Temple) temple was built in the 15th century by Lama Namkha Samdrup, a contemporary of Pema Lingpa.

Despite the rustic and decrepit exterior, the interior contains some lovely statues and paintings. Look also for the saddles by the entrance. The primary statue is of Guru Rinpoche, flanked by his two consorts, Yeshe Tsogyal from Tibet and Mandarava from India. There is a mural of the Zhabdrung on the wall opposite the altar and an image of Guru Rinpoche on a lotus surrounded by swans.

The upper chapel is a *goenkhang*, with statues of Tsepame, Chenresig, Vijaya and Drolma. The statue of Guru Rinpoche to the bottom right was fashioned by Pema Lingpa. Protector deities lurk in the shadows. Hanging from the rafters are masks used in the three-day Ngang Shey, a festival held here in the 10th month in honour of the temple's founder.

It's possible to drive here with a 4WD but it's a much nicer walk along the true left bank of the river. You could walk one way and arranged to be picked up at nearby Damphey. For a map of the region see p230.

## Eastern Side of the Valley

The best way to visit the eastern side of the Chokhor valley is to walk a couple of hundred metres north from Kurjey Lhakhang then follow a path east to cross a footbridge, then uphill to a trail on the opposite side. Downstream of the bridge you can see a natural formation named **Do Zam**, said to be the remains of a stone bridge that was built by a goddess who was trying to meet Guru Rinpoche, but the bridge was destroyed by a demon.

From here you can follow the east-bank trail south for 30 minutes to Tamshing Goemba. A

---

### TERTON PEMA LINGPA

Pema Lingpa (1450–1521) was one of the five great *tertons* (treasure-finders) of Nyingma Buddhism, and the most important *terton* in Bhutan. The texts and artefacts he found, the dances he composed and the art he produced have significantly shaped Bhutan's cultural heritage. He is also considered a reincarnation of Guru Rinpoche.

He was born in the hamlet of Drangchel in Bumthang's Tang valley, near Kunzangdrak Goemba. As a boy he learned the craft of blacksmithing from his grandfather; indeed two of the chainmails he forged are still on display at Tamshing and Thangbi goembas.

At age 25 he discovered his first *terma* after he dreamed a monk handed him a scroll in dakini script that gave instructions on how to find a treasure chest deep in a pool in the Tang valley (see p177). Pema eventually managed to translate the scroll but this was a huge project, because in dakini script each word stands for 1000 human words. Later, assisted by the *khandromas* (dakinis), he used the text as a basis for teachings. His residence at the time was in Kunzangling, which is on a cliff above the Tang valley and is now the site of the Kunzangdrak Goemba (see p178).

During Pema Lingpa's life he found a total of 34 statues, scrolls and sacred relics in Bhutan and as far away as Samye in Tibet. Many of the statues and relics he discovered are preserved in lhakhangs throughout Bhutan, including Bumthang's Tamshing and Kunzangdrak goembas, which he founded.

In his visions, Pema Lingpa often visited Zangto Pelri, Guru Rinpoche's celestial paradise. During these visions he observed the dances of the *khandromas* and *yidam* (tutelary deities). He taught three of these dances, called *pa-cham,* to his disciples, and several of these are still performed as part of Bhutan's tsechu festivals.

After his death he was reincarnated in three forms, consisting of *ku* (body), *sung* (speech) and *thug* (mind) and these lineages continue to this day.

Through his six sons, one daughter and numerous reincarnations, Pema Lingpa left behind a legacy that still influences much of Bhutan. His most important son, Dawa Gyeltshen, was born in 1499 and settled in Chhume, one of Bumthang's valleys. Another of his sons, Pema Thinley, was a reincarnation of Pema Lingpa himself. This incarnation founded Gangte Goemba in the Phobjikha valley (see p152), and the Gangte Trulku lineage continues there, with Kuenzang Pema Namgyal, born in 1955, as the ninth 'mind' reincarnation.

Another of his sons, Kuenga Wangpo, born in 1505, settled in Lhuentse (known then as Kurtoe), where his great-grandsons founded Dungkhar Dzong, north of Lhuentse Dzong. The royal family of Bhutan, the Wangchuck dynasty, is descended from this line.

more interesting 45-minute detour is to take a left after the bridge for ten minutes to an impressive **rock painting** of Guru Rinpoche in the form of Dorje Drolo, astride a tiger. From here, head uphill to the **Dorji Bi Lhakhang** with its large white chorten, and then descend past a former country mansion, across a stream, to the turn-off to Pema Sambhava Lhakhang and then Tamshing Goemba. You can send your vehicle back through Jakar to meet you here.

The major influence in the temples on this side of the valley was Pema Lingpa, the great *terton* of the 16th century.

## TAMSHING GOEMBA

This goemba, formally the Tamshing Lhendup Chholing (Temple of the Good Message), is at the northern end of the eastern road, 5km from Jakar. It was established in 1501 by Pema Lingpa and is the most important Nyingma goemba in the kingdom. Pema Lingpa built the unusual structure himself, with the help of *khandromas,* who made many of the statues. On the inner walls are what are believed to be original unrestored images that were painted by Pema Lingpa, though recent research has uncovered even older paintings underneath.

The entrance to the lhakhang is via an inner courtyard lined with monks' quarters. To the left is the small Mani Dungkhor Lhakhang, built in 1914 to hold a huge prayer wheel.

The main lhakhang has an unusual design with the key chapel screened off in the centre of the assembly hall, almost like a separate building. In the chapel are three thrones for the three incarnations (body, mind and speech) of Pema Lingpa. During important ceremonies the reincarnations sit here, although a photograph is substituted if one of the incarnations is not present.

The primary statue in the inner sanctuary is of Guru Rinpoche flanked by Jampa (Maitreya, the Buddha of the Future) and Sakyamuni. This statue is particularly important because it was sculpted by the *khandromas*. The statue's eyes are looking slightly upward, following the angels in their flight; another unique aspect of the statue is that the Guru is not wearing shoes. Above the altar are two *maksaras* (mythological crocodiles) and a *garuda*. On the walls are the eight manifestations of Guru Rinpoche, four on each side. A small statue of Pema Lingpa occupies a glass case in front of the chapel.

At the far end of the inner *kora* path is a suit of chain-mail armour made by Pema Lingpa. It weighs about 25kg and it is an auspicious act to carry it around the goemba three times.

The upper floor forms a balcony around the assembly hall. Pema Lingpa was a short man and it is said that he built the low ceiling of the balcony to his exact height. Around the outside are 100,000 old paintings of Sakyamuni. In the upper chapel is a statue of Tsepame, the Buddha of Long Life, and a large collection of masks that are used for lama dances. Also here, but closed to visitors, is a statue of Pema Lingpa fashioned by the man himself.

There are good views from Tamshing back across the river to Kurjey Lhakhang.

## KONCHOGSUM LHAKHANG

Just 400m below Tamshing is a small rural-looking **temple** – the source of many interesting stories. It was renovated in 1995 and looks quite new, but it is in fact very old, probably dating back to the 6th or 7th century. The current structure, however, dates from the 15th century, when Pema Lingpa restored it; the pillar outside the building is attributed to him. Pema Lingpa revealed *terma* on the hillside behind this goemba, and also in the lake said to be beneath the lhakhang.

There is a pedestal in the courtyard upon which a large and ancient bell used to sit. It is said that when this bell was rung, it could be heard all the way to Lhasa in Tibet. A 17th-century Tibetan army tried to steal the bell, but the weight was too great and they dropped it, which cracked the bell. It is said to comprise 10% gold, 20% silver, 50% bronze and 20% tin. After a period on display in the National Museum in Paro a fragment of the bell is now back inside the lhakhang.

The small statues of the three Buddhas (past, present and future) in the sanctuary (locked in the safe) are said to have flown here straight from Khaine Lhakhang in Dungkhar (in eastern Bhutan). Hence the name of this lhakhang is Konchogsum – *konchog* (divine being), *sum* (three).

The central figure in the lhakhang is Nampa Namse (Vairocana, one of the five Dhyani buddhas). On Vairocana's left is Chenresig, and to the right is Guru Rinpoche. Other statues are of Pema Lingpa (right), the great Nyingma scholar Longchenpa (left) and, in the far corner, the protector deity Beker Gyalpo.

### PEMA SAMBHAVA LHAKHANG

At the end of the road a short steep climb above the valley floor leads to the small **Pema Sambhava Lhakhang**. The original lhakhang was built in 1490 by Pema Lingpa around the cave where Guru Rinpoche meditated and assumed his manifestation of Padmasambhava. It was expanded by Jigme Namgyal, the father of the first king, and restored in the early 1970s.

There are several rock paintings here, as well as a representation of the local protector Terda Norbu Zangpo, and the cave itself is painted in rainbow colours. The interesting round bamboo weaving that looks like a shield is an unusual representation of the bodhisattva Chenresig. The extremely elderly caretaker has lived in this chapel since he was 15.

## TANG VALLEY

Tang is the most remote of Bumthang's valleys. As it is higher than Chokhor and the soil not as rich, there's not much agriculture here, although the valley turns bright pink with buckwheat flowers in October. The people of this valley raise sheep and, at higher elevations, yaks. For a map of the region, see p230.

From Jakar it's 10.5km to the unpaved road that branches north up the Tang valley. This road climbs past the trail to Membartsho (1.3km from the turn-off) and the new Pema Tekchok Chholing Nunnery (currently under construction), to reach the jumping-off point for the hike to Kunzangdrak, 7km from the turn-off. The road then climbs high above the river, crossing the bridge at Pangshing and then passing **Gemtshong**, a particularly

picturesque village and lhakhang perched on a ridge. After a short descent to the river it's 3km to a school at Mesithang (Tang) and 1km further to the Tang Rimochen Lhakhang.

The road becomes rougher as it approaches the bridge at **Kizum** (Ki Zam), 22km from the road junction. This is generally the end point of the Bumthang Cultural trek, though the increasingly rough road does continue a few kilometres further to Gamling and Wobtang.

You can take in all the sites in this section in a good day trip from Jakar, or on the drive back to Jakar at the end of the Bumthang Cultural trek. Better still, overnight at the secluded Ogyen Chholing Guest House.

### Membartsho

A five-minute walk from a parking spot at a bend in the road leads to a picturesque pool in the Tang Chuu that is known as **Membartsho** (Burning Lake). Pema Lingpa found several of Guru Rinpoche's *terma* here. It's a lovely spot, where nature, religion and mythology blur into one.

A wooden bridge crosses the prayer-flag-strewn river gorge and offers a good vantage point over the 'lake'. Only the enlightened will spot the temple that lurks in the lake's inky depths. The sanctity of the site is made obvious by the numerous small clay offerings called *tsha-tsha* piled up in various rock niches.

Under a rock shrine with a carving of Pema Lingpa and his two sons is a cave that virtuous people can crawl through, no matter how big they are. Beware: it's quite small, and very dusty.

**CENTRAL BHUTAN**

---

### THE BURNING LAKE

Two of Pema Lingpa's most celebrated discoveries took place at Membartsho.

The first took place when a dream told him to go to a point where the river forms a large pool that looks like a lake. After a while, standing on a large rock, he saw a temple with many doors, only one of which was open. He plunged naked into the lake and entered a large cave where there was a throne, upon which sat a life-sized statue of Lord Buddha and many large boxes. An old woman with one eye handed him one of the chests and he suddenly found himself standing on the rock at the side of the lake holding the treasure.

Pema Lingpa's second treasure find was the most famous. His previous *terma* had instructed him to return to the lake but when he did so many people gathered to watch the event and the sceptical *penlop* of the district accused him of trickery. Under great pressure to prove himself, Pema Lingpa took a lighted lamp and proclaimed: 'If I am a genuine revealer of your treasures, then may I return with it now, with my lamp still burning; if I am some devil, then may I perish in the water.' He jumped into the lake, was gone long enough that the sceptics thought they were proven right, and then suddenly emerged back on the rock with the lamp still burning and holding a statue and a treasure chest. The lake became known as Membartsho, or Burning Lake.

## Kunzangdrak Goemba

A stiff hour-long, Stairmaster-style climb up the hillside above Drangchel leads to one of the most important sites related to Pema Lingpa. He began construction of the **goemba** in 1488, and many of his most important sacred relics are kept here.

The first chapel has a *kora* path around it, with Chenresig, Guru Nazey (a form of Guru Rinpoche) and Namkhai Ningpo inside. Walk around the back of the building to the gravity-defying Khandroma Lhakhang, spectacularly situated against a vertical rock face that seeps holy water. Ask to see the stone anvil bearing the footprint of Pema Lingpa. Finally, cross over the small bridge, past a fire-blackened cleft in the cliff, to the spooky *goenkhang*.

Figure on three to four hours for the return trip.

## Tang Rimochen Lhakhang

**Tang Rimochen Lhakhang** was built by Pema Lingpa in the 14th century to mark a sacred place where Guru Rinpoche meditated. The original name 'Tag (or Tak) Rimochen' (an impression of tiger's stripes) is derived from the tiger stripes that appear on a rock cliff behind the building.

There are footprints of the Guru and his consort Yeshe Tsogyal on the cliff face and at the top of the concrete steps leading to the temple. The two huge rocks below the lhakhang represent male and female *jachung*, as well as the bathing spot of the Guru.

Just a couple of hundred metres away, by a two-legged *khonying*, is an important cremation site.

## Ogyen Chholing Palace

From either Gamling or Kizum it's a 45-minute climb to this hilltop 16th-century **nagtshang**, or country manor, originally built by Deb Tsokye Dorje, the one-time *penlop* of Trongsa and a descendant of the terton Dorji Lingpa. The present structures, including the *tshuglhakhang* (main temple), *utse* (central tower), *chamkhang* (dance house), *shagkor* (servants' quarters) and *nubgothang* (guest house) are more recent, having been rebuilt after their collapse in the 1897 earthquake.

The family that owns Ogyen (or Ugyen) Chholing has turned the complex into a **museum** (www.geocities.com/ogyencholingmuseum; admission Nu 100) to preserve its legacy and provide a place for religious studies, research and solitude. The fas-

cinating and well-captioned exhibits offer real insights into the lifestyle of a Bhutanese noble family. Highlights include a book of divination, a dakini dance costume made of bone and the revelation that petrified yak dung was one of the ingredients for Bhutanese gunpowder. Bring a torch. The complex is supported through the Ogyen Chholing Trust, which produces an excellent museum booklet (Nu 180).

The superbly rustic **Ogyen Chholing Guest House** ( ☎ 03-631221; r Nu 500-1000) in the palace grounds has two excellent suites and four smaller basic rooms and offers a tranquil overnight retreat. Proceeds go to the trust.

If you walk to the palace from Kizum it's well worth returning via the lovely village of Gamling. A 4WD track reaches the palace but at the time of research there was no road bridge over the river, due to a dispute between villagers over its proposed location.

## Thowadrak Hermitage

The remote hermitage of **Thowadrak** (or Thowa Drak) clings to the highest rocks above the north end of the Tang valley. It is said to have been founded by Mandarava, the Indian consort of Guru Rinpoche, and the Guru himself is believed to have meditated here. The goemba was built by Dorji Lingpa. There are numerous small meditation retreats on the hillside above (don't disturb the hermits) and dramatic views over the valley. Texts relate that the upper valley conceals a sealed gateway to one of Bhutan's *bey-yul*. The only sounds here are of rushing water and the rustle of bamboo.

The six-hour return hike could be done as a day trip from the Ogyen Chholing Guest House or can be tagged on to the end of the Bumthang Cultural trek (see p230). From Jakar you'd have to leave very early, figuring in a two-hour drive each way, plus an hour at the site. Bring a packed lunch. The hike is probably only really worthwhile for those with a spiritual leaning.

The trail starts near the suspension bridge to Karap, though with a 4WD you could cut off the first 45 minutes' walk. After an hour or so walking along the dirt road, five minutes past a white chorten, take the trail branching to the right, down to a wooden bridge across the river. Follow the lovely riverside trail for 20 minutes to a second bridge beside a Bhutanese-style chorten. The trail climbs to the right, past well-tended *mani* walls to a white chorten surrounded by lush dense forest. The trail continues uphill, past trailside shrines, dakini marks, carved mantras and a stone lion-print. The last 40 minutes is a killer climb, up increasingly steep steps.

Just before the main Pema Osel Chholing chapel is a pilgrim's shelter and sin-testing rock. At the back of the chapel a log ladder leads down around the cliff face to a holy spring.

## URA VALLEY

Southeast of Jakar, Ura is the highest of Bumthang's valleys and is believed by some to have been the home of the earliest inhabitants of Bhutan.

### Jakar to Ura

**48km / 1½ hours**

The road crosses the bridge to the east of Jakar, then travels south along the east bank of the Chamkhar Chhu, winding around a ridge past the turn-off to the Tang valley. Just past the turn-off is an impressive new chorten. As the road climbs, look back at excellent views up the Chokhor and Chhume valleys.

The few houses and potato fields that make up Tangsibi are 24km from Jakar. The road climbs to 3420m, where there is a monument with a cross, in memory of a Indian road supervisor who died here in a 1985 road accident.

The road reaches a false summit, then finally crosses the Shertang La (3590m), also known as the Ura La. Just before the pass you'll get a view of Gangkhar Puensum (7541m) to the northwest and the yellow-roofed lhakhang of Somrang village to the south.

It's then a long descent into the Ura valley to the village of Ura, which lies below the road. The descent on foot from the pass makes for a nice hour-long walk into the village.

A couple of kilometres before the turn-off to Ura is the turn-off to Shingkhar (see right).

### Ura

**☎ 03 / elev 3100m**

Ura is one of the most interesting villages in Bhutan. There are about 40 closely packed houses along cobblestone streets, and the main lhakhang dominates the town, giving it a medieval atmosphere. In colder weather Ura women wear a sheepskin shawl that serves as both a blanket and a cushion. Yet change is afoot; the number of people living in the village has decreased in recent years, as young people move to the towns for jobs or education, and there is now a labour shortage in the village.

Ura gets a rush of visitors during the Ura *yakchoe,* a notoriously unreliable festival that regularly changes dates at the last minute, leaving behind lots of disappointed tour groups on tight schedules. If you do decide to visit the festival, normally in May, it would be wise to budget a couple of days' leeway in your itinerary. The three days of masked dances starts on the 12th day of the third month with a procession carrying an image of Vajrapani from the nearby Geyden Lhakhang down to the main lhakhang. The eve of the festival sees the frantic brewing of *singchang* (made from millet, wheat or rice) and late-night rites of excorcism.

### SLEEPING & EATING

**Hotel Arya Zambala** (azherbal05@yahoo.com) Situated alongside the main road, before the turn-off to Ura, this tavern has rooms for rent, some with attached bathrooms, and can provide basic meals. Their main business is in herbal medicines and dried mushrooms.

During the Ura festival even camping spots are at a premium and some groups commute from Jakar, 90 minutes' drive away.

### Around Ura

#### SHINGKHAR

The traditional village of **Shingkhar** (elevation 3400m, population 250), made up of only 35 households, is 9km up a good gravel side road from Ura. The small **Rinchen Jugney Lhakhang,** on a hill 50m from the Shinkhar Guest House, was founded by the Dzogchen master Longchen Rabjampa (1308–63).

The village's central **Dechen Chholing Goemba** is headed by Shingkhar Lama, whose predecessor featured prominently in the Bhutanese novel *Hero with The Thousand Eyes,* by Karma Ura. The central lhakhang has its floorboards exposed to show the stone teaching throne of Longchen. The protector deities are appropriately fierce, except for Rahulla who looks embarrassed wearing a gorilla mask. The Shingkhar *Romney* (festival) held here in the ninth month (October) features an unusual yak dance, without the tour groups that often crowd out Ura.

There are several good hiking options in the valley. Day hikes lead up to the Singmu La, along the former trade route to Lhuentse and bordering the Thrumshing La National Park, or try the four- to five-hour return hike to the cliff-hanging Shamsul Lhakhang.

CENTRAL BHUTAN

**Shingkhar Guest House** ( ☎ 323206; fax 323718; masagang@druknet.bt; www.masagang.com; r Nu 800-1200) is a great base from where to explore the village. The rooms are basic but cosy, with mud walls and solar electricity. Meals are available. For bookings, tours and more information on the region contact Ugyen Wangdi at Masagang Tours, who can also arrange homestays in the village. You can contact Masagang through Shingkhar Guest House.

# SOUTHERN DZONGKHAGS

Two dzongkhags lie on the southern border of central Bhutan. For a few years now tourists have not been permitted to travel in these regions because of the threat posed by Assamese separatist groups, but moves are afoot to reopen the region to tourism. When that happens, the Royal Manas National park in particular will offer a unique nature experience in an area of extreme biodiversity.

## ZHEMGANG DZONGKHAG

Zhemgang, along with neighbouring Mongar, was once a collection of tiny principalities, collectively known as Khyeng, absorbed into Bhutan in the 17th century. Panbang, near the Indian border, is known for its round baskets called *bangchung*.

A two-day walk from Zhemgang town leads to Nabji, where a stone pillar commemorates the settlement of the dispute between the Sindhu Raja and Naochhe that was mediated by Guru Rinpoche. (See the boxed text, p173).

## SARPANG DZONGKHAG

Sarpang is on the southern border and a large part of the district is protected within the Royal Manas National Park. Kalikhola in the far west is a border town that has no road connection with the rest of Bhutan; all travel here involves passing through Indian terri-

tory. There is talk of building an airport in Gelephu.

## Gelephu
☎ 06

The large border town of Gelephu is the gateway to the south and to the Manas area. There's a good *tsachhu* (hot spring) in nearby Shershong, 15km from town and you could also check out the town's whisky distillery. A bomb exploded in the Sunday vegetable market here in September 2004, killing two and injuring 27.

There are a few hotels, including the **Hotel Chorten** ( ☎ 251252), (**Hotel Dechen** ☎ 251293) and, best of all, **Dragon Guest House** ( ☎ 251019; Nu 800).

## Royal Manas National Park

There are simple lodges at Kanamakra, Rabang and Panbang, and, if the area is reopened, a tented camp can be established at Pantang. A 25km road leads from Gelephu to Kanamakra at the southwestern corner of the park. There is also a road from Tingtibi on the Trongsa–Gelephu road. This 40km road passes along the northern boundary of the park from Gomphu to Panbang village.

---

**THE NABJI TRAIL**

In late 2006 the Department of Tourism launched a community tourism program in Nabji in an attempt to bring tourist income directly to remote local communities, through the employment of local guides, community-owned camping grounds and local cultural activities. The proposed six-day winter trek leads through the Jigme Singye Wangchuck National Park and passes through several Monpa villages. It's only feasible from November to March due to the low elevations. The region only opened in 2006 and only one group is allowed on the trail at a time so you can be sure you won't bump into anyone else here. For more details, see www.abto.org.bt.

---

*CENTRAL BHUTAN*

# Eastern Bhutan

Even though it is the most densely populated region, eastern Bhutan remains the kingdom's hinterland. Roads reach the major towns, but most settlements are hidden in the steep hillsides of remote and isolated valleys, some of which are home to minority ethnic groups comprising less than 1000 people.

The dominant language here is Sharchop (language of the east), although there are many local languages and dialects. Sharchop is different enough from Dzongkha that people from eastern and western Bhutan usually have to use English or Nepali to communicate. If you visit a particularly remote village your guide may have to resort to sign language.

Eastern Bhutanese love their home-brewed *arra* (rice wine) and locally grown green chillies. Because of the slash-and-burn system of shifting cultivation called *tseri*, the forest cover at lower elevations is less extensive than in other parts of Bhutan. The lower altitudes mean that spring and summer here are hot, humid and sweaty.

The general quality of hotels, food and service in eastern Bhutan is lower than it is in Thimphu and Paro. Don't venture into this part of the kingdom unless you have a sense of humour and are able to take a possible lack of hot water and Western toilets in your stride.

It's a *looong* drive out to the far east. The good news for tourists is that the border crossing at Samdrup Jongkhar is once again open to foreigners (though for exit only), so you can avoid the winding three-day drive back to Thimphu, with Guwahati and direct flights to Bangkok just a two-hour drive away.

EASTERN BHUTAN

## HIGHLIGHTS

- Visit **Trashigang** (p190), one of the most attractive and lively towns in Bhutan
- Fasten your seatbelt for the dramatic cliff-hugging road over the 3750m **Thrumshing La** (p184)
- Take the picturesque drive up to **Lhuentse Dzong** (p187) in the remote and ancient region of Kurtoe
- Watch some of Bhutan's finest cloth being woven at the remote and traditional weaving village of **Khoma** (p188)
- Check your sin levels at the picturesque pilgrimage spot of **Gom Kora** (p193)
- Walk around the impressive Chorten Kora and watch handicrafts made at the National Institute for Zorig Chusum in remote **Trashi Yangtse** (p195)

# EASTERN BHUTAN

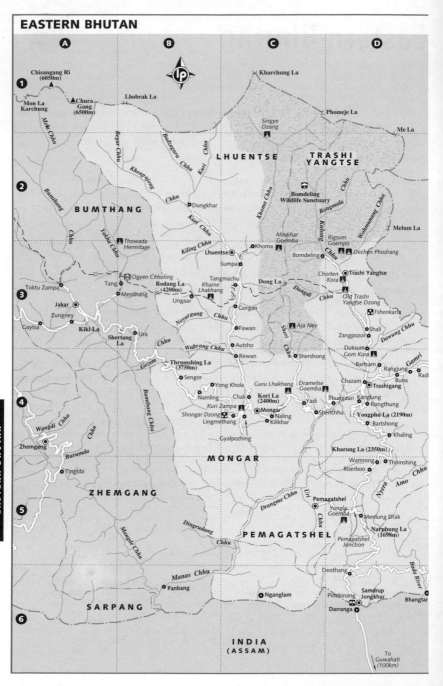

**EASTERN BHUTAN**

## Geography

Eastern Bhutan is separated from the rest of the country by a large and extremely steep chain of hills that runs from the Tibetan border almost to the Indian border. The road from Bumthang crosses these hills over the Thrumshing La (3750m). Other than trails, this one road is the region's only link to the rest of the country.

The Manas river system, Bhutan's largest river and a major tributary of the Brahmaputra, drains most of eastern Bhutan. The Kuri Chhu (with its headwaters in Tibet), the Drangme Chhu (with part of its source in the Indian state of Arunachal Pradesh), and the Kulong Chhu (which drains the Trashi Yangtse valley) all flow into the Manas. Just before it exits Bhutan, the Manas is joined by the Mangde Chhu, which drains Trongsa and most of central Bhutan.

## History

In ancient times eastern Bhutan was ruled by a collection of separate petty kingdoms and an important trade route between India and Tibet. Goods flowed via Bhutan through what is now Singye Dzong in the Lhuentse district to the Tibetan town of Lhodrak.

The most important figure in this region's history was Chhogyel Mingyur Tenpa. When he was *penlop* (governor) of Trongsa he led his armies to eastern Bhutan to quell revolts in Bumthang, Lhuentse, Trashigang, Mongar and Zhemgang. His efforts were responsible for bringing eastern Bhutan under the rule of the *desi* (secular ruler of Bhutan) and went a long way towards the ultimate unification of the country. Mingyur Tenpa built the dzong at Trongsa and was responsible for the construction of most of the dzongs in eastern, as well as central, Bhutan. In 1668 he was enthroned as the third *desi* and ruled until 1680.

# MONGAR DZONGKHAG

The Mongar district is the northern portion of the ancient region of Khyeng. Shongar Dzong, Mongar's original dzong, is in ruins, and the new dzong in Mongar town is not as architecturally spectacular as others in the region. Drametse Goemba, in the eastern part of the district, is an important Nyingma monastery, perched high above the valley.

EASTERN BHUTAN

## JAKAR TO MONGAR (193KM)

It takes about seven hours to travel between Jakar and Mongar, crossing two passes and passing numerous sheer drops on what is one of the most spectacular drives in the country, descending 3200m in a distance of 84km. During winter the Thrumshing La is occasionally closed for a day or two during heavy snowfall.

### Ura to Thrumshing La
36km / 1¼ hours

Beyond the office of the Thrumshing La National Park and the Japanese-funded hydroelectric plant, the road crosses the small Lirgang Chhu on a bridge called Liri Zam to enter the territory of the national park. It climbs past overhanging cliffs and cedar trees, more often than not framed in mist, and crosses a ridge that is labelled Wangthang La on some maps. It then drops into the Gayzam Chhu valley and starts climbing again past a road workers' camp. Because the soil is very sandy, the road is unstable and has left a large scar on the hillside.

Three kilometres before the pass is a small park that features over 40 species of rhododendron. It's possible to follow the trail inside the park and hike up through the forest for 40 minutes to the pass. If you have a keen interest in rhododendrons it's often possible to get the park ranger to accompany you and point out the different species; mention this to your guide in advance and ask at the national park office in Ura.

If you are lucky enough to travel on a clear day, watch for a view of Gangkhar Puensum (7541m) as you approach the pass. A *mani* wall and prayer flags adorn the pass and a fallen sign proclaims: 'You are at highest point'. This is Thrumshing La (3750m), 85km from Jakar, and the border of Mongar Dzongkhag; you are now officially in eastern Bhutan.

### Thrumshing La to Sengor
22km / 1 hour

The eastern side of the pass is much rockier; the road switchbacks down through a fir forest past a road sign that says 'Life is a journey, complete it'. At about 3000m, 20km from the pass, the route emerges from the trees and enters the pastures of the Sengor valley. The settlement at Sengor has a few houses near the road, although the main part of the village, about 20 houses, is in the centre of the valley. If you're carrying a picnic lunch and have not already eaten it,

this is an excellent place to do so – there is no good place to stop for the next two hours. A sign in Dzongkha adorns the rustic **Kuenphen Hotel** ( ☎ 03-635002) where you can get a simple local-style meal. A large road-construction contingent here toils to keep the pass open.

### Sengor to Kuri Zampa
62km / 1¾ hours

The next stretch of road is the wildest in Bhutan. Five kilometres beyond the Sengor valley the road begins a steep descent into the Kuri Chhu valley, clinging to the side of a rock cliff, with numerous streams and waterfalls leaping out onto the road. The frequent fog and cloud on this side of the pass makes it difficult to see what's below – for which you should be profoundly grateful, since more often than not, there's nothing.

There are several chortens here – erected as memorials to the almost 300 Indian and Nepali contract labourers who were killed during the construction of this portion of the road. As you drive along the narrow track that was hacked into the side of a vertical cliff, it's hard not to be concerned that you might well join them soon. Prayer plaques and Shiva tridents offer some limited spiritual protection. There are no settlements here except for a camp at **Namling**, 22km from Sengor, where a crew works frantically to protect the road from tumbling down the mountainside.

About 17km from Namling, after a long descent that traverses the side of a cliff, the road reaches safer ground and leaves the territory of the Thrumshing La National Park. At Yong Khola it emerges into the upper part of a large side valley of the Kuri Chhu, a lush land of bamboo, ferns and leeches (and good bird-watching). You pass cornfields and descend to the valley floor on a road that winds around like a pretzel. Rice terraces appear and tropical fruits such as mango and pineapple start to flourish.

Atop a hill on the opposite side of the river, near the kilometre marker 123, is a view of the ruined **Shongar Dzong**. There's not much to see – just some stone walls almost hidden by trees on the top of a hillock – but this is believed to have been one of the earliest and largest dzongs, perhaps built as early as 1100. Like Trongsa, Shongar was powerful because the dzong was ideally situated to control movements between eastern and western Bhutan. The new dzong was built in Mongar town

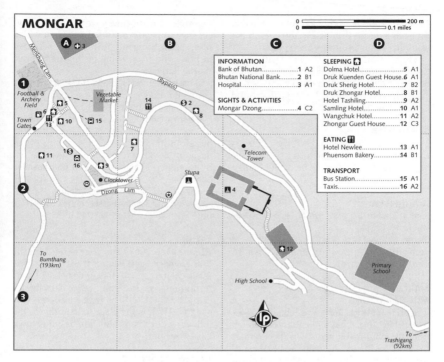

when the old one was destroyed by fire in 1899. You can hike to the dzong on a sweaty overgrown trail rich with birdlife.

A few kilometres further, Lingmethang (650m) has a large Public Works Department (PWD) station, some small rough wooden shops, a pig farm and a big sawmill.

The road turns north at a chorten that marks the junction of the main Kuri Chhu valley. At Kuri Zampa (570m) you finally hit the valley floor with a bump – an amazing descent of 3200m from the pass. Step out of your vehicle and breathe in the thick syrupy air before frantically stripping off three layers of clothing. On the east side of a prayer flag–strewn Bailey bridge is a large concrete **chorten** that is patterned after Bodhnath in Nepal; it is said to contain relics from the original Shongar Dzong. Beside the bridge is a deserted factory that used to extract oil from lemongrass, before the funding ran out.

A secondary road leads downstream to the new town of Gyalpozhing and the Kuri Chhu power project. The government is in the process of building an entire town similar to Khuruthang here, including a 64km-long road down the Kuri Chhu valley to Nanglam on the Indian border.

## Kuri Zampa to Mongar
### 25km / 45 mins
The road to Mongar climbs through chir-pine forests up the eastern side of the Kuri Chhu valley. To the north you can see the road to Lhuentse traversing the side of the valley. This road leaves the Mongar road at Gangola, 12km before Mongar, and travels 65km to Lhuentse (see p186).

The Mongar road climbs up and up through cornfields towards a cluster of houses on top of the hill. A final switchback leads into Mongar.

## MONGAR
☎ 04 / elev 1600m

Most towns in the west of Bhutan are in valleys. In eastern Bhutan most towns, including Mongar, are on the tops of hills or ridges. A row of large eucalyptus trees protects the town from the wind.

There is little of real interest to see in Mongar, but many people spend a night here before continuing to Trashigang. It takes about

11 hours to drive from Jakar to Trashigang. This often means driving at night, which is a waste in such interesting countryside.

The pleasant main street is lined with traditionally painted wooden Bhutanese buildings decorated with colourful potted plants. Archers sharpen their aim on the football ground most afternoons.

## Orientation

Mongar was redesigned in 1997 when a bypass road was constructed and a large part of the bazaar razed and rebuilt. The dzong is on a ridge above the town.

## Information

**Bank of Bhutan** (Map p185; ☎ 641123; ☷ 9am-1pm Mon-Fri, to 11am Sat)
**Bhutan National Bank** (Map p185; ☎ 641495)
**Hospital** (Map p185; ☎ 641112) Eastern Bhutan's new main hospital should open here in 2007.

## Sights
### MONGAR DZONG

The present **Mongar Dzong** was rebuilt in 1953; unusual because it has two entrances and because the monk and administrative bodies share the same courtyard. The dzong was established here in 1930 to replace the original Shongar Dzong, although the original *utse* (central tower) dates from an earlier age. There are 250 monks in the dzong, many of them young boys aged eight to 10 years old. The week-long Mongar tsechu is held here in November. The main Sangay Lhakhang is probably the only chapel in Bhutan equipped with comfy sofas!

## Sleeping

Several new tourist hotels should have opened by the time you read this, including the top-end **Wangchuk Hotel** (Map p185) and **Druk Sherig Hotel** (Map p185), and these will be the hotels of choice.

**Druk Zhongar Hotel** (Map p185; ☎ 641587; fax 641590; r Nu 1800, ste Nu 2200; ⌨) Until the new hotels open, this well-run modern hotel is easily the best place in town. Rooms are excellent, with a balcony and satellite TV, though some are larger than others. The Phuntso Delek Restaurant here is also good and a steam room is planned.

**Zhongar Guest House** (Map p185; ☎ 641107; s Nu 500-1200, d Nu 800-1400) This government guesthouse is in a charming traditional-style wooden building, complete with royal quarters, great views over the dzong and a fabulous sense of history. Unfortunately staying here is a bit of

a gamble; if at any time government employees turn up, you'll be turfed out, even with a reservation, so agents are naturally reluctant to book you here. Some of the rooms have shared bathrooms.

**Dolma Hotel** (Map p185; ☎ 641508; d Nu 500) A clean and modern place in a shopping plaza, with a balcony and private bathrooms.

There are numerous small local-style hotels in Mongar because the Trashigang–Thimphu bus stops here on the first night of its three-day journey. The only place occasionally used by foreigners is the overpriced **Druk Kuenden Guest House** (Map p185; ☎ 641240; r Nu 400-900), though there's also the **Hotel Tashiling** (Map p185; ☎ 641207) and **Samling Hotel** (Map p185; ☎ 641111), both with rooms from Nu 250 to 350.

## Eating

Almost everyone eats in their hotel. Both the **Druk Kuenden Guest House** ( ☎ 641127) and the **Samling Hotel** ( ☎ 641111) have cosy lodge-style restaurants, as does the nearby **Hotel Newlee** (Map p185; ☎ 621240). The **Phuensom Bakery** (Map p185; ☎ 641143) is the place to load up for the following day's picnic lunch. The entire town closes by 8pm.

## Getting There & Away

Buses run daily to Trashigang (6am) and Lhuentse (1pm), and on Tuesday, Thursday and Saturday to Thimphu (two days, 6am) and Samdrup Jongkhar (6.30am).

# LHUENTSE DZONGKHAG

Formerly known as Kurtoe, the isolated district of Lhuentse is the ancestral home of Bhutan's royal family. Although geographically in the east, it was culturally identified with central Bhutan, and the high route over Rodang La was a major trade route until the road to Mongar was completed. Many Lhuentse women have looms at home and Khoma is especially famous for its *kushuthara* (brocade) weaving.

## MONGAR TO LHUENTSE (76KM)

Lhuentse is 63km from the junction at Gangola and a three-hour drive from Mongar. It's a dramatic trip, frequently taking you alongside cliffs high above the river valley, but it's a comfortable ride if there have not been any recent landslides.

EASTERN BHUTAN

## Mongar to Autsho
**38km / 1¼ hours**

It is 12km down the hill from Mongar to the junction of the Lhuentse road at Gangola (1110m). The Lhuentse road winds around the hill to Chali and passes the few houses of Palangphu and then the new suspension bridge to Banjor village (the previous bridge further upstream was washed away when a glacial lake burst, sending floodwaters surging down the valley). The road descends through an unstable slide area to the banks of the Kuri Chhu and the two shops that make up the village of Rewan. Passing a large Tibetan-style brick chorten surrounded by 108 smaller chortens, the road reaches the extensive cornfields and impressive riverside location of **Autsho** (920m). Near the river you may be able to spot rhesus monkeys playing on stones, and black cormorants looking for fish.

## Autsho to Tangmachu
**26km / 1 hour**

The road passes towering cliffs, half hidden in the mist, en route to Fawan. The road switchbacks 100m above the river to the scruffy roadside settlement of Gorgan opposite the large valley of the Noyurgang Chhu, which enters from the west. Near this part of the road, in Umling, are said to be the remains of an ancient underground stone castle built by Bangtsho Gyalpo in about 1500 BC.

After a while the Kuri Chhu valley begins to widen. Beyond a large white chorten the road crosses to the west bank of the river on a suspension bridge. On the hillside high above the bridge locals are building a 41m-high statue of Guru Rinpoche, above the improbably located settlement of **Tangmachu** (known locally as Darkila). The statue will be one of the world's tallest and will cost 100 million ngultrum. A rough unpaved road leads 10km up to the village and high school, 600m above the road, but the road is often impassable if it's been raining.

## Tangmachu to Lhuentse
**13km / 30 mins**

The road traverses the foot of the Tangmachu valley for about 6km, passing a road construction camp and a hydrology station at Sumpa. Rounding a corner there's a view of **Lhuentse Dzong**, which dominates the head of the valley. A small suspension bridge leads across the river here, providing access to the trail to Khoma and Singye Dzong (see p188).

A short distance on the valley narrows and the road begins climbing towards the town. As the road passes the hospital there is an excellent view of the dzong perched dramatically atop a bluff. The road to Dongkhar branches off by the hospital.

## LHUENTSE
☎ 04 / elev 1440m

There is little to see in Lhuentse and there's no actual village here, but the dzong is one of the most picturesque in Bhutan. The series of concrete terraces you see as you enter the town, just above the current collection of wooden shops and bars, is the site for yet another of Bhutan's new towns. The pillared pavilion nearby is a cremation ground.

The road terminates in front of the dzong. Adjoining the parking lot are quarters for government officials working in Lhuentse who have been posted to this remote area where housing is scarce.

It's worth driving up to the Royal Guest House for views of the dzong and the snow peaks at the head of the Kuri Chhu valley. The peak at the head of the valley to the northwest of the guesthouse is Sheri Nyung.

As you leave Lhuentse for Mongar, look out for the ancient ruined bridge down in the valley below, just before the bend in the river.

### Sights
#### LHUENTSE DZONG

Lhuentse Rinchentse Phodrang Dzong, as it is correctly known, sits high on a rocky outcrop overlooking the Kuri Chhu valley, with near-vertical drops on all sides.

Although Pema Lingpa's son Kuenga Wangpo established a small goemba on this site early in the 16th century, the dzong itself was built by the Trongsa *penlop* Mingyur Tenpa in 1654. It has been renovated several times and numerous lhakhangs have been added. A three-day tsechu fills the dzong to capacity in December/January.

Visitors can visit seven lhakhangs, assuming you can find someone with the keys. The 100 or so resident monks see few tourists and are very friendly, which perhaps explains why visitors here have more freedom to explore than they do in any other dzong in Bhutan.

## Sleeping & Eating

**Royal Guest House** ( ☎ 545102; bed Nu 120-200) Lhuentse's only hotel is this government guesthouse, on a hill 100m above the town. It's possible to get a booking here but it's a hassle (the local *dzongkhag* administration prefers you have permission from the Home Ministry in Thimphu) and you could get bumped by visiting officials.

It's best to arrive in Lhuentse with a packed lunch, otherwise you can get Bhutanese dishes and perhaps *momos* (dumplings) at the basic **Shangrila Hotel** ( ☎ 545123) or nearby and slightly nicer **Karma Hotel**.

## Transport

Buses run three times a week to Thimphu, overnighting in Bumthang.

## AROUND LHUENTSE
### Khoma

If you are interested in weaving (and even if you're not) it's worth making the hike up to this traditional weaving village. The village produces some of Bhutan's most sought-after and expensive *kushutara* weavings and almost all of the 30 houses in the village have traditional back-strap looms set up in their porches. The weavings are so elaborate that they resemble embroidery and are generally used as *kiras* (women's traditional dress), though bags and other pieces are produced. The village's comparative wealth has translated into Sony TVs and Hoyt bows, and mule caravans frequently shuttle consumer goodies up to the well-stocked shops. The Zangto Pelri Lhakhang sits on a spur overlooking the river junction.

It's an easy 90-minute hike up to the village, passing the Drak Kharpo (White Hermitage Cave) of Guru Rinpoche, visible high on the far cliffs.

A few Bhutanese travel companies offer three-day tours of surrounding weaving villages, including Gonpokarpo, Chenling, Minje and Nyilamdun (Ngangladung)

### Dungkhar

An unpaved road runs from Lhuentse for 39km to the small village of Dungkhar, named because the ridge upon which it sits is shaped like a conch (*dungkhar*). Pema Lingpa's son Kuenga Wangpo settled here, and it is through him that Bhutan's royal family, the Wangchucks, trace their ancestry to the Kurtoe region. Jigme Namgyal, father of the first king, was born here in 1825 and left home when he was 15 to eventually become Trongsa *penlop* and the 51st *desi*.

Special permission is required to visit Dungkhar, although check with your travel agency as this may soon change. The Jigme Namgyal Naktshang and the renovated 16th-century Dungkhar Naktshang are above the village. (A *naktshang* is a temple dedicated to a warlord or protective deity.) Also here is the renovated Dungkhar Choeje, the birthplace of the first king. Guru Rinpoche meditated in a cave overlooking Dungkhar, and Pema Lingpa visited the area many times and built Goeshog Pang Lhakhang near the river below the village.

### Singye Dzong

Singye Dzong is on the old trade route from Bhutan to Lhobrak in Tibet. Guru Rinpoche meditated here and it's an important pilgrimage place for Bhutanese. The trek takes three days in each direction, but is off-limits to tourists. Yeshe Tsogyal, the consort of Guru Rinpoche who concealed many *terma* here, founded the goemba.

# TRASHIGANG DZONGKHAG

Trashigang is the heart of eastern Bhutan and was once the centre of important trade with Tibet. There are several goembas and villages that make a visit worthwhile, but a lot of driving is required to reach this remote region.

## MONGAR TO TRASHIGANG (92KM)

The Mongar to Trashigang stretch is easier and shorter than the journey from Jakar to Mongar, but you still need about 3½ hours to cover the 92km between the two towns, plus an extra two hours if you detour to Drametse Goemba. The road crosses one low pass, then follows a river valley before making a final climb to Trashigang.

### Mongar to Kori La
**17km / 30 mins**

Leaving Mongar, the road climbs past fields of corn to the power substation and *shedra* (Buddhist college) at Kilikhar, then through rhododendron and blue-pine forests to the few houses in the scattered settlement of Naling. Soon the road is clinging to the side of a cliff, passing through a deep forest of rhodo-dendrons and orchids.

About 3km past a forest nursery is Kori La (2400m), where there is an array of prayer flags and a small *mani* wall. The forest surrounding the pass is under a management plan regulating the harvest of trees and bamboo.

## Kori La to Yadi
**21km / 1 hour**

The road drops from the pass into the upper reaches of the extensive Manas Chhu drainage, switchbacking down through broadleaf forests to the small private Guru Lhakhang, near the village of **Naktshang**. Above the road are several small buildings used by monks as retreat and meditation centres.

The road continues its descent past fence-like prayer flags (the Bhutanese equivalent of road safety barriers) and through fields of corn and mustard, past the road-crew camp at Ningala, finally reaching the substantial village of **Yadi** (1480m). The **Choden Restaurant** ( ☎ 04-539113) here is a good place to break for a cup of tea and a look at the village lhakhang just across the road.

Below Yadi a dirt road branches off 17km to Shershong (or Serzhong) and, for Bhutanese pilgrims only, a two-day walk to Aja Ney. The 'A' of Aja is a sacred letter and 'ja' means 'one hundred'. Guru Rinpoche placed one hundred letter As on rocks here, and for devotees it's like a spiritual treasure hunt: the more you see the more merit you gain. Those without sin usually find the most.

## Yadi to Thungdari
**33km / 1 hour**

Beyond Yadi a long stretch of prayer flags lines the road; below are numerous switchbacks, nicknamed the **Yadi Loops**, that lead down through a forest of chir pine, dropping 350m in 10km. There is a good viewpoint where you can see the road weaving down the hill; pictures taken from here often appear in books and brochures to illustrate just how circuitous Bhutan's roads are. The unpaved road that heads west before the loops begin leads to the village and hydro plant of Chaskhar.

After more switchbacks, the road crosses a bridge painted with the eight auspicious symbols and continues for 10km to the nondescript bazaar of Sherichhu (600m). Climb out of the Sherichhu valley to a chorten and cross a ridge to meet the large Drangme Chhu, which flows from the eastern border of Bhutan and is a major tributary of the Manas Chhu. The road winds in and out of side valleys for 12km to Thungdari, 71km from Mongar, where a side road leads to Drametse Goemba.

## Drametse Goemba

Drametse is the biggest and most important monastery in eastern Bhutan. It's an 18km, hour-long detour on a dirt track off the main road, gaining 1350m, and you'll need a 4WD vehicle if it's been raining.

There are about 60 *gomchen* (lay or married Nyingma monks) at Drametse. The monastery was founded in 1511 by the great-granddaughter of Pema Lingpa, Ani Chhoeten Zangmo, and her husband, Yeshe Gyalpo, in a place she named Drametse, which means 'the peak where there is no enemy'.

The monastery is famous as the home of the Nga Cham drum dance that features in many tsechus and which was proclaimed a masterpiece of oral and intangible heritage by Unesco in 2005.

The murals of the guardian kings in the entryway were painted in the 1950s and re-painted in 1982. In the main chapel, to the right of a central Guru Rinpoche, is the gold chorten of Chhoeten Zangmo, next to a statue of her great-grandfather.

The middle floor has chapels dedicated to the protectors Palden Lhamo (Sri Devi) and the 'horse-necked' Tamdrin (Hayagriva). The upstairs **Goenkhang Chenmo** (Great Protector Chapel) is jam-packed with weapons, a stuffed lynx, a dead flying fox (that looks like it's been blown up with a foot pump), lots of arrows and the three local protector deities of Gyelpo, Drametse and Tsong Tsoma. Make an offering and you'll be blessed with a sacred thread. The next-door Tseringma Lhakhang houses the black hats used in the annual tsechu in September/October (see p247), as well as five versions of Tseringma, all riding different mythological beasts. Finally the Kanjur Lhakhang houses a box of sacred relics, including bowls and *drilbu* (Tantric bells).

This is wonderful potato-growing country. In the autumn there are huge piles of potatoes waiting for trucks to carry them down to the market for eventual sale in India and Bangladesh. In the distance to the southeast you can see the college at Kanglung (see p196).

**EASTERN BHUTAN**

## Thungdari to Chazam
**11km / 30 mins**

Back down on the main road you'll catch glimpses of Trashigang Dzong high above the south bank of the Drangme Chhu. Much of the hillside beside the road is made up of loose alluvial deposits. Boulders embedded in the sand often break loose during rainstorms and fall onto the road, causing delays while road crews scramble to remove them.

After passing a PWD camp at Rolong, the road reaches a new 90m-long bridge at Chazam (710m). This place was named after the original chain-link bridge here, said to have been built by the Tibetan bridge builder Thangtong Gyalpo (see the boxed text, p131) in the 15th century (*cha* means 'iron', *zam* means 'bridge'). The large building that formed the abutment of the old bridge has been partially restored and can be seen a short distance upstream of the new bridge. Look for the ruins of watchtowers on the ridge above the old bridge.

## Chazam to Trashigang
**9km / 15 mins**

On the south side of the bridge is an immigration checkpoint where police inspect your travel permit. The road north from here follows the Kulong Chhu valley and then climbs to Trashi Yangtse (p195).

The road switchbacks up through cornfields towards Trashigang, passing a turn-off that leads down to the small settlement of Chenary. The Druk Seed Corporation here produces seeds for subtropical fruit.

At the top of the hill is a collection of motor workshops and a road junction. The road to southern Bhutan leads to the right. The left fork leads to Trashigang, 3km away. Go round a bend where there's a good view of Trashigang Dzong, then follow the road into Trashigang, which is well hidden in a wooded valley.

## TRASHIGANG
☎ 04 / elev 1070m

Trashigang is one of Bhutan's more interesting towns and a good base for excursions to Trashi Yangtse, Khaling, Radi, Phongme and elsewhere in eastern Bhutan.

Accommodation here is fairly limited, but there is a variety of restaurants and you're bound to find at least one amusing place to drink among the town's 21 bars. Not many tourists make it to Trashigang, but there used to be many Canadian teachers working here

and the people of Trashigang are used to Westerners.

Villagers come to town on holy days, which occur on the first, 10th and 15th of the Bhutanese month, to trade and sample the local *arra*.

## Orientation

Trashigang is at the foot of a steep wooded valley with the tiny Mithidang Chhu channelled through it. The road crosses the stream on a substantial bridge near a chorten. A side road leads downhill from the chorten past a handsome collection of shops, bars and small restaurants, then through trees and bougainvillea past a chorten to the dzong.

The town's focal point is a central plaza and parking area. A large prayer wheel sits in the centre of the square. The pedestal on the covered structure, holding the prayer wheel, is a favourite sleeping place for villagers waiting for buses. Surrounding the parking area are several hotels and restaurants, a bakery and the main liquor outlet.

The road north of here quickly branches, left to Rangjung, Radi and Phongme, or right to the upper town's main administrative offices.

## Information

**Bank of Bhutan** (Map p191; ☎ 521294; ◷ 9am-1pm Mon-Fri, to 11am Sat)

**Bhutan National Bank** (Map p191; ☎ 521129; ◷ 9am-1pm Mon-Fri,to 11am Sat) On the ground floor of the post office.

**Jigme Wangmo Photo Studio** (Map p191) Sells *Kuensel* as well as print film.

**Kuenphen Medical Store** (Map p191; ☎ 521175) For medical supplies.

**Pelden Digital Café and Gift Corner** (Map p191; ◷ 8am-9pm; per min Nu 3) Internet access.

**Post Office** (Map p191; ◷ 9am-5pm Mon-Fri, to 1pm Sat) Above the town, near the high school.

## Sights
### TRASHIGANG DZONG

The **dzong** is on a high promontory that overlooks the confluence of the Drangme Chhu and the Gamri Chhu. It was built in 1667 by Mingyur Tenpa, Bhutan's third *desi*. The entire eastern region was governed from this dzong from the late 17th century until the beginning of the 20th century.

This dzong is unusual in that both the administrative and monastic bodies face onto a single *dochey* (courtyard). As always, the

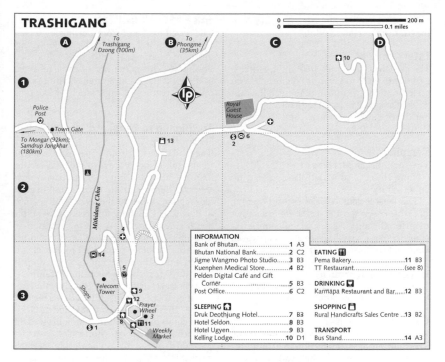

## TRASHIGANG

INFORMATION
Bank of Bhutan..........................1 A3
Bhutan National Bank................2 C2
Jigme Wangmo Photo Studio......3 B3
Kuenphen Medical Store............4 B2
Pelden Digital Café and Gift
  Corner...................................5 B3
Post Office...............................6 C2

SLEEPING
Druk Deothjung Hotel...............7 B3
Hotel Seldon............................8 B3
Hotel Ugyen.............................9 B3
Kelling Lodge..........................10 D1

EATING
Pema Bakery...........................11 B3
TT Restaurant......................(see 8)

DRINKING
Karmapa Restaurant and Bar.....12 B3

SHOPPING
Rural Handicrafts Sales Centre ..13 B2

TRANSPORT
Bus Stand...............................14 A3

---

*gorikha* (porch) has paintings of the Four Guardian Kings. Inside the Kunrey Lhakhang is a statue of the deity Gasin-re or Yama, the wrathful aspect of Chenresig. He is a protector of the faith, the god of death and the king of law, and the one that weighs up the good and evil at the end of a person's life. You can see him in the vestibule of most lhakhangs holding the Wheel of Life in his mouth. Many lama dances are performed in Trashigang to appease Yama, especially during the four-day tsechu in November/December.

### Sleeping & Eating

An alternative to staying in Trashigang is to continue 16km east of town and overnight at the pleasant guesthouse of the Rangjung Wodsel Chholing Monastery (see p192).

**Druk Deothjung Hotel** (Map p191; ☎ 521214; fax 521269; s/d Nu 1150/1500; 🖵 ) This family-run hotel near the central prayer wheel is the best in town. It's comfortable, with satellite TV and hot-water showers, and is an authentic Bhutanese hotel unlike many of the ones that tourists get herded into, but it's far from luxurious, with concrete grills in the walls that let in bugs and

street noise. The pleasant al-fresco dining area serves up the best food in town. The owner is planning a 20-room hotel 1km west of town but has yet to gain permission to build.

**Kelling Lodge** (Map p191; ☎ 521145; s/d Nu 150/300, deluxe s/d Nu 250/450) Travellers can in theory obtain permission to stay at this slightly neglected government guesthouse. The two top-floor deluxe rooms are perfect for a group of four.

**Hotel Ugyen** (Map p191; ☎ 521140; s/d Nu 100/200) Formerly the Sonam Wangchuck, this basic place is very much a third or fourth choice. It has rooms that are similar in standard to a trekking lodge in Nepal, with basic bathrooms down the corridor.

**Hotel Seldon** (Map p191; ☎ 521362; s/d Nu 500/800) This also has some basic overpriced rooms for rent upstairs, if you are desperate.

**Pema Bakery** (Map p191; ☎ 521196) Next-door to the Druk Deothjung Hotel, this bakery serves bread and pastries, as well as a good range of imported goodies from Pringles to Coffee Mate.

**TT Restaurant** (Map p191; ☎ 521184) For a quick meal of rice, *ema datse* (chillies with cheese)

EASTERN BHUTAN

and meat try this busy place, downstairs in the back of the Hotel Seldon.

## Entertainment

The garden of the Druk Deothjung Hotel is a favourite place to savour a cold beer. If you prefer something more Bhutanese in flavour, try the **Karmapa Restaurant and Bar** (Map p191) but drink quickly, because the entire town starts to close at 8pm.

## Shopping

The small **handicrafts shop** at the Druk Deothjung Hotel is your last place to load up on souvenirs.

The **Rural Handicrafts Sales Centre** (Map p191; ☎ 521150; ✆ 9am-1pm & 2-5pm, Mon-Fri) is a showroom for Khaling's National Handloom Development Project, so is the place to pick up woven *kiras*, table runners and scarves, particularly if you can't make it to the weaving centre in Khaling (see p196). *Kiras* aren't cheap (Nu 4000 to 16,000) but bear in mind that an elaborate piece can take up to six months to weave.

## Getting There & Away

From Trashigang it's 281km to Bumthang, 349km to Trongsa and 551km to Thimphu.

The local jeep drivers that wait at the bus stand say that if you leave Trashigang at 3.30am, you can reach Thimphu at 8.30pm, a total of 17 hours' gruelling driving.

There are daily local buses to Thimphu, Samdrup Jongkhar and Radhi, as well as less-frequent services to Mongar (Monday to Saturday), Trashi Yangtse (Wednesday and Saturday) and Phongme (Wednesday, Friday and Sunday). On many of these services the 'bus' is actually a converted truck, which provides a very bumpy and dusty ride.

## FAR EASTERN BHUTAN

The paved road east from Trashigang travels up the valley of the Gamri Chhu to Rangjung, and then continues as a dirt track to Radi and Phongme. This is the end of the line, as far east as you can go in Bhutan. If you're short on time, you won't miss much by skipping this route.

## Trashigang to Rangjung
### 16km / 45 mins

The road descends from Trashigang, weaving in and out of side valleys to the banks of the Gamri Chhu at 820m. A side road crosses the river here and leads 19km uphill in great zigzagging gashes to the town and goemba at Bartsam. The Rangjung road stays on the south side of the river, passing through an area affected by flooding in 2005 (the chorten in the middle of the plain that protects against floods didn't do a very good job…). Shortly afterwards is the village of Lungtenzampa.

After traversing fields for 6km, past the large Vocational Training Institute at Buna, the road crosses the small Kharti Chhu and makes a short climb to **Rangjung** at 1120m. Beyond the high school an elaborate chorten dominates the pleasant centre of town. The weekly vegetable market is sheltered by a huge mango tree. The new road layout for a planned expansion is in place just to the north of the village.

Above the town is the **Rangjung Woesel Chholing Monastery**, a large Nyingma goemba founded in 1990 by Garub Rinpoche. The main chapel has some impressive *torma* (sculptures of barley and butter), including one depicting the five senses, with eyeballs, earlobes, nostrils, a tongue and skin. The lower courtyard hosts *cham* dancing at the end of a 10-day *drup* (festival) in the 12th month.

---

### MIGOI – THE BHUTANESE YETI

Naturally, Bhutanese yetis have different characteristics from yetis found (or not found) in Tibet and other Himalayan regions. The Bhutanese name for a yeti is *migoi* (strong man) and they are believed to exist throughout northern and northeastern Bhutan, particularly in Sakten Wildlife Sanctuary.

The *migoi* is covered in hair that may be anything from reddish-brown to black, but its face is hairless, almost human. It is similar to the yetis of Nepal and Tibet in that the breasts of the female are large and sagging, and both sexes have an extremely unpleasant smell. But Bhutanese *migoi* are special because they have the power to become invisible, which accounts for the fact that so few people have seen them. Another feature that helps them escape detection is that the feet of many yetis face backwards, confusing people who try to follow them.

The book *Bhutanese Tales of the Yeti* by Kunzang Choden is a wonderful collection of tales told by village people in Bhutan who have seen, or have met people who have seen, a *migoi*.

The monastery has a good new **guesthouse** ( ☎ 04-561145; s/d Nu 600/800) just up the hill that is occasionally booked by tourists and particularly Buddhist groups. The modern concrete bungalows smell like a hospital but have private bathrooms and offer great views over the goemba.

## Rangjung to Phongme
**17km / 1 hour**
The road continues east, climbing through large rice terraces and fields of corn to Radi (1570m).

For an unusual outing, hike downhill for about 30 minutes from the Yeshi Lhundup shop, at a hairpin loop just before Radi (kilometre marker 23), to the small village of **Tzangkhar**. Most of the women here are weavers who specialise in fabrics made from *bura* (raw silk), and it's fun to walk from house to house to see the results. Enough cloth to make a *gho* or *kira* costs about Nu 30,000 for a flower design and about Nu 10,000 for a plainer pattern. It's a stiff uphill climb back to the road, gaining 130m.

Beyond Radi the road climbs past terraced hillsides and above the large modern **Thakcho Kunzang Choeden Anim Goemba**. A few kilometres later, past Khardung village, is the collection of shops that is Phongme (1840m).

On the hill above the village is the 150-year-old **Phongme Lhakhang**. The central statue is of Chenresig with 1000 arms and 11 heads. A rolled-up *thondrol* (building-sized *thangka*) hangs from the rafters and *cham* masks are stored in boxes at the foot of the statues.

## Sakten Wildlife Sanctuary
From Phongme a trail leads east to the remote minority villages of **Merak** and **Sakten**, which are inhabited by seminomadic tribesmen called Brokpa. Tourists were permitted to make this three-day trek in the past, but since 1995 the route has been closed to foreigners out of concern for the unique culture of the people living there. Tall Brokpa men often come into Phongme, Khaling and Trashigang to trade. You can recognise them by their sheepskin and yak-hair clothing and unusual yak-felt hats called *shamo,* which have hanging spider-like legs that act as rainspouts.

Katie Hickman gives a good description of her visit to the region on horseback in her travelogue *Dreams of the Peaceful Dragon* (see p17).

Apart from the Brokpas, the sanctuary's most famous resident is the *migoi*, or yeti, for whom the park was allegedly established in 2002. The sanctuary office is 1km east of Phongme, at the end of the motorable road.

# TRASHI YANGTSE DZONGKHAG

Previously a *drungkhag* (subdistrict) of Trashigang, Trashi Yangtse became a fully fledged *dzongkhag* in 1993. It borders the Indian state of Arunachal Pradesh, and there is some cross-border trade. The old trade route between east and west Bhutan used to go through Trashi Yangtse, over the mountains to Lhuentse and then over Rodang La (4200m) to Bumthang. This difficult route fell into disuse when the road from Trashigang to Bumthang via Mongar was completed. The district lies at the headwaters of the Kulong Chhu, and was earlier known as Kulong.

## TRASHIGANG TO TRASHI YANGTSE (53KM)
The drive from Trashigang to Trashi Yangtse takes about 1¾ hours' driving time, but you should budget extra time to visit Gom Kora on the way. There's lots to see en route and it's a great day trip from Trashigang. Even if you don't have time to drive all the way to Chorten Kora, do make the effort to make the short trip to Gom Kora.

To get from Trashigang to Chazam (9km, 15 minutes), follow the switchbacks down to the bridge at Chazam. Just past Chazam, an unpaved side road leads steeply uphill to Gangthung and Yangnyer. The complex that is visible a short distance up this road is a jail.

From Chazam, the road is level as it winds its way through sparse clumps of chir pine above the west bank of the Drangme Chhu to Gom Kora (13km, 30 minutes). A couple of kilometres before Gom Kora, by the side of the road, is a *nye* (holy spot), where a rock shrine is covered in *tsha-tshas* (small images moulded in clay) and brass images of the Rigsum Goempo.

## Gom Kora
Gom Kora is an extraordinarily picturesque temple to the east of the road, 13km north of Chazam. The lush green of the fields, the red

robes of the monks and the yellow roof of the temple combine with colourful painted Buddhist carvings and the rushing of the nearby river to create an idyllic atmosphere.

The correct name for the site is Gomphu Kora. Gomphu denotes a sacred meditation site of Guru Rinpoche and *kora* means 'circumambulation'. The Guru meditated here and left a body impression on a rock, similar to that in Kurjey Lhakhang in Bumthang.

The central figure in the goemba is Guru Rinpoche. To the right is Chenresig in his 1000-armed aspect. To the far right is an image of the snake demon Gangan Yonga Choephel, who holds a golden mirror in his right hand. The murals on the walls of the goemba are believed to date from the 15th century.

On a shelf below Chenresig are numerous sacred objects that either miraculously appeared here or were brought by the Guru. The largest item is a *garuda*'s egg, which is a very heavy, perfectly shaped, stonelike egg. Other relics include the traditional bootprint of the Guru, the footprint of his consort Yeshe Tsogyal (aged eight), the hoofprint of Guru Rinpoche's horse and a phallus-shaped rock belonging to Pema Lingpa.

Gom Kora's celebrated old *thondrol,* unique because it is painted, not appliquéd, is now kept in Chorten Kora. Gom Kora has a new *thondrol,* which is displayed at the tsechu in the second lunar month (March/April). This festival is different from most other tsechus and pilgrims circumambulate the goemba and sacred rock throughout the night (one article in *Kuensel* salaciously suggests that the evening's activities result in many marriages!).

Behind the goemba is a fantastical large black rock. It is said that Guru Rinpoche was meditating in a small cave near the bottom of the rock when a demon in the shape of a cobra suddenly appeared. The Guru, alarmed, stood up quickly (as you would), most likely swore and left the impression of his pointed hat at the top of the cave. The Guru then made an agreement with the demon to stay away until the end of his meditation. The contract was sealed with thumb prints, which are still visible on the rock. The serpent also left a print, with his hood at the top of the rock.

A small sin-testing passageway leads from the cave to an exit below the rock – one successful participant reported that you must indeed move like a snake to get through the cave. Visitors also test their sin levels and rock climbing

skills by trying to climb up the side of the rock (the 'stairway of the dakinis'); only the virtuous can make it. On certain auspicious days holy water, believed to be the Guru's nectar of immortality, flows down from a crevice in the rock and pilgrims line up to spoon it into empty Sprite bottles. You may also see childless women carrying a holy stone around the *kora* path to boost their chances of conceiving.

The monastery is home to 25 student monks.

## Gom Kora to Trashi Yangtse
**28km / 1¼ hours**

Two kilometres from Gom Kora is the sleepy village of **Duksum** (860m), the roadhead for many large villages higher in the valley. A couple of shops (try the 'Shantimo Tsongkhag and Cum Bar Shop') sell colourful patterned cloth and belts woven by the local women using back-strap looms. Duksum's iron chain-link bridge, believed to be the last surviving example of those built by Thangtong Gyalpo (see the boxed text, p131) was tragically washed away by flooding in 2004, but some links were recovered and used in the reconstructed bridge at Tamchhog Lhakhang (see p131). Duksum has had a difficult few years; a rockfall recently caused the villagers to abandon the upper section of the bazaar.

The road turns northwest and follows the Kulong Chhu valley towards Trashi Yangtse. The eastern fork of the river flows from Arunachal Pradesh in India and is known as the Dawung Chhu. There are proposals to build a dam along this section of the Kulong Chhu.

Climbing high above the Kulong Chhu, at Zangpozor the road passes the junction of a paved road that leads 9km to the village of Tshenkarla. Above the village school are the ruins of **Tshenkarla dzong**, which was built in the first half of the 9th century by Prince Tsangma, the eldest son of Tibetan king Trisong Detsen. The prince established himself in eastern Bhutan after he was banished from Tibet. The old name of this town is Rangthang Woong.

Beyond the small settlement of Shali the habitation gets more sparse as the valley becomes steeper and less suitable for cultivation. Snowy peaks at the head of the valley come in an out of focus. After traversing along a rocky cliff, a house-like building appears on a promontory where a side stream, the Dongdi Chhu, joins the valley. This is the original **Trashi Yangtse Dzong**, built by Pema Lingpa alongside the former trade route, and now houses the town's community of 100 monks. The *dratshang* (monastic college) has a dramatic main assembly hall and an *utse*, which holds the dzong's most precious relic, a statue of Chenresig that flew here from Ralung in Tibet. The dzong is 1.5km up a side road, past a wonderful traditional cantilevered bridge.

## TRASHI YANGTSE

☎ 04 / elev 1700m

The new settlement of Trashi Yangtse is near the Chorten Kora, 3km from the old dzong. The new dzong and rapidly growing town occupies a large bowl in one of the furthest corners of the kingdom, 550km from Thimphu. The dzong was inaugurated in 1997 and, being new, has little historical or architectural significance.

The town is known for the excellent wooden cups and bowls made here from avocado and maple wood using water-driven and treadle lathes. Trashi Yangtse is also a centre of paper making. They use the *tsasho* technique with a bamboo frame, which produces a distinctive pattern on the paper.

### Orientation

The road enters from the south near the large Chorten Kora. North of the chorten is a bazaar area with a few shops and a tall, elaborately decorated Bhutanese-style chorten. From here one road leads to the impressive headquarters of the Bomdeling Wildlife Sanctuary and another climbs to the new dzong and administrative offices, on a ridge 130m above the town.

The turn-off to the local hospital and Institute for Zorig Chusum is in the south of town, just before you pass the Chorten Kora.

### Sights

#### CHORTEN KORA

Chorten Kora is large, but not nearly as large as the stupa of Bodhnath, after which it was patterned. It was constructed in 1740 by Lama Ngawang Loday in memory of his late uncle, Jungshu Phesan, and to subdue local spirits. The lama went to Nepal himself and brought back a model of Bodhnath carved in a radish. He had it copied here so that people could visit this place instead of making the arduous trip to Nepal. The reason that Chorten Kora is not an exact copy of Bodhnath is because the radish shrank during the trip and distorted the carving.

During the second month of the lunar calendar there is a *kora* here, whereby people gain merit by walking around the chorten. It is celebrated on two separate dates, 15 days apart. The first day is for the people from the Dakpa community in Arunachal Pradesh, India, who make the three-day pilgrimage here to celebrate the sacrifice of an eight-year-old girl from Arunachal Pradesh who was enshrined in the chorten during its construction to appease a troublesome demon. The second *kora* is for the Bhutanese, who come from all over eastern Bhutan. A month before the festival the chorten is whitewashed anew, with funds earned from rice grown in the fields immediately surrounding the chorten.

In front of the chorten is a natural stone stupa, the *sertho*, which is referred to as the 'mother' of the chorten. There's also a small goemba here. A popular recent Bhutanese film of the same name was shot at the chorten.

#### NATIONAL INSTITUTE FOR ZORIG CHUSUM

This red-roofed **institute** ( ☎ 781141; fax 781149; ☽ 9am-noon & 1-3.30pm Mon-Fri, to 12.30pm Sat) was opened in June 1997 to provide opportunities in vocational training for those who do not continue in the system of higher education. The school strives to produce technically proficient craftspeople, while providing them with a basic educational foundation. Six of the Zorig Chusum (13 arts and crafts) are studied here, including *thangka* painting, sculpture, metalwork and woodcarving. You can visit the school, watch the 96 students at work and take photographs, though the selection of crafts for sale was disappointing during our recent visit. The students are on holiday from December to March and for two weeks in July.

### Sleeping & Eating

**Dzongkhag Guest House** ( ☎ 781148; r Nu 300-500) If you have connections, you might be able to stay at this tin-roofed government guesthouse, just below the dzong and Royal Guest House (off-limits to visitors). All rooms have a bathroom but only half have hot water.

**Karmaling Hotel and Bakery** ( ☎ 781113; s/d Nu 600/800) With attached western bathrooms, a veranda and a bakery restaurant, this place could be nice if it weren't for the hard beds and bare concrete walls.

**Sonam Chhoden Hotel** ( ☎ 781152; s/d Nu 120/160) This hotel has basic rooms and you can get a simple meal here, but don't upset the owner – he's the school's tae kwan do instructor.

EASTERN BHUTAN

The Bomdeling Wildlife Sanctuary office (see below) has a couple of basic rooms in its **guesthouse** (r Nu 300-400), which you could use as a base to visit the sanctuary. Upper-floor rooms are the best. It's also possible to **camp** near Chorten Kora.

### Transport
Public buses run to Thimphu on Monday and Friday and to Trashigang on Wednesday and Saturday.

## AROUND TRASHI YANGTSE
### Bomdeling Wildlife Sanctuary
Bomdeling is a two- to three-hour walk or a 13km 4WD drive north of Chorten Kora. It is the winter (November to early March) roosting place of a flock of black-necked cranes (see p88). The flock of 141 cranes, smaller than the flock in Phobjikha, returns here year after year, though the recent flooding of roosting habitat reduced crane numbers considerably in 2006. The sanctuary is also home to red pandas, tigers and snow leopards.

The **visitor centre** ( ☎ 781155; bws@druknet.bt; ⏰ 9am-5pm Mon-Fri) in Trashi Yangtse has some good displays on the 1445-sq-km sanctuary and the manager can advise on hiking and camping options (in the central part of the sanctuary only). Apart from crane-watching, there are possible hikes up to the Buddhist sites of Rigsum Goempo, Dechen Phodrang and Minkhar Goemba.

# SAMDRUP JONGKHAR DZONGKHAG

The only reason to make the tortuous drive into southeastern Bhutan is to leave it, at the recently reopened border crossing with India at Samdrup Jongkhar.

## TRASHIGANG TO SAMDRUP JONGKHAR (180KM)
The winding drive from Trashigang to Samdrup Jongkhar takes at least six hours.

### Trashigang to Kanglung
22km / 45 mins
Three kilometres from Trashigang bazaar the southern road turns off the Mongar road and climbs past the petrol station.

Climbing around a ridge and heading south the road passes the settlement of Pam. There are few houses near the road, but there is an extensive settlement and a lhakhang on the hillside above. The narrow unpaved road that leads uphill from here goes to Rangshikhar Goemba.

Descend into a side valley, cross a stream and climb through rice terraces to the prosperous farming community of Rongthung, 17km from Trashigang. The road then climbs to a ridge and enters Kanglung (1870m), where you can see the clock tower and extensive campus of Sherubtse College.

The late Father William Mackey, a Jesuit priest, was instrumental in setting up Sherubtse (Peak of Knowledge), Bhutan's only college, in the late 1970s. India aided the construction of the original school in 1964 as part of the construction of the road from Trashigang to the Indian border. Most foreigners know of the college through reading Jamie Zeppa's *Beyond the Sky and the Earth*, which chronicles her time teaching here as a Canadian volunteer. The clock tower and green lawns give the town the feel of a Himalayan hill-station.

### Kanglung to Khaling
32km / 1 hour
The road climbs through fields of corn and potatoes, then switchbacks around a line of eight chortens. There are fine views down over the college and as far as Drametse Goemba (p189), far across the valley. Above the road is the Yongphula army camp and further on is Yongphu Goemba. Hidden on a ridge above the road is Bhutan's second airstrip. There is occasionally talk that this small military airstrip might eventually be served by domestic flights, which would make eastern Bhutan much more accessible, but weather patterns would make any flights highly unreliable.

The road crosses the **Yongphu La** (2190m), offering you a last glimpse of the Himalaya, and swoops along the top of the Barshong valley, cuts across a ridge into another valley, then winds down again. A short climb leads over yet another ridge marked by chortens. It then descends to Gumchu, below which is a pretty valley, with several traditional houses surrounded by large, lush meadows.

Rounding a corner, the road enters Khaling, spread out in a large valley high above the Drangme Chhu. Above the valley is a small lhakhang. In the centre of the valley below

Khaling is the **National Institute for the Disabled**. This is a very well-organised institution that tries to assimilate students from all over Bhutan who are blind or otherwise disabled into the local educational system by providing special resources and training. One of their accomplishments is the development of a Dzongkha version of Braille. The school was originally set up by missionaries but has been run by the government since 1987.

Three kilometres beyond Khaling is the **National Handloom Development Project** ( ☎ 04-581122; nhdp@druknet.com ⏱ 9am-1pm & 2-5pm Mon-Fri), operated by the National Women's Association of Bhutan (NWAB). It contracts out weaving and provides cotton yarn on credit to about 400 villagers, who then return the finished product to be sold here, in Trashigang or at Handicraft Emporiums in Thimphu, Paro and Bumthang. It has samples of about 300 designs and, although it doesn't have fabric from every design in stock, it will take orders.

Particularly interesting are samples of the plants that are used to produce the natural dyes, including rhododendrons (pale yellow), an insect secretion called *lac* (purple) and the stem of the madder creeping plant (pale pink). Photography of the workshops and of the design samples is strictly prohibited. Prices for a length of woven cloth vary from Nu 950 up to Nu 12,000 and there are also shawls. Most of the basic cotton is imported from Kolkata.

## Khaling to Wamrong
### 27km / 45 mins
Beyond Khaling the road traverses above scattered houses and cornfields before climbing to the head of a rhododendron-filled valley and crossing the Kharung La at 2350m. There's a short descent through lots of loose rock, then another climb to another pass at 2430m.

Curling around the valley, the route descends past a side road to Thrimshing then curves round the **Zangto Pelri Lhakhang**. This may well be the last Bhutanese goemba you see, so check out the unique and wonderfully detailed murals and ceiling mandalas for old times' sake. Two kilometres below the lhakhang is the pleasant town of **Wamrong** (2130m), where you can get a good lunch at the local-style **Dechen Wangdi Restaurant** ( ☎ 04-571103). Wamrong is a *drungkhag* and so has a small dzong.

## Wamrong to Pemagatshel Junction
### 20km / 45 mins
The road here descends for 6km to Riserboo and its Norwegian-funded hospital. There is a good view down the huge valley as the road traverses in and out of side valleys past the hamlet of Moshi, halfway between Trashigang and Samdrup Jongkhar. At a bend in the road at kilometre marker 77 you get your first glimpse of the Assam plain below.

Before long you meet the junction to Pemagatshel, from where you can see Yongla Goemba on a hill across the valley.

## Pemagatshel Junction to Deothang
### 55km / 1¾ hours
Below the junction comes the day's most dangerous section of road, the **Menlong Brak** (*brak*, or *brag*, means cliff in Sharchop), high above the upper Bada valley. The fragile road passes prayer flags, prayer plaques and chortens to reach the Dantak-sponsored Hindu shrine at Krishnagiri, where your car will get a tikka from the resident sadhu. It's an amazing descent, with sheer drops putting the fear of Shiva into you.

From the two-road village of **Narphung** (with its one-way system!) the road passes a checkpoint to the Narphung La at 1698m. It crosses a ridge and climbs to 1920m before beginning the final descent to the plains.

The road weaves down, reaching the PWD camp at Morong at 1600m, whose workers are responsible for the Indian-style homilies that line the roads here: 'speed thrills but kills', 'no hurry, no worry', and our favourite 'it is not a rally, enjoy the valley'.

The Choekey Gyantso Institute for Advanced Buddhist Philosophy marks the outskirts of **Deothang** at 850m. The town's old name town was Dewangiri, and it was the site of a major battle between the Bhutanese and the British in 1865. The town is dominated by a large Royal Bhutan Army (RBA) camp and to the south is a chorten with the names of all those who died building Bhutan's roads. A side road branches off here to Bhangtar, a border town not open to foreigners.

## Deothang to Samdrup Jongkhar
### 18km / 30 mins
The road eventually hits the valley floor with a thud, as a rock painting of Guru Rinpoche marks the end of the Himalayan foothills. The road curves past Bhutan Chemical Industries to the fairly cursory **customs and immigration**

**EASTERN BHUTAN**

check at Pinchinang, 4km or so before Samdrup Jongkhar. It is here that you will get your exit stamp from Bhutan, even if you are spending the night in town before heading on to India.

## SAMDRUP JONGKHAR

☎ 07 / elev 170m

There's little reason to linger in this sweltering border town. The streets are jammed with Tata trucks and every morning and afternoon a tide of Indian workers crosses the border to work in the town. A Bhutanese-style gate decorated with a dragon and *garuda* bids you farewell as you cross into the heat and chaos of India.

Electricity is rather haphazard in Samdrup Jongkhar.

### Orientation

The highway enters the town from the north, passing the small modern dzong, post office, Dzongkhag (former Hifi) Guest House and Bank of Bhutan. The main road crosses a bridge then turns left by an internet café into the compact bazaar area, where you'll find the hotels, shops and restaurants. If you go straight instead of turning left, you will hit the border, with the Indian town of Darranga 400m beyond.

### Information

**Bank of Bhutan** ( ☎ 251149; ⏰ 9am-1pm Mon-Fri, to 11am Sat) Will change ngultrum into Indian rupees but not US dollars.

**PCO & Internet** ( ⏰ 8am-9pm; per min Nu 1.50)

### Sleeping & Eating

No hotels in Samdrup Jongkhar offered air-conditioning at the time of research.

**TLT Guesthouse** ( ☎ 251470; fax 251502) This Indian-style place next to the bazaar is probably the best option, with clean attached bathrooms and a decent restaurant.

**Hotel Menjong** ( ☎ 2511094; s/d Nu 650/850) The former Peljorling Hotel has spacious rooms but check the mattresses as these vary. There's a decent lobby restaurant and bar.

Other options include the basic Indian-style **Hotel Shambhala** (s Nu 210-260, d Nu 260-360) and **Hotel Friends** ( ☎ 251544, r Nu 300), where some rooms come with an 'air cooler', as well as bathroom and satellite TV.

### Getting There & Away

The easiest way to get to Guwahati is to arrange an Indian taxi through your hotel. A Bolero jeep costs US$40 for the 100km drive. Buses from the Indian town of Darranga, a 10-minute walk or rickshaw ride over the border, depart for Guwahati (Rs45 to 55) at 6.30am and 2pm.

Due to security concerns, all Bhutanese vehicles have to travel in a convoy as far as Ragiya (convoys do not run on Thursday or Sunday), 49km from the border. Indian vehicles face no such restrictions. For more on onward travel into India, see p261.

# PEMAGATSHEL DZONGKHAG

The name Pemagatshel means 'blissful land of the lotus'. This rural dzongkhag in the southeastern part of the country is Bhutan's smallest district. Its headquarters, Pemagatshel, is reached via a side road that leads off the Samdrup Jongkhar to Trashigang road.

### Yongla Goemba

Yongla Goemba is one of the holiest shrines in eastern Bhutan. It was founded in the 18th century by Kheydup Jigme Kuenduel, who was advised by the great *terton* Rigzin Jigme Lingpa to establish a monastery on a mountain that looked like a *phurba* (ritual dagger) and overlooked the vast plains of India. Later the goemba was used as a base for religious ceremonies by Trongsa *penlop* Jigme Namgyal during the great Duar War with the British in 1865.

# Trekking

Towns, dzongs and temples are one aspect of Bhutan, but the majority of the country is deep forests with a scattering of tiny settlements and high grazing lands. A trek provides the best opportunity to experience the real heart of Bhutan and to get insight into the rural culture of the kingdom through contact with people in remote villages and the staff accompanying you.

Many places feel so remote that you can imagine you are the first person ever to visit. As you sit contemplating this, read about the invading armies or royal processions that preceded you decades – or centuries – ago and you will be amazed at what these people accomplished.

## TREKKING IN BHUTAN

Government rules dictate that all treks must be arranged as camping trips. This also happens to be the only practical solution because there are few villages in the high country and no lodges or hotels in the hills.

A Bhutanese crew treks with you to set up camp, cook and serve meals. You carry a backpack with only a water bottle, camera and jacket. The rules specify that a licensed guide accompany all trekkers, but there is still a very limited number of guides who

are seasoned trekking guides. The Department of Tourism (DOT) operates a guide training and registration program to try to overcome this shortage, but you might still find that you have more camping experience than your guide.

Treks in Bhutan do not use porters. All your personal gear, plus tents, kitchen and food, is carried by pack horses or, at higher elevations, yaks. There are so few villages and facilities along trek routes that the people driving the pack animals carry their own food and tents and camp each night alongside you.

You will sleep in a tent with foam pads placed on the floor as a mattress. All your gear goes into the tent with you at night. Because there are also tents for the Bhutanese guides and the packers, you do not need to camp near villages and can trek comfortably to remote regions and high altitudes.

Often you will arrive at your camp at 3pm and will not dine until 6pm or 7pm. Unless you choose to do some exploring, there will be several hours of sitting around before dinner. It can also be quite cold in the dining tent, so you will need to dress warmly for meals.

For information on trekking companies abroad and on Bhutanese tour companies, see p257.

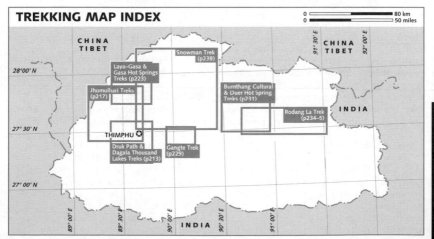

**TREKKING MAP INDEX**

0 — 80 km
0 — 50 miles

CHINA
TIBET

CHINA
TIBET

Snowman Trek (p238)

Laya–Gasa & Gasa Hot Springs Treks (p223)

28°00′ N

Jhomolhari Treks (p217)

Bumthang Cultural & Duer Hot Spring Treks (p231)

Rodang La Trek (p234–5)

INDIA

27° 30′ N

THIMPHU

Druk Path & Dagala Thousand Lakes Treks (p213)

Gangte Trek (p229)

27° 00′ N

89° 00′ E

89° 30′ E

90° 00′ E

90° 30′ E

91° 00′ E

91° 30′ E

92° 00′ E

INDIA

## A Trek is...

### A WILDERNESS EXPERIENCE

Most of Bhutan's landscape is covered with forests, and nowhere is this more obvious than on a trek. All treks climb up and down hills, passing through various vegetation zones with a great variety of trees. As there is a lot of wildlife in the hills of Bhutan, and most treks are in protected areas, there is a chance, albeit small, of seeing wildlife in its native habitat.

Once you step off the road to start the trek you are in true wilderness much of the time. Although there are established trails, there are no planes flying overhead, no roads and very few villages; instead there are views of snowcapped peaks and forested hillsides stretching to eternity.

### LONG

A short trek in Bhutan is three or four days in duration, an average trek is a week, but a trek of 25 days or more is possible. Every day your walk leads you one day further into the hills and you will have to walk that same distance to get back to a road. Make proper preparations before you start so that three days into the trek you don't find that you are ill-equipped, exhausted or unable to cope with the thought of walking all that distance back.

### PHYSICALLY DEMANDING

A Bhutan trek is physically demanding because of its length and the almost unbelievable changes in elevation. If you add all the climbing in the 14-day Laya–Gasa trek, for example, it is more than 6800m of elevation gain and loss during many steep ascents and descents. On most treks, the daily gain is less than 500m in about 18km, although 1000m ascents are possible on some days. You can always take plenty of time during the day to cover this distance; the physical exertion, although quite strenuous at times, is not sustained. You can take time for rest, but the trek days in Bhutan are long, requiring seven to nine hours of walking and you do have to keep moving to get to camp before dark.

Many of the climbs and descents are on rocky trails. Bhutan is amazingly rocky and on many routes the trail traverses long stretches of round river rocks. It requires some agility to hop between these. The trail is often extremely muddy, sometimes requiring a diversion to keep your feet dry. It can be a tricky balancing act on stones and bits of wood to get across stretches that have been ground into sloppy mud by the hooves of passing horses, yaks and cattle.

Many of the treks are on old trade routes that fell into disuse once a road was built. Some trails, especially in eastern Bhutan, have had little or no maintenance for 20 or 30 years. It's always possible to encounter snow, especially on high passes.

Probably the only physical problem that may make a trek impossible is a history of knee problems on descents. Throughout the Himalaya the descents are long, steep and unrelenting. There is hardly a level stretch of trail in the entire Himalayan region. If you are an experienced walker and often hike 20km to 25km a day with a backpack, a trek should prove no difficulty. You will be pleasantly surprised at how easy the hiking can be if you carry only a light backpack and do not have to worry about setting up a camp, finding water and preparing meals.

Previous experience in hiking and living outdoors is, however, helpful as you plan your trek. The first night of a two-week trek is too late to discover that you do not like to sleep in a sleeping bag.

Another unpleasant aspect of a trek in Bhutan is attacks by leeches during the rainy season. Leeches are rare during the normal trekking seasons, but if you want to see alpine flowers you need to come during July and August when the rain and leeches make life more difficult.

### NOT A CLIMBING TRIP

A Bhutan trek will not allow you to fulfil any Himalayan mountaineering ambitions. Bhutan's regulations prohibit climbing any peak higher than 6000m because of local concerns for the sanctity of the mountain peaks, which are revered as the home of deities.

## WHEN TO TREK

The most important consideration as you decide when to trek is weather. Most trekkers come in autumn; spring is the second most popular season. The high tourist season is during the period of best weather in autumn. Flights and hotels are fully booked and you will probably meet other trekkers on the popular routes.

Winter snow and summer rain limit the ideal trekking season in Bhutan to two brief periods. Late September to mid-November is

---

## MOUNTAINEERING

The mountains of Bhutan are ruggedly beautiful and though there are no 8000m-high peaks they are still largely unexplored. Also, there remains uncertainty over the name, location and height of many peaks. Jhomolhari was a famous landmark on the trip to Everest for early mountaineers. On the approach march for the 1921 British Everest Expedition, George Leigh Mallory described it as 'astounding and magnificent', but he remained 'cold and rather horrified' by the mountain. It was climbed from Tibet in 1937 by F Spencer Chapman and Passang Lama and again in 1970 by a joint Indian-Bhutanese team.

Michael Ward and Dr Frederic Jackson made an extensive survey of Bhutan's mountains in 1964–65. Climbing several peaks of around 5500m, they categorised the Bhutan Himalaya as a defined group of mountains. Bhutan opened its mountains to climbers for a short period from 1983 to 1994. A Bhutanese expedition scaled the 4900m-high Thurigang, north of Thimphu, in 1983. Jichu Drakye was attempted three times before it was successfully climbed in 1988 by an expedition led by Doug Scott. In 1985 Japanese expeditions climbed Gangri (7239m), Kari Jang, Kang Bum (6526m) and Masang Gang (7165m). Gangkhar Puensum (7541m) remains the highest unclimbed peak in the world after unsuccessful attempts by Japanese and British teams in the 1980s.

The government decided to prohibit mountain climbing after villagers living near the peaks asked it to for religious reasons.

---

recognised as the best time for trekking and the March to April period is the next best time. No matter when you trek you will have rain.

During autumn, nights are cold in the mountains, but the bright sun makes for pleasant daytime temperatures – in the high 20s, falling to 5°C at night, between 1000m and 3500m. At higher altitudes, temperatures range from about 20°C down to minus 10°C. Mornings are usually clear with clouds building up after 1pm, but they typically disappear at night to reveal spectacular starry skies. Most high passes are snowbound from late November until around February and in some years the snow does not disappear until April or May.

Late March to mid-May affords warmer weather and blooming rhododendrons, but there is a higher chance of rain or snow if you trek during this time and high country treks in March are often snowed out. There will be long periods of constant rain during a monsoon trek between May and August. Alpine wildflowers are in bloom during August and September, but the mud is deep and there are no mountain views. The ardent botanist (or the insane) might select July and August for a trek.

## GUIDES & CAMP STAFF

A small but efficient number of trek staff will accompany you. If you are trekking with a small group, the guide and cook will team up to handle the logistics. With a large group, the team will include a 'trek organiser' who will see that the loads are packed, tents set up and pack animals loaded on time. English names, not Dzongkha, are used for the various job titles. In addition to the cook and guide, there will be one or more 'waiters' who serve food and handle the kitchen chores.

### Pack Animals

There is a well-organised system for arranging pack animals in Bhutan. Contractors at the starting point of each trek arrange for horses to carry the gear. The animals' owners accompany the trek to arrange the loads and see that they get where they are supposed to each day. The ancient *dolam* system in Bhutan allocates specific grazing grounds to each village. For this reason, pack animals don't cross *dzongkhag* boundaries. Messages are sent ahead so that replacement animals are, hopefully, waiting at the boundary. At higher elevations, yaks carry the loads.

Food, tents and camp gear are packed in large, rectangular, covered baskets called *zhim*, which are then lashed to a wooden pack saddle. Trekkers' duffel bags are usually placed inside a jute sack for protection and then tied onto the animals. The process of saddling and loading the animals in the morning is a slow and tedious chore.

You won't have much to do with your pack animals, except at camp, but you will probably pass them, and other pack animals, along the trail. Stand off to the side to let horses pass, but with yaks you must get as far as possible off to the side of the trail because they are much

**TREKKING**

---

**YAKS**

Westerners tend to oversimplify the many manifestations of the yak into this single word, yet it is only the full-blooded, long-haired bull of the species Bos grunniens that truly has the name yak. In Bhutan the name is pronounced 'yuck' and females of the species are called jim. Females are prized for their butterfat-rich milk, used to make butter and cheese.

Large, ponderous and clumsy looking, yaks have the ability to move very quickly when startled. They are used as pack animals for seasonal migration to alpine pastures in Laya and other high regions of western Bhutan. If you are trekking with yaks, give them a wide berth, and don't put anything fragile in your luggage. If an animal becomes alarmed, it charges up a hill and your baggage falls off and gets trampled as the yak bucks and snorts when its keeper tries to regain control.

Though some yaks are crossbred with local cows, there are many purebred yaks in Bhutan – massive animals with thick furry coats and impressive sharp horns.

---

more skittish and won't pass if you are close to them. Yaks are dangerous, especially their sharp horns. Stand on the uphill side of the trail so you don't get pushed off as the animals pass.

## TREKKING FOOD

You can rely entirely on the camp meals and not carry any food with you to Bhutan. You might carry a small supply of chocolate bars or trail mix for snacks, or a few packets of seasoning to liven up soups, but it's not necessary. Your cook can look after any special dietary requirements if given advance notice.

Because there is almost no fresh food available on trek routes, the entire supply must be carried from the start of the trek. As you begin the trek, fresh vegetables and meat are available and camp meals tend to be even better than those available in Thimphu. On a longer trek, the fresh food goes off after the first week or so and you are largely reduced to tinned food.

Meals usually include a rice dish, a potato dish or, frequently, both. The cook prepares meals over stoves fuelled by bottled gas, and most Bhutanese trekking cooks are adept at producing a reasonable variety of Western and Asian dishes. They often add interesting Bhutanese touches, such as cheese sauces, but know to avoid hot chillies unless you specifically request them.

The midday meal is often a packed lunch and may consist of fried rice or noodles, boiled potatoes or chapatis. It is normally accompanied by tea from a large flask. Sometimes the cook loads a lunch horse with a gas cylinder and a basket of food and produces a hot lunch on the trail, but this is infrequent because on most trekking days there is not a good place to cook and eat at the right time.

## CLOTHING & EQUIPMENT

There is no trekking gear available in Bhutan; you must bring all your equipment. Everything on the Personal Equipment Check List (p207) is useful, and most of it necessary, on a long trek. All of this gear (except perhaps the sleeping bag) will pack into a duffel bag weighing less than 15kg.

Some gear will not be necessary on your trek. You might be lucky enough to trek during a rare warm spell and never need a down jacket. It might be so cold and rainy that you never wear short pants. However, these are unusual situations, and you should be prepared for extremes.

Make a special effort to reduce the weight of the baggage you bring on the trek. Each pack animal carries 30kg and it is expected that one animal will carry the luggage of two trekkers. Hence, any baggage over 15kg is a complication.

### What is Provided

The trek operator will provide two-person tents with foam mattresses, as well as eating utensils and kitchen equipment. Government rules specify that the trek operator should also provide a first-aid kit and a pressure bag (Portable Altitude Chamber) for high-altitude treks, but you should still carry your own supply of basic medical needs.

Trek operators expect you to bring your own sleeping bag. There are no sleeping bags available for rent in Bhutan.

### General Trekking Clothing
#### DOWN- OR FIBRE-FILLED JACKET
You should bring a good jacket on a trek. Most ski jackets are not warm enough and

---

**DIFFERENCES BETWEEN TREKS IN NEPAL & BHUTAN**  *Robert Peirce*

People used to trekking in Nepal will find that conditions are generally similar in Bhutan. The differences that do exist are mostly due to geography. The hillsides in Bhutan tend toward the near-vertical. This means there are fewer farms, villages and reasonable camp sites.

Because geographical considerations make the distance between camp sites greater than the average distance between camps in Nepal, trekking days tend to be longer. Side-hill climbing on steep slopes also means that you do more up-and-down climbing to get around vertical cliffs, avalanche tracks and side canyons. The trails are generally good but, through centuries of use, in many places they have been worn down to paths of scattered rounded rocks or just plain mud.

You may not see other trekkers on the trail but, because camp sites are designated, you are likely to share your camp spot with other parties on the popular Jhomolhari and Laya–Gasa treks. On other treks you probably won't see another group at all. Generally speaking, the trekkers are older than those trekking in Nepal. This, I assume, is because older, settled people are better able to afford the high cost of travel in Bhutan. In some camp sites there are huts that can serve as kitchens for your crew, or used as dining rooms, but most of the time meals are served in a dining tent. There are no Nepali-style teahouses or trekkers' lodges in Bhutan.

In my experience, trekkers' meals in Bhutan compare well with restaurant meals. If you are used to Nepal's two-hour-plus lunch breaks, you'll learn to adjust to a much shorter midday stop here. In Nepal, the crew takes time to cook a hot meal while the members nap. In Bhutan, they bring along a hot dish in an insulated container (with other goodies) for what amounts to a glorified trail lunch. The crew tends to be much smaller than crews in Nepal. Three or four people do the work of five to seven or more. Maybe one reason for this is that there are fewer security problems in Bhutan and thus no need for extra people to guard the camp.

In most places in Nepal, the local people have become accustomed to trekkers but in Bhutan you are still a curiosity. People stare at you with open, friendly faces or greet you warmly as you pass – even come up to you and shake your hand. You become used to kids running to greet you, shouting, 'Bye-bye'. Some have not learnt that it is a no-no to ask for pens. Others startle you by bowing low and bidding, 'Good morning, sir'.

---

most so-called expedition parkas are too heavy and bulky.

Your jacket can serve many functions on the trek. It will become a pillow at night and on long car trips and can also protect fragile items in your backpack or duffel bag. If you are extremely cold, wear your down jacket to bed inside your sleeping bag.

Artificial-fibre jackets (filled with Polargard, Thinsulate or Fibrefill) are a good substitute for down and much cheaper.

**JUMPER OR PILE JACKET**

Two light layers of clothing are better than a single heavy layer, and one or two light jumpers (sweaters), shirts or polypropylene layers are superior to a heavy jacket.

Pile jackets made of polyester fleece come in a variety of styles and thicknesses. They are light, warm (even when wet) and easy to clean.

**HIKING SHORTS OR SKIRT**

Most treks are at altitudes where it is cool, even during the day, so most people are com-

fortable in long pants. Pants, however, pull at the knees and are hot, so some prefer shorts. Either cut-offs or hiking shorts with big pockets are fine, but only for men. Skimpy track shorts are culturally unacceptable.

Women should consider a skirt, perhaps over a pair of shorts. Many women who have worn skirts on treks are enthusiastic about them. The most obvious reason is the ease in relieving yourself along the trail. There are long stretches where there is little chance to drop out of sight, and a skirt solves the problem. A wrap-around skirt is easy to put on and take off in a tent. Long 'granny' skirts are not practical because you will be walking through mud. Slacks are also culturally correct.

**RAIN GEAR**

It is almost certain to rain at some time during your trek. The condensation inside a waterproof jacket can make you even wetter than standing out in the rain. Gore-Tex jackets are supposed to keep you dry by allowing the jacket to breathe, but in Bhutan you'll sweat a lot on the steep hills and jackets don't always work as advertised.

One way to keep dry while hiking in the rain is to use a poncho – a large, hooded tarp with a hole in the centre for your head.

Another way of keeping dry is an umbrella. This is an excellent substitute for a poncho (except on windy days) and can serve as a sunshade, a walking stick, an emergency toilet shelter and a dog deterrent.

### T-SHIRTS OR BLOUSES

You'll spend a lot of time walking in short sleeves – what the equipment catalogues call the first layer. Cotton garments are fine, but if you can afford (and find) a synthetic T-shirt, you will be much more comfortable. You will perspire excessively, and a polypropylene shirt (with brand names such as Capilene and Thermax) wicks the moisture away from your skin.

### SWIMWEAR

The only reasonable places to bathe on a trek are in hot springs. Skinny dipping is taboo if you are more than 10 years old. Bring along swimwear or use shorts or a skirt when you go into the hot spring.

## High-Altitude Clothing

### INSULATED PANTS

Insulated pants are a real asset on a trek that goes above 4000m. You can bring pile pants, ski warm-up pants or down pants and put them on over your hiking pants or under a skirt when you stop. You can also wear them to bed for extra warmth when the nights become particularly cold.

### NYLON WINDBREAKER

Strong winds are rare in the places most treks visit, but a windbreaker is helpful in light wind, light rain and drizzle, when a poncho is not necessary. If you already have a waterproof jacket as your 'outer layer', you don't need another shell garment. Your windbreaker should breathe, otherwise perspiration cannot evaporate and you will become soaked. A windbreaker is more in the line of emergency gear. If there is a strong wind, you must have it, otherwise you will probably not use it. If you can afford it, or spend a lot of time in the outdoors, a Gore-Tex parka is a good investment.

### NYLON WIND PANTS

If you prefer to hike in shorts wear a pair of wind pants over your shorts or under your skirt in the morning, then remove them to hike in lighter gear during the day. Most wind pants have special cuffs that allow you to remove them without taking off your shoes.

You can substitute ski warm-up pants, or even cotton jogging pants, for both wind pants and down-filled pants. The cost will be lower and there is hardly any sacrifice in versatility or comfort.

### LONG UNDERWEAR

Long johns are useful. A complete set makes a good, warm pair of pyjamas and is also useful during late-night emergency trips outside your tent. You can bring only the bottoms and use a woollen shirt for a pyjama top. Cotton underwear is OK, although wool or polyester is warmer.

### WOOLLEN HAT OR BALACLAVA

A balaclava is ideal because it can serve as a warm hat or you can roll it down to cover most of your face and neck. You may even need to wear it to bed on cold nights. Because much of your body heat is lost through your head, a warm hat helps keep your entire body warm.

### GLOVES

Warm ski gloves are suitable for a trek. You might also consider taking along a pair of woollen mittens, in case your gloves get wet.

### GAITERS

There is an enormous amount of mud on Bhutan's trails, and a pair of high gaiters is a must to help keep your boots and socks clean and dry.

## Footwear

Proper footwear is the most important item. Your choice will depend on the length of the trek and the terrain.

### TREKKING OR RUNNING SHOES

Tennis or running shoes are good, even for long treks, provided you won't be walking in snow. There are numerous brands of lightweight trekking shoes that have stiffer lug soles and are available in both low- and high-top models. High-top shoes provide ankle protection, but low-cut shoes are cooler to walk in. Most trekking shoes are made of a leather-and-nylon combination and many have Gore-Tex waterproofing, but they are expensive.

### MOUNTAIN TREKKING BOOTS
Wherever there is snow (likely anywhere above 4000m), proper waterproof boots can become an absolute necessity. Since animals are carrying all your gear, you have the luxury of carrying two sets of shoes and swapping them from time to time.

### SOCKS
Nylon-wool blend socks are fine, but polypropylene hiking socks (which cost astronomical prices) are the best. Several manufacturers make special hiking socks designed to prevent blisters by wicking moisture away from your feet. Bring more socks than you think you will need because it's sometimes difficult to wash clothes on a trek.

### DOWN BOOTIES
Many people consider these excess baggage, but they are great to have and weigh little. If they have a thick sole, preferably with Ensolite insulation, they can serve as camp shoes at high elevations. They're also good for midnight trips outside in the cold.

## Other Equipment
### BACKPACK
A backpack should have a light internal frame to stiffen the bag and a padded waistband to keep it from bouncing around and to take some weight off your shoulders. Bring a small pack so you won't try to carry too much during the day and the pack will fit easily inside your tent at night.

### SLEEPING BAG
Buy the best sleeping bag you can afford and be sure it is large enough. Nights are quite cold during trekking season, so a warm sleeping bag is a very worthwhile investment.

### WATER BOTTLE
By day your bottle provides the only completely safe source of cold drinking water. If you use iodine, fill your water bottle from streams, add the iodine and have cold, safe water 30 minutes later.

### TORCH (FLASHLIGHT)
Almost any torch will do, although many people prefer a headlamp – which is particularly useful for reading or when using a toilet. Spare batteries are almost impossible to find during a trek, so bring a supply with you.

### DUFFEL BAG
You will need a strong duffel bag in which to pack your gear. Get one with a zip along the side for easy entry. This is not an item to economise on; get a bag that is durable and has a strong zip. A duffel 35cm in diameter and about 75cm long is large enough to carry your gear and will usually meet the weight limit of pack animals – typically 15kg.

Your duffel bag will sit on the back of a horse or yak all day; when it rains, it will get wet. Pack it in such a way that important items stay dry during rainstorms. It is unlikely that you will be able to find a completely waterproof duffel bag or backpack, so you might want to pack your gear in a waterproof river bag. Use coated nylon stuff bags to separate your gear, or you can also use plastic garbage bags, but these are much more fragile.

Use a small padlock that will fit through the zip pull and fasten to a ring sewn to the bag. The lock will protect the contents from pilferage during the flight to and from Bhutan and will help protect the contents on your trek.

### EXTRA DUFFEL BAG OR SUITCASE
When starting a trek, you will leave your city clothes and other items in the storeroom of your hotel or travel agent. Bring a small suitcase or extra duffel bag with a lock for this purpose.

### SUNGLASSES OR GOGGLES
The sun reflects brilliantly off snow, making good goggles or sunglasses with side protection essential. At high altitude they are so essential you should have an extra pair in case of breakage or loss. A pair of regular sunglasses can serve as a spare if you rig a side shield to them. The lenses should be as dark as possible. At 5000m, the sun is intense and ultraviolet rays can severely damage unprotected eyes. Store your goggles in a metal case as, even in your backpack, it is easy to crush them.

### SUNSCREEN
During April and May and at high altitude throughout the year, sunburn can be severe. Use a protective sunscreen; those with sensitive skin will need a total sunscreen such as zinc oxide cream. Snow glare at high altitude

is a real hazard; you'll need a good sunscreen, not just suntan lotion.

To protect your lips at high altitude you need a total sunscreen such as Dermatone or Labiosan.

### CAMERA

A trek is long and your gear will be subjected to heat, dust, blowing sand, and moisture. Carry lens caps, lens tissue and a brush to clean the camera and lenses as frequently as possible.

A telephoto (or zoom) lens is more useful than a wide angle, because it will allow close-up pictures of wildlife, mountains and portraits of shy people. A polarising filter is a useful accessory. Insure your camera equipment.

### ADDITIONAL ITEMS

If there are two people travelling, divide a lot of this material to save weight and bulk.

Bars of Indian laundry soap are available in Bhutan. This avoids an explosion of liquid or powdered soap in your luggage.

Premoistened towelettes are great for a last-minute hand wash before dinner. Frequent washing helps avoid many stomach problems. If you bring these, check the way they are packaged. Buy them in a plastic container and avoid leaving a trail of foil packets in your wake.

A pair of scissors on your pocketknife is useful. Also bring a sewing kit and some safety pins.

Put all your medicines and toiletries in plastic bottles with screw-on lids.

Bring a cigarette lighter or matches to burn your used toilet paper. You might also bring a small trowel to dig a toilet hole when you get caught on the trail with no toilet nearby.

Always carry items to deal with blisters. It's important to treat blisters as soon as you discover them.

If you own a satellite phone, bring it. These are legal in Bhutan and are useful in emergencies.

## MAPS

The entire country has been mapped by the Survey of India at 1:50,000. These maps are restricted and difficult to obtain. There is a related series of topo maps produced by the Survey of Bhutan, but these are also restricted. The US Army Map Service produced a set of now-outdated maps in the 1950s (Series U502 at 1:250,000, sheets NG45-4 and NH46-1), based on the Survey of India maps. The to-

pography is extremely inaccurate and they, too, are difficult to obtain. Another series is the 1:200,000 Russian Military Topographic set which takes 10 sheets to cover Bhutan, but its text is in Russian.

In cooperation with an Austrian project, DOT produced large-scale contour maps of the Jhomolhari and Dagala Thousand Lakes treks based on the Survey of Bhutan series. These are the best (although not entirely accurate) trekking references available and can be purchased from the DOT office in Thimphu for Nu 300 each.

## TREKS IN THIS BOOK

In this chapter, 12 of the 13 officially permitted trekking routes in Bhutan are described. The other trek, in Cheli La, is described briefly in the Paro section of the Western Bhutan chapter (p131). Other trekking routes may be possible with prior negotiation between tour operators and DOT, but the major treks offer everything that a trekker could want, including what is described as the world's most difficult trek. Numerous variations are possible, even within the prescribed itineraries. Most of the routes can be trekked in the reverse direction, although this sometimes causes logistical problems because horses are not always available at the standard trek end points.

Several other treks are possible, including the Nabji Trail (p180) and several routes in the Haa district. Treks to Gangkhar Puensum base camp may become officially permitted, which would allow the reopening of the extension of the Snowman trek from Thanza to Gangkhar Puensum base camp and on to join the Duer Hot Spring trek.

### Route Descriptions

The trek descriptions in this book provide a general explanation of the lie of the land and cultural background, but are not self-guiding trail descriptions. Although some treks follow old trade routes, people don't use many of them today. Because there is usually no-one around to ask for directions, you need to stay reasonably close to the guide or horsemen to ensure you are on the correct path.

### DAILY STAGES

The route descriptions are separated into daily stages. This helps to make them readable and gives a quick estimate of the number of days

## PERSONAL EQUIPMENT CHECK LIST
### FOR ALL TREKS

**Clothing**
down- or fibre-filled jacket
jumper or pile jacket
hiking shorts (for men) or skirt
waterproof jacket, poncho or umbrella
hiking pants
T-shirts or blouses
long-sleeved shirt
underwear
sun hat
swimwear (optional)

**Footwear**
trekking or running shoes
camp shoes, thongs or sandals
socks (polypropylene)

**Other Equipment**
backpack
sleeping bag
water bottle
torch (flashlight), batteries & bulbs

**Miscellaneous Items**
toiletries
toilet paper & cigarette lighter
small knife
sunscreen (SPF 15+ or 30+)
towel
laundry soap

medical & first-aid kit
premoistened towelettes
sewing kit
bandanna
goggles or sunglasses
sunscreen for lips
binoculars
books
duffel bag with a padlock, a few stuff sacks and lots of
   plastic bags
another duffel bag or suitcase to leave your city clothes in

**Photograph Equipment**
camera & lenses
lens-cleaning equipment
film (about 20 rolls)

### FOR TREKS ABOVE 4000M

**Clothing**
insulated pants
nylon windbreaker
nylon wind pants
long underwear
woollen hat or balaclava
gloves
gaiters

**Footwear**
mountain trekking boots
socks (wool)
socks (light cotton) to wear under wool socks
down booties (optional)

required for each trek. The stages are those defined by DOT as designated camp sites, and the rules state that you must camp at these places. This doesn't usually create any hardship because in most cases the designated sites are the only spots with water and a space flat enough for making a camp.

Be sure you have the itinerary, including rest days, worked out in advance. Messages are sent ahead to arrange pack animals. If you don't meet them on the specified day, they might not wait for you.

As you discuss the trek with your guide and horsemen, be particularly careful to ensure that everyone agrees on the place you will camp the following night. More than once the horsemen have set off for a camping place beyond the destination the trekkers expected.

Some Bhutanese trekking staff have a very relaxed approach to schedules and late morning starts are common. Because many daily stages are quite long, this can result in late arrivals to camp, sometimes after dark. Always carry a torch in your backpack.

### TIMES & DISTANCES
The route descriptions list approximate walking times. These are estimates based on personal experience and information produced by DOT. The times and daily stages are 'tourist times' and offer a leisurely, comfortable trek with plenty of time for rest, sightseeing or just viewing the mountains. Bhutanese horsemen and over-enthusiastic trekkers can reduce these times to less than those shown here.

The distances shown are those published by DOT. They are estimates and have not been determined by any accurate method of measurement.

## SCHEDULE CHANGES

Despite all the preplanning and the complicated advance arrangements, there are still numerous factors that can upset a trek schedule. Rain and mud can make the trail slippery and the camping miserable. Snow can block trails, horses can fail to appear on schedule or the horse drivers may consider the trail too dangerous for their animals. These things happen more frequently than you might imagine. There is little recourse when the trek cannot proceed and you should always be prepared for possible disappointment.

### REST DAYS

The route descriptions are based on a reasonable number of days needed to complete the trek. You will enjoy the trek more if you add the occasional day for rest, acclimatisation or exploration – even at the cost of an extra US$200.

## Maps in this Chapter

The maps included in this chapter are based on the best available maps of each region. To make them legible, only those villages and landmarks mentioned in the text are shown on the maps. The maps show elevations for peaks and passes only – other elevations, including each camp, are given in the descriptions. Trails and roads follow the general direction indicated on the maps, but maps this size cannot show small switchbacks and twists in the trail.

Instead of contour lines, the maps depict ridge lines. This is the line of the highest point on a ridge. If the trail crosses one of these lines, you will walk uphill. If the trail leads from a ridge line to a river, you walk downhill.

### CONSIDERATIONS FOR RESPONSIBLE TREKKING

Trekking places great pressure on wilderness areas and you should take special care when trekking to help preserve the ecology and beauty of Bhutan. The following tips are common sense, but they are also mandated by the government, and you, or your guide, could be fined for not observing them.

#### Rubbish

- Carry out all your rubbish. If you've carried it in you can carry it out. Don't overlook those easily forgotten items, such as silver paper, cigarette butts and plastic wrappers. Empty packaging weighs very little and should be stored in a dedicated rubbish bag. Make an effort to carry out rubbish left by others.

- Minimise the waste you must carry out by reducing packaging and taking no more than you will need. If you can't buy in bulk, unpack small packages and combine their contents in one container before your trek. Take reusable containers or stuff sacks.

- Sanitary napkins, tampons and condoms should also be carried out despite the inconvenience. They burn and decompose poorly.

#### Human Waste Disposal

- Contamination of water sources by human faeces can lead to the transmission of hepatitis, typhoid and intestinal parasites. It can cause severe health risks not only to members of your party, but also to local residents and wildlife. A toilet tent will be set up at each camp; please use it.

- Where there is no toilet tent, bury your waste. Dig a small hole 15cm deep and at least 100m from any watercourse. Consider carrying a lightweight trowel for this purpose. Cover the waste with soil and a rock. Use toilet paper sparingly and burn it or bury it with the waste. In snow, dig down to the soil otherwise your waste will be exposed when the snow melts.

## Altitude Measurements

The elevations given in the route descriptions are composites, based on measurements with an altimeter or GPS and checked against maps. There is no definitive list of the elevations or names of peaks and passes in Bhutan, and various maps and publications differ significantly. In most cases the peak elevations are those defined in the mountain database produced by the Alpine Club in Britain. All other elevations are rounded to the nearest 10m.

## Place Names & Terminology

Bhutan is a maze of valleys and rivers that wind around in unexpected turns. It is, therefore, difficult to define in which compass direction a river is flowing at a particular spot. Instead of referring to the north or south bank of rivers, the slightly technical term of 'river right' or 'river left' has been used. This refers to the right or left side of the river as you face downstream, which is not necessarily the direction you are walking. In the route descriptions, right and left in reference to a river always refers to river right or river left.

The route descriptions list many mountains and places that do not correlate with names in other descriptions of the same route or with names on maps. The variance occurs because most maps were made before the Dzongkha Development Commission produced its guidelines for Romanised Dzongkha. This book uses the Romanised Dzongkha standards for all place names throughout Bhutan.

Many streams and landmarks remain nameless in the trail descriptions. Most trekking routes go through sparsely populated country, where there is less formality about place names. Although some places have official, historically accurate names, many camping places are in meadows or yak pastures. Local herders, or perhaps trekking guides, made up

---

### Washing

- Don't use detergents or toothpaste, even if they are biodegradable, in or near watercourses. For personal washing, use biodegradable soap and a basin at least 50m away from any watercourse. Widely disperse the waste water to allow the soil to filter it fully before it finally makes it back to the watercourse.

### Erosion

- Hillsides and mountain slopes, especially at high altitude, are prone to erosion. It is important to stick to existing tracks and avoid short cuts that bypass a switchback. If you blaze a new trail straight down a slope it will turn into a watercourse with the next heavy rainfall and eventually cause soil loss and deep scarring.

- If a well-used track passes through a mud patch, walk through the mud: walking around the edge of the patch will increase the size of the patch.

- Avoid removing the plants that keep the topsoil in place.

### Wildlife Conservation

- Don't assume animals found in huts to be nonindigenous vermin and attempt to exterminate them. In wild places they are likely to be protected native animals.

- Discourage the presence of wildlife at the camp by not leaving food scraps behind.

- Do not disturb or feed wildlife or do anything to destroy their natural habitat.

### Cultural Conservation

- Respect the culture and traditions of local people, whether they are villagers, your camp staff or your horse drivers.

- Do not give sweets, money, medicines or gifts to local people, particularly children, as this encourages begging.

- Do not buy local household items or religious artefacts from villagers.

TREKKING

names for some of these places and these now appear on maps. Numerous small streams, valleys and other landmarks do not have any names at all or, if they do have local names, there is usually nobody living nearby to ask.

In some places there is a facility that the Bhutanese call a 'community hall'. This is a stone building that the staff can use for cooking and shelter and may be available for trekkers to use as a dining room or emergency shelter.

## Route Finding

It isn't easy to get totally lost in the hills, but it has happened to some trekkers, and there are few people around who can help you find the correct trail. If you are on a major trekking route, the trail is usually well defined and there is only one route, although there may be a few confusing short cuts. Watch for the lug-sole footprints of other trekkers or for arrows carved into the trail or marked on rocks by guides with trekking parties. You can also use the hoofprints and dung of your pack animals to confirm that you are on the correct trail. If you find yourself descending a long way when the trail should be going up, if the trail vanishes, or if you suddenly find yourself alone ahead of the rest of your party, *stop and wait for the other trekkers and guides to catch up*. If you noticed a trail junction some distance back, retrace your steps to try to find where you went wrong.

## RESPONSIBLE TREKKING

Bhutan's trekking rules require that your staff carry a supply of fuel for cooking. Until 1996, the use of wood was allowed. The horsemen and yak drivers sometimes violate the code and cook their own meals over wood. Although theoretically prohibited, it's a hard rule to enforce.

## Fires

Campfires are prohibited and you should decline the offer if your staff suggest one. Bring enough warm clothing and you won't need to stand around a fire. It's a dilemma if the packers build a fire, or if one appears as part of a 'cultural show' in a village. Don't get too upset, however; as long as they burn dead wood the impact is minimal.

### GARBAGE FIRES

Burning garbage is offensive to deities, especially within sight of a sacred mountain such as Jhomolhari. Be aware of this cultural issue and try to arrange for rubbish to be packed out with you, burned or disposed of in a way that does not cause offence.

## What You Can Do to Help

Try to follow the guidelines in the boxed text, pp208–9. If your trek staff are not digging the toilet pits deep enough, or not filling them in properly, the time to solve that problem is on the spot. It does no good to go home and write a letter complaining about something that could have been easily solved by some simple assistance and guidance from you.

## HEALTH & SAFETY

For general advice on medical issues see p267. For information on high altitudes and acclimatisation, see p272.

Trekking in Bhutan involves multiple long ascents and descents. This can prove physically tiring, especially as the altitude increases. The best training is to walk up and, in particular, down hills as much as possible. If you have a busy life, with little access to hiking on weekends, you should train with exercise machines (such as 'Stairmasters'), ride a bicycle or jog. If you have no hills to train on, try putting a pack on your back to increase the strength training associated with walking or jogging. Take stairs whenever possible in preference to a lift (elevator).

People over 45 often worry about altitude and potential heart problems. There is no evidence that altitude is likely to bring on previously undiagnosed heart disease. If you are able to exercise to your maximum at sea level, you should not have an increased risk of heart attack while trekking at altitude. However, if you have known heart disease and your exercise is already limited by symptoms at low altitude, you may have trouble at altitude. If you have a history of heart disease, you should consult a doctor who has some knowledge of high altitude before committing yourself to a trek.

## Common Ailments
### TREKKERS' KNEE

If your legs have not been gradually accustomed to walking uphill and downhill through training, there is a chance that you will develop some knee soreness after a long descent. The pain generally comes from mild trauma repeated thousands of times on the descent. The two areas most affected are the outer side of the knee and the area under the kneecap.

You may experience difficulty walking and have to rest for a few days before continuing. Anti-inflammatory pills are helpful, as are ski poles or a walking stick. The pain can take several weeks to go away completely, but there are no long-term consequences.

### BLISTERS

The repeated rubbing of the skin against the inside of your shoe or boot can cause blisters. The superficial surface of the skin eventually gets lifted off its base and fluid collects in the resulting bubble. Blisters can usually be avoided by conscientious attention to your feet as you hike. You should immediately investigate any sore spot on your foot and put some form of protection over the area that is being rubbed. There are many commercial products that protect your feet from blisters. Moleskin is the most popular item, but adhesive tape also works. Newer products, utilising soft gels, have recently been added to the mix. Using a thin inner sock inside a thicker sock can provide a sliding layer that reduces the friction on the foot. Try not to begin a trek in brand-new shoes or boots.

Blisters are not infected when they first form, but after the bubble breaks infection can develop. Wash the area and keep it clean. If swelling and redness develop, you should take oral antibiotics.

### SNOW BLINDNESS

This is a temporary, painful condition resulting from sunburn of the clear surface of the eye (the cornea). It comes from heavy exposure to ultraviolet radiation, almost exclusively when walking on snow without sunglasses. If you are in a party of trekkers attempting to cross a high pass covered with snow, try to make sure everyone has something to protect their eyes, even if it means using pieces of cardboard with narrow slits cut in them.

The treatment is simply to try to relieve the pain. Cold cloths held against the outside of the eyelids can bring relief. Antibiotic eye drops are not necessary and anaesthetic drops should be avoided as they slow the healing and make the eyes vulnerable to other injuries. The cornea will be completely repaired within a few days and there are no long-term consequences.

## Rescue

If you find yourself ill or injured in the mountains, don't panic. If someone falls, take some time to assess the situation: suspected broken bones may only be bruises, and a dazed person may wake up and be quite all right in an hour or two. In most areas of Bhutan, some kind of animal, either horses or yaks, will be available to help transport a sick or injured trekker.

Sometimes either the seriousness of the injuries or the urgency of getting care will make land evacuation impractical. If this is the case, the only alternative is to request a helicopter rescue flight. Fortunately, this is a reasonably straightforward process, but once

### OVERVIEW OF TREKS

| Trek | Start | Finish | Number of days | Maximum elevation (m) | Standard |
|------|-------|--------|----------------|-----------------------|----------|
| Druk Path | Paro Ta Dzong | Motithang | 6 | 4210 | medium |
| Dagala Thousand Lakes | Geynikha Primary School | Chamgang | 6 | 4720 | medium |
| Jhomolhari | Drukgyel Dzong | Dodina | 9 | 4930 | medium–hard |
| Jhomolhari 2 | Drukgyel Dzong | Drukgyel Dzong | 8 | 4520 | medium |
| Laya–Gasa | Drukgyel Dzong | Tashithang | 14 | 5005 | medium–hard |
| Gasa Hot Spring | Tashithang | Tashithang | 5 | 2430 | easy |
| Gangte | Phobjikha | Tikke Zampa | 3 | 3480 | easy |
| Bumthang Cultural | Thangbi Goemba | Kizum | 3 | 3360 | easy–medium |
| Duer Hot Spring | Duer | Duer | 8 | 4700 | medium–hard |
| Rodang La | Thangbi Goemba | Trashi Yangtse | 10 | 4160 | medium–hard |
| Snowman | Drukgyel Dzong | Sephu | 25 | 5320 | hard |
| Samtengang Winter | Punakha | Chhuzomsa | 4 | 1500 | easy |

TREKKING

you ask for a helicopter, you will be charged for the service. Prices start at US$1500 and can go much higher, especially if weather conditions are bad and the chopper has to make several attempts to rescue you.

Rescue helicopters in Bhutan come from the Indian air-force base in Hasimara or the Indian army facility at Bagdogra airport. If there is a need for an evacuation during a trek, the guide will send a message to the appropriate tour operator. The tour operator contacts DOT to request a helicopter, DOT forwards the request to the Royal Bhutan Army and it, in turn, requests the Indian Army to send a chopper. It's a well-organised and efficient chain of communication and a helicopter is usually dispatched within a day.

## DRUK PATH TREK

The Druk Path trek has two possible starting points. Yours will depend on what arrangements have been made with the horse owners. The traditional start is in Dambji, near a gravel pit on the eastern side of the Do Chhu at 2300m. Most groups opt to save 140m of climbing, starting at a trailhead outside the gate of the National Museum at 2470m.

The trek is usually possible from late February to June and from September to December, although snow sometimes closes the route in late autumn and early spring. Days are normally warm, but nights can be very cold and you should always be prepared for snow. Avoid the monsoon season of July and August.

It is possible to shorten the trek to four days, but to do this you must walk more than eight hours a day. With the shorter schedule you would camp at Jili La, Jimilang Tsho

---

**THE TREK AT A GLANCE**

**Duration** 6 days
**Max Elevation** 4210m
**Standard** Medium
**Season** February to June, September to December
**Start** Paro Ta Dzong
**Finish** Motithang
**Access Towns** Paro, Thimphu
**Summary** One of the most scenic and popular treks in Bhutan, following a wilderness trail past several remote lakes. Although it is a short trek, it still goes to a high altitude, making it moderately strenuous.

---

and Phajoding, arriving in Motithang on the morning of the fourth day. Some agents modify the Druk Path trek into a four-day trek in the reverse direction, starting at the youth centre in Motithang and finishing by hiking down from Jimilang Tsho to the roadhead at Tsaluna in the Bemang Rong Chhu valley. If you're a masochist you can even race through the trek in a single day. An old punishment for Bhutanese soldiers was a forced one-day march along this route from Thimphu to Paro.

### Day 1: National Museum to Jili Dzong
10km / 4-5 hours / 1090m ascent

The first day is a long climb as you gain more than 1000m of elevation. The trek follows a gravel road past a few farms for about 30 minutes and then climbs steeply up a ridge on the first of many short cuts that avoid road switchbacks, passing Kuenga Lhakhang at 2640m. A further climb past cultivated fields leads back to the road and another 30 minutes of walking through blue-pine forest takes you to a big stone house at **Damchena** (2880m), where the road ends.

The wide trail climbs through blue-pine and fir forest to a *mani* (carved stone) wall in a clearing known as **Damche Gom**, at 3020m. It's then a long, but not steep, climb through forests to a meadow at 3260m where it's possible to camp. It is better to keep climbing for another hour to a camping place in a large pasture just before Jili La, marked by a cairn at 3560m.

If you are in a small group you can cross the pass and drop to an excellent camping place in a meadow below **Jili Dzong** at 3480m.

### Day 2: Jili Dzong to Jangchhu Lakha
10km / 3-4 hours / 310m ascent, 50m descent

This is a short day, which allows time to visit Jili Dzong, atop a promontory at 3570m. If the weather is clear, there is an excellent view of Paro town and the upper Paro valley far below, with Jhomolhari and other snowcapped peaks in the distance.

Jili Dzong was the residence of Ngawang Chhogyel (1465–1540), the cousin of Lama Drukpa Kunley. The large *lhakhang* (temple) contains an impressive statue of Sakyamuni almost 4m high. Once in a state of disrepair, the walls of the lhakhang have been replastered and painted. One wonders what kinds of mischief the young monks must have perpetrated to warrant banishment to such a high and isolated monastery.

From the dzong the route begins a long ridge walk, first climbing on the west side of the ridge in a rhododendron forest to a saddle at 3550m, then descending through a forest of trees ravaged by bark beetles. Climb again and traverse around the west side of a cone-shaped hill to a meadow. There are views of Jhomolhari and other snow peaks, and you are likely to see or hear some monal pheasants during the day. Cross to the east side of the ridge and make a long traverse through rhododendrons and cedars to Jangchhu Lakha, a pasture at 3760m. There is another good camping spot 10 minutes beyond at **Tshokam**, a yak-herder camp at 3770m.

## Day 3: Jangchhu Lakha to Jimilang Tsho
11km / 4 hours / 230m descent, 330m ascent

Beyond Tshokam there is a choice of trails. The high trail follows the ridge, making many ups and downs, and is said to be difficult and about two hours longer than the normal route. From the ridge there are good views of Jhomolhari and 6989m Jichu Drakye, the peak representing the protective deity of Paro.

The normal route descends from Tshokam through forests to the foot of a valley and crosses the upper part of the Bemang Rong Chhu, here only a stream, at 3540m. Trek upstream past a yak pasture called Langrithang. The trail is difficult to see as it traverses muddy bogs, but eventually becomes more distinct as it follows the east side of the stream (river left) to a small

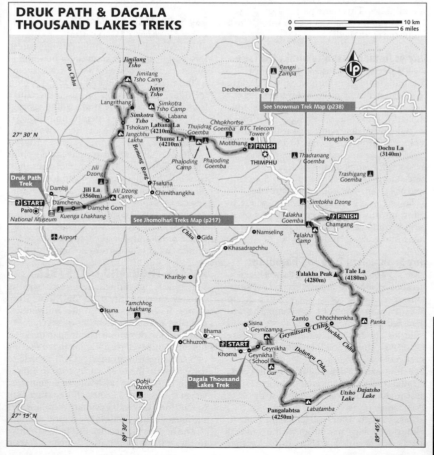

DRUK PATH & DAGALA THOUSAND LAKES TREKS

bridge at 3670m. A short distance above the bridge the high route rejoins after a descent from the ridge. The trail then climbs through forest and finally makes a steep ascent through large rocks and dwarf rhododendrons to a crest, then traverses a short distance to Jimilang Tsho, an isolated lake at 3870m. There is a pleasant camping place at the far end of the lake.

Jimilang Tsho means 'Sand Ox Lake', and was named for a bull that emerged from the lake and joined the cattle of a family that uses the area as a summer grazing ground. The lake is also known for its giant trout, which were introduced in the 1970s.

It is possible to cut the trek short by descending towards the southeast through a forest of blue pine to the road at Tsaluna, but the route is not obvious and crosses the river several times. This route passes Tsalu Ney, a 14th-century lhakhang at a cave where Guru Rinpoche meditated.

### Day 4: Jimilang Tsho to Simkotra Tsho
11km / 4 hours / 820m ascent, 400m descent

The trail climbs from the lower end of the lake to a ridge at 4010m, makes a traverse along the side of the ridge, then descends to a single stone shelter. Climb to another ridge, then make several ups and downs to a crest at 4050m overlooking Janye Tsho. Descend to a yak herders' camp near the lake and walk along the shore at 3950m before climbing to a ridge at 4150m and descending to some stone ruins and a camp spot at 4110m, overlooking **Simkotra Tsho**.

Be sure you have agreement on where to camp on this day. The horse drivers often push to continue over the next pass to a better camp and grazing land at **Labana**.

### Day 5: Simkotra Tsho to Phajoding
10km / 3-4 hours / 130m ascent, 680m descent

It's another long climb past several false summits, then a long rocky traverse to a group of cairns atop Labana La at 4210m. The trail descends gently and traverses above a broad valley to another crest at 4210m. There are views of Dochu La and Jhomolhari along this stretch of trail.

Below Labana La, a side trail descends through rocks to a camping place at 4110m, near a stone hut beside an almost-dry lake at Labana.

Pass a rough stone wall and soon come to some prayer flags on a hill above the trail that mark a seldom-used sky burial site. Another

long traverse leads to a crest at 4120m, then drop and cross a final ridge at Phume La (4080m). Weather permitting, there are views of Gangkhar Puensum and other Himalayan peaks. Below sprawls the entire Thimphu valley. A trail leads northeast and descends steeply towards Phajoding. An alternative trail leads southeast and descends to Thujidrag Goemba, a meditation centre that hangs on the side of a precipitous rock face at 3950m.

Another steep descent on a maze of eroded trails through juniper and rhododendron leads to a camp site above Phajoding at 3750m. Meditation centres and lhakhangs are scattered across the hillside. The large buildings of Phajoding Goemba are a short distance below the camp. See p117 for details of Phajoding Goemba.

### Day 6: Phajoding to Motithang
4-5km / 2½ hours / 1130m descent

This day's trek is all downhill through forest. Descend to the main monastery building at 3640m and start down on a wide trail, passing a Bhutanese *chorten* (stone Buddhist monument) at 3440m. Just below the chorten there is a trail junction. The trail leading straight goes to Chhokhortse Goemba and the BTC telecom tower, offering an alternative way to end this trek.

The normal route turns right and descends towards Motithang. There are numerous short cuts, but they all eventually lead to the same place. Pass another chorten at 3070m and descend steeply to a stream, crossing it at 2820m. Climb to a rough road and follow it down, skirting around the wooden buildings of the royal bodyguard camp and on to the Motithang youth centre at 2520m.

## DAGALA THOUSAND LAKES TREK
This trek is not difficult and most trekking days are short but there are some long, steep climbs. It is not a popular route, and you will probably encounter no other trekkers.

It's a 29km drive from Thimphu to the junction of an unpaved road leading to the starting point. It's best to arrange a 4WD vehicle to drive 8km up the steep, rocky road to a Basic Health Unit (BHU) at Khoma, high above the Geynitsang Chhu at 2850m. It's another 1km to the small Geynikha primary school where the horses usually wait to meet groups.

The best way to arrange this trek is to drive to the starting point after lunch and then

**THE TREK AT A GLANCE**

**Duration** 6 days
**Max Elevation** 4720m
**Standard** Medium
**Season** April, September to October
**Start** Geynikha Primary School
**Finish** Chamgang
**Access Town** Thimphu
**Summary** A short trek, near Thimphu, to a large number of lovely, high-altitude lakes (far fewer, however, than the name suggests).

make the short descent to the first camp in the late afternoon.

The recommended times for this trek are April and late September through October. Snow in the high country often blocks the route and makes it necessary to retrace your steps to the starting point.

## Day 1: Geynikha to Geynizampa
**2km / 1 hour / 150m descent**
Start walking along the road, which soon turns uphill towards a Geologic Survey of India mining site in Sisina, high on the hillside above. Leave the road and follow the trail that leads straight and level for about 500m to a chorten overlooking the fields of Geynikha (2950m). Make your way through the picturesque village and head for the ruins of a house on the ridge to the northeast. The route descends to a small stream, the Chhokosen Chhu, and follows it down to a chorten and an excellent camping place in a forest of blue pines alongside the Geynitsang Chhu at 2800m. There are two villages, Zamto and Chhochhenkha, further up the valley, which are the destination for a day hike described in the Royal Society for the Protection of Nature *Mild and Mad Hikes* book.

## Day 2: Geynizampa to Gur
**5km / 4 hours / 550m ascent, 60m descent**
Crossing a suspension bridge, the trail turns south along the east side of the Geynitsang Chhu (river left) to a side stream, the Dolungu Chhu. Cross the stream on a log bridge and start uphill on an eroded trail through an oak forest. The trail is used only by yak herders, woodcutters and a handful of trekkers, but it was once a major trading route between Thimphu and **Dagana**, headquarters of Dagana Dzongkhag. This accounts for the walls, well-

crafted stone staircases and other developments along portions of the route.

A long climb leads to an outstanding lookout point at 3220m. The climb becomes gentler as it ascends towards the top of the ridge where it makes a hairpin turn at 3350m. Be careful here; the trail to the camp site is an inconspicuous path that leads south through the forest to **Gur**, some yak pastures in the trees at 3290m.

## Day 3: Gur to Labatamba
**12km / 5 hours / 1040m ascent, 110m descent**
After climbing back from the camp to the main trail the route continues gently up the ridge on a wide track. A long, stiff climb through blue pines leads to a rocky outcrop where the vegetation changes to spruces, dead firs and larches. The trail traverses into a side valley, crosses a stream at 3870m and begins a long, gentle climb through scattered birches and rhododendrons towards the pass, weaving in and out of side valleys and crossing several tiny streams. At **Pangalabtsa**, a pass marked by cairns at 4250m, there is a spectacular view of the whole Dagala range. This is now yak country and there are numerous herders' camps scattered across the broad Labatamba valley. Descend from the pass to the first herders' hut at 4170m and traverse around the head of a small valley to the main valley floor. Climb beside a stream to **Labatamba**, a camp at 4300m near Utsho Tsho, where there are said to be plenty of golden trout. The high-altitude area near the lakes is a mass of alpine wildflowers in September.

You should schedule an extra day here to walk to the numerous lakes in the vicinity and perhaps do some trout fishing.

## Day 4: Labatamba to Panka
**8km / 6-7 hours / 260m ascent, 520m descent**
There are two possible routes and the pack animals will take the lower one. The trekking route is not well marked and is more of a cross-country traverse. It climbs along the western side of the lake Dajatsho to a saddle at 4520m, where there are good mountain views. If you want a better view, you could scramble to the top of a 4720m peak to the east. From the pass the trail descends past several herders' camps, then drops to the Dochha Chhu, rejoining the trail at about 4200m. Follow the trail as it climbs over three ridges and descends to **Panka** at 4000m. Because there is a water problem here during spring, it may be necessary to descend to an alternative camp 20 minutes below.

## Day 5: Panka to Talakha
8km / 6-7 hours / 180m ascent, 1100m descent

The route leads north to a crest at 4100m where several trails lead off in different directions. The trail to Talakha climbs steeply up a slate slope to the ruins of a house. It's then a long traverse to **Tale La** at 4180m. From here, there is a view of the Dagala range and of Thimphu, far to the north. It is then a long descent through bamboo forests to the *goemba* (Buddhist monastery) at **Talakha** (3080m).

## Day 6: Talakha to Chamgang
6km / 3 hours / 440m descent

There is a steep, eroded trail that leads to Simtokha, but there are numerous fences surrounding apple orchards along the way and there is no longer a direct route.

You can arrange to have vehicles pick you up at Talakha, but it's a long, rough, muddy road suitable only for 4WDs. It's best to walk three hours down the road, with a few short cuts where trails avoid switchbacks, to **Chamgang** at 2640m and meet your vehicle there.

# JHOMOLHARI TREK

The first three days of this trek follow the Paro Chhu valley to Jangothang, climbing gently, but continually, with a few short, steep climbs over side ridges. It crosses a high pass and visits the remote village of Lingzhi, then crosses another pass before making its way towards Thimphu. The last four days of the trek cover a lot of distance and require many hours of walking. The trek also affords an excellent opportunity to see yaks.

There are two versions of this trek and DOT counts them as two separate treks. About 40% of Bhutan's trekkers follow one of the

---

**THE TREK AT A GLANCE**

**Duration** 9 days
**Max Elevation** 4930m
**Standard** Medium–hard
**Season** April to June, September to November
**Start** Drukgyel Dzong
**Finish** Dodina
**Access Towns** Paro, Thimphu
**Summary** Bhutan's most popular trek offers spectacular views of the 7314m-high Jhomolhari from a high camp at Jangothang.

---

Jhomolhari trek routes, but this represents fewer than 25 groups a year.

The trek is possible from April to early June and September to November, but the best chance of favourable conditions is April or October. Days are normally warm, but nights can be very cold, especially above Jangothang. There is a lot of mud on this trek and it can be miserable in the rain. Snow usually closes the high passes in mid- to late November and they don't reopen until April.

## Day 1: Drukgyel Dzong to Sharna Zampa
17km / 4-6 hours / 360m ascent, 80m descent

The trek starts from Drukgyel Dzong at 2580m. On a clear day you can see the snow-covered peak of Jhomolhari in the distance. There is a rough unpaved road that travels a few kilometres up the valley. If you are travelling in a 4WD vehicle, you can drive to Mitshi Zampa and start the trek there.

If you're walking from Drukgyel Dzong, the trek starts with a short downhill walk on the road. After descending about 80m, you reach the river. Look back and see how well positioned the dzong was to keep watch over this valley.

A short distance upriver is the small settlement of Chang Zampa, where there's an outreach clinic and a little shop. A *zam* (bridge) crosses to river left here. Don't cross it. The trek stays on the south bank (river right). The fields on this side of the river are planted with potatoes and wheat; on the opposite side of the river, it's red rice.

Thirty minutes of walking takes you to the settlement of Mitshi Zampa. Here the route leaves the road and crosses to the left bank of the clear, fast-flowing Paro Chhu via a Swiss-built suspension bridge at 2540m.

The trail climbs very gently, traversing through well-maintained rice terraces and fields of millet. It's a well-worn trail with lots of round stones and irrigation water running down it. A short walk through a forest of blue pine leads to a small stream and a white chorten. Beyond is Sangatung, a pleasant farmhouse surrounded by fields.

The route now enters an area of apple orchards and blue-pine and fir forests, and the trail is littered with rocks sticking out of the mud. On some parts of the trail, logs have been placed in washboard fashion. In other places it's necessary to leap from rock to rock to keep your feet dry. If you are lucky, your guide will lead you along a less-muddy, alter-

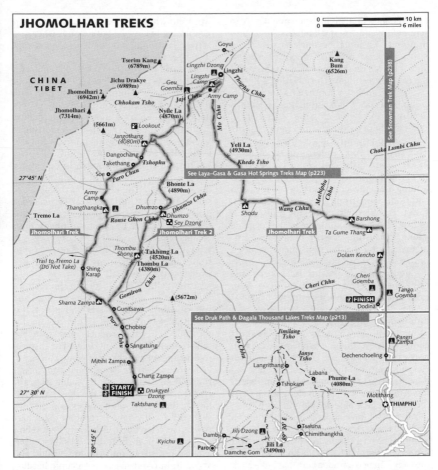

## JHOMOLHARI TREKS

native route that cuts across fields, following a telephone line. Don't cross the cantilever bridge that leads to the south; stay on river left, climbing gently to Chobiso, a single house at 2800m.

Soon the valley widens and you reach the army post of Gunitsawa at 2810m. There is also a primary school and a shop here. This is the last stop before Tibet; all army personnel and civilians are required to report to the checkpoint. The trek permit that your tour operator arranged will be checked and endorsed here; wait for your guide so the registration formalities can be completed. The large dormitory-style buildings across the river are quarters for enlisted men and their families.

Below the shop at Gunitsawa the trail crosses the Paro Chhu to river right on a wooden cantilever bridge at 2790m. It then climbs to **Sharna Zampa**, a camping place in meadows surrounded by trees at 2850m. On the opposite side of the river you can see a helicopter pad and archery field.

### Day 2: Sharna Zampa to Thangthangka
22km / 7-8 hours / 770m ascent, 10m descent

This is a long, hard day with lots of short ups and downs of 10m to 20m. It's made more strenuous because of all the rock-hopping necessary to avoid mud holes.

The trail continues its gradual climb alongside the Paro Chhu through conifers and rhododendrons. In places it is quite close to

**TREKKING**

the river; if the water is high you might have to scramble over a few small hills to get around it. About 15 minutes beyond Sharna Zampa are the remnants of an old bridge with a house and a chorten on the other side. At this point the route enters Jigme Dorji National Park.

The trail makes a continuous, but gentle, climb on a rocky trail through oaks, rhododendrons and ferns, crossing several small streams. About two hours from camp is Shing Karap, a stone house and a clearing at 3110m. This is where most guides choose to serve lunch. Some distance beyond is the route to Tremo La, which is the stone-paved trail leading off to the left. This is the old invasion and trade route from Phari Dzong in Tibet. Don't take this inviting-looking trail; several trekkers have done so in the past and made a long, exhausting side trip to nowhere. Immediately after the trail junction is a wooden bridge over a substantial side stream.

Climb a short set of switchbacks over a little ridge, then descend and cross the Paro Chhu to river left on a wooden cantilever bridge at 3230m. The route up this side of the river goes up and down on a rocky trail through forests of birch and fir. There are numerous short climbs and descents, and in one place the trail crosses an old landslide. There is only a 300m elevation gain, but the continual little ups and downs add up to a fair amount of uphill walking. Among the tree species along this part of the trail are blue pine, maple and larch.

After about three hours of trekking there's a bridge back to river right of the Paro Chhu at 3560m. The trail climbs to a place where you can see a white chorten on the opposite side of the river. There is a bridge here that leads back across the river, but don't cross it. That trail leads up the Ronse Ghon Chhu towards **Chora**, the camp on Day 6 of the Jhomolhari trek 2.

Follow the trail on river right as it turns a corner where there is an outstanding view of Jhomolhari. Climb over a small ridge as the Paro Chhu makes a noticeable bend. Fifteen minutes from the bridge is a lovely meadow with Jhomolhari looming at the head of the valley. This is **Thangthangka** (3610m) where there is a small stone shelter and a Bhutanese-style house in a cedar grove at the edge of the meadow.

## Day 3: Thangthangka to Jangothang
19km / 5-6 hours / 480m ascent

This is not a long day, but there is a significant elevation gain at high altitude, and you will be worn out when you reach camp. Jhomolhari was probably covered with clouds when you arrived last night, but you'll get a good view if you get up early.

As you climb beyond the camp, Jhomolhari disappears behind a ridge. Less than an hour from camp, at 3730m, is an army post with rough stone barracks housing personnel from both the Bhutan army and the Indian Military Training Team (IMTRAT). It's depressing to see the number of trees that have been carelessly felled to keep the post going.

The trail crosses a wooden bridge over a fast-flowing stream a short distance beyond the army post. The hillside on the opposite side of the Paro Chhu is a near-vertical rock face with a few trees clinging to it. Along this stretch the trail can be extremely muddy; there are lots of big stones you can use to rock-hop around mud holes. At 3770m, about one hour from camp, the trail turns sharply right at a whitewashed *mani* wall.

A short climb leads to a small chorten on a ridge. You are now entering yak country and you will see these huge beasts lumbering across the hillsides and lazing in meadows alongside the trail. One of the products made from yak milk is dried cheese called *chugo*. The cheese is sold strung on a necklace of white blocks.

There are two trails, an upper and a lower route. Both contour up the valley from the chorten and end up near the river bank, following the bottom of the valley as it makes a sharp bend to the right. Parts of the hillside are covered with larches, which turn a light yellow in autumn. Above the trail is the village of **Soe**. You cannot see it until you are beyond and above it, but you may meet people herding yaks near the river.

One hour beyond Soe is the settlement of **Takethang**, a cluster of stone houses on a plateau at 3940m. The villagers grow barley and a large succulent plant called *kashaykoni* that is fed to the yaks during winter.

The trail follows straight across the plateau, high above the river. It then crosses a little stream on a bridge made of big stones laid on logs. On the opposite side are a white chorten, an outreach clinic and the few houses of **Dangochang**. The people of this village raise yaks and a few sheep, and some households grow potatoes, turnips and radishes. This area is snowbound from mid-November until the end of March; one resident said the snow can be so deep they have to pee out of the second-floor windows, but this sounds like another Bhutanese myth.

It is slow going uphill beside a side stream to the camp at **Jangothang** (4080m) and a spectacular view of Jhomolhari. The ruins of a small fortress sit atop a rock in the middle of the side valley that leads northwest to Jhomolhari. A chain of snow peaks forms the eastern side of the Paro Chhu valley and it's often possible to spot blue sheep on the lower slopes.

There's a community hall with a kitchen and several large flat spots for camping. This is a popular trek route and Jangothang is one of the most spectacular camping places in the entire Himalaya. You are unlikely to have the camp to yourself.

The guidelines for pack animals require that you now exchange your horses for yaks from Soe or horses from Dangochang. Don't be alarmed when your loads get dumped at the camp and the animals disappear down the valley, leaving you alone with a mountain of baggage. If all goes well, the replacement pack animals will show up on schedule when you are ready to leave.

## Day 4: Acclimatisation Day & Exploration of Jangothang

If going on to Lingzhi, you should spend a day here for acclimatisation. If you are returning to Drukgyel Dzong on the Jhomolhari trek 2, a day in Jangothang is the highlight of the trek; the views don't get any better than here. There are lots of day hikes you can make and a day here is very well spent.

There are four major possibilities for day hikes. The first, and best, is a three- to four-hour excursion up the ridge to the north of the camp. There's no trail, but it's a broad open slope and you can just scramble up it. The ridge is endless, but after an hour or so of climbing there is a good view of **Jichu Drakye**, although the upper part of the ridge blocks the view of Jhomolhari unless you continue to the highest point at 4750m. You are likely to encounter grazing yaks, and occasionally blue sheep, on the upper slopes.

A second alternative, which can be combined with the walk up the ridge, is to trek up the main valley towards the last house, then continue up the valley towards Jichu Drakye. You will see much of this country if you trek over Nyile La to **Lingzhi**.

A third hike is to go up towards the head of the valley in the direction of **Jhomolhari**.

There is a very rough overgrown trail that cuts across moraines and through brush that leads to the foot of the mountain. You can't get very far, but there are good views in the upper part of the valley.

The last alternative is an expedition to **Tshophu**, a high-altitude lake. High on the opposite side of the river to the east is a bowl with a lake that has a good supply of spotted trout. To get to the lake, follow the trail north to the last settlement in the valley (as described in Day 5 of the Jhomolhari trek 2). It takes about one hour to get to the top of the ridge and then another 30 minutes following a stream to the lake.

## Day 5: Jangothang to Lingzhi

18km / 6-7 hours / 840m ascent, 870m descent

If you are having problems with the altitude at Jangothang, don't go on to Lingzhi.

Ten minutes beyond the camp are three stone houses inhabited by park rangers and a few elderly people. This is the last settlement in the valley and it's an extremely isolated place. Near the houses the trail turns a corner and there's a spectacular view of Jichu Drakye.

Descend and cross a log bridge at 4160m to the left bank of the Paro Chhu, then start up a steep traverse that heads back downstream. The trail crests at the foot of a large side valley and follows the valley eastwards. Jichu Drakye towers above the Paro Chhu valley and soon the top of Jhomolhari appears over the ridge above the camp at Jangothang. The snow peak in the middle is a secondary summit of Jhomolhari.

At 4470m the trail traverses under the big rocks that were visible from the camp, leads to the left and enters a large east–west glacial valley with numerous moraines. The trees have been left far below; there are a few small gentians, but otherwise it's just grass, tundra and small juniper bushes. You may spot blue sheep on the hillside above and see fat marmots darting into their burrows.

There is a false summit with a cairn at 4680m. As the trail approaches the ridge you can see Jichu Drakye to the northwest. After a very short downhill stretch the trail climbs further up a moraine and offers spectacular views of the sharp ridge that juts out from Jichu Drakye. You can see the prayer flags on the pass far above.

The final pull is up a scree slope to **Nyile La** (4870m), about four hours from the camp.

If you're ambitious you can climb the ridge to the northwest and go even higher. On one side of the ridge you can see the peaks of Jhomolhari 2 and Jichu Drakye; on the other side is Tserim Kang (6789m).

As Nyile La is frequently very windy, you probably won't stay long on the pass. The descent is through more scree along the side of the hill. This makes it awkward and uncomfortable to walk because the trail slopes outward as it traverses the side of the hill.

It's a long descent to a stream on the valley floor at 4450m. There is some vegetation here, mostly grass, juniper and cotoneaster. This is an excellent place to stop for lunch.

The trail now travels north, contouring along the side of the hill high above the valley. The opposite hillside is completely covered with rhododendrons. It is a long traverse on a good trail with a couple of little ups, but mostly down and level. Eventually you can see an army camp near the river below; the white tower of Lingzhi Dzong is visible on the top of a ridge in the distance.

It is a long walk in and out of side valleys to a lookout at 4360m, then the trail descends steeply into the large Jaje Chhu valley. There are many switchbacks on the rocky trail as it makes its way down through the heavy stands of rhododendron and birch to a yak pasture on the valley floor. Jichu Drakye and Tserim Kang tower over the head of the valley and you can see some remarkable examples of moraines on their lower slopes. Much of the rest of the trek gives you an outstanding lesson in geography, with several good examples of both terminal and lateral moraines.

The camp is at **Chha Shi Thang** near a large stone community hall (4010m) used by both Bhutanese travellers and trekking groups. Perched on a cliff on the north side of the valley is the small Geu Goemba, but it's not visible from the trail. Lingzhi is up the obvious trail on the opposite side of the Jaje Chhu.

If you take a spare day here, you can make an excursion to Chhokam Tsho at 4340m near the base camp of Jichu Drakye. During the hike you may encounter blue sheep and musk deer. If you are continuing to Thimphu, schedule a rest day here. The village and dzong at Lingzhi are worth visiting, and it's useful to rest up for the following strenuous trek day.

## Day 6: Lingzhi to Shodu
22km / 8-9 hours / 940m ascent, 920m descent

Start early because this day is long and tiring. Climb towards a white chorten on a ridge above the camp, then turn south up the deep Mo Chhu valley. The trail stays on the west side of the largely treeless valley, climbing steadily and crossing numerous side streams, most without bridges. About three hours from camp the trail crosses the Mo Chhu. There is no bridge and the river has broken into many small channels, presenting a tedious route-finding exercise, jumping among hummocks of grass and slippery rocks.

The trail climbs steeply up the side of the main valley and crosses into a large side valley, climbing above a stream. It then makes an impressive climb up the headwall, switchbacking through rocks to a large cairn atop Yeli La at 4930m. Try to avoid walking with the pack animals because the trail is carved into a rock cliff near the pass and is quite narrow. From the pass, on a clear day, you can see Jhomolhari, Gangchhenta and Tserim Kang.

It's a steep descent into a hanging valley, passing a small lake at 4830m. The trail follows the outflow from the lake, descending into another huge valley and another, larger lake, Khedo Tsho, at 4720m. Watch for blue sheep grazing alongside the lake. The trail then crosses the upper reaches of the Jaradinthang Chhu and descends along the valley, following the river southwards for a very long distance, crossing several side streams. After crossing back to the east bank on a log bridge at 4340m, the trail reaches a chorten at 4150m where it turns eastwards into the upper Wang Chhu valley. Descending and crossing to the south bank (river right) of the Wang Chhu on a log bridge, the trail traverses a narrow, sandy slope to a camping place at **Shodu** (4080m), just at the tree line.

## Day 7: Shodu to Barshong
16km / 5-6 hours / 250m ascent, 670m descent

Upon leaving Shodu the trail crosses to river left and passes an abandoned army camp and a small alternative camp site. The trail traverses under steep yellow cliffs with a few meditation caves carved into them. It is believed that the Zhabdrung spent some time in these caves. Descending on a steep stone staircase, the trail reaches the river, crossing it on a log bridge at 3870m. For the next three hours the trail crosses the river five more times, slopping through muddy cypress forests on the south slope and hugging the steep canyon walls and crossing large side streams on the north slope, eventually ending up on the north bank (river left) at 3580m.

The route climbs gradually for one hour to **Barshong**, where there is a dilapidated community hall and the ruins of a small dzong. The designated camp is below the ruins at 3710m, but it is in a swampy meadow and most groups elect to continue to a better camp by the river, about 1½ hours beyond (see below).

## Day 8: Barshong to Dolam Kencho
**15km / 4-6 hours / 290m ascent, 640m descent**
The trail descends gently through a dense forest of rhododendron, birch and conifers, then drops steeply on a rocky trail to meet the Wang Chhu. Thirty minutes of walking through a larch forest leads to a clearing known as **Ta Gume Thang** (Waiting for Horses) at 3370m. Most groups camp here or 15 minutes further on at **Dom Shisa** (Where the Bear Died) instead of Barshong.

Stay on river left, climbing over ridges and descending to side streams. The route then makes a steep climb to 3340m. After traversing for about 30 minutes in rhododendron forests, a trail leads off to the right. This descends to **Dolam Kencho**, a pleasant camp in a large meadow at 3320m. If your group has elected to shorten the trek and continue on to Dodina, stay on the left-hand trail, bypassing Dolam Kencho, and climb to a crest at 3430m.

## Day 9: Dolam Kencho to Dodina
**8km / 3-4 hours / 500m ascent, 930m descent**
From the camp the trail climbs back to the trail, reaching a crest with a cairn at 3430m. The trail descends to a stream at 3060m, then climbs again to a pass at 3120m. Another short descent and climb through bamboo forest leads to a rocky stream bed, which the trail follows down to the remains of a logging road along the Wang Chhu at 2720m. It is then a 15-minute walk south along a rocky route to the roadhead at **Dodina** (2640m), opposite the bridge that leads to Cheri Goemba.

## JHOMOLHARI TREK 2
If you want to avoid high altitude it's best to return from Jangothang to Drukgyel Dzong

---

### THE TREK AT A GLANCE
**Duration** 8 days
**Max Elevation** 4520m
**Standard** Medium
**Season** April to June, September to November
**Start/Finish** Drukgyel Dzong
**Access Town** Paro
**Summary** The shorter and easier version of the main Jhomolhari trek goes to the Jhomolhari base camp at Jangothang, returning either via the same route or by an alternative trail.

---

by the same route. The trek described here is an alternative route that is less strenuous than the classic Jhomolhari trek, but still reaches an elevation that could cause altitude problems.

## Days 1-4: Drukgyel Dzong to Jangothang
Follow days 1 to 4 of the main Jhomolhari trek (see p216).

## Day 5: Jangothang to Chora
**16km / 6-7 hours / 810m ascent, 1090m descent**
The trail leads north to the last settlement in the valley and drops to the Paro Chhu, crossing it on a wooden bridge. Switchback up the side of the hill to a large cirque and the lake of Tshophu (4380m), which is inhabited by a flock of ruddy shelducks. Climb high above the eastern side of the lake, passing a second lake as the trail climbs across a scree slope to a crest. Descend into a hidden valley and climb steeply to **Bhonte La** at 4890m.

From the pass the route descends a scree slope, then winds down a ridge with a lot of crisscrossing yak trails. It finally switchbacks down to the Dhumzo Chhu. Trek downstream below the few houses of Dhumzo to a bridge, cross to the south side of the river and make a short climb to a camp in a meadow at **Chora**, 3800m.

## Day 6: Chora to Thombu Shong
**11km / 4-5 hours / 720m ascent, 340m descent**
The trail climbs 100m over a ridge, then drops to another stream. Crossing that stream, the trail heads up the hillside, dropping into a small side valley before emerging onto a ridge. Here the route turns south, ascending past a few huts to **Takhung La** (4520m). A short descent leads to **Thombu Shong** (4180m), with three yak herders' huts.

## Day 7: Thombu Shong to Sharna Zampa

13km / 4-5 hours / 200m ascent, 1650m descent

Climb out of the valley to Thombu La at 4380m, then drop gradually to about 4000m. The trail then makes a steep descent, switch-backing down the ridge, finally reaching the helipad at **Gunitsawa** (2730m). Camp here or cross the river and go upstream to camp at **Sharna Zampa**, the same place as Day 1.

## Day 8: Sharna Zampa to Drukgyel Dzong

17km / 4-6 hours / 80m ascent, 360m descent

Follow Day 1 of the Jhomolhari trek in reverse to **Drukgyel Dzong**.

## LAYA–GASA TREK

This trek begins in the Paro valley and follows the same route as the Jhomolhari trek as far as Lingzhi, then heads north into the high country. Snow can close the high passes, but they are generally open from April to June and mid-September to mid-November. The best trekking month in the Laya region is April.

The trek will introduce you to the unusual culture of the Layap people and offers a stop at a natural hot spring in Gasa. If you are lucky, you may also see takins and Bhutan's national flower, the blue poppy.

## Days 1-5: Drukgyel Dzong to Lingzhi

Follow Days 1 to 5 of the Jhomolhari trek (see p216).

## Day 6: Lingzhi to Chebisa

10km / 5-6 hours / 280m ascent, 410m descent

Cross the stream below the Chha Shi Thang camp on a wooden bridge and climb up the opposite side to a chorten below Lingzhi Dzong. In the valley to the east is a cluster of wood-shingled houses that is one part of

---

**THE TREK AT A GLANCE**

**Duration** 14 days
**Max Elevation** 5005m
**Standard** Medium–hard
**Season** April to June, September to November
**Start** Drukgyel Dzong
**Finish** Tashithang
**Access Towns** Paro, Punakha
**Summary** This trek is an extension of the Jhomolhari trek. It offers diverse flora and fauna, as well as a good opportunity to spot blue sheep.

---

**YUGYEL DZONG**

The third *druk desi*, Mingyur Tenpa, who ruled from 1667 to 1680, built the dzong in Lingzhi. It is on a hill about 200m above Lingzhi village and is quite close to the Tibetan border. The dzong was destroyed in the 1897 earthquake, but was rebuilt in the 1950s to serve as an administrative headquarters.

It's quite small, with a few offices along the outside wall and a two-storey *utse* (central tower) in the centre. Some years ago the basement was used as a jail to house murderers and temple robbers, but the facilities were quite primitive and the dzong is no longer used for this purpose. There are only a few monks staying in the dzong.

---

Lingzhi village. There is a medicinal-plant collection centre there. If you look back at Tserim Kang you can see a very distinct rock pinnacle sticking up at the end of the east ridge.

There is a direct route that stays level along the side of the hill, but you can take a short diversion and climb to Lingzhi Dzong, which sits at 4220m atop a ridge that separates the main valley from a side valley.

Walk down the ridge from the dzong and rejoin the lower trail. The Lingzhi La at the head of the valley was a trade route between Punakha and the Tibetan town of Gyantse and was also used by Tibetan armies during various attacks on Bhutan. The name of Lingzhi's dzong is **Yugyel Dzong**; it was built to control travel over the Lingzhi La.

The largest part of Lingzhi village is hidden in a valley formed by the ridge upon which the dzong was built. There are fields of wheat and barley in the upper part of the side valley. The trail crosses the lower part, where there are a few houses, a school and post office (with a telephone) at 4080m. The Lingzhi region has a wide variety of herbs, many of which have medicinal value. The National Institute of Traditional Medicine in Thimphu has a large herb collecting and drying project here. Because of the high elevation, the only other major crop that grows well is barley.

After a look around the village, walk out of town on a level trail. It's a pleasant hike on a good trail along a hillside covered in wildflowers and junipers. Far to the north you can see

Jhari La and some of the sharp hills you must cross to get to Laya.

The trail traverses high above the river, which flows in a valley so steep that there are very few houses. The path descends to cross a small stream, then continues along the side of the valley, climbing gently. This area is the source for many plants of medicinal value and the entire hillside looks like a colourful herb garden.

About one hour from Lingzhi the trail reaches a cairn and prayer flags on a ridge at 4140m. The route turns into another side valley and makes a long gradual descent to the pleasant settlement of **Goyul** (3870m). In this compact village the stone houses are clustered together, unusual in Bhutan. Surrounding the village are large fields of barley.

Goyul is at the side of a stream with dramatic rock walls towering above. Leaving Goyul, the trail climbs then traverses for an hour to a chorten that overlooks another side valley. A short descent leads into the spectacular Chebisa valley, with a frozen waterfall at its head. The camp site is on a meadow opposite **Chebisa** (3880m). Upstream of the camp is the twin village of **Chobiso**.

## Day 7: Chebisa to Shomuthang
**17km / 6-7 hours / 890m ascent, 540m descent**
The route climbs the ridge behind Chebisa, passing a few houses above the main part of the village, then makes a long, steep climb up a featureless slope. There are large herds of blue sheep living in the rocks above, which

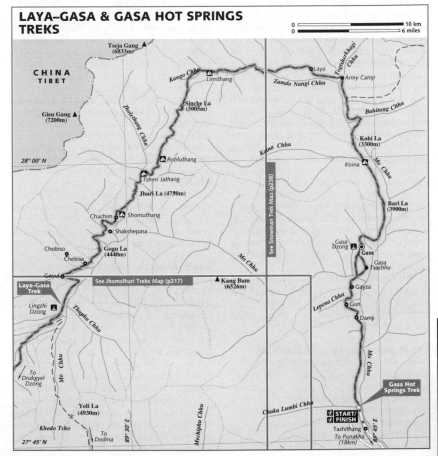

### LAYA–GASA & GASA HOT SPRINGS TREKS

CHINA
TIBET

Tseja Gang ▲ (6833m)

Kango Chhu

Limithang

Laya

Topchurkhagi Chhu

Army Camp

Zamdo Nangi Chhu

Bahitung Chhu

Sinche La (5005m)

Phokethang Chhu

Gieu Gang ▲ (7200m)

28° 00' N

Robluthang

Tsheri Jathang

Jhari La (4750m)

Koina Chhu

Kohi La (3300m)

Koina

Mo Chhu

See Snowman Trek Map (p238)

Bari La (3900m)

Chachim

Shomuthang

Shakshepasa

Gasa Dzong

Gasa

Gasa Tsachhu

Chobiso

Gogu La (4440m)

Chebisa

Goyul

Laya–Gasa Trek

See Jhomolhari Treks Map (p217)

Kang Bum (6526m)

Mo Chhu

Gayza

Lepena Chhu

Lingzhi Dzong

Thiughu Chhu

Gun

Damji

Mo Chhu

To Drukgyel Dzong

Mo Chhu

Yeli La (4930m)

Khedo Tsho

To Dodina

Mechiphu Chhu

89° 30' E

Chaka Lumbi Chhu

Gasa Hot Springs Trek

START/FINISH

Tashithang
To Punakha (18km)

89° 45' E

27° 45' N

0 ——— 10 km
0 ——— 6 miles

**TREKKING**

you are sure to spot. Watch for bearded vultures and Himalayan griffons flying overhead. At about 4410m the trail levels out and traverses to **Gogu La** (4440m). It's not really a pass; it just crosses a ridge that leads off the top of the hill. From the ridge the trail descends into a side valley through a deep forest of rhododendrons.

It's a long descent to a stream at 4170m, then the trail climbs again over a small ridge through a cedar forest, passing several places where the hillside has been burned. The trail crests the ridge at 4210m and descends on a muddy path into the main Jholethang Chhu valley in a deep forest of fir and birch. There's a little climb past some yak herders' huts and then over the side of the valley and down to **Shakshepasa** (3980m) and a helipad, marked by a big H.

At the bottom there's a marsh and a fairly messy stream crossing with many little channels to jump across on hummocks of moss, muddy earth and rocks. On the opposite side is a good spot for lunch.

There are yak herders' huts downstream, but otherwise the valley is uninhabited. The trail now goes quite steeply up the northern side of the valley. At about 4200m it levels and heads into a side valley, passing a couple of yak herders' huts and traversing high above the valley floor on river right to Chachim, a yak pasture at 4260m.

The camp is in a cluster of brush beside a stream at the bottom of the valley. There is a path that leads directly to the camp from Chachim, but it's a steep, rough trail with a lot of bushwhacking. A longer, but better, route follows a larger trail that contours up the side of the valley past the camp. You can then drop down a side trail to **Shomuthang** (4220m).

This deserted spot is not a particularly good camp site but by camping here you get a head start on tomorrow's pass. If you're travelling in the opposite direction, you should camp down by the river at Shakshepasa.

## Day 8: Shomuthang to Robluthang
**18km / 6-7 hours / 700m ascent, 760m descent**
The trail climbs from the camp up the valley, starting on river right, crossing to river left and then crossing back again at 4360m. The white flowers are edelweiss and the snow peak visible to the southeast is Kang Bum (6526m).

The trail climbs out of the valley through pretty desolate country to Jhari La (4750m),

about two hours from camp. There are four cairns and some prayer flags here. In the distance to the northeast you can see Sinche La, the next obstacle on the route to Laya. The big snow peak to the north is 6840m Gangchhenta (Great Tiger Mountain; ta means tiger). Tserim Kang and the top of Jhomolhari are visible if the weather is clear.

On the north side of the pass the trail switchbacks down to a little stream at 4490m, then becomes a rough, rocky route through rhododendrons on the stream's left. Soon the vegetation changes to big rhododendrons, birches and firs and there are lots of slippery loose rocks on the trail. There is a pleasant lunch spot at the bottom beside a log bridge and stream at 4050m.

Follow the stream gently downhill through bushes on river left as it makes its way to the main valley. It's a gradual descent to a meadow by the Jholethang Chhu at 3990m, which you cross on a log bridge that is about 1km upstream. A yak trail leads west up the valley towards Tibet.

There is a camp called **Tsheri Jathang** by the river. Herds of takin migrate to this valley in summer and remain for about four months. Takins are very disturbed by the presence of other animals. The valley has been declared a special takin sanctuary and yak herders have agreed not to graze their animals in the valley when the takins are here.

The trail climbs steeply on the northern side to a crest at about 4150m. It then traverses into a side valley past a tiny lake. There are good camping places in a rocky meadow named **Robluthang** at 4160m.

## Day 9: Robluthang to Limithang
**19km / 6-7 hours / 850m ascent, 870m descent**
This is a long, hard day, crossing Sinche La, the last and highest pass on the trek.

Over the hill above the camp is a little stone house where a Laya woman lives. She'll be happy to sell you trinkets if you are in the mood for shopping; she is also the person responsible for the local *arra* (spirit) your guide was drinking last night. The trail climbs through the remnants of a burned forest and up the hillside through some boggy patches. It follows a set of steep switchbacks to a shelf at 4390m, then turns into another large glacial side valley. From here the pass looks a long way away – and it is.

Follow a stream for a while, crossing to river right on an icy log bridge at 4470m, then climb onto a moraine and traverse past lots of marmot holes. You may be able to spot blue sheep high on the slopes to the north before the trail crosses back to stream left. Another climb through rocks leads to the foot of the pass at 4720m.

It's a tough climb from here to the pass because the high altitude will slow you considerably. Passing a false summit with a cairn, the trail levels out a little before reaching some rock cairns and prayer flags on Sinche La (5005m), about five hours from camp. The snow-covered peak of Gangchhenta fills the horizon to the north.

The descent is on a rough, rocky trail that follows a moraine into another glacial valley. Small rocks on the path keep sliding out and threatening to twist your ankle. Eventually you arrive at the Kango Chhu, a stream below a terminal moraine that forms the end of another valley to the west.

Cross the Kango Chhu to river left on a small log bridge at 4470m. A short distance beyond the stream crossing is a yak pasture and camping spot next to a huge rock. It's best to continue to Limithang to camp; follow the valley northwards, staying high as the stream falls away below you.

The valley from Gangchhenta enters from the northwest and provides more lessons in glaciology. There is a huge terminal moraine and a glacial lake at the foot of the valley. You can see classic examples of lateral moraines where the glacier has pushed rocks up on both sides of the valley.

Beyond an uninhabited stone house the trail starts a steep descent to the valley floor. It switchbacks down with the terminal moraine looming above, crossing the Kango Chhu on a bridge at 4260m. After a short climb through rhododendrons the trail levels out on a plateau above the Zamdo Nangi Chhu. It's then a short walk on a good trail through a cedar forest interspersed with small meadows to Limithang (4140m), a lovely camp site in a big meadow by the river. The peak of Gangchhenta towers over the camp site, even though it's quite a distance away.

## Day 10: Limithang to Laya
**10km / 4-5 hours / 60m ascent, 340m descent**
After 20 minutes of walking, the trail crosses to river left and enters a deep cedar forest, crossing many little, muddy side streams.

After a while there is a stone herders' hut with a sod roof; here the vegetation changes to fir trees draped with lichen.

Cross a large stream that flows in from the north and make a steep rocky descent down the side of the valley to the river at 3800m, then cross to river right on a wooden cantilever bridge. A short distance later, cross back and make a stiff climb.

It's a long walk through the heavily wooded, uninhabited valley. Descend, then cross a waterfall that flows across the trail, then traverse with many small ups and downs. Near a point where you can see a single house on a ridge-top to the east, there is an inconspicuous trail junction. It's not important which trail you choose: the upper trail leads to the top of Laya, and the other leads to the lower part of the village.

If you take the upper trail you will cross a ridge and see the stone houses and wheat fields of **Laya** laid out below you with some abandoned houses and a goemba above.

Gangchhenta dominates the skyline to the west of the village and from some places you can get a glimpse of Masang Gang (7165m). In the village centre is a community school, hospital, archery field and the first shop since the Paro valley. You can camp in the fields below the school at 3840m.

## Day 11: Laya to Koina
**19km / 6-7 hours / 260m ascent, 1070m descent**
Layaps are not noted for their reliability and punctuality, and the horses may arrive late. Below the village, the trail drops back to the river. The trail exits the village through a *khonying* (arch chorten), then passes another chorten at Taje-kha as it descends on a muddy trail to a stream. There are a few houses near the trail, but it's mostly deep forest all the way to the river.

There is an alternative camping place on a plateau at 3590m, next to the large Togtsherkhagi Chhu, which flows in from the northeast. Cross the river on a wooden bridge and climb to the stone buildings of the army camp on the opposite side. At the army post is a wireless station and a checkpoint where the guide registers the trekkers' names; you'll have to wait here until the formalities are completed. The peak of Masang Gang is barely visible at the head of the side valley.

The route now follows the Mo Chhu downstream all the way to Tashithang. Beyond the army camp the trail goes uphill, crossing a few streams and making little ups and downs.

## LAYA

The people of Laya have their own language, customs and distinct dress. Laya language is similar to Dzongkha, but if people speak fast, Dzongkha speakers cannot understand them. The Layap language is said to use very respectful form of speech.

The women keep their hair long and wear peculiar conical bamboo hats with a bamboo spike at the top, held on by a beaded band that reaches to the back of the head. They dress in a black woollen jacket with silver trim and a long woollen skirt with a few stripes in natural earth colours like orange and brown. They wear lots of silver jewellery on their backs; on many women this display includes an array of silver teaspoons.

Spread out over a hillside near the Tibetan border, Laya is one of the highest villages in the country, at 3700m. The peak of the daunting Tsenda Gang (7100m) towers over the village. Villagers raise turnips and mustard and produce one wheat or barley crop a year before the region is snowed in for the winter.

This is Bhutan's primary yak-breeding area; during the summer, people move to the high pastures and live in black tents woven from yak hair.

The village women are easily encouraged to stage an evening 'cultural show', which consists of Bhutanese circle dancing accompanied by traditional Bhutanese and Layap songs.

Women often offer to sell their bamboo hats for Nu 150 or so. It's fine to buy these because they are made locally from native materials, but don't buy ones with beads as these are often family heirlooms and, once sold, cannot be replaced except with cheap plastic beads. Layap women also sometimes come around to trekking camps selling jewellery; most of this is made in Nepal. Unless you particularly want to contribute to the Laya economy you'll probably get less value than what you pay for.

Zhabdrung Ngawang Namgyal passed through Laya and in a small meadow below the village is a chorten with the footprints of the Zhabdrung and his horse.

The region is believed to be a *bey-yul* (hidden land) protected by an ancient gate that leads to Laya village. The Layaps perform a ceremony each year in honour of the protective forces that turned all the stones and trees around the gate into soldiers to repel Tibetan invaders.

About 30 minutes from the army post is an inconspicuous trail junction at 3340m. The route for the Snowman trek leads uphill from here on a tiny path. The route to Gasa keeps going downstream on a muddy trail. After a while it turns a corner into a side valley, goes a short distance up the valley and crosses the Bahitung Chhu at 3290m. This is the traditional lunch spot for this day.

The trail travels alongside the Mo Chhu to an overhanging rock that forms a cave, then crosses to river right at 3240m on a cantilever bridge. The canyon closes in and the trail makes several major climbs over side ridges as it makes its way downstream. Beyond another cave formed by a large overhanging rock the first long, steep climb starts, cresting at the top of a ridge at 3390m. It's a 150m descent to a clear side stream, then the trail wanders up and down near the river as it runs fast through some big cascades in a gorge. After some more ups and downs through bamboo about 100m above the river there is another serious climb to the Kohi Lapcha at 3300m.

The muddy trail stays high for about 30 minutes until it reaches a stone staircase, where it turns into a side valley, traversing for a bit, then dropping to the large Koina Chhu. Welcome to **Koina** (3050m), a muddy bog in the forest by the bridge. There is a single stone house with some muddy camping places scattered around. Because of the deep black mud you must wade through and the damp, soft ground upon which you must pitch your tent, this is the worst camp on the whole trek and perhaps the most unpleasant camp in the Himalaya. There is talk of developing an alternative camping place nearby.

## Day 12: Koina to Gasa

**14km / 6-7 hours / 900m ascent, 1710m descent**

You may think that because you are headed downstream the climbs on this trek are finished, but there's another major ascent ahead – Bari La.

Cross the bridge at Koina and start up the hill. Parts of the trail are so muddy that logs have been placed to form little bridges.

There are also places where the trail follows the side of a ridge and you walk gingerly across logs that dangle out into space. The muddy trail keeps going through a deep forest of fir, in and out of side valleys, for almost three hours to a small rock cairn and a few prayer flags atop Bari La (3900m). Then it's a reasonably level walk to another chorten. There are few good places to stop along this part of the trail, so lunch will probably be an impromptu event.

The route starts down again, sometimes steeply, through a bamboo forest to a stream. At 3080m it rounds a corner where you can finally see Gasa Dzong on the opposite side of a large wooded side valley. The trail descends past an old chorten, then crosses a ridge into a big side valley. It drops and crosses a large stream at 2780m, then traverses along the side of the valley to four chortens on the ridge at 2810m.

The chortens mark the southern boundary of **Gasa town** (2770m). The trail traverses above the soccer and archery ground, past several small teashops, then intersects Gasa's main street, a stone-paved path that leads uphill to the dzong, school and a BHU. Trek downhill to the bazaar, which consists of about nine shops and a police checkpoint. The police post checks permits, providing a perfect excuse to stop for a soft drink or beer at one of the shops.

You can camp in a field near the town, or continue downhill for 1½ hours to the *tsachhu* (hot spring). Many trek itineraries schedule an extra day to laze around in the hot springs – a useful activity after the last two days of strenuous mud walking. See Day 2 of the Gasa Hot Spring trek (p228) for details of the springs. If it is raining, the

remainder of this trek is perfect country in which to meet leeches.

## Day 13: Gasa to Damji
**18km / 5-6 hours / 470m ascent, 280m descent**

Follow the trail generally south, passing a few houses and *mani* walls, as it descends to the primary branch of the Mo Chhu, which has flowed through the mountains from Lingzhi to join the other branch of the Mo Chhu that flows from Gasa. Look back for a good view of the dzong, sitting on top of the hill. Be careful as you follow this trail; near a chorten there is a fork where a second trail leads steeply downhill to the hot spring. The trail towards Damji goes straight here.

After a long descent, cross the river at 2360m on a cable suspension bridge high above the water. The trail starts climbing on the opposite side. At 2510m there's a picnic table at a lookout, from where you can see down to the hot spring and back to a large part of yesterday's trail, although it's all in the forest. Gasa Dzong with its distinctive rounded front wall is visible, glued to the valley wall and seeming to float in space.

There's a crest at 2330m where the trail turns south along the Mo Chhu (from here downstream there is only one river known as the Mo Chhu) and then goes up and down on the side of the valley, high above the river. It descends through bamboo to a stream, then starts climbing back again to a meadow at 2530m. Gasa Dzong and the snow peaks towards Laya are still visible.

The trail stays high, crossing a meadow and descending to the small village of **Gayza** at 2500m. The trail then drops into a deep subtropical ravine filled with trees and ferns, crossing the Lepena Chhu on a spectacular suspension bridge high above a narrow wooded gorge at 2300m.

The trail climbs to another crest and traverses around the top of a side valley to the four houses of Gun at 2400m, then drops again and climbs back up to a chorten. Then it's a short walk to the large village of Damji (2430m), in a huge side valley with an amphitheatre of rice terraces. Pass the school and traverse to the southern end of the village where there is a large cluster of houses and a little chorten at 2380m. A road from Tashithang is slowly being built towards Damji and is planned to continue on to Gasa, the only *dzongkhag* headquarters that is not reached by a road.

---

**TRASHI THONGMOEN DZONG**

This dzong in Gasa lies on the old trade route to Tibet. The Zhabdrung built it in 1646 after his victories over the Tibetans. Originally called Drukgyel (Victorious) Dzong, it saw a lot of activity when defending the country against Tibetan invasions in the 17th and 18th centuries. It lay in ruins after being destroyed by fire, but has been renovated and now serves as the *dzongkhag* administrative headquarters.

## Day 14: Damji to Tashithang
16km / 5 hours / 250m ascent, 870m descent

Until the road from Tashithang to Damji is complete you'll have to walk, meeting the road at whatever point the construction has been completed.

Trek past a few more houses and fields as the trail climbs to a chorten at the southern end of Damji. The trail begins a long descent to the river, first winding down gently in the jungle past a few streams, then switchbacking steeply down on a rocky trail in the shadow of a huge rock. After a long descent you will cross a wooden bridge over a side stream at 1960m. There is an alternative camp site here near the banks of the river, about one hour below Damji.

The trail follows the Mo Chhu downstream through forests where you may encounter rhesus monkeys and takins alongside the river. You'll have to stick close to your guide as he inquires where the route joins the road. At some point you'll climb from the river to the unfinished road. If you're lucky, vehicles will be waiting there to take you to Punakha, otherwise you will walk down to **Tashithang** at 1840m. It's then an 18km (one-hour) drive to Punakha; it's a good road, but the first 5km is unpaved.

# GASA HOT SPRING TREK
Being at a reasonably low elevation, this trek is possible from February to March and October to December. There are leeches in the lower part of the trek, which make it particularly unpleasant during the rainy season.

## Day 1: Tashithang to Damji
16km / 5-6 hours / 870m ascent, 250m descent

Follow Day 14 of the Laya–Gasa trek in reverse, driving as far as possible from Tashithang, dropping to the trail and climbing

---

> **THE TREK AT A GLANCE**
>
> **Duration** 5 days
> **Max Elevation** 2430m
> **Standard** Easy
> **Season** February to March, October to December
> **Start/Finish** Tashithang
> **Access Town** Punakha
> **Summary** This trek is the last part of the Laya-Gasa trek in reverse. The hot springs are fun, but there is a lot of climbing to get there.

---

steeply to the terraced rice fields of **Damji** (2430m).

## Day 2: Damji to Gasa Tsachhu
16km / 4-5 hours / 470m descent

Follow Day 13 of the Laya–Gasa trek in reverse along the side of the valley, then drop to the large stream below Gasa. A trail leads north from here, following the stream directly to the hot spring at 2240m. The Jigme Dorji National Park administers the hot-spring complex and offers various kinds of accommodation in a grove of large birch trees. There are some houses that can be rented, a few buildings that can be used as kitchens, a dormitory and numerous good camping places. It is a pleasant place to spend a day.

The hot springs are by the bank of the stream, below the hotel complex. There are five concrete pools and a shower room. The water temperature is 40°C, which is comfortably warm, but not scalding.

You may encounter women selling souvenirs; it's mostly Tibetan-style jewellery made in Nepal.

## Day 3: A Day at Gasa Tsachhu
You can laze around in the hot springs or take a packed lunch and climb about two hours to Gasa village and the dzong.

## Days 4-5: Gasa Tsachhu to Tashithang
Follow Days 13 to 14 of the Laya–Gasa trek and drive back to Punakha or Thimphu.

# GANGTE TREK
This trek is recommended from March to May and September to November, although it's usually possible to trek here throughout winter. It is especially beautiful in April, when rhododendrons are in bloom.

## Day 1: Phobjikha to Zasa
15km / 6-7 hours / 610m ascent, 410m descent

The trek starts near the village of Tabiting, a short distance up the road from the Dewachen Hotel, just before the Black Mountain National Park warden's office at 2890m. Follow a wide trail uphill beside a stream that climbs above a fenced-in potato field. Climb through a sparse forest of blue pine to **Kelwag**, a large meadow of scrub bamboo at 3120m. The climb becomes steeper as it switchbacks up a ridge to a few prayer flags at 3370m.

It's then a gentle ascent through pines and rhododendrons to **Tsele La** at 3430m.

From the pass the trail descends through scrub bamboo into the huge Kangkha Chhu valley and traverses above a single wooden house at **Tsele Pang** (3280m). Descend further into a forest of cypress, juniper, rhododendron and daphne to the small village of **Tserina** at 3120m. There is a trail junction here; if you are in a large group, follow the lower trail to the camping place at Dzomdu Gyakha. The upper route to Gogona crosses two small streams and, after a few minutes, reaches the extensive sheep pastures and potato fields of Gankakha at 3030m. It's then a long traverse through forests to a few houses at Gogona (3090m).

Gogona Lhakhang is dominated by statues of Chenresig, Atisha and several manifestations of Guru Rinpoche. The walls are covered with elaborate paintings and on the *gorikha*

---

**THE TREK AT A GLANCE**

**Duration** 3 days
**Max Elevation** 3480m
**Standard** Easy
**Season** March to May, September to November
**Start** Phobjikha
**Finish** Tikke Zampa
**Access Towns** Phobjikha, Wangdue Phodrang
**Summary** A short trek at relatively low elevations, visiting several remote villages and monasteries.

---

(porch) is a painting of Lama Drukpa Kunley. Most of the *gomchens* (lay monks) from Gogona travel to Thimphu for winter.

Camping is not allowed at the monastery, therefore it's necessary to trek around the ridge to a large side valley and the pretty village of **Dangchu** (3040m). The women here weave blankets and speak a different dialect called Bjop-kha (language of the nomads). The usual camping place is near the head of the grassy valley beside a small stream in a yak pasture known as **Zasa** (3130m). This is a small camping place; larger groups usually camp below in the valley at Dzomdu Gyakha or near the cheese factory at Sha Gagona, a community-based dairy farm that produces Gouda-style cheese.

## Day 2: Zasa to Chorten Karpo

16km / 5-7 hours / 450m ascent, 860m descent

An inconspicuous trail leads up the large meadow above Zasa, eventually entering forests on the northwest corner. Climb into a forest of fir, oak, spruce, dwarf rhododendron, miniature azaleas, cypress and juniper. A large area of this forest was burned by a fire that was probably caused by lightning. Much of the undergrowth consists of daphne (the plant used for handmade paper), which may be identified by its sweet-smelling, whitish-cream-coloured flowers. Climb for about two hours to a crest at 3360m high, then again for another 30 minutes to **Shobe La**, a forested ridge marked by a rock cairn at 3480m. A rocky trail

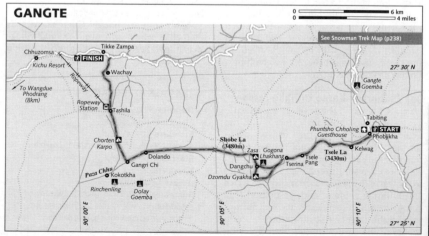

TREKKING

leads down through a forest of cypress, juniper and rhododendron to a clearing at 3270m that offers a good lunch spot.

Descend further on a rocky trail to join a rough forest road at 2970m. The trek from here to the Tashila ropeway strays on and off this road, which is used by tractors to transport the timber harvested in this region. Follow the road across a stream, then through an oak forest, following a few trails that provide short cuts to avoid long loops in the road, eventually arriving at **Dolando**, an isolated sawmill and several wooden houses at 2790m. The road makes a small detour around a rock that is said to be the remains of a demon. If you look closely you may be able to see the marks left when Guru Rinpoche beat the demon with his stick.

Follow the road alongside a stream, crossing to river right at 2730m, and continue to another sawmill at the edge of the broad Karte Thang valley near Gangri Chi village at 2670m. Below is the village of Kokotkha, with about 60 rustic houses. The large Kokotkha valley to the southwest was once considered as a site for a domestic airport to serve Wangdue Phodrang and Punakha, but this plan never materialised.

Atop a ridge to the southwest is the large Rinchenling monastery. It's about a 15-minute walk. High above to the south is Dolay Goemba. The trek route turns north here and follows the small Paza Chhu, then climbs over a ridge on a narrow trail, re-crosses the road and climbs gently to Chorten Karpo, four chortens in a forest of blue pines at 2680m. The Nepali chorten is in honour of a Je Khenpo. The next one commemorates a rich merchant from Kokotkha; next is a *kani* (archlike chorten) with its middle filled in; and the southernmost chorten was built by a Kokotkha flour merchant.

### Day 3: Chorten Karpo to Tikke Zampa
12km / 4-5 hours / 120m ascent, 1340m descent
The trail climbs from the camp to join the forest road at 2720m. It's then an easy walk to the top of the ridge at 2800m. You can take a trail that cuts across the top of the ridge, but it's more interesting to continue a few minutes to the top of the **Tashila ropeway** and watch rice and building supplies coming up and logs going down. It's not officially allowed, but you may be able to get a ride down the 6km-long cableway and save yourself a knee-cracking

descent, but note the warning: 'The passenger who travels by Tashila ropeway will be at their own risk'. For more about the ropeway see the Wangdue Phodrang to Pele La section (p151).

The walk down is through a beautiful forest, with the undergrowth changing from rhododendrons and magnolias to ferns and dwarf bamboo. Experts claim that this stretch of trail is one of the finest bird-watching areas in Bhutan. Among the birds found here are laughing thrushes, shrikes, magpies and woodpeckers.

There's a trail junction at 2250m. Take the right-hand fork and keep descending until you reach the houses and fields of Wachay at about 1880m. You may need to rely on a guide to traverse through fields and farmyards as the trail plunges down past steep terraced wheat fields to two shops at 1460m on the road about 300m east of the bridge at **Tikke Zampa**.

## BUMTHANG CULTURAL TREK
Although it is a short trek, the Bumthang trek is strenuous, featuring a 500m climb to Phephe La. This trek is usually possible from March to May and again from September to November. The start of the trek is a 3km drive up the unpaved road from Kurjey Lhakhang to Toktu Zampa at 2540m, then a short drive to Thangbi Goemba. With luck, the packhorses will be waiting and you can start walking with a minimum of delay.

### Day 1: Thangbi Goemba to Sambitang
10km / 2-3 hours / 170m ascent
The road continues up the valley, but you will probably stop at Thangbi Goemba, with its distinctive yellow roof, near the small village of Thangbi. See p174 for a brief description of this goemba.

---

**THE TREK AT A GLANCE**

**Duration** 3 days
**Max Elevation** 3360m
**Standard** Easy–medium
**Season** March to May, September to November
**Start** Thangbi Goemba
**Finish** Kizum
**Access Town** Jakar
**Summary** This trek is so named because the opportunities to visit villages and lhakhangs are greater than on most other treks in Bhutan.

The trail follows a broad ledge above the river past a 70m-long painted *mani* wall and a *khonying* with a mandala painted on the roof inside. Just beyond the arched chorten is a trail junction. Take the trail that leads to a suspension bridge across the Bumthang Chhu (known locally as the Choskhor Chhu). On the opposite side the route traverses.

Follow the left bank of the Bumthang Chhu through pleasant meadows and forests of blue pine and scrub. After about an hour of walking you pass the Zangling Lhakhang on the hill to the right. From here it's 15 minutes to a trail junction next to a chorten and prayer wheels. The left branch leads to Ngang Lhakhang; if you follow the right branch it's about 15 minutes to the camp site at Sambitang.

To visit Ngang Lhakhang, make a short, steep climb to a settlement of old-looking houses at 2800m. There are two water-driven prayer wheels; the water comes down an interesting sluiceway of carved wooden pipes. This is Ngang Lhakhang, the Swan Temple. See the description of this interesting temple on p174.

From Ngang Lhakhang it's a 30-minute walk to the camp at **Sambitang**.

## Day 2: Sambitang to Ogyen Chholing

18km / 6-7 hours / 750m ascent, 670m descent

The day's walk starts out across meadows, with a lot of dwarf bamboo and several little streams to cross. The trail cuts across the top of some fields, goes over a small hill and down to a stream. Soon you will be convinced that

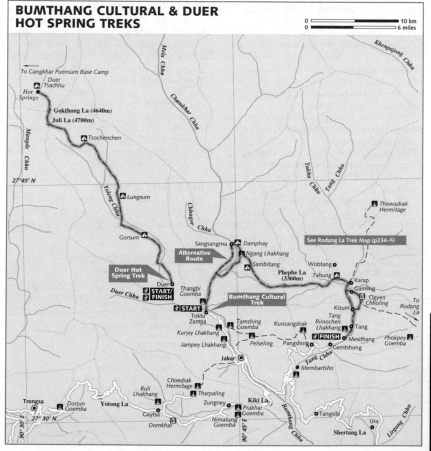

**BUMTHANG CULTURAL & DUER HOT SPRING TREKS**

0        10 km
0        6 miles

this cannot be the correct trail and you are hopelessly lost. Don't worry; stick with your guide or the horsemen because it is a narrow, indistinct trail through forests.

After crossing a stream the trail starts climbing, crossing back and forth across the stream on a series of slippery logs and stones. Birches, sycamores, dwarf bamboo and lots of tall bamboo form a cold, sunless forest. Spanish moss drapes from the ancient trees, giving an eerie feel to the steep climb.

Finally, the stream disappears and the climb continues through a rhododendron forest in a dry gully to a rock cairn and a little stone shrine stuffed with offerings of branches and a few ngultrum notes. Tattered prayer flags stretch across the path atop Phephe La (3360m). There is no view from the pass; it is a forested ridge with big birch and fir trees.

There is more deep forest on the opposite side; the trail leads down to a stream at 3200m, then into a side valley covered in dwarf bamboo, passing a small *mani* wall and a *khonying* chorten. Much of the walk is delightful, breaking out of the forest into broad meadows full of grazing yaks and cows.

It continues through ploughed fields and wide meadows and then into a broad valley, surrounded by rounded, treeless hills. Near a herders' hut the trail becomes indistinct as it crosses a meadow. To stay on track, just aim for the trees on the right side of the meadow.

The route keeps going downhill. As it approaches the bottom of the valley, there are several side trails that lead to pastures and buckwheat fields. Take the most prominent trail, which leads downhill to a large stream and a substantial wooden bridge at 2790m near the village of **Tahung**. Behind Tahung is the Australian-assisted Wobtang sheep development project. A rough road suitable only for tractors follows the right bank of the Tang Chhu from the project all the way down the valley to Tang village. The trekking route leads downstream in meadows next to the river, sometimes on the road and sometimes on a footpath. It crosses the stream you have been following on a road bridge and turns a corner into the main valley of the Tang Chhu at 2640m.

Cross the Tang Chhu near Gamling, a large, wealthy village noted for its *yathra* weaving, about 45 minutes downstream.

Walk downstream from Gamling, crossing a stream and following the trail around a farmyard. Soon it starts climbing onto a ridge, reaching four chortens and several large houses at 2760m. **Ogyen Chholing** is on the top of the hill to the right. You can camp near the palace or splurge on a room in the guest house. For more information about Ogyen Chholing Palace and its fascinating museum, see p178.

### Day 3: Ogyen Chholing to Kizum
**16km / 1 hour / 130m descent**
It's a short walk downhill to **Kizum** where the vehicles should be waiting. It's then a 25km drive to the junction of the paved road near Membartsho.

## DUER HOT SPRING TREK
With special permission, it might be possible to extend this trek to the base camp of Gangkhar Puensum itself, although this is a rough, difficult route. It is also possible to vary either the upward or return route to travel via the Mangde Chhu valley to meet a gravel road that leads west from Trongsa.

Snow covers the route during winter so the trek is considered open from March to April and from September to early November. Its starting point, Duer village, is one hour (5km) of rough driving from Toktu Zampa. This trek includes a visit to a *tsachhu*.

### Day 1: Duer to Gorsum
**18km / 6-7 hours / 380m ascent**
The route follows the valley of the Yoleng Chhu, which is famous for trout, up to **Gorsum** at 3120m.

### Day 2: Gorsum to Lungsum
**12km / 5 hours / 40m ascent**
The route travels through a forest of cypress, juniper, spruce, hemlock and maple. The trail

---

**THE TREK AT A GLANCE**

**Duration** 8 days
**Max Elevation** 4700m
**Standard** Medium–hard
**Season** March to April, September to November
**Start/Finish** Duer
**Access Town** Jakar
**Summary** This trek is the old expedition route to Gangkhar Puensum.

is muddy and climbs gradually to the camp at
**Lungsum** (3160m).

## Day 3: Lungsum to Tsoc henchen
15km / 6-7 hours / 620m ascent
Trek through more forest to a camp at Tso-chenchen, above the tree line at 3780m.

## Day 4: Tsochenchen to Duer Tsachhu
18km / 8-9 hours / 1340m ascent, 1530m descent
The day starts with a long climb to a small
lake and on to Juli La (4700m), a rocky sad-dle with a few prayer flags and a good view
of the surrounding mountains. After crossing
the pass the trail descends to a lake at 4220m,
climbs again to Gokthong La (4640m), then
switchbacks steeply down through jungle to
a camp near the **Duer hot springs** at 3590m. It
may be possible to see musk deer, Himalayan
bears and blue sheep.

## Day 5: A Day at Duer Tsachhu
Take a rest day to relax in the *tsachhu*. There
are several wooden tubs set into the ground
inside a rough wooden shelter.

## Day 6: Duer Tsachhu to Tsochenchen
18km / 6 hours / 1530m ascent, 1340m descent
Return via the same route to Tsochenchen.

## Day 7: Tsochenchen to Gorsum
27km / 9 hours / 660m descent
Follow the route back down the valley.

## Day 8: Gorsum to Duer
18km / 6 hours / 380m descent
Return to the road.

# RODANG LA TREK
Although it was an important trade route
before the National Hwy was built, few people
travel this path any more. Most trekkers com-bine this route with the Bumthang cultural
trek, starting at Thangbi Goemba. Alterna-tively, you can start the trek by driving up
the Tang valley to Kizum, saving two days
of walking.

Rodang La is subject to closure because of
snow; this trek is best planned in October and
early November as well as late spring.

The trek crosses the road near Lhuentse,
which breaks up the continuity of the trek-king experience, but offers a chance to visit
the remote dzong.

**THE TREK AT A GLANCE**

**Duration** 10 days
**Max Elevation** 4160m
**Standard** Medium–hard
**Season** October to November
**Start** Thangbi Goemba
**Finish** Trashi Yangtse
**Access Town** Jakar
**Summary** This trek across eastern Bhutan is tough
and involves a tremendously long, steep descent.
The logistics are complicated and horses are often
difficult to obtain for the final four days of the trek.

## Days 1-2: Toktu Zampa to Ogyen Chholing
Follow Days 1 to 2 of the Bumthang cultural
trek to **Ogyen Chholing**, at an elevation of 2760m
(see p178).

## Day 3: Ogyen Chholing to Phokpey
17km / 5-6 hours / 920m ascent
The long climb to Rodang La takes two days.
Above Ogyen Chholing the trail is rutted with
the hoof prints of cattle. If it's wet, this is a
very muddy, miserable, slippery climb. The
trail levels out at about 2900m and meets a
stream. At about 3000m the cow trails end and
it becomes a small footpath through muddy
fields and dwarf bamboo.

At 3400m the trail crosses a meadow with
more dwarf bamboo. High on the opposite
hill you can see the recently built Phokpey
Goemba. Climb through the meadow and
traverse through forest to another steep, high
meadow, finally turning a corner into a side
valley. The opposite side is all big firs.

The trail leads up a draw towards the head
of the valley and **Phokpey**, a camp in a meadow
at 3680m. This is a summer pasture and there
is the frame for a house that herders cover
with a plastic sheet to use as a shelter. The
meadow is surrounded by forest and the
ground is dotted with tiny blue alpine flow-ers. Once the sun goes down, the temperature
plummets.

## Day 4: Phokpey to Pemi
20km / 6-7 hours / 480m ascent, 1160m descent
The trail goes through a small notch and onto
another ridge at 3700m. It traverses the east
side of the ridge, passing big rhododendrons
with large leaves that curl up in the cold. Soon
you will see the pass up ahead. After a long

## RODANG LA TREK

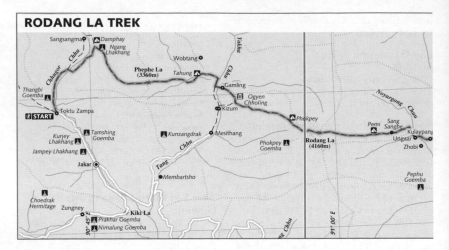

traverse at 3770m, the trail begins the final climb to the pass up big stone slabs and a steep stone staircase. **Rodang La** (4160m) is about a two-hour climb from camp. There's a small stone chorten here.

Once across the pass it's a steep descent of nearly 2500m to the valley floor. The descent starts on some rough rocks and an unbelievably long and steep stone staircase that was built when this was the only route between eastern and western Bhutan. This is the same near-vertical slope that the road descends on the eastern side of Thrumshing La, which is only 20km to the south.

You can see the trail far below, snaking down the ridge to the east. This is a tough route for horses, and it is said that even the king walked downhill here.

Part of the route is along a vertical face and the trail is on wooden galleries fastened into the side of the cliff. There are a few small meadows as the trail winds its way down on a complex route through a region where sightings of ghosts and yetis have been reported. Leaving the rhododendrons and conifers, it makes a gentle descent through a forest of broad-leafed species along a ridge to the east to a big meadow called **Pemi** at about 3000m. After a short walk through some dwarf bamboo you reach the ruins of a house and a camp site at 2950m. This is not an ideal camping place because the water is 15 minutes down the side of a hill; go easy on the washing here. The ruined stone building was the grain storehouse during the time of the first and second

kings, when royal parties travelled regularly between Bumthang and Kurtoe.

## Day 5: Pemi to Khaine Lhakhang
**21km / 7-8 hours / 350m ascent, 1340m descent**

From Pemi the trail tumbles into the valley of the Noyurgang Chhu. The route leads from the camp through dwarf bamboo, then heads down a damp, rock-filled gully with lots of leaves, moss and wet rocks to pick your way through.

At about 2600m the vegetation changes to ferns and more tropical species and there is a long level stretch through the mud. It then goes down steeply again, working its way out towards the end of a side ridge and a meadow called Sang Sangbe (2300m), where a ghost is said to live. High on the hillside on the opposite side of the valley is Yamalung Goemba, hidden behind a bunch of very tall trees planted in a circle. The trail drops off the side of the ridge to a bridge over a stream at 1700m. The village of Ungaar is on a ridge above the stream and downstream is another small village named Zhobi. It's then a short walk across rice fields in the bottom of the valley to a suspension bridge over the Noyurgang Chhu at 1660m.

Cross to river left and start climbing through ferns and tropical jungle to Bulay (1800m). The trail passes above the rice terraces of the village, turns a corner and climbs up a little draw. The valley below is covered with rice and temporary shelters used by planters.

The trail makes a long climb as it heads along the valley, traversing in and out of side

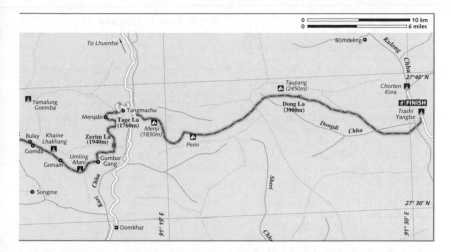

valleys and passing numerous villages. Ku-laypang (1930m) is a few simple houses and some cornfields. There's an inviting-looking trail that goes down and cuts across the next ridge but the correct trail goes up.

The trail passes below the settlement of Gomda (2040m). The language spoken in these villages is Kurtepa, which Dzongkha speakers cannot understand. After passing a chorten, the trail drops to cross a stream at 2000m, then climbs to a *mani* wall at 2020m. Then it's a level walk past cornfields to the few houses of Gongdra and a Tibetan-style chorten.

Beyond Chanteme, a spread-out village with extensive cornfields, the trail crosses a

---

**KHAINE LHAKHANG**

Some people believe that the remote Khaine Lhakhang is one of the 108 temples built by King Songtsen Gampo in AD 659. Three small statues from here are said to have flown of their own accord to Konchogsum Lhakhang in Bumthang, which is said to have been built at the same time.

The primary statue is a 2.5m-high Sakyamuni figure. A statue of Karmapa is on his right and Zhabdrung Rinpoche is above him on the left. There are also smaller statues of Milarepa and Guru Rinpoche. The main protective deity is a ferocious god named Taxan, who is depicted riding on a horse. A two-day festival is celebrated here in mid-November.

---

stream and makes a climb to **Khaine Lhakhang**. Follow the cement irrigation canal for a while and then climb onto the ridge where the temple sits at 2010m. There are two tall cedars by the monastery and fields of soya beans surrounding it.

You can see a goemba and a village at the eastern end of the ridge on the opposite side of the river. Pephu Goemba is high above and the town below is Songme.

## Day 6: Khaine Lhakhang to Tangmachu
**18km / 6-7 hours / 520m ascent, 810m descent**

The trail goes down to a stream and up to a BHU and community school in **Gorsam**. It then goes in and out of more side valleys and climbs to 2130m. It's level for about 15 minutes, then starts climbing gently through trees. You can see a glimpse of the road at the bottom of the Kuri Chhu valley.

The Tibetan-style Umling Mani at 2180m is at the corner between the Noyurgang Chhu and the Kuri Chhu valleys. It was built by a lama from Tibet and marks the boundary between the two gewogs (administrative blocks). Here the route turns north up the Kuri Chhu.

The next stretch of trail traverses through four large side valleys, descending to a stream and climbing to the next ridge. The trail emerges from the first valley at Gumbar Gang (2120m). After a long, almost level, stretch the trail goes down and up to a chorten on Zerim La (1940m).

The route contours down to the head of a valley at 1840m, where there is a little chorten and a prayer wheel, then immediately starts climbing back through chir pines to 1890m. It traverses grassy slopes in the main valley to another ridge and several herders' huts.

There's one more big side valley to traverse. Descend to a *mani* wall, and pass the fields and houses of Menjabi, a pretty village with large, white Bhutanese houses. Cross the stream at 1540m, then start a long, hot climb on a grassy slope dotted with chir pines to some chortens and a *mani* wall on Tage La (1760m). Southeast of the pass is the Tangmachu High School, where 400 students study on the top of this windswept ridge. It may be possible to camp near the school or, better yet, have vehicles waiting to drive you down to the valley.

It's 8km down the dirt road to the paved road, and 13km from the road junction to Lhuentse. The best way to handle the logistics is to arrange for a vehicle to meet you at **Tangmachu**, take you to Lhuentse to visit the impressive dzong and then drop you off at the bottom of the hill to finish the last of the trek. The vehicle can then drive on to Trashi Yangtse to pick you up four days later.

## Day 7: Tangmachu to Menji
16km / 4-5 hours / 690m ascent, 620m descent
From the bridge (1140m) below Tangmachu, the trek starts gradually up through rice terraces and cornfields to Chusa. It then becomes a steep haul up a treeless slope, although the path is beautifully scented with wild mint, lemon grass and artemisia. Camp is at 1830m, above **Menji**, beside the Darchu Pang Lhakhang. The lhakhang's well-kept garden is full of flowers – marigolds, geraniums, dahlias and nasturtiums – and has a vegetable patch of tomatoes and huge cucumbers. There are banana trees, too, and dozens of long-tailed birds in the trees.

## Day 8: Menji to Pemi
20km / 3-4 hours / 620m ascent
Continue uphill through the thick, humid forest packed with a dense foliage of ferns and creepers and a constant whistle of cicadas. The trail is narrow, steep and rutted. Climb steadily for two hours to a ridge-top meadow, then plunge back into the forest to reach some herders' huts at **Pemi** (2450m) on a narrow ridge-top clearing with a view to a forested gorge. There's not a village or house in view, although Menji villagers use this area as a summer pasture. Much of the trail for the next two days has fallen into disuse and is narrow and slippery.

## Day 9: Pemi to Taupang
21km / 7-8 hours / 1450m ascent, 1450m descent
The trail stays in damp, cold forest, with occasional summer pastures with bamboo herders' shelters. The climb goes on and on, but the area is a botanist's delight, with shrubs of every kind, pungent with a sweet fermented smell, thick with humus. The next stretch of trail traverses nine passes, nicknamed the Nine Sisters, the highest of which is **Dong La** (3900m). Cross several ridges to Dong La, where there are good mountain views and a few prayer flags on a pile of rocks.

Cross the remaining ridges, each adorned with prayer flags, and descend steeply through thick evergreen forests on a trail strewn with rocks, logs and slippery leaves to a ridge-top meadow called Lisipang. The last part of the trek starts easily enough, turning right and down through a pasture at Yesupang, but then becomes increasingly rocky and muddy as it nears the Dongdi Chhu. There's no bridge, so you either rock- hop across or, if you're lucky, find a tree trunk balanced on rocks.

The path on the other side of the river is even muddier and rockier; parts of it are layered with a makeshift washboard-style log path. It's more like jungle than forest here, with ferns and creepers above and the river roaring nearby. The camp is at **Taupang** (2450m), a clearing in the forest with a wooden cowherds' shelter.

## Day 10: Taupang to Trashi Yangtse
24km / 8-9 hours / 720m descent
The path through the forest beside the river is damp and muddy with huge ferns, red-berried palms and occasional leeches. The forest is alive with birds and monkeys. Two hours of sloshing through mud or springing from stone to log to stone brings you to **Shakshing**, a cluster of houses on the hillside, surrounded by corn and millet fields, banana trees and grazing cows.

The trail stays on the ridge on the northern side of the valley, passing above the village of Tongshing. It then descends past some swampy areas and crosses to the southern bank of the Dongdi Chhu on a large bridge. The small, old **Trashi Yangtse** dzong suddenly appears at the end of the valley on a hill top above the river. The trail crosses back to the north side of the river below the dzong on an old cantilever bridge. Finally cross the Kulong Chhu at 1730m where, with luck, your vehicles will be waiting, or climb to the road and walk 3km into Chorten Kora.

## SNOWMAN TREK

The combination of distance, altitude, remoteness and weather makes this a tough journey, and when trekking fees were set at US$200 a night, it suffered a sharp decline in the number of trekkers who attempt it. Even though there are reduced rates for long treks, few people can afford a 25-day trek for US$4280.

If you plan to trek this route, double-check your emergency evacuation insurance (see p248). If you get into Lunana and snow blocks the passes, the only way out is by helicopter, an expensive way to finish an already expensive trek. Another obstacle that often hampers this trek is bridges in remote regions that get washed away.

The Snowman trek is frequently closed because of snow, and is impossible to undertake during winter. The season for this trek is generally considered to be from late September to mid-October. Don't plan a summer trek; this is a miserable place to be during the monsoon.

This classic trek follows the Jhomolhari and Laya–Gasa treks to Laya. Many walking days can be saved by starting in Tashithang and trekking north up the Mo Chhu, following the Laya–Gasa trek in reverse.

### Days 1 to 5: Drukgyel Dzong to Lingzhi

Follow Days 1 to 5 of the Jhomolhari trek (see p216).

### Days 6 to 10: Lingzhi to Laya

Follow Days 6 to 10 of the Laya–Gasa trek (see p222).

---

**THE TREK AT A GLANCE**

**Duration** 25 days
**Max Elevation** 5320m
**Standard** Hard
**Season** September to October
**Start** Drukgyel Dzong
**Finish** Sephu
**Access Town** Paro
**Summary** The Snowman trek travels to the remote Lunana district and is said to be one of the most difficult treks in the world. Fewer than half the people who attempt this trek actually finish it, either because of problems with altitude or heavy snowfall on the high passes.

---

### Day 11: Rest & Acclimatisation Day in Laya

If you have trekked from Drukgyel Dzong you should spend a day recuperating from the trek to Laya and preparing for the rest of this rigorous trek. If you've trekked from Tashithang, you should also walk up to Laya to acclimatise. The army post below Laya has a radio; you will need to send a runner here with a message in an emergency.

### Day 12: Laya to Rodophu

**19km / 6-8 hours / 1030m ascent, 70m descent**

The trek leads gradually downhill to the Lunana trail junction, then climbs steeply for 30 to 40 minutes to a hilltop with good views over the Mo Chhu and the Rhodo Chhu. Much of the forest cover here was burned. The rough trail continues to climb gradually up the Rhodo Chhu valley, first through mixed conifers, then through rhododendron shrubs above the tree line. At the top of a large rock slide there is a view of the broad glacial valley and a massive glacier on Tsenda Kang (7100m), towering overhead. The **Roduphu** camp is just beyond a wooden bridge across the Rhodo Chhu at 4160m.

If you have time in the afternoon, or are taking an acclimatisation day here, you have a choice of several short hikes. A small trail leads up the valley for about 2km to a knoll with excellent views of the valley and surrounding mountains. You could continue further to the base of the glacier. Another option is to follow a small trail that starts about 500m upstream from the camp and switchbacks up the hill to the north, ending in a small yak pasture with a hut at 4500m.

### Day 13: Rodophu to Narethang

**17km / 5-6 hours / 720m ascent**

The path crosses the wooden bridge and follows the river for about 20 minutes through rhododendron shrubs before turning right up the hill. Climb steadily to a high open valley at 4600m then more gradually through meadows to **Tsomo La** (4900m), which offers good views towards the Tibetan border and Jhomolhari. The route then crosses a generally flat, barren plateau at about 5000m with yak trails crisscrossing everywhere. Hopefully you'll have a knowledgeable guide and won't get lost. The camp is at **Narethang** (4900m), below the 6395m peak of Gangla Karchung.

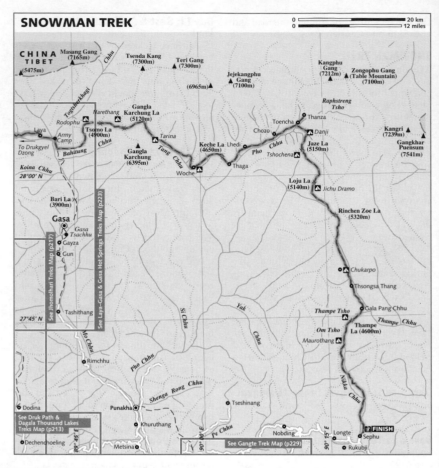

**SNOWMAN TREK**

## Day 14: Narethang to Tarina

18km / 5-6 hours / 270m ascent, 1200m descent

From camp it takes about one hour to climb to 5120m **Gangla Karchung La**. Mountain views from the pass are excellent with distant Kang Bum (6526m) to the west and the rugged peaks of Tsenda Kang, Teri Gang (7300m) and Jejekangphu Gang (7100m) on the northern horizon.

The path descends along a large moraine to the edge of a near-vertical wall. Views from the edge of the wall are breathtaking – among the best along the entire trek. A massive glacier descends from Teri Kang to a deep turquoise lake at its foot, 1km below you. The glacial lake to the left burst through its dam in the early 60s, causing widespread damage downstream, and partially destroying Punakha Dzong.

Now the path becomes very steep (almost vertical in places) as it descends into the valley. In the lower half of the descent it passes through thick rhododendron shrubs and trees. When wet, this stretch can be rather nasty, with lots of roots and slippery mud.

At the bottom of the large, U-shaped valley the trail turns right, following the Tang Chhu downstream. There are several good camp sites along the river, both before and after the trail crosses the river at **Tarina**.

## Day 15: Tarina to Woche

17km / 6-7 hours / 275m ascent, 330m descent

The walk leads through conifer forest down the Tang Chhu on river left, passing some impressive waterfalls cascading down both sides of the valley. The trail climbs gently out of the valley past several huge landslides and eventually climbs steeply to the northeast into the high side valley of **Woche**. Woche is a small settlement of five houses at 3940m and is the first village in the Lunana region.

Looking up the valley you can see the following day's route to Lhedi. There have been reports of theft of hiking equipment or clothing here; keep all your gear safely inside your tent.

## Day 16: Woche to Lhedi
**17km / 6-7 hours / 980m ascent, 950m descent**
The path to Lhedi begins below the camp and climbs the Woche valley, crossing a stream and climbing over a moraine before descending to a wooden bridge across the Woche Chhu. It then climbs on a wide trail past an extremely clear lake to **Keche La** (4650m). From the pass there are excellent views of the surrounding mountains, including Jejekangphu Gang's triple peak, the source of the Woche Chhu.

The route descends steeply into the Pho Chhu valley, the heart of the Lunana district. In the small village of Thaga (4050m) the farmers grow buckwheat, potatoes, turnips and radishes. From Thaga the path drops towards the Pho Chhu, then turns northeast towards Lhedi, which is visible in the distance above the river.

In 1994 a moraine holding back a large glacial lake north of Thanza burst, hurling millions of litres of water down the Pho Chhu. The resulting flash flood caused considerable damage, which is still visible along this stretch of trail.

Passing a few scattered settlements and crossing below a waterfall on a wooden bridge, the trail descends to the banks of the Pho Chhu. Continue along the river bed until you reach Lhedi at 3700m.

Lhedi is a district headquarters with a school, BHU and wireless station, but there is no shop here (or anywhere else in the Lunana district). Everything is carried in by yak trains across 5000m passes. Strong winds blow up the valley in the late afternoon, making it bitterly cold in autumn and winter.

## Day 17: Lhedi to Thanza
**17km / 7-8 hours / 400m ascent**
The trail follows the north bank of the Pho Chhu past several small farms. In clear weather there are excellent views of Table Mountain (7100m) to the north and Tangse Gang across the river. Floods have destroyed parts of the trail so a temporary path winds its way among

massive boulders in the river bed, crossing small, rickety bridges across several channels of the river. Around lunch time the trail passes the small village of **Chozo** at 4090m. The village has a small dzong, which is still in use.

If you are pressed for time, you can gain a day or two by stopping here and taking a direct trail to Tshochena, but most trekkers continue to Thanza (4100m), a couple of hours further up the valley. The first part of the trail to Thanza leads through lush yak pastures on the wide river flats, but soon the grass gives way to a large expanse of fine glacial sand. Protect your camera; if it is windy the sand will enter any little opening.

Eventually the trail leaves the river bed and climbs a bluff overlooking the villages of **Thanza**, straight ahead, and **Toencha**, on the other bank of the river. Table Mountain forms an immense, 3000m-high wall of snow and ice only a few kilometres behind Thanza. Most groups camp in Toencha (4150m), but there are places to camp in Thanza as well.

## Day 18: Rest Day in Thanza
Schedule a rest day here. This is as far as the yak drivers from Laya go. It takes time to round up enough yaks for the rest of the trek and you may get a rest day even if you have not scheduled one. This provides a good opportunity to explore the villages and glacial lakes up the valley. The closest lake, Raphstreng Tsho, is 100m deep and caused the 1994 flood. A large crew of Indian workers dug a channel through the moraine to prevent a recurrence, but there are several more glacial lakes in the area that could burst through their moraines at any time.

## Day 19: Thanza to Danji
**8km / 3-4 hours / 80m ascent**
If your party is very fit, you can do the hike to Tshochena in one day, but it's a long, hard walk at high altitude and it's better to split it into two half-days.

The route climbs from Toencha to a large boulder on the hill south of the village. From the boulder there are excellent views of Thanza, Toencha, Chozo and the surrounding mountains. The path then turns east up a side valley. After a couple of hours of relatively flat and easy walking, the trail enters **Danji**, a yak meadow with some herders' huts. This is an excellent camping spot; there are often blue sheep on the hills above, and they have been known to walk into camp.

TREKKING

If you stop here, there is ample opportunity to explore the area. A few hundred metres up the valley, a small trail climbs the ridge to the left, leading to a higher valley. The top of the ridge offers excellent views of the surrounding mountains.

## Day 20: Danji to Tshochena
12km / 5-6 hours / 490m ascent, 240m descent
There is a trail junction near the camp site at Danji. The trail up the valley leads to Gangkhar Puensum base camp and to Bumthang. The path to the end of the trek crosses the creek and leads up a rocky side valley. It is a long climb across several false summits to **Jaze La** at 5150m, which offers spectacular mountain views in all directions. From the pass, the path descends between snow-covered peaks past a string of small lakes. The camp is near the shore of **Tshochena** lake at 4970m. This is the first of two nights' camping above 4900m.

## Day 21: Tshochena to Jichu Dramo
14km / 4-5 hours / 230m ascent, 140m descent
The trail follows the shore of the blue-green lake before climbing to a ridge at 5100m. On top you are surrounded by a 360-degree panorama of snowy peaks while, far below, the Pho Chhu descends towards Punakha. Below the ridge, the road and microwave tower at Dochu La are just visible in the distance.

The path makes several ups and downs over small rounded hills, but because of the altitude, walking can be slow. The trail descends past a glacial lake before climbing up to Loju La at 5140m. Many trails wander around high-altitude yak pastures in this region, and it's easy to go astray. The correct path will lead you across a small saddle at 5100m into a wide glacial valley. The trail descends gradually to the camp at **Jichu Dramo** (5050m), a small pasture on the east side of the valley.

## Day 22: Jichu Dramo to Chukarpo
18km / 5-6 hours / 320m ascent, 730m descent
After leaving camp the trail climbs through a moraine to Rinchen Zoe La (5320m), which divides the Pho Chhu and Mangde Chhu drainages. The pass is surrounded by breathtaking mountain scenery. Rinchen Zoe peak (5650m) towers above the pass to the west and major Himalayan mountains

stretch along the northern horizon. To the east the western flank of Gangkhar Puensum is visible above the closer ranges, while the Thampe Chhu valley stretches below you to the south.

From the pass the trail descends into a broad, marshy valley with a string of lakes. The trail generally follows the left (east) side of the valley, which narrows the lower you go. Eventually the trail descends steeply down the face of a moraine to a yak pasture in the upper reaches of the Thampe Chhu. There are trails on both sides of the river, but you should cross to the west bank (river right) here, as there is no bridge further down. The vegetation gradually begins to thicken, first to rhododendron and juniper shrubs and eventually to trees of both species, the first real trees since Lhedi. After a couple of hours you reach the camp at **Chukarpo** (4600m), or you can continue to a better site at **Thsongsa Thang** (4400m), one hour down the trail.

## Day 23: Chukarpo to Thampe Tsho
18km / 5-6 hours / 400m ascent, 640m descent
The trail continues to descend along the right bank of the river until it reaches a yak pasture at Gala Pang Chhu (4010m). You might be lucky enough to spot some takins on the hills across the river. From this point, the path begins to climb quite steeply through junipers and silver firs towards **Thampe Tsho**. The path generally follows a stream to the beautiful, clear, turquoise lake, set in a bowl and surrounded by steep mountain walls. The camp is at the far end of the lake at 4300m.

## Day 24: Thampe Tsho to Maurothang
14km / 5 hours / 280m ascent, 1020m descent
The trail climbs steeply to **Thampe La** at 4600m. You may see blue sheep high on the slopes above the trail.

The path descends to Om Tsho, sacred because Pema Lingpa found a number of *terma* (sacred texts and artefacts) here. The path then skirts the northwestern shore of the lake before crossing its outlet, marked by a string of prayer flags. From here the path drops steeply past a waterfall to a smaller lake, about 100m lower.

From the second lake, the path descends steeply to the headwaters of the Nikka Chhu. It's so steep that even yaks are reluctant to come down this stretch. The drainage of the second lake also forms a waterfall, which can only be seen once you have descended almost to the bottom. The path levels out, following the left bank of the Nikka Chhu. After approximately 2km, it reaches a large open glade near the confluence of a major tributary coming from the east. A wooden bridge crosses the Nikka Chhu to river right, then a broad path follows through mixed forest to **Maurothang** (3610m), a large clearing on the banks of the river beside a few yak herders' huts.

## Day 25: Maurothang to Sephu
18km / 5-6 hours / 990m descent

If horses are not available at Maurothang, your guide will probably send someone ahead to arrange for them further down. Yaks cannot walk all the way to the road because of the low altitude and the many cows in the area.

A well-used trail continues down the west side of the Nikka Chhu for about 30 minutes before crossing to the east bank into a mixed deciduous and bamboo forest. It then descends gradually through forests interspersed with pastures. Eventually it emerges into a large grassy area, overlooking the road and the village of Sephu. The path becomes somewhat confusing at this point, as there are many trails. Look for a large trail about 20m to 30m above the river and you'll soon pass a large suspension bridge over the Nikka Chhu, which you shouldn't cross. Soon the trail turns into a narrow tractor road that emerges onto the main road at Sephu, next to the Nikka Chhu bridge at 2600m, where there are several stores as well as a small restaurant.

---

**THE TREK AT A GLANCE**

**Duration** 4 days
**Max Elevation** 1500m
**Standard** Easy
**Season** April, September to October
**Start** Punakha
**Finish** Chhuzomsa
**Access Town** Punakha
**Summary** A low-altitude trek southeast of Punakha. Low elevation makes this trek possible throughout the winter, but miserable when it's hot. This route sees few trekkers.

---

# SAMTENGANG WINTER TREK
## Day 1: Punakha to Limukha
12km / 4 hours / 880m ascent

Cross the footbridge over the Pho Chhu from Punakha Dzong and walk to Shengana. The trek begins with a gradual climb through a forest of chir pine to **Limukha**.

## Day 2: Limukha to Chhungsakha
14km / 5 hours / 430m descent

The trail descends through rhododendron and oak forests to **Chhungsakha**.

## Day 3: Chhungsakha to Samtengang
13km / 5 hours / 650m ascent, 270m descent

Trek down to the Pe Chhu, crossing it at 1420m, then climb through the village of Sha to **Samtengang**.

## Day 4: Samtengang to Chhuzomsa
15km / 5-6 hours / 730m descent

The trail leads steeply downhill on a treeless slope to the road at **Chhuzomsa**.

# Directory

## CONTENTS

| | |
|---|---|
| Accommodation | 242 |
| Activities | 243 |
| Business Hours | 244 |
| Children | 244 |
| Climate Charts | 245 |
| Courses | 246 |
| Customs | 246 |
| Dangers & Annoyances | 246 |
| Embassies & Consulates | 247 |
| Festivals & Events | 247 |
| Food | 247 |
| Gay & Lesbian Travellers | 248 |
| Holidays | 248 |
| Insurance | 248 |
| Internet Access | 249 |
| Legal Matters | 249 |
| Maps | 249 |
| Money | 250 |
| Photography & Video | 251 |
| Post | 252 |
| Shopping | 252 |
| Solo Travellers | 253 |
| Telephone & Fax | 254 |
| Time | 254 |
| Toilets | 254 |
| Tourist Information | 254 |
| Travellers with Disabilities | 254 |
| Visas | 255 |
| Volunteering | 256 |
| Women Travellers | 256 |

## ACCOMMODATION

Tour operators should book you into Department of Tourism (DOT) approved hotels. Since most visitors effectively pay the same rate whether staying in a budget or midrange

---

**BOOK ACCOMMODATION ONLINE**

For more accommodation reviews and recommendations by Lonely Planet authors, check out the online booking service at lonelyplanet.com. You'll find the true, insider lowdown on the best places to stay. Reviews are thorough and independent. Best of all, you can book online.

---

hotel, it makes sense to ask for the best when you make your travel arrangements. During the high season, particularly at *tsechu* (festival) time, you may not get the hotel you have asked for, and you may be accommodated in a hotel that caters primarily to local travellers. Still, these can be comfortable, though the toilet facilities may not be what you're used to.

The prices in this book are for standard rooms at normal foreign-tourist rates and do not include the usual 10% tax and 10% service charge. For a guide to price ranges used in this book, see the inside front cover.

### Hotels

There is a variety of hotels in Bhutan, ranging from simple huts that cater to Bhutanese yak herders to five-star luxury resorts. All rooms in the DOT-approved, midrange hotels in Thimphu, Paro and Phuentsholing have electricity, telephone, private bathroom and hot water. Every hotel has a restaurant that serves buffet meals when a group is in residence and à la carte dining at other times. Restaurants invariably serve alcohol and often have a bar. Several hotels advertise IDD, but this can mean that the phones simply connect to the front desk and the hotel operator will then dial the international number.

All the hotels publish their room rates, which usually just apply to Bhutanese, Indians and project staff. Many have various rates for standard, deluxe or suite accommodation, although the difference between standard and deluxe in most hotels is minimal. When you book a trip, you may specify which hotel you wish, but unless you are particularly charming to the agent, you'll probably get a standard room. If you want fancier accommodation or a single room, you may be asked to pay a little more than the standard tourist tariff. If you are travelling off season you can often pay less for a special room; if it's tsechu time, you may pay more. The handful of top-end hotels all provide international-standard accommodation and services and charge a substantial additional cost to the usual tourist tariff.

A confirmed hotel reservation does not always guarantee a booking in hotels as small as those in Bhutan. A large tour group can exert

**PRACTICALITIES**

- The biweekly national newspaper of Bhutan, *Kuensel* (www.kuenselonline.com) is available on Wednesday and Saturday mornings in English, Dzongkha and Nepali editions. The *Bhutan Times* (www.bhutantimes.com) is a privately owned newspaper published every Sunday in English. The *Bhutan Observer*, the second private newspaper, is published on Fridays in Dzongkha and English. Indian newspapers and magazines are available in Phuentsholing and Thimphu two to three days after publication.

- Bhutan Broadcasting Service (www.bbs.com.bt) broadcasts radio from 4pm to 8pm on the 60MHz band (5030kHz) and FM 96 Monday to Saturday. On Sunday it broadcasts from 10am to 4pm on the 49MHz band (6035kHz) and FM 96. Programmes are in Dzongkha, English, Nepali and Sharchop. The English news is at 11am and 2pm daily. BBS TV broadcasts from 6pm to 11pm daily with news in English and Dzongkha, and additional locally produced programming. Cable companies serve Thimphu and other large towns with feeds from satellite broadcasts including the BBC, CNN and a vast array of Hindi channels.

- The voltage in Bhutan is the same as India: 230V, 50 cycles AC. Bhutan uses the standard Indian round-pin sockets and multi-adapters are available in Thimphu.

- The metric system is used throughout the country. In villages, rice is sometimes measured in a round measure called a *gasekhorlo*. There is a scale called a *sang* that is used for butter and meat.

a powerful influence and you may discover that there is an extended negotiation taking place between your guide and the desk clerk when you check in. Don't worry; *something* will be arranged.

It's *cold* at night in Bhutan and central heating is rare. In Thimphu and Paro there are small electric heaters, and in Bumthang many hotel rooms are heated by a wood stove called a *bukhari*, which often has a pile of rocks on the top to retain the heat. All hotels provide sheets, blankets or quilts, and a pillow. Unless you are trekking, you won't need to carry bedding or a sleeping bag, but in the winter you may find yourself wearing all your clothing to bed. Hotel pillows tend to be extra firm and mattresses on the thin side.

If there is an electric water heater (called a geyser) in the room, turn it on as soon as you check in. The water flasks in hotel rooms are not always filled, and there is no assurance that the water they contain is boiled (see p272).

Some hotels have a *dotsho* (traditional hot-stone bath), a simple wooden structure containing water warmed with fire-heated rocks. The red-hot rocks tumble and sizzle into the water and a grill protects the bather's skin. Expect to wait up to two hours for the rocks to heat up and to pay extra for the experience.

## ACTIVITIES

There are lots of things to do in Bhutan after you have had your fill of dzongs and temples, and several tour operators are developing activities in an effort to convince visitors to stay longer and discover more about Bhutan. For details of companies offering activity-based tours in Bhutan, see p262.

There are many possible day hikes, particularly in Thimphu, Paro and Bumthang, and these are described in the relevant destination chapters. For serious treks ranging from three to 25 days, see the Trekking chapter (p199). Horse riding is available in Paro and on some treks, but remember the Bhutanese adage: It is not a horse that cannot carry a man uphill, and it is not a man who cannot walk downhill.

### Bird-Watching

Bhutan is rightly celebrated for its wintering populations of the vulnerable black-necked crane, but with over 600 recorded species and a spectacular range of habitats (see p87) this tiny country is a bird-watchers' paradise.

Although several companies specialise in bird-watching tours (see p262), Bhutan's plentiful mature forests and lack of hunting makes any travel a bird-spotting opportunity.

General wildlife viewing is generally confined to Royal Manas National Park in the south, currently off-limits because of the dangers posed by separatist groups in India,

**DIRECTORY**

but the closure was under review at the time of research.

## Fishing

Fishing with lure or fly for brown trout is possible in many rivers, though it is frowned upon by many Bhutanese. A licence (Nu 500 per day) is required and fishing is prohibited within 1km of a monastery, temple, dzong or *shedra* (religious school). A closed season applies from October to December and fishing is banned on many religious days throughout the year. The most popular lure is the Tasmanian Devil available in general shops in Thimphu. Yangphel Adventure Travel (www .yangphel.com) operates fly-fishing tours and encourages a 'catch and release' approach.

## Golf

There's an international-standard golf course in Thimphu and there are small courses in Haa and Deothang. The Thimphu course is used mainly by Bhutanese and expatriates, though it welcomes tourists playing there. It is popular with Japanese golfers both for the experience and because it's very inexpensive

compared with green fees in Japan. For details see p107.

## Cycling

Mountain biking is rapidly gaining popularity with Bhutanese and expats, who have formed the **Bhutan Bicycle Club** ( ☎ 02-321905; www.bhutanmtb .com), which has mountain bikes for hire (see p107). Some adventure travel companies have organised trips that allow bikers to bring their own cycles and travel throughout Bhutan accompanied by a 'sag wagon' for support. Long journeys are challenging because there's a lot of uphill peddling and approaching vehicles roar around corners, not expecting cyclists. Local cycling excursions in the Paro, Thimphu and Bumthang valleys offer a safer and less strenuous mountain-biking experience. A number of dedicated trails have been developed in Phobjikha (see p153) and Punakha (see p148).

## Rafting & Kayaking

Though rafting in Bhutan is in its infancy, those who have scouted the rivers feel that it has the potential for some of the best rafting on earth.

### RIVERS FOR RAFTING & KAYAKING

| River (chhu) | Location | River section | km | Grade | Recommendation |
|---|---|---|---|---|---|
| Amo | Haa | middle & lower | 35 | III & IV | rafting & kayaking |
| Bumthang | Bumthang | Thankabi | 5 | II & III | rafting & kayaking |
| Dang | Wangdue Phodrang | upper Dang Chhu | 3 | IV & V | kayaking |
| Dang | Wangdue Phodrang | middle Dang Chhu | 5 | IV & V | rafting with an experienced team & kayaking |
| Dang | Wangdue Phodrang | lower Dang Chhu | 5 | III | rafting & kayaking |
| Kuri | Lhuentse | upper run | 14 | IV & V | kayaking |
| Kuri | Lhuentse | middle run | 20 | IV with a couple of V | kayaking |
| Kuri | Lhuentse | lower run | 10 | III | rafting & kayaking |
| Mangde | Trongsa | Ema Datsi Canyon | 7 | III & IV at medium flow | kayaking |
| Mo | Punakha | upper Mo Chhu | 3 | IV & V | kayaking |
| Mo | Punakha | Sonam's put-in | 5 | III & IV | rafting & kayaking |
| Mo | Punakha | lower Mo Chhu | 6 | I & II | rafting & kayaking |
| Paro | Paro | Mitsi Zam | 10 | III & IV | kayaking |
| Paro | Paro | lower Paro Chhu | 7 | III with 1 class IV | kayaking |
| Pho | Punakha | upper Pho Chhu | 7 | III & IV | rafting & kayaking |
| Pho | Punakha | lower Pho Chhu | 7 | III | rafting & kayaking |
| Puna Tsang | Tsirang | Wakley Tar | 15 | III & IV | rafting & kayaking |
| Tang | Bumthang | Mesithang Tang | 10 | III | kayaking |
| Upper Wang | Chhuzom | Chhuzom to Tam Chhu | 4 | IV & V | kayaking |
| Lower Wang | Tam Chhu | Tam Chhu | 4 | III | rafting & kayaking |

From small alpine runs like the Paro Chhu to the big-water Puna Tsang Chhu, the white water of Bhutan is as diverse as its topography. Since 1997 small groups of paddlers have been exploring 14 rivers and over 22 different runs that vary from class II (beginner with moderate rapids) to class V (expert only).

There are two superb day trips on the Pho Chhu and the Mo Chhu. The trip on the Pho Chhu combines a hike up the side of the river through forest and farmland to the put-in at Samdinka. The raft trip has a couple of class III rapids and ends in a bang with the 'Wrathful Buddha' rapid next to the Punakha Dzong.

The second trip, a very easy scenic float on the Mo Chhu, is suitable for all abilities and is a good introduction for the novice. The run starts about 6km above the Punakha Dzong at the Khamsum Yuelley Namgyal Chorten. As the river meanders through the wide valley you float past one of the queen's winter residences, the king's weekend retreat and some beautiful farmland before taking out just below the dzong.

The fees for river rafting are the same as cultural tours and trekking, though there are extra charges for hiring equipment. Presently only one overseas operator, Needmore Adventures (see p263), and one Bhutanese operator, Lotus Adventures (see p263), has trained river guides and equipment for river running in Bhutan.

## BUSINESS HOURS

Government offices open at 9am and close at 5pm in the summer and 4pm in the winter, Monday to Friday. Banks are open from 9am to 3pm Monday to Friday and 9am till noon Saturday. Shops are usually open from 8am to 8pm or 9pm. In Phuentsholing shops are open on Saturday and Sunday, but closed Tuesday. Some restaurants in Thimphu stay open as late as 10pm, but many close earlier. Nightclubs and discos stay open till the early morning on Wednesday, Friday and Saturday and most bars are closed on Tuesday – the national 'dry' day. Reviews in this book mention business hours only if different from these standards.

## CHILDREN

As there are discounts for children travelling in Bhutan, it needn't break the bank if you bring kids along. Up to the age of five, children are free, and kids from six to 12 accompanied by parents or guardians receive a 50% discount on the daily rate. Kids may become bored with long, monotonous drives, limited availability to TV and little other 'entertainment' available. On the other hand, they will be immediately accepted by local kids and their families, and they could make many new friends. Lonely Planet's *Travel with Children* has lots of useful advice and suggestions.

## CLIMATE CHARTS

Bhutan is at the same latitude as Miami and Cairo. The climate varies widely depending on the elevation. In the southern border areas it is tropical; at the other extreme, in the high Himalayan regions, there is perpetual snow. Temperatures in the far south range from 15°C in winter (December to February) to 30°C in summer (June to August). In Paro the range is from -5°C in January to 30°C in July, with 800mm of rain. In the high mountain regions the average temperature is 0°C in winter and may reach 10°C in summer, with an average of 350mm of rain. For more on Bhutan's climate see p13.

Rain occurs primarily during the southwest monsoon season from June to September. Bhutan bears the brunt of the monsoon, receiving more rainfall than other Himalayan regions – up to 5.5m a year. During the monsoon, heavy rain falls almost every night; in the day there may be long periods without rain. Low clouds hang on the hills, obscuring views and, if they are too low, forcing the cancellation of flights at Paro airport.

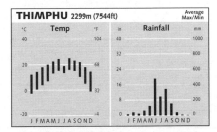

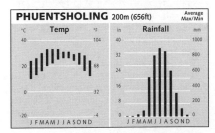

**DIRECTORY**

Precipitation varies significantly with the elevation. The average rainfall varies from region to region.

**Himalayan regions** Less than 500mm per year.
**Inner central valleys** 500mm to 1000mm per year.
**Southern foothills** 2000mm to 3500mm per year.
**Southern border area** 3000mm to 5000mm per year.

## COURSES

There are no formal courses offered in Bhutan but your tour operator may be able to arrange programs (meditation, Buddhism, cooking etc) to meet your particular interest. Given sufficient notice, the Dzongkha Development Commission can arrange brief courses and lectures on language and music.

With prior arrangement through your tour operator, **WWF** (www.wwfbhutan.org.bt; see p92) and **RSPN** (www.rspn-bhutan.org; see p87) can arrange lectures and discussion groups on wildlife and environmental issues, and the Folk Heritage Museum (see p104) can provide courses in Bhutanese cooking and paper making.

## CUSTOMS

You will receive a baggage declaration form to complete when you arrive in Bhutan. For tourists, the main purpose of this form is to ensure that you re-export anything you bring into the country. List any expensive equipment that you are carrying, such as cameras and portable computers. Customs officials usually want to see the items that you list, and then they endorse the form and return it to you. Don't lose it as you must return it when you leave the country.

Duty-free allowances include 2L of liquor but cigarettes attract a 200% duty upon arrival and your limit is 200 (ie one carton). There are no restrictions on other personal effects, including trekking gear, brought into the country.

Departure formalities are straightforward, but you'll need to produce the form that you completed on arrival and may need to show all of the items listed on it. A lost form means complications and delays. If you lose the form, let your guide know as soon as possible so that special arrangements can be made to avoid any inconvenience.

The export of antiques and wildlife products is prohibited. If you purchase a souvenir that looks old, have your guide clear it as a nonantique item with the **Division of Cultural Properties** ( ☎ 02-322284; fax 02-323286). Customs authorities pay special attention to religious statues. It would be prudent to have any such statue cleared, old or not.

## DANGERS & ANNOYANCES

Fortunately, travel in Bhutan is still largely immune to the major banes of travel in Asia – theft and begging. It does, however, have some irritations of its own.

### Altitude

The maximum elevation that you can reach on a Bhutanese road (3140m in the west and 3750m in the east) is lower than that which causes altitude problems for most people. There are rare individuals who can suffer from altitude problems even at elevations as low as Thimphu (2320m); if you have had previous altitude problems at these elevations, avoid travelling to Bhutan.

Most treks go to extremely high elevations. If you are planning a trek, see p272 for advice about acclimatisation.

### Dogs

Those same cute dogs that wag their tails for you during the day turn into barking monsters at night. Don't forget to bring earplugs. There is little danger of dog bites, but occasional rabies outbreaks occur in rural Bhutan, and if you are going trekking, be wary of big dogs guarding properties.

### Weather

You are always close to nature in Bhutan, and often this proximity affects your travel schedule, especially Druk Air flights. Even on a cultural tour you will be windblown in towns such as Paro, Wangdue Phodrang and Jakar. Clouds often obscure the mountain views that you made such an effort to see. Rain can turn trails and paths into a sea of mud, and flights are often delayed by bad weather. Leeches inhabit the lower valleys and can be a real irritation in the monsoon season. A rainstorm can turn small streams into torrents, moving huge boulders and smashing bridges.

### Winding Roads & Breakdowns

If you venture east of Thimphu, you will spend hours driving on rough, winding roads. Even those who have never been carsick before can get squeamish with the constant bouncing and motion, especially in the back seat of a van or bus. Vehicles do break down, no matter how well maintained they are, and there is no emergency road service. It's unlikely, but not impossible, for you to be forced to spend a night sleeping in a vehicle at the side of the road, or hitch a ride in a crowded bus to the next town.

## EMBASSIES & CONSULATES

It is not possible to apply for a Bhutanese visa through a Bhutanese embassy. All tourist visas must be channelled through a tour company and the Department of Tourism (DOT) in Thimphu, and from there through the Ministry of Foreign Affairs.

### Bhutanese Embassies & Consulates

Bhutan does not have a wide network of resident embassies abroad.

**Bangladesh** ( ☎ 02-882 6863, 882 7160; fax 882 3939; House No 12 (CEN), Rd No 107, Gulshan Ave, Dhaka 1212)

**India** ( ☎ 011-26889807, 26889230; fax 2687 6710; Chandragupta Marg, Chanakyapuri, New Delhi 100021)

**Kuwait** ( ☎ 2516640; fax 2516550; Adailiya-Block 3, Essa Abdul Rahman Al-Assoussi St, Jaddah No 32, Villa No 7, Kuwait)

**Switzerland** ( ☎ 022-799 0890; fax 799 0899; Palais des Nations, 17-19 Champ d'Avier, CH-1209 Geneva)

**Thailand** ( ☎ 02-274 4740; fax 274 4743; 375/1 Soi Ratchadanivej, Pracha-Uthit Rd, Samsen Nok, Huay Kwang, Bangkok 10320)

**USA** ( ☎ 212-682 2268; fax 661 0551; 763 United Nations Plaza, 1st Ave, New York, NY 10017)

### Embassies & Consulates in Bhutan

Only a handful of foreign countries have an official presence in Bhutan. Bhutan's relations with other countries are handled through its embassies in Delhi and Dhaka.

**Bangladesh** ( ☎ 322539; fax 322629; Thori Lam, Thimphu)

**India** Phuentsholing ( ☎ 252635, 252992) Thimphu ( ☎ 322280; www.eoithimphu.org; India House, Zhung Lam)

**Korea** ( ☎ 02-323027; fax 323666; PO Box 423 GPO Thimphu; Clocktower Sq, Thimphu) Inside Tashi Tours & Travel.

**Thailand** ( ☎ 02-323978; fax 323807; PO Box 1352 GPO Thimphu; Doendrup Lam, Thimphu)

## FESTIVALS & EVENTS

The New Year is called Losar, and is celebrated according to the lunar Bhutanese calendar. Losar usually falls between mid-January and mid-March. To complicate matters further, there are different dates for the New Year in various parts of the country.

On an auspicious day near the end of the monsoon season the people celebrate Blessed Rainy Day. This is the day when *khandromas* (celestial beings) shower blessings on the earth in the form of rain to wash away bad luck. People wash their hair and shower to help wash off evil and sins.

On the first day of the 10th month the Thimphu *rabdey* (district monk body) moves to Punakha. The procession includes the Je Khenpo (the Chief Abbot of Bhutan), the four *lopons* (senior monks) and the entire monk body. The Khamsum Zilnoen, a sacred image of the Zhabdrung, and other relics are also moved with the monks. Local people line up outside the dzong to get blessed with the image and relics. The *rabdey* returns to Thimphu on the first day of the fourth month.

The Black-Necked Crane Festival in Phobjikha (see p154) is always held on 12 November, the day after the king's birthday.

## FOOD

Since most travel in Bhutan is via an all-inclusive package, you can expect to eat most of your meals in your hotel dining room. Most hotels cater to groups and habitually provide buffet-style meals. There is usually a continental dish, and sometimes an Indian, Chinese or Bhutanese dish. There is almost always rice, either white or the local red variety, and dal. If you are in a small group, or have booked your tour directly, you can specify that you want to order from the menu, though sometimes the buffet meals offer a wider selection. Most experienced Bhutan travellers recommend that you stick to Bhutanese or Indian food rather than Western fare.

Drinks, including mineral water, are usually charged as extras, and payment is collected at the end of the meal or the following morning when you check out of the hotel.

On long drives or hikes you will not return to your hotel for lunch, and most tour operators arrange packed lunches from the hotel. These tend to be an uninspired collection of sandwiches, boiled potatoes, eggs, fruit and a small carton of juice. Consider a visit to a bakery for some bread or rolls and perhaps buy some biscuits to make your picnic more interesting.

The other way to liven up lunch is to forego the packed lunch and eat in a local roadside restaurant. As long as you stick to cooked food that is served hot, it should be safe to eat.

The food in hotels is often the best in town, but if you want to sample local restaurants, your guide can arrange it so that the tour

**DIRECTORY**

## FESTIVAL DATES

The following are the festival dates according to the Bhutanese calendar and the estimated corresponding months in the Western calendar. Dates for subsequent years can vary by two weeks or more, especially if they are adjusted to conform to auspicious dates. Before you schedule a trip around a specific festival, check with a tour operator or the **Department of Tourism** (DOT; www.tourism.gov.bt) for the correct dates for the year in which you plan to travel.

| Festival | Bhutanese month | Days | Place | Western months |
|---|---|---|---|---|
| Punakha Domchen | 1 | 5-9 | Punakha | Feb/Mar |
| Chorten Kora | 1 | 13-15 | Tashi Yangtse | Feb/Mar |
| Gom Kora | 2 | 8-10 | Tashi Yangtse | Mar/Apr |
| Chhukha tsechu | 2 | 8-10 | Chukha | Mar/Apr |
| Paro tsechu | 2 | 11-15 | Paro | Mar/Apr |
| Ura Yakchoe | 3 | 13-15 | Bumthang | Apr/May |
| Nimalung tsechu | 5 | 8-10 | Bumthang | Jun/Jul |
| Kurjey tsechu | 5 | 10 | Bumthang | Jun/Jul |
| Wangdue tsechu | 8 | 8-10 | Wangdue Phodrang | Sep/Oct |
| Thimphu tsechu | | 5-11 | Thimphu | Sep/Oct |
| Tamshing Phala Choepa | 8 | 9-11 | Bumthang | Sep/Oct |
| Thangbi Mani | 8 | 14-16 | Bumthang | Sep/Oct |
| Jampey Lhakhang Drup | 9 | 15-18 | Bumthang | Oct/Nov |
| Prakhar tsechu | 9 | 15-18 | Bumthang | Oct/Nov |
| Ngang Lhakhang Shey | 10 | 15-17 | Bumthang | Nov/Dec |
| Mongar tsechu* | 10 | 7-10 | Mongar | Nov/Dec |
| Trashigang tsechu* | 10 | 8-11 | Trashigang | Nov/Dec |
| Lhuentse tsechu | 10 | 9-11 | Lhuentse | Dec/Jan |
| Trongsa tsechu* | 11 | 9-11 | Trongsa | Dec/Jan |

\* The first day is Cham Ju. *Cham* means 'dance' and *ju* means 'ending'; it is the last day of the rehearsal and the dances are performed without masks.

operator pays for your restaurant meals. For more information see p94.

## GAY & LESBIAN TRAVELLERS

Like most Asians, the Bhutanese believe that what one does in private is strictly a personal matter, and they would prefer not to discuss such issues. Public displays of affection are not appreciated and everyone, regardless of orientation, should exercise discretion. Officially, male homosexuality is illegal.

## HOLIDAYS

Public holidays follow both the Gregorian and lunar calendars and are announced by the **Royal Civil Service Commission** (www.rcsc.com.bt). Bhutan's national day is 17 December, the date of the establishment of the monarchy in 1907. Other important holidays are the king's birthday on 11 November and Coronation Day on 2 June. The birth of third king is commemorated on

2 May following the Gregorian calendar, while the anniversary of his death is also a holiday but it follows the lunar calendar and changes from year to year.

## INSURANCE

A travel insurance policy to cover theft, loss and medical problems is always highly recommended. Most policies will cover costs if you are forced to cancel your trip because of flight cancellation, illness, injury or the death of a close relative. If you have such a problem, travel insurance can help protect you from major losses due to Bhutan's prepayment conditions and hefty cancellation charges.

Some policies specifically exclude 'dangerous activities', and these can include motorcycling and even trekking. Read your policy carefully to be sure it covers ambulance rides or an emergency helicopter airlift out of a remote region, or an emergency flight home.

---

**BHUTANESE CALENDAR**

The Bhutanese calendar is based on the Tibetan calendar, which evolved from the Chinese. In the 17th century the Bhutanese scholar Pema Karpo developed a new way of computing the days of the week. This caused a divergence between the Tibetan and Bhutanese calendars, and dates do not agree between the two systems.

In the Bhutanese system, months have 30 days, with the full moon on the 15th. The eighth, 15th and 30th days of the month are auspicious. The fourth is also auspicious: Buddha first preached his religious principles on the fourth day of the sixth month.

Years are named according to the Tibetan system of five elements and 12 animals, producing a 60-year cycle. For example, the year 1998 is Earth-Tiger year, and 1974, the year of King Jigme Singye Wangchuck's coronation, is the Wood-Tiger year.

The calendar operates according to a very flexible system that allows bad days to be avoided. Astrologers sometimes add a day if it's going to be an auspicious one or lose a day if it's not. They can even change months. In some years, for example, there may be no October because it has been deemed an inauspicious month, or there may be two Augusts because that happens to be a good month.

Bhutanese include the nine months in the womb in the calculation of their age. Everyone considers themselves a year older on Losar, New Year's day, and thus people can be nearly two years younger than they say they are.

---

If you have to stretch out you may need two seats. Many travel insurance policies include repatriation and evacuation through the worldwide network of International SOS Assistance.

You may prefer a policy that pays doctors or hospitals directly rather than your having to pay on the spot and claim later. If you have to claim later make sure you keep all documentation. Some policies ask you to call back (they suggest reversing the charges, an impossibility from Bhutan) to a centre in your home country where an immediate assessment of your problem is made.

It's a good idea to photocopy your policy in case the original is lost. If you are planning to travel for a long time, the insurance may seem very expensive – but if you can't afford it, you certainly won't be able to afford to deal with a medical emergency overseas.

## INTERNET ACCESS

Full international internet service was inaugurated on 2 June 1999, the 25th anniversary of the king's coronation. You can access **Druknet** (www.druknet.bt), Bhutan's internet provider, from any telephone in Bhutan by dialling ☎ 100 or ☎ 101. At the time of research Bhutan had not yet joined any of the global internet roaming agreements, so a local Druknet account was needed to log in. There are internet cafés in many large towns. For more info on internet resources, see p18.

## LEGAL MATTERS

Although you will probably notice cannabis growing in any bit of spare dirt, even in the towns, there is not a tradition of use and possession is illegal. Bhutan recently implemented restrictions on smoking and the sale of tobacco products. Don't sell any cigarettes brought into the country. The age of consent is 18 years.

## MAPS

There is a dearth of maps on Bhutan and a good map can be hard to source outside the country. Kathmandu bookshops are the best bet for finding a map. **International Travel Maps** (www.itmb.com) produce a 1:380,000 *Bhutan* and Nepa Maps produce two maps: 1:380,000 *Bhutan* and *Bhutan Trekking Routes*. The laminated Berndtson & Berndtson 1:500,000 *Bhutan Road Map* is hard to find inside Bhutan but available in Kathmandu and (with some difficulty) elsewhere.

In Bhutan, bookshops sell Thimphu and Paro city maps as well as country maps published by the Survey of Bhutan. The Survey publishes a large 1:250,000 country map that is a composite of Landsat Images overlaid with roads and major towns and district boundaries, as well as several specialised maps showing historical places and points of interest. The Trekking chapter (p199) lists details of topographical maps and their availability.

DIRECTORY

# MONEY

The unit of currency is the *ngultrum* (Nu), which is equivalent to one Indian rupee. The ngultrum is further divided into 100 *chetrum*. There are coins to the value of 25 and 50 chetrum and Nu 1 and notes of Nu 1, 5, 10, 20, 50, 100 and 500. The Nu 1 coin depicts the eight auspicious symbols (see p64), while each note depicts a different dzong. Indian rupees may be used freely anywhere in Bhutan (don't be surprised if you get change in rupees), but ngultrums are not welcome in India.

It is OK with the Bhutanese if you bring a reasonable amount of Indian currency into Bhutan, though Indian regulations prohibit currency export. Consult the inside front cover for exchange rates and p15 for information on costs.

## ATMs

At the time of research, the few Bhutan National Bank ATMs could only be used by local customers. The bank does have plans, however, for extending the network and providing credit-card facilities.

## Black Market

There is no black market in Bhutan. The Indian rupee is a convertible currency, and the rate is set by market conditions, not by the Indian government. Subject to some restrictions, Indians and Bhutanese can buy dollars officially to purchase goods from abroad. Therefore, there is not much difference between the market rate and the official rate for the Indian rupee, and thus, the ngultrum.

It's sometimes possible to buy Indian rupees at a slightly better rate in Bangkok or Hong Kong and then bring them to Bhutan, but the small gain is hardly worth the hassle.

## Cash

If you plan to make a major purchase, for example textiles or art, consider bringing US dollars in cash. Most shops will accept this, and it can save you the hassle of exchanging a large quantity of money in advance and then attempting to change it back if you don't find the exact piece you were looking for.

## Credit Cards

You should not count on using a credit card in Bhutan. Credit cards are accepted at the government-run Handicrafts Emporium, a few other handicraft shops and some of the larger hotels in Thimphu, but these transactions do take time. The credit-card companies charge high fees and the verification office is only open from 9am to 5pm. This precludes paying your hotel bill at night or when you check out early in the morning. The Bhutan National Bank has plans for rolling out point of sale credit-card facilities, so check with your tour agent for the latest news.

## Moneychangers

Since your trip is fully prepaid, theoretically you could manage in Bhutan without any local money at all, though you'll probably want some to pay for laundry, drinks, souvenirs and tips.

The exchange counters at the airport, larger hotels and the banks in Thimphu and Phuentsholing can change all the currencies listed on the inside front cover, and sometimes Scandinavian currencies. If you are heading to central and eastern Bhutan, you will do better with more common currencies such as US dollars or pounds sterling. In smaller towns foreign-currency exchange may be an unusual transaction so be prepared for delays.

You may change your unused ngultrums back to foreign currency (though usually only into US dollars) on departure from Thimphu or Paro. Travellers departing via Samdrup Jongkhar don't have this facility at the time of research. You will need to produce your original exchange receipts. Ngultrums are useless outside of Bhutan (except as a curiosity).

Bhutan has two banks, the Bank of Bhutan and the Bhutan National Bank, each with branches throughout the country where money can be exchanged. The Bank of Bhutan's main branches are open 9am to 1pm Monday to Friday and 9am to 11am on Saturday, though the branches in Trongsa, Trashigang and Mongar are open on Sunday and closed Tuesday. It also has a branch in Thimphu that stays open later for the convenience of office workers (and travellers).

## Tipping

Tipping is officially discouraged in Bhutan, but it's becoming a common practice and it's OK to do so if you want to reward good service.

You will usually be accompanied throughout your visit to Bhutan by the same tour guide and probably the same driver. Though it's against the official DOT policy, these people expect a tip at the end of the trip. Many leaders on group tours take up a collection at the conclusion of the trip and hand it over in one packet. With a large group this can be a substantial amount and the practice has created high expectations on the part of Bhutanese guides.

If you've been trekking, it's appropriate to tip the guide, cook and waiter. Horsemen also expect tips, but this can be minimal if they are the owners of the horses or yaks and are making money by hiring out their animals. The stakes go up, however, if they have been especially helpful with camp chores and on the trail.

## Travellers Cheques
You can cash travellers cheques at any bank, most hotels and the foreign-exchange counter at the airport. There are bank charges of 1% for cheque encashment. You should carry only well-known brands such as American Express, Visa, Thomas Cook, Citibank or Barclays. There is no replacement facility for travellers cheques in Bhutan.

## PHOTOGRAPHY & VIDEO
### Film & Equipment
A limited supply of colour print film is available in Bhutan and is sold in shops throughout the country. If you are shooting transparencies, bring all your film with you, as slide film is not readily available. Memory cards are still hard to find, but you will have no problem finding an internet café in Thimphu that can burn digital images to a CD.

There are colour-printing facilities in Thimphu and Phuentsholing. **Kuenphen Colour Lab** ( ☎ 02-324058; Norzin Lam) in Thimphu has an automatic machine. No lab in Bhutan has facilities to process colour slides.

Many of the dzongs and mountain peaks are best photographed at a distance with a telephoto lens. Bear in mind that there will be little or no opportunity for photography inside buildings, therefore you don't need to organise a flash attachment and tripod for that purpose. A polarising filter will help make your mountain pictures more dramatic by increasing the contrast between the sky and the white peaks and clouds. Carry spare batteries, as these are hard to find in rural Bhutan.

In Thimphu the **Sony Shop** ( ☎ 02-324414; Norzin Lam) below the NT Hotel and **Jimmy Bros Stationery** (Map pp102-3; ☎ 02-323388; Clocktower Sq) sell blank video cartridges. Grab a copy of Lonely Planet's *Travel Photography* for tips and advice.

## Restrictions
Bhutan is generally liberal about photography by tourists. There are a few places with signs prohibiting photography such as the telecom tower above Thimphu and it would also be prudent to refrain from taking pictures of military installations.

There are no restrictions on photographing the outside of dzongs and goembas, but photography is *strictly* prohibited inside goembas and lhakhangs. There are several reasons for this. One is that tourists in the past have completely disrupted holy places with their picture taking. Another is the fear that photos of treasured statues will become a catalogue of items for art thieves to steal. And thirdly, some early tourists made photographs of religious statues into postcards that were then sold, which is unacceptable to the Bhutanese religious community.

During festivals you may enter the dzong courtyard where the dances take place. This provides an excellent opportunity to photograph the dzongs, people and local colour. Remember, however, that this is a religious observance and that you should behave accordingly. Use a telephoto lens without a flash. Don't intrude on the dance ground or on the space occupied by local people seated at the edge of the dance area. If you do end up in the front row, remain seated.

There is an extensive set of rules and restrictions, including payment of royalties, for commercial movie making in Bhutan. DOT publishes a booklet that details all these rules.

## Photographing People
Always ask permission first. Bhutanese people are naturally shy but will usually allow you to take a photograph, especially if you ask them first. Many people, especially children, will pose for you, and a smile or joke will help to make the pose a little less formal. Remember that almost everyone understands English, even if they are too embarrassed to try to speak it.

After you take a picture, many people will write down their address so that you may send them a copy. Don't take pictures of people unless you are prepared to honour your promise to send a copy (many people leave their best intentions at Paro airport on their way home). Don't photograph a member of the royal family, even if you happen to be at a festival or gathering where they are present.

## POST
### Postal Rates
Airmail postage rates for the first 20g of ordinary (nonpackage) mail are Nu 20 for most countries (Nu 4 for India, Nepal and Bangladesh).

### Sending Mail
You can send mail from hotels and post offices. The mail service from Bhutan is reliable, and no special procedures are necessary. It would be better, however, to avoid sending important letters, money or film through the mail.

If you mail cards or letters from the Thimphu post office, you can buy exotic postage stamps from the philatelic bureau.

Bhutan Post offers both outgoing and incoming Expedited Mail Service (EMS), which is a reliable and fast international mail delivery facility that is cheaper than courier services. It also has a Local Urgent Mail (LUM) service for delivery within Thimphu.

If you have made a purchase and want to send it home, it's best to have the shop make all the arrangements for you. Keep the receipt and let your guide know what you are doing so they can follow up in case the package does not arrive. Send all parcels by air; sea mail, via Kolkata, takes several months.

**DHL** ( ☎ 02-324730; dhl@druknet.bt; Thori Lam, Thimphu) provides efficient international courier service to and from Bhutan. There are several smaller courier companies that specialise in service to India.

### Receiving Mail
The best way to receive mail is to have it sent to the post office box of the Bhutanese tour operator that is handling your trip. Unless you are on a long trek, you will probably not be in Bhutan long enough for a letter to reach you.

## SHOPPING
Bhutan boasts a variety of handicrafts. Until recently, nothing in Bhutan was made especially for sale to tourists and it was possible to find high-quality arts and crafts almost everywhere. Now there is a fair amount of tourist schlock on offer; one of the worst places for this is alongside the trail to Taktshang Goemba. A few creative souvenir items, such as Dragon Kingdom T-shirts, coin purses shaped like *bangchung* (round covered bamboo baskets) and mini *atsara* (clown) masks are available.

There are many handicraft shops in Thimphu and Paro, and most hotels have a shop selling Bhutanese crafts. As you shop, remember that it is illegal (and immoral) to export antiques.

Some of the crafts sold in Bhutan are actually made in Nepal or India; if in doubt, ask. Most shopkeepers will be honest with you, and your guide can probably offer some independent advice.

### Thangkas
*Thangkas* are Buddhist paintings, usually on canvas. Traditionally, they are mounted on a background of brocade and hung by a dowel sewn across the top. You can also buy an unmounted painting and roll it up to take home. If you buy an expensive one and don't want it damaged in your luggage, stop at a hardware shop and get a short length of plastic pipe to protect it. Prices vary tremendously, with small paintings made by students selling for Nu 500 and large mounted *thangkas* starting at Nu 30,000. The price depends on size, quality of work and detail.

### Textiles
Hand-woven fabric is the most traditional and useful item you can buy in Bhutan. The quality is almost always good, but the price will vary depending on the intricacy of the design and whether any expensive imported silk was used in the weaving. Hand-woven fabric is sold in 'loom lengths' that are 30cm to 45cm wide and 2.5m to 3m long. Bhutanese sew three of these lengths together to make the traditional dress of *gho* and *kira*. You can find handmade cloth in the Khaling handloom project in eastern Bhutan (see p196), in handicraft shops or in ordinary fabric shops. Also check out the National Textile Museum (p105), the Gagyel Lhundrup Weaving Centre (p113) and the Handicrafts Emporium (p114) in Thimphu. Indian machine-made cloth, in a variety of Bhutanese designs, is also sold at a price far lower than handmade cloth.

Hand-woven woollen cloth is also available. *Yathras* are lengths of rough woollen cloth that can be sewn together to make sweaters, scarves or blankets. A length costs Nu 1000 to 3000, depending on the tightness of the weave and whether wool or cotton threads were used for the weft. The best place to shop for *yathras* is in Zungney in Bumthang's Chhume valley (see p166).

## Other Items

Brass statues and Buddhist ritual items, such as prayer wheels, bells, cymbals, trumpets and *dorjis* (stylised thunderbolts) are available from handicraft shops and at the weekend market in Thimphu (p103).

Jewellery and other silver items are best purchased from a reputable shop or from the artisans themselves. Much of the low-priced silverwork sold in Bhutan is actually made in Nepal from white metal.

If you have lots of space in your luggage, you can choose from a variety of carved wooden pieces. Useful items such as picture frames and furniture are available, as are wooden masks similar to those used in the tsechu dances. Wooden bowls, either plain or lined with silver, are a speciality of eastern Bhutan.

Bamboo work is available in most of the handicraft shops and sometimes at roadside stalls. The round *bangchung* baskets, which some people have nicknamed 'Bhutanese Tupperware', can easily be stuffed into a bag or suitcase. The large baskets called *zhim* that are fastened on horses to carry gear on treks are hard to find, but a smaller version is available in many shops. Another unusual item is the large bamboo pipes covered with weaving that are used for carrying local liquor.

Handmade paper is available in large sheets and sometimes is packaged into handy packets of letter-writing size. Several local artists sell their paintings in small art galleries in Thimphu and Paro, and sometimes in hotel shops.

Carpet manufacturing is a recent innovation in Bhutan; traditionally most carpets in Bhutan were imported from Tibet or Nepal.

There is a large factory in Phuentsholing and a small carpet workshop in the Phobjikha valley. Carpets are available in most handicraft shops, and a limited supply is on hand at the workshop behind the Phuntsho Chholing Guest House in Phobjikha (see p154).

Some of Bhutan's minority groups wear 'interesting' hats, which make for curious gifts and conversation pieces. If you look carefully, you can find bamboo hats from Laya, Brokpa yak-hair 'spider' hats and conical bamboo Bumthang hats in shops throughout Bhutan.

Traditional Bhutanese songs can be haunting, if monotonous. The popular songs are an interesting combination of Bhutanese, Tibetan and Indian influences. You can find recordings of both classical and popular Bhutanese songs in most towns. Locally produced CDs cost Nu 200 to 400.

## Bargaining

Bargaining is not a Bhutanese tradition, and you won't get very far with your haggling skills here, except with trailside vendors on the hike to Taktshang and in the local handicrafts section of the Thimphu weekend market (p103). Shops, restaurants and hotels all have fixed prices.

## SOLO TRAVELLERS

Solo travellers attract a hefty surcharge (US$40) on the daily tariff (see p15 for details) and may find that larger groups get priority at hotels and restaurants. But apart from these inconveniences they should enjoy the personal service and potential flexibility of travelling solo. For issues related to women travellers see p256.

---

### BIZARRE BHUTANESE STAMPS

You probably won't strike it rich by buying postage stamps from Bhutan, but they make a colourful addition to any collection. Some items are issued specifically for sale to collectors by an agency in New York, and others are locally produced by the government itself. There is not much demand for Bhutanese stamps and the value is generally low. However, the number of stamps issued in each series is generally so small that any increase in demand sends prices skyrocketing.

The price of 3D mushroom stamps shot up when topical collectors of mushroom stamps discovered them and exhausted the supply. The issue of playable record stamps sold out quickly in Bhutan, and only a few thousand were produced because of the expense. These are now worth hundreds of dollars a set. Most stamps, however, are available in adequate quantities at a reasonable mark-up over face value. Bhutanese stamps often are auctioned on the internet through eBay.

Some shops sell older issues and handsome souvenir sheets, but the philatelic counter in the Thimphu post office has the largest selection. For more information on Bhutanese stamps check the websites at www.bhutan.org and www.bhutanpost.com.bt.

# TELEPHONE & FAX

There are numerous public call offices (PCOs) throughout the country from which you can make STD (long-distance) calls within Bhutan or to India at a standard rate of 30% above the normal tariff. Some PCOs also offer international subscriber dialling (ISD) calls overseas. Most hotels can arrange both local and international calls, though very few have in-room direct-dial facilities.

International telephone rates are Nu 47 per minute with a 10% discount from 6pm to 9am. Domestic direct-dial calls cost Nu 8 per minute, also with a 10% discount from 6pm to 9am. Directory inquiries is ☎ 140 for Bhutan and ☎ 116 for international numbers. Trunk calls may be booked through the operator on ☎ 117 for international numbers, ☎ 119 for domestic numbers and ☎ 118 for calls to India.

**Bhutan Telecom** (www.telecom.net.bt) also provides satellite phones using the Thuria system, which allows direct dialling from anywhere in the country, even on a trek. Some tour operators have these phones and can rent them, though the charges are higher than for normal calls. Check the website for information of all phone tariffs from satellite to mobiles.

## Fax

Nearly all hotels and some PCOs have facilities to send and receive faxes. Tour operators in Bhutan rely on email for most of their communications, but will use fax for documents such as visa authority letters if they don't have a scanner.

## Mobile Phones

You can buy a pre-paid mobile phone kit (SIM card and phone number) from numerous outlets. That is, when demand doesn't outstrip supply! As B-Mobile keeps expanding it will be easier to get a SIM card in towns other than Thimphu and the arrival of a new service provider in late 2006 will further advance the service. The cost of a B-Mobile SIM is Nu 600 (Nu 400 is the activation charge and then you get a balance of Nu 200). Refills for Nu 100 to Nu 2000 are available.

## Phone Codes

The country code for Bhutan is ☎ 975. The international access code is ☎ 00. Local dialling codes:

**Bumthang** ( ☎ 03)
**Mongar** ( ☎ 04)
**Paro** ( ☎ 08)
**Phuentsholing** ( ☎ 05)
**Samdrup Jongkhar** ( ☎ 07)
**Thimphu** ( ☎ 02)
**Trashigang** ( ☎ 04)
**Trongsa** ( ☎ 03)

# TIME

Bhutan time is GMT/UTC plus six hours; there is only one time zone throughout the country. The time in Bhutan is 30 minutes later than in India, 15 minutes later than Nepal, and one hour earlier than Thailand. When it is noon in Bhutan, standard time is 6am in London, 4pm in Sydney, 1am in New York and 10pm the previous day in San Francisco.

# TOILETS

Most hotels provide Western toilets and loo paper, though there are some exceptions, particularly in eastern Bhutan. There are very few public toilets so take full advantage of hotel and restaurant facilities before that long drive. There is an excellent pay'n'pee facility outside Paro airport, but the few public loos in Thimphu, near the market and on Norzin Lam, are less salubrious. Most are of the Asian squat variety and toilet paper isn't available, though a container of water may be present.

Keep an eye out for traditional Bhutanese long-drop toilets hanging precariously off the side of the upper story of old houses and goembas. This is a strange hobbyhorse commode featuring a large square pipe leading straight down to a pit. There's an example in the Folk Heritage Museum in Thimphu.

# TOURIST INFORMATION

The **Department of Tourism** (DOT; ☎ 02-323251, 323252; fax 02-323695; www.tourism.gov.bt; PO Box 126, Thimphu) has a very limited amount of literature available. However, it has a comprehensive website and it can refer you to tour operators who can assist with arrangements to visit Bhutan. There is no official government tourist office outside Bhutan.

# TRAVELLERS WITH DISABILITIES

A cultural tour in Bhutan is a challenge for a traveller with physical disabilities, but is possible with some planning. The Bhutanese are eager to help, and one could arrange a strong companion to assist with moving about and getting in and out of vehicles. The roads are rough and pavements, where they exist, often have holes and sometimes steps. Hotels and public buildings rarely have wheelchair access or lifts, and only the newest will have bathrooms designed to accommodate wheelchairs.

For further general information there is a website for and by disabled travellers at www .travelhealth.com/disab.htm.

# VISAS

Most countries issue visas from their embassies abroad and stamp it in your passport, but not Bhutan. Visas are issued only when you arrive in the country, either at Paro airport or (if entering by road) at Phuentsholing. You must apply in advance through a tour operator and receive approval before you travel to Bhutan.

All applications for tourist visas must be initialised by a Bhutanese tour operator and are approved by the Ministry of Foreign Affairs in Thimphu. The operator submits the visa application to DOT in Thimphu. It, in turn, checks that you have completely paid for your trip and then issues an approval letter to the tour operator. With this approval in hand, the tour operator then makes a final application to the Ministry of Foreign Affairs, which takes up to a week to process the visa.

It's not necessary to fill in a special visa application form. Just provide the following information to the operator in Bhutan: your name, permanent address, occupation, nationality, date and place of birth, passport number and its date and place of issue and date of expiration. If any item is missing the whole process is delayed. Double-check that the information you send is correct; if there are any discrepancies when you arrive in Bhutan, there'll be further delays and complications in issuing the visa.

When the visa clearance is issued by the Ministry of Foreign Affairs, it sends a visa confirmation number to the tour operator and to Druk Air. Druk Air will not issue your tickets to Paro until it receives this confirmation number and then rechecks the visa information when you check in for the flight.

The actual visa endorsement is stamped in your passport when you arrive at one of the two ports of entry for tourists. You will receive a visa for the exact period you have arranged to be in Bhutan. If some unusual event requires that you obtain a visa extension, your tour operator will arrange it.

It's surprisingly efficient considering all the time, distance and various levels of bureaucracy involved. When you arrive in Bhutan, the

visa officer will invariably be able to produce your approval form from the file and the visa will be issued on the spot. It's helpful, however, to have the reference number or even better a faxed/emailed scan copy of the visa authority available to aid the immigration officials and Druk Air to find your information quickly.

## Visa Extensions

A visa extension for a period not exceeding six months costs Nu 510. Since tourist visas are issued for the full period you have arranged to stay in Bhutan, it's unlikely that you would need a visa extension.

## Visas for Indian Nationals

Upon arrival, Indian visitors are issued a 14-day permit, which may be extended in Thimphu. No passport or visa is required, but some form of identification such as a passport, driving licence or voter's registration card is necessary. Indians arriving by road at Phuentsholing need five photos: three for the Indian certificate and two for the Bhutanese permit. Those arriving by air need two photos for the arrival permit in Paro.

## Visas for Neighbouring Countries
### INDIA
Nationals of most countries need a visa to visit India. If you are travelling overland to or from Bhutan via the border post in Phuentsholing you will need an Indian visa.

The government of India strongly prefers that you obtain your Indian visa in the country that issued your passport. It's usually a simple task to get your Indian visa before you leave home, but it's complicated to get one overseas. It is possible to obtain a seven-day transit visa overseas if you have confirmed flights in and out of India and can produce the appropriate tickets. Otherwise, you must pay a fee to the overseas embassy to send a fax to the Indian embassy in your own country and wait up to a week for a reply.

Tourist visas are issued for six months, are multiple entry, and are valid from the date of issue of the visa, not the date you enter India. This means that if you first enter India five months after the visa was issued, it will be valid for one month.

### NEPAL
Visas for Nepal are available on arrival at Kathmandu airport or at land border crossings,

including Kakarbhitta, the road crossing nearest to Bhutan. Normal visas are valid for 60 days. If you are making a side trip to Bhutan from Kathmandu, get a double-entry visa the first time you arrive in Nepal. You can obtain a visa for Nepal in advance from embassies abroad or from the Nepali embassy or consulate in the gateway cities of Bangkok, Delhi, Dhaka or Kolkata.

## Travel Permits
### RESTRICTED-AREA PERMITS
All of Bhutan outside of the Paro and Thimphu valleys is classified as a restricted area. Tour operators obtain a permit for the places on your itinerary, and this permit is checked and endorsed by the police at immigration checkpoints strategically located at important road junctions. The tour operator must return the permit to the government at the completion of the tour, and it is scrutinised for major deviations from the authorised program.

There are immigration checkpoints in Hongtsho (east of Thimphu), Chhukha (between Thimphu and Phuentsholing), Rinchending (above Phuentsholing), Wangdue Phodrang, Chazam (near Trashigang), Wamrong (between Trashigang and Samdrup Jongkhar), and in Samdrup Jongkhar. All are open from 5am to 9pm daily.

### PERMITS TO ENTER TEMPLES
Tourists are allowed to visit the courtyards of dzongs and, where feasible, the *tshokhang* (assembly hall) and one designated lhakhang in each dzong, but only when accompanied by a licensed Bhutanese guide. This provision is subject to certain restrictions, including visiting hours, dress standards and other rules that vary by district. Permits are issued by the National Commission for Cultural Affairs and all the necessary paperwork will be negotiated by your tour company. If you wish to know which dzongs and goembas are included in your itinerary, or you wish to make specific requests, contact your tour company well in advance. If you are a practising Buddhist, you may apply for a permit to visit certain dzongs and religious institutions usually off limits. The credibility of your application will be enhanced if you include a letter of reference from a recognised Buddhist organisation in your home country.

Dzongs are open to all during the time of a tsechu, when you may visit the courtyard, but not the lhakhangs.

## VOLUNTEERING
Bhutan is selective about the type of projects it wants in the country and disdains indiscriminate assistance. Each donor or charitable agency is limited to specified projects or activities, and is allowed only a certain number of volunteers. The opportunities for volunteer work in Bhutan are therefore limited. Americans will find it difficult to get a position because the US Peace Corps does not have a Bhutan programme.

The UN has numerous programmes in Bhutan, all coordinated through the UN Development Programme (UNDP). Different agencies feed into the programme.
**UN Capital Development Fund** (UNCDF)
**UN Children's Fund** (UNICEF)
**UN Educational, Scientific, and Cultural Organization** (Unesco)
**UN Volunteers** (UNV)
**World Food Program** (WFP)

Other agencies that operate programmes in Bhutan include the following:
**ACB** (Austria)
**Danida** (Denmark)
**GTZ** (Germany)
**Helvetas** (Switzerland)
**JOCV & JICA** (Japan)
**Save the Children**
**SNV** (Netherlands)
**VSA** (New Zealand)

## WOMEN TRAVELLERS
Women, both foreign and Bhutanese, are not usually subject to harassment and do not need to take any special precautions. Men have a reasonably liberated attitude towards their relations with women. There are several opportunities for misunderstanding if you don't make your intentions clear from the very outset. Female travellers should be aware that romantic liaisons between tourists and Bhutanese guides are quite common. You might also be invited to a 'party' at the home of a Bhutanese male, and discover too late that you are the only guest.

For information on women's groups and the status of Bhutanese women, see p53.

# Transport

## CONTENTS

| | |
|---|---|
| **Getting There & Away** | **257** |
| Entering the Country | 257 |
| Air | 257 |
| Land | 260 |
| Tours | 262 |
| **Getting Around** | **264** |
| Bicycle | 264 |
| Bus | 265 |
| Car & Motorcycle | 265 |
| Hitching | 265 |
| Local Transport | 266 |

# GETTING THERE & AWAY

## ENTERING THE COUNTRY

There are only two entry points to Bhutan open to foreigners. Most travellers arrive by air at Bhutan's only international airport in Paro. The alternative is to travel through the Indian state of West Bengal and enter Bhutan by road at Phuentsholing on the southern border of Bhutan. At the time of research, it was possible for foreigners to depart but not enter Bhutan via Samdrup Jongkhar in the east of the country. Furthermore, unless you are an Indian national, foreigners are required to fly in or out of Bhutan using Druk Air, the national carrier. Most travellers will choose to fly both routes.

## Passport

You need a passport to enter Bhutan and its neighbouring countries. You should ensure that it has sufficient empty pages for stamps, especially if you are travelling via India or Nepal. If your passport has less than six months of validity left, it is worth getting a new one, because many countries in this region will not issue visas to persons whose passports are about to expire.

Keep your passport safe. No country other than India has the facility for issuing a replacement passport in Bhutan. If you lose your passport, you must travel 'stateless' to another country to get it replaced. You should carry some additional form of identification and a photocopy of your passport to help in such an event.

For details of how to organise a Bhutanese visa, see p255.

## AIR
### Airports & Airlines

Bhutan has one airport, **Paro** (PBH; ☎ 08-271423) and one airline, Druk Air.

The schedule changes by season, but normally there are three flights per week from New Delhi (via Kathmandu) and a daily flight from Bangkok via Dhaka or Kolkata, depending on the day of the week. To allow for extra visitors to the Thimphu *tsechu* (festival) in October and the Paro tsechu in April, the airline usually provides extra flights.

Reconfirm your Druk Air flight with your tour operator a few weeks before departure to ensure that the schedule has not changed, and also check the flight time the day before your departure. Druk Air is quite good about announcing schedule changes at least a week in advance in *Kuensel* and on BBS TV. Check in early for Druk Air flights as they occasionally depart before the scheduled time, especially if the weather starts to change for the worse. Flights are often delayed because of weather and Druk Air recommends that you travel on nonrestricted tickets and allow at least 24 hours transit time with your connecting

**THINGS CHANGE**

The information in this chapter is particularly vulnerable to change: prices for international travel are volatile, routes are introduced and cancelled, schedules change, special deals come and go, and rules and visa requirements are amended. You should check directly with the airline or a travel agency to make sure you understand how a fare (and ticket you may buy) works and be aware of the security requirements for international travel. The details given in this chapter should be regarded as pointers and are not a substitute for your own careful, up-to-date research.

TRANSPORT

flight in order to minimise the complications of delays. When flights cannot land in Paro there is no charge for the unscheduled tour of Bagdogra, near Siliguri, or Kolkata.

There are only a few aircraft that can operate on a runway that is as short and high as Paro's. All landings and takeoffs in Paro are by visual flight rules (VFR), which means the pilot must be able to see the runway before landing, and see the surrounding hills before takeoff. No flights can be operated at night or in poor visibility. When Paro valley is clouded in, flights are delayed, sometimes for a few days. When this happens your tour program will have to be changed and everything rebooked. The up side of such a delay is that you can probably put some spontaneity into your schedule in Bhutan and make a few modifications as you go, depending on what you find interesting.

Druk Air is not allowed to issue tickets to Paro for foreign visitors until they receive a 'visa clearance' from the Ministry of Foreign Affairs in Thimphu. When the visa is authorised, the information is entered into the computer record for your reservation even though the actual visa will not be issued until you arrive at Paro airport. Druk Air will issue your ticket once it receives this number. For this reason, it's difficult to get tickets for Paro flights issued along with your other international air tickets.

Because Druk Air has no interline agreements with other carriers, your ticket to Paro will be separate from your other international tickets. This means you cannot check your baggage all the way through to Paro via a connecting flight. You will need to reclaim your baggage and recheck it at the Druk Air counter. Similarly, when you depart from Bhutan, you can only check baggage as far as you are travelling with Druk Air, not all the way through to your final destination.

It is useful to have a photocopy of the visa clearance, or at least the visa number, to expedite the visa process.

In Bhutan contact **Druk Air** Paro ( ☎ 08-271856; fax 271861; www.drukair.com.bt; Nemizampa, Paro) Thimphu ( ☎ 02-322215; fax 322775; Chang Lam Plaza, Chang Lam, Thimphu).

Overseas offices include:

**Aeroglobal** ( ☎ 852-2868 3231; fax 2845 5078; RM, 22-24, New Henry House, 10 Ice St, Hong Kong)

**Danfe Travel Centre** ( ☎ 01-4239988, airport office ☎ 4471712; Woodlands Hotel; Durbar Marg, Kathmandu)

**Druk Air Corporation** India ( ☎ 033-240 2419, airport office ☎ 511 9976; fax 247 0050; 51 Tivoli Court, 1A Ballygunge Circular Rd, Kolkata); Thailand ( ☎ 02-535

---

## CLIMATE CHANGE & TRAVEL

Climate change is a serious threat to the ecosystems that humans rely upon, and air travel is the fastest-growing contributor to the problem. Lonely Planet regards travel, overall, as a global benefit, but believes we all have a responsibility to limit our personal impact on global warming.

### Flying & Climate Change

Pretty much every form of motorised travel generates CO2 (the main cause of human-induced climate change) but planes are far and away the worst offenders, not just because of the sheer distances they allow us to travel, but because they release greenhouse gases high into the atmosphere. The statistics are frightening: two people taking a return flight between Europe and the US will contribute as much to climate change as an average household's gas and electricity consumption over a whole year.

### Carbon Offset Schemes

Climatecare.org and other websites use 'carbon calculators' that allow travellers to offset the level of greenhouse gases they are responsible for with financial contributions to sustainable travel schemes that reduce global warming – including projects in India, Honduras, Kazakhstan and Uganda.

Lonely Planet, together with Rough Guides and other concerned partners in the travel industry, support the carbon offset scheme run by climatecare.org. Lonely Planet offsets all of its staff and author travel.

For more information check out our website: lonelyplanet.com.

1960; fax 535 3661; Room 3237, Central Block, Bangkok International Airport, Bangkok)

**Druk Air Corporation Ltd** ( ☎ 011-5653207, 5652011, ext 2238; Indira Gandhi International Airport, Terminal Bldg, New Delhi, India)

**Mams Aviation** ( ☎ 02-986 2243; fax 882 8439; mams@ bdmail.net; 33 Gulshan Ave Rd No 45, Gulshan-2, Dhaka 1212, Bangladesh)

**Oriole Travels & Tours** ( ☎ 02-237 9201; fax 2379200; oriole@samart.co.th; 5th fl Skulthai Suriwong Tower, 141 Suriwong Rd, Bangkok 10500, Thailand)

**Unique Air Travels** ( ☎ 033-2474333; fax 2476167; G2, Circular Centre, 222 AJC Bose Rd, Kolkata 700017, India)

**Yale Air Service** ( ☎ 02-26523362; fax 2643 9614; Hangang Bldg, Yangcheon-Gu, Seoul, Korea)

## Tickets

Because there is no competition with other airlines for flights to Paro, Druk Air fares are expensive. Check the latest fares at www.drukair .com.bt. There are no discounts or student fares except for citizens of Bhutan. The Druk Air rules say that if fares are increased after the ticket is issued, they may collect the difference when you check in.

Thai International can issue tickets on Druk Air; the Bangkok offices know how to do this, but most of the overseas offices are not familiar with the procedures. Once your Bhutanese agent has confirmed the flight and the visa authority has been issued, allow another week for the reservation information to make its way to Thai International's computers. You'll probably still have to communicate several times with your agent in Thimphu to get Druk Air to send a confirmation message to Thai.

Many overseas agents that arrange groups to Bhutan have the tickets issued in Kathmandu, Bangkok or Delhi. A local representative waits at the Druk Air counter to deliver the tickets and check you in for your flight. If you have booked directly with a Bhutanese tour operator, you can send payment for the air fare directly to the agent in Thimphu as a separate bank transfer, not as part of the payment for the tour. The agent can then issue the Paro ticket and mail or courier it to you.

You will need to buy a ticket to and from the place where you will connect to Druk Air. Bangkok is the best place to connect if you are coming from North America, Australia or Asia. Delhi is the best place to connect if you are coming from Europe or the Middle East. A connection via Kathmandu will give you a taste of the Himalaya and of Tibetan

Buddhism before you fly to Bhutan (but you might find all the window seats taken by passengers who embarked in Delhi). Other connections via Kolkata or Dhaka are possible, but these are off the routes of direct flights for major airlines, and few discounted air fares are available to these places. The airport tax on departure from Paro is Nu 500, which is included in the price of the ticket.

## Africa

There are plenty of flights between East Africa and Mumbai. From Mumbai you can make your way to Delhi or Kathmandu to connect to Paro with either Ethiopian Airlines, Kenya Airways, Air India or Pakistan International Airlines (PIA; via Karachi). **STA Travel** (www.statravel .co.za) and **Rennies Travel** (www.renniestravel.com) have offices throughout southern Africa.

## Asia

Bangkok and Hong Kong are discount-ticket capitals of the region. Be wary of bucket shops and ask the advice of other travellers before buying a ticket. **STA Travel** (Bangkok ☎ 02-236 0262; www.statravel.co.th; Hong Kong ☎ 27361618; www.statravel .com.hk; Singapore ☎ 67377188; www.statravel.com.sg) has branches throughout Asia. In Japan try **No 1 Travel** ( ☎ 03-32056073; www.no1-travel.com).

## Australia

Two well-known agencies for cheap fares are **STA Travel** ( ☎ 1300 7333 035; www.statravel.com.au) and **Flight Centre** ( ☎ 133133; www.flightcentre.com.au), both with offices throughout Australia. Quite a few agents specialise in discount air tickets, some advertise cheap air fares in the travel sections of the major weekend newspapers. For online bookings, try www.travel.com.au.

## Canada

From Canada most flights to Delhi are via Europe but reasonable fares to Asia are also available from Vancouver. Canadian consolidators' air fares tend to be about 10% higher than those sold in the USA. **Travel CUTS** ( ☎ 800-667 2887; www .travelcuts.com) is Canada's national student travel agency and has offices in all major cities.

## Continental Europe

From Europe, travellers will need to get to Delhi where they can connect with flights up to Bhutan. Although London is the best for good fare deals, most major European cities have fairly competitive deals via the Middle East.

TRANSPORT

TRANSPORT

**THE FLIGHT FROM KATHMANDU TO PARO**

The Druk Air flight from Kathmandu to Paro provides the most dramatic view of Himalayan scenery of any scheduled flight. (Get a window seat on the left if you can.) After the plane climbs out of the Kathmandu valley a continual chain of peaks appears just off the left wing. The captain usually points out Everest (a black pyramid), Makalu (a grey chair-shaped peak) and Kanchenjunga (a huge massif), but if you have trekked in Nepal and are familiar with the mountains you can pick out many more. The elusive Shishapangma (8013m) is visible inside Tibet. Other easily recognisable peaks are Gauri Shankar (7185m), with its notch shape, Cho Oyu (8153m), Nuptse (7906m), with its long ridge, Lhotse (8501m) and Chhamlang (7319m). With a sharp eye, you can even spot Lukla airstrip and the town of Namche Bazaar at the foot of Khumbila (5761m) in Nepal.

When you pass Kanchenjunga, look for the dome-shaped peak on the western skyline. That is Jannu (7710m), which some French climbers have described as a 'peak of terror'; the Nepalis have renamed it Khumbakarna. Once past Kanchenjunga, the peaks are more distant. This is the Sikkim Himalaya; the major peaks, from west to east, are Chomoyummo (6829m), Pauhunri (7125m) and Shudu Tsenpa (7032m).

As the plane approaches Paro you may be able to spot the beautiful snow peak of Jhomolhari (7314m) and the grey ridge-shaped peak of Jichu Drakye (6989m). The plane then descends, often through clouds, into the wooded valleys of Bhutan.

The captain may announce that you are about to see the mountains closer than you have ever seen them before. He's not joking. Depending on the approach pattern that day, you may drop into the Paro valley and weave through the hills, with goembas and prayer flags on the hillsides above. If you are on the left side of the plane, look for Taktshang Goemba and Paro Dzong as you descend towards the airport, before using almost the entire 1830m of the runway to stop. On other occasions you may overfly the airport, then bank, skim over a few tree-covered ridges and the roofs of houses, and make a gut-wrenching plunge into the valley before turning for the final approach to the runway.

**Airfare** (Netherlands; ☎ 020 620 5121; www.airfare.nl)
**Anyway** (France; ☎ 0892 893 892; www.anyway.fr)
**CTS Viaggi** (Italy; ☎ 06 462 0431; www.cts.it)
**Just Travel** (Germany; ☎ 089 747 3330; www.justtravel.de)

### New Zealand
**STA Travel** ( ☎ 0508 782 872; www.statravel.co.nz) and **Flight Centre** ( ☎ 0508 782 872; www.flightcentre.co.nz) have many branches throughout the country.

### UK
As for continental Europe the cheapest fares are usually with Middle Eastern or Eastern European airlines, though Thai International always seems to have competitive fares. Various excursion fares are available from London to both India and Thailand, but you can get better prices through London's many cheap-ticket specialists.

Discount air travel is big business in London. Advertisements for many travel agencies appear in the travel pages of the weekend broadsheet newspapers, in *Time Out*, the *Evening Standard* and in the free magazine *TNT*.

**ebookers** ( ☎ 0870 010 7000; www.ebookers.com)
**Flight Centre** ( ☎ 0870 890 8099; www.flightcentre.co.uk)
**STA Travel** ( ☎ 0870 160 0599; www.statravel.co.uk)
**Trailfinders** (www.trailfinders.co.uk)

### USA
The best connections from the US west coast to Bhutan are via Bangkok. Discount travel agencies in the USA are known as consolidators (although you won't see a sign on the door saying 'Consolidator'). San Francisco is the ticket consolidator capital of America, although some good deals can be found in Los Angeles, New York and other big cities.
**American Express Travel** (www.itn.net)
**Expedia** (www.expedia.com)
**STA Travel** ( ☎ 800 781 4040; www.statravel.com)
**Travelocity** (www.travelocity.com)

### LAND
Unless you are an Indian national, the Department of Tourism (DOT) rules require that you either enter or exit Bhutan on a Druk Air flight. This limits the overland option to travelling one direction by air and the other by land, perhaps visiting Darjeeling and Sikkim en route.

## Border Crossings

The two border crossings from India into Bhutan that are permitted to foreigners are at Phuentsholing, on the border with the Indian state of West Bengal, and at Samdrup Jongkhar, on the border with the state of Assam. At the time of research, foreigners could only use the Phuentsholing border crossing for entering Bhutan. Foreigners could depart but not enter via Samdrup Jongkhar.

## India

### TO/FROM PHUENTSHOLING

If you are travelling to or from Bhutan by land, all roads lead through Siliguri, West Bengal, the major transport hub in northeast India. Heading into India, you can make road connections from Phuentsholing or Jaigaon (just across the border) to the train station in Siliguri (169km, six hours) or the airport in Bagdogra. From Siliguri there are convenient connections to Kolkata, Delhi or the Nepali border at Kakarbhitta. You can also travel on to the Indian hill stations of Kalimpong, Gangtok and Darjeeling. Bhutanese vehicles may travel freely in India and a Bhutanese tour operator can easily arrange a vehicle to any of these destinations. There are also taxis and shared hire cars available in both Phuentsholing and Siliguri.

The best places to stay in Jaigaon are these air-conditioned hotels:

**Hotel Anand** ( ☎ 03566-63783, 03566-263290, 263990; ashokagarwall@hotmail.com; M.G. Rd; s/d Rs 300/375-1000) You can get a double with air-con for Rs 1000.

**Hotel Kasturi** ( ☎ 03566-363035; fax 263254; N.S. Rd; s/d Rs 300/375-1000) Next to the immigration checkpoint.

Several Bhutanese transport companies operate a direct bus service twice a day between Siliguri and Phuentsholing; buses leave at 8am and 2pm and cost Rs 60 for the 3½-hour journey. In Siliguri the booking office is on Tenzing Norgay Rd (also known as Hill Cart Rd), opposite the Shree Punjab Hotel. You can sometimes find Bhutanese taxis (yellow-roofed minivans with numberplates beginning with 'BT') looking for a return fare; you might buy a seat for Rs 200, but usually you will have to charter the whole taxi for about Rs 750. Indian bus companies also operate services between Siliguri and Jaigaon on the Indian side of the Bhutanese border.

The gate between Phuentsholing and Jaigaon closes at 9pm for vehicles, but people can cross on foot until 10pm.

### Foreigners

Don't forget to get your passport stamped when leaving India. The Indian immigration office, open 24 hours, is in a compound on the east side of the main road in the centre of Jaigaon, next door to the Hotel Kasturi and about 400m south of the Bhutan entrance gate. (There is a plan to relocate the office.) If your transport has already deposited you in Bhutan, you can simply walk back across the border to complete the paperwork.

To obtain a Bhutanese visa, foreigners need to present their passport, two photos and a US$20 fee to the visa officer in the *drungkhag* (subdistrict) office near the east end of town. The visa is issued here, but the arrival details will be stamped in your passport when you pass the immigration checkpoint at Rinchending, 5km away.

Foreigners may cross back and forth across the border during the day but are required to leave by 10pm unless staying in a hotel – a useful facility in case you neglected to complete Indian departure formalities before you crossed into Bhutan.

### Indian Nationals

At the time of research Indian nationals needed a total of five photos, to fill in two copies of a form and present two photographs and photocopies of an identification document such as a driving licence or voter card to the office of the **Indian embassy** ( ☎ 05-252635, 252992; India House, Zhung Lam; ☿ 9.30-11.30am & 3.30-5pm Mon-Fri), near the post office in Phuentsholing. You then receive a request form to be presented to the Rinchending immigration officer along with three photographs. On weekends and holidays when the office is closed, Indian nationals who have either a voter registration card or a passport may go directly to the entry station in Rinchending.

Indian nationals may wander freely into Phuentsholing during the day, but are required to leave by 10pm unless staying in a hotel.

### TO/FROM DELHI & KOLKATA

The nearest main-line Indian train station to Phuentsholing is in New Jalpaiguri. From there it's a 12-hour rail journey to Kolkata and a 33-hour trip to Delhi. You can travel by road direct to New Jalpaiguri from Phuentsholing or drive to Siliguri where you can connect to a local train to New Jalpaiguri.

**TRANSPORT**

From Siliguri it's easy to arrange a share-taxi or bus to Darjeeling, 77km away, or to Gangtok in Sikkim, 114km away. If you are travelling to Sikkim, arrange a permit in Siliguri at the **Sikkim Tourist information Centre** ( ☎ 0353 2512646; Tenzing Norgay Rd; 10am-4pm Mon-Sat).

### TO/FROM SAMDRUP JONGKHAR
At the time of research foreign tourists were allowed to depart Bhutan at Samdrup Jongkhar, and Indian nationals may enter or leave via Samdrup Jongkhar. It is prudent to check with Bhutanese or Indian authorities on the current status of Assamese separatist groups before you decide to travel by land through Assam.

The primary reason you would want to exit this way is to avoid the long drive back over the mountains to Thimphu after visiting eastern Bhutan. The easiest connection from Samdrup Jongkhar is to overland to Guwahati in Assam and fly to Kolkata, Delhi, Bangkok or Bagdogra or get a train connection to numerous Indian destinations. Due to security concerns, all Bhutanese vehicles have to travel in a convoy as far as Rangiya (there's no convoy on Thursday or Sunday), 49km from the border. (Indian vehicles face no such restrictions.) Four kilometres from the border there is a border post, open 24 hrs, where you must get a police registration/ entry stamp. There is a train station at Rangiya for connection to Guwahati. Alternatively, it is an 80km, 2½-hour drive from the Bhutanese border all the way to Guwahati. It is then a further 20km from Guwahati to the airport.

Another alternative is a 400km drive through the Indian duars to Siliguri. On this route you could visit Kaziranga National Park, famous for its rhino population, 233km east of Guwahati.

### Nepal
Panitanki (aka Raniganj), in northern West Bengal, is opposite the eastern Nepal border town of Kakarbhitta. A long bridge separates the two towns across the Mechi River. Bhutanese tour operators can pick you up or drop you at Panitanki or you can arrange for them to take you to Bhadrapur or Biratnagar to catch a flight to Kathmandu.

Panitanki is only one hour (35km) from Siliguri (India). Buses run regularly on this route (IRs 20) and taxis are easy to arrange (IRs 400). A cycle-rickshaw across the border to Kakarbhitta costs Rs 20. Buses depart Kakarbhitta daily at 5pm for Kathmandu (17 hours, NRs 500), a long rough drive via Narayanghat, Mugling and the Trisuli River valley. See Lonely Planet's *Nepal* for details of what to see and do along this route.

A better option is to take a one-hour bus or taxi ride from Kakarbhitta to Bhadrapur and take a domestic flight to Kathmandu. There is a larger airport at Biratnagar, a four-hour drive from the border. Several airlines have offices in both towns, but airlines come and go and schedules change frequently. **Jhapa Travel Agency** ( ☎ 977-23-562020) in Kakarbhitta will be able to book a flight.

## TOURS
There are several travel agencies and adventure travel companies that specialise in Bhutan, but most operate their Bhutan trips only as part of a series of programs. In addition to removing the hassle of faxing Thimphu and transferring money, they will also arrange your tickets on Druk Air.

Most group tours to Bhutan fly to Paro together, often collecting their tickets at the check-in counter in Bangkok, Delhi or Kathmandu. The agent should also be able to either recommend a group flight or arrange air transportation, hopefully at a reasonable rate, on flights that they have prebooked to the connecting point for the flight on to Paro.

The following tour and adventure travel companies organise overland and cultural tours as well as treks in Bhutan. Their group treks are escorted by a leader, though some can also organise private trips.

### Australia
**Peregrine Adventures** ( ☎ 1300 854 444; www.peregrine.net.au)
**World Expeditions** ( ☎ 1300 720 000; www.worldexpeditions.com.au)

### Continental Europe
**Explorator** (France; ☎ 01-53 45 85 85; fax 42 60 80 00; www.explorator.fr)
**Hauser Exkursionen** (Germany; ☎ 089-235 0060; www.hauser-exkursionen.de)
**Horizons Nouveaux** (Switzerland; ☎ 027-771 7171; www.horizonsnouveaux.com)

### UK
**Abercombie & Kent** ( ☎ 0845 0700 600; www.abercrombiekent.co.uk)
**Exodus** ( ☎ 0870 240 5550; www.exodus.co.uk)
**Explore Worldwide** ( ☎ 01252-344161; www.explore.co.uk)

**Himalayan Kingdoms** ( ☎ 0845-3308579; www
.himalayankingdoms.com)
**World Expeditions** ( ☎ 0800-074 4135; www.world
expedition.co.uk)

## USA & Canada
**Above the Clouds** ( ☎ 802-482 4848; www.above
clouds.com)
**Adventure Center** ( ☎ 800-227 8747; www.adventure
-center.com)
**Asian Pacific Adventures** ( ☎ 1800-825 1680; www
.asianpacificadventures.com)
**Bhutan Travel** ( ☎ 800-950 9908; www.bhutan
travel.com)
**Far Fung Places** ( ☎ 415-386 8306; www.farfung
places.com)
**Geographic Expeditions** ( ☎ 1800-777 8183; www
.geoex.com)
**Journeys International** ( ☎ 1800 255 8735; www
.journeys-intl.com)
**Mountain Travel Sobek** ( ☎ 1888 687 6235; www
.mtsobek.com)
**Wilderness Travel** ( ☎ 1800 368 2794; www
.wildernesstravel.com)

## Thailand
**Oriole Travel & Tours** ( ☎ 02-237 9201; oriole@
samart.co.th)

## Specialised Tours
Guided mountain-bike tours are arranged by
**Bicycle Sambhava** (www.bicyclesambhava.com). Motor-
cycle trips can be arranged through **Himalayan
Roadrunners** (www.ridehigh.com) and **Saffron Road
Motorcycle Tours** (www.saffronroad.com).

The only overseas company specialising in
river trips in Bhutan is **Needmore Adventures**
( ☎ 888-900 9091; www.excellent-adventures.net).

Photography enthusiasts should check out
the expert-guided itineraries of **Rainbow Photo
Tours** ( ☎ 1800 685 9992; www.rainbowphototours.com).
The following companies specialise in tours
for twitchers (bird-watchers).
**Sunbird** ( ☎ 01767-262522; www.sunbirdtours.co.uk)
**Wings** ( ☎ 888-293 6443, 520-320 9868; www.wings
birds.com)

## Bhutan-Based Tour Operators
It is relatively easy to make your own arrangements if you choose to use a Bhutanese
operator. When tourism was privatised the
state-run Bhutan Tourism Corporation was
disbanded. Many of the ex-employees used
their expertise to set up their own operations,
and there are now more than 200 licensed

tour companies. They range from one-person
operations to large and professional organisa-
tions such as Etho Metho Tours and Treks
and Bhutan Tourism Corporation Limited
(BTCL), which have fleets of vehicles and, in
some places, their own hotel facilities.

The following list includes a selection of
the largest companies. For a complete list see
the DOT website at www.tourism.gov.bt and
the Association of Bhutanese Tour Operators
website at www.abto.org.bt.
**Bae-Yul Excursions** ( ☎ 02-324335; fax 323728; www
.baeyul.com.bt; PO Box 437, Thimphu)
**Bara Lynka Tours and Travels** ( ☎ 02-271 698; fax
272 447; baralynka@druknet.bt; www.baralynka.com; PO
Box 1010, Thimphu)
**Bhutan Footprints Travel** ( ☎ 02-334960; fax 334961;
www.tourbhutantravel.com; PO Box 732, Thimphu)
**Bhutan Kaze Tours and Treks** ( ☎ 02-326623; fax
323178; wings@druknet.bt; PO Box 715, Thimphu)
**Bhutan Mandala Tours and Treks** ( ☎ 02-323676; fax
323675; www.bhutanmandala.com; PO Box 397, Thimphu)
**Bhutan Tourism Corporation Limited** (BTCL; ☎ 02-
324045, 322647; fax 323292; www.kingdomofbhutan.com;
PO Box 159, Thimphu)
**Bhutan Travel Bureau** ( ☎ 02-321749; fax 325100;
www.btb.com.bt; PO Box 959, Thimphu)
**Bhutan Travel Service** ( ☎ 02-325785; fax 325786;
www.bhutantravel.com.bt; PO Box 919, Thimphu)
**Chhundu Travels and Tours** ( ☎ 02-322592; fax
322645; www.chhundu.com.bt; PO Box 149, Thimphu)
**Dechen Cultural Tours and Trekking Co.** ( ☎ 02-
321358; fax 324408; dechen@druknet.bt; PO Box 818,
Thimphu)
**Diethelm Travel Bhutan** ( ☎ 02-324063; fax 323894;
dwpenjor@druknet.bt; PO Box 666, Thimphu)
**Dragon Trekkers and Tours** ( ☎ 02-323599; fax
323314; dragon@druknet.bt; PO Box 452, Thimphu)
**Etho Metho Tours and Treks** ( ☎ 02-323162; fax
322884; www.ethometho.com; PO Box 360, Thimphu)
**Gangri Tours and Trekking** ( ☎ 02-323556; fax
323322; www.gangri.com; PO Box 607, Thimphu)
**International Treks and Tours** ( ☎ 02-326847; fax
323675; www.intrekasia.com/bhutan.htm)
**Jamphel Tours and Travels** ( ☎ /fax 02-321111;
jamphel@druknet.bt; PO Box 289, Thimphu)
**Jojo's Adventure Tours** ( ☎ 1711 0305; fax 02-333940;
www.jojos.com.bt; PO Box 816, Thimphu)
**Lhomen Tours and Trekking** ( ☎ 02-324148; fax
323243; www.lhomen.com.bt; PO Box 341, Thimphu)
**Lingkor Tours and Treks** ( ☎ 02-323417; fax 323402;
www.lingkor.com; PO Box 202, Thimphu)
**Lotus Adventures** ( ☎ 02-322191; fax 325678;
equbhu@druknet.bt; PO Box 706, Thimphu) Whitewater
rafting specialist.

TRANSPORT

**Masagang Tours** ( ☎ 02-323206; fax 02-323718; masagang@druknet.bt; www.masagang.com) Tours based in the Ura Valley.

**Namsey Adventure** ( ☎ 02-325616; fax 324297; namsay@druknet.bt; PO Box 549, Thimphu)

**Passage to Himalayas** ( ☎ 02-321726; fax 321727; lekid@druknet.net.bt; PO Box 1068, Thimphu)

**Rainbow Tours and Treks** ( ☎ 02-323270; fax 322960; rainbow@druknet.bt; PO Box 641, Thimphu)

**Sakten Tours and Treks** ( ☎ 02-323899; fax 323545; sakten@druknet.bt; PO Box 532, Thimphu)

**Snow Leopard Trekking Co.** ( ☎ 02-321822; fax 325684; www.snowleopardtreks.com; PO Box 953, Thimphu)

**Snow White Treks and Tours** ( ☎ 02-323028; fax 321696; www.snowwhitetours.com.bt; PO Box 112, Thimphu)

**Tashi Tours and Travels** ( ☎ 02-323027; fax 323666; bhutantashitours.com; PO Box 423, Thimphu)

**Thoesam Tours and Trekking** ( ☎ 02-365101; fax 365073; thoesam@druknet.bt; PO Box 629, Thimphu)

**Thunder Dragon Treks** ( ☎ 02-321999; fax 321963; www.thunderdragontreks.com; PO Box 303, Thimphu)

**White Tara Tours and Treks** ( ☎ 02-333224; fax 326942; wtara@druknet.net.bt; PO Box 467, Thimphu)

**Windhorse Tours** ( ☎ 02-326026; fax 326025; www .windhorsetours.com; PO Box 1021, Thimphu)

**Yangphel Adventure Travel** ( ☎ 02-323293; fax 322897; www.yangphel.com; PO Box 236, Thimphu) One of the largest, also specialising in fishing tours.

**Yu Druk Tours and Treks** ( ☎ 02-323461; fax 322116; www.yudruk.com; PO Box 140, Thimphu) Bicycling and trekking specialists.

**Zhidey Bhutan Tours and Treks** ( ☎ 02-328324; fax 327511; zhidey@druknet.bt; PO Box 841, Thimphu)

All operators in Bhutan are subject to government regulations that specify services, standards and rates. You are quite safe no matter which company you choose, though the large companies do have more clout to obtain reservations in hotels and on Druk Air.

In addition to Etho Metho and BTCL, the largest operators are Yangphel, International Treks and Tours, Rainbow and Gangri.

There are both advantages and disadvantages in dealing with the largest companies. One Bhutanese hotelier suggested that the following companies would be large enough to handle overseas queries, but still small enough that the owner would pay personal attention to your program: Bae-yul, Bhutan Kaze, Bhutan Mandala, Chhundu, Sakten, Tashi, Thunder Dragon, Windhorse, Yodsel and Yu Druk.

Chhundu is renowned for its high-quality personal service, and it's responsible for looking after many VIP clients. Other companies known for their personal attention and quality service are Lhomen, Namsey, Yu Druk and Bhutan Travel Bureau. Bhutan Kaze and Bhutan Mandala specialise in service to Japanese clients.

If you are planning to go trekking, you might consider one of the companies that specialises in this area. The biggest trek operators are Yangphel, International, Yu Druk, Lhomen, Tashi and Namsey.

# GETTING AROUND

Because Bhutan has no domestic air service, doesn't yet possess any helicopters and does not have a centimetre of railway track, the only way to see the country is either by foot or by road.

There is one main road: the National Highway, a 3.5m-wide stretch of tarmac that winds its way up and down mountains, across clattering bridges, along the side of cliffs and over high mountain passes. Rivers, mudflows and rockfalls present continual hazards, especially when it rains. The road can easily become blocked due to snow or landslides and can take anywhere from an hour to several days to clear. Take plenty of reading material.

Unless you want to walk, the only way to travel between towns in the south of Bhutan is via India, because there are no roads. Currently this is impractical for foreigners since the only road entry point that foreigners are allowed to use is Phuentsholing.

Tour operators use Japanese-made buses, minivans and cars, depending on the size of the group. These vehicles can take you almost anywhere in the country, but for trips to central and eastern Bhutan during winter (December to February) or the monsoon (June to September) a 4WD vehicle is an advantage, and often a necessity.

If you are travelling on a tourist visa, the cost of all transport is included in the price of your trip and you'll have a vehicle available for both short- and long-distance travel. You'll only have to rely on public transport if you are an Indian national or if you are working with a project that does not provide you with a vehicle.

## BICYCLE

Some travellers have ridden mountain bikes in Bhutan, and DOT (Department of Tourism) are promoting this kind of travel. Good routes include the upper parts of the Paro and Thimphu valleys. For a wild ride, get dropped off at the top of the Cheli La, above Paro, and ride 35km nonstop downhill. For more information, including dedicated mountain biking trails, see p153 and p148.

## BUS

Public buses are crowded and rattly, and Bhutan's winding roads make them doubly uncomfortable. The government's **Bhutan Post Express** ( ☎ 02-322381), **Dawa Transport** ( ☎ 02-324250) and plenty of other companies operate minibuses and so many passengers suffer from motion sickness that these have earned the nickname 'vomit comets'. Some private operators, including **Leksol Bus Service** ( ☎ 02-325232) and **Karma Transport** ( ☎ 02-332412), use more comfortable Toyota Coasters at about 50% more than the minibus fare. In eastern Bhutan you might arrive at the bus stop to discover that your bus is actually a truck with seats in the back!

There are three or four buses a day between Thimphu and the major centres of Phuentsholing, Paro and Punakha. Fares and schedules are all monitored by the Road Safety and Transport Authority.

### Costs

Public buses are cheap. A minibus fare between Thimphu and Paro is Nu 40, Thimphu and Phuentsholing Nu 120, and Thimphu and Jakar Nu 202.

## CAR & MOTORCYCLE

Since all transport is provided by tour operators, you normally do not have to concern yourself with driving. If for some reason you are arranging your own transport, you are still far better off using the services of a hired car and driver or a taxi. Driving in Bhutan is a harrowing experience. Roads are narrow and trucks roar around hairpin bends, appearing suddenly and forcing oncoming vehicles to the side. Because most roads are only about 3.5m wide, passing any oncoming vehicle involves one, or both, moving onto the verge.

If you don't already have one at your disposal, the best way to hire a car is through a tour company (see p263). It's unlikely that you'll find a motorcycle for rent; however, you can join an organised motorcycle tour; see p263.

### Bring Your Own Vehicle

If you drive a vehicle into Bhutan, you can get a 14-day permit at the Phuentsholing border. You will need the help of a tour operator to handle the paperwork. If you are driving a vehicle that is registered overseas, you will need a carnet in order to get through India.

Indian visitors may travel throughout most of Bhutan in their own vehicle, but need a permit from the Road Safety and Transport Authority at the border. Traffic regulations are the same as in India and are strictly enforced.

### Driving Licence

If you insist on driving in Bhutan, you should obtain a driving licence issued by the Road Safety and Transport Authority. Bhutanese licences are also valid throughout India.

An International Driving Permit is not valid in Bhutan. An Indian driving licence is valid in Bhutan, and it's possible for Indian nationals to drive in Bhutan; but unless you are an accomplished rally driver or are from a hill station such as Darjeeling and have experience in motoring in the mountains, it's safer with a professional driver.

### Road Rules

Traffic keeps to the left and is much more orderly than in most other south Asian countries. Speeds are low in towns and on rural roads; you will be lucky to average more than 30km/h on the roads in the hills.

As is the case throughout Asia, it is important that the police establish who was at fault in any traffic accident. This means that the police must arrive and make the decision before any of the vehicles can be moved, even if the vehicles are blocking a narrow road. A relatively minor fender-bender can block the road for hours while everyone waits patiently for the police to arrive from the nearest town.

## HITCHING

Most people pay for a ride, either in a bus or cab or back of a truck. But bus services are limited, especially in the east, and it's not unusual to see someone flagging down a vehicle asking for a ride. If you have paid for a vehicle, you will only need to hitch if that vehicle has broken down and you are stranded on a mountain road. Hitching is never entirely safe in any country in the world, and we don't recommend it, but if you do have to hitch because of a break-down, Bhutan is about as safe a place as you could find.

## LOCAL TRANSPORT
### Taxi
There are taxis in Phuentsholing and Thim-phu. Taxis have meters, but drivers rarely use them. For long-distance trips they operate on a flat rate that is rarely open to negotiation.

You should expect to pay Nu 50 for a local trip within Thimphu, Nu 700 for a full day and Nu 1200 (Maruti) to Nu 2000 (Mahindra Jeep or Bolero) from Thimphu to Phuentshol-ing. If you are travelling between Thimphu and Phuentsholing, look for a taxi that is from the place to which you want to go (vehicles with BT-2 numberplates are from Phuentshol-ing and those with BT-1 numberplates are from Thimphu or Paro) – you may be able to negotiate a lower price.

# Health

## CONTENTS

| | |
|---|---|
| **Before You Go** | **267** |
| Insurance | 267 |
| Vaccinations | 267 |
| Medical Checklist | 268 |
| Internet Resources | 268 |
| Further Reading | 269 |
| **In Transit** | **269** |
| Deep Vein Thrombosis (DVT) | 269 |
| Jet Lag & Motion Sickness | 269 |
| **In Bhutan** | **269** |
| Availability of Health Care | 269 |
| Infectious Diseases | 269 |
| Traveller's Diarrhoea | 271 |
| Environmental Hazards | 272 |
| Women's Health | 274 |

The main health concerns in Bhutan are similar to those in other south Asian destinations: the relatively high risk of acquiring traveller's diarrhoea, a respiratory infection, or a more exotic tropical infection. If you go trekking, there are also risks associated with accidents and altitude sickness. The infectious diseases can interrupt your trip and make you feel miserable, but they are rarely fatal. Falling off trails, or having a rock fall on you as you trek, is rare but can happen.

The following advice is a general guide only and does not replace the advice of a doctor trained in travel medicine.

# BEFORE YOU GO

Pack medications in their original, clearly labelled containers. A signed and dated letter from your physician describing your medical conditions and medications, including generic names, is also a good idea. If carrying syringes or needles, be sure to have a physician's letter documenting their medical necessity. If you have a heart condition, bring a copy of your ECG taken just prior to travelling.

If you take any regular medication, bring double your needs in case of loss or theft. You can't rely on many medications being available from pharmacies in Bhutan.

## INSURANCE

Even if you are fit and healthy, don't travel without health insurance – accidents do happen. Declare any existing medical conditions you have – the insurance company *will* check if your problem is pre-existing and will not cover you if it is undeclared. You may require extra cover for adventure activities such as rock climbing. If your health insurance doesn't cover you for medical expenses abroad, consider getting extra insurance – check Lonely Planet's website (lonelyplanet.com) for more information. If you're uninsured, emergency evacuation is expensive; bills of over US$100,000 are not uncommon.

Find out in advance if your insurance plan will make payments directly to providers or reimburse you later for overseas health expenditures. (In many countries doctors expect payment in cash.) You may prefer a policy that pays doctors or hospitals directly rather than you having to pay on the spot and claim later. If you have to claim later, make sure you keep all documentation. Some policies ask you to call back (reverse charges) to a centre in your home country, where an immediate assessment of your problem is made.

## VACCINATIONS

Specialised travel-medicine clinics are your best source of information; they stock all available vaccines and will be able to give specific recommendations for you and your trip. The doctors will take into account factors such as past vaccination history, the length of your trip, activities you may be undertaking and underlying medical conditions, such as pregnancy.

Most vaccines don't produce immunity until at least two weeks after they're given, so visit a doctor four to eight weeks before departure. Ask your doctor for an International Certificate of Vaccination (otherwise known as the yellow booklet), which will list all the vaccinations you've received.

### Recommended Vaccinations
The World Health Organization recommends the following vaccinations for travellers to

Bhutan (as well as being up to date with measles, mumps and rubella vaccinations):

**Adult diphtheria and tetanus** Single booster recommended if none in the previous 10 years. Side effects include sore arm and fever.

**Hepatitis A** Provides almost 100% protection for up to a year, a booster after 12 months provides at least another 20 years' protection. Mild side effects such as headache and sore arm occur in 5% to 10% of people.

**Hepatitis B** Now considered routine for most travellers. Given as three shots over six months. A rapid schedule is also available, as is a combined vaccination with Hepatitis A. Side effects are mild and uncommon, usually headache and sore arm. Lifetime protection occurs in 95% of people.

**Polio** Bhutan's last case of polio was reported in 1986, but it has been reported more recently in nearby Nepal and India. Only one booster required as an adult for lifetime protection. Inactivated polio vaccine is safe during pregnancy.

**Typhoid** The vaccine offers around 70% protection, lasts for two to three years and comes as a single shot. Tablets are also available; however, the injection is usually recommended as it has fewer side effects. Sore arm and fever may occur.

**Varicella** If you haven't had chickenpox, discuss this vaccination with your doctor.

These immunisations may be recommended for long-term travellers (more than one month) or those at special risk:

**Japanese B Encephalitis** Three injections in all. Booster recommended after two years. Sore arm and headache are the most common side effects. Rarely, an allergic reaction comprising hives and swelling can occur up to 10 days after any of the three doses.

**Meningitis** Single injection. There are two types of vaccination: the quadrivalent vaccine gives two to three years' protection; meningitis group C vaccine gives around 10 years' protection. Recommended for long-term backpackers aged under 25.

**Rabies** Three injections in all. A booster after one year will then provide 10 years' protection. Side effects are rare – occasionally headache and sore arm.

**Tuberculosis** A complex issue. Adult long-term travellers are usually recommended to have a TB skin test before and after travel, rather than vaccination. Only one vaccine given in a lifetime.

## Required Vaccinations

The only vaccine required by international regulations is yellow fever. Proof of vaccination will only be required if you have visited a country in the yellow-fever zone within the six days prior to entering Bhutan. If you are travelling to Bhutan from Africa or South America you should check to see if you require proof of vaccination.

## MEDICAL CHECKLIST

Recommended items for a personal medical kit:

- Antifungal cream, eg Clotrimazole
- Antibacterial cream, eg Muciprocin
- Antibiotic for skin infections, eg Amoxicillin/Clavulanate or Cephalexin
- Antibiotics for diarrhoea include Norfloxacin or Ciprofloxacin; for bacterial diarrhoea Azithromycin; for giardiasis or amoebic dysentery Tinidazole
- Antihistamine – there are many options, eg Cetrizine for daytime and Promethazine for night
- Antiseptic, eg Betadine
- Antispasmodic for stomach cramps, eg Buscopa
- Contraceptives
- Decongestant, eg Pseudoephedrine
- DEET-based insect repellent
- Diarrhoea – consider an oral rehydration solution (eg Gastrolyte), diarrhoea 'stopper' (eg Loperamide) and antinausea medication (eg Prochlorperazine)
- First-aid items such as scissors, Elastoplasts, bandages, gauze, thermometer (but not mercury), sterile needles and syringes, safety pins and tweezers
- Ibuprofen or another anti-inflammatory
- Indigestion medication, eg Quick-Eze or Mylanta
- Iodine tablets (unless you are pregnant or have a thyroid problem) to purify water
- Laxative, eg Coloxyl
- Migraine sufferer – take your personal medicine
- Paracetamol
- Permethrin to impregnate clothing and mosquito nets
- Steroid cream for allergic/itchy rashes, eg 1% to 2% hydrocortisone
- Sunscreen and hat
- Throat lozenges
- Thrush (vaginal yeast infection) treatment, eg Clotrimazole pessaries or Diflucan tablet
- Ural or equivalent if you're prone to urine infections

## INTERNET RESOURCES

There is a wealth of travel health advice on the internet. For further information, **Lonely Planet** (lonelyplanet.com) is a good place to start. The **World Health Organization** (WHO; www.who.int/ith/) publishes a superb book called *International*

*Travel & Health,* which is revised annually and is available free online. Another website of general interest is **MD Travel Health** (www.mdtravelhealth.com), which provides complete travel health recommendations for every country and is updated daily. The **Centers for Disease Control and Prevention** (CDC; www.cdc.gov) website also has good general information.

## FURTHER READING

Lonely Planet's *Healthy Travel – Asia & India* is a handy pocket-size book that is packed with useful information including pretrip planning, emergency first aid, immunisation and disease information and what to do if you get sick on the road. Other recommended references include *Traveller's Health* by Dr Richard Dawood and *Travelling Well* by Dr Deborah Mills – check out the website www.travellingwell.com.au.

# IN TRANSIT

## DEEP VEIN THROMBOSIS (DVT)

Deep vein thrombosis (DVT) occurs when blood clots form in the legs during plane flights, chiefly because of prolonged immobility. The longer the flight, the greater the risk. Though most blood clots are reabsorbed uneventfully, some may break off and travel through the blood vessels to the lungs, where they may cause life-threatening complications.

The chief symptom of DVT is swelling or pain of the foot, ankle or calf, usually but not always on just one side. If a blood clot travels to the lungs it may cause chest pain and difficulty in breathing. Travellers with any of these symptoms should immediately seek medical attention.

To prevent the development of DVT on long flights you should walk about the cabin, perform isometric compressions of the leg muscles (ie contract the leg muscles while sitting), drink plenty of fluids and avoid alcohol.

## JET LAG & MOTION SICKNESS

Jet lag is common when crossing more than five time zones; it results in insomnia, fatigue, malaise or nausea. To avoid jet lag try drinking plenty of fluids (nonalcoholic) and eating light meals. Upon arrival, seek exposure to natural sunlight and readjust your schedule (for meals, sleep etc) as soon as possible.

Antihistamines such as dimenhydrinate (Dramamine) and meclizine (Antivert, Bonine) are usually the first choice for treating motion sickness. Their main side effect is drowsiness. A herbal alternative is ginger, which works like a charm for some people.

# IN BHUTAN

## AVAILABILITY OF HEALTH CARE

There are no private health clinics or physicians in Bhutan, but all district headquarters towns have a hospital, and will accept travellers in need of medical attention. The best facility is the Jigme Dorji Wangchuk National Referral Hospital in Thimphu. It has general physicians and several specialists, labs and operating rooms. Treatment is free, even for tourists. If you are seriously ill or injured you should consider evacuation to the excellent medical facilities in Bangkok. It is difficult to find reliable medical care in rural areas. Your embassy and insurance company are good contacts.

Self-treatment may be appropriate if your problem is minor (eg traveller's diarrhoea), you are carrying the appropriate medication and you cannot attend a recommended clinic. If you think you may have a serious disease, especially malaria, do not waste time – travel to the nearest quality facility to receive attention. It is always better to be assessed by a doctor than to rely on self-treatment.

In most large towns there are shops that sell medicines. Most of the medical supplies mentioned in this section are available without a prescription in these medicine shops.

## INFECTIOUS DISEASES
### Coughs, Colds & Chest Infections

Respiratory infections usually start as a virus and are exacerbated by environmental conditions such as urban pollution, or cold and altitude in the mountains. Commonly a secondary bacterial infection will intervene – marked by fever, chest pain and coughing up discoloured or blood-tinged sputum. If you have the symptoms of an infection seek medical advice or commence a general antibiotic.

### Dengue Fever

This mosquito-borne disease is becomingly increasingly problematic throughout the tropical world, especially in the cities. As there is no vaccine available it can only be prevented by avoiding mosquito bites. The mosquito that carries dengue bites day and night, so use insect avoidance measures at all times. Symptoms include high fever, severe headache and body ache (dengue was previously known as 'breakbone fever'). Some people develop a rash and experience diarrhoea. There is no specific treatment, just rest and paracetamol – do not take aspirin as it increases the likelihood of haemorrhaging. See a doctor to be diagnosed and monitored.

### Hepatitis A

A problem throughout the region, this food- and water-borne virus infects the liver, causing jaundice (yellow skin and eyes), nausea and lethargy. There is no specific treatment for hepatitis A, you just need to allow time for the liver to heal. All travellers to Bhutan should be vaccinated against hepatitis A.

### Hepatitis B

The only sexually transmitted disease that can be prevented by vaccination, hepatitis B is spread by body fluids, including in sexual contact. The long-term consequences can include liver cancer and cirrhosis.

### Hepatitis E

Hepatitis E is transmitted through contaminated food and water and has similar symptoms to hepatitis A, but is far less common. It is a severe problem in pregnant women and can result in the death of both mother and baby. There is currently no vaccine, and prevention is by following safe eating and drinking guidelines.

### HIV

HIV is spread via contaminated body fluids. Avoid unsafe sex, unsterile needles (including in medical facilities) and procedures such as tattoos.

### Influenza

Present year-round in the tropics, influenza (flu) symptoms include high fever, muscle aches, runny nose, cough and sore throat. It can be very severe in people over the age of 65 or in those with underlying medical conditions such as heart disease or diabetes; vaccination is recommended for these individuals. There is no specific treatment, just rest and paracetamol.

### Japanese B Encephalitis

This viral disease is transmitted by mosquitoes and is rare in travellers. Like most mosquito-borne diseases it is becoming a more common problem in affected countries. Most cases occur in rural areas and vaccination is recommended for travellers spending more than one month outside cities. There is no treatment, and a third of infected people will die, while another third will suffer permanent brain damage.

### Malaria

For such a serious and potentially deadly disease, there is an enormous amount of misinformation concerning malaria. You must get expert advice as to whether your trip actually puts you at risk. For most rural areas, the risk of contracting malaria far outweighs the risk of any tablet side effects. Before you travel, seek medical advice on the right medication and dosage for you.

Malaria is caused by a parasite transmitted by the bite of an infected mosquito. The most important symptom of malaria is fever, but general symptoms such as headache, diarrhoea, cough or chills may also occur. Diagnosis can only be made by taking a blood sample.

Two strategies should be combined to prevent malaria – mosquito avoidance and antimalaria medications. Most people who catch malaria are taking inadequate or no antimalarial medication.

Travellers are advised to prevent mosquito bites by taking these steps:

- Use a DEET-containing insect repellent on exposed skin. Wash this off at night, as long as you are sleeping under a mosquito net. Natural repellents such as citronella can be effective, but must be applied more frequently than products containing DEET.
- Sleep under a mosquito net impregnated with pyrethrin
- Choose accommodation with screens and fans (if not air-conditioned)
- Impregnate clothing with pyrethrin in high-risk areas
- Wear long sleeves and trousers in light colours
- Use mosquito coils
- Spray your room with insect repellent before going out for your evening meal

There are a variety of medications available. The effectiveness of the **Chloroquine and Paludrine** combination is now limited in many parts of south Asia. Common side effects include nausea (40% of people) and mouth ulcers.

The daily tablet **Doxycycline** is a broad-spectrum antibiotic that has the added benefit of helping to prevent a variety of tropical diseases, including leptospirosis, tick-borne disease and typhus. The potential side effects include photosensitivity (a tendency to sunburn), thrush (in women), indigestion, heartburn, nausea and interference with the contraceptive pill. More serious side effects include ulceration of the oesophagus – you can help prevent this by taking your tablet with a meal and a large glass of water, and never lying down within half an hour of taking it. It must be taken for four weeks after leaving the risk area.

**Lariam (Mefloquine)** has received much bad press, some of it justified, some not. This weekly tablet suits many people. Serious side effects are rare but include depression, anxiety, psychosis and having fits. Anyone with a history of depression, anxiety, another psychological disorder, or epilepsy should not take Lariam. It is considered safe in the second and third trimesters of pregnancy. Tablets must be taken for four weeks after leaving the risk area.

The new drug **Malarone** is a combination of Atovaquone and Proguanil. Side effects are uncommon and mild, most commonly nausea and headache. It is the best tablet for those on short trips to high-risk areas. It must be taken for one week after leaving the risk area.

### Rabies

Rabies is considered to be highly endemic in Bhutan. This uniformly fatal disease is spread by the bite or lick of an infected animal – most commonly a dog or monkey. You should seek medical advice immediately after any animal bite and commence post-exposure treatment. Having pre-travel vaccination means the post-bite treatment is greatly simplified. If an animal bites you, gently wash the wound with soap and water, and apply iodine based antiseptic. If you are not pre-vaccinated you will need to receive rabies immunoglobulin as soon as possible.

### STDs

Sexually transmitted diseases most common in south Asia include herpes, warts, syphilis, gonorrhoea and chlamydia. People carrying these diseases often have no signs of infection. Condoms will prevent gonorrhoea and chlamydia but not warts or herpes. If after a sexual encounter you develop any rash, lumps, discharge or pain when passing urine, seek immediate medical attention. If you have been sexually active during your travels, have an STD check on your return home.

### Tuberculosis

While rare in travellers, medical and aid workers, and long-term travellers who have significant contact with the local population should take precautions. Vaccination is usually given only to children under the age of five, but adults at risk are recommended pre- and post-travel tuberculosis testing. The main symptoms are fever, cough, weight loss, night sweats and tiredness.

### Typhoid

This serious bacterial infection is also spread via food and water. It gives a high and slowly progressive fever, headache and may be accompanied by a dry cough and stomach pain. It is diagnosed by blood tests and treated with antibiotics. Vaccination is recommended for all travellers spending more than a week in Bhutan. Be aware that vaccination is not 100% effective so you must still be careful with what you eat and drink.

## TRAVELLER'S DIARRHOEA

Traveller's diarrhoea is by far the most common problem affecting travellers – between 30% and 50% of people will suffer from it within two weeks of starting their trip. In over 80% of cases, traveller's diarrhoea is caused by a bacteria (there are numerous potential culprits), and therefore responds promptly to treatment with antibiotics. Treatment with antibiotics will depend on your situation – how sick you are, how quickly you need to get better, where you are etc.

Traveller's diarrhoea is defined as the passage of more than three watery bowel-actions within 24 hours, plus at least one other symptom such as fever, cramps, nausea, vomiting or feeling generally unwell.

Treatment reequires staying well-hydrated; rehydration solutions like Gastrolyte are the best for this. Antibiotics such as Norfloxacin, Ciprofloxacin or Azithromycin will kill the bacteria quickly.

Loperamide is just a 'stopper' and doesn't get to the source of the problem. It can be helpful, for example if you have to go on a long bus ride. Don't take Loperamide if you have

---

**DRINKING WATER**

- Never drink tap water
- Bottled water is generally safe – check the seal is intact at purchase
- Avoid ice
- Avoid fresh juices – they may have been watered down
- Boiling water is the most efficient method of purifying it
- The best chemical purifier is iodine. It should not be used by pregnant women or those with thyroid problems.
- Water filters should also filter out viruses. Ensure your filter has a chemical barrier such as iodine and a small pore size, eg less than four microns.

---

a fever, or blood in your stools. Seek medical attention quickly if you do not respond to an appropriate antibiotic.

## Amoebic Dysentery

Amoebic dysentery is very rare in travellers but is often misdiagnosed by poor quality labs. Symptoms are similar to bacterial diarrhoea, ie fever, bloody diarrhoea and generally feeling unwell. You should always seek reliable medical care if you have blood in your diarrhoea. Treatment involves two drugs: Tinidazole or Metronidazole to kill the parasite in your gut and then a second drug to kill the cysts. If it's left untreated, complications such as liver or gut abscesses can occur.

## Giardiasis

*Giardia lamblia* is a parasite that is relatively common in travellers. Symptoms include nausea, bloating, excess gas, fatigue and intermittent diarrhoea. 'Eggy' burps are often attributed solely to giardiasis, but work in Nepal has shown that they are not specific to this infection. The parasite will eventually go away if left untreated but this can take months. The treatment of choice is Tinidazole, with Metronidazole being a second-line option.

## ENVIRONMENTAL HAZARDS
### Food

Eating in restaurants is the biggest risk factor for contracting traveller's diarrhoea. Ways to avoid it include eating only freshly cooked food, and avoiding shellfish and food that has been sitting around in buffets. Peel all fruit, cook vegetables and soak salads in iodine water for at least 20 minutes. Eat in busy restaurants with a high turnover of customers.

## High Altitude

If you are going to altitudes above 3000m you should get information on preventing, recognising and treating Acute Mountain Sickness (AMS). AMS is a notoriously fickle affliction and can also affect trekkers and walkers accustomed to walking at high altitudes. AMS has been fatal at 3000m, although 3500m to 4500m is the usual range.

### ACCLIMATISATION

With an increase in altitude, the human body needs time to develop physiological mechanisms to cope with the decreased oxygen. This process of acclimatisation is still not fully understood, but is known to involve modifications in breathing patterns and heart rate induced by the autonomic nervous system, and an increase in the blood's oxygen-carrying capabilities. These compensatory mechanisms usually take about one to three days to develop at a particular altitude. Once you are acclimatised to a given height you are unlikely to get AMS at that height, but you can still get ill when you travel higher. If the ascent is too high and too fast, these compensatory reactions may not kick into gear fast enough.

### SYMPTOMS

Mild symptoms of AMS are very common in travellers visiting high altitudes, and usually develop during the first 24 hours at altitude. Most visitors to Tibet will suffer from some symptoms; these will generally disappear through acclimatisation in several hours to several days.

Symptoms tend to be worse at night and include headache, dizziness, lethargy, loss of appetite, nausea, breathlessness and irritability. Difficulty sleeping is another common symptom.

AMS may become more serious without warning and can be fatal. Symptoms are caused by the accumulation of fluid in the lungs and brain, and include breathlessness at rest, a dry irritative cough (which may progress to the production of pink, frothy sputum), severe headache, lack of coordination (typically leading to a 'drunken walk'), confusion, irrational behaviour, vomiting and eventually unconsciousness.

The symptoms of AMS, however mild, are a warning – be sure to take them seriously! Trekkers should keep an eye on each other as those experiencing symptoms, especially severe symptoms, may not be in a position to recognise them. One thing to note is that while the symptoms of mild AMS often precede those of severe AMS, this is not always the case. Severe AMS can strike with little or no warning.

### PREVENTION

To prevent acute mountain sickness:

- Ascend slowly. Have frequent rest days, spending two to three nights at each rise of 1000m. If you reach a high altitude by trekking, acclimatisation takes place gradually and you are less likely to be affected than if you fly directly to high altitude.
- Trekkers should bear in mind the climber's adage 'Climb high, sleep low'. It is always wise to sleep at a lower altitude than the greatest height reached during the day. High day climbs followed by a descent back to lower altitudes for the night are good preparation for trekking at high altitude . Also, once above 3000m, care should be taken not to increase the sleeping altitude by more than 400m per day. If the terrain won't allow for less than 400m of elevation gain, be ready to take an extra day off before tackling the climb.
- Drink extra fluids. The mountain air is dry and cold, and moisture is lost as you breathe. Evaporation of sweat may occur unnoticed and result in dehydration.
- Eat light, high-carbohydrate meals for more energy.
- Avoid alcohol as it may increase the risk of dehydration, and don't smoke.
- Avoid sedatives.
- When trekking, take a day off to rest and acclimatise if feeling over-tired. If you or anyone else in your party is having a tough time, make allowances for unscheduled stops.
- Don't push yourself when climbing up to passes; rather, take plenty of breaks. You can usually get over the pass as easily tomorrow as you can today. Try to plan

your itinerary so that long ascents can be divided into two or more days. Given the complexity and unknown variables involved with AMS and acclimatisation, trekkers should always err on the side of caution and ascend mountains slowly.

### TREATMENT

Treat mild symptoms by resting at the same altitude until recovery, usually a day or two. Take paracetamol or aspirin for headaches. If symptoms persist or become worse, however, *immediate descent* is necessary – even 500m can help.

The most effective treatment for severe AMS is to get down to a lower altitude as quickly as possible. In less severe cases the victim will be able to stagger down with some support; in other cases they may need to be carried down. Whatever the case, do not delay, as any delay could be fatal.

AMS victims may need to be flown out of Bhutan as quickly as possible – make sure you have adequate travel insurance.

The drugs acetazolamide (Diamox) and dexamethasone are recommended by some doctors for the prevention of AMS. However, you should be aware that their use is controversial. They can reduce the symptoms, but they may also mask warning signs; severe and fatal AMS has occurred in people taking these drugs. Drug treatments should never be used to avoid descent or to enable further ascent.

## Insect Bites & Stings

Bedbugs don't carry disease but their bites are very itchy. They live in the cracks of furniture and walls and then migrate to the bed at night to feed on you. You can treat the itch with an antihistamine. Lice inhabit various parts of your body but most commonly your head and pubic area. Transmission is via close contact with an infected person. They can be difficult to treat and you may need numerous applications of an antilice shampoo such as Permethrin. Pubic lice are usually contracted from sexual contact.

Ticks are contracted after walking in rural areas. Ticks are commonly found behind the ears, on the belly and in armpits. If you have had a tick bite and experience symptoms such as a rash at the site of the bite or elsewhere, fever, or muscle aches you should see a doctor. Doxycycline prevents tick-borne diseases.

Leeches are found in humid rainforest areas. They do not transmit any disease but their bites are often intensely itchy for weeks afterwards and can easily become infected. Apply an iodine-based antiseptic to any leech bite to help prevent infection.

Bee and wasp stings mainly cause problems for people who are allergic to them. Anyone with a serious bee or wasp allergy should carry an injection of adrenaline (eg an Epipen) for emergency treatment. For others pain is the main problem – apply ice to the sting and take painkillers.

### Skin Problems

Fungal rashes are common in humid climates. There are two common fungal rashes that affect travellers. The first occurs in moist areas that get less air such as the groin, armpits and between the toes. It starts as a red patch that slowly spreads and is usually itchy. Treatment involves keeping the skin dry, avoiding chafing and using an antifungal cream such as Clotrimazole or Lamisil. *Tinea versicolor* is also common – this fungus causes small, light-coloured patches, most commonly on the back, chest and shoulders. Consult a doctor.

Cuts and scratches become easily infected in humid climates. Take meticulous care of any cuts and scratches to prevent complications such as abscesses. Immediately wash all wounds in clean water and apply antiseptic. If you develop signs of infection (increasing pain and redness), see a doctor.

### Sunburn

Even on a cloudy day sunburn can occur rapidly. Always use a strong sunscreen (at least factor 30), and always wear a wide-brimmed hat and sunglasses outdoors. Avoid lying in the sun during the hottest part of the day (10am to 2pm). If you become sunburnt stay out of the sun until you have recovered, apply cool compresses and take painkillers for the discomfort. One per cent hydrocortisone cream applied twice daily is also helpful.

## WOMEN'S HEALTH

Pregnant women should receive specialised advice before travelling. The ideal time to travel is in the second trimester (between 16 and 28 weeks), when the risk of pregnancy-related problems are at their lowest and pregnant women generally feel at their best. During the first trimester there is a risk of miscarriage and in the third trimester complications such as premature labour and high blood pressure are possible. It's wise to travel with a companion. Always carry a list of quality medical facilities available at your destination and ensure you continue your standard antenatal care at these facilities. Avoid rural travel in areas with poor transportation and medical facilities. Most of all, ensure travel insurance covers all pregnancy-related possibilities, including premature labour.

Malaria is a high-risk disease in pregnancy. WHO recommends that pregnant women do *not* travel to areas with Chloroquine-resistant malaria. None of the more effective antimalarial drugs is completely safe in pregnancy.

Traveller's diarrhoea can quickly lead to dehydration and result in inadequate blood flow to the placenta. Many of the drugs used to treat various diarrhoea bugs are not recommended in pregnancy. Azithromycin is considered safe.

Although not much is known about the possible adverse effects of altitude on a developing foetus, many authorities recommend not travelling above 4000m while pregnant.

In the urban areas of Bhutan, supplies of sanitary products are readily available. Birth-control options may be limited so bring adequate supplies of your own form of contraception. Heat, humidity and antibiotics can all contribute to thrush. Treatment is with antifungal creams and pessaries such as Clotrimazole. A practical alternative is a single tablet of Fluconazole (Diflucan). Urinary tract infections can be precipitated by dehydration or long bus journeys without toilet stops; bring suitable antibiotics.

# Language

## CONTENTS

Pronunciation 275
Conversation & Essentials 276
Directions & Transport 276
Health & Emergencies 276
Numbers 276
Shopping & Services 277
Time & Date 277
Trekking & Country Life 277

The official language of Bhutan is Dzongkha. While Dzongkha uses the same 'Ucen script as Tibetan – and the two languages are closely related – Dzongkha is sufficiently different that Tibetans cannot understand it. English is the medium of instruction in schools, so most educated people can speak it fluently. There are English signboards, books and menus throughout the country. Road signs and government documents are all written in both English and Dzongkha. The national newspaper, *Kuensel*, is published in three languages: English, Dzongkha and Nepali. In the monastic schools Choekey, the classical Tibetan language, is taught.

In eastern Bhutan most people speak Sharchop (meaning 'language of the east'), which is totally different from Dzongkha. In the south, most people speak Nepali. As a result of the isolation of many parts of the country, a number of languages other than Dzongkha and Sharchop survive. Some are so different that people from different parts of the country can't understand each other. Bumthangkha is a language of the Bumthang region, and it's common for regional minorities have their own language. Other tongues in Bhutan's Tower of Babel are Khengkha from Zhamgang, Kurtoep from Lhuentshe, Mangdep from Trongsa and Dzala from Trashi Yangtse.

The Dzongkha Development Commission has established a system for transliterating Dzongkha into Roman script. This official system uses three accent marks: the apostrophe to represent a high tone (eg *'ne*) or a 'soft' consonant (eg **g'**); a circumflex accent (eg **ê**) to represent long vowels; and a diaeresis (eg **ö**), which alters pronunciation in different ways, depending on the vowel (see Vowels, below). The system also attempts to represent sounds in Dzongkha that don't occur in English, such as retroflex and aspirated consonants. In this language guide a simplified system is used, with the primary aim being ease of communication at the risk of imperfect pronunciation. In the rest of this book, no accent marks are used in the Romanisations.

## PRONUNCIATION
### Vowels

| | |
|---|---|
| **a** | as in 'father' |
| **ä** | as the 'a' in 'hat' |
| **e** | as the 'ey' in 'hey' |
| **i** | as in 'hit' |
| **o** | as in 'go' |
| **ö** | as the 'ir' in 'dirt' (without the 'r' sound) |
| **u** | as in 'jute' |
| **ü** | like saying 'i' with the lips stretched back |

### Consonants

Most consonants in Roman Dzongkha are pronounced as in English. The following list covers letters and sounds that might prove troublesome.

An 'h' after the consonants **c, d, g, l, p** and **t** indicates that they are 'aspirated' (released with a slight puff of air) – listen to the 'p' sounds in 'pip'; the first is aspirated, the second is not. While getting aspiration wrong can have a direct impact on the meaning, it shouldn't be a problem with the words and phrases in this guide.

| | |
|---|---|
| **c** | as the 'ch' in 'church' |
| **ng** | as in 'sing'; practise using the 'ng' sound at the beginning of a word, eg *ngawang* (a name) |
| **sh** | as in 'ship' |
| **t, th** | 'dental' consonants, pronounced with the tongue tip against the teeth |
| **zh** | as the 's' in 'measure' |

LANGUAGE

## CONVERSATION & ESSENTIALS

| | |
|---|---|
| Hello. | *kuzuzangbo la* |
| Goodbye. | |
| (person leaving) | *läzhimbe jön* |
| (person staying) | *läzhimbe zhü* |
| Good luck. | *trashi dele* |
| Thank you. | *kadriche* |
| Yes. | *ing/yö* |
| No. | *mê* |
| Maybe. | *im ong* |
| (Hello) How are you? | *chö gadebe yö?* |
| I'm fine. | *nga läzhimbe ra yö* |
| Where are you going? | *chö gâti jou mo?* |
| What's your name? | *chö meng gaci mo?* |
| My name is ... | *ngê meng ... ing* |
| Where are you from? | *chö gâti lä mo?* |
| I'm from ... | *nga ... lä ing* |
| I'm staying at ... | *nga ... döp ing* |
| What is this? | *di gaci mo?* |
| It's cold today. | *dari jâm-mä* |
| It's raining. | *châp cap dowä* |
| I know. | *nga shê* |
| I don't know. | *nga mi shê* |
| Can I take a photo? | *pâ tabney chokar la?* |
| May I take your photo? | *chögi pâ ci tapge mä?* |
| That's OK. | *di tupbä* |

| | |
|---|---|
| mother | *ama* |
| father | *apa* |
| daughter | *bum* |
| son | *bu* |
| elder sister | *azhim* |
| younger sister | *num/sïm* |
| elder brother | *phôgem* |
| younger brother | *nucu* |
| friend | *totsha/châro* |

| | |
|---|---|
| happy | *gatokto* |
| enough | *tupbä/lâmmä* |
| cheap | *khetokto* |
| expensive | *gong bôm* |
| big | *bôm* |
| small | *chungku* |
| clean | *tsangtokto* |
| dirty | *khamlôsisi* |
| good | *läzhim* |
| not good | *läzhim mindu* |
| heavy | *jice* |
| this | *di* |
| that | *aphidi* |
| mine | *ngêgi* |

| | |
|---|---|
| yours | *chögi* |
| his/hers | *khogi/mogi* |

## DIRECTIONS & TRANSPORT

| | |
|---|---|
| What time does the bus leave? | *drülkhor chutshö gademci kha jou inna?* |
| I want to get off here. | *nga nâ dögobe* |
| Is it near? | *bolokha in-na?* |
| Is it far? | *tha ringsa in-na?* |
| Go straight ahead. | *thrangdi song* |

| | |
|---|---|
| left | *öm* |
| right | *yäp* |
| here | *nâ/nâlu* |
| there | *phâ/phâlu* |
| where | *gâti* |
| which | *gade* |
| in front of | *dongkha* |
| next to | *bolokha* |
| behind | *japkha* |
| opposite | *dongko/dongte* |
| north | *bjang* |
| south | *lho* |
| east | *shâ* |
| west | *nup* |

## HEALTH & EMERGENCIES

| | |
|---|---|
| I'm ill. | *nga nau mä* |
| I feel nauseous. | *nga cûni zum beu mä* |
| I feel weak. | *nga thangchep mä* |
| I keep vomiting. | *nga cûp cûsara döp mä* |
| I feel dizzy. | *nga guyu khôu mä* |
| I'm having trouble breathing. | *nga bung tang mit shubä* |
| doctor | *drungtsho* |
| fever | *jangshu* |
| pain | *nazu* |

## NUMBERS

| | |
|---|---|
| 1 | *ci* |
| 2 | *nyî* |
| 3 | *sum* |
| 4 | *zhi* |
| 5 | *nga* |
| 6 | *drû* |
| 7 | *dün* |
| 8 | *gä* |
| 9 | *gu* |
| 10 | *cuthâm* |
| 11 | *cûci* |
| 12 | *cunyî* |
| 13 | *cûsu* |
| 14 | *cüzhi* |
| 15 | *cänga* |

| | |
|---|---|
| 16 | *cùdru* |
| 17 | *cupdü* |
| 18 | *côpgä* |
| 19 | *cügu* |
| 20 | *nyishu/khächi* |
| 25 | *nyishu tsanga* |
| 30 | *sumcu or khä pcheda nyî* |
| 40 | *zhipcu/khänyî* |
| 50 | *ngapcu or khä pcheda sum* |
| 60 | *drukcu/khäsum* |
| 70 | *düncu or khä pcheda zhi* |
| 80 | *gepcu/khäzhi* |
| 90 | *gupcu or khä pcheda nga* |
| 100 | *cikja/khänga* |
| 1000 | *ciktong or tongthra ci* |
| 10,000 | *cikthri* |
| 100,000 | *cikbum/bum* |
| 1,000,000 | *saya ci* |

## SHOPPING & SERVICES

The word *khang* means building; in many cases it's only necessary to add the kind of building.

| | |
|---|---|
| **Where is a ...?** | *... gâti mo?* |
| **bank** | *ngükha* |
| **book shop** | *pekha* |
| **cinema** | *loknyen* |
| **hospital** | *menkha* |
| **market** | *throm* |
| **monastery** | *goemba* |
| **police station** | *thrimsung gakpi mâkha* |
| **post office** | *dremkha* |
| **public telephone** | *manggi jüthrin tangsi* |
| **shop** | *tshongkha* |
| **temple** | *lhakhang* |
| **toilet** | *chapsa* |

| | |
|---|---|
| **Where is the toilet?** | *chapsa gâti in-na?* |
| **How far is the ...?** | *... gadeci tha ringsa mo?* |
| **I want to see ...** | *nga ... tagobe* |
| **I'm looking for ...** | *nga ... tau ing* |
| **What time does it open?** | *chutshö gademci lu go pchiu mo?* |
| **What time does it close?** | *chutshö gademci lu go dam mo?* |
| **Is it still open?** | *datoya pchidi ong ga?* |
| **What is this?** | *di gaci mo?* |
| **I want to change money.** | *nga tiru sôgobä* |

Bargaining is not a Bhutanese tradition, but if you are buying Bhutanese handicrafts at the weekend market, you might be able to lower the price a bit.

| | |
|---|---|
| **How much is it?** | *dilu gadeci mo?* |
| **That's too much.** | *gong bôm mä* |
| **I'll give you no more than ...** | *ngâgi ... anemci lä trö mitshube* |
| **What's your best price?** | *gong gademcibe bjinni?* |

## TIME & DATE

| | |
|---|---|
| **What is the time?** | *chutshö gademci mo?* |
| **Five o'clock.** | *chutshö nga* |
| **today** | *dari* |
| **tomorrow** | *nâba* |
| **day after tomorrow** | *nâtshe* |
| **yesterday** | *khatsha* |
| **sometime** | *retshe kap* |
| **morning** | *drôba* |
| **afternoon** | *pchiru* |
| **day** | *nylm, za* |
| **night** | *numu* |

| | |
|---|---|
| **Sunday** | *za dau* |
| **Monday** | *za mìma* |
| **Tuesday** | *za lhap* |
| **Wednesday** | *za phup* |
| **Thursday** | *za pâsa* |
| **Friday** | *za pêm* |
| **Saturday** | *za nyim* |

## TREKKING & COUNTRY LIFE

| | |
|---|---|
| **Which trail goes to ...?** | *... josi lam gâti mo?* |
| **Is the trail steep?** | *lam zâdra yö-ga?* |
| **Where is my tent?** | *ngê gû di gâti in-na?* |
| **What's the name of this village?** | *Ani ügi meng gaci zeu mo?* |

| | |
|---|---|
| **house** | *chim* |
| **steep uphill** | *khagen gâdra* |
| **steep downhill** | *lam khamâ zâdra* |
| **tired** | *udû/thangche* |
| **cold (weather)** | *sîtraktra* |
| **warm (weather)** | *drotokto/tshatokto* |
| **alpine hut** | *bjobi gâ* |
| **alpine pasture** | *la nogi tsamjo* |
| **bridge** | *zam* |
| **hills** | *ri* |
| **lake** | *tsho* |
| **mountain** | *gangri* |
| **mountain pass** | *la* |
| **mule track** | *ta lam* |
| **plain or meadow** | *thang* |
| **prayer flag** | *dâshi* |
| **river** | *chhu/tsangchhu* |
| **stone carved with prayers** | *dogi mani* |

| trail | lam/kanglam |
| village | ü |

## Animals & Crops

| bird, chicken | bja |
| cow | ba |
| dog | rochi/chi |
| horse | ta |
| pig | phap |

| water buffalo | mahe |
| yak (male/female) | yâ/jim |
| barley | nâ |
| buckwheat | bjô |
| corn (maize) | gäza/gesasip |
| millet | membja |
| standing rice | bjâ |
| husked rice | chum |
| wheat | kâ |

# Glossary

**ABTO** – Association of Bhutanese Tour Operators
**anim** – Buddhist nun
**anim goemba** – nunnery
**arra** – home-made spirit distilled from barley, wheat or rice
**ashi** – title for a queen or lady of aristocracy
**atsara** – masked clown that badgers the crowd at a tsechu

**bangchung** – round bamboo basket with a tight-fitting cover
**bey-yul** – Hidden land of the Himalaya and a Buddhist refuge in times of trouble
**BHU** – Basic Health Unit
**bodhisattva** – a being who has the capacity of gaining Buddhahood in this life, but who refuses it in order to be reincarnated in the world to help other beings
**Bon** – ancient, pre-Buddhist, animistic religion of Tibet; its practitioners are called Bon-po
**Brokpa** – minority group in eastern Bhutan
**BTCL** – Bhutan Tourism Corporation Limited
**bukhari** – wood-burning stove
**bumpa** – vase, usually used to contain holy water in *goembas*

**cairn** – pile of stones marking a trail or pass
**carom** – a game similar to snooker or pool played on a small wooden board using checkers instead of billiard balls
**cham** – dance
**chang** – north
**chapati** – flat unleavened bread
**chhang** – beer made from rice, corn or millet, pronounced 'chung'
**chhu** – river, also water
**chilip** – foreigner
**chimi** – member of the National Assembly
**Choekey** – classical Tibetan (the language of religion)
**choesham** – altar or shrine room
**choesum** – chapel
**chorten** – stone Buddhist monument, often containing relics
**chugo** – hard, dried yak cheese

**dal** – lentil soup
**Dantak** – Indian Border Roads Task Force
**dasho** – honorary title conferred by the king
**datho** – astrological calendar
**datse** – traditional archery
**deb raja** – British term for the *desi* during the period 1652–1907

**desi** – secular ruler of Bhutan
**dharma** – Buddhist teachings
**dharma raja** – British name for the Zhabdrung, the religious ruler, during period 1652–1907
**dochey** – inner courtyard of a *dzong*
**dotsho** – hot-stone bath
**doma** – betel nut, also known by its Indian name, *paan*
**dorji** – a stylised thunderbolt used in rituals; *vajra* in Sanskrit
**DOT** – Department of Tourism
**drak** – cave or hermitage
**dratshang** – central monk body
**driglam chhoesum** – code of etiquette
**driglam namzha** – traditional values and etiquette
**drubda** – meditation centre for monks
**Druk Gyalpo** – the king of Bhutan
**Drukpa Kagyu** – the official religion of Bhutan, a school of tantric *Mahayana* Buddhism
**drungkhag** – subdistrict
**dukhang** – assembly hall in a *goemba;* also called a *tshokhang*
**dungpa** – head of a subdistrict
**dzong** – fort-monastery
**dzongdag** – district administrator
**Dzongkha** – national language of Bhutan
**dzongkhag** – district
**dzongpen** – old term for lord of the *dzong*

**gakpa** – police
**gangri** – snow mountain
**gewog** – block, the lowest administrative level
**gho** – traditional dress for men
**global positioning system (GPS)** – a device that calculates position and elevation by reading and decoding signals from satellites
**goemba** – a *Mahayana* Buddhist monastery
**goenkhang** – chapel devoted to protective and terrifying deities, usually *Mahakala*
**gomchen** – lay or married monk
**gorikha** – porch of a *lhakhang*, literally 'mouth of the door'
**GSI** – Geological Survey of India
**gup** – elected leader of a village
**Guru Rinpoche** – the common name of Padmasambhava, the founder of *Mahayana* Buddhism
**gyalpo** – ruler or king

**himal** – Sanskrit word for mountain

**IMTRAT** – Indian Military Training Team

**Je Khenpo** – Chief Abbot of Bhutan
**jogyig** – Bhutanese cursive script

**kabney** – scarf worn over the shoulder on formal occasions
**khandroma** – a female celestial being; dakini in Sanskrit
**khenpo** – abbot
**khonying** – archway chorten
**kira** – traditional dress for women
**kora** – circumambulation
**kuru** – a game played with large darts thrown 20m to a small target

**la** – mountain pass
**lam** – path or road
**lama** – *Mahayana* Buddhist teacher or priest
**lha** – god or deity
**lhakhang** – temple, literally 'god house'
**lhentshog** – commission
**lho** – south
**Lhotshampa** – southern Bhutanese people, mainly Nepali-speaking
**lopon** – Senior monk or teacher
**Losar** – Bhutanese and Tibetan New Year
**lu** – serpent deities, called *naga* in Sanskrit
**lyonpo** – government minister

**Mahakala** – Yeshe Goenpo, the guardian god of Bhutan, who manifests himself as a raven
**Mahayana** – school of Buddhism, literally 'great vehicle'
**mandala** – cosmic diagram; *kyilkhor* in *Dzongkha*
**mani stone** – stone carved with the Buddhist mantra *om mani peme hum*
**mantra** – prayer formula or chant
**momo** – a steamed or fried dumpling
**moraine** – ridge of rocks that a glacier pushed up along its edges (a medial moraine) or at its foot (a terminal moraine)

**nakey** – fiddlehead fern frond
**naktshang** – temple dedicated to warlord or protective deity, literally 'place of vows'
**NCCA** – National Commission for Cultural Affairs
**ney** – sacred site
**NGO** – nongovernment organisation
**ngultrum** – unit of Bhutanese currency
**nup** – west
**NWAB** – National Womens' Association of Bhutan
**Nyingma** – lineage of Himalayan Buddhism; its practitioners are Nyingmapa

**om mani peme hum** – sacred Buddhist mantra, roughly translates as 'hail to the jewel in the lotus'
**outreach clinic** – health posts in remote villages

**PCO** – Public Call Office
**penlop** – regional governor, literally lord-teacher
**phajo** – priest
**prayer flag** – long strips of cloth printed with prayers that are 'said' whenever the flag flaps in the wind
**prayer wheel** – cylindrical wheel inscribed with, and containing, prayers
**PWD** – Public Works Department

**rabdey** – district monk body
**rachu** – shoulder cloth worn by women on formal occasions
**RBA** – Royal Bhutan Army
**RBG** – Royal Body Guard
**RBP** – Royal Bhutan Police
**rigney** – name used for a school for traditional studies
**rinpoche** – reincarnate lama, usually the abbot of a *goemba*
**river left** – the left bank of a river when facing downstream
**river right** – the right bank of a river when facing downstream
**RSPN** – Royal Society for Protection of Nature

**SAARC** – South Asia Association for Regional Cooperation. This includes the seven countries of Bangladesh, Bhutan, India, Maldives, Nepal, Pakistan and Sri Lanka.
**Sakyamuni** – one name for Gautama Buddha, the Historical Buddha
**shar** – east
**shedra** – Buddhist college
**shing** – wood
**shunglam** – highway
**sonam** – good luck
**stupa** – hemispherical Buddhist structure from which the *chorten* evolved

**terma** – texts and artefacts hidden by *Guru Rinpoche*
**terton** – discoverer of *terma*
**thang** – plain
**thangka** – painted or embroidered religious picture
**thondrol** – huge *thangka* that is unfurled on special occasions, literally 'liberation on sight'
**thos** – a heap of stones representing the guardians of the four directions
**thukpa** – noodles, often served in a soup
**torma** – ritual cake made of *tsampa,* butter and sugar
**trulku** – a reincarnation; the spiritual head of a *goemba*
**Tsa-Wa-Sum** – Government, Country and King
**tsachhu** – hot spring
**tsampa** – barley flour, a staple food in hill villages
**tseri** – the practice of shifting cultivation
**tshamkhang** – small meditation quarters
**tsha-tsha** – small images moulded in clay
**tsho** – lake

**Tshogdu** – National Assembly
**tshokhang** – assembly hall in a *lhakhang*
**tsip** – lay monk

**UNCDF** – UN Capital Development Fund
**utse** – the central tower that houses the *lhakhang* in a *dzong*

**WWF** – World Wide Fund for Nature (known as the World Wildlife Fund in North America)

**yak** – main beast of burden and form of cattle above 3000m elevation
**yathra** – strips of woven woollen cloth
**yeti** – the abominable snowman

**Zangto Pelri** – the celestial abode or paradise of *Guru Rinpoche*
**Zhabdrung, the** – title of the reincarnations of the Zhabdrung Ngawang Namgyal

# Behind the Scenes

## THIS BOOK

The 1st and 2nd editions of Bhutan were researched and written by Stan Armington. This 3rd edition was researched and written by Lindsay Brown and Bradley Mayhew, and Stan updated the Trekking chapter. Richard Whitecross wrote the Bhuddism in Bhutan and The Culture chapters. This guidebook was commissioned in Lonely Planet's Melbourne office, and produced by the following:

**Commissioning Editors** Janine Eberle, Lucy Monie, Sam Trafford
**Coordinating Editor** Sarah Stewart
**Coordinating Cartographer** Jolyon Philcox
**Coordinating Layout Designer** Katie Thuy Bui
**Senior Editor** Helen Christinis
**Managing Cartographer** Shahara Ahmed
**Assisting Editor** Melissa Faulkner
**Assisting Cartographers** Joshua Geoghegan, Amanda Sierp
**Layout Designer** Jacqui Saunders
**Cover Designer** Rebecca Dandens
**Project Manager** Rachel Imeson
**Language Content Coordinator** Quentin Frayne

**Thanks to** Carol Chandler, Sin Choo, Sally Darmody, Eoin Dunlevy, Nicole Hansen, Michelle Lewis, Kate McDonald, Lyahna Spencer, Celia Wood

## THANKS
### LINDSAY BROWN

I am very grateful for the assistance, guidance and wisdom of Lonely Planet author and trekking guru Stan Armington who introduced me, along with countless others, to the magical Himalaya all those years ago and who blazed the trail with the first two editions of this title.

It was wonderful to receive so much enthusiastic support from so many people in Bhutan. The following people provided invaluable information, advice and assistance with great grace and patience: Rinzin Ongdra Wangchuk, Sonam Wangmo and Robin Pradhan of Yu Druk Tours and Treks; Dasho Lhatu Wangchuk, Thuji Dorji Nadik and Megan Ritchie at the Department of Tourism; Foreign Secretary Yeshey Dorji and Pema Choden at the Foreign Ministry; Wangchuk Wangdi of Thunder Dragon Treks; Tshering Tashi of JoJo's Adventure Tours; Sonam Tobgay of Lotus Adventures; Ashi Khendum Dorji of Chuundu Travels and Tours; and Dasho Paljor J Dorji of Bara Lynka Tours and Travels. Also I thank Kinley Dorji of Kuensel and Siok Sian Pek-Dorji for sharing a fraction of their vast knowledge, and Chophel Dayang (WWF Bhutan), Karma Gelay (Druk Heritage Consultancy), Tiger Sangay (Nature Conservation Program), Dilu Giri, Anuj Chettri, Robin Joshi, Tsering Yonten, Kesang Dorji and Michelle Hogan, for their specialist knowledge and great tips.

Last but not least, thanks to legendary fellow authors Bradley Mayhew, Stan, and Buddhism expert Dr Richard Whitecross; LP commissioning editors Marg, Lucy and Sam; and Jenny, Pat and Sinead at home.

### BRADLEY MAYHEW

My thanks to Chimmy at Bae-yul Excursions (www .baeyul.com.bt) who arranged my trip to Bhutan,

---

### THE LONELY PLANET STORY

The story begins with a classic travel adventure: Tony and Maureen Wheeler's 1972 journey across Europe and Asia to Australia. There was no useful information about the overland trail then, so Tony and Maureen published the first Lonely Planet guidebook to meet a growing need.

From a kitchen table, Lonely Planet has grown to become the largest independent travel publisher in the world, with offices in Melbourne (Australia), Oakland (USA) and London (UK). Today Lonely Planet guidebooks cover the globe. There is an ever-growing list of books and information in a variety of media. Some things haven't changed. The main aim is still to make it possible for adventurous travellers to get out there – to explore and better understand the world.

At Lonely Planet we believe travellers can make a positive contribution to the countries they visit – if they respect their host communities and spend their money wisely. Every year 5% of company profit is donated to charities around the world.

and to Daza Jigme (www.tourbhutantravel.com), who was a truly superb guide, from the Haa valley all the way to Samdrup Jongkhar. Thanks to all the team at Bae-yul, including drivers Kinley and Tashi, and chef extraordinaire Tashi.

Special thanks to Stan Armington, whose excellent original text I was merely updating and who offered help and advice throughout research. Cheers to coordinating author Lindsay, with whom it is always a pleasure to work. Thanks to Rebecca Chau for helping me fit *Bhutan* around China work commitments.

In Bhutan thanks to Nanda Ritsma, Megan Ritchie and Mr Thuji Dorji at the Department of Tourism. Tsering Chuki helped out with information on ecotourism in Phobjikha.

Most of all thanks to Kelli who did without me for three long months on this trip.

### RICHARD W WHITECROSS

I would like to thank Alan Masson, Shiona Whitecross and my mother, the late Margaret Whitecross, for their unfailing support. Michael Aris encouraged me to pursue my studies, and I received invaluable advice from Michael Rutland. Françoise Pommaret has been a peerless mentor and her research has been invaluable to me. Tim and Prue Sutton, Chris Faris and Sue Robertson provided friendship and an audience. Particular thanks to the Permanent Mission of the Kingdom of Bhutan, Geneva, and to the Royal Court of Justice. I cannot thank all my Bhutanese friends individually, so I offer my thanks to all who know

me and have assisted me in various ways. To you all, I offer my heartfelt thanks – *kadinche*.

## OUR READERS

Many thanks to the travellers who used the last edition and wrote to us with helpful hints, useful advice and interesting anecdotes:

**B** Peter & Rosemary Balmford, Paul Barnetson, Inger-Anne Becker Wold, Gaelle Bellec, Megan Berkle, David Birch **C** Amanda Cheng, Andrea Cohen, Garth Coverdale **D** Gun Dalmia, Alex & Kate Davis, Koen de Boeck, Axel de la Forest Divonne, Sergio de Souza, Lucia Alvarez de Toledo, Bill Devanney **E** Mel Ehlers **F** Krzysztof Fedorowicz, Carolynn & Patrick Fischer **G** Arne Georgzen, Maurizio Giuliano **H** Johan Haentjens, Wally Hampton, Dilys Harlow, Barbie Hawkins, Bill & Lynda Hohenboken, Mark Huntington, Antonio Hyder **I** Takashi Iwakiri **K** Lang Kidby **L** Bavo Lauwaert, Alessandro Liverani, Gerd Loacker **M** Andrew & Christine McPherson, Tobias Micke, Susan Morin **N** Patrick Naish **P** Dawn Penso, Leonardo Pereira **R** Pedro Ribeiro **S** Monica Schmitz-Salue **T** Janette Tollis, Bettina Tondury **U** Brian Underwood **V** Paulien van der Linden, Elien van Dille, Peter van't Westeinde, Narayan Vinodh

## ACKNOWLEDGMENTS

Many thanks to the following for the use of their content:

Quotes from *Political Missions to Bootan* © Eden, Pemberton and Baboo, 2002. Used by permission of Asian Educational Services.

Quote from *The Divine Madman: The Life and Songs of Drukpa Kunley*, trans., Rider & Co., London, 1982 and Dawn Horse Press, U.S.A. and Pilgrim's Publishing, Kathmandu 2000.

# Index

## A

acclimatisation 246, 272
accommodation 125-6, 242-3, *see also individual locations*
hotels 15, 242-3
Thimphu 108-10
activities 243-5, *see also individual activities*
Acute Mountain Sickness 272-3
agriculture 24, 45
air travel 257-60
airlines 257-9
airports 257-9
climate change 258
Himalayan scenery 260
altitude 246, 272
ambulance, *see inside front cover*
animals 85-8, *see also individual animals*
animism 25, 26
archery 62, 113, **139**
Changlimithang Stadium & Archery Ground 105
architecture 78-82
phalluses 78, 136, **144**
area codes 254, *see also inside front cover*
Aris, Michael 17, 27, 36
arts 54-62, *see also handicrafts, weaving*
Assam Duars 34-5, 38-9, 84
astrology 42, 249
ATMs 250
Autsho 187

## B

bamboo 161
bargaining 253
bars
Thimphu 112
Barshong 220-1
basketball 62
bathrooms 254
baths, hot-stone 243
bears 86-7
beer 171
Bengal Duars 38-9, 84
bharals, *see blue sheep*
Bhutanese calendar 248, 249

Bhutan Souvenir Production Training Centre 147
bicycle travel, *see cycling*
birds 87-8
bird-watching 184, 230, 243-4
black-necked cranes 87, 88, 152, 153, 154, 196
blue poppies 89
blue sheep 85, 219, 223, 225, 239
bodhisattvas 75-6
Bodo groups 43
Bogle, George 33, 34, 36
Bomdeling Wildlife Sanctuary 91, 196
Bon 25, 26
Bondey 131-2
books 17-18, *see also literature*
Aris, Michael 17, 27 36
Dowman, Keith 136
Lumley, Joanna 18
National Library 104-5
Pommaret, Françoise 45, 58, 74
sacred texts 28-9, 177, 240
border crossings 257, 261-2
customs & immigration checks 197-8
Gelephu 180
Indian separatist movement 43, 90
Phuentsholing 156
Samdrup Jongkhar 181, 198
botanical gardens
Serbithang Royal Botanical Garden 116
bridges 29, 131, 132
British, the
Assam Duars 34-5, 38-9, 84
Bengal Duars 38-9, 84
Bogle, George 33, 34, 36
East India Company 33, 34
Eden, Ashley 18, 36-8
explorers 18, 36-8, 201
treaty of Punakha 39
Ronaldshay, Earl of 18, 33, 34, 121
Turner, Samuel 36
White, John Claude 18, 37, 46
Brokpa 193
Buddha, the 63-4, 75
manifestations of 48
Buddhism 26, *see also deities, Guru Rinpoche, tsechus*
concepts 64-7

domestic rituals 73-4
eight manifestations 28-9, 61
Eight-Fold Path 66
Four Mind Turnings 67
Four Noble Truths 64
history 27-9, 63-4
important figures 75-7
introduction to Bhutan 27-9
in Bhutan 45, 68, 72-3
leaders 27-9
Nyingmapa 68-9, 166, 169
prayer flags 65, 79, **139**
schools 67-9
Wheel of Life 46, 191, **144**
*bukhari* 243
Buli Lhakhang 166
Bumthang Dzongkhag 165-80, **142**
hiking 170
itineraries 21
tsechu 167
Bumthang valley 165-80, **142**
Bunakha 155
business hours 245, *see also Inside front cover*
bus travel 265

## C

Cabral, Father 36
Cacella, Father 36
calendar, Bhutanese 248, 249
cafés 112, *see also food*
camping 196, 199, 210
carpets 158
car travel 265
roads 246-7
central Bhutan 160-80, **162**
Chakhar Lhakhang 173
Chakkar 167-71, **168**
Chamgang 216
Chana Dorje 76
Changangkha Lhakhang 106
Changlimithang Stadium & Archery Ground 105
Chazam 190
Chebisa 222-3
Cheli La 131, 133
Chendebji Chorten 161-2
Chenresig 75-6, 147, 191
Cheri Goemba 115-16, **7**
Chhoeten Lhakhang 124

**INDEX**

Chhukha 155
Chhukha Dzongkhag 155-9
Chhundu Lhakang 134
Chhuzom 131-2, 134
children, travel with 15, 245
chillies 94
Chimi Lhakhang 145
Chirang Dzongkhag 159
Chokhor valley 168, 171-7, **172**
   itineraries 21
Chora 221
Chorten Karpo 229-30
Chorten Kora 195
chortens 82
   Chendebji Chorten 161-2
   Chorten Lhakhang 164
   Chorten Karpo 229-30
   Chorten Kora 195
   Khamsum Yuelley Namgyal
      Chorten 148
   National Memorial Chorten 104, 7
cinema, see film
climate 13-14, 200-1, 245-6, **245**
   change 258
conservation 24, 88, 89-90, 209 see
   also environmental issues
consulates 247
Cooch Behar 33, 35
costs 15-17
courses 246
cranes, black-necked 87, 88, 152, 153,
   154, 196
credit cards 250
crocodiles 158
culture 45-62
customs regulations 197-8, 246
cycling 107, 244, 264-5

**D**
Dagana Dzongkhag 159
dakinis 166, 175
Dalai Lama 31
Dalay Goemba 145
Damji 227
dance 60-2, **141**, see also tsechus
dangers 246-7
Darkila 187
Dechen Chholing Goemba 179
Dechen Phodrang 106
Dechenphu Lhakhang 115
deer 85

**000** Map pages
**000** Photograph pages

deities
   Chenresig 75-6, 147, 191
   protective 71, 72, 76-7
   Shelging Kharpo 173
delogs 58, 74
democratic constitution 41
Demoness, the 129
Deothang 197
Deothang Goemba 174
disabled travellers 254-5
discounts 15-16
Divine Madman, the, see Kunley,
   Lama Drukpa
Dochu La 135
Dodina 221
dogs 101, 246-7
Dolam Kencho 221
doma 46, 89, 95-6
Domkhar Trashi Chholing Dzong 166
dotsho 243
Drametse Goemba 189
driglam namzha 42-3, 50, 52
drinks 95
   beer 171
   water 272
driving 246-7, 265
driving licenses 265
Drolay Goemba 117
Drubthob Goemba 106
Drukgyel Dzong 130-1, 216-17
Drukpa Kagyu lineage 27-9
Druk Choeding 124
Duer Tsachhu 233
Duksum 194
Dumtse Lhakhang 124-5
Dungdung Nyels 152
Dungkhar 188
dzoe 74
Dzongkha 50, 52, 275-8
dzongs 79-80
   Domkhar Trashi Chholing 166
   Drukgyel 130-1
   Jakar 168-9
   Lhuentse 187
   Mongar 186
   Paro (Rinpung) 122-3
   Punakha 146-7, **144**
   Shongar 184-5
   Simtokha 116-18
   Singye 188
   Ta Dzong 164
   Trashi Chhoe 101-3, **6**, **139**
   Trashi Thongmoen 227
   Trashigang 190-1
   Trongsa 163, 164, **144**

Wangchulo 133
Wangdichholing 169
Wangdue Phodrang 149-50
Yugyel 222

**E**
earthquake of 1897 26, 34, 41
eastern Bhutan 181-98, **182-3**
   itineraries 22
East India Company 33, 34
economy 47
   gross national happiness 41
   hydroelectricity 24, 40
Eden, Ashley 18, 36-8
education 47
Eight-Fold Path 66
eight manifestations of Guru Rinpoche
   28-9, 61
electricity 243
elephants 86
email services 249
embassies 247
emergencies, see also inside front
   cover
   trekking 211-12
environmental issues 92-3
   climate change 258
   conservation 24, 88, 89-90, 209
   endangered species 86, 88
   global warming 92
   poaching 93
etiquette 50-1
   driglam namzha 42-3, 52
   food 95-6
   names & titles 49
   photography 251
   temple 50
Eundu Chholing 165
exchange rates, see inside front cover
explorers 18, 36-8, 201
   Bogle, George 33, 34, 36
   Eden, Ashley 18, 36-8
   Ronaldshay, Earl of 18, 33
   Turner, Samuel 36
   White, John Claude 18, 37, 46

**F**
fax services 254
festivals 14, 23, 247-8, see also
   tsechus
   Black-Necked Crane festival 154
   Jampa Lhakhang drup 173
   Punakha domchoe 147
   Shingkhar Romney 179
   Ura yakchoe 179

film 18, 59
  cinemas 113
fires
  campfires 210
  in dzongs 26, 146
fishing 244
five-year plan 40
flags, prayer 65, 79, **139**
Folk Heritage Museum 104
food 94-5, 247-8
  cafés 112
  *doma* 46, 89, 95-6
  etiquette 95-6
  hygiene 272
  restaurants 111
  self-catering 112
  trekking 202
  vegetarian travellers 95
football 62, 113
foreign exchange 250
Four Friends 57
Four Mind Turnings 67
Four Noble Truths 64
fungus 86, 90

**G**

Gampo, King Songtsen 129, 172, 235
  Kyichu Lhakhang 127-8, 5
Gangchhenta 225
Gangkhar Puensum 135
Gangla Karchung La 238
Gangte 152
Gangte Goemba 152-3
Gasa 159, 227
Gasa Dzongkhag 159
Gasa *tsachhu* 228
gay travellers 248
Gedu 156
Gelephu 180
geography 24, 83-5, *see also* glacial
  lakes, mountains
Geynikha 215
Geynizampa 215
*ghos* 49, 113-14, 158
glacial lakes 92, 238, 239
gods, *see* deities
goembas 80-2, *see also* chortens,
  dzongs, lhakhangs, temples
  Cheri 115-16, 7
  Dalay 145
  Dechen Chholing 179
  Deothang 174
  Drametse 189
  Drolay 117
  Drubthob 106

Gangte 152-3
Kharbandi 156
Khuruthang 145
Kunzangdrak 178
Lamey 169
Lungchuzekha 117
Namkhe Nyingpo 169
Nimalung 167
Phajoding 117
Prakhar 167
Taktshang 128-30, 5
Talakha 117
Talo 145
Tamshing 176
Tango 115-16
Thadranang 117
Thangbi 174
Tharpaling 166
Trashigang 117
Wangditse 117
Yongla 198
golf 62, 107, 244-5
*gomchen* 73, 174, 189
Gom Kora 193-4
government 24, 31-2
  democracy 41
  five-year plan 40
  gross national happiness 41
  refugees 42-4
Goyul 223
gross national happiness 41
Guardians of the Four
  Directions 80
guides, trekking 199, 201
Gur 215
Guru Rinpoche 77
  arrival in Bhutan 26-7
  eight manifestations of 28-9
  footprints of 166, 178
  Kurjey Lhakhang 173, 5
  meditation sites 174, 194, 188,
    214
  predictions of146
  Taktshang Goemba 128-30, 5
  tsechus in honour of 60, 61, 174
Gyalpo, Thangtong 131, 132, 190

**H**

Haa 133-4
Haa Dzongkhag 133-4
handicrafts
  Sangay Arts & Crafts 167
  shopping 252-3
  Thimphu 114
  Trashigang 192

weaving 188, 193, **137**
  *yathra* 58, 166, 167
health 267-74
  Acute Mountain Sickness 272-3
  books 269
  high altitude 272-3
  insurance 267
  internet resources 268-9
  malaria 270-1
  medical services 269
  rabies 271
  snow blindness 211
  typhoid 271
  vaccinations 267-8
  water 272
Henke 152
hiking 153, *see also* trekking,
  walking
Himalayas 83-5, 246
  glacial lakes 92, 238, 239
Hinduism 74
history 25-44, **25**
  Buddhism 27-9, 63-4
hitching 265-6
holidays 14, 248
horses 201-2
hot-stone baths 243
hotels 15, 242-3
hot springs 228, 233
human rights 42-4
hydroelectricity 24, 40

**I**

immigrants 43-4
India
  consulate offices 247
  Jaigaon 156
  travel to/from 155, 255, 261-2
Indian nationals 16, 261
  visas 255
insurance 248-9, 267
internet access 53, 249
internet resources 18
  health 268-9
itineraries 19-23, 100

**J**

Jaigaon 156
Jakar 167-71, **168**
Jakar Dzong 168-9
Jampey Lhakhang 172-3
Jangchhu Lakha 212-13
Jangkhaka 134
Jangothang 218-19
Jetshaphu village 131

Jigme Singye Wangchuck National Park 152
Jili Dzong 212
Jimilang Tsho 213-14
Jumja 156
Juneydrak 134

**K**
Kagyupa 69
karma 66
Kathmandu 260
kayaking 244-5
Khaine Lhakhang 235
Khaling Wildife Santuary 91
Khamsum Yuelley Namgyal Chorten 148
*khandromas* 166, 175, 176
Kharbandi Goemba 156
Kharibje 132
Khoma 188
Khuruthang 145-9, **146**
Khuruthang Goemba 145
Kila Nunnery 133
kings, *see individual kings*, royal family, Wangchuck, Jigme Singye
*kiras* 50-1, 113-14
Koina 226
Konchogsum Lhakhang 176
Kori La 188-9
Kuenga Rabten 165
Kulha Gangri 135
Kunley, Lama Drukpa 77, 87, 136
Kunzangdrak Goemba 178
Kuri Zampa 184-5
Kurjey Lhakhang 173-4, 5
Kurtoe, *see* Lhuentse
Kyichu Lhakhang 127-8, 5, *see also* Kunley, Lama Drukpa

**L**
Labatamba 215
Lamey Goemba 169
languages 52-3, 275-8
    Dzongkha 50, 52, 275-8
    Henke 152
    Layap 226
    Lhotshampa 42-4, 52-3
    Nepali 42-4, 52-3
    Sharchop 181
langurs 85, 86
Laya 159, 225, 226

Layap 226
legal matters 249
leopards, snow 86
lesbian travellers 248
lhakhangs 80-2, *see also* chortens, dzongs, goembas, temples
    Buli 166
    Chakhar 173
    Changangkha 106
    Chhoeten 124
    Chhundu 134
    Chimi 145
    Dechenphu 115
    Dumtse 124-5
    Jampey 172-3
    Khaine 235
    Konchogsum 176
    Kurjey 173-4, 5
    Kyichu 127-8, 5
    Ngang 174-5
    Pema Sambhava 177
    Potala 162
    Sey 172
    Tang Rimochen 178
    Zangto Pelri (Kurjey Lhakhang) 174
    Zangto Pelri (Phuentsholing) 158
    Zangto Pelri (Taktshang Goemba) 130
    Zangto Pelri (Thimphu) 106
    Zangto Pelri (Wamrong) 197
Lhedi 239
Lhotshampa 42-4, 52-3
Lhuentse 187-8
Lhuentse Dzong 187
Lhuentse Dzongkhag 186-8
Limithang 225
Lingpa, Pema 77
    burial 147
    Burning Lake 177
    chain-mail armour 176
    paintings by 176
    *terma* 166, 175
Lingzhi 159, 219-20, 222-3
literature 17-18, 58-9, *see also* books
Longchen Rabjampa 166
Lungchuzekha Goemba 117
*luso* 74, *see also* Buddhism, religion

**M**
Machig Labdrom 134
Mackey, Father William 196
*mani* walls 82
maps 98, 206, 249

markets
    Paro Sunday market 125
    Thimphu weekend market 103-4, **138**, **141**
Masang Gang 135
measures 243
media 53
medical services 100, 269, *see also* health
Membartsho 177
Menji 236
metric conversions, *see inside front cover*
*migois* 192, 193, *see also* yetis
Milarepa 69, 77
mobile phones 254
monasteries, *see also* dzongs, goembas, lhakhangs, temples
    Thowadrak Hermitage 178-9
money 15-17, 250-1, *see also inside front cover*
Mongar 185-6, **185**
Mongar Dzong 186
Mongar Dzongkhag 183-6
monkeys 85-6
monks 72-3
    *gomchen* 73, 174, 189
    processions 135
Motithang 106, 214
Motithang Takin Preserve 106
motorcycle travel 265
mountain biking 244
mountains 201
    Black Mountains 84, 90, 119
    Gangchhenta 225
    Gangkhar Puensum 83, 135
    Jhomolhari 83, 119, 219, 8
    Jichu Drakye 83
    Kulha Gangri 83, 135
    Masang Gang 135
museums
    Folk Heritage Museum 104
    National Museum 124
    National Textile Museum 105
    Ogyen Chholing Palace 178
    Ta Dzong 164
music 59-60, 114
    live 112-13
mythology
    dragons 27
    Four Friends 57

**N**
Nabji 180
Namgyal, Ngawang, *see* Zhabdrung, the

Namkhe Nyingpo Goemba 169
Narphung 197
National Institute for Zorig Chusum
    Thimphu 104, **137**
    Trashi Yangtse 195
National Institute of Traditional
    Medicine 105, *see also* traditional
    medicine
National Library 104-5
National Memorial Chorten 104, 7
National Museum 124
national parks **91**, *see also* wildlife
    sanctuaries & reserves
    Jigme Dorji 86, 90
    Jigme Singye Wangchuck 90,
        152
    Royal Manas 43, 85, 86, 90,
        160, 180
    Thrumshing La 91
National Textile Museum 105
Nepal
    travel to/from 255-6, 262
Nepali
    language 52-3
    speakers 42-4
newspapers 243
Ngang Lhakhang 174-5
Nimalung Goemba 167
Nyingmapa 68-9, 166, 169

**O**
Ogyen Chholing Palace 178, 232
opening hours 245, *see also inside
    front cover*

**P**
paan, 46, 89, 95-6
Padmasambhava 77, *see also*
    Rinpoche, Guru
painting 55, 56-7, see also *thangkas,
    thondrols*
    Four Friends 57
palaces
    Domkhar Trashi Chholing Dzong
        166
    Eundu Chholing 165
    Ogyen Chholing Palace 178
    Ugyen Pelri Palace 124
    Wangdichholing Dzong 169
pandas 86-7
Pangri Zampa 115
Panka 215
parks
    Serbithang Royal Botanical Garden
        116

Paro 122-32, **123**, **141**
    accommodation 125-6
    attractions 122-5
    entertainment 127
    food 126-7
    internet access 122
    itineraries 19-20
    shopping 127
    travel to/from 127
Paro Dzong 122-3
Paro Dzongkhag 121-32
    upper Paro valley 127-31, **128**,
        **140**
passports 257, *see also* travel
    permits
Pele La 151-2, 161-3
Pemagatshel Dzongkhal 198
Pema Sambhava Lhakhang 177
*penlop* of Trongsa 36, 161, 183
permits, *see also* travel permits
    Dungkhar 188
    Jampey Lhakhang 173
    Taktshang monastery 130
    temple 256
Phajo Drugom Zhigpo 70
Phajo Drukpa 70
Phajoding 214, **137**
Phajoding Goemba 117
phalluses 78, 136, **144**
Phibsoo Wildife Sanctuary 90
Phobjikha 228-9
Phobjikha valley 152-4, **143**
    accommodation 154
    cranes, black-necked 154
    hiking 153
    travel to/from 154
Phokpey 233, **142**
photography 251
Phuentsholing 156-9, **157**
    climate 245
planning 13-18, 208, *see also*
    permits
plants 88-9, *see also individual plants*
poaching 93
police services, *see inside front cover*
politics 24, *see also* government
Pommaret, Françoise 45, 58, 74
population 24, 51-2, 181
postage stamps 114, 253
postal services 252
Potala Lhakhang 162
potatoes 189
Prakhar Goemba 167
prayer flags 65, 79, **139**
prayer wheels 81, 106, 167, 231 7

Punakha 145-9
    *domchoe* 147
    floods 92
    treaty of 39
Punakha Dzong 146-7, **144**
Punakha Dzongkhag 134-49
    upper Punakha valley 147-8

**R**
Radak Natshang 150
radio 243
rafting 244-5
Rangjung 192-3
rebirth 66
refugees 42-4
religion 63-77, *see also* Buddhism
restaurants 111, *see also* food
rhododendrons 89, 91, 135, 184
*rigsar* 59-60
Rinchending 156
Rinchengang 151
Rinpoche, Guru 77
    arrival in Bhutan 26-7
    eight manifestations of 28-9
    footprints of166, 178
    Kurjey Lhakhang 173, 5
    meditation sites 174, 188, 194,
        214
    predictions of 146
    Taktshang Goemba 128-30, 5
    tsechus in honour of 60, 61, 174
Rinpung Dzong 122-3
rivers 84-5, 183
    Chhuzom 132
roads 246-7, 265
Robluthang 224
rock climbing 107
Rodang La 233-7
Rodophu 237
Ronaldshay, Earl of 18, 33, 34, 121
Royal Academy of Performing Arts
    106
royal family 164, 169, 172, 188, *see
    also* Wangchuck
Royal Manas National Park 43, 85, 86,
    90, 160, 180
Rukubji 161

**S**
SAARC building 105
sacred texts 28-9, 177, 240
Sakten Wildlife Sanctuary 91, 193
Sakyamuni 75, *see also* Buddha, the
Sakya Pandita 69
Sakyapa 69

Samchi Dzongkhag 159
Samdrup Jongkhar 198
Samdrup Jongkhar Dzongkhag 196-8
Samtse Dzongkhag 159
Sarpang Dzongkhag 180
self-catering 112
Sengor 184
separatist groups 43
Serbithang Royal Botanical Garden 116
Sey Lhakhang 172
Shakshepasa 224
Sharchop 181
Sharna Zampa 216-17
Shingkhar 179-80
Shodu 220
Shomuthang 224
Shongar Dzong 184-5
shopping 252-3
Simkotra Tsho 214
Simtokha 116-18
Simtokha Dzong 116-18
Sindhu Raja 173
Singye Dzong 188
snow blindness 211-2
snow leopards 86
snowlions 173
So-ba Rig pa 48, *see also* traditional medicine
soccer 62, 113
solo travellers 15, 253
sports 62
    archery 113, 139
    cycling 107, 244
    fishing 244
    football 62, 113
    golf 62, 107, 244
    kayaking 244-5
    rafting 244-5
    rock climbing 107
    soccer 62, 113
    swimming 107
springs 228, 233
Sunday market, Paro 125
swimming 107
Swiss Farm 171

**T**
Tabiting 153
Tahung 232

takins 87, 224
    Motithang Takin Preserve 106
Taktshang Goemba 128-30, 5
Talakha 216
Talakha Goemba 117
Talo Goemba 145
Talung 134
Tamshing Goemba 176-7
Tamshing Lhendup Chholing 176
Tang Rimochen Lhakhang 178
Tang valley 177-9
    itineraries 21
Tangmachu 187
Tango Goemba 115-16, 136
Tashila ropeway 151, 230
tashi tagye 64, 65, 66, 67, 68, 69
Tashithang 228
taxis 115, 266
telephone services 254
temples, *see also* chortens, dzongs, goembas, lhakhangs
    Dechen Phodrang 106
    Druk Choeding 124
    Gom Kora 193-4
    Kuenga Rabten 165
    Radak Natshang 150
*tendo* 74
Tenpa, Chhogyel Mingyur 32, 161, 183
Tenzin Drugyey 32
*terma* 28-9, 177, 240
*tertons, see* Lingpa, Pema
textiles 105, 252
Thadranang Goemba 117
Thangbi Goemba 174
*thangkas* 55, 57, 252
Thangthangka 217-18
Thanza 239
Tharpaling Goemba 166
theatre 60-2
Thimphu 97-118, 134-5, **99**, **102-3**, **115**, **138**
    accommodation 108-10
    attractions 101-6
    bars 112
    climate 245
    dogs 101
    emergencies 98
    entertainment 112-13
    festivals 107-8
    food 110-12
    internet access 98, 100
    itineraries 19-20, 100, 117
    maps 98
    shopping 113-14
    travel to/from 114

travel within 114-15
    walking tour 107
Thinleygang 135
Thirteen Arts, the 55-6, 104, 195
Thombu Shong 221
*thondrols* 57, 194
Thowadrak Hermitage 178-9
Thrumshing La 184
Thungdari 189
Tibet 31, 167
Tikke Zampa 230
time 254, **294-5**
tipping 250-1
toilets 254
Torsa Strict Nature Reserve 91, 92
tourism 15-17, 24, 42
    Nabji trail 180
tourist information 254
tours 15, 262-4
    Bhutanese operators 263-4
traditional dress 49-51, *see also ghos, kiras*
traditional medicine 86, 87, 222
    National Institute of Traditional Medicine 105
    So-ba Rig-pa 48
    poaching 93
traffic lights 97
Trashi Chhoe Dzong 101-3, 6, 139
    Dechen Phodrang 106
Trashi Thongmoen Dzong 227
Trashi Yangtse 195-6
Trashi Yangtse Dzongkhag 193-6
Trashigang 190-2, **191**
Trashigang Dzong 190-1
Trashigang Dzongkhag 188-93
Trashigang Goemba 117
travellers cheques 251
travel permits
    daily tariff 15-17
    Indian Nationals 16, 255, 261
treaty of Punakha 39
trekking 199-241, *see also* hiking, walking
    in Bhutan 203
    Bumthang valley 170
    clothIng & equipment 114, 202-6, 207
    considerations 208-9, 210
    guides 199, 201
    health & safety 200, 210-12
    itineraries 23
    maps 206, 208
    Nabji trail 180

pack animals 201-2
Phobjikha valley 153, 143
rescue 211-12
routes 206-10, 211
weather 200-1
trekking routes **199**
Bumthang Cultural trek 230-2, **231**
Dagala Thousand Lakes trek 214-16, **213**, 8
Druk Path trek 212-14, **213**
Duer Hot Spring trek 232-3, **231**
Gangte trek 228-30, **229**, 143
Gasa Hot Spring trek 228, **223**
Jhomolhari trek 216-21, **217**, 143
Jhomolhari trek 2 221-2, **217**
Laya-Gasa trek 222-8, **223**
Rodang La trek 233-7, **234-5**
Samtengang Winter trek 241
Snowman trek 237-41, **238**
Trongsa 160, 162-5, **163**
penlop of 36
tsechu 164
Trongsa Dzong 163, 164, **144**
Trongsa Dzongkhag 161-5
trout 232
tsechus 23, 60, 154
Bumthang 167
Drametse 189, 6, 140
Guru Rinpoche 60, 61, 174
Lhuentse 187
Thimphu 107-8
Trashigang 191
Trongsa 164
Ura 179
Zungney 167
Tsheri Jathang 224
Tsirang Dzongkhag 159
Turner, Samuel 36
TV 243
Tzangkhar 193

**U**
Ugyen Pelri Palace 124
Umling 187
United Liberation Front of Assam, the 43
United Nations 256

Ura 179-80
Ura valley 179-80

**V**
vacations, 14, 248
vegetarian travellers 95
visas 255-6, see also passports, travel permits
Voluntary Artists Studio Thimphu 105-6, 7
volunteering 16, 256

**W**
walking 107, **108** see also hiking, trekking
Wangchuck, Ashi Kesang 174
Wangchuck, Jigme Dorji 40-1
Wangchuck, Jigme Khesar Namgyal 41
Wangchuck, Jigme Namgyal 36, 38-9
Wangchuck, Jigme Singye 24
Wangchuck, Lam Ngagi 163, 164, 168
Wangchuck, Ugyen 38-9
Wangdi 149-51, **150**
Wangdichholing Dzong 169
Wangditse Goemba 117
Wangdue Phodrang 149-51, **150**
Wangdue Phodrang Dzong 149-50
Wangdue Phodrang Dzongkhag 149-154
wars
Assam Duars 34-5
Bengal Duars 38-9
civil 32-3
water 272
weather 13-14, 200-1, 245-7, **245**
weaving 56, 57-8, 252, **137**
bura 193
khushutara 188
National Handloom Development Project 197
yathra 58, 166, 167
websites, see internet resources
weekend market, Thimphu 103-4, **138, 141**
weights 243, see also inside front cover
western Bhutan 119-59, **120-1**
Wheel of Life 46, 191, **144**
wheels, prayer 81, 106, 167, 231, 7

White, John Claude 18, 37, 46
wildlife see animals, birds, plants, individual species
wildlife sanctuaries & reserves **91**
Bomdeling Wildlife Santuary 91, 196
Khaling Wildlife Sanctuary
Motithang Takin Preserve 106
Phibsoo Wildife Sanctuary 90
Sakten Wildife Santuary 91, 193
Torsa Strict Nature Reserve 92
Woche 239
Wolakha 145
women in Bhutan 53-4, 226
women travellers 256, 274
health 274
wood-block printing 58
work, see volunteering

**Y**
Yadi 189
yaks 201-2
yathra 58, 166, 167, 252
Yatong La 166-7
yetis 93, 192, 193
Yongla Goemba 198
Younghusband expedition 37, 39
Yuelay Namgyal Dzong 168-9
Yugyel Dzong 222

**Z**
Zangto Pelri Lhakhang (Kurjey Lhakhang) 174
Zangto Pelri Lhakhang (Phuentsholing) 158
Zangto Pelri Lhakhang (Taktshang Goemba) 130
Zangto Pelri Lhakhang (Thimphu) 106
Zangto Pelri Lhakhang (Wamrong) 197
Zasa 229
Zeppa, Jamie 196
Zhabdrung, the 29-31, 71, 77
Pangri Zampa 115
Punakha Dzong 146-7, **144**
traditional medicine 48
Zhemgang Dzongkhag 180
Zorig Chusum 55-6, 104, 195, **137**
Zungney 166-7